ISLAM IN SOUTH ASIA IN PRACTICE

ISLAM IN
SOUTH ASIA

IN PRACTICE

Barbara D. Metcalf, Editor

PRINCETON READINGS IN RELIGIONS

PRINCETON UNIVERSITY PRESS

PRINCETON AND OXFORD

Published by Princeton University Press, 41 William Street,
Princeton, New Jersey 08540
In the United Kingdom: Princeton University Press, 6 Oxford Street,
Woodstock, Oxfordshire OX20 1TW

Library of Congress Cataloging-in-Publication Data

Islam in South Asia in practice / Barbara D. Metcalf, editor.

p. cm. — (Princeton readings in religions)

ISBN 978-0-691-04421-7 (hardcover : alk. paper) — ISBN 978-0-691-04420-0 (pbk. : alk. paper)

1. Islam—South Asia. I. Metcalf, Barbara Daly, 1941–

BP63.A37I864 2009   297.054—dc22   2008052340

British Library Cataloging-in-Publication Data is available

This book has been composed in Berkeley

Printed on acid-free paper. ∞

press.princeton.edu

Printed in the United States of America

1 3 5 7 9 10 8 6 4 2

PRINCETON READINGS

IN RELIGIONS

Princeton Readings in Religions is a series of anthologies on the religions of the world, representing the significant advances that have been made in the study of religions in the last thirty years. The sourcebooks used by previous generations of students, whether for Judaism and Christianity or for the religions of Asia and the Middle East, placed a heavy emphasis on "canonical works." Princeton Readings in Religions provides a different configuration of texts in an attempt better to represent the range of religious practices, placing particular emphasis on the ways in which texts have been used in diverse contexts. The volumes in the series therefore include ritual manuals, hagiographical and autobiographical works, popular commentaries, and folktales, as well as some ethnographic material. Many works are drawn from vernacular sources. The readings in the series are new in two senses. First, very few of the works contained in the volumes have ever been made available in an anthology before; in the case of the volumes on Asia, few have even been translated into a Western language. Second, the readings are new in the sense that each volume provides new ways to read and understand the religions of the world, breaking down the sometimes misleading stereotypes inherited from the past in an effort to provide both more expansive and more focused perspectives on the richness and diversity of religious expressions. The series is designed for use by a wide range of readers, with key terms translated and technical notes omitted. Each volume also contains a substantial introduction by a distinguished scholar in which the histories of the traditions are outlined and the significance of each of the works is explored.

Islam in South Asia in Practice is the fifteenth volume in the series. It has been designed, organized, and edited by the eminent historian of South Asia, Barbara Metcalf. The twenty-nine contributors include many of the leading scholars of South Asian Islam, from North America, Europe, India, and Pakistan. Each scholar has provided one or more translations of key works, many of which are translated here for the first time. These works include prayers, meditation manuals, lives of saints, treatises on Islamic law, sermons, and political manifestos, beginning from the period of the introduction of Islam into South Asia and continuing to the present century. Each chapter begins with a substantial introduction in which the translator discusses the history and influence of the work, identifying points of particular difficulty or interest. Barbara Metcalf, who contributes several chapters, opens the book with a general introduction to the world of South Asian Islam and also provides introductions to each of the thematic sections of the volume.

The volumes *Zen in Practice* and *Yoga in Practice* are forthcoming in the series.

Donald S. Lopez, Jr.
Series Editor

NOTE ON TRANSLATION, TRANSLITERATION, AND ACKNOWLEDGMENTS

———

Unless otherwise indicated, all translations are by the contributors of each chapter. In part because of the variety of languages of the original texts, contributors have been largely free to transliterate according to their preferred systems.

I wish to thank Azfar Moin, who not only contributed a chapter to the volume but also played a key role in preparing the manuscript for submission. Warm thanks also to Catherine Asher and Frederick Asher for providing several photographs reproduced in this book. I am also grateful to the staff of Princeton University Press, especially Fred Appel for his invitation to prepare this volume and for his confidence in the project over its many delays. Eva Jaunzems, one of the most careful readers I've ever worked with, brought formidable editing skills to the manuscript. It is far better for having been in her hands.

CONTENTS

Princeton Readings in Religions   v
Note on Translation, Transliteration, and Acknowledgments   vii
List of Illustrations   xiii
Contributors   xv
Preface: Islam in South Asia in Practice · *Barbara D. Metcalf*   xvii
Maps   xxvi

Introduction: A Historical Overview of Islam in South Asia
· *Barbara D. Metcalf*   1

Devotion and Praise: To Allah, Muhammad, Imams, and Elders

Introduction · *Barbara D. Metcalf*   43
  1. Satpanthi Ismaili Songs to Hazrat Ali and the Imams · *Ali S. Asani*   48
  2. The Soul's Quest in Malik Muhammad Jayasi's Hindavi Romance
       · *Aditya Behl*   63
  3. Pilgrimage to the Shrines in Ajmer · *Catherine B. Asher*   77
  4. Women's Grinding and Spinning Songs of Devotion in the
       Late Medieval Deccan · *Richard Eaton*   87
  5. Qawwali Songs of Praise · *Syed Akbar Hyder and Carla Petievich*   93
  6. *Na't*: Media Contexts and Transnational Dimensions of a Devotional
       Practice · *Patrick Eisenlohr*   101
  7. Shi'i Mourning in Muhurram: *Nauha* Laments for Children Killed
       at Karbala · *Syed Akbar Hyder and Carla Petievich*   113
  8. Islam and the Devotional Image in Pakistan · *Jamal J. Elias*   120

Holy and Exemplary Lives

Introduction · *Barbara D. Metcalf*   135
  9. Ibn Battuta Meets Shah Jalal al-Din Tabrizi in Bengal
       · *Barbara D. Metcalf*   138
  10. Narratives of the Life of Haider Shaykh in Punjab
       · *Anna Bigelow*   144

11. The Daily Life of a Saint, Ahmad Sirhindi, by Badr
al-Din Sirhindi · *Carl Ernst*   158

12. Sufi Ritual Practice among the Barkatiyya Sayyids of U.P.:
Nuri Miyan's Life and 'Urs, Late Nineteenth–Early Twentieth
Centuries · *Usha Sanyal*   166

13. Transgressions of a Holy Fool: A *Majzub* in Colonial India
· *Nile Green*   173

The Transmission of Learning

Introduction · *Barbara D. Metcalf*   187

14. Saving Tamil Muslims from the Torments of Hell:
Vannapparimalappulavar's Book of One Thousand Questions
· *Ronit Ricci*   190

15. The *Taqwiyyat al-Iman* (Support of the Faith) by Shah Isma'il
Shahid · *Barbara D. Metcalf*   201

16. The Brilliance of Hearts: Hajji Imdadullah Teaches Meditation
and Ritual · *Scott Kugle*   212

17. Studying Hadith in a Madrasa in the Early Twentieth Century
· *Muhammad Qasim Zaman*   225

18. Jihad in the Way of God: A Tablighi Jama'at Account of a Mission
in India · *Barbara D. Metcalf*   240

19. A College Girl Gives a Qur'an Lesson in Bangladesh
· *Maimuna Huq*   250

Guidance, Sharia, and Law

Introduction · *Barbara D. Metcalf*   265

20. Ibn Battuta as a Qadi in the Maldives · *Barbara D. Metcalf*   271

21. Guiding the Ruler and Prince · *Muzaffar Alam*   279

22. A Colonial Court Defines a Muslim · *Alan M. Guenther*   293

23. Maulana Thanawi's Fatwa on the Limits of Parental Rights
over Children · *Fareeha Khan*   305

24. Shari'at Governance in Colonial and Postcolonial India
· *Ebrahim Moosa*   317

25. Two Sufis on Molding the New Muslim Woman: Khwaja Hasan
Nizami (1878–1955) and Hazrat Inayat Khan (1882–1927)
· *Marcia Hermansen*   326

26. Fatwa Advice on Proper Muslim Names · *Muhammad Khalid
Masud*   339

27. A Rallying Cry for Muslim Personal Law: The Shah Bano Case
and Its Aftermath · *Sylvia Vatuk*   352

Belonging

Introduction · *Barbara D. Metcalf* 371

28. Forest Clearing and the Growth of Islam in Bengal · *Richard Eaton* 375

29. Challenging the Mughal Emperor: The Islamic Millennium according to 'Abd al-Qadir Badayuni · *Ahmed Azfar Moin* 390

30. Custom and Conversion in Malabar: Zayn al-Din al-Malibari's *Gift of the Mujahidin: Some Accounts of the Portuguese* · *Engseng Ho* 403

31. Muslim League Appeals to the Voters of Punjab for Support of Pakistan · *David Gilmartin* 409

32. Advocating a Secular Pakistan: The Munir Report of 1954 · *Asad Ahmed* 424

33. Maulana Yusuf Ludhianvi on the Limits of Legitimate Religious Differences · *Naveeda Khan* 438

34. The Indian Jama'at-i Islami Reconsiders Secular Democracy · *Irfan Ahmad* 447

Glossary 457
Index 461

ILLUSTRATIONS

———

Maps

Map 1: South Asia and surrounding regions with key towns, cities,
and geographical features mentioned in the text   xxvii

Map 2: South Asia, with contemporary national borders, in its larger
geographic context   xxviii

Figures

Fig. I.1: Nakhuda Mithqal Masjid (Mithqalpalli) at Calicut (Kozhikode)   2

Fig. I.2: The Nagore Dargah, Nagapatnam, Tamilnadu   3

Fig. I.3: The Qutb Minar, Delhi   7

Fig. I.4: Qawwals performing at the shrine of Muʿinuddin Chishti in Ajmer 9

Fig. I.5: The Sarkhej Roza, Ahmadabad   11

Fig. I.6: The Emperor Shah Jahan standing upon a globe   16

Fig. I.7: A *taʿzia* inside the Husainabad Imambara, Lucknow   19

Fig. I.8: Portrait of Sir Sayyid Ahmad Khan   23

Fig. I.9: Islamic chromolithographs for sale near the Tablighi Jamaat
center, New Delhi   33

Fig. I.10: Tablighis departing for a tour, New Delhi   34

Fig. I.11: Offerings for sale at the shrine of Hazrat Nizamuddin, New Delhi 35

Fig. I.12: The *dargah* of Hazrat Inayat Khan, Basti Nizamuddin, New Delhi 36

Fig. 3.1: The Tomb of Muʿinuddin Chishti   78

Fig. 3.2: Shah Jahan's mosque, Delhi   80

Fig. 8.1: Footprint of the Prophet   122

Fig. 8.2: Sandalprint of the Prophet   123

Fig. 8.3: Girl in prayer   125

Fig. 8.4: Shahbaz Qalandar   126

Fig. 8.5: Data Ganj Bakhsh and Khwaja Muʿinuddin   127

Fig. 8.6: Girl at Tomb of Data Ganj   127

Fig. 8.7: Sakhi Sarvar   129

Fig. 8.8: Shah ʿAbdul Latif Bhitai   130

Fig. 8.9: Truck with Sufi and other religious motifs   131

CONTRIBUTORS

Asad Ahmad is an Assistant Professor in the Department of Anthropology, Harvard University.

Irfan Ahmad is an anthropologist and Assistant Professor of Politics in the School of Political and Social Inquiry at Monash University in Australia where he is also affiliated with the Centre for Islam and the Modern World.

Ali Asani is a Professor in the Department of Near Eastern Languages and Civilizations at Harvard University.

Muzaffar Alam is G. V. Bobrinskoy Professor in South Asian Languages at the University of Chicago.

Catherine B. Asher is a Professor in the Department of Art History at the University of Minnesota.

Aditya Behl is an Associate Professor in the Department of South Asia Studies, University of Pennsylvania.

Anna Bigelow is an Assistant Professor in the Department of Philosophy and Religion, North Carolina State University.

Richard M. Eaton is a Professor in the Department of History, University of Arizona.

Patrick Eisenlohr is Professor of Cultural Anthropology at Utrecht University.

Carl Ernst is Kenan Distinguished Professor in the Department of Religious Studies at the University of North Carolina, Chapel Hill.

David Gilmartin is a Professor in the Department of History, North Carolina State University.

Nile Green is an Associate Professor of History at the University of California, Los Angeles.

Alan Guenther is an Assistant Professor of History at Briercrest College and Seminary in Saskatchewan, Canada

Marcia Hermansen is Professor of Islamic Studies and Director of Islamic World Studies at Loyola University, Chicago.

Engseng Ho is Professor of History and Professor of Anthropology at Duke University.

Maimuna Huq is an Assistant Professor in the Department of Anthropology at the University of South Carolina.

Syed Akbar Hyder is Associate Professor of Asian Studies and Islamic Studies at the University of Texas at Austin.

Fareeha Khan is Assistant Professor of Religious Studies at Georgia State University.

Naveeda Khan is an Assistant Professor in the Department of Anthropology at Johns Hopkins University, Homewood Campus.

Scott Kugle is an independent scholar who received a doctoral degree in Religious Studies from Duke University and is currently based in Hyderabad, India.

Muhammad Khalid Masud was the founding director of the International Institute for the Study of Islam in the Modern World, Leiden University, and is currently Chairman of the Council of Islamic Ideology, Islamabad.

Barbara D. Metcalf is Alice Freeman Palmer Professor of History at the University of Michigan, Ann Arbor.

A. Azfar Moin is a PhD candidate in the Department of History at the University of Michigan, Ann Arbor.

Ebrahim E. I. Moosa is Associate Professor of Islamic Studies in the Department of Religion and Director of the Center for the Study of Muslim Networks at Duke University.

Carla Petievich is Professor of History and Women's Studies at Montclair State University.

Ronit Ricci recently received her PhD in Comparative Literature from the University of Michigan, Ann Arbor, and is currently a post-doctoral fellow in the Asia Research Institute, National University of Singapore.

Usha Sanyal is a Visiting Assistant Professor in the History Department, Wingate University, Wingate, North Carolina.

Sylvia Vatuk is Professor Emerita of Anthropology at the University of Illinois at Chicago.

Muhammad Qasim Zaman is Robert H. Niehaus '77 Professor of Near Eastern Studies and Religion at Princeton University.

Islam in South Asia in Practice

Barbara D. Metcalf

کافر عشقم مسلمانی مرا درکار نیست

هر رگ من تار گشته حاجت زنار نیست

Kafir-i ishqam musalmani mara darkar nist

Har rag-i man tar gashta hajat-i zunnar nist

I am an idolater (*kafir*) of love,

The mark of Muslim I do not need;

Every fiber of mine is tuned like a string,

The [*kafir's*] thread I do not need.

—Amir Khusrau (1253–1325)

The South Asian subcontinent is a particularly rich site for the study of Islam. Muslims in this region constitute roughly a third of the entire Muslim population worldwide. They are divided among seven nation states whose demographic and political characteristics vary widely. Among them, Pakistan is the only state in the world created explicitly on the basis of its population's Muslim identity. Bangladesh, Afghanistan, and the tiny Maldives also have populations that are primarily Muslim. The majority population of India, in contrast, is non-Muslim, but its Muslim population is still the third largest in the world (following Indonesia and

Pakistan). In Sri Lanka and Nepal, Muslims are also today a political "minority." Muslims in this area have in fact typically lived in a context of considerable religious pluralism. That this condition in today's globalized world is increasingly true for all Muslims—and indeed all religious traditions—makes the Islamic thought and practice of South Asia's Muslims the more significant.

Islam in South Asia has been characterized by its richness and variety of expression throughout history. This diversity has in part been shaped by the subcontinent's multiple linguistic and cultural traditions and its distinctive networks beyond the region. At any given time, and nowhere more evidently than in modern times, differences have also emerged from disagreements among Muslims over what should be the correct standard for cultural and political life.

In terms of Islamic practice, Sufism in some form has been at the heart of Islamic devotional and spiritual life in South Asia, as the epigraph above suggests. Typically glossed as "Islamic mysticism," Sufism (*tasawwuf*) may embrace the inculcation of ethical norms, the cultivation of an inner life, and the encouragement of devotion to elders and holy men, living and dead, who may serve as teachers, guides, exemplars, intercessors, and conduits of charisma. Sufism's core institution is a master-to-disciple relationship (*silsila*) that can be traced back over time to the Prophet Muhammad himself, the different strands representing distinctive paths (*tariqa*) of devotional practices and teachings. In this institutionalized form, Sufism is a product of the centuries coinciding with sustained Muslim rule in the subcontinent, and its foundational patterns take shape here as they do elsewhere. As two figures discussed below make clear—Mahmud Ghaznavi in the eleventh century and Ibn Battuta in the fourteenth—Sufism flourished in these centuries from North Africa to Central Asia.

At the same time, however, and often hand-in-hand with the loyalties, disciplines, and devotion of the Sufi traditions, the Indian Subcontinent has long been a center of great scholarly traditions, above all in recent centuries the study of hadith, the sacred texts that communicate the Prophet Muhammad's teachings and example. In the modern period, moreover, this geographic area has given rise to one of the most important schools of Islamic "modernist" reinterpretation (the other being Egypt), and it has also produced many of the Muslim world's foremost political theorists, whether articulating an "Islamist" perspective or providing a theological underpinning to secular democracy. Historically, in fact, the subcontinent has offered a virtual laboratory to explore multiple expressions of Islam in political life, given a history of forms of government from kingdoms, sultanates, and empires, to democracies of various kinds as well as authoritarian military regimes. For all these reasons, the Indian Subcontinent should be thought of not as a periphery of Islam and Muslim life, but as a center. Throughout history, the area has never been sealed off from the larger world. Relationships of trade, political regimes, colonial and neocolonial interventions, and Muslim networks of scholarship, pilgrimage, and patronage have sustained flows of people, goods, and ideas back and forth from South Asia for centuries.

The voices of Muslims of the South Asian region included in this volume are intended to enrich the reader's understanding of how Islamic religious thought, symbols, practices, and institutions have provided meaning, ethical guidance, structures of belonging, and pleasure to millions of people over more than a millennium. With the words "in practice" in the title of the volume, we hope to counter the assumption, one perhaps particularly pervasive in the case of Islam, that a given religion presents timeless universals or positions that hold in all times and places. With the phrase "in practice," we shift the lens toward Muslims and away from "Islam," and recognize that "Islam" is always processed through human eyes. Thus in this volume it is not "Islam" that has an answer to the question of the proper forms of prayer, or the nature of moral obligations, or the risk of idolatry in devotion to prophets and saints, but rather a modernist judge in a colonial court, or an upwardly mobile Bangladeshi college girl giving a Qur'anic lesson to her fellow students, or working-class Muslims in Mauritius following their Pakistani guide — all engaging with the historic Islamic tradition as they themselves practice it.

It is, however, not easy to hear Muslim voices across distances of time, language, and culture. The term and subject of "Islam" everywhere bears the burden of heavily politicized distortion both in scholarship and public life. Many scholars, above all Edward Said in his path breaking *Orientalism* (1978), have identified blinders that have shaped understandings of Islam. These have been forged in the context of Western colonialism and neocolonialism, and they have shaped the enduring historical narratives and ideologies of the colonizers and the colonized alike. South Asia, by the mid-nineteenth century, was for the most part contained within the boundaries of "British India," an area characterized by the longest and most intensive experience of European colonial rule anywhere.

The Colonial Legacy: The Story of "Conquest"

Stories about Muslims and about Islam have played important roles for those who tell them. The *locus classicus* for the colonial story is the *History of India as Told by Its Own Historians*, first published in 1849, a compilation of translated selections in eight substantial volumes, taken from Persian (and some Arabic) sources. Purporting to convey a story about Muslims in India, it told instead a story about the British. As Sir Henry M. Elliot wrote in his preface, the publication was intended to confirm that Britain's colonial subjects had been delivered from oppression and granted the free gift of enlightened rule—a familiar colonial trope to the present day. A view of Islam was central to that story:

> The common people must have been plunged into the lowest depths of wretchedness and despondency. The few glimpses we have, even among the short Extracts in this single volume, of Hindus slain for disputing with Muhammadans, of general prohibitions against processions, worship, and ablutions, and of other intolerant measures, of idols mutilated, of temples razed, of forcible conversions and marriages, of proscriptions and confiscations, of murders and massacres, and of the sensuality and drunkenness of the tyrants who enjoined them, show us that this picture is not overcharged.

These published translations, Elliot wrote, "[would] make our native subjects more sensible of the immense advantages accruing to them under the mildness and the equity of our rule" (Elliott n.d., 1:xxii, xxvii).

One of the key actors in Elliott's drama, the mid-eleventh-century Sultan Mahmud, head of a Turkish-Afghan kingdom based in Ghazna (present-day Afghanistan), became paradigmatic for the colonial view of the Muslim presence in South Asia. Mahmud was a favorite of British historians as well of later Hindu nationalist histories, who all fixated on the story of Mahmud's raids into the subcontinent, particularly the destruction of a particular temple located at Somnath in Gujarat. This episode was a handy metonym for nothing less than the imagined destruction of "Hindu civilization" by the Muslim people as a whole on behalf of a rigid and iconoclastic "Islam."

Why did Mahmud become so important? To be sure, *later* chroniclers of the Turko-Afghan rulers, two to three hundred years after the fact, embroidered Mahmud's career to make him a great iconoclast and hero of Islam and to add legitimacy to the heritage of their respective sultans. Not only were these texts read off as fact in the positivist historical style of the colonial era, but Mahmud was brought back to life, so to speak, beyond the covers of the book. In the midst of the unmitigated disaster of the First Afghan War (1839–1842), for example, India's Governor-General Ellenborough ordered one of his generals to secure a set of gates from Ghazna on the grounds that these were the very gates looted from the temple at Somnath. Ellenborough issued a triumphant declaration that with the return of these gates an "insult of 800 years is at last avenged." The idea that a category of people called "Indian" had harbored this grievance continuously over eight centuries, as Richard Davis notes, is hardly plausible (1997, 201–202). It imputes an anachronistic nationalist homogeneity to the subcontinent, and it imagines geographic borders that did not then exist. It also implies that Muslims were not part of the "people of India." It soon became apparent (even if kept under wraps) that the gates had no connection with Gujarat at all (209).

Somnath periodically reappeared as an important symbol in the idealization of "pre-Islamic" India in nationalist political rhetoric, social reform movements, and in the vernacular historical fiction of the colonial era that attributed India's current problems to Muslim rule. Shortly after Indian independence, a project was undertaken to actually "rebuild" a temple at Somnath. Over the objections of Prime Minister Nehru, who insisted upon India's commitment to secularism, even Dr. Rajendra Prasad, the president of India, attended the ritual inauguration of the temple. The language used on that occasion about Muslims as foreign and the recovery of Indian self-respect, as well as the implications in the whole undertaking that Hindus were the real natives and the real citizens of India, was little different from that of the British a century before.

The histories created in the colonial period are thus not academic. Mahmud's story reached its climax, in a sense, with an even more dramatic post-colonial reenactment. This was a procession in 1990, organized by Hindu nationalists, that depicted the god Ram in a "chariot" driven from Somnath to Ram's purported birthplace in Ayodhya, the site of a sixteenth-century Mughal mosque. A campaign to destroy the mosque, of which the procession was a key element, culminated two years later when a well-organized crowd of hundreds of participants demolished it by hand. The retelling and reenactment of these historical stories do not occur in a vacuum but serve functional ends in specific social and political contexts. The episode of the mosque's destruction, for example, was told to generate Hindu unity in order to deflect lower-caste demands for affirmative action and to challenge the ruling government. It led to an anti-Muslim pogrom the impact of which was felt most dramatically in far-off Mumbai.

Recently, the distinguished historian of early India, Romila Thapar (2005), has rewritten the story of Somnath. What she does, in a sense, is to make Mahmud *simply ordinary*. For starts, she places Mahmud's eleventh-century raids in the context of the culture of the times when genealogies, epics, and folklore celebrated warfare and valor on all sides. Mahmud and the Ghaznavids at one end of the subcontinent were, after all, contemporaries of the great Chola Dynasty of the southeast, a Hindu dynasty whose conquests at this point extended from the Maldives across the south, with raids as far north as Orissa and eastwards toward Southeast Asia.

At the time Mahmud's raids were not at all the defining event they became in modern nationalist ideology. This is clear, Thapar argues, from contemporaneous texts and epigraphy. Mahmud did indeed seize the wealth of Hindu temples, but he was only one of many marauders, including pirates, Hindu rajas, and others, who were lured by the prosperous coast and fertile hinterland of the northwest. Temples, as sites of accumulation and investment of wealth, were always major magnets for raids. It is also noteworthy, lest one assume, as nationalist histories do, a monolithic "Islam," that Mahmud justified his incursions into the subcontinent on the grounds that some of the rulers of the area adhered to the Shi'i Isma'ili and Qarmatian heresies—so his targets were many. Moreover, while he raided eastwards toward Punjab and Gujarat, he also raided and conquered toward Muslim-ruled lands to the west and the north at a time when today's national borders had no meaning. Yet Muslims in the colonial period were anachronistically imagined as "foreigners" in a homogeneous India.

A Competing Narrative: "Domestication"

In response to the accounts that emphasized Muslims as foreign conquerors, many scholars and others have insisted that the real weight of Muslim experience in South Asia has not been that story at all, but rather a peaceful story of accommodation to local practices summed up by terms like "syncretic," "hybrid," or "tolerant." One must note at the outset, however, that this story too often shares the premise of two-sided homogeneity expressed as the encounter of "India" with "Islam." Such a formulation assumes an "Islam" already fully formed rather than as a historic tradition, like all others, taking on distinctive shapes in local contexts. This story of "accommodation" emphasizes the importance of Sufi shrines, devotional music, the customary celebration of life-cycle rituals, languages like Urdu, and always, always, the sixteenth-century Mughal Akbar, whom Amartya Sen—the Nobel prize–winning economist and public intellectual—turns into a modern liberal (Sen 2005).

The political scientist Partha Chatterjee, reflecting on these two characteristic approaches to studying South Asian Islam, has aptly written that nationalism is the key to understanding the enduring power of this conceptual duality: "The idea of the singularity of national history has inevitably led to a single source of Indian tradition, namely ancient Hindu civilization. *Islam here is either the history of foreign conquest, or a domesticated element of everyday popular life.*" (Chatterjee 1993, 115; italics added). Pakistani historian Muhammad Ikram, embracing this theme of duality, wrote in the preface to his influential history of "Muslim Civilization in India" that the story of Islam in this region was one of two "heterogeneous elements," the Islamic and the indigenous or "native," that always produced either assimilation or reaction when they came into contact (Ikram 1964, 295–296). In this schema he is able to place rulers and thinkers on one side or the other of a ledger: e.g. Mahmud on one side; on the other, Akbar. Official Pakistani ideology was founded on this binary.

In a celebrated debate in the 1980s, those emphasizing syncretism were led by the anthropologist Imtiaz Ahmad, who was responsible for an important series of edited volumes on South Asian Muslims published in the 1970s and early 1980s. For Ahmad, it was axiomatic that "the Islamic theological and philosophical precepts and principles on the one hand and local, syncretic elements on the other" were integrated in Indian Islam (Ahmad 1981, 14). The historian Francis Robinson (1983), in contrast, intervened to underline a historical trend toward what he called "the high Islamic tradition" by stripping Islam of local deviations. Robinson saw Ahmad's stance as more political than academic, attributing his argument for syncretism to his wish to show that Indian Muslims had their roots deep in Indian society and that they were good and loyal citizens. Indeed, a recent collection of essays, *Lived Islam in South Asia* (2004), edited by Ahmad along with Helmut Reifeld, argues explicitly the political importance of an emphasis on accommodation. As Reifeld explained in the introduction, after 9/11 "[it] seemed to us . . . extremely important to dispel [the connection of Islam to violence] . . . and try to counterbalance negative stereotypes." (Reifeld in Ahmad and Reifeld, eds. 2004, vii–viii).

At the time of the debate in the 1980s, the sociologist Veena Das joined the discussion. She worried that Robinson seemed to favor repressive regimes that enforced "a pattern of [Islamic] perfection," a concern that made clear the political stakes in a purportedly academic discussion (Das 1984). In more recent years, a further political implication of the debate, Peter van der Veer suggests, is that any suggestion that the "popular" practices of Muslims are not "really" Islamic but an expression of a Hindu substratum with only an Islamic veneer plays into Hindu nationalist efforts to obliterate any religious difference at all (Van der Veer 1994).

Beyond Binaries

In the earlier debate, Das aptly noted that Ahmed and Robinson, despite their apparent differences, assumed that their categories—"native," to use Ikram's problematic term again, and "Islamic," respectively—each had an enduring and transparent continuity. This, one might add, is the same problem as dogs the term "syncretism," which, as van der Veer points out, similarly assumes some kind of fixed list of what it is that is somehow mixed or melded. Thus, even while challenging politically negative accounts of Muslim history, those telling a story of purported syncretism are implicitly imaging an "Islam" that is always foreign and outside. Das urged that the binaries themselves be studied by focusing on the shifting issues of difference generated by Muslims in each specific historical context. Such an approach means shelving the labels that scholars and politicians have frequently used in favor of attending to Muslims' own distinctions.

A corollary to this requires abandoning stereotypical sociological categories that correspond to each side of the binary. Sultan Mahmud, for example, is primarily remembered as a warrior. But he is cherished in legend and in Persian literary and mystic tradition as the besotted seeker of the Divine, the ideal Beloved, whose earthly form was Mahmud's cherished slave Ayyaz. Conversely, the stories told by followers of the legendary Ghazi Miyan of Bahraich are redolent of local, nonsectarian tropes of gods and holy men, cherished by Hindu and Muslim devotees alike. Local folklore invokes his identity as a warrior—as the nephew of Mahmud, no less—only to celebrate his defending the cows and women of his town (Amin 2002). Such stories fit uneasily into the compartmentalization of Sufi assimilation on the one hand and conquest on the other.

There are in this volume many examples of the blurring of presumed boundaries, of which the most common is that of Islamic scholar and Sufi. In a pattern that is suggestive of Islamic systems of knowledge and authority generally, scholars and Sufis alike in practice often claimed both textual and spiritual knowledge even as, at times, they competed with each other for superiority. Rhetoric like that of Khusrau's verse, quoted above, seeming to condemn the knowledge and practice of the learnèd (across traditions), is thus not reflective of actual social and religious practice. Nor, on the other hand, is condemnation of certain Sufi practices to be understood as dismissal of the tradition of inner cultivation in its entirety. The mainstream 'ulama of the colonial period, well represented in this volume, are a good example of these blurred boundaries, and so unlike the "Wahhabis" colonial officials at times thought them to be.

As a result of this binary, "Islam"—in the sense of traditional scholarly learning and practice rooted in the Arabic classics—all too often simply drops out of South Asian studies (as it does, one might add, in African and Southeast Asian studies as well). There are at least two reasons for this. One is that defining classical Islam as foreign means, in the style of European Orientalist scholarship, that it is properly studied in its place of origin. But a second reason is that, as Chatterjee also notes, "The classical heritage of Islam remains external to Indian history" (Chatterjee 1993, 114). One is in any case implicitly better off closing one's eyes to South Asia's traditions of Islamic scholarship, canonical rituals, *shari'a* institutions, and so forth, for to do otherwise would disrupt the theory of domestication that seems to offer so much hope. Such a strategy is of course no solution since, even if ignored, "Islam" lurks outside, confirming by its absence the rigidity, lack of adaptation, and alien practice "true" Islam is assumed to represent.

The entries below on such subjects as the canonical rituals, traditions of scholarly learning, and the guidance of the learnèd, show them to be far from unchanging. The failure to study all these subjects in their specific contexts has implications beyond South Asia and is relevant to understanding contemporary Islamic practices and movements as well. Today's interpretations far too often imagine that whatever Muslims do is derived from an enclosed set of beliefs that serves as explanation for all Muslim behavior. This "culture talk," as Mahmood Mamdani reminds us in his aptly titled book, *Good Muslim, Bad Muslim* (2004), all too often precludes attention to geopolitical (and, one might add, social) realities. Instead, all is reduced to "good," or moderate, Islam versus "bad," or extremist, Islam. The entries below, in contrast, introduce Muslims engaged with a whole array of human projects: living a moral life, embracing higher-status practices as a route to social mobility, marking the transitions of family life, looking for healing, attempting to secure minority rights, or seeking a spiritual guide fully deserving one's trust. Trying to understand the specific ways in which Islamic symbols and institutions work does not make for simple narratives, but, given the implications of such stories, one ought to welcome narratives that place Muslims in specific contexts, constructing boundaries in different ways at different times.

Further Reading

Imtiaz Ahmad, *Ritual and Religion among Muslims in India* (New Delhi: Manohar, 1981); Imtiaz Ahmad and Helmut Reifeld, eds., *Lived Islam in South Asia: Adaptation, Accommodation and Conflict* (Delhi: Social Science Press, 2004); Shahid Amin, "On Retelling the Muslim Conquest of North India," in eds. Partha Chatterjee and Anjan Ghosh, *History and the Present* (Delhi: Permanent Black, 2002), pp. 24–43; Partha Chatterjee, *The Nation and Its Fragments: Colonial and Postcolonial Histories* (Princeton, NJ: Princeton University Press, 1993); Veena Das, "For a Folk-theology and Theological Anthropology of Islam," *Contributions to Indian Sociology* 18 (1984): 293–300; Richard H. Davis, *Lives of Indian Images* (Princeton, NJ: Princeton University Press, 1997); H. M. Elliot and John Dowson, trans. and eds., *The History of India as Told by Its Own Historians*, 8 vols. (Allahabad: Kitab Mahal, n.d.); S. M. Ikram, *Muslim Civilization in India* (New York: Columbia University Press, 1964); Mahmood Mamdani, *Good Muslim, Bad Muslim: America, the Cold War, and the Roots of Terror* (New York: Pantheon, 2004); Francis Robinson, "Islam and Muslim

Society in South Asia," *Contributions to Indian Sociology* 17 (1983), pp. 185–203; Amartya Sen, *The Argumentative Indian: Writings on Indian History, Culture and Identity* (New York, Farrar, Straus, Giroux, 2005); Romila Thapar, *Somanatha: The Many Voices of a History* (London: Verso, 2005); Peter van der Veer, "Syncretism, Multiculturalism and the Discourse of Tolerance," in Charles Stewart and Rosalind Shaw, eds., *Syncretism/Anti-Syncretism: The Politics of Religious Synthesis* (London: Routledge, 1994).

Map 1 South Asia and surrounding regions

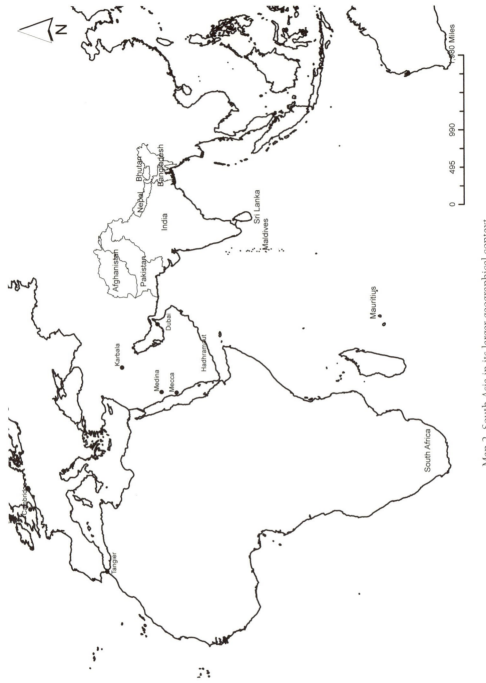

Map 2 South Asia in its larger geographical context

ISLAM IN SOUTH ASIA IN PRACTICE

INTRODUCTION

A Historical Overview of Islam in South Asia

Barbara D. Metcalf

Sri Lanka and the Southern Coasts

For long centuries, India, in a memorable phrase, was "on the way to everywhere" (Abu Lughod 1989). Trade brought Arabs to India's southern seacoasts and to the coasts of Sri Lanka, where small Muslim communities were established at least by the early eighth century. These traders played key economic roles and were patronized by non-Muslim kings like the Zamorin of Calicut (Kozhikode) who welcomed diverse merchant communities. The coastal areas had long served as nodal points for the transshipment of high value goods between China, Southeast Asia, the Middle East, and Europe, in addition to the spices, teak, and sandalwood locally produced. The Muslim populations grew through intermarriage, conversion, and the continued influx of traders.

The Portuguese, who controlled the Indian Ocean by the early sixteenth century, labeled the Sri Lankan Muslim population "Moro" or "Moors." Sri Lankan Muslims are still known by this term, whether they are by origin Arabs, locals, Southeast Asians (who came especially during the Dutch dominance from the mid-seventeenth to the end of the eighteenth century) or Tamils from south India (whose numbers increased under the British Crown Colony, 1796–1948).

One account of early Islam in Malabar on the southwestern coast is the *Qissat Shakarwati Farmad*, an anonymous Arabic manuscript whose authenticity may be disputed by contemporary historians but which continues to be popular among the Mapilla ("Moplahs") of the region. In this account, Muslims claim descent from the Hindu king of Malabar, who was said to have personally witnessed the miracle of the Prophet Muhammad's splitting of the moon (Friedmann 1975). Similarly, Tamil-speaking Muslims of the eastern coast claim that they too represent a community whose members embraced Islam during the lifetime of the Prophet; mosques in the area date at least from the early eighth century. Figure I.1 shows a mosque built in the local style, located in the west coast city of Calicut.

Not only traders, but also rulers, scholars, and literati in the south looked more

Fig. I.1: Nakhuda Mithqal Masjid (Mithqalpalli) at Calicut (Kozhikode). Fourteenth
century, rebuilt in 1578/79, with subsequent additions. *Photo: Sebastian Prange.*

toward their Indian Ocean connections than toward those of Central Asia that
dominated the north. They used Arabic over Persian and the Shafi'i jurispruden-
tial tradition rather than the Hanafi law of Central Asia. The cosmopolitan world
of Arabic-speaking traders on the western coast in the twelfth century is vividly
evoked in the story of an Arabic-speaking North African trader of Jewish origin
that is retold in Amitav Ghosh's *In an Antique Land* (1992), a story pieced together
from fragments of letters and other papers preserved in a Cairo synagogue. Among
the Sufis, whose influence was also widespread in the south, was Shahul Hamid
Nagori (1504–1570), popularly known as "Qadir Wali" because of his power to
protect seafarers and others who sought his aid. His vast shrine on the coast south
of Madras, shown in Figure I.2, draws not only local pilgrims but also others from
Malaysia, Sri Lanka, and beyond, where Tamil Muslims have carried his tradition.
The ritual at this shrine is of a pattern with that performed at nearby Hindu and
Catholic sites (Narayanan 2004).

Two entries in this volume depict the world of these coastal Muslims. A selection from a sixteenth-century Arabic tract from the western coast demonstrates the
deep interrelationships that existed locally, even among transnational traders, in
the face of Portuguese aggression (Chapter 30). A pedagogic Tamil text, also orig-

Fig. I.2: The Nagore Dargah; in front, a display of silver offerings representing body parts, vehicles, and other concerns for which the saint's intercession is sought. Nagapatnam, Tamilnadu, January 2007. Smaller replicas of this shrine have been built by Tamil devotees in Singapore and Penang. *Photo: Barbara D. Metcalf.*

inally from the sixteenth century, exemplifies the way that Tamil-language Muslim texts typically utilize the larger traditions of Tamil literature in their vocabulary, tropes, and descriptions of the local terrain (Chapter 14).

The distinctive cultures of the south, shaped in large measure by their oceanic connections, are a reminder that historical cultural and political regions do not map onto the areas defined by today's nation states. Kingdoms in the northwest for centuries spread over what are now international borders. The coastal areas of the south often had far closer connections via ocean routes than they did with many parts of inland India. This point is particularly important because of the routine description of those originating west of contemporary Pakistan, or even of all Muslims, as "foreigners" on the Indian Subcontinent. This anachronistic perspective reads into the past modern geopolitical loyalties (Asher and Talbot 2006, 5–7).

The Northwest in the Seventh to Twelfth Centuries

By the mid-seventh century Muslim armies had reached the Hindu Kush, and by 711 an Arab dynasty had established itself in the northwest of the Indian Subcontinent, the area defined by the lower delta of the Indus River, which was then still known by its Arab name, Sindh. The subcontinent as a whole was at this time still thinly populated, covered with dense forests and vast expanses of scrubland. The population included nomads, shifting cultivators, and hunters and gatherers, as well as settled farmers. There were, however, increasing numbers of local kingdoms as new dynastic centers were established through the more energetic use of irrigation and subsequent settled agriculture. Transportation and communication by land and sea were increasing, not least as part of ocean networks, like that of the seaborne trade that apparently stimulated the Arab campaign in Sindh.

Although the ruler of Sindh in the early eighth century was a Brahmin, there were also Buddhists and Jains in the area, as well as people following a range of local cults not linked to any larger tradition. Contrary to the widespread assumption that South Asian Muslims are largely "Hindu converts," this more complex situation was probably characteristic of those areas, like Sindh, where over the centuries the majority of the population would come to identify itself as Muslim. Muslims, as noted in the Preface, added one more strand to an already heterogeneous population. According to an Arab chronicle of the period, the Umayyid caliph in Baghdad, using the pretext of a ship seized by the local ruler, sent out an expedition under the youthful Muhammad bin Qasim (695–715). He was supported by an overland army as well as by a second contingent arriving by sea.

What did a change of dynasty in Sindh mean? Dynastic rulers in this period in the subcontinent depended on establishing relationships with subordinates, giving rise to "layered sovereignties," the boundaries of their reach shifting as alliances stabilized or were undone. Thus, rather than suppress old local rulers, a dynast would seek a local alliance, looking not to deepen control but to extend dominion. In so doing, the early Arab rulers of Sindh, who were far from being the first rulers from outside the area, followed a pattern established by the Greeks, the Mauryans from the eastern Indo-Gangetic plain, and, more recently, the Central Asian Huns. Early sources document both Buddhist and Brahmin rulers allying themselves with the Arabs in order to be confirmed in their local kingships. There were frequent changes of governors, factional feuds among Arabs, and conflicts with Jats and other segments of the local populations.

The Arab rulers, in contrast to common assumptions about Muslim conquerors, had no interest in, let alone a program for, conversion. This was also true of their conquests elsewhere. Later texts tell us that the local populations of Sindh were assimilated to the Islamic category of *zimmi*, protected peoples who were in principle to pay a special tax (the *jizya*) but who would in return be exempted from military service and guaranteed safety; in some cases limitations were placed on the height of places of worship or other kinds of sumptuary regulations were imposed. This was the model pioneered in earlier Arab conquests of Jews, Christians, and Zoroastrians, who were all three understood to be the (flawed) inheritors of a shared revelation. Thus, after the initial destruction of selected places of worship, deemed symbols of the legitimacy of the now-defeated ruler, other temples and the rituals associated with them continued as before. On the basis of one later textual source, the *Chachnama*, it seems that *zimmi* regulations were in fact deployed to preserve the existing social structure, with Brahmins exempted from tax, and the unruly Jats obliged to continue such practices as going barefooted and bareheaded, as they had under the previous dynasty (Friedmann 1984, 32).

Ultimately the Sindhi population would become largely Muslim. Since the colonial period, the common explanation for this identification with Islam has been the desire on the part of the downtrodden to escape the trammels of caste. This theory seems to be a reflection of modern ideologies, one that gives conversion legitimacy. In many areas, however, Brahmanic institutions had not yet penetrated deeply into the society by medieval times, nor did Muslim rulers challenge the social hierarchies that existed. There is no evidence in Sindh, or indeed elsewhere in the subcontinent, of Sufi holy men or others preaching the concept of equality to non-Muslims. In fact, at an even later period in south India conversion to any religion typically had the goal not of escaping hierarchy but of improving one's standing in the hierarchic ladder (Bayly 1990). What evidence there is for Sindh—some of it surely legendary—suggests that those who did convert in the early centuries of Arab rule were at the top, not the bottom, of local society, opting through shared religious identity to be part of powerful Muslim rule.

The year 711 may figure prominently in contemporary Pakistani history text books as the founding date of Muslim rule on the Indian Subcontinent, but Muhammad bin Qasim's conquest seems to have been taken for granted at the time and in no sense formed a watershed in subcontinental history. Turko-Afghans, however, who began to establish settled kingdoms in the northern heartlands of the subcontinent in the early thirteenth century, by contrast began to imagine themselves as inaugurating an era of continuous Muslim rule. After the fragmentation of caliphal rule in Baghdad in the tenth century, Turks, moving westward out of Central Asia, some of them military slaves (*mamluk*) of Muslim rulers, others immigrant tribes that settled and assimilated, had begun to reinvigorate Muslim expansion. As early as the eleventh century, some of them launched raids into the subcontinent, among them Mahmud of Ghazna, whose regional significance was sketched in the Preface.

Mahmud presided over an urbane and sophisticated court. His patronage produced Firdausi's great Persian epic, the *Shahnama*, the scientific work of al-Biruni (973–1048), and major works on Sufism as well. The first Persian text on Sufism in the subcontinent was the *Kashf al-Mahjub* (The Disclosure of the Hidden) of Shaykh Abul Hasan 'Ali Hujwiri (d. 1071), written in Ghaznavid Lahore, which became a major source for early Sufi thought and practice. Hujwiri's tomb in Lahore stands today as one of the major Sufi shrines of the subcontinent.

The writings of the great scientist, traveler, and writer known as al-Biruni encompass scientific, ethnographic, and philosophical subjects, in contrast to the devotional topics that typically hold pride of place for this era. Al-Biruni visited many of the towns of northwestern India and wrote an encyclopedic work on the history, religion, and sciences of the region. He was a remarkable scholar whose work on geography, astronomy, and comparative religion was innovative and wide-ranging.

He learned Sanskrit in order to converse with Brahmans and read their texts, and he concluded that their traditions were fundamentally monotheistic. Although not included in the selections below, al-Biruni's writings represent a cosmopolitan "Islam in practice" that give witness to an extraordinary intellectual curiosity.

The Delhi Sultans

In the late eleventh century, a new wave of Persianized Turks under the leadership of Muhammad of Ghor (1162–1206), began a series of conquests of Ghaznavid centers in Punjab, taking Delhi in 1192, and subsequently the Hindu-ruled kingdoms of Ajmer and Kanauj. Key features of their war arsenal were their superior horses and their skilled horsemanship. Upon Ghori's death in 1206, Qutbuddin Aibek (d. 1210), a *mamluk* (military slave), took independent control of Delhi. He and his successors, who rapidly expanded control across the north, would be known as the "Slave Dynasty" (1206–1290). The Khiljis (1290–1316) extended the reach of Delhi into the Deccan, with excursions reaching beyond into the deep south. The Tughluq Dynasty followed (1316–1413), but was in decline by the end of the century, falling victim to the devastating raids of the Turko-Mongol founder of a vast Central Asian empire, Timur ("Tamerlane," 1336–1405), who moved through the Punjab and into Delhi in 1398.

The celebrated Qutb Minar, with its adjoining Jami' (congregational) Mosque (Figure I.3), located in what is now south Delhi, dates from the reign of Qutbuddin Aibak. Conventionally today the soaring minaret is interpreted as a proclamation of Islamic victory, intended to impress the vanquished, as the mosque's name, the "Might of Islam," and its use of the rubble from demolished temples, suggest. According to historian Sunil Kumar, however, the mosque was meant to convince factions among the conquerors of Aibek's claim at a time when divisions ran high among urbane Persianized aristocrats, military slaves of the Turkic army, and members of various nomadic tribes, all of whom represented people drawn from different areas and with different loyalties. The local population would in any case not have been allowed inside the mosque and hence could not have seen the re-used materials, whether they signaled deliberate destruction or simply an expedient use of rubble whose design may well have been appreciated. At least one similar tower (the minaret of Jam) was earlier built by the Ghorids in the course of establishing themselves in what is now Afghanistan.

Today's name for the mosque, the "Might of Islam," moreover, dates only from a colonial period misreading of a historic name for Delhi that dates to the late thirteenth century, namely, "Sanctuary of Islam," a name extended to the mosque complex and to the near-by shrine of the saint Qutbuddin Bakhtiyar Kaki (d. 1236) as well. The word "sanctuary" (*qubba*) was heavy with meaning, as refugees fled Mongol depredations for the relative peace of India. The colonial misreading of *qubba* as *quwwa* (power) helped fit the site into a negative image of Muslim marauders, an image that would serve both colonialist and some strands of nationalist ideol-

Fig. I.3: The Qutb Minar, Delhi, early thirteenth century.
Photo: Catherine B. Asher and Fredrick M. Asher.

ogy. In travel and folklore accounts of the eighteenth and nineteenth centuries, furthermore, the inhabitants of the area called the minaret "Qutb Sahib ki Lath" (the staff of Qutb, the saint), removing it from the story of conquest completely and focusing on it as a symbol of reaching toward heaven. Kumar's work is a reminder of how symbols take on different meanings at different times (Kumar 2002).

As in Sindh, the lives of most of the population in sultanate lands, apart from those of the displaced elites, at first continued much as before. But the rule of the new sultans ultimately brought significant changes. They established networks throughout the subcontinent and into Central Asia; they created a new urban presence; and they cultivated a new religious and classical culture in the Arab and Persian traditions. Their military strength allowed them to provide substantial protection for the subcontinent from the thirteenth-century upheavals of the Mongols that spread across Asia and to create a "sanctuary" for scholarly luminaries and others fleeing their depredations. Gradual conversions in this period seem to have included urban artisans, like weavers, in the context of the new urban settings where the ruling elites were based, as well as the beginnings of conversions of newly settled agrarian populations in areas like Punjab and Bengal, as texts from the latter region indicate (Chapter 28).

The sultans of this period justified their rule as a source of order and patronage that allowed Islamic life to flourish. Court texts of the period provided models for an ideal king, however, that were in actual practice more pragmatic than ideological (Chapter 21). As for the power of an Islamic judge, or *qazi*, the case of the Tughluq-period Ibn Battuta (1304–1377) provides an example of an arbiter of Islamic behavior who showed some stringency but also considerable tolerance for locally condoned practices, from women rulers to topless female dress, and an overall appreciation of the population's piety (Chapter 20).

It is impossible to over emphasize the importance in the subcontinent of Sufis, both culturally and politically, in these centuries. The sultans patronized them as inheritors of charisma (*baraka*) derived through "chains of succession" (*silsila*) from the Prophet himself. Their blessing was regarded as essential to a ruler's power. The Sufi elder (known as pir, *shaykh*, or *murshid*) was an instructor in spiritual disciplines, a guide to the moral way and discipline (*tariqa*) that led to the inner realization of the Divine, an intercessor for his followers, and a conduit of divine intervention or miracles (*karamat*) in everyday life. The lodges of the elders were ideally places of prayer, discipline, and guidance for disciples, but also served for teaching, intercession, and as an open kitchen for all who came. Some were intermediaries for their followers to worldly power and some played key roles in agrarian expansion. Their graves, or *dargahs*, became power-charged places of pilgrimage for blessings and intercession.

There had been Sufis in the subcontinent early on, among them, as noted above, Hujwiri in Ghaznavid Lahore, and, of enduring importance, Khwaja Hasan Mu'inuddin Chishti (d. 1236) who, as instructed in a dream, reached the subcontinent in the 1190s and settled in Ajmer in Rajasthan (Chapter 3). The Chishti lineage, founded and centered in the subcontinent, produced key figures in the spiritual and political life of the sultanate, among them Hazrat Qutbuddin Bakhtiyar Kaki, mentioned above, and Shaykh Nizam al-Din Auliya (d. 1325), the Sufi *shaykh* of Amir Khusrau, the courtier, poet, and musician whose verse introduced the Preface. Other active orders in this period included the Suhrawardiyya, the Firdausiyya, and the Mahdawi (Chapter 29), as well as those outside formal lineages who were known by such names as *qalandar* or *malamati,* and whose defiance of convention was understood as their own route to God. Such figures offer a precedent for the colonial era *majzub* (madman) represented in Chapter 13 as a "holy fool."

The relationship of the Sufis to the sultans was a matter of contestation. The Sufis ideally disdained worldly power but at the same time they were understood to be essential to its success. The Chishtis in particular eschewed accumulation of wealth, and some withdrew from family life, but they were, ideally, conduits of material generosity to those who came to them. Their practices elicited debate, even if, like the unconventional holy men, they did not seek it. Especially controversial was their use of music (like the qawwali introduced in Chapter 5) that could culminate in ecstasy and trance (*sama',* as exemplified in Chapter 9). Figure 4 shows the celebrated qawwals at the Chishti shrine in Ajmer. The celebration of the saint's death anniversary, the *'urs,* has also been a contested practice, especially targeted by reformers in the modern period. Yet specific practices aside, as models of piety and intercession, Sufis have been central to mainstream Islam in South Asia and have interacted with both women and men from all levels of society.

Fig. I.4: Qawwals performing at the shrine of Mu'inuddin Chishti in Ajmer.
Photo: Catherine B. Asher and Fredrick M. Asher.

The Regional Kingdoms of the Long Fifteenth Century

The emergence of regional states in the fifteenth and early sixteenth centuries provided fertile ground for cultural efflorescence and local diversity. There were still sultans in Delhi, the Sayyids (1414–1451) and the Lodhis (1451–1526), but their territorial sway was limited. Malwa, south of Delhi, with its magnificently built capital of Mandu, became independent in 1406. Jaunpur under the Sharqi Dynasty, to the east, soon became more important than Delhi. Bengal had become independent as early as the beginning of Firoz Shah Tughluq's reign, as Ibn Battuta comments in his travels there (Chapter 9). The capitals of these newly independent kingdoms saw the building of splendid monuments that drew on local architectural skills and styles. As Alka Patel writes, the Gujarati buildings of the period were a continuation of the always-fluid architectural traditions of the region, adapted now to Islamic ritual requirements. This, she suggests, is a more useful line of analysis than notions of "synthesis" derived from the colonial classification of architecture as either "Hindu" or "Islamic" (Patel 2004). Part of the fifteenth-century Sarkhej complex of mosques, tombs, pavilions, a palace, and a pool, which was built in Sultan Ahmad's new Gujarat capital of Ahmadabad, is shown in Figure 5.

All of these regional kingdoms were centers of intellectual life and, above all, of influential Sufi personalities. As Ali Asani notes in his introduction to Isma'ili ginan (of which all but one included in this volume date from this fifteenth-century period), this was an era characterized by an intense devotional style that was shared across religious traditions. The "sant" teachers and poets, like Kabir (b. 1398?) and Guru Nanak (1469–1539), focused on the believer's direct relationship with a beloved Divine and sought to go beyond the formal symbols and rituals of Muslims and Hindus. Vaishnava *bhakti* also flourished in this period, as exemplified by the great saint Chaitanya (d. 1575) in Bengal. There was as well fruitful interaction with the theories and techniques of bodily discipline of the Nath yogis, coupled with the embrace of local languages in poetry. Both of these features are elegantly exemplified in the Sufi romance excerpted in Chapter 2. Shaykh Sadruddin (d. 1515) was one of the Sufis of the time who played an important role in regional political and spiritual life (Chapter 10).

Others Sufi teachers were primarily scholars, who focused not only on spiritual issues and practices but also on the core Islamic disciplines of hadith study, Qur'anic interpretation, and law (*fiqh*). One remarkable figure of this era who brought together the spiritual, the intellectual, and the political was Sayyid Muhammad Kazimi (1443–1505) who was born in the kingdom of Jaunpur. In 1495, in the course of a pilgrimage to Mecca, he declared himself the promised Mahdi who was to come at the end of time. Upon his return to Ahmadabad in Gujarat, he was condemned by 'ulama who demanded his banishment; he died in exile in Khurasan. Followers were nonetheless drawn to his knowledge, piety, and charisma. Despite episodes of persecution, small groups, some putting into practice his utopian teaching by sharing their worldly goods, continued his tradition for centuries in Guja-

Fig. I.5: The Sarkhej Roza, Ahmadabad, 1457, including saintly and noble tombs.
It is part of a palace complex of the kingdom's rulers, built in a distinctive
regional style. *Photo: Catherine B. Asher and Fredrick M. Asher.*

rat, Rajasthan, the Deccan, and Sindh. Rather than see Muhammad Kazimi as a
unique figure, and place "Mahdavis" in opposition to "orthodox," it is important
to recognize the extent to which millenarian discourses were part of mainstream
thought during the Mahdi's lifetime and afterward (as shown in Chapter 14). The
author of the Sufi romance included in Chapter 2 was himself attached to the
Mahdavi (as well as the Chishti) Sufi lineages.

By the mid-fourteenth century, the Bahmanid Dynasty in the Deccan had established itself independently of Delhi. At the turn of the sixteenth century, the kingdom split into five regional kingdoms that would persist well into the Mughal era.
The cultivation of the language of Dakhni Urdu was one of the major cultural
achievements of this period. In Bijapur and Golconda in particular, Dakhni Urdu
Sufi verse flourished, notable for its use of the image of a woman in quest of the
Divine as a symbol of the soul, a device shared with non-Muslim devotional traditions across South Asian vernaculars (and exemplified in the Isma'ili verses of
Chapter 1). Chapter 4 includes translations of Dakhni folk songs, sung by women
while grinding and spinning.

The kingdoms fought with and against each other, as well as in opposition to
or, at times, in alliance with the great kingdom of Vijayanagar under its local
Hindu rajas, the largest state ever created in the south. They also interacted with

and fought the Portuguese, now established along the southwest coast and centered in Goa. Vijayanagar's political and economic structure mirrored that of the Muslim sultans, and, like them, it participated in the growing militarism of this era across Eurasia. Lines in this period were not drawn on religious grounds as many have wrongly concluded. Cynthia Talbot has shown from Vijayanagar documents that the great rivals of this era were identified in terms of their military specialization: the Vijayanagar warriors as "Lords of Men"; the "Turks" (identified on ethnic grounds), as "Lords of the Horse"; and the Orissans to the northeast, as "Lords of the Elephant" (Talbot 1995).

The "long" fifteenth century conventionally comes to an end in 1526 with the defeat of the last Lodhi sultan by Muhammad Zahiruddin Babur (1483–1530), scion of Timur and the Mongols, who turned to India when his own Central Asian territorial ambitions faltered. He would later be reckoned the founder of one of the great early modern agrarian empires, known to history as the Mughals, the most powerful and richest polity the subcontinent had ever known. Muslims and Islamic institutions of rule, education, Sufism, and belles lettres were by then well entrenched. The landscape boasted not only the forts and palaces of the rulers, but mosques, madrasas, *khanaqas*, sarais, and tombs, as well as homes of Muslims large and small. Such buildings served as sites of prayer, instruction, devotion, intercession, and a range of other activities that cemented common bonds. One should imagine the venues and sounds of the texts of this period as they were repeatedly put into practice in these many sites.

The Mughals

In the late sixteenth and seventeenth centuries, the Mughals ruled an empire far greater in population, wealth, and power than any of the other contemporaneous empires with which they shared Turko-Mongol heritage: the Safavids, Uzbeks, and Ottomans. In Mughal India, the fundamental transformations of the preceding centuries—the expansion of the agricultural frontier, the growth of commercial networks, and incremental technological change—continued apace under stronger and more unified rule. This was across Eurasia an era of increased global contacts, population growth, and political strength. As had been the case in the sultanates before them, the core military and economic institutions of these early modern empires were not specifically "Islamic" but rather shared characteristic patterns common across Asia.

The court language of the Mughal ruling elite continued to be Persian, a language that fostered networks into central and southwest Asia as well as distinctive cultural traditions in political theory, literature, and religious styles. The Mughal system flourished with the participation of a wide range of notables: military figures, traders, bankers, and cultural experts representing extraordinarily diverse ethnic, linguistic, and religious origins. As the empire matured in the late sixteenth century, the high nobility included not only Afghans, Turks, and Uzbeks of Central Asian origin, but also Persians (who as Shi'a differed from the majority Sunni Muslims), some Arabs, and locally born Muslims, as well as Hindu Rajputs, Brahmins, and Marathas. They were unified by a common culture defined by mastery of the Persian language and culture. Hindu and other non-Muslim scribal, trading, and military communities made the workings of the empire possible.

Babur's rule in Delhi lasted only a brief four years (r. 1526–1530). His daughter Gulbadan would describe his death as owed to a specific ritual practice: his circling the sickbed of his son Humayun, praying that he, not the son, would be taken (Gulbadan n.d.). Humayun lost out after a decade of rule to the rival Afghan Sur Dynasty (1540–1555), but succeeded in briefly reclaiming power after long exile in Persia. As the most commonly told story goes, only six months after his return to power, while hastening to prayer, he slipped and fell to his death from his library steps. This was a sad denouement, but showed the emperor as a model of canonical "Islam in practice."

The Surs had laid a foundation for the bureaucratic and military regime that Humayun's remarkable son Akbar (r. 1556–1605) consolidated. Akbar's conquests extended Mughal control north to Kabul and Kashmir, east to Bengal and coastal Orissa, south to Gujarat and parts of the Deccan, and southwest from Delhi to Rajasthan. Akbar incorporated new lineages into the ruling structure, significantly, those of the Hindu Rajputs whose allegiance was secured by imperial marriages to Rajput women (who did not convert to Islam), among them Jodh Bai, mother of Akbar's son and successor, Jahangir (r. 1605–1627).

The Mughals continued the patronage of the holy men of the Sufi orders. Babur initiated the patronage of the Central Asian Naqshbandi Sufis, who soon expanded into India from their base in Kabul. Akbar (like other notables of the court) was long devoted to Khwaja Mu'inuddin Chishti, and his visits to Delhi typically entailed pilgrimage to the shrine of Hazrat Nizam al-Din Chishti and to the tomb of his father, Humayun, which had been built under Akbar's direction in the shadow of the saint's shrine. Monumental in size, surrounded by a garden embodying a vision of paradise, Humayun's tomb was meant as a site for multiple dynastic graves linked at once to a vision of heaven and to saintly charisma. Humayun himself had been particularly devoted to Muhammad Ghawth Gwaliori (d. 1562), known for his treatises on astrology, including one that linked astral features to the Divine Names of God. Muhammad Ghawth also translated (or had translated) the Hatha yoga Sanskrit text, the *Amrtakunda*, whose breathing and other techniques of bodily discipline would be widely embraced by Sufi practitioners (Ernst 2003). Jahangir in turn honored both the Sufi Mian Mir Qadiri (d. 1635) and the Hindu ascetic, Gosain Jadrup.

The Mughals, however, not only sought out the charisma and wisdom of the holy along eclectic paths, but, like monarchs across Eurasia in this period, also sought cosmological and divine sanctions for their aspirations to unparalled power. Akbar, after experimenting with a decree asserting his unassailable right to make judicial pronouncements, primarily presented himself as the focus of elaborate ceremonial and even Sufi allegiance on the part of selected court disciples who shared the ritual he formulated for his "divine faith" (*din-i ilahi*). His courtier Abu al-Fazl associated him with images of immanent light, a special light communicated directly by God to kings in the Mughals' cherished Turko-Mongol lineage (reaching back to the mythical Mongol queen Alanqua, impregnated by a ray of light). Abu al-Fazl also celebrated Akbar as a model of the human perfectibility cultivated by some Shi'i and Sufi thinkers (1997). Later historians, as the Preface notes, have taken Akbar as an example of "syncretism" and "tolerance," thus implicitly and misleadingly setting him apart from other "orthodox" Mughals. Of these, modern historians have taken the courtier 'Abdul Qadir Badayuni as preeminent example. But Badayuni turns out of have wholly shared, for example, the millenarian perspective of Akbar and others of his day with its notions of cyclical time and even of a form of reincarnation, ideas that make clear the complexity and variety of what was taken at the time as mainstream Islamic thought (Chapter 29).

Jahangir, and his successors, Shah Jahan (r. 1627–1658) and Aurangzeb (r. 1658–1707), were all depicted with halos in miniature paintings of the day, a motif denoting sanctity borrowed from European art that had been brought to the court. Jahangir, like his father, enrolled his closest courtiers as his spiritual disciples, a relationship symbolized by their shared practice of ear piercing and wearing pearl earrings. Shah Jahan's claims to legitimacy were made material and visible in the architectural projects for which he is famed, above all the best-known artifact of the Mughals, the Taj Mahal, the tomb of his beloved wife, Mumtaz Mahal. The art historian Wayne Begley has argued that the tomb not only recreated a paradisiacal garden layout, but, as demonstrated in the calligraphy of the site, also presented Shah Jahan himself as nothing less than the analogue of the Divine (Begley 1979), claims that are echoed in epigraphy at Ajmer (Chapter 3).

In keeping with the "orthodox" vs. "liberal" binary, conventional historiography has blamed the last of the great Mughals, Aurangzeb, for destroying the Mughal Empire through his exclusionary "orthodox" religious policies. To be sure, Aurangzeb chose to cultivate an Islamic image different from that of his predecessors, presenting himself as a man of abstemious habits and personal piety, and as a patron of Islamic scholars. He supported a group of scholars who compiled Islamic rulings in the Hanafi tradition, the *Fatawa-yi 'alamgiri*; he also patronized an important family of Lucknow 'ulama, known by the name of the dwelling he gave them, "Farangi Mahall." Even so, the Mughals in general stand in contrast to the Ottomans in their relative lack of engagement with the 'ulama. The emperors' Islamic legitimacy derived more from their own charismatic image, their links to holy men, and their patronage—often left in the hands of women of the royal family—of mosques, gardens, and sarais, as well as the *dargahs* of the Sufis.

As for Aurangzeb, whatever his personal behavior, or his particular patronage of a group of 'ulama, he did not, in fact, change the broad contours of Mughal religious policy. All the emperors extended patronage to Islamic thinkers, holy men, and sites, even as, in their capacity as rulers of culturally plural polities, they also patronized the religious specialists and places of worship of non-Muslims.

Indeed, as Catherine Asher has argued, the temples of a Hindu noble like the Rajput Man Singh, built with Mughal patronage, should be seen as "imperial projects," reflecting the bonds between nobles and king and making visible empire-wide architectural styles. It is, moreover, in these terms that one must understand Aurangzeb's destruction of temples in Varanasi, Mathura, and Rajasthan. Such destruction was not the fruit of iconoclasm, since the emperor continued to patronize other Hindu temples, but rather a response to the disloyalty of nobles associated with these sites, nobles who no longer saw their interests served by the empire at a time when it was geographically overstretched and financially precarious (Asher 1992). Even as Aurangzeb applied differential taxes to non-Muslims (a source of revenue for his hard-pressed regime), his leading general was a Rajput, among his enemies were other Muslims, and a quarter of the most powerful nobles were Hindu. The Mughals were guided throughout by pragmatic ideologies intended to secure their rule and, ideally, to give priority to the well-being of their domains (Chapter 21).

What in any case was "Islamic?" Among the most celebrated cultural products of the Mughal court are paintings, some recording and glorifying the court, others large-scale illustrations of legendary Islamic stories or of translations of Hindu epics. According to Abu al-Fazl, Akbar replied to those who brought up the conventional Islamic objection to depicting human forms: "It appears to me as if a painter had quite peculiar means of recognizing God: for a painter in sketching anything that has life, and in devising its limbs, one after the other, must come to feel that he cannot bestow individuality upon his work, and is thus forced to think of God, the giver of life, and will thus increase in knowledge" (Schimmel 1980, 84). Figure 6 shows Shah Jahan in a painting of the mid-seventeenth century, standing on a globe imagining his ordered realm in which lion and lamb are at peace. A halo and cherubs point to his lofty status.

There was on the part both of Akbar and of Jahangir in particular, an expectation that all religious traditions contained elements of value. This is suggested not only by Akbar's dialogues and Jahangir's links to a Hindu ascetic, noted above, but also by an active program of the translation of Sanskrit texts into Persian. In his memoir, Jahangir wrote about his father:

> Followers of various religions had a place in the broad scope of his peerless empire—unlike other countries of the world like Iran, where there is room for only Shi'ites. . . . Just as all groups and the practitioners of all religions have a place within the spacious circle of God's mercy, in accordance with the dictum that a shadow must follow its source, in my father's realm, which ended at the salty sea, there was room for practitioners of various sects and beliefs, both true and imperfect, and strife and altercation were not allowed. Sunni and Shi'ite worshipped in one mosque and Frank and Jew in one congregation. (Jahangir 1999 ed., 40)

This is, of course, an imagined ideal, but it represents nonetheless an important theme in the cultural world of the court.

Fig. I.6: The Emperor Shah Jahan standing upon a globe. The emperor is depicted as a semidivine figure, with halo and cherubs; a lion and lamb sleep at his feet. Mid-seventeenth century, Hashim, Mughal Dynasty, India. Color and gold on paper. H: 25.1 W: 15.8 cm. *Freer Gallery of Art, Smithsonian Institution, Washington, D.C.: Purchase, F1939.49a.*

Conversion

By the Mughal era, certain patterns in the distribution of the Muslim populations on the subcontinent begin to be clear. Muslims continued as a significant presence along the southwestern coast; in modern times they would form roughly one-quarter of the population as a whole in that region. In the old Mughal heartlands of the north, including the regions around imperial cities like Delhi and Agra, as well as in the Deccan, there was no correlation between the presence of Mughal elites and conversion: in these areas; the Muslim population would never be more than some 15 to 20 percent, often represented not only by rulers but by crafts-people, like weavers, and others in the service of the courts. Throughout most of the subcontinent, Muslims lived widely distributed among far larger non-Muslim populations. The two exceptions would be in the northwest and the northeast, where Muslims had become by the British colonial period the majority population. The presence of Muslims in the northeast is particularly striking, given the relative remoteness of the area. It is largely attributable to the role of court-sponsored Sufis in organizing local populations into an expanding frontier of settled agriculture (Chapter 28).

The Eighteenth Century and British Colonial Rule

By the early eighteenth century, Mughal power had begun to contract in favor of a wide range of regional states. Some were breakaway provinces of the empire. Others were led by locally rooted lineage heads and chieftains whose power had grown during the prosperous seventeenth century and who, typically, had gained ruling experience through Mughal institutions. The most prominent of these locally based polities were the Rajputs, some of whom had already challenged the center under Aurangzeb; the Marathas of the Deccan; the Sikhs in the Punjab; and the Jats, southeast of Delhi. Breakaway provinces, led initially by their Mughal-appointed governors and continuing to pay formal allegiance to the center, included Bengal, Hyderabad in the Deccan, and Awadh, east of Delhi, with its capital of Lucknow. The establishment of the new, non-Muslim polities was often interpreted in modern colonial and nationalist historiography as an assertion of "native" Hindu (or Sikh in the case of Punjab) power against "foreign" Muslims. In fact, the non-Muslim dynasts engaged in strategic cooperation and even alliances with Muslim rulers, both at the center and in other regional polities, and were never united among themselves. Similarly, the brutal invasions of Persians (1739) and Afghans (1748–1767) from the northwest made no distinction on the grounds of religion; they attacked Muslims and non-Muslims alike.

Afghanistan, competed over by the Safavids and Mughals, took enduring shape in this period, notably under the empire of Ahmad Shah Abdali (r.1747–1772). Afghan power grew in part thanks to burgeoning trade into Russia and China sustained substantially by Hindu bankers and traders based in cities like Shikarpur in

Sindh. The Afghan kingdom at its peak reached into former Mughal territories in the northwest, but it was never able to establish itself in the Indian heartland despite its defeat of the Marathas at Panipat in 1761, a battle that showed the limits of each of these newly powerful regimes. By the end of the nineteenth century, the British succeeded in making Afghanistan into a "buffer state" and fostered the authoritarian centralization of the so-called "Iron Amir," 'Abdurrehman Khan (r. 1880–1901).

Despite the upheavals in the region around Delhi, the eighteenth century was overall a period of population growth, urbanization, and the establishment of new markets. The new regional kingdoms were centers of effective state-building, particularly in the Maratha case reaching deeply into their populations with effective bureaucracies and sustaining powerful armies. An innovation with far-reaching implications for the new system of regional states was their recruitment of professional infantry forces on the European model, efficient at handling artillery, and subject to new kinds of disciplined fighting. Such troops, who were initially often trained by European adventurers, had to be paid regularly, and they had to be paid in cash. The resultant "military fiscalism," as David Washbrook has called it, created at once the need for extracting more revenue from the peasantry and the services of bankers, traders, and revenue intermediaries who developed increasingly strong networks and played key political roles (Washbrook 1988).

The regional states also provided a context for new directions in poetry, art, architecture, music, and religious thought. Islamic traditions were among those that found new expressions in the regional settings. Across India in the eighteenth century there was a renewed attention to devotion, evident, for example, in a reinvigoration of the Chishti Sufis, particularly in the Punjab and in areas of Afghan dominance. Sindhi and Punjabi poets in this period produced masterpieces of vernacular poetry that reinterpreted local folk stories in terms of the human soul, symbolized as a woman searching for the Divine. The Punjabi story of *Hir Ranjha*, composed by Waris Shah (b. c. 1730), would prove one of the most enduring and popular of these accounts. At the Delhi and Lucknow courts, Urdu was adapted to Persian poetic genres, and Urdu poetry attained its classic form. This was also a period of Shi'a efflorescence, not only in Lucknow and Awadh, but also in other Shi'a-led states, including for a time Bengal. The Shi'a rulers of Lucknow undertook massive building projects, among them *imambaras* for the rituals of their mourning month of Muhurram, and celebrated Lucknow poets wrote elegies (*marsiyas*), like "The Battle of Karbala" by Anis, to recount the events commemorated during that month (Anis 2003). Figure 7 shows an *imambara*, a site used for mourning assemblies and for the storage of ta'zias (replicas of the tombs of the martyrs), some towering, which are carried in procession during Muhurram, some miniature, like the ones pictured here. Replicas of permanent material are used over and over, in contrast to others whose use culminates in being submerged, like Hindu images, in water.

A central figure in creative Islamic thought in the eighteenth century was Shah Waliullah (1703–1762), whom many later Islamic movements in modern India

Fig. I.7: A *ta'zia* inside the Husainabad Imambara, Lucknow, carried in procession during the Shi'a mourning festival of Muhurram. *Photo: Catherine B. Asher and Fredrick M. Asher.*

would claim as their forebear. His father had been one of those involved in Aurangzeb's *Fatawa 'Alamgiri* project, and his own scholarship was enriched by extended study with hadith scholars in the Hijaz. Later scholars have commonly assumed that figures associated with these eighteenth-century Arabian hadith circles represented a single movement, all sharing the spirit of the radical Arabian reformer, Ibn 'Abdulwahhab (1700–1791). As Ahmad Dallal argues, however, the many reform movements of the century are deeply imbedded in their local contexts and vary profoundly. Thus, in contrast to the Arabian Wahhabis, associated with what Dallal calls "a grim and narrow theory of unbelief," Shah Waliullah represented a tolerant and rich synthesis incorporating the approach and teachings of all the law schools and, in the tradition of al-Ghazali (d. 1111), he ambitiously attempted to reconcile Sufism with tradition (Dallal 1993).

If much in this period had a dynamic of its own, increasingly cultural life and all else would take place in a context shaped by the English East India Company. By the end of the century, the Company had abandoned its pattern, dating back to the first years of the seventeenth century, of trading out of coastal enclaves, in favor of acting itself as a landed, regional power in the rich province of Bengal. Increasingly driven by the nationalism that defined its relationship (in particular to France), Britain had succeeded in edging out other rivals to the European trade in India. It had done so in part by involving itself in the internal politics of states in ways that made them ripe for takeover. Company ties with the newly powerful banking and financial groups were key to this success. In this, as David Washbrook has argued, the eighteenth century witnessed a "conjunction" not of a "progressive" Europe and a "declining" India, but of two thriving commercial worlds. It was India's flourishing institutions that drew and sustained European penetration.

Islam in Colonial India: Law, Jihad, and Mutiny

The British focus on the "rule of law" as a principle for ordering society and justifying their authority took shape by the end of the eighteenth century. British efforts to systematize personal law—laws related to marriage, inheritance, adoption, and so forth—had particularly far-reaching implications for religious practice across communities. Laws were to be homogenized into categories, "Hindu" and "Muslim," and derived from texts whose teachings were assumed to have been lost. This was only one of many administrative measures that served to delineate, if not actually to create, social categories that were erroneously supposed to already exist.

By the early decades of the nineteenth century, the process of transforming the Indian economy into a raw-material exporter, in return for manufactured goods from the metropolis, was underway. Nowhere did this classic colonial trading pattern fall earlier or more heavily than in Bengal with its large Muslim peasant population. The East India Company developed the production of opium, illegally smuggled into China at substantial profit. Peasant cultivators who faced an uncertain market grew indigo, often through coercion. Artisanal production declined with the loss of overseas markets and the advent of machine-made cloth, which was especially devastating for skilled weavers in the great weaving centers like Dacca and Murshidabad.

Throughout, the weightiest burden was a heavy land revenue, rigorously collected in cash, and ultimately used to pay the cost of the colonial presence. In an important decision in Bengal in 1793, those recognized as landlords were guaranteed possession of their lands in return for a fixed payment. That payment, initially high, led to a turnover of perhaps one-third of the land of the province. Those who profited were largely those who were familiar with the new regime and had prospered under it, especially Brahman and Kayastha employees of the Company, who along with the old landlords enjoyed what would soon become a low taxation payment relative to the demands they levied on the peasants. Having seen the shortcomings of this experiment, British land policy was different elsewhere, but the cost to the Bengal peasant, especially when coupled with a depression from the 1820s to the 1840s, was high.

In 1821, a charismatic scholar, Shari'atullah (d. 1840), returned to Bengal after two decades in the Hijaz, preaching a renewed commitment to spiritual life and ritual obligations. By the 1830s he had gained a large following in the eastern Bengal countryside for what had become known as the Fara'izi movement (from farz, obligation). The movement joined religious consciousness to class antagonism. Participants refused to pay the customary levies used by Hindu landlords to support their temples and festivals. Shari'atullah's son, Dudu Miyan (d. 1862), organized the Fara'izis to assert their rights not only against Hindu landowners, but against moneylenders and British indigo planters as well. For several decades, the Fara'izis conducted agrarian protest activities throughout the region while operating within the fundamental boundaries set by the colonial state. In contrast, a movement led by Titu Mir (d. 1831), similarly focused both on both renewed spiritual and ritual life and on peasant rights, was crushed militarily when it resorted to violent jihad.

A second focus of militant jihad in this period was on the northwestern frontier in opposition to the Sikh warrior state that was deemed oppressive of Muslims. Its leader, Sayyid Ahmad Barelwi (1786–1831), was part of the circle of Shah 'Abdul Aziz (1746–1823), who was the distinguished son of Shah Waliullah and himself a great scholar of hadith and a charismatic guide to many disciples. Shah 'Abdul Aziz's *fatawa* defining India as *darul harb*, a site of war, has been taken by later anticolonial nationalists as evidence that the jihad was launched against the British. In fact, Shah 'Abdul Aziz had cordial relations with East India Company officials posted in Delhi, and he intended his *fatawa* to give guidance in relation to practical matters, such as interest rates, that were different in a context of *darul harb*. He did not regard militancy against British power as legitimate given that Muslims were free to practice their religious rituals in British territories (Masud 2000).

Like his mentor, Sayyid Ahmad Barelwi was deeply committed to teaching and practicing religious renewal, including reform of what were regarded as Sufi and Shi'i deviations. He undertook his militant campaign in the state-building spirit of the times, hoping to carve out a place of correct and unhampered Muslim rule and practice. Two of the reformist tracts of the movement, the *Taqwiyyatul Iman* and the *Siratul Mustaqim*, were disseminated through the new and inexpensive medium of printing, and they were to prove enduringly influential throughout the region (Chapter 15). Once on the frontier, the fighters were defeated as much by the Muslim Afghans, who did not share their reformist concerns, as by the Sikhs. With the East India Company's own conquest of the Sikhs in 1849, the entire Indian Subcontinent was essentially under its control.

Less than a decade later, in 1857, an army mutiny joined civil unrest to sweep across northern and parts of central India, disrupting British control for over a year. The grievances that fed this revolt were many, from army conditions to taxation to the arbitrary removal of princely rulers. Both Bengal and Punjab remained quiet. The soldiers marched to Delhi, claiming the aged Mughal at Delhi, Bahadur Shah Zafar (1775–1862), as their symbolic leader. Hindu army sepoys predominated in the initial mutiny, and Hindu Marathas were among the fiercest rebels. Some Islamic clerics invoked jihad against unjust rule, but theirs was a minor stand in the uprising. Nonetheless, in the brutal, bloodthirsty reprisals that followed, the British hand fell particularly hard on Muslims who were stereotyped as "fanatics" seeking to restore Mughal rule. Large parts of Delhi were laid waste, its inhabitants killed indiscriminately, mosques were destroyed, and Shah Jahan's great congregational mosque was made for a time into a stable.

With the end of conflict, the East India Company was abolished in favor of direct crown rule. The new order, put in place after 1857, was geared to creating stability. In 1858 a Queen's Proclamation declared that there would be no interference on the part of the government in the religious lives of her subjects. Moreover, the Crown entered into agreements with a range of landlords and various princes, preeminent among them the Muslim Nizam of Hyderabad, who were guaranteed their tenure and expected to become a conservative bulwark for the regime. The post-1857 regime also took for granted that India was comprised of groups so diverse that only a foreign power could contain them. This assumption, translated into administrative practice, helped to create the diversity it was meant to counter, not least by drawing a sharp line drawn between Hindu and Muslim. An example of the reasoning of a colonial court anomalously adjudicating nothing less than a case of Islamic identity is provided in Chapter 22.

Renewal and Community

A second-generation employee of the Company, Sayyid Ahmad Khan (1817–1898), who had himself protected the British during the uprising, devoted himself in the decades following to fostering intellectual and political reconciliation between the Muslim service elite and the colonial power. In 1875, he established the Muhammadan Anglo-Oriental College at Aligarh (now Aligarh Muslim University), an English-style institution that cultivated gentlemanly skills in Muslims who could play a role in the kind of polity he imagined, one that welcomed "native" consultation and demonstrated respect for its subjects, as the Company had failed to do. Within two decades, Muslim elites had, in fact, come to be seen, like the princes, as a pillar of loyalty, a role not uncommon for "minorities" in authoritarian settings. Figure 8 shows a portrait of Sayyid Ahmad, wearing the Turkish fez he popularized at Aligarh as a symbol of the modern Muslim, as well as medals he had received from the British government, his very dress a demonstration of Muslim, if not "Islamic," modernity in practice.

Fig. I.8: A portrait of Sir Sayyid Ahmad Khan, educational reformer and modernist Islamic thinker. Note his Turkish fez, popularized at Aligarh as a symbol of modernity, and his medals from the British government. http://www.twf.org/bio/SAKhan.JPEG

Sayyid Ahmad and the circle that grew around him at Aligarh were, however, also intellectual pioneers of Islamic modernism. Part of Sayyid Ahmad's intellectual project was to demonstrate a special spiritual bond between Christians and Muslims as monotheists, an analogue to the bond he sought in political life. (This argument is somewhat parallel to the nineteenth-century racial "Aryan" identity posited by high-caste Hindus and the British as a foundation for their imagined bond.) Central to Sayyid Ahmad's modernism was a rejection of the commentarial tradition of the traditional law schools and the specialized knowledge of the 'ulama in favor of the belief that any educated Muslim could turn to the sacred texts, to the Qur'an above all and in some cases to the hadith, in order to interpret Islamic principles appropriately for the current day. Sayyid Ahmad's denial of all miracles, and his insistence that Islam and western science were in perfect harmony, gained little support, but this perspective helped cast an aura of "superstition" over practices associated with tombs and holy men (see Chapter 13), which, nonetheless, continued in widespread use.

In part, Sayyid Ahmad's work, and the work of the modernists generally, sought to refute Western critiques of Islam on such issues as jihad, the status of women, and negative depictions of the moral character of the Prophet Muhammad. They accepted the judgment that Indians were "backward," and that modern education was crucial to their future, as did many Indian reformers, across religious backgrounds. It was to modern education for Indian Muslims that Sayyid Ahmad primarily dedicated his career. There were now two strands of education for Muslims: that of the British-style school and college; and that of the Islamic madrasa, which in the post-Mutiny period began to be organized on the contemporaneous European model of a school with a formal staff and a common curriculum organized by classes (Chapter 17). The British-style schools, which used English as their medium of instruction, produced not only government servants and professionals, but also new "lay" claimants to Islamic authority, who had neither a saintly reputation nor the classical scholarly training that continued to flourish. (For examples of these new claimants, see Chapters 22, 25, 27, and 34).

The importance of newly available printing presses for disseminating religious texts contributed to the work not only of the challengers but of the 'ulama as well. Printed texts made possible access to sacred knowledge without the personal relationships to lineages of teachers that the traditionalists valued (Robinson 2000). But the traditionalists also benefited, using the presses both within the madrasas and for disseminating their own works to colleagues and to a general public. Examples include selections from a seminal reformist tract of the early nineteenth century (Chapter 15), a late nineteenth-century manual of Sufi practice (Chapter 16), a biography of a major family based at a saintly shrine (Chapter 12), a memoir by a former madrasa student (Chapter 17), and a mid-twentieth-century tract of guidance on family relationships (Chapter 23). As many of these texts make clear, this was a period of considerable intellectual dynamism, not only among the better-known modernists but among traditionalist thinkers as well. Spiritual guides also flourished, some representing a composite model of spiritual and scholarly learning (Chapters 12, 17, 23, and 26). Into this mix came as well the colonial authorities, who, as the example of the army-based "holy fool" evocatively suggests, could reduce a conduit to the divine to being a "madman," properly confined to a modern asylum (Chapter 13).

Of increasing importance in the twentieth century was the sense that personal identity was linked to public identity as a "Muslim" or a "Hindu." With the gradual introduction of Indian participation in the country's administration, the population numbers within each community became an issue of contention; Muslims and Hindus competed for a larger share in the seats the colonial authorities granted to each group in governing councils and for positions in schools, in public employment, and so forth. The protection of mosques, the right to conduct religious processions, and the status of Urdu all were made public symbols of Muslim rights (Freitag 1988; Gilmartin 1988). Urdu, written in Arabo-Persian script, had become an official provincial language across the north in the mid-nineteenth century. Its displacement in 1900 as the sole vernacular official language in the United Provinces (where Hindi, written in the Sanskrit-based Devanagari script, now shared official status) was taken as a blow to Muslim interests, as was British policy toward the Ottoman Empire in the early twentieth century, which was viewed as inimical to Muslims. Sayyid Ahmad's hope for a privileged relationship between the British and Muslims was short-lived.

The denouement of the administrative partition of the large province of Bengal in 1905 was a further blow. The division outraged politically active Bengali nationalists, who saw their base narrowed, but it provided an unexpected boon to some of the Muslim Bengali leaders who now had a majority province of their own in the east. In the face of protests and violence, in 1912 the British reunited the province and, as with the policy on Urdu, the Muslim elite felt betrayed.

In the course of the Bengal episode, a delegation of Muslims, composed of landed and aristocratic leaders from across India, petitioned the viceroy to acknowledge the presumed political needs of Muslims. This was the foundation of the Muslim League, a party focused on the protection of Muslim interests. The initiative was clearly welcomed by the British rulers. In the subsequent Indian Councils Act (1909), not only were seats in councils "reserved" for Muslims, but "separate electorates" were established in which only Muslims could vote for Muslim representatives. This pattern persisted in the subsequent reforms of 1919 and 1935, and it contributed significantly to the creation of a separate political identity for Muslims. By World War I, there was a distinct Muslim intelligentsia making demands on the colonial power and disseminating their causes in politically-oriented newspapers that emerged in this period.

These Muslim causes were initially led by western-educated Muslims, but in 1919 influential 'ulama organized the Jamiat Ulama-e-Hind (Association of Indian Ulama) to join in as well, radicalized in particular by the cause of defense of the Ottoman caliphate. This issue soon found supporters in Gandhi and others of the Indian National Congress who regarded post-war colonial Middle Eastern policy as another case of European deceit and aggrandizement. The Khilafatists in turn enthusiastically supported Gandhi's call for peaceful non-cooperation, even as some nationalist politicians, notably Muhammad Ali Jinnah (1876–1948), demurred from resort to any other than legal means. The Khilafat Movement did not survive for long: in 1924 the Turks themselves abolished the caliphate under Ataturk's modernizing policies. The nationalist 'ulama, however, continued their allegiance to the nationalist movement and to the Congress.

The first non-cooperation movement had by then collapsed, and the decade of the 1920s was increasingly troubled by Hindu-Muslim violence. The aggressive conversion movement of the Hindu revivalist Arya Samaj intensified in this period, and, in response, Muslim movements of proselytization (*tabligh*), education, and guidance spread (including the movement later known as Tablighi Jama'at, Chapter 18). At best, such cultural strengthening was seen not as divisive but as integral to the independence movement, fostering each religious community as a strong component of the whole. This rationale influenced, for example, the foundation of non-governmental courts (Chapter 24).

At the end of the 1930s, Muslim political activists faced not only the struggle for India's freedom but full-out conflict among rivals for Muslim allegiance. The Muslim League gained little electoral support until the very end of the colonial period. In the elections following the Government of India Act of 1935, it was the Indian National Congress that dominated most of the provincial assemblies. Congress, however, did little to address Muslim League concerns. At that point, Mohammad Ali Jinnah, a Bombay lawyer who had for the most part cooperated with the Congress, determined to assert the League and himself as Indian Muslims' "sole spokesman." His cause was helped by his expressions of loyalty during World War II when the Congress leadership refused to support a war they had not entered independently. The verses of the Islamic modernist, Muhammad Iqbal (1877–1938), whose poetry celebrated Islamic history, denounced colonialism, and imagined a just society, helped fuel a separate Muslim nationalism (1993). Emphasizing this influence, Annemarie Schimmel, in her history of Islam in the subcontinent, calls the period from 1906 to Partition, "The Age of Iqbal" (Schimmel 1980).

For Jinnah and many other leaders of the League, "Islam" meant commitment to the Muslim community as an overriding identity. To secure that, he sought at all times constitutional strategies that would allow, above all, protection of Muslim minority interests. Ironically, for Jinnah it was only by creating autonomous areas of Muslim population that the religious identities and symbols that had come to dominate political life could, he believed, give way to the liberal, secular ideal of politics he espoused. Islam, for him, was a moral spirit that supported democratic and egalitarian goals. Other supporters of the Pakistan movement and participants in the new state, however, came to imagine a Muslim polity as one fundamentally shaped by some version of Islam, a cause evident in the final election campaign before independence (Chapter 31), as well as in debates and political strategies within Pakistan in the decades that followed (Chapters 32 and 33). Would Pakistan be a state for Muslims or an Islamic state?

A divided India gained independence on 15 August 1947. Many hands were involved in that outcome. Political and cultural movements had long drawn sharper boundaries around communities. Politicians had long negotiated on the basis of community. Some Congress leaders saw Partition as a way to avoid the decentralized federalism that they thought would impede the strong center needed for a development-oriented state. Some Hindu Bengali politicians welcomed a "second partition" that removed the Muslim majority that challenged their dominance. Partition unleashed one of the most horrific bloodlettings of the twentieth century. Perhaps a million people were killed; as many as ten million migrated, often in forced evacuations fueled by "ethnic cleansing."

Islam in the New Nation States

The ruptures of 1947, and subsequent changes in political regimes elsewhere in the subcontinent, could not but change many expressions of Islamic thought, practice, and patterns of belonging given the intensity of national identities in the twentieth century. Muslims in Pakistan would now live in the only state ever created to be a "Muslim" homeland. The Bengali citizens of that homeland, however, would soon reject religion as an adequate base for national identity. Muslims in India and other minority contexts like Sri Lanka would find themselves in polities where nationalists at least implicitly challenged the notion that being Muslim was compatible with national identity. South Asia since the mid-twentieth century thus offers an opportunity for studying Islam in a wide range of modern political contexts: from democracy to military rule; from a majority status to that of a small and large minority.

Pakistan and Afghanistan

During the decades that preceded Partition, Muslim politicians and many others had negotiated ways to secure a Muslim voice in politics through such strategies as separate electorates, reserved seats, "weightage" to secure representation that exceeded the proportion of the population in minority provinces, and the establishment of Muslim-majority provinces. They had, however, not tied their focus on community identity to a romanticized relationship with a specific geographic territory in the style of modern nationalism. Indeed, as the idea of some kind of separate polity or polities (perhaps within an encompassing Indian nation) emerged in the 1930s, there was not even consensus on where that polity would be. The new citizens of Pakistan were thus in many ways unprepared when the decision in favor of Partition was made and the territorial lines of the new state drawn.

Moreover, Pakistan lacked for the most part the national institutions that India had inherited, from its newly built capitol in Delhi to its functioning bureaucracies to the well-established Indian National Congress itself. Bengali East Pakistan, some thousand miles of Indian territory distant from the western wing, differed profoundly in language, culture, and economic level from the dominant west. The princely state of Hyderabad in the center of India, with its Muslim ruler and largely Hindu population, which some had imagined as Muslim territory, was forcibly integrated into India. The princely state of Kashmir, adjoining West Pakistan, was claimed by India on the grounds that its Hindu ruler had "acceded" to India despite its majority Muslim population. Fought over on several occasions, it remains a tragic and unresolved legacy of the Partition.

Included within West Pakistan were two provinces, Baluchistan and the North West Frontier Province (NWFP), whose populations spilled over into the adjoining countries of Iran and Afghanistan. The Pathans (now more typically known as "Pashtuns") of the NWFP came uneasily into Pakistan given their political mobilization around a charismatic figure known as "The Frontier Gandhi" whose organization, the Khuda'i Khidmatgar (Servants of God), had mobilized the population in support of the Indian National Congress and nonviolence. The Pashtuns, moreover, chafed at a boundary that divided them from their fellow Pashtuns in Afghanistan, and their commitment to an autonomous Pashtun polity persisted well after independence. It would be East Bengal, however, that posed the greatest challenge to the new state, primarily in protesting their neocolonial economic and cultural position within the larger state.

Pakistan's strongest inherited institution was its military, thanks to the colonial policy of recruiting substantially from the Muslim populations of the northwest.

Support for the military was justified in the name of protection against India and fears over provincial separatism. Military coups have ushered in three long periods of army dominance, which together equal over half of the period since independence. Each coincided with significant international support. Pakistan was a Cold War ally of the West during the first two periods, from 1958 to 1971 and then again from 1977 to 1988, when the country (reduced to its western wing after a civil war in 1971) served as a conduit for U.S. and Saudi support to Afghan refugees fighting a jihad against Russian invaders. In the third period, under General Pervez Musharraf (1999–2008), Pakistan became a U.S. ally against the Afghan Taliban after their role in the attacks on the United States in 2001. Such geopolitical realities more than "Islam" contribute to Pakistan's democratic failures.

Two perspectives on the appropriate ideological path the nation ought to pursue have competed throughout Pakistan's history. The secular position that the state was created to serve Muslim political and economic interests was evident in a much-quoted speech of Muhammad Ali Jinnah to the Constituent Assembly of Pakistan:

> You are free; you are free to go to your temples, you are free to go to your mosques or to any other place or worship in this State of Pakistan. You may belong to any religion or caste or creed; that has nothing to do with the business of the State. As you know, history shows that in England, conditions, some time ago, were much worse than those prevailing in India today. The Roman Catholics and the Protestants persecuted each other. . . . We are starting with this fundamental principle that we are all citizens and equal citizens of one State. (11 August 1947, available at http://www.pakistani.org/pakistan/legislation/constituent_address_11aug1947.html)

Islam from this perspective was an identity and a culture with values relevant to the state as well as a focus for unity, as the electoral campaign represented in Chapter 30 shows. Sacred texts did not serve as a blueprint for state organization or legislation, nor did religious affiliation provide a basis for citizenship.

In contrast, there were 'ulama and others who imagined Pakistan as an "Islamic state" embodying distinctive forms and laws in accordance with sacred teachings and distinguishing Muslims from non-Muslims. This conception of an "Islamic State" is a fundamentally modern one, as even a brief review of earlier Muslim-led politics and texts of the premodern period, discussed above, makes clear. The influence of the "Islamists," those favoring a modern state organized on Islamic principles, can be traced in successive constitutions, criminal laws, and legal practice, all of which form a significant dimension of "Islam in practice" in South Asia.

Of increasing influence in Pakistan has been the thought of Maulana Abul A'la Maududi (1903–1979), the foremost Islamist thinker of the subcontinent, who had initially opposed the idea of the new state. For an Islamist, Islam is "a system" and "a complete way of life," not a secular state for Muslims. Maududi opposed the traditionalist 'ulama's adherence to the historic law schools in favor of his own direct interpretation of the Qur'an in the style of the modernists. And he opposed their *de facto* acceptance of Islam as primarily restricted to the compass of private life. His organization, the Jama'at-i Islami, founded in 1941, appealed primarily to the modern-educated, not to graduates of the madrasas. His ideas were, however, increasingly shared by the Pakistani 'ulama, which formed political parties, as did the Jama'at-i Islami. Chapter 32 includes excerpts from the classic text on the secular vision of Pakistan, the Munir Report (1954), and Chapter 33 introduces recent writings of a leading Pakistani Islamic scholar on the rampant sectarianism that has produced violent confrontations in the country, particularly intense since the 1980s.

The 1980s ushered in a period in which the politics of Pakistan were intimately tied to the politics of its neighbor, Afghanistan. In 1979, a coup led to a communist government (1978–1989) supported by direct Soviet military intervention. International resources then flowed to Pakistan's military ruler, General Ziaul Haq, from both the United States and Saudi Arabia. Some three million refugees flooded into the border provinces of Pakistan, bringing with them guns, opportunities for drug dealing, and soon a commitment to jihad on the part particularly of young Afghans educated in the madrasas whose numbers began to soar. Ziaul Haq saw his regime strengthened militarily and ideologically as he introduced Islamic criminal laws and other Islamic regulations. Under Ziaul Haq, the Jama'at-i Islami first attained political influence, including cabinet seats. Both the secular Pakistani army and the non-Muslim United States saw their interests served by fostering jihadi Islam.

There were unforeseen consequences of Zia's authoritarianism, Islamic policies, and the encouragement of jihad, of which the growth of sectarianism was one. Shi'a groups, for example, resisted what they saw as Sunni fiscal and other policies imposed from above. A second stimulus was a kind of competitive funding, as Saudi money flowed to Sunni institutions and Islamist parties like the Jama'at-i Islami in the 1980s, while Iranian money, in the wake of the Iranian revolution of 1979, flowed to Shi'a. Sectarianism also served as a platform for involvement in public life at a time when an authoritarian regime precluded other forms of political engagement.

Within Afghanistan, a further unforeseen consequence was the extent to which rival groups that had emerged in the anti-Russian jihad fought each other for control after Russian withdrawal. Of these groups, the Taliban, led by students of an NWFP Deobandi seminary, gained control of most of the country by the mid-1990s. Their accommodation to al-Qaeda jihadis, who traded support to the regime for training sites, coupled with news reports on their draconian legal system, elicited international opposition to their regime. The Taliban at this point had no international goals of their own; they were nationalists. Al-Qaeda in contrast was committed to a global jihad and after bombings of U.S. embassies in Africa by terrorists linked to al-Qaeda in 1998, the United States retaliated with an attack on Afghan territory. After al-Qaeda-linked terrorists crashed aircraft into the World Trade Center and the Pentagon on 11 September 2001, the United States and its allies retaliated again, this time with all-out attacks that destroyed the Taliban's hold on government power. At this point, Pakistan again became a somewhat reluctant ally of the United States in its continuing struggle to control Afghanistan and destroy terrorist networks.

Pakistan was then again led by a general, Pervez Musharraf, who had come to power in a military coup in 1999. Musharraf, unlike Zia, was not himself committed to furthering Islamic legislation, but during his tenure support for religious parties grew, especially in the two provinces that border Afghanistan. In part this support filled a vacuum created by Musharraf's restrictions on the major political parties; in part it also served as a protest against Musharraf's anti-democratic, pro-U.S. policy as the religious parties called for free and democratic elections. Musharraf in fact used the fear of Islamist power as leverage for gaining international support for his "moderate" and anti-terrorist policies. When elections were finally held in early 2008, support went neither to Musharraf nor to the religious parties but to the major political parties that were once more permitted to operate.

Bangladesh

Many citizens of East Pakistan, the Muslim-majority districts of Bengal assigned to Pakistan at Partition, soon became disillusioned with their position in the new state. Bengalis came to feel themselves virtually a colony of the Punjabi-dominated army and bureaucracy. The privileged place of Urdu and English as official languages, despite the fact that Bengali speakers were a majority in the country as a whole, particularly rankled. Urdu was in fact the mother tongue of only some seven percent of the entire population, but it had been the official language in Punjab for roughly a century and had become a symbol of Muslim cultural identity. Bengal had a much more highly developed sense of linguistically and geographically based cultural unity than did West Pakistan, not least because the latter was comprised of four ethnically distinct provincial areas (Punjabi, Sindhi, Pashtun, and Baluch).

In 1971 the Bengali Awami League, led by Shaykh Mujibur Rahman (1920–1975), won the majority of votes but was denied the opportunity to form a ministry. East Pakistan seceded. In the brutal civil war that followed, India intervened on the side of Bengal, whose refugees were flooding across the international border. About 17% of Bangladesh's population is currently non-Muslim, largely Hindu, in contrast to Pakistan where a full 97% of the population is Muslim.

Bangladesh's first constitution declared it a secular state and prohibited religiously based parties, a reaction in part to the participation of groups like the Bengali Jama'at-i Islami on the side of Pakistan during the war. The mid-1970s, however, saw the beginnings of a turn toward much greater visibility of Islam in public life and debate. This was something of a world-wide phenomenon, evident in Pakistan as well; it was in part a response to the oil boom of the 1970s, which brought both support and job opportunities abroad for many poorer Muslim countries. Islam also provided a rhetoric for more populist regimes. In 1975, a coup against the increasingly dictatorial regime of Mujibur Rahman (who was assassinated) ushered in governments that fostered links to other Muslim countries and support to religious institutions. In 1988 a constitutional amendment declared Islam "the state religion."

Two parties have dominated politics in Bangladesh, the Awami Party and its rival Bangladesh Nationalist Party, the latter including the Jama'at-i Islami (as well as a second, very small, Islamic party, the Islami Oikya Jote) in its ruling alliance from 2001 to 2006. Although acknowledging that the number of militants is small, many observers believe that the expansion of the number of madrasas and some episodes of violence in recent years suggest the potential for a new level of radical Islam in Bengal, in part as a response to the corruption endemic throughout the government. But all Islamic action is not the same, as a Qur'an class, led by a woman college student participant in an organization loosely linked to the Jama'at-i Islami, suggests (Chapter 19). This entry is a caution against conflating all forms of Islamic dress and piety with extremism.

India

Some sense of the dislocations and violence that took place in parts of India after Partition is evident in an account dictated by a small group of illiterate Muslims, affiliated with the Tabligh movement, who went to the Punjab in 1950 to try to reconvert Muslims who had apostatized (Chapter 18). Experiences like this, of course, do not reflect the tenor of everyday life for most Muslim Indians, although strands of Hindu nationalism, reinforced by an international situation that made Pakistan an enemy, persisted. India, however, was unusual among the new nations of the mid-century in its success at sustaining open debate and a vibrant democracy, in which Muslims actively participated. There emerged no single party or organization to speak for Muslim interests in independent India. Through the 1960s, Muslims, like most Indians, supported the Congress Party, which deliberately sought Muslim votes, but since that time Muslims, again like everyone else, have participated in electoral politics largely by voting for whatever party seems most likely to serve their interests.

As described in the Preface, there was violence against Muslims, who were all too often seen not only with the classic negative stereotypes of a minority group but also as disloyal citizens with Pakistani sympathies, especially from the 1980s on. This was in part a surrogate, it would seem, for opposition to the state, as well as a strategy to unite Hindus at a time of mounting social pressure from below that came with democracy, affirmative action, and, increasingly, economic "privatization." Muslims were presented as a vested interest whose "appeasement" proved governmental immorality and whose culture and politics were risks to the moral and political unity of the nation.

Fueled by a range of Hindu nationalist organizations, and with the connivance of government officials, a campaign focused on the symbol of a particular Mughal mosque, the Babri Majid in Ayodhya, allegedly built on the birthplace of the god Ram. The movement culminated in 1992 in mass participation in tearing down the mosque, followed by anti-Muslim pogroms in Bombay and elsewhere. In 2002 a second pogrom was unleashed in the state of Gujarat, one that shocked the world with its genocidal brutality. The work of many Indian human rights organizations and journalists in documenting the Gujarat tragedy represented humane voices that actively dissented from these crimes.

The defeat of the Hindu nationalist party (Bharatiya Janata Party [BJP]) in 2004 brought into power a government more attuned to addressing the problems faced by Muslim citizens, as signaled by their creation of a Prime Minister's Committee on the Social, Economic, and Educational Status of Muslim Indians. The committee's report, known as the Sachar Report (after Justice Rajinder Sachar who chaired the committee), was issued in 2007 and has seemingly put to rest any talk of Muslim "appeasement" by showing the depressed status of Indian Muslims. As a whole, Muslim Indians were demonstrated to be poor; below the national average in literacy; underrepresented in government, the army, and the police; and underserved by the public education and health infrastructure. There are, to be sure, individual success stories of people of Muslim background, with figures in "Bollywood" and the world of cricket particularly well known. Three Muslims have served since Independence in the largely symbolic role of India's president. There are also great regional and class differences that are masked by gross measures of socioeconomic status. Nonetheless, the Report indicates that India's enormous Muslim population has suffered considerable handicaps.

At the same time, a great deal in Islamic life in India is vibrant and open. India's cultural pluralism contributes to that variety, as does the fact of democracy rather than authoritarianism. The Indian Jama'at-i Islami, with its Islamist roots, provides a particularly striking example of creative change in having moved, in contrast to sister organizations elsewhere in the subcontinent, toward a program of education, social service, and ecumenical outreach. Although Muslim spokesmen have clung to the preservation of Muslim Personal Law (Chapter 27), in recent years multiple "law boards," including ones representing women, have emerged to assert appropriate standards for such matters as marriage contracts. And Islamic symbols here, as everywhere, are products of their local contexts. An ethnographic film, for example, "Banaras Muharram and the Coals of Karbala" (2004), depicts the Shi'a mourning rituals of Muhurram. At times, the Muharram story has been interpreted as a charter for rebellion against injustice. In the film on Banaras, in contrast, it is taken as a profound symbol of peace and brotherhood. The Indians interviewed in the film explain that the very blood of ritual flagellation is a sign of willingness to hurt oneself before another. This interpretation is particularly poignant in the contemporary Indian context.

Nizamuddin

The area surrounding the tomb of the beloved fourteenth-century saint, Hazrat Nizamuddin Auliya Delhi contains the burial sites of his successors and disciples as well as those of a wide range of princes and paupers who over the centuries longed to share his charisma. Today, the busy site and its market spill into a neigh-

Fig. I.9: A display of Islamic chromolithographs for sale near the Tablighi Jamaat center, New Delhi, December 2006. *Photo: Barbara D. Metcalf.*

borhood of both middle-class housing and a slum, a railroad station, a near-by police *thana*, and the noisy streets characteristic of this densely populated capital city. To visit this neighborhood is an opportunity to witness many forms of "Islam in practice."

In Figure 9, a poster-seller offers chromolithographs representing devotional images, much like those that circulate in Pakistan (Chapter 8). His modest stall stands close to the historic center of the Tablighi Jama'at (Chapter 18). The center draws not only Indians but participants from throughout the world, some of whom come to study at the adjoining madrasa, which provides the traditionalist Hanafi teaching associated with Deoband; most come to worship, learn, and, possibly, venture out on preaching tours. The vendor of the posters has hung on the wall uncontroversial subjects, like pictures of Mecca and of pious children, keeping below a two-foot stack that includes more exuberant Sufi devotional posters illustrating saintly miracles or other subjects that reformers might find deviant.

Given the vendor's location, such discretion is not surprising. Figure 10 depicts Tablighis, with their travel gear on their backs, setting off to try to persuade other Muslims of the importance of prayer and other canonical obligations. Close by

Fig. I.10: Tablighis departing for a tour, New Delhi, December 2006.
Photo: Barbara D. Metcalf.

(but out of the camera's range) is the shop of a major publisher of books in Urdu, Hindi, English, French, Arabic, and other languages where visitors, including an international mix of Tablighis, browse as they make their way among great bundles wrapped for mailing to purchasers around the world.

Other passers-by may be en route to the shrine of Hazrat Nizamuddin Auliya itself, frequented for the blessings of the saints, living and dead, and the singing of the famous hereditary qawwals on Thursday nights. On the way they might purchase rose petals, puffed rice, or a velvet cloth to offer at the shrine (Figure 11). As the sign above the rose petals indicates (in Urdu and English), someone else

Fig. I.11: Offerings for sale at the shrine of Hazrat Nizamuddin, New Delhi,
December 2006. *Photo: Barbara D. Metcalf.*

going in the same direction might be making a pilgrimage of another sort, to the
tomb of the great Urdu poet of the nineteenth century, Ghalib, and the adjacent
hall named for him, which is often used for literary events. Ghalib's verses are
quoted by lovers of Urdu of all religious backgrounds and taken as evidence of a
secular "composite culture" shared across religious boundaries.

Someone else, a South Asian or a visiting European, might be arriving at Nizamuddin at the same time to visit the tomb, hear a lecture, or consult the library at
the pristine, modern complex built in honor of Hazrat Inayat Khan (Figure 12),
the twentieth-century Baroda musician who carried "Sufism without Islam" to Europe (as discussed in Chapter 25). These four photographs (Figures 9–12) are
from India, but similar diversity of practice may be found in any of the countries
of the region.

Islamic Practice across Borders

Apart from this diversity, a great deal else in relation to Islamic practice is shared
across borders in contemporary South Asia. Like the photographs above, many of
the entries in the following text point to new forms of transnationalism that link
the identity issues of diasporas and home communities into reciprocal relationships that tie South Asian Muslims to Muslims of other backgrounds. This trans-

Fig. I.12: The *dargah* of Hazrat Inayat Khan, Basti Nizamuddin, New Delhi,
December 2006. *Photo: Barbara D. Metcalf.*

nationalism is clearly expressed in the strong worldwide presence of Tablighis and
in the international stature of Inayat Khan. Transnational networks have, of
course, always existed, but they are intensified today by new modes of transportation and communication. A particular challenge in recent times for all religious
traditions has been the reconciliation of competing truth claims as all religions are
dispersed throughout the world.

Other characteristics of contemporary Islamic practice are evident in these selections as well. One is the fact of extraordinary sectarian competition, whether
affixed to old labels like Sunni and Shi'a; new denominations, like Deobandi and
its Tablighi offspring, and Barelvi, more sympathetic to shrine-based rituals; or
new-style associations, formal or loose, like that represented by the followers of
Inayat Khan. In the last, as in the Tabligh movement, one witnesses another common feature: leaders who claim Islamic authority without a base in either traditionalist scholarship or in a saintly lineage of their own. All of these characteristics
may be observed in the practices of modern Hindu and other religious groups as
well. In relation to transnationalism, sectarian competition, and "lay" leadership,
the importance of print that makes available translations and other texts continues to be of great importance.

In yet another way, a common pattern across national boundaries, as sketched in the sections on separate countries above, has been the growth of religiously based nationalisms, whether Muslim, Hindu, or, one might add, in Sri Lanka, Buddhist as well. All religious practice today takes place in a context of more bounded and self-conscious communities. The categories that define the five Parts of this volume—"Devotion and Praise," "Holy and Exemplary Lives," "The Transmission of Learning," "Guidance, Sharia, and Law," and "Belonging"—have all been constant themes in Islamic practice, but all today mark self-conscious, and often contested, "Muslim" identities in social and political life. The manifestations of Islamic practice at Nizamuddin, however, preclude any simple characterization or easy evolutionary trajectory for what goes on. The site is a reminder of the sociological diversity, the rich variety of practice and belief, the edginess among competing views, and the movement of people, institutions, and ideas that have characterized South Asia's Muslims throughout. We will meet these themes many times in the contributions that follow, as we attempt to sample "Islam in practice in South Asia."

Bibliography

Abu al-Fazl ibn Mubarak. *Ain-i Akbari*. Trans. H. Blochman. Ed. D. C. Philott. Delhi: Low Price Publications, 1997.

Abu Lughod, Janet. *Before European Hegemony: The World System, 1250–1350*. New York: Oxford University Press, 1989.

Al-Biruni. *Alberuni's India*. Trans. Edward C. Sachau. New York: Norton, 1971.

'Ali ibn Uthman al-Hujwiri. *Kashful Mahjub: The Oldest Persian Treatise on Sufism*. Trans. Reynold A. Nicholson. Lahore: Islamic Book Society, 1971.

Anis. *The Battle of Karbala: A Marsiya of Anis*. Trans. and ed. David Mathews. New Delhi: Rupa, 2003.

Asher, Catherine B.. "The Architecture of Raja Man Singh: A Study in Sub-imperial Patronage." In Barbara Stoler Miller, ed., *The Powers of Art: Patronage in Indian Culture*. New Delhi: Oxford University Press, 1992: 183–201.

"Banares Muharram and the Coals of Karbala." Film. University of Wisconsin Center for South Asian Studies, 2004. See also their 1984 film, "Being Muslim in India," for the routines of worship, work, and family life of a Muslim family in Lucknow, culminating in the happy occasion of the initiation into learning (the *bismillah* celebration) of the beaming, bedecked four-year-old granddaughter of the family.

Bayly, Susan. *Saints, Goddesses and Kings: Muslims and Christians in South Indian Society, 1700–1900*. Cambridge: Cambridge University Press, 1990.

Begley, Wayne. "The Myth of the Taj Mahal and a New Theory of Its Symbolic Meaning." *Art Bulletin* 61:1 (1979): 7–37.

Dallal, Ahmad."The Origins and Objectives of Islamic Revivalist Thought, 1750–1850." *Journal of the American Oriental Society* 113:3 (1993): 341–359.

Ernst, Carl. "Lives of Sufi Saints." In Donald S. Lopez Jr., ed., *Religions of India in Practice*. Princeton, NJ: Princeton University Press, 1995: 495–512.

———. "The Islamization of Yoga in the *Amrtakunda* Translations." *Journal of the Royal Asiatic Society*, Series 3, 13:2 (2003): 1–23.

Freitag, Sandria. "The Roots of Muslim Separatism in South Asia: Personal Practice and Public Structures in Kanpur and Bombay." In Edmund Burke, III, and Ira Lapidus, eds., *Islam, Politics, and Social Movements.* Berkeley, CA: University of California Press, 1988: 115–145.

Friedmann, Yohanan. "Qissat Shakarawati Farmad." *Israel Oriental Society* 5 (1975): 233–258.

———. "The Origins and Significance of the Chach Nama." In Yohanan Friedmann, ed., *Islam in South Asia.* Jerusalem and Boulder, CO: Magnes Press and Westview, 1985: 23–37.

Ghosh, Amitav. *In an Antique Land: History in the Guise of a Traveler's Tale.* New York: Random House, 1992.

Gilmartin, David. "The Shahidganj Mosque Incident: A Prelude to Pakistan." In Edmund Burke, III, and Ira Lapidus, eds., *Islam, Politics, and Social Movements.* Berkeley, CA: University of California Press, 1988: 146–168.

Iqbal, Muhammad. *Iqbal: A Selection of the Urdu Verse.* Text and trans. D. J. Matthews. London: University of London, School of Oriental and African Studies, 1993.

Jahangir. *The Jahangirnama, Memoirs of Jahangir, Emperor of India.* Annotated, ed., and trans. Wheeler M. Thackston. Oxford: Oxford University Press, 1999.

Kumar, Sunil. *The Present in Delhi's Past.* Delhi: Three Essays Collective, 2002.

Masud, Muhammad Khalid. "The World of Shah 'Abd al-'Aziz (1746–1824)." In Jamal Malik, ed., *Perspectives of Mutual Encounter in South Asian History, 1760–1860.* Leiden: E. J. Brill, 2000: 298–314.

Narayanan, Vasudha. "Nagore: Dargah of Hazrat Shahul Hamid." In Mumtaz Currim and George Michell, eds., *Dargahs: Abodes of the Saints.* Mumbai: Marg Publications, 2004: 135–147.

Patel, Alka. *Building Communities in Gujarat: Architecture and Society during the Twelfth through Fourteenth Centuries.* Leiden: E. J. Brill, 2004.

Robinson, Francis. "Islam and the Impact of Print in South Asia." In Nigel Crook, ed., *Transmission of Knowledge in South Asia: Essays on Education, Religion, History and Politics.* SOAS Studies on South Asia. New Delhi: Oxford University Press, 2000: 62–97.

Schimmel, Annemarie. *Islam in the Indian Subcontinent.* Leiden: E. J. Brill, 1980.

Talbot, Cynthia. "Inscribing the Other, Inscribing the Self: Hindu-Muslim Identities in Precolonial India." *Comparative Studies in Society and History* 37:4 (1995): 692–722.

Thapar, Romila. *Somanatha: The Many Voices of History.* New York: Viking, 2004.

Van der Veer, Peter. "Syncretism, Multiculturalism and the Discourse of Tolerance." In Charles Stewart and Rosalind Shaw, eds., *Syncretism and Anti-Syncretism.* London: Routledge, 1994: 196–212.

Waris Shah. *The Adventures of Hir and Ranjha.* Trans. Charles Frederick Usborne. Karachi: Lion Art Press, 1966.

Washbrook, D. A. "Progress and Problems: South Asian Economic and Social History, c.1720–1860." *Modern Asian Studies* 22:1 (1988): 57–96.

Further Reading

The Oxford Encyclopedia of the Modern Islamic World, 4 vols., John Esposito, ed. (New York: Oxford University Press, 1995), includes many entries relevant to this chapter, accompanied by annotated bibliographies. Annemarie Schimmel's *Islam in the Indian Subcontinent* (Leiden: E. J. Brill, 1980) is a classic survey with extensive bibliographies.

The following works provide general historical background: Catherine B. Asher and Cynthia Talbot, *India before Europe* (Cambridge: Cambridge University Press, 2006); Peter Hardy, *The Muslims of British India* (Cambridge: Cambridge University Press, 1972); David Ludden, *India and South Asia: A Short History* (Oxford: Oneworld, 2002); and Barbara D. and Thomas R. Metcalf, *A Concise History of Modern India*, 2nd ed. (Cambridge: Cambridge University Press, 2006).

Devotion and Praise:
To Allah, Muhammad,
Imams, and Elders

DEVOTION AND PRAISE:
TO ALLAH, MUHAMMAD,
IMAMS, AND ELDERS

Introduction

Barbara D. Metcalf

No extant texts are more characteristic of the early centuries of the Muslim presence in South Asia than the devotional stories and songs preserved by diverse traditions. Typically written in regional languages, the selections below are translated from Hindi (or Hindavi), Gujarati, Awadhi, Dakhni, and Urdu. This section includes as well a chapter related to the practice, well established by the thirteenth century and widely current today, of pilgrimage and patronage to the tombs of holy men. The final entry shifts emphasis toward the visual with its reproductions of the inexpensive, colorful devotional chromolithographs that over the past century have become such an important part of pious practice across religious traditions throughout South Asia.

The Isma'ili verses translated by Ali Asani in Chapter 1 serve as a good introduction not only to this section but also to the volume as a whole. The enduring presence of the Isma'ili sectarian denomination in South Asia aside, their influence appears to have been extensive. One can, for example, point to the centrality of 'Ali (the Prophet's son-in-law and the focus of Shi'i devotion) in the devotionalism of Sufis like the Chishtis, whose areas of influence were initially shared with the Isma'ili.

The Isma'ili texts also offer striking examples of language, symbols, and styles of worship that were shared across denominational bounds. The Isma'ili preachers called their teachings by the Indic term *satpanth* (the true path) and expressed their beliefs and ritual in the local cultural idiom, for example by presenting their first Imam, 'Ali, as an *avatar* (incarnation) of Vishnu. In their verses in praise of the imam, the authors used the idiom, common to Sufi and *bhakti* poetry both, of the devoted woman separated from her beloved.

These verses are also a reminder of the great diversity of Islamic expressions on the subcontinent, and of the disputes that at times have arisen between competing sects and interpretations. Muslims were in no sense a monolithic whole. It was ostensibly to defeat Isma'ili heresy that Mahmud of Ghazna in the eleventh century tried to extend his influence into the area. Among Isma'ili themselves, moreover, Ali Asani explains, reformers in the colonial period challenged community practices in order to align Isma'ili doctrines and expressions with less sectarian-oriented and regionally specific beliefs and practices.

A distinctive genre of devotional expression was that of the *prem kahani*, "the love story," like the sixteenth-century Awadhi poem by Muhammad Ja'isi, of which a selection is translated by Aditya Behl in Chapter 2. While building on the Persian *masnawi* form and sharing its devotional focus, the Indian romances recreated that genre in local languages, shaping their stories through local idioms (preeminently, Behl argues, that of the Nath yogis) and telling local stories, in this case that of a northern prince's passion for a princess of legendary beauty on the paradise-like island of Singhala. The marvelous passage translated by Behl evokes a dream image of all the most beautiful, paradisiacal elements of South Asia with its trees and flowers, its birdsong, its waters, and its fragrant air.

These tales seem to have been read and heard at many levels, from that of the simple romance to symbolic expressions of esoteric theories about spiritual realization. Saintly figures can be, as Behl explains, "teaching *shaykhs*," who would instruct their disciples in morality and spiritual disciplines. For example, they might interpret a story such as the one presented in Behl's chapter in the subtle terms of the struggles and satisfactions of the soul's assent. But the stories were recounted in many other contexts as well, from the courtly palace to the military camp, at a saintly shrine, or at a mother's knee. As we have already noted, such writings were a form familiar across religious traditions. As the local version of the Persian *masnawi* developed, it became the model for such texts as the story of Lord Ram in the Awadhi *Ramcharitmanas* of Tulsidas (1532–1623), perhaps the most cherished poem of north Indian Hindus today.

Whether a simple mound, perhaps covered by a tinseled piece of cloth, or a great complex, like that of Shahul Hamid Nagore in Tamilnad (pictured in Figure I.2), South Asia is filled with the graves of the holy. As for Muslims in other lands, these sites in South Asia are places of resort for spiritual peace and material intercession. The saints are widely believed to continue alive in their graves, able to hear and to intercede for their devotees. In the course of the independence movement, a narrow nationalist ideology claimed that only Hindus recognized the soil of India as sacred. However, as the site of centuries of holy graves it was for Muslims more, not less, charismatic than for anyone else.

In Chapter 3, Catherine Asher presents texts relevant to the subcontinent's most important Sufi shrine, that of Mu'inuddin Chishti (d. 1236) at Ajmer. Mu'inuddin was the founder of a lineage centered in the subcontinent that produced key figures in the spiritual and political life of the sultanate rulers, among them Hazrat Qutbuddin Bakhtiyar Kaki, and Shaykh Nizamuddin Auliya, who are mentioned in the Preface.

The texts translated here give a sense of the great numbers of those who sought to honor the shrine through their devotion and patronage. Particularly interesting among the inscriptions are ones that make clear the extent to which the encomiums that focused on the saint and those directed toward an emperor were similar. Just as royal metaphors indicated the saint's power, saintly ones made clear, in a style that was familiar across Eurasia, the elevated status claimed by these early modern rulers.

At the opposite sociological extreme from the court are the women imagined as performing their household tasks in the devotional Dakhni poems translated by Richard Eaton in Chapter 4. By the mid-fourteenth century, the Bahmani rulers in the Deccan plateau had declared their independence from the Delhi rulers. Cultural life there flourished thanks to both reinvigorated ties to Arabs and Persians across the Indian Ocean and deeper roots into the local cultures, as the creation of Dakhni as a distinctive local language suggests. The Bahmani rulers continued the practice of close ties to Sufis, among them those associated with the Chishti lineage. One of these was Muhammad Gesudaraz (d. 1422), who was celebrated for his knowledge of hadith as well as for his engagement with the monistic ontological and theological issues of *wahdat al-wujud* in his writings, including his Persian poetry on the themes of mystical love. The concept of *wahdat al-wujud*, formulated by the Andalusian thinker, Ibn al-'Arabi (1165–1240), found rich elaboration in the Indian Subcontinent. An almost legendary figure, Gesudaraz was (erroneously) credited with one of the devotional Dakhni songs translated here. Even these verses engage the great theological issues debated in that era concerning divine transcendence and immanence.

Among the shrine-based practices that were particularly controversial was that of ecstatic music and singing at the Sufi shrines, which was conducted above all on the part of the Chishtis. Listening to such music could culminate in trance and ecstasy (*sama'*). Families of musicians, qawwals, have crossed over in modern times from the shrine to the stage, to recordings, and even film scores, and their modern renditions enjoy great popularity. Akbar Haidar and Carla Petievich provide an example of modern qawwali verse in Chapter 5, and Figure I.4 shows a photograph of the celebrated qawwals at the Chishti shrine in Ajmer. The celebration of a saint's death anniversary, the *'urs*, has also been a contested practice, but it remains vibrant nonetheless (consider for example, the early twentieth-century celebration described in Chapter 12).

In Chapter 6 Patrick Eisenlohr presents translations of *na't* songs that eulogize the Prophet, another popular form of devotional expression. These particular songs were produced by Mauritian performers trained by Indian and Pakistani imams residing in Mauritius, their source and medium guaranteeing their authenticity in both origin and performance style to their listeners. Their engagement with this music, moreover, aligns the participants with the modern Ahl-i Sunnat wa Jama'at or Barelwi sectarian denomination, which has a reach that extends beyond South Asia to populations of subcontinental Muslim origin abroad (see Chapter 12). A defining feature of this denomination is precisely its embrace of devotional practices related to the Prophet Muhammad, his descendants, and holy men. This entry is a particularly valuable reminder that while devotional songs may seem timeless, the role they play in people's lives and societies varies greatly. In this case, they at once cement a tie with "home" and assert a contested sectarian orientation.

Similarly controversial have been the many practices of Shi'a devotion to the imams, whose succession the Shi'a regard as properly embodying legitimacy following the death of the Prophet. In Chapter 7, Akbar Haidar and Carla Petievich translate mourning verses focused on the deaths of children during the great battle at Karbala in 680, when the third Imam and his band of followers were martyred. Commemoration of that event takes place during the mourning month of Muharram, which is marked by processions, reproductions of the standards and tombs of the martyrs, and compositions in a range of genres that recount and lament the tragic stories of the event. Reformers since the late eighteenth century have singled out Shi'a practices among a whole range of devotional practices as acts that compromise the "Unity of Allah" and the honor due to him alone (as the influential nineteenth-century text, the *Taqwiyyat al-Iman*, included in Chapter 15, illustrates).

It is often argued that the forms of Muslim devotional practices in South Asian Sufism, even the use of vernacular languages, were expedient means to lure "Hindus" to "Islam" or attempts by Muslims to disguise their differences from Hindus. Apart from the artificiality of such tightly bounded categories (which we explained in our Preface), Ali Asani rejects this idea on the grounds that the Isma'ilis, at the time that they ruled Egypt and had no need for subterfuge, similarly expressed themselves in local forms and metaphors. An explicit reason that polyglot authors embraced local languages for their devotional writings was the essentially literary one that languages like Avadhi were best for expressing ideas of beauty and longing. Arguments of expedience, such as the imputation of "liberalism" or "tolerance," project into the past contemporary concerns about Hindu-Muslim relations.

Thus devotional texts and practices persist, but changing contexts impute different meanings to them. In Pakistan, for example, Zulfiqar 'Ali Bhutto (Prime Minister from 1971 to 1977) invoked the antinomian Sufi folk tradition of his native Sindh in the face of Islamic criticism of his behavior. One of Pakistan's most popular rock bands, Junoon (Madness), similarly turned to Punjabi devotional poetry as an escape from Zia al-Haq's Islamicizing policies in the 1980s. They sing, for example, a spinning-wheel song by Shah Husayn (1538–1599) that is virtually identical to the one included in Chapter 4, which is attributed to a fifteenth-century Deccani saint (http://www.junoon.com/jeemography_files/lyrics_files/Parvaaz/Ghoom.htm). Junoon also sings a verse by Bulhe Shah (1680–1758) that recalls the words of Amir Khusraw in the Preface (e.g. http://www.youtube.com/watch?v=uBsD3pfLL8s):

> Bulleya, who am I?
> I am no believer in a mosque
> And I have no pagan ways
> I am not pure. I am not vile
> I'm no Moses and I'm no Pharaoh
> Bulleya, who am I?

The political/spiritual project of these songs, as well as their media of distribution, marks them as a part of our times, not their authors'.

To represent religious practices by the written word alone, as a volume like this one inevitably does, is especially limiting for these texts in Part I. The Web, including sites like YouTube, today allow us to hear the group repetitions of Sufi *zikr* (sometimes in settings like an *'urs*), devotional songs, the chanting of regional Sufi stories, and the mourning assemblies of the Shi'a. The sounds of practices described in other sections of the book are also available on the Web. One can readily find, for example the call to prayer (the *azan*)—a sound that many Muslims living in Europe and North America remember from their original homes with particular nostalgia— and the voices of preachers and guides. These bring to life the words on the printed pages that follow.

—— 1 ——

Satpanthi Ismaili Songs to Hazrat Ali
and the Imams

Ali S. Asani

Among the Muslim communities of South Asia, the Nizari Ismailis constitute a distinctive minority. As Shia Muslims, they believe that after the Prophet Muhammad authority over the Muslim community was inherited by imams who are direct descendants of the Prophet through his daughter Fatima and son-in-law Ali ibn Abi Talib (d. 661). Currently, they acknowledge Shah Karim al-Husseini, Aga Khan IV, as their forty-ninth Imam, or spiritual leader, on account of which they are sometimes referred to as Aga Khanis.

Residing predominantly in western India (Gujarat and Maharashtra) and in southern (Sind) and northern Pakistan, they have also settled in East Africa, Europe, and North America. The Nizari Ismailis and the Aga Khanis are well known in contemporary South Asia for their philanthropic activities and their prominence in the financial and commercial sectors. In the political sphere, the present Aga Khan's grandfather, Sir Sultan Muhammad Shah Aga Khan III (d. 1957), played a leadership role among Muslims in pre-Partition India and in the creation of Pakistan. In addition, he served for a short time as president of the League of Nations, the precursor to the United Nations. Muhammad Ali Jinnah, the founder of Pakistan, also has his ancestral roots in this community.

This chapter examines two literary genres of this small but influential Muslim community: the ginan (a hymn of wisdom, from the Sanskrit jnana) and the git (a song of praise). The ginans are attributed to one of several medieval preacher-poets, referred to as pirs and sayyids whom, traditions assert, Ismaili Imams, then living in Iran, sent to the subcontinent in order to propagate Ismaili doctrines from the tenth century onwards. In the process, they composed songs as a way of providing instruction on a variety of doctrinal, ethical, and mystical topics. Eventually, these songs crystallized into the corpus known as the ginans. Today, the corpus is "frozen," with the last ginans being those composed in the mid-nineteenth century by the female *sayyida*, Imam Begum. Although written several hundred years ago, ginans are recited daily in *jama'at khanas* (houses of congregation) wherever Nizari Ismailis from the subcontinent have settled. In contrast to the ginans, gits are songs composed by individual Ismailis to express their devotion to the imams and are usually sung during religious celebrations and festivals. They are a less formally constituted genre representing a "living" tradition of devotional expression.

Background

The strand of the Nizari Ismaili tradition primarily associated with the ginans and gits developed in the western regions of the subcontinent, specifically in Punjab, Sind, Gujarat, and Rajasthan. In this area, the pirs and sayyids preached their doctrines under the name *satpanth*, an Indic term meaning "the true path," rather than "Nizari Ismaili" or "Ismaili," both terms being conspicuously absent in their compositions. Historically, the Satpanthis, as they were known, came to be further divided into various caste-like subgroups such as the Khojas, Momans, Shamsis, Nijyapanthis (Nizarpanthis), and Imamshahis. Over the centuries, Satpanthis have defined and redefined their identities, beliefs, and practices. The most significant redefinition took place in the late nineteenth and early twentieth centuries when various Satpanthi groups realigned their religious and caste identities within the new frameworks prevalent in colonial and postcolonial South Asia. Today, most Khojas, for example, identify themselves as Nizari Ismaili Muslims, while those who broke away in the "reform" movements in the early twentieth century consider themselves to be Ithna Ashari (Twelver) Shia or even Sunni Muslims.

The central concern in the propagation of Satpanth was the expression of Nizari Ismaili beliefs and rituals within local religious and cultural frameworks. Wherever the Ismaili tradition has developed, it has engaged itself with the tools of various philosophical and religious systems as a means of articulating fundamental aspects of its theology. Consequently, the tradition has been remarkably adaptable to different religious and political environments. It is true that acculturation may have been a form of *taqiyya* (dissimulation of religious beliefs) traditionally used by Shia groups in order to avoid persecution. And yet, the impulse to acculturate seems to have been innate in the ethos of Ismaili tradition. Thus, in the ninth and tenth centuries, when Ismaili Imams ruled over the Fatimid Empire centered in Cairo, Ismaili philosophers drew on elements from the Gnostic, Neoplatonic, Manichean, and Zoroastrian traditions to formulate their conceptions of the imam.

Not surprisingly, in the subcontinent, the pirs and sayyids exhibited the same ethos when they presented the Satpanth tradition within the frameworks of a variety of indigenous religious and philosophical currents—such as the Bhakti, Sant, Sufi, and yogic traditions. The classic example of this formulation was the creation of an ostensible equivalence between the Vaishnava Hindu concept of *avatara* and the Ismaili concept of *imam*. Kalki, the messianic tenth incarnation (*dasa avatara*) of Vishnu, renamed in the Satpanth tradition as Nakalanki, "the stainless one," was identified with Ali, the first Shi'i Imam. The pirs represented themselves as guides who knew the whereabouts of the long awaited tenth *avatara* of Vishnu, meaning the Ismaili Imam, thus portraying their path as the culmination of the Vaishnavite Hindu tradition. In this manner, they were able to create a synthesis that was uniquely Satpanthi. Although drawing from seemingly disparate traditions, the worldview of the ginans is remarkably coherent. However, in contemporary South Asia religious identities have been so highly politicized and cultural differences between Hindus and Muslims so rigidly polarized that pluralistic doctrinal formulations such as those of Satpanth have been difficult, if not impossible, to sustain.

The Ginans: Hymns of Wisdom

The corpus of ginans consists of nearly one thousand compositions, of varying length, in a variety of languages indigenous to Punjab, Sind, and Gujarat. Employing local or folk poetic forms and meters, the ginans are meant to be sung in specific melodies or ragas. The ginans were composed during two periods: the first, from approximately the middle of the eleventh century to the end of the fifteenth century, is the period of the "great" pirs about whom there is, unfortunately, little reliable historical information; the second, the period of the sayyids, was initiated when the imam in Iran, Mustansir bi'llah II (d. 1480), designated a Persian book, the *Pandiyat-i Jawanmardi* (The counsels of chivalry) as a pir, rather than appointing a person. As a result, from the sixteenth to the nineteenth centuries, sayyids, respected as descendants of the family of the Prophet, guided Satpanth communities and continued the tradition of composing ginans.

Traditionally, many Nizari Ismailis have accorded the ginans a scriptural status, regarding them as conveying, in the vernacular, the inner meaning of the Arabic Qur'an. This understanding is reflected in their tendency, even today, to match ginan verses with Qur'anic ones. In this sense, the ginans play a role similar to that of "scriptural" vernacular poetic texts such as Rumi's *Masnavi* among Persian-speaking Muslims, or Shah 'Abdu'l Latif's *Risalo* and Bullhe Shah's poems among Sindhi and Punjabi speakers, respectively.

Singing ginans alongside the performance of prescribed ritual prayers is one of the principal forms of worship. Usually, a solo singer leads the singing with the congregation joining in so that the act of singing becomes a communal act of worship. A ginan recitation can evoke powerful emotions, particularly when there is a large congregation singing in unison. Indeed, community tradition records the redemption of one Ismail Gangji (d. 1883) of Junagadh, who on one occasion was so moved by this singing that he tearfully sought forgiveness of his sins. Frequently, entire ginans, or a selection of verses from specific ginans, are associated with particular rituals. Certain ginans are also designated for religious festivals such as the birthday of the Prophet Muhammad, of imams, and so on. Finally, ginanic verses are often used by preachers as proof texts in their sermons. Ginans also permeate the daily lives of individuals. They are quoted as proverbs and sung while performing domestic tasks in the style of the Dakhni songs translated in Chapter 4. Occasionally, they are recited in informal musical gatherings, called *ginan mehfils* or *ginan mushairas*. In recent decades, recordings of ginans by various artists have been widely circulated by means of cassettes, CDs, and even over the Internet.

Key Themes in the Ginans

The ginans translated below exemplify two key themes. First, the role of the imams and pirs as guides to the spiritual or the esoteric (*batin*). Satpanth, in common with most traditions of Islamic mysticism, seeks to foster the spiritual development of a disciple (*murid*) through control over the *nafs*, or ego self, a task best accomplished under the guidance and supervision of a spiritual preceptor (pir, *murshid*). The goal is to realize the ultimate experience for Muslim mystics—the "face to face meeting with God" or *didar*, "seeing the Divine." Many ginans emphasize a form of inward spirituality by employing vocabulary from contemporaneous Indian religious movements, particularly that of the Sants, a group of lower caste "poet-saints" who represented a powerful anti-ritual and anti-caste movement that swept across medieval India. Challenging the efficacy of ritualism and rote learning as paths to salvation, these ginans urge the faithful to adopt a righteous lifestyle and recognize the transitory nature of the world (*maya*) in which the soul is entrapped in endless cycles of rebirth. Mindless performance of religious rituals is of no use in liberating the soul. The only means of breaking these cycles is through regular repetition/remembrance (*sumiran*) of the Divine Name (*nam/shabd*), which is given to those who follow the True Path by the *Satguru*, the "True Guide," ambiguously identified in most ginans as either the pir or the imam. The ultimate goal of this inward meditation is enlightenment (*darshan*) in which one "sees," spiritually, the light (*nur*) of the imam who is frequently referred to as Ali, the historic person and a symbol of all the imams.

A second theme is the relationship between disciples and the imam, who is a repository of knowledge and the inheritor of a pre-eternal and cosmic light. These ginans draw on love symbolism from the Bhakti tradition, the movement of devotionalism that swept across North India at approximately the same time as the Sant movement. In particular, they utilize the central symbol used to express love and devotion in Bhakti poetry—the *virahini*, the woman longing for her beloved, best exemplified by Radha and the *gopis* (cowmaids) in their yearning for Krishna. In the ginans, the *virahini* becomes symbolic of the human soul who is experiencing *viraha* (painful longing) for the Beloved, almost always identified as the imam. As a result, ginans often portray the believer as a *virahini* employing the feminine voice, although their authors are predominantly male. Some ginans mention a promise (*kol*) of love between the female bride-soul and the imam, represented as the promise of marriage and marital bliss (*suhag*). This may, in fact, be an allusion to the primordial covenant of love between creation and God that is so central to Sufi love mysticism. Notwithstanding the highly evocative language of unfulfilled love and waiting, the ginans emphasize that the True Beloved can only be found after searching within the depths of one's own soul.

SELECTIONS FROM *SALOKO NANO*

FROM THE SECTIONS ON LOVE, FAITH, THE BELIEVER, AND WORSHIP, ATTRIBUTED
TO PIR SADR AD-DIN (LATE FOURTEENTH–EARLY FIFTEENTH C.); IN HINDI/GUJARATI

The True Guide proclaims:
When true faith is manifest in a heart, all negligence is dispelled;
What room is there for the darkness [of ignorance] where the light of
    the True Master radiates?

The True Guide proclaims:
Construct a boat from the name of Ali and fill it with Truth.
When the winds of Love blow, the True Master will surely guide it to
    the shore of salvation.

The True Guide proclaims:
Color yourself with the pigment of Truth; just like *patola* silk,
Which may fall to tatters, yet its color remains steadfast.

The True Guide proclaims:
Place your hope in the Truth; adorn yourself with the Truth;
Apply the collyrium (*kajal*) of Love to your eyes, let the Beloved be the
    garland around your neck.

The True Guide proclaims:
The entire world appears to be poor, no one seems wealthy;
Wealthy, indeed, is one who is in love with the Beloved.

The True Guide proclaims:
Distance yourself from the seemingly enchanting world, keeping your
    soul away from its delusion and allure;
If you surrender your life to Love; you will find the Beloved.

The True Guide proclaims:
When love rises on the horizon, one feels its wounds;
When the sickness of love takes hold, no sleep comes to the eyes.

The True Guide proclaims:
Love does not grow in a garden nor is it sold in a store;
Love grows in the heart; a heart consumed by intense yearning [for the
    Beloved].

The True Guide proclaims:
Whosoever has tasted the nectar of Ali, will never turn away from it;
Whosoever dies a death of Love drinks the nectar of Love.

The True Guide proclaims:
"Beloved! Beloved!" all cry out, but none finds the Beloved.

If the Beloved were to be found simply by uttering His name, what need would there be to sacrifice one's self [*literally*, what need would there be for bargaining with heads?].

The True Guide proclaims:
If you want to sacrifice your self (ego), then stay awake (in meditation) at night;
If you dedicate your life to remembrance [of Him], then the true Creator will be with you.

The True Guide proclaims:
"Beloved! Beloved!" all creatures cry out, but none finds the Beloved.
If the Beloved were to be found by simply repeating His name with the tongue, then the heron would become a swan.

The True Guide proclaims:
The heron and the swan are clearly different although they may seem alike;
But the heron eats whatever it fancies, while the swan feeds on pearls.

The True Guide proclaims:
Glass and gems are clearly different; only testing reveals their true value.
Dealing in glass accumulates only poison; through gems comes enlightenment.

The True Guide proclaims:
Those without and with a guide are clearly different; although outwardly they may appear to be alike;
Those without a Guide lust for wealth; those with a Guide desire only His name.

"FROM HIS LIGHT HE CREATED THE EARTH"

ATTRIBUTED TO PIR HASSAN SHAH (D. 1470); IN GUJARATI

From His Light He created the earth and the heavens, suspended without any support.

He revealed His power, manifest in the imam (leader) of the faith.

Follow the path of the Five Holy Persons [Muhammad, Ali, Fatima, Hasan, Husayn] and have faith in the True Path (Satpanth).

Believers, abide by the Truth and follow the Truth; keep your attention firmly on the True Path (Satpanth).

O careless one! Beware of the material world; you will not be misled if
   you follow the straight Path.

Countless foolish and helpless souls have blindly wasted their lives.

Pir Hasan Shah has recited this hymn of wisdom (ginan).
Friends! Whoever seeks the Lord, finds Him.

"YOU COME FROM AN EXALTED PLACE"

ATTRIBUTED TO PIR SHAMS (LATE THIRTEENTH–EARLY FOURTEENTH C.);
IN HINDI-GUJARATI

You come from a highly exalted place; why then do you pay attention
   to the low?
Your stay in the world is as short as four days, why then do you accrue
   falsehood?
What do you gain from sin?

Refrain:
Do not be misled by the illusionary world;
Walk the path of humility for, in the end, you have to die.
Seek the intercession of the Messenger, the intercession of the
   Prophet.
Fear evil, fear falsehood.
Do not be misled by the illusionary world.
Walk the path of humility, for in the end, you have to die.

Born naked into the world, you will be covered with cloth [when
   you die].
What you earn in one moment, why do you squander in the next?
Why do you sin and abandon the true faith?

Do not be misled by the illusionary world . . .

Those who abandon the true faith are ensnared by deceit;
They stray from the true path and stand with sinners.
Following their egotistical desires, they cast their lives into hell.

Do not be misled by the illusionary world . . .

Only the few who are brave and courageous follow this path
That Prophet Muhammad has shown;
Pir Shams teaches true knowledge.

Do not be misled by the illusionary world . . .

"KNOW YOUR [TRUE] SELVES"

ATTRIBUTED TO PIR IMAM AD-DIN (D. 1531); IN HINDI/GUJARATI. THE TITLE
IS AN ALLUSION TO THE SAYING OF THE PROPHET MUHAMMAD:
"HE WHO KNOWS HIMSELF, KNOWS HIS LORD."

Know your [true] selves, O believers, by meditating on the name
(*naam*) of the Lord.

Keep away from the five vices [lust, anger, greed, temptation, and pride]
by forsaking the ego; focus your heart only on "except God" [a phrase
from the *shahadah*].

The believers who have found the [path of] Truth and righteousness,
they have earned the reward of their virtuous acts.

The believers who have dissolved themselves in righteousness, they
have merged within the Light as light.

Those who are so united have become eternal; they have found within
themselves the splendor of the Lord.

Pay heed: [For the sake of] love of the world, why do you devote your
life to such [lowly] purposes?

Those who are attached to greed, desire, and temptation; they have gone
astray from the path of faith.

Believers! Those who are ensnared in obeying their egos, they will be
burnt between the armies of temptation.

O believer in the Five Persons [Muhammad, Ali, Fatima, Hasan,
Husayn]! One who does not share his wealth, he has wasted his life
in a false business.

Know that [giving] one-fortieth [of income to the pir] is an obligation;
escape from the trap of the world.

O believers! If you do not recognize the Perfect Guide, you will wander
blindly in the world.

When you recognize Him within your inner self, your heart will shine
as pure as the moon.

Obey the Guide with an attentive mind, [then you will realize that] the
Lord is ever-present in your heart.

Pir Imam ad-din says: "O righteous ones listen to these words; the Light
is to be found in the interior cavity behind the eyebrows" [a yogic site
of energy; a focus for Satpanthi meditation leading to vision of the
light of the imam].

"O FRIEND, THE SAVIOR OF MY SOUL"

ATTRIBUTED TO PIR SADR AL-DIN (LATE FOURTEENTH–EARLY FIFTEENTH C.);
IN GUJARATI

> O friend, the savior of my soul,
> Do not abandon me and stay apart from me.
> I have built such a beautifully decorated house for you,
> Come and reside in it.
>
> O friend, I have prepared for you a bed of incomparable beauty;
> Return (to rest) on this bed.
> (Lying) next to the Beloved, overwhelmed by love,
> I forget all of my sorrows.
>
> O friend, the bed-swing sways back and forth,
> With [the rhythm of] my every breath.
> What ecstasy is aroused in the body,
> When I am with the Beloved.
>
> O friend, to whom can I describe
> The pangs of separation (*viraha*) from the Beloved?
> [Perhaps if] I were to meet a wise sage
> He would understand.
>
> O friend, the Creator of the creation
> Is the One who has saved me.
> Pir Sadr ad-Din, grasping me by the hand,
> Takes me across the ocean (to salvation).

"HOW TIRED ARE MY EYES FROM WAITING EXPECTANTLY"

ATTRIBUTED TO PIR FAZAL SHAH (D. 1659); IN GUJARATI

> How tired are my eyes from waiting expectantly:
> When will my Lord come?
> So that knowing Him to be present before me, I may touch his feet.
> Beloved, bowing humbly, I will greet you.
>
> Sweet Lord, I remember your name,
> O Lord, I remember your name,
> O Master, I remember your name.
>
> My Master, I have been in love with you since childhood;
> I am in love with the Lord of the Light.
> How can the ignorant possibly understand this?

Sweet Lord, I remember your name,
O Lord, I remember your name,
O Master, I remember your name.

Pir Fazal Shah humbly pleads:
O Merciful One, have mercy on me!
Only your mercy will redeem my honor!
I, your slave, am sinful; You are the Savior.

Sweet Lord, I remember your name,
O Lord, I remember your name,
O Master, I remember your name

Gits: Songs of Praise

Gits represent a vibrant tradition of literature among Nizari Ismaili communities of South Asian origin. They are the principal literary form through which the individual believer can express religious devotion in a personal voice. At the same time, they permit those who listen to them to participate in this devotion. The historical origins of gits are obscure, but it would be reasonable to assume that this important tradition dates back several centuries. Today, cassettes and CDs of gits are common and seem to be particularly appealing to the younger generation, as their lilting lyrics, rhythmic melodies, and musical instrumentation reflect contemporary cultures and tastes. More importantly, since most gits are written in modern vernaculars, their lyrics are more comprehensible to contemporary audiences than those of the ginans, which often employ grammatical forms and vocabulary from various medieval dialects.

Both men and women have been actively engaged in composing and singing gits. The majority of them are neither professional musicians nor songwriters, although in several cases involvement with the git tradition is a family affair. Alongside individual composers, various community institutions have been active in promoting the git tradition by sponsoring performances and recordings both of talented "star" singers and of community-based groups.

Traditionally, gits commemorate festive events such as Imamat Day (the anniversary of the imam's accession) or the birthday of the imam, or they may celebrate the imam's official visits to followers in particular countries. In 1982/3 dozens of gits were composed during the Silver Jubilee of Karim al-Husayni, Aga Khan IV's reign as imam. Gits have also been recited on general Muslim festivals such as the two Muslim 'ids. In addition to such celebrations, gits are also sung in special musical concerts, called git mehfils or mushairas. Frequently, gits are composed to accompany the performance of dances popular in the community, such as the traditional Gujarati dandiya (stick dance), raas, and garba. More recent innovations include gits with a fast-paced tempo for use during "disco" dandiyas.

In terms of their formal structures, gits draw on a variety of eclectic sources: the folk traditions of Gujarat and Sind, particularly the Gujarati *garbi* and *raas*; Bollywood songs from India's popular cinema industry; *bhajans*, or devotional songs attributed to poets associated with the Bhakti and Sant traditions; and genres of Urdu poetry, in particular the *ghazal*. Hindi, Urdu, Gujarati, and Sindhi predominate as major languages. Occasionally, entire Arabic phrases, usually from the Qur'an or having some theological import (such as the *salwat*, the formulaic blessing on the Prophet Muhammad and his family) are also incorporated to create bilingual gits. Among Nizari Ismaili communities in East Africa, gits have also been composed in Swahili.

The relationship between the imam and his followers forms a central theme within the gits. According to Ismaili teachings, an individual believer's progress on the path of spiritual development is possible only by means of the relationship that exists between the inner reality of the believer and the spiritual reality of the imam as the locus of divine light (*nur*). As keeper of the mysteries of the *batin* (the esoteric), the imam becomes not only the guide but also the object of the spiritual quest for the attainment of the spiritual vision (*didar*) and union for which the believer yearns. The gits depict this relationship in a variety of ways, depending on the temperament of the poet. One of the most interesting and intriguing portrayals of this relationship takes place within the complex of images associated with the *virahini*, a loving and yearning woman tormented by the absence of her beloved or her husband. As we have seen above, the *virahini*, who enjoys great popularity in a wide variety of South Asian religious traditions, is conspicuous in the ginans as well. That she should appear in gits devoted to the imam, the longed-for Beloved, hardly comes as a surprise, for such usage is entirely in keeping with Indic literary conventions according to which the human soul is always represented as feminine before the Divine.

The gits translated below contain a kaleidoscope of images associated with the typical *virahini*. To stress the humility of the disciple before the spiritual guide, the *virahini* is represented as a simple village woman who is afflicted by the fiery pangs of yearning for the beloved imam. She is convinced that out of love for her, the Beloved will overlook her inferior social status, as well as her numerous faults, and will visit her humble abode. To tempt him, she offers him the best hospitality that someone of her status can provide, proposing that she prepare for him freshly cooked bread and other delicacies. She thirsts and pines for even a single glance from her elusive Beloved, calling out to her girlfriends for help as she searches desperately for him. Highlighting her longing is the use of rain imagery, for in Indian literary traditions the season of rain is the season for lovers, always involving the theme of *viraha*, or love in separation, and the yearnings of the *virahini*. Her happiness in anticipating the coming of the imam is shared by creation: the birds, the flowers, and even the rivers rejoice. The heavens, too, join in celebrating this event as the moon smiles radiantly in the sky. Notwithstanding the imagery borrowed from the realm of yearning human love and nature, the poet is aware that the relationship with the imam is a spiritual one. Thus, the *virahini*, though searching outwardly, realizes that the real search has to be an inner one, within the depths of her heart, which is where the Beloved truly resides.

The gits translated below were composed by the prominent git writer, Hassanali Rammal (d. 1990), under the pen name Suman. Born in Karachi in 1906, Suman composed over one hundred and thirty gits in Gujarati, Sindhi, and Urdu/Hindi, some of which were published in 1970 in a book titled *Suman Sangrah*. His compositions have been sung by prominent singers, including the famous Khursheed Noor Ali (Bhaloo), originally of Karachi but now living in Vancouver. Through a proliferation of recordings, the most famous being *Prem Sandesh* (A Message of Love), Suman's songs have become popular among Nizari Ismailis worldwide, particularly those living in the United Kingdom and North America. Suman was a versatile and talented writer, contributing articles and poems to a variety of periodicals and newspapers. In addition, he was a playwright for two drama clubs in the Ismaili community in Karachi. A member of the Theosophical Society in Karachi, he composed songs in praise of Krishna, the Buddha, Zoroaster, and the founder of the society, Madame Blavatsky, which were regularly sung at the society's meetings. Clearly a talented individual with a cosmopolitan outlook, he was particularly well versed in Bhakti and Sufi devotional poetry in various vernacular languages, a familiarity that is readily apparent in the pluralist ethos of his compositions.

"WON'T YOU COME TO MY LITTLE VILLAGE JUST ONCE, O OUR LORD!"

IN GUJARATI

Won't you come to my little village just once, O our Lord!
Come, O beloved Karim Shah;
O star of our eyes, the *jamats* await expectantly for you to bestow *didar*
  [the ultimate goal of Ismaili mysticism is enlightenment in which one
  "sees" (*didar*) spiritually the light (*nur*)].
Come, O beloved Karim Shah.

Come, so that I can give you cupfuls of milk to drink,
And serve you warm delicious *rotla* [flat bread] with butter,
And dishes drippingly rich in *ghee* [clarified butter],
And sumptuous sweet juicy fruits.
We are simple and naive village folk;
But we will host you heart and soul.

Gathering extraordinarily fragrant jasmines and red roses,
I weave a garland for you;
With the deepest sentiments of devotion in my heart,
I place it around the neck of our beloved imam,

O Bestower of blessings,
The light of everyone's eyes.

My eyes gaze expectantly waiting for my Master,
And with the light of knowledge, I awaken my soul;
In my heart I spread a bed adorned with "Suman" [flowers]
And lay my beloved Karim lovingly to sleep.
Deflect all our sorrows,
    O knower of the secrets of the heart!
    Oh, where should I look for you, O beloved?

You are the Prophet's progeny and beloved of Ali;
Whenever I have asked a question, I have never returned
    empty-handed.
Oh, where should I look for you, O beloved,
Karim Shah, my beloved?

Into which lane has beloved Karim Shah gone,
O girlfriend, won't you please tell me?
I have searched the heavens and under the earth.
Truly, he resides in the believer's heart.
Oh where . . .

To behold the day of the Silver Jubilee
My eyes are thirsting.
My heart pines, O beloved,
Won't you show me that sweet sight?
Oh where . . .

Your place is in these eyes,
Your name pulsates in my heartbeats.
"Suman" thirsts for a glimpse of your face,
So that the heart dances in rapture.
Oh where . . .

"GENTLY IT RAINS"

IN GUJARATI

O friend, here comes the colorful cloud of the rainy season; gently it
    rains. Yes, friend, thunder roars, lightning flashes, and gently it rains.
O friend, listen to the gushing of rivers, gurgling of streams, and the
    chattering of countless birds.
Friend, the lakes are overflowing; the earth is soaked; all creation is
    beautifully adorned.

O friend, this is not an ordinary stream of rain, rather the gates of
heavenly blessings have opened, and gently it rains.

O friend, the Jubilee has come to our front yard with anklet bells
jingling, our hearts are filled with boundless happiness.
O friend, let's welcome beloved Karim Shah with a shower of flowers:
he is our support.
O friend, let's celebrate this occasion with heart's love, and gently it
rains.
O friend, everywhere there is lush greenery with an exuberance of
nectar-laden flowers, "Suman" blossoming in the garden.
O friend, with the colorful rainy season and the company of friends,
spring enters my life.
O friend, with delicious waves every part of my body sways, and gently
it rains.

"IN THE TOWN SQUARE OF THE SKY, THE MOON IS SMILING"

IN GUJARATI

Spring has blossomed fragrant with the sweet scent of flowers;
With eyes anxiously searching the path by which Shah Karim will arrive,
The moon is smiling, O girlfriend, the moon is smiling.
In the town square of the sky, the moon is smiling.

The Shah has arrived at our front yard.
Let us lovingly welcome him with flowers on this occasion.
I have strung flowers onto every thread of my heart.
Oh, girlfriend, what a sweet and delightful fragrance comes forth!
In the town square . . .

O king bird, do tell us the tale of the heavens:
How is the celebration up there? Is it magnificent?
Surely much more glorious than on the earth:
Full of grandeur are the festivities in paradise.
    In the town square . . .

Bravo, bravo, O Ismaili! Bravo to your love.
Magnificent is your heart; awe-inspiring are your sentiments.
    Due to your beloved, the sitar of love plays;
And the entire universe is dazzled.

How delightful are these bonds of love.
"Suman," the wasps are bowing before the nightingales.
Wherever you step, I would spread my eyes for you to walk upon.
The Shah's brilliance radiates from every step.

Sources

Ginans

Saloko Nano, Saloko Moto (Nairobi, Kenya: H.H. The Aga Khan Shia Imami Ismailia Association for Kenya, n.d.), pp. 4–9; *Ginan-e-Sharif: Our Wonderful Tradition* (Vancouver: The Shia Imami Ismaili Tariqah and Religious Education Board for Canada, n.d.) 2, pp.10–11, 100; *Ginan-e-Sharif: Our Wonderful Tradition* (Vancouver: H.H. The Aga Khan Shia Imami Ismailia Association for Canada, 1977), pp. 88–89; *Ginan-e-Sharif: bhag pahelo, 105 ginans*, 1st rev.ed. (Bombay, 1978), p. 109; *Pachas ginan, bhag bijo* (Bombay: Ismailia Association for India, 1980), pp. 5–6.

Gits

Suman Sangrah (Karachi,1970).

Further Reading

For an account of the history of the pirs and sayyids, see Azim Nanji, *The Nizari Ismaili Tradition in Hind and Sind* (Delmar, NY: Caravan Press, 1978) and Wladmir Ivanow, "Satpanth (Indian Ismailism)," in W. Ivanow, ed., *Collectanea* 1 (Leiden: E. J. Brill, 1948). For the evolution of the identity of Khojahs and other Satpanthi groups in the late nineteenth and twentieth centuries, see Ali S. Asani, "The Khojahs of South Asia: Defining a Space of Their Own," *Cultural Dynamics* 13 (2001): 155–168; and Dominique Sila Khan, *Conversions and Shifting Identities: Ramdev Pir and the Ismailis in Rajasthan* (New Delhi: Manohar, 1997). Detailed studies of the corpus of the ginan literature include: Ali Asani, *Ecstasy and Enlightenment: The Ismaili Devotional Literatures of South Asia* (London: I. B. Tauris, 2002); Christopher Shackle and Zawahir Moir, *Ismaili Hymns from South Asia: An Introduction to the Ginans* (London: School for Oriental and African Studies, University of London, 1992); and Tazim Kassam, *Songs of Wisdom and Circles of Dance: Hymns of the Satpanthi Ismaili Muslim Saint, Pir Shams* (Albany, NY: State University of New York Press, 1995).

2

The Soul's Quest in
Malik Muhammad Jayasi's
Hindavi Romance

Aditya Behl

Not much is known about the life of Malik Muhammad Jayasi (*fl.* 1540), the poet of the *Padmavat*, except that he was a practicing Sufi attached to both the Chishti and Mahdavi lineages. The verse romance that has assured his enduring fame is the *Padmavat*, a quest narrative written in eastern Hindavi or Avadhi in the first half of the sixteenth century. The *Padmavat* is the premier text of the genre of the Hindavi Sufi romance, an Indian Islamic literary tradition created in the late fourteenth century in the eastern part of the Ganga-Jamuna *doab*. The poets of these romances drew on the model of Persian verse romances (*masnavi*), most notably in prefacing their works with elaborate prologues in praise of Allah, the Prophet Muhammad, and their political patrons and spiritual guides. They also drew on local languages of asceticism and devotion, drawing symbolism and imagery from Gorakhnathi yogis and worshippers of Krishna. These Sufi poets produced a sophisticated Indian Islamic literary tradition, employing a set of *desi* (indigenous) literary and religious terms and a romantic narrative universe to express their distinctive spiritual agenda in the local landscape of Avadh and Bihar.

The first poets of these romances, the Chishti Sufis, were powerful figures in the cultural and religious life of the Delhi Sultanate. At the core of their mystical activity and contemplation was the transcendental monotheism of belief in Allah, the invisible center, cause, and creator of the visible world. In order to achieve closeness to Allah, the Chishtis aimed at transforming themselves through ascetic practice, which involved a hard regimen of spiritual exercises, fasting, and extra prayers performed at night. They tried to resolve the intractable dilemma posed by a transcendental godhead within a material world. Since this strictly monotheistic, invisible God created the physical, sensible world and yet was apart from the world, how could a seeker have access to divine presence? The objective of Sufi asceticism was to open the seeker up to the invisible yet powerful world of divine presence, watched over by invisible agents of Allah and by Sufi *shaykhs* who were "friends of God." Ultimately, the novice had to transform himself into a devoted lover of Allah, spending his life in mystical absorption trying to understand the secrets of the invisible world that lay behind ordinary physical reality.

In conjunction with this emphasis on self-mortification, the discourses of the Chishti *shaykhs* frequently used exceedingly erotic language and imagery. Eroticism was understood as embedded within the ladder of transformation that links *majazi* (worldly love) with *haqiqi* (spiritual love). On this ladder each object of desire is loved for the sake of the one higher than itself, all the way up to Allah. The Hindavi romances were sung aloud in evening gatherings or courtly assemblies, but most ideally in Sufi hospices and shrines. Here the novice was exposed to poetry and music with the aim of opening up his consciousness and directing it towards God, thus initiating his own inner journey. The Sufis were operating in a landscape marked by multiple competing spiritual agendas and technologies of the self. Preeminent among these was the path followed by the yogis of the legendary guru Gorakhnath, with whom the Sufis vied for control over sacred sites while borrowing many of their ascetic practices. In the Sufi romances, the seeker has always to assume the guise of a yogi to attain the divine Beloved, the object of his quest. The Sufis also appropriate the Sanskritic language of *bhava* (emotion) and *rasa* (the juice or essence of aesthetic and devotional experience), and use it to frame their own mystical instruction. The absence of a stated allegorical principle in the romances is directly related to the presence of a teaching *shaykh* who could explicate the secret clues in these romances to guide the spiritual quests of his disciples. This was, however, a private exercise, and in public the romances were performed to great acclaim as entertaining and lushly erotic love stories.

The passage translated here is from the opening pages of the *Padmavat*, in which the poet Jayasi sets the scene for the seeker's internal quest. He describes the paradise-like island Singhala-dipa, the home of the Princess Padmavati. Singhala is not to be confused with the actual island of Sri Lanka, but is rather an imaginary landscape on which the seeker's inner journey is played out. This landscape conceals many levels of signification, and Jayasi uses symbols and coded vocabulary to suggest that the hero Ratansen's progress is also the interior progress of a Sufi along the ascetic path. The ultimate goal is imagined as a city within this paradise. The seeker will have to traverse many stages of this interior landscape before he can conquer the fortress of Singhala, his own subtle or spiritual body. This is the paradise within, an imaginary landscape that transcreates in Hindavi poetic terms the Qur'anic notion of paradise as a garden. Here the supernatural plane of divinity in its mysterious, pre-manifest state intersects with the physical plane of a lush Indian garden with lakes, mango orchards, sandalwood trees, and beautiful pavilions set among colorful flowerbeds.

Jayasi recasts into Hindavi the charming and widespread Sufi convention that the birds of the world praise their Creator in their different tongues. Each bird has its own way of praising Allah, and Jayasi uses Indian birds and their special calls. Peacocks and cuckoos, whose calls ordinarily signify the monsoons and the summer, join a chorus of birds proclaiming the message of Islamic monotheism. Jayasi goes on to place within his imaginary Sufi landscape a full range of Indian seekers—including devotees of Rama, worshippers of Siva, and naked Jains—making it clear that the Chishti Sufis are one among a range of competitors. All of them come to the Sufi Singhala-dipa in order to pray and to mortify themselves at its holy sites, hoping to gain salvation at its fords and step-wells. Jayasi represents the spiritual center of Singhala as a holy lake, the Manasarodaka or Manasarovara. In Indian poetic convention, the Manasa lake near Siva's mountain home Kailasa (*Hind.* Kabilasa) is the true home of the soul, imagined as a migratory *hamsa* bird or goose. However, the Manasarovara is also an internal station in the yogic body, just below the tenth door or *dasama dvara* (the tenth door or secret opening, a place to which we shall return). The geese playing on the lake, suggesting human souls in paradise, are "pictures etched in gold" among the crimson lotuses. The flowering lotuses have a thousand petals, a reference to the thousand-petalled lotus (*sahasra-dala kamala*) of the yogic body, where the ascetic can taste the rain of nectar through the control and redirection of spiritual energies. The blossoming of this lotus allows the practitioner to cross through into the world within, the primordial egg (*brahmanda*) from which creation sprang.

Jayasi's spatialization of the subtle body in the technical language of yoga creates the effect of the internalization of vision through the tropes of a built and embodied landscape. He uses the figure of the body as a city with nine gates, a reference to the nine openings of the body: the mouth, eyes, ears, nostrils, and the organs of excretion and reproduction. The tenth door is the secret opening (*brahma-randhra*) between and above the eyes in the subtle body, through which the practitioner can enter the microcosmic universe within. Jayasi's description of the nine-storied city of Singhala is both a description of the subtle body and of a lofty fortress. The five captains suggest the five senses that guard the body. The four days suggest, obliquely, the four stages of the Sufi path: *shari'at* (following the law), *tariqat* (the Sufi way), *ma'rifat* (gnosis), and *haqiqat* (realizing the truth). Alternatively, they could be a reference to the four states of existence: *nasut* (the human world), *malakut* (the angelic world), *jabarut* (the heavenly realm), and *lahut* (absolute divinity).

Jayasi uses also the symbol of the royal water-clock or clepsydra that marks time for the fort/body. In yogic texts, the clock marks the unstruck or mystic sound within. Jayasi turns the symbol to issue a stern warning to his heedless listeners to wake up to the reality of time passing and to turn towards God. He employs here his given name, Muhammad, as a poetic name, and the image of the waterwheel to mark the finitude of life. The next verse refers ambiguously to two rivers of milk and water that flow in the fort. At the center of the garden of paradise in the Qur'an flow rivers of milk, water, wine, and honey. The lake of crushed pearls suggests the *amrita-kunda,* or pool of nectar, that is located between the eyes in the symbolic geography of the yogic body. If the body is a fort, its king is the soul (*ruh*), and he can be transformed through the appropriate spiritual practices and drink the water of immortality. In Jayasi's text, the king is well established in his city, with vassals who are lords of horses, elephants, forts, and men. The interlinear Persian gloss of an important early manuscript interprets these as the equivalents of the four chief Islamic angels: Jibril, Mika'il, Israfil, and Azra'il. Jayasi uses this vision of orderly rule in his own symbolic geography of the body, adding elements to the basic image of the body as city to create his interior landscape of the isle of paradise.

At the holy lake, the Manasarodaka, flowers a golden tree. The celestial tree suggests the Qur'anic *sidrat al-muntaha,* or lote-tree, of the furthest extremity, the magical tree that is radiant with Allah's light and is the point of demarcation between the manifest world and the unseen. The tree is here translated into Hindavi as the *kalpataru* or wishing-tree of Indra's heaven, where the creeper of immortality (*amarabeli*) grows. Depending on the audience, this polysemous poetic symbol can be understood either as Indra's wishing-tree or as the Islamic lote-tree. Jayasi's adaptation of elements from Gorakhnathi notions of the subtle body, from the Qur'anic idea of paradise, and from Indian mythologies of heaven are all fitted into the framework of a Sufi ascetic body which has its own logic of transformation into immortality. It is on this landscape that the Sufi seeker has to undertake his quest. The landscape of paradise that is poetically described here can refer simultaneously to Singhala, a fabled island; to the Qur'anic idea of heaven; and to the interior geography of the symbolic body, Jayasi's distinctive embodied city.

King Ratnasena, the hero of the story, sets out for this island in the guise of a yogi and conquers the seven levels of the embodied city. After joining with Padmavati, the divine princess, in mystical union, he brings her back home to his native city of Chittaur. Here lives Nagmati, Ratnasena's first wife, who is intensely jealous of Padmavati. The two wives fight, but Ratnasena manages to make peace between them. In the narrative code of the genre, this signifies the seeker's need to balance spiritual and material aspects of existence. To this elaborate articulation of the formulaic narrative pattern of the genre, Jayasi adds a concluding section containing an account of the siege and capture of Chittaur by wicked Sultan 'Alauddin Khalji, the ruler of Delhi. The sultan lusts after the beautiful Padmavati, and captures her husband by treachery. When the King escapes, aided by his loyal warriors, the sultan launches his mighty army against Chittaur. Despite a heroic last stand by the Rajputs, the fortress falls and the women of the city commit suicide by throwing themselves on a flaming pyre (*jauhar*). This fictive motif, which here encodes a pacifist critique of the violence attendant on the Islamic conquest of north India, has ironically become a commonplace of Hindu nationalist thinking about the premodern period. In Jayasi's romance, the *jauhar* of Padmavati signifies the inability of violence and brutality to capture the true spiritual essence that was first incarnate on the fabled isle of Singhala.

"THE ISLE OF SINGHALA"

FROM THE *PADMAVAT*

And if anyone ever comes to that isle,
it is as if he enters Paradise: on every side
are planted thick mango groves,
rising from the earth to meet the sky.
Everywhere there are fragrant sandalwood trees,
world-shadowing, they make day into night.
Scented breezes blow in their pleasant shade,
and even the hot month of Jeth feels wintry.
Their dark shade is so much like night
that the blue sky seems green under them.
When a traveler comes there, faint from sun,
he forgets his troubles, rests at ease.
Whoever finds this matchless shade,
never goes out to face the sun's rays.
    Such dense mango groves lie there that I cannot describe where they
      end.
    They blossom and bear fruit through the six seasons, as if in eternal
      spring. [27]

Mango trees bore fruit, dense and pleasant.
As they grew heavier, they bowed their heads.
Jackfruit trees ripened from branch to bole.
The yellow *badahal* fruit looked matchless.
Khirni berries matured, sweet as cane sugar.
Rose-apples clustered together, looking like black bees.
Coconuts grew full, and the *khurhuri* figs were as ripe
as if they had sprung forth in Indra's heavenly city.
And the *mahua* tree dripped yet sweeter liquor,
luscious as honey, scented as with flowers.
And many other edibles, hard to name,
could be seen in these lovely orchards.
All hung on branches, sweet as nectar.
Whoever tasted them remained enchanted.
    Areca and betel-nut and nutmeg, all these fruits abounded there in
      plenty.
    All around the tamarind grew thick, and dense the palmyra and
      date-palm. [28]

Birds dwell there, singing in many tongues,
exulting at the sight of those branches.

At dawn, the honey-suckers draw the scent
from the flowers, and the doves cry out,
"One alone, only You." The mynahs
and parrots play about chirping.
Pigeons also create a tumult.
"My love, my love!" cries the *papiha*,
and the warbler sings, "Just You, just You!"
The cuckoo coos, "Ku-hu, ku-hu!"
The drongo calls out in many tongues.
"I burn, I burn!" says the *mahari*.
The green pigeon, plaintive, cries his woe.
The peacocks shrill pleasantly,
and crows caw, creating a tumult.
    As many birds as I have named, all sit in the mango orchard.
    Each in its own tongue sings the praises of the supreme Lord. [29]

At every step, there are wells and step-wells,
adorned with seats and broad steps.
Everywhere there are lakes and pools,
all holy, and named after the fords of pilgrimage.
In four directions are temples and pavilions built fine.
Holy men and ascetics all sit there in meditation.
Some are great sages, some are renunciants.
Some focus on Rama, others follow their vow
for a month at a time. Some stay celibate,
others are Digambaras, who remain naked.
Some are accomplished adepts, others *jogis*.
Those disappointed in love focus there on God.
Saivas and wanderers and mendicants are there,
and those who try the rites of the Goddess.
    White-clad *sadhus*, Jains, and forest-dwellers, adepts, seekers, and
        *avadhuta*s,
    all sit there in meditation, searing body and soul with austerities. [30]

How can one look at Manasarodaka, the holy lake?
It is fuller than the ocean, and fathomless.
Its water is pure and lustrous as pearls,
nectar-like, scented with camphor.
They brought lapis lazuli from the isle of Lanka
to make the broad *ghats* around the lake,
and set winding stairs on all its sides
for people to climb up and down.
Crimson lotuses flower there,
and each bloom has a thousand petals.
When a shell opens up to yield a pearl,

beautiful geese peck it up and play,
golden birds swimming on the water,
like pictures etched in gold.
   On all four sides are high banks, where every tree bears ambrosial
      fruit.
   Whoever sees the beauty of that lake, feels no hunger, nor thirst. [31]

The women are coming to draw water.
Each one is lovely, a Padmini or lotus-woman.
Their limbs exude the scent of lotuses.
Bees cling to them and follow them about
With waists like lionesses, doe-eyed,
they glide like geese and sing like cuckoos.
They walk in a group, arrayed in ranks,
their varying gaits delighting the eye.
Storm-cloud tresses fall from head to foot,
and white teeth flash like lightning.
Their breasts are golden pitchers,
adding luster to their moon-faces.
They play blissfully as they come and go.
When a woman's eye falls on a man,
he is as if killed by the dagger of her glance.
These heavenly houris were the image of Love, all nymphs of matchless
   kinds!

   If these were the water-carriers, imagine the beauty of their
      Queen! [32]

Those lakes and pools cannot be described.
One cannot decide where they begin or end.
The lilies that blossom in those pools,
are radiant as stars risen in the sky.
Rain-clouds come down to those pools,
to drink their water, then ascend.
Fish gleam in the water, like lightning.
Birds swim there, flocked together
in divers colors, white, yellow and red.
The *caka* and its mate play with each other,
spending nights apart, but together by day.
The Sarus cranes cry out in delight,
"In life or death, we are bound together!"
Water fowl: the *keva*, the *sona*, the crane, the stork,
and the *ledi* abound there, and fish pierce the deeps.
   Priceless gems lie in these lakes, shining in the daylight like lamps.
   Whoever dies to life and dives in, finds the shell with the pearl. [33]

Then there are ambrosial gardens planted
with peerless fruit, watched over carefully.
Limes fresh in color, and orange-citrons,
and almond trees, willows, and figs grow there.
In fruit are huge citrons, grapefruits and lemons,
and oranges, red and full of juice.
Grapes ripen, and apples fresh in leaf.
Pomegranates and vines please the eyes.
The Indian gooseberries are delightful,
and the banana clusters, hanging low.
Mulberries, averrhoa and red currants bear fruit,
as do the corinda, jujube, and *cironji* nut.
One can see both sorrel and date,
and other edible fruits, both sweet and sour.
 The wells yield water like sherbet, as if mixed with sugar in the
  channels.
 It flows through the clay pots of waterwheels, and soaks the
  ambrosial vine. [34]

In all four directions are planted flower-gardens
which imbue the trees with the scent of sandal.
The *ghana-valli* bears its many blossoms.
The screw-pine flowers, and golden magnolia,
and the Indian and Arabian jasmines.
There are red roses and *kadamba* blossoms,
large *kuja*-roses and the scented white *bakavali*
which King Gandhrapasena offers in worship.
Rose-chestnut, marigold, and jessamine,
and the weeping nyctanthes blow in these glades.
Oleasters and dog-roses blossom here,
and night-jasmine and "bouquet of beauty."
Bunches of fragrant jasmine are planted here,
and the rose-apple flowers please the eye.
The *maulasiri*, the vine, and the citron,
are all in bloom with flowers of many colors.
 Whoever is crowned with these blossoms owns the jewel of fortune.
 They remain eternally fragrant, as if celebrating the rites of
  spring. [35]

Then, look at Singhala, the city well-founded!
Fortunate is the King who is situated there.
Sheer are its gates, and high its abodes,
like heavenly Kabilasa, the home of Indra.
Kings and beggars are happy in their houses.
Whoever one sees has a smiling face.

The public platforms have seats of sandal,
plastered with aloes, *meda* and screw-pine.
All the pavilions have pillars of sandal.
Lords, reclining, preside there in assemblies.
The assemblies seem like the councils of gods
one sees in the celestial city, Indra's seat.
Everyone is a skilled pandit, and learned.
Sanskrit is heard from every mouth.
> They adorn their earthly thoroughfares as in the matchless heaven
> of Siva.
> In every house, lovely lotus-women bewitch with their beauty and
> form. [36]

Now look at the market of Singhala, stocked
with the nine treasures of Goddess Lakshmi.
The goldsmiths' shops are anointed with saffron.
There sit the merchants of Singhala-dipa.
They shape the silver into bracelets for the hand,
adorned with many images and cutwork forms.
Gems of essence, rubies, pearls, diamonds, coral,
all sparkle with varied brilliance.
Gold and silver are spread out everywhere.
They paint the houses and doors gleaming white.
Camphor and vetiver and musk,
sandal and aloes are in abundance here.
Can any other market be profitable
for the man who does not buy in this bazaar?
> Some people come to buy, others are here to sell their goods,
> some leave with profit earned, others lose all their capital. [37]

In that country, the bazaar of beauty is blessed!
The courtesans sit there, much-adorned—
their mouths red with *pan* juice,
the saris on their bodies bright orange,
jeweled golden ear-studs in their lobes.
At the music from the *bins* in their hands,
even deer are enchanted, and men
cannot move a single step. Their eyebrows are bows,
their eyes keen hunters. They shoot arrow-glances,
sharpened on the whetstone. They laugh,
with curls dancing on their cheeks,
and their sidelong glances cut to the quick.
Their bodiced breasts are paired game-pieces.
They let slip their veils seductively in the game.
Whoever throws the dice against them

goes away defeated, with empty hands.
> They seduce with their magic, enslaving the heart, all till there's money in the purse!
> Once spent, the traveler leaves, for there's no more friendship, nor meeting. [38]

There are flower sellers there with flowers,
with superb *pan* spread out before them.
Perfume sellers sit with all their fragrant wares,
many packets of catechu and camphor.
Here, there are pandits reciting the scriptures,
discoursing on the holy path of paths.
There, someone tells a tale, another something else.
Some perform fine dances and marvels.
Here, the market of illusion puts on a show,
or someone deceives by making puppets dance!
Here, there are auspicious songs and stories,
there, a drama or a display of magic.
Here, some practice the art of thuggee,
there, they drive humans mad.
> Confidence men, thieves, pickpockets, knaves, all put on their dance.
> Only the one who is on to the dance, can save his purse and capital. [39]

After that one comes to the fort of Singhala.
How can I describe it? It seems to touch the sky!
Below, it rests on the backs of the tortoise
and Vasuki, serpent of the nether world.
Above, its glance reaches Indra's heaven.
A moat stretches out around it, vertiginous.
One cannot look over the precipice, it makes
the thighs tremble! An abyss so deep,
it defies the gaze, makes one fearful
of falling into the seven circles of hell.
It has nine crooked gateways, nine levels,
and whoever climbs up to the ninth one
escapes into the cosmos within, Brahman's egg.
A golden fortress, its ramparts studded with gems,
as if filled with constellations flashing lightning.
The castle appears taller than Ravana's Lanka.
One cannot look, it wearies both eye and mind.
> The heart cannot contain it, the gaze cannot span it, it stands there like Sumeru.
> How can I depict its height? How far can I describe its circumference? [40]

The sun and moon always avoid that fort,
else their chariots would crash into dust.
Nine gates it has, made of adamant,
with a thousand foot-soldiers at each.
Five captains of the guard make their circuit.
The gates shake at the tread of their feet.
At each door are carved lions rampant.
Kings are afraid seeing them standing there.
With great care are those images carved,
as if roaring, and ready to attack one's head.
They shake their tails and stretch out their tongues.
Elephants fear that they'll roar and capture them!
Gold and lapis lazuli are carved into stairways
that sparkle to the very top of the fortress.

> The castle has nine stories and nine gates, each with its doors of
> adamant.
> Four stages it takes to reach the top. If one climbs with truth, one
> arrives! [41]

Above the nine stories is the tenth door,
where the royal clepsydra strikes.
There are men there to mark the hours,
taking their turn through the watches.
When each hour passes, they strike the bell.
The clock chimes out from hour to hour.
When the rod strikes, the whole world is warned:
"O vessel of clay, how can you remain uncaring?
You became raw clay and climbed on the wheel!
You have come to spin around, and cannot save yourself
by staying still. When an hour passes, your life lessens.
Wayfarer, why do you sleep so heedlessly?
From watch to watch, the bell always rings out.
Only the one whose heart is free of care does not wake!"

> Muhammad, life is but the filling of water into a clock or waterwheel.
> The hour strikes, and it empties its load, and so passes away life. [42]

At the fort, two rivers of milk and water
flow perpetually, like Draupadi's platter.
And there is a lake of crushed pearls,
its water like nectar, camphor its clay.
Only the King drinks its water,
and never grows old as long as he lives.
Near the lake is a golden tree,
like the wishing-tree from Indra's heaven.
Its roots go down to the nether world,

and its branches up to heaven. Who can reach it?
Who can taste the vine of immortality?
Its leaves are like the moon, its fruit, the stars.
Its radiance spreads till the limits of the city.
Only the one who performs austerities
can taste its fruit, become a youth from an old man.
   Rajas have become beggars on hearing of that ambrosial delight!
   Whoever gets it, becomes immortal. He does not sicken, nor age. [43]

In the fortress are four lords of the city,
in charge of horses, elephants, and men.
All their palaces are decorated with gold,
and each is the lord in his own castle.
They are handsome, wealthy, and fortunate,
their doorsteps studded with philosophers' stones.
All enjoy eternal delight and pleasure.
All through their lives no one knows grief, nor care.
On every palace, there are open pavilions.
All the Princes sit there and play with the pieces.
The dice fall, and the game moves briskly.
No one can match them at generosity or swordplay.
Minstrels sing aloud their glorious fame,
and get in reward horses and Singhali elephants.
   In every palace is a flower-garden, sunk in sandal and mingled
      fragrance.
   Night and day it is springtime there, all six seasons and twelve
      months. [44]

Then I went forth and saw the royal gate.
One could wander the world and not gain that door!
There are Singhali elephants tied at the gate,
like mountains alive, all standing there.
Some were white, some sorrel or bay,
others tawny or smoky gray or black.
Their colors were varied as clouds in the sky.
They seemed to hold up the heavens on their backs.
Singhala is famed for Singhali elephants,
each one stronger than the last.
They thrust aside mountains, hills, and peaks.
Uprooting trees, they shake them
and carry them in their mouths.
Elephants in heat and in control,
all roaring loudly, are tied up there.
Night and day, mahouts stay on their shoulders.

> The earth cannot bear their weight; it trembles when they put down
>   their feet.
> When they walk the shell of the tortoise cracks, and the serpent's
>   hood is split. [45]

And gallant steeds were tied at the royal gate.
How can I tell you of the glory of their colors?
The iron-gray and pale horses are famed for their gait.
Some are bay with black points, some jet,
and some are dark brown, as I describe.
Some are golden sorrel, others dark bay.
There are chestnuts of many hues,
and lines of roans, whites, and yellow-manes.
Keen Tocharian horses, fiery and skittish,
curvet and rear up without the whip.
They respond to the reins faster than the mind.
They let out their breath and their heads touch the sky.
As they gain their wind, they gallop on the sea.
Their hooves do not sink, but carry them across and back.
They don't stand still, but bite the steel spiritedly.
They lash their tails and throw up their heads.
> I saw they were all Tocharian steeds, such as draw the chariot of the
>   mind.
> In just the blink of an eye, they reach their rider's intended
>   destination! [46]

Then I saw the royal assembly seated there.
It seemed my gaze had fallen on Indra's court.
Blessed the King who adorns such a court,
like a flower-garden in full bloom.
All the crowned kings sit there, at whose gates
drums and kettle-drums always ring out.
They are handsome, with jewels sparkling at their foreheads.
Above them are parasols, and they sit on royal thrones.
They are like lotuses blossoming in the lake.
Those who see the beauty of that court lose their minds.
The court is full of luscious scents in plenty:
betel, camphor, cooling *meda* and fragrant musk.
There is a high heavenly throne amidst them,
where King Gandhrapasena sits in state.
> His parasol reaches up to the sky. His radiance shines forth like the
>   sun itself.
> His court blossoms like a lotus from the great brilliance of his
>   brow. [47]

The royal palace was adorned like Kabilasa,
all made of gold, from earth to heaven.
Seven stories high was the palace built.
Only such a King could construct it.
The bricks were diamonds, the mortar, camphor.
Studded with jewels, the palace reached heaven.
All the patterns were depicted there,
inlaid in mosaics, with various jewels.
Everywhere there were divers traceries.
Pictures stretched out, row upon row.
Pillars were encrusted with rubies and jewels.
They blazed bright like lamps by day.
Seeing the radiance of that royal palace,
the sun, moon, and stars hid away in shame.
   Just like the fabled seven paradises was the seven-storied palace.
   As you went up level by level, the mood of the decorations
      changed. [48]

Sources

The text for this selection has been taken from V. S. Agravala, ed., *Malik Muhammad Jayasi krita Mahakavya: Mula aur Sanjivini Vyakhya* (Chirganv, Jhansi: Sadan, 1957). I have also consulted the edition of Mataprasad Gupta (Allahabad: Bharati Bhandar, 1973), and the 1675 manuscript of the *Padmavat,* copied by Muhammad Shakir of Amroha, preserved in the Rampur Raza Library (RRL Hindi Ms. 1).

Further Reading

For a brief survey of the genre, see R. S. McGregor, *Hindi Literature from its Beginnings to the Nineteenth Century* (Wiesbaden: Otto Harrassowitz, 1984), pp. 26–28, 65–73, and 150–154. Ramiya Sreenivasan's *The Many Lives of a Rajput Queen: Heroic Pasts in India, c. 1500–1900* (Seattle: University of Washington Press, 2007) traces many versions of the Padmavat story, from the one discussed here to nationalist versions of the late nineteenth century. For a more detailed discussion of the genre, and a modern verse translation of a Hindavi Sufi romance, see Mir Sayyid Manjhan Shattari Rajgiri, *Madhumalati: An Indian Sufi Romance,* trans. Aditya Behl and Simon Weightman (Oxford: Oxford University Press, 2000). For a reading of a different Hindavi romance, see Aditya Behl, "The Magic Doe: Desire and Narrative in a Hindavi Sufi Romance," in Richard M. Eaton, ed., *India's Islamic Traditions, 711–1750* (Delhi: Oxford University Press, 2003), pp.180–208.

—3—

Pilgrimage to the Shrines in Ajmer

Catherine B. Asher

Khwaja Mu'inuddin Chishti (d. 1236) was one of the Sufis of the early Delhi Sultanate recognized for his immediate and personal relationship with God. Figures like him often served as bridges between Muslim authorities and the larger Indic population. There were always debates about some practices of the Sufis, of which their use of ecstatic music (like that exemplified in Chapter 5) was one. The early Chishti Sufis in fact were particularly known for employing *sama'* (music and song) as a means to spiritual union with God. Nonetheless, their many followers in no way saw them as deviant, but rather sought them out as teachers, mediators, intercessors, and guides who were intimates of God. Sufis were central to the religious and social life of the day,

By the sixteenth century, Khwaja Mu'inuddin Chishti's shrine (*dargah*) in the Rajasthani city of Ajmer had become popular not only with Muslims but with Hindus as well. It remains India's most widely visited Muslim shrine, especially during the annual celebration of the *'urs*, the anniversary of the saint's death and union with God. Pilgrims come, when possible, not only from within India but from Pakistan, Bangladesh, and beyond.

The text reproduced below, in three sections, comes from a chronicle about the sixteenth-century Mughal emperor Akbar, who was, for a period of his life, deeply influenced by devotion to Mu'inuddin Chishti. Abu al-Fazl, the text's author, notes the Khwaja's origin in Chisht (in modern Afghanistan) and provides as well a record of his distinguished lineage. Little is known, however, from this or other sources about the saint's day-to-day life and his manner of practicing Sufism. What is known is the story of his relationship with Akbar. According to Abu al-Fazl, in 1562 the young Mughal emperor was setting off to hunt when he heard qawwali songs being sung in honor of Khwaja Mu'inuddin, songs that so moved Akbar that he decided to go on pilgrimage to Ajmer (Figure 3.1). This commenced a seventeen-year period during which Akbar made annual pilgrimages to the shrine in complete devotion to the saint. Akbar also established a relationship with a living Chishti holy man, Shaykh Salim Chishti (1418–1572), who predicted the birth of

Fig. 3.1: The Tomb of Mu'inuddin Chishti. *Photo: Catherine B. Asher and Fredrick M. Asher.*

the son and heir that the emperor lacked. Akbar attributed the subsequent birth of his son Salim to the saint's miraculous power, and rewarded him by providing a splendid *khanqah* in the courtyard of the congregational mosque at Fatehpur Sikri.

In addition, in thanksgiving, Akbar walked for sixteen days over two hundred kilometers to the shrine of Mu'inuddin Chishti where he then spent several days.

Akbar's activities at the shrine parallel those of many devout pilgrims who visit the Ajmer *dargah* today. He first prayed at the saint's white marble tomb. In Abu al-Fazl's words, Akbar then "placed the forehead of sincerity on that spot and implored for help." These words are undoubtedly more than metaphors of intense devotion. In this same manner, a seventeenth-century Mughal princess, author of an eloquent biography of Mu'inuddin, wrote that she rubbed her face at the tomb's threshold and swept the tomb's floor with her eyelashes. The practice of these royal devotees is repeated by pilgrims today who touch their foreheads on the silver railing inside the tomb as an act of piety. The emperor distributed gifts, surely meaning money, to the attendants of the shrine, a practice also widely observed today.

Abu al-Fazl also records that the emperor was sufficiently annoyed that the shrine's main attendant, Shaykh Husayn, had mismanaged the *dargah's* funds that he removed the *shaykh* from his position. Inscriptional evidence at the shrine indicates that after some time the *shaykh* returned to Ajmer, most probably having spent the intervening time undertaking the mandatory hajj pilgrimage to Mecca. Probably as a further effort to make amends, the *shaykh* (who later calls himself Khwaja Husayn) funded the rebuilding of the dome of Mu'inuddin's tomb.

The eleven-lined inscription written in Persian verse, reproduced below in translation, comes from inside the tomb. Its imagery replicates much of the imagery that would be found in Abu al-Fazl's description of Akbar as a perfect enlightened ruler. Here it is Mu'inuddin who is described as the "sun of the universe" and likened to the light of the sun and the moon. The sun and moon, like long-ago royal pilgrims and pilgrims today, "rub their forehead" at the tomb's entrance. Another verse praises the saint as a precious pearl, a reference to the pearl-like quality of the tomb's marble fabric and dome. We can imagine that while only the elite could actually read this inscription, the luminous quality of the tomb itself might evoke images of light and all its implications of spiritual enlightenment for many.

At his death in 1637, Shaykh Husayn, like many other pious Muslims, wished to be buried close to his beloved Mu'inuddin so that he might be in the presence of his *baraka*, his spiritual charisma. A five-line inscription praising the spiritual leader embellishes the tomb. A chronogram in the final line, consisting of the Persian word *maghz*, gives the tomb's date according to the *abjad* calculation, which assigns a numerical value to each letter of the Arabic script. (The sum of the numbers is 1047 corresponding to 1637 c.e.) The word *maghz*, "brain" or "essence," is important not only for its date but for its further meaning as a special kind of "pearl."

Akbar's successors continued patronage of the shrine of Mu'inuddin Chishti. The fifth Mughal ruler, Shah Jahan, added a magnificent white marble mosque to the west of the tomb itself, built, according to a long inscription on the mosque, in thanksgiving for a military victory against a long-standing foe (Figure 3.2). While reference is made to Mu'inuddin and his tomb, the inscription focuses more on the emperor himself and his newly constructed mosque, likening both the king and the mosque to the Ka'ba in Mecca, Islam's holiest building. This inscription no doubt reveals how Shah Jahan wished to be thought of, but it is not particularly visible as it is under the main eave of the mosque's façade. More visible are medal-

Fig. 3.2: Shah Jahan's mosque. *Photo: Catherine B. Asher and Fredrick M. Asher.*

lions placed between the verses, each of which is inscribed with one of the ninety-nine "beautiful names" of God. Chances are that those single words, often recognizable rather like a logo, are what the faithful could recognize much more than the elaborate Persian verses. Even more so today as fewer and fewer Muslims in India can read Persian/Arabic script, these single epitaphs telling of God's everlasting compassion and goodness are probably all that most are able to recognize.

The Ajmer *dargah* of Mu'inuddin is visited by over two hundred thousand people just for the *'urs* alone, and the shrine is packed the rest of the year as well, especially on Fridays. The sorts of activities that took place at the shrine in the sixteenth and seventeenth centuries continue even today, although most who visit lack the formidable resources of royalty. However, the number of pilgrims who pay homage at the shrine has increased considerably over recent years, so the quantity of offerings may compensate for the loss of royal largess.

Akbar made it the obligation of the wealthy and elite to build in Ajmer, both at Ajmer's various shrines and in the city generally. Thus over time there was considerable construction, including mosques, city walls, wells, and more. According to the inscriptional record left at Ajmer's shrines, it seems that as popular as was Mu'inuddin Chishti's shrine, the privilege of building there was the prerogative of only a few. The lesser elite instead focused their patronage on the *dargah* of Sayyid Husayn Khing Sawar, also a Chishti, located high on a hill above Mu'inuddin's shrine. Sayyid Husayn Khing Sawar was a contemporary of Mu'inuddin and probably his disciple. It was only in the Mughal period that substantial attention was given to his shrine, almost surely a direct result of Akbar's interest in the tomb below. The inscription reproduced below indicates that Shah Quli Khan, an officer associated with important nearby towns, renewed the enclosure surrounding the ancient tombs. Now a paved road provides access to the hilltop, but until only a few years ago pilgrims reached the shrine by means of an arduous winding path. The *dargah* of Sayyid Husayn Khing Sawar is commonly visited during the '*urs* of Mu'inuddin Chishti after the pilgrim has paid homage at the main shrine.

SELECTIONS FROM THE AKBARNAMA

The Khwaja [Mu'inuddin Chishti] came from Sistan, and they call him Sijzi, which is the Arabic for Sigzi. His honored father who was named Khwaja Hasan and who was a contented husbandman died when he was in his fifteenth year. Shaykh Ibrahim Majzub of Qanduz's attention was drawn to him and, by the blessing of his glance, the pains of inquiry seized the Khwaja's soul and cut away outward ties. He hastened to Samarqand and Bukhara and for a time applied himself to the acquisition of knowledge. From there he went to Khurasan, and there he grew up. In Haran, which is a dependency of Nishapur, he made the acquaintance of Shaykh Osman Haruni and became his disciple. For twenty years he practiced strenuous austerities in the *shaykh's* company, and he undertook journeys and sojournings in strange lands. He became acquainted with many saints of the time, such as Shaykh Najm al-Din Kubri. In short, he is one of the great men of the Chishti order. He is three removes from Khwaja Maudud Chishti and nine from Ibrahim Adham. Before Mu'izz al-Din, the son of Sam, came from Ghazni to India, he took leave from his pir (spiritual master) and came to that country.

He established himself in Ajmer, where Rai Pithora, the ruler of India, resided. Certainly the Khwaja was a lord of austerities and spiritual conflicts and had waged great wars with his carnal spirit. Though many miracles are related of him, what miracle can be more glorious than the contest with the desires of this carnal spirit which is the father of excesses? Khwaja Qutbuddin Ushi of Andijan became, in Baghdad, in the month of Rajab 522 [1128 c.e.], in the mosque of Imam Abu-i Laith of Samarqand and in the presence of Shaykh Shihab al-Din Suhrawardi, of Shaykh Uhad al-Din of Kirman and of a number of other saints, the disciple of Khwaja Mu'inuddin. Shaykh Farid Shakrganj, who is buried in [Pak]patan, is a disciple of this Qutbuddin, and Shaykh Nizamuddin Auliya, who was the pir of Amir Khusrau, gave his hand of discipleship to Shaykh Farid. In short, many of the perfect masters have risen up from under the skirts of the Khwaja's teaching. May God sanctify their souls!

One night His Majesty went off to Fatehpur to hunt and passed near by Mandhakar, which is a village on the way from Agra to Fatehpur. A number of Indian minstrels were singing enchanting ditties about the glories and virtues of the great Khwaja, Khwaja Mu'inuddin, may his grave be hallowed, who sleeps in Hazrat Ajmer. Often had his perfections and miracles been the theme of discourse in the holy assemblies. His Majesty, being a seeker after Truth who in his zealous quests sought for union with travelers on the road of holiness and showed a desire for enlightenment, conceived a strong inclination to visit the Khwaja's shrine. The attraction of a pilgrimage thither seized his collar.

As the holy understanding of the King desires inspiration from saints, he, at the time when he was seeking for a son, had made a vow to his God that if this blessing should be attained, he would perform an act of thanksgiving that should be personal to himself, viz., that he would walk from Agra to the shrine of Khwaja Mu'inuddin Chishti, and there pay his devotions to God. It was set-tled in Rajab (the seventh month), which was the month of the saint's anniver-sary ('urs), that this intention should be carried into practice. When such a night-gleaming jewel of the casket of the Caliphate arrived at the shore of hope, he recognized his obligation and set out on foot from Agra on the day of Aban 10 Bahman, the divine month, corresponding to Friday 12 Shaban (the eighth month) [20 January 1570], and traversed stages and deserts. Each day he jour-neyed ten or twelve kos [roughly two miles], less or more.

There follows a list of the stages of the journey from Agra (culminating in the holy dwelling of the Khwaja in Ajmer).

Then he straightway went to the shrine and placed the forehead of sincerity on that spot and implored help. He spent several days there in devotion and good works. He distributed gifts among the attendants of the shrine. As on the occasion of the division of the gifts, which came to a large amount, those who claimed to be descendants of the Khwaja, and who had the superintendence of the shrine—their chief was Shaykh Husayn—took possession of the whole of the money, and there were disputes and quarrels between Shaykh Husayn and the attendants of the shrine, and there was the allegation that the shaykhs who had charge of the shrine had told falsehoods with regard to their descent, and as this dispute had gone on a long time, His Majesty appointed trustworthy per-sons to inquire into the matter and to report thereon. After much investigation it was found that the claim of legitimacy was not genuine. Accordingly the charge of the shrine was made over to Shaykh Muhammad Bukhari, who was distinguished among the Sayyids of Hindustan for knowledge and fidelity. His Majesty also arranged for the management of the shrine, and for the treatment of pilgrims and for the erection of mosques and khanqahs in the territory. In fine [i.e., in conclusion], after having made over the presents he set out on his re-turn and proceeded to visit the shrines of the saints of Delhi. He went there, and in Isfandarmaz, the divine month corresponding to Ramadan [February–March 1570], he arrived at Delhi. He spent some days in that pleasant spot, in visiting the shrines and in the administration of justice, and he gladdened the hearts of friends and strangers.

INSCRIPTIONS AT THE AJMER SHRINE OF MU'INUDDIN CHISHTI

REBUILDING OF THE DOME OF THE TOMB BY KHWAJA HUSAYN IN 1579

> Lord of the Lords, Mu'inuddin. Most eminent of all the saints of the
>   world [is he],
> Sun of the sphere of the universe, king of the throne of the dominion of
>   Faith,
> What room is there for doubt as regards his beauty and perfection? This
>   is evident from the fortified citadel.
> I have composed a verse in his praise which, in its style, is like a
>   precious pearl.
> Oh ye whose door is an altar for the faithful, [even] the sun and the
>   moon rub their forehead at your threshold.
> It is at thine door that the foreheads are rubbed by hundred thousands
>   of kings like the emperor of China.
> The attendants of thy shrine are all like Rizwan [the gatekeeper of
>   paradise] [while] in sanctity thy shrine is like the sublime heaven;
>   a particle of its dust is like ambergris in nature; a drop of its water
>   is like limpid [pure] water.
> The locum tenens of Mu'in [namely] Khwaja Husayn, for the
>   embellishment said this:
> That the old may assume fresh hue anew, the dome of Khwaja
>   Mu'inuddin
> Oh Lord! As long as the sun and moon endure, may the lamp of the
>   Chishtis possess light!

INSCRIPTION ON THE TOMB OF KHWAJA HUSAYN, DATED 1637

> God is great.
> By the favor of the guide and my spiritual instructor for certain
> The emperor of both of the worlds [namely] Khwaja Mu'inuddin
> The holy mausoleum of Khwaja Husayn was constructed.
> The year of its completion has been found in the word *maghz* [1047 A.H./
>   1637 C.E.].

INSCRIPTION OF SHAH JAHAN'S MOSQUE, DATED 1637

> I have heard from the elite of happy omen that prior to [his] eternity-
>   bound accession
> Faith-cherishing refuge of religion, of heavenly dignity, Shah Jahan, the
>   king,
> Asylum of nations, lord of throne and crown, in whose reign the Divine
>   Law prevails

After scoring victory over the Rana, pitched his tent at Ajmer, with great
   dignity, pomp and felicity

For paying a visit to the shrine of the truthful, Mu'in [helper] of the
   world, Khwaja [lord] of the age

The refuge of truths, the receptacle of divine knowledge to whom the
   heaven has awarded the title of Qutb-i 'Alam [the Axis of the World].

As there was no mosque in [the enclosure of] that holy mausoleum,
   a desire for [constructing] a mosque arose in his heart.

Between the lord [Shah Jahan] and God it was ratified that there should
   be a mosque in memory of him.

After many revolutions of the sphere were not yet over when that altar of
   monarchs and angels [Shah Jahan]

Occupied the seat of emperorship and sovereignty, through divine favor

He girded up his loins and went ahead, not by way of formality, but
   through sincere intention [to put desire into reality].

By the grace of God, the work was done as desired. He laid the
   foundation of this mosque and it was completed.

How excellent is the mosque of the king of the world [Shah Jahan's name
   literally means "the king of the world"], which bears the stamp of the
   Bayt al-Muqaddas [the name of the holy mosque in Jerusalem].

How happy is the dignity of this house that on account of its sanctity is
   the second of the two of the Holy Houses [a reference to the Ka'ba].

It is a sacred shrine like the sanctuary of Ibrahim [the prophet
   Abraham]; the tongue is dedicated to honorable mention for its
   description.

It is considered the twin of the Ka'ba; who has beheld a mosque with
   such splendor and grandeur?

The sun makes a handle out of its eyelashes in order that he might get
   the honorific of "sweeper" at this place.

The Ka'ba is visible therein at the time of prayer, having opened the door
   of its niche towards the Holy Sanctuary [the Ka'ba].

When you rub your fortunate face on its floor, your book of deeds
   becomes white as marble [pure].

The indigent seeker has his heart attached therein; its *guldasta* [a
   bouquet or mosque finial] is the springtime of prayers.

When the king of the world [Shah Jahan] turned the face of supplication
   towards its niche at the time of prayer,

Through divine favor he made an altar on both sides; he turned his face
   to one [the qibla (the direction of prayer) of the mosque] and his back
   to the other [the saint's tomb].

There are two eyes that sit in the pupil of the world; one is the house of
   the Ka'ba and the other is this [the mosque].

The emperor of the faith sits in this mosque, may the Ka'ba [Shah Jahan]
   occupy the mosque forever!

Prayer is favored with response; [therefore] happy is one who offers
prayers here!

The soul can be burnt as an incense on its [the mosque's] pulpit,
where the name of the king of the world [Shah Jahan] is recited
[referring to the reading of the ruling monarch's name in the Friday
prayer].

To the throng of people who offer prayers [here] its gate is always open,
as is the gate of penitence.

In order that the sermon of the king may be worthy of it, it is befitting
that its pulpit should be made out of wings of angels.

Its reservoir is full to the brim with the water of Zum Zum [the well at
Mecca]; through its niche it embraces the Ka'ba.

Its limpid water has drawn a sword of waves in order to sever relations
[with everything mundane].

The joints of the stone have been so finely set together that you may say
it was carved from a single piece.

Since at the behest of the Shadow of God [Shah Jahan] destiny raised
this edifice,

Men of faith recorded for its chronogram, the words "the edifice of the
emperor of the world." 1047 [1637]

Between the verses are medallions inscribed with the traditional ninety-nine
beautiful names of God, among them the following:

The Compassionate, the Merciful, The King, The Holy, The Source of Peace,
The Protector, The Mighty, The Compeller, The Majestic, The Creator, The
Fashioner, The Great Forgiver, The Dominant, The Bestower, The Provider, The
Opener, The All-Knowing, The Retainer, The Expander, The Exalter, The Honorer, The Dishonorer, The All-Hearing, The Just.

INSCRIPTION ON THE *DARGAH* OF SAYYID HUSAYN KHING SAWAR,
TARAGARH, AJMER

Shah Quli Khan Mahram by way of truthful intention

Performed the circumambulation of Ganj-i Shahidan ["Treasure of
Martyrs," i.e., Sayyid Husayn Khing Sawar's shrine at Taragarh] in the
region of Ajmer.

He raised the edifice of this mausoleum afresh

For the pleasure of God, the Omniscient, the Omnipotent.

In the year nine hundred and seventy-nine [1571] it was completed,

During the reign of the king, the conqueror of dominions [Akbar].

Written by Muhammad Baqir.

Sources

Passages from the *Akbarnama* are from Abu al-Fazl, *Akbarnama*, trans. H. Beveridge (Delhi: Rare Books, 1972) vol. 2, pp. 237, 238–239, 510–511; a reprint of the original three-volume edition published in Calcutta by the Asiatic Society, 1907–1939. Inscriptions from Ajmer are from S.A.I. Tirmizi, *Ajmer through Inscriptions, 1532–1852,* (New Delhi: Indian Institute of Islamic Studies, 1968), pp. 28–29, 31–32, 43–49. I have made some modifications for clarity and have standardized spellings.

Further Reading

See P. M. Currie, *The Shrine and Cult of Mu'in al-Din Chishti of Ajmer* (Delhi: Oxford University Press, 1989). Carl W. Ernst and Bruce B. Lawrence provide an extensive study of the Chishtis generally in *Sufi Martyrs of Love: The Chishti Order in South Asia and Beyond* (New York: Palgrave Macmillian, 2002); an excerpt on the Mughal princess's visit to Ajmer is included in the text.

— 4 —

Women's Grinding and Spinning Songs of Devotion
in the Late Medieval Deccan

Richard Eaton

One of the challenges facing historians of South Asia is the difficulty of explaining why and how Islam became the dominant popular religion in some parts of the subcontinent but not in others. Attempting to explain Islamization in premodern India generally, nineteenth and twentieth-century commentators often stressed the presumed "missionary" activities of peaceful or charismatic Sufi *shaykhs*. Such persons were construed as having labored in "spreading" Islam among low-caste Hindus in areas that later became Muslim-majority regions.

However, peaceful or charismatic Sufi *shaykhs* are found *throughout* the subcontinent in the medieval period, and not just in those parts of it that, by the nineteenth century, had Muslim majorities. Contemporary biographies of Sufis, moreover, give no hint that *shaykhs* were interested in non-Muslims or in making Muslim converts of them. Endeavoring to transcend the norms of conventional Islamic piety without actually violating those norms, Sufis of medieval India generally accepted as their followers persons who were already Muslim. And when they put their thoughts to paper, Sufis in India usually wrote in Persian, a language not likely to have been familiar to the non-Muslim masses to whom they presumably preached. Yet despite all this evidence to the contrary, the myth that Sufis played a major role in "converting" large parts of the subcontinent remains very much alive.

On the other hand, one unique body of popular literature found in the late medieval Deccan does suggest a possible link between Sufism as a practical dimension of Islam, and the culture of everyday rural society. This body of literature consists of two categories of folk song—the *chakki-nama*, "grindstone song," and the *charkha-nama*, "spinning-wheel song"—written in Dakani, one of the Deccan's vernacular languages. Spoken Dakani can be traced to the speech of Muslim immigrants from north India who had settled in the northern Deccan in the early fourteenth century, when the Delhi sultanate was trying to colonize the region. It did not appear as a literary medium until the fifteenth century, when it was called

"Hindavi" or "Hindi," owing to its remembered association with north India, or "Hind." But by the seventeenth century, authors began referring to the language as "Dakani," thereby asserting both the language's rootedness in the Deccan plateau and its literary independence from the two great classical languages of the day, Sanskrit and Persian.

Most Dakani poets were patronized by the courts of the two most illustrious dynasties of the sixteenth and seventeenth centuries: the 'Adil Shahi sultans of Bijapur (1490–1686), and the Qutb Shahi sultans of Golkonda (1510–1687). Several of the more cultivated rulers of these states were themselves authors of Dakani poetry, which typically treated themes of romance or aesthetics. These two courts were not, however, the only foci of Dakani literature. The tomb-shrines of famous Sufi saints—men popularly venerated and thought capable of interceding with God—were also centers of Dakani literary production. But the themes of this *dargah* (tomb-shrine) literature differed significantly from those found in the more refined courtly poetry. Most of the *chakki-nama*s and *charkha-nama*s associated with Sufi shrines were intended to be sung by village women while engaged in various household chores, in particular grinding meal at a grindstone, or *chakki*, and spinning thread at a spinning-wheel, or *charkha*. Both of these activities involved steady, rhythmic hand motions that could be readily synchronized with songs sung in a regular meter.

While it is difficult to date the composition of these poems with any certainty, their style seems to belong to the seventeenth or early eighteenth century. Most are attributed to well-known *shaykh*s of the Chishti Sufi order who had resided in Bijapur and whose *dargah*s are located there, such as Amin al-Din A'la (d. 1675). Several *chakki-nama*s are attributed to the most famous *shaykh* of the Deccan, Muhammad Gisu Daraz (d. 1422), whose shrine is in Gulbarga. But these attributions are certainly spurious, as they are signed by an epithet never used by Gisu Daraz himself.

The dominant theme of these poems is devotion to God and respect— indeed, veneration—for one's pir, a spiritual guide descended from, or associated with, one of the Chishti *shaykh*s of Bijapur. One of these *shaykh*s, Shah Burhan al-din Janam (d. 1597), actually alluded to the principal subject of the *chakki-nama*, the grindstone, in one of his mystical treatises. "In the case of the *chakki*," he wrote,

> some other power is required—somebody's hand must be applied to move the wheel. There are many people who use the *chakki*, yet only the power hidden in the hand actually turns the wheel. That hand is 'arif al-wujud ("knower of existence," i.e., God), and those who see that the power is in the hand are witnesses of the light; thereby they witness the essence, which is God.

Even if great *shaykh*s like Burhan al-Din did not write *chakki-nama*s themselves, passages like the above suggest their familiarity with the conceptual link between spiritual themes and ordinary housework. For it is precisely this link that characterizes these poems. While proclaiming spiritual connections between God, the Prophet Muhammad, one's own pir, and the reciter herself, *chakki-nama*s and *charkha-nama*s also conceptually connected the Sufis' *zikr*, or spiritual exercise, to various phases of the woman's work, inasmuch as such exercises regulated those phases of work. Above all, the poems sought to establish the pir as the mediator between God and the singer-devotee, and to enhance the latter's spiritual dependency on her pir.

This sort of folk literature no doubt deepened the Islamic identity of those rural women who used it. Whether or not it also served to facilitate the initial Islamization of households in the rural Deccan, however, is more difficult to say. At the very least, it seems likely that children dwelling in households where these songs were sung would have absorbed their religious worldview. Although such a process could hardly be construed as "conversion," a term connoting a self-conscious and sudden change of faith, one can nonetheless imagine how, in this manner, the rudiments of Islamic piety could have quietly infiltrated households of the rural Deccan.

CHAKKI-NAMA OF SHAH HASHIM KHUDAWAND HADI

The first example of this literary genre establishes the link between God and a woman at the grindstone. It also elaborates in simplified form the Chishti theory of Creation and of God's relationship to the material world. The poem is attributed to Shah Hashim Khudawand Hadi (d. 1704/05), who was one of the closest initiates (*khalifa*) of the Bijapur Chishti, Shah Amin al-Din A'la.

> First was God's name,
> And then His qualities.
> In my mind I keep the name,
> And with each breath,
>> [refrain] Say *la ilaha* ("There is no god"),
>> Dwell in *illa'l-lah* ("but God").
>
> God Himself from the hidden treasure,
>> Has created the whole world artistically.
> He has created it with his own power—
>> [refrain] Say *la ilaha* ("There is no god"),
>> Dwell in *illa'l-lah* ("but God").
>
> God Himself came out from the hidden treasure
> And showed Himself in the guise of the Prophet.
>> [refrain] Say *la ilaha* ("There is no god"),
>> Dwell in *illa'l-lah* ("but God").
>
> In the presence of God, the Prophet is chief,
> Whose teachings have given us support in both worlds.
>> [refrain] Say *la ilaha* ("There is no god"),
>> Dwell in *illa'l-lah* ("but God").

The Prophet's *khalifa* is 'Ali, who is dear to Him,
And whose disciples are our pirs.
>[refrain] Say *la ilaha* ("There is no god"),
>>Dwell in *illa'l-lah* ("but God").

Allah, Muhammad, and 'Ali
Are our leaders whom we trust most and obey as slaves.
>[refrain] Say *la ilaha* ("There is no god"),
>>Dwell in *illa'l-lah* ("but God").

Our pir has taken our hands in his;
>He has given us connections whole-heartedly.
May he keep this connection forever.
>[refrain] Say *la ilaha* ("There is no god"),
>>Dwell in *illa'l-lah* ("but God").

. . . .

As the *chakki* turns, so we find God.
>It shows its life in turning as we do in breathing.
>[refrain] Say *la ilaha* ("There is no god"),
>>Dwell in *illa'l-lah* ("but God").

CHAKKI-NAMA ATTRIBUTED TO SHAYKH GISU DARAZ

The following *chakki-nama*, spuriously attributed to Shaykh Muhammad Gisu Daraz (d. 1422), effectively weaves together three elements: the parts of the grindstone, the specific tasks in which the woman is engaged, and the simplest precepts of Islam. In this way the poem transforms the components of a common household device into religious metaphors.

See that our body is also a *chakki*,
>And be careful in grinding.
The devil is my *saukan* [co-wife?]
>Which prevents me from working and tires me.
>>[refrain] *Ya bism Allah*, hu hu Allah.

The *chakki*'s handle resembles *alif*, which means Allah;
>And the axle is Muhammad, and is fixed there.
In this way the truth-seeker sees the relationship.
>[refrain] *Ya bism Allah*, hu hu Allah.

. . . .

We put the grains in the *chakki*,
>To which our hands are witnesses.
The *chakki* of the body is in order
>When you follow the *shari'at* [Islamic Law].
>>[refrain] *Ya bism Allah*, hu hu Allah.

The name of Allah comes from *alif*.
    Know that pirs and murshids [teachers] can direct our lives.
Grind the flour and then sift it—
    [refrain] *Ya bism Allah*, hu hu Allah.
        .   .   .   .   .   .

Grind the flour and make stuffed *puri*;
    Put in it heavenly fruits and sugar,
The seven qualities of God must be taken in the body
    As the seven ingredients fill the *puri*, oh Sister.
        [refrain] *Ya bism Allah*, hu hu Allah.

CHARKHA-NAMA OF SALAR

The final example in this genre is a *charkha-nama* attributed to an unidentified *shaykh* named Salar. Once again, specific parts of a household device, in this instance a spinning wheel, are directly linked to the terms used by Sufis when performing spiritual exercises intended to bring them closer to God. These include the *zikr-i jali*, or vocalized recitation; the *zikr-i qalbi*, or the recitation of the heart; and the *zikr-i 'aini*, or the recitation of the essence.

Imagine that your body is a spinning wheel, Oh Sister.
    We should get rid of our negligence
    And give up worldly differences, Oh Sister.
        .   .   .   .   .   .

The tongue is the unspun thread for the message of God;
    The tongue is the rim of the spinning wheel.
    Bring out the thread of breath and show it, Oh Sister.

Both of these memories should be in our throat:
    God has given us the ability to turn our hand,
    And it is that which moves the wheel, Oh Sister.

Faith must be for you what the drive-rope is for the wheel.
    Perhaps you know of the two wheels connected by the rope;
    Then you will know how the wheel turns, Oh Sister.

As you take the cotton, you should do *zikr-i jali*.
    As you separate the cotton, you should do *zikr-i qalbi*,
    And as you spool the thread you should do *zikr-i 'aini*.

Zikr should be uttered from the stomach through the chest,
    And threaded through the throat.

The threads of breath should be counted one by one, Oh Sister.
    Up to twenty-four thousand.
Do this day and night,
    And offer it to your pir as a gift.

Sources

The quote from Shah Burhan al-din Janam in the introduction is from Burhan al-Din Janam, *Kalimat al-haqayiq*, M. Akbaruddin Siddiqi, ed. (Hyderabad: Idara-e-Adabiyat-e-Urdu, 1961), p. 53. The *chakki-nama* of Shah Hashim Khudawand Hadi is taken from Hashim Khudawand Hadi, *Chakki-nama 'Irfan,* Dakani manuscript (Hyderabad: Idara-e-Adabiyat-e-Urdu, no. 93-B), fols. 126b–128a. The *chakki-nama* attributed to Shaykh Gisu Daraz [d. 1422] can be found in Khwaja Bandanawaz Gisu Daraz, *Chakki-nama*, Dakani manuscript (Hyderabad: Idara-e-Adabiyat-e-Urdu, no. 120-B) The *charkha-nama* of Salar is from Salar, *Charkha-nama,* Dakani manuscript (Hyderabad: Salar Jung Museum, Tasawwuf and Akhlaq, No. 35).

Further Reading:

For a good study of the Sufi shrines, where such women's devotional songs were produced, see Christian Troll, ed., *Muslim Shrines in India: Their Character, History, and Significance* (Delhi: Oxford University Press, 1989). For surveys of medieval Indo-Muslim literature generally, see Shamsur Rahman Faruqi, *Early Urdu Literary Culture and History* (Oxford: Oxford University Press, 2001); and A. Schimmel, *Islamic Literatures of India* (Wiesbaden: Harrassowitz, 1973). For medieval Deccani literature in particular, see Carla Petievich, "Dakani's Radha-Krishna Imagery and Canon Formation in Urdu," in Mariola Offredi, ed., *The Banyan Tree: Essays on Early Literature in New Indo-Aryan Languages* 1 (Delhi: Manohar, 2000), pp. 113–128; and Carla Petievich, "The Feminine and Cultural Syncretism in Early Dakani Poetry," *The Annual of Urdu Studies* 8 (Madison, WI: Center for South Asia, University of Wisconsin, 1993): 119–130.

For studies of medieval Sufis and their role in converting non-Muslims, see Raziuddin Aquil, "Conversion in Chishti Sufi Literature, 13th–14th Centuries," *Indian Historical Review* 24, nos. 1–2 (1997–1998): 70–94; see also Richard M. Eaton, *Sufis of Bijapur: Social Roles of Sufis in Medieval India* (Princeton, NJ: Princeton University Press, 1978). For a comprehensive overview of Islam in South Asia, see A. Schimmel, *Islam in the Indian Subcontinent* (Leiden: E. J. Brill, 1980).

—5—

Qawwali Songs of Praise

Syed Akbar Hyder and Carla Petievich

Qawwali are songs of devotion and supplication, mostly written in Urdu, Hindi, Persian, Punjabi, and Sindhi. Many qawwalis use a mixture of languages, and they are often sprinkled with Qur'anic verses or sayings of the Prophet (hadiths/qawls). Frequently, qawwalis combine various genres of devotional literature: *hamd* (praise of God), *na't* (praise of the Prophet), and *manqabat* (praise of revered Islamic personalities). Traditionally qawwalis began with the words of the Prophet (*qawl*) and were sung at Sufi shrines, but in the past hundred years or so they have become increasingly popular in household celebrations, musical concerts, commercial recordings, and even South Asian films. Many qawwals (qawwali performers), like Meraj Ahmed of Delhi or Aziz Ahmed Khan Warsi of Hyderabad (whose qawwali is translated in this chapter), are rigorously trained in Sufi practices and poetics; others are novices who are drawn to this literature because of its celebratory and ecstatic tones. Qawwals like Nusrat Fateh Ali Khan (d. 1997) have been pivotal in promoting this genre in the West and thereby bringing greater awareness globally to Sufism in particular and to South Asian devotional and musical traditions in general. The appeal of qawwalis is not to Muslims alone; because of the manner in which they upset rigid religious and social hierarchies, they are immensely popular in non-Muslim circles.

They are also accessible, a trademark of Sufi writings and songs from the earliest days of Islam in the Indian Subcontinent: their language is generally vernacular, and often employs literary tropes drawn from the local environment, so that in form they can resemble expressions from popular Indic devotionalism (*bhakti*). Thus, at this popular level of expression and consumption, boundaries between two great and theologically distinct religious traditions are blurred. Such blurring doubtless contributes to the great appeal of Sufi religious traditions.

Many qawwalis also undermine the rigid gender polarities that characterize orthodox culture and religion, as does *bhakti*. While "high" Islamic devotional and lyric texts address the divine in the masculine and also speak in the masculine voice, Aziz Ahmed Khan Warsi's qawwali in this chapter, an Indian composition, addresses God in the feminine voice, as is normative in Indic devotional literatures (and is also represented in the Isma'ili git in Chapter 1). Mystical devotion is based on love of the Divine. Indeed, love for God is understood as "true love" (*'ishq-i haqiqi*), while love between humans is seen as merely metaphorical (*majazi*). Since the Beloved is God—who is imagined as male—the narrator/devotee speaks to "Him" in the feminine voice. The refrain here is that of a woman who lets her beloved know that she is so steeped in love for him that she knows, understands, and sees through every gesture, every artifice of his, and still recognizes him to be her beloved. These gestures (*ada*) range from playful to deceptive to expressions of the beloved's intrinsic nature:

I've come to know your every gesture, haven't I, my dear?

Though this is sadly lost in translation, the gender of the beloved in the poem is grammatically ambiguous. Though "he" is addressed in the super-familiar second person, it is not clear whether this particular beloved is human or divine. Because of this, generic lines are blurred between *hamd* (praise of Allah) and *na't* (praise of the Prophet Muhammad); either might be this narrator's beloved.

The Prophet Muhammad is unambiguously human in theological terms, but he has evolved over the centuries into such a perfect human in popular imagination as to be understood as almost more than human, certainly not the same as the rest of us. He is described, for example, as casting no shadow. According to a hadith tradition, even his own shadow dares not come near him, for that would compromise his uniqueness, might spoil or sully him. Moreover "shadow" means reflection, which, in turn, presupposes duality, whereas Muhammad was unique. In spite of all this, he is concerned only about his community's well-being. Wearing the crown, he intercedes on their behalf. He covers their sin under his cloak. He spreads his mercy so as to shelter all sinners. Though King of Kings, he remains humble: he is described as having a black *kambal*, a humble palm leaf mat typical of mendicants. He also provides a model for worldly conduct, as is pointed out toward the close of the qawwali: he is a helper of the less fortunate, regal in charity, a speaker of truth. He embraces modesty and poverty. A friend of all sinners, he is merciful toward even the bloodthirsty and gracious toward the foulmouthed.

Muhammad is the model that commands the love and affection of the Muslim community. It is for the sake of this model that they are willing to sacrifice their lives, and it is as their spokesperson that the qawwali's narrator speaks when he says, "I've sacrificed myself for the Prophet, given myself up for my Prophet." The extreme to which he is sometimes venerated can make the orthodox uncomfortable. But such extremes are conventional for Sufi poetry's divine Beloved; devotion to Muhammad is intimately bound up with devotion to Allah.

In Indian love poetry, where gods can take human form and love humans back, extremes of (eroticized) devotion are common. With God as the (male) Beloved, the feminine narrator became normative in Indian poetry, and this trope was picked up by Sufis. Here, "she," coupled with the language of the *virahini* (a woman suffering in separation from her beloved), makes this qawwali specifically Indian, while simultaneously drawing Indian devotional poetry into an Islamic cultural world. Many of these themes also evoke the devotional songs that flourish in honor of the groom par excellence of *bhakti* tradition, Lord Krishna. Clearly, the turbaned bridegroom in this poem calls to mind the familiar image of the turbaned Krishna as he plays his flute.

The background to this poem consists of a number of theological axioms. Among them is the mystical truth (*haqiqat*) that no real separation exists between God and the self. The seeker who realizes this follows in the footsteps of the tenth-century ecstatic Sufi, Mansur al-Hallaj, who drank from the goblet of intoxicating insight and understood *ana al-haq* (I am the Truth). He went behind the curtain separating human reality from divine reality and saw there what he had seen here. There was nothing separating the two! Proclaiming this insight, he dismayed and outraged those (the orthodox) who perpetuated the notion of distance between the mortal and divine realms (here *vs.* there). Mystical truth is dangerous to the worldly status quo, and Hallaj was sent to the gallows.

Like al-Hallaj this qawwali particularly challenges the orthodox notion that the Divine is unseeable and unknowable. When the prophet Moses on Mt. Sinai made the request to Allah, "Show me your self," the reply that came told Moses that he would be incapable of seeing Allah, even if Allah showed himself. But in the redaction of Qur'anic legend on which this qawwali builds, the contract between God and humans has changed somewhat. Through mystical relationship the divine Beloved softens, promising what the Qur'anic version assured would be impossible, namely that Muhammad would be able to see God. In fact, the narrator in this qawwali asserts that "she" not only sees her divine Beloved, but she sees *through* him, sees through his elusive behavior, understanding it to be more flirtation than his essence.

Another underlying theme here is that of the value for the mystic of *majazi* (metaphorical) love. It is invoked through the famous romance of Qays, or Majnun ("the crazy") and his beloved Laila. Qays's love and longing for Laila are so profound that he is transported from the state of normal perception into the realm of the love-crazed. His attachment approximates devotion, and he sees the Divine in Laila, for her beauty is nothing but a metaphor for the beauty of the Divine. A line in this poem says, "You possessed Laila and drove Majnun mad." Here, interestingly (and unusually), Allah can be imagined in feminine form.

Another beloved manifestation of divine beauty in human form was Joseph, who was sold as a slave in the marketplace of Egypt. Joseph has long stood for the Beloved, his lover being Zulaykha, Potiphar's wife. This love story recounted in the Qur'an is called the "most beautiful story" that God told. The four lines recalling this story seem to be in praise of Allah's omnipotence and immanence. Furthermore, to recognize that God himself was sold as a slave reiterates the merciful and egalitarian message of Islam: no human is better than any other, and even the lowliest servant is a manifestation of the Divine.

The third stanza begins with allusions to Qur'anic chapters 91 and 92, *ash-Shams* (the Sun) and *al-Lail* (the Night). God's praise is evoked by referring first to the radiant sun and the splendor it exudes, and then to the calm night that complements the sunny day. Not only has Allah been spoken of through light imagery, but the Prophet Muhammad himself has been praised through this imagery. From the ninth century onwards, those engaged in theosophical discussions have spoken of the cosmos as manifest through the "light of Muhammad." The great Andalusian mystic, Ibn al-'Arabi (1165–1240) ties the radiance of the very first light to Muhammad's glory; and the Qur'an itself speaks of Muhammad as *siraj al-munir*, a glowing lamp (33:46). If the Prophet's face is like the radiant sun, then his tresses are like the calm night. Certainly such a Being could not be comprehended by the intellect (*'aql*), that faculty so scorned in the world of mysticism. Even though Muhammad called himself a human, according to this qawwali, the (wise) world— his lover—knows he is not only human, but also much more.

Towards the midway point of the qawwali, the linguistic register switches from standard Urdu to a more colloquial Hindi/Urdu/Dakani/Purabi. Such language switching is common in qawwalis, where didactic purposes are served by lines in Persian and/or Arabic, while those in vernaculars encourage emotional, experiential contemplation of the Divine (also a goal of the vernacular devotion poetry excerpted in chapters 1 and 2). With this shift, the poet creates resonance with the ethos of a north Indian Krishna *bhajan*. The object of praise (Muhammad/Allah) is now spoken of as Hari/Shyam, which are primary epithets for Krishna, *bhakti* poetry's romantic hero. Some medieval Sufis did speak of Muhammad as an *avatara* of Vishnu, perhaps as the Tenth Awaited *Avatara*. The mention of *birha/viraha* (separation from one's lover—referred to here in standard terms as a scorching fire) is bound to conjure up images prevalent in the devotional *virahini* tradition, wherein the lover speaks as a pining woman awaiting her beloved's advances. The register briefly switches back to Arabic again before proceeding to speak in the Urdu voice once again: "Whenever you encounter my beloved . . ." is the second *misra* of a medieval Perso-Arabic verse, the first being "*Saba ba gulshan-i ahbab agar hami guzari* ("Saba! Were you to blow through my Friend's garden . . ."). In an interview with Syed Akbar Hyder, one qawwal claimed that by invoking Arabic and Persian, the qawwali reinforces the hierarchy rooted in mystical knowledge. Not all audience members can comprehend the Arabic elements; gnosis is not available to all, certainly not immediately: it must be apprehended through spiritual practice.

Muhammad is also figured into Islam's cosmology in a more direct manner: Allah and Muhammad in this qawwali are separated by a curtain, but beyond the curtain they are really the same. This is a lesson that Muhammad teaches Gabriel, the best of angels. Muhammad is thus not only superior to all other prophets, but he is also Gabriel's teacher. Muhammad is then referred to as *yar* (friend/beloved), and those who are concerned about his book-message (*khat*) only and not about the Messenger are chastised as foolish or ignorant (*aghyar*). Then the Prophet is described with the standard metaphor of the bridegroom. The community sings in the bridal voice. This groom is chaste and virgin: untouched by evil, unlettered (*ummi* being a common epithet for the Prophet), a symbol one might liken to the virginity of Mary, which permits the Divine to enter the human. Mary is at times compared to the Prophet Muhammad, because just as Mary needed to be a virgin for Jesus to inhabit her womb, the Prophet needed to be unlettered so that the Qur'an could descend in all its purity and not be sullied by any worldly knowledge.

One of the strikingly Indian aspects of this qawwali is the interplay between a message of profound awe and the playful intimacy of the female lover toward her elusive beloved. This narrative voice blurs distinctions between "high" Arabicized mysticism and vernacular *bhakti*. Yet the *virahini's* playful voice is not that of some innocent sixteen-year-old; rather it is that of a mature woman, practiced in love, who can recognize and *see through* every gesture/mannerism/ploy (*ada*). Hers is a voice tied to knowledge. Thus, intellect becomes associated with women, challenging the conventional understanding that women are lacking in '*aql*.

Finally, this qawwali also beautifully demonstrates aspects of Sufi pedagogy. It asks such questions, at least implicitly, as "What/Who is Muhammad? What/Who is Allah? What qualities should we love and be devoted to?" Here they are laid out, enumerated in didactic fashion, and answered.

Teri har ek ada ko main jan gain na

I've come to know your every gesture, haven't I, my dear?
I've figured out your ways and means,
haven't I, my dear?
It's not just my heart I've lost, my dear,
it's life itself, is it not, my dear?

You appeared on Mt. Sinai and knocked Moses senseless,
You possessed Laila and drove Majnun mad,
gave Mansur the goblet and got him drunk;
and wasn't that you, sold off in Egypt's marketplace?

Your radiant countenance
is but the promised sun,
its splendor lighting up the universe

Those glorious night-black locks of yours
bring the world repose.

Your stature casts no shadow:
how can mere mortals grasp it?

Insist a hundred thousand times that you are but human—
humanity apprehends that you're much more.

I know your every gesture,
Each and every one.
I've come to know each move of yours,
Each sign, each blandishment.

It's not just my heart I've lost is it, now?
I've lost my life and soul.

The townsfolk have started to ask,
"[And] who might this one be to you?"

Who can know my heart's secrets?
You, after all: my heart's master.

Why talk of losing my heart;
I've lost my life to you, haven't I, dear?

Loving you, Hari, is secret strife,
A disease that's laid me low.
And now I can't think straight.

Even cooling sighs inflame
the soul-scorching fire of Separation;
day and night I lament my love for you.

If you meet my beloved please give him my desperate news:

It's not just my heart that I've lost,
it's life itself.

So he came enshrouded
in a beggar's black mantle;
so he altered his form, disguised himself;
could I fail to recognize who it was?

As he stood tying his bridal turban
the King who Bestows Dignity
commanded Gabriel: "O my friend,
my soulmate, go look and see
what mystery lies behind
that veil of Unity
calling out to you!"
Gabriel submitted in humble reply:
"How is it within me to do so?"

The Beloved answered,
"Go, for I grant you leave."

He lifted the curtain and saw naught there
than what he'd seen on this side;
behind the curtain it was not God
but God's Beloved [standing there]
tying his turban in just the same way.
The Beloved came as a messenger,
but those not in the know were
confounded with his Word.

Ask not [about] my bridegroom's purity:
my groom is as chaste as green grass.

Angels are only angels, but
the Immaculate Master says:
"Do not dare question my bridegroom,
my groom is as chaste as green grass."

Prince of the Excellent,
King of the world,
king of the world who wears the crown,
the crown of Intercession,
spreads wide his mantle of mercy
before his fortunate people!
Over all the sinners he has spread
the mantle of his mercy.

Enshrouded in his black beggar's mantle,
even in an altered form
could I fail to know it was he?

Behold the bedroll
of the King of Creation:
a meager mat of palm leaves,
a blackened beggar's shroud,
and yet what enchantment lay in his words!
So many lives lost in the mists/web of those words . . .

Blessings on him who succored the friendless,
Blessings on him who was humble, though King,
Blessings on him who was ever truth-telling,
Blessings on him who in exile lived destitute,
Blessings on him who bestowed robes on the bloodthirsty,
Blessings on him who blessed those who cursed [him],
Blessings on him who casts pearls of graciousness,
Blessings on him who claimed evil-doers as his own.

How many lives lost in his words!
Zulaikha was possessed by Yusuf,
But I've given myself up for my Prophet

Haven't I, dear?

Sacrificed for the blanket-clad Prophet,
For the prophet who loves his people,
For my beloved prophet,
For the prophet who's my very own.

Even your slightest gesture . . .

Sources

The source of this qawwali is an audio recording, in the form of a CD, in the private collection of Syed Akbar Hyder. The text has been transcribed from a private performance in 1974 in Hyderabad, India by the qawwal Aziz Ahmad Khan Warsi.

Further Reading

The best place to begin is Annemarie Schimmel's *My Soul Is a Woman,* trans. Susan H. Rey (New York: Continuum, 1997). Her explanations are lucid, and she draws in many relevant sources on the issues raised here, especially that of how Sufi love expression is gendered. See also Ali Asani and Kamal Abdel-Malek, *Celebrating Muhammad* (Columbia, SC: University of South Carolina Press, 1995). Lexical definitions are taken from Ali Akbar Dihkhuda, *Lughatnama* (Tehran: Tehran University Press, 1946), entry #18990. Regula Qureshi's *Sufi Music of India and Pakistan: Sound, Context and Meaning in Qawwali* (New York: Cambridge University Press, 1986) is a key work on South Asian devotional music, especially in its qawwali form.

— 6 —

Na't: Media Contexts and
Transnational Dimensions
of a Devotional Practice

Patrick Eisenlohr

Na't is a devotional performance genre frequently encountered in South Asian Muslim settings, most commonly in Urdu. It consists of recitations of poems in praise of the Prophet Muhammad, and also of other Islamic authorities, such as the prominent Sufi teachers Mu'inuddin Chishti (d. 1235, popularly known as Khwaja Gharib Nawaz), 'Abd al-Qadir Gilani (d. 1166), and even members of the *Ahl-i Bayt* (the family of the Prophet and their descendants), such as the Prophet's grandson Husayn. Nevertheless, *na't* is most strongly associated with the intense devotion to and veneration of the Prophet which, for many Muslims in South Asia and its diasporas, are key to proper Islamic conduct. The performance of these devotional poems and hymns addressed to the Prophet enacts a special relationship between Muslims and the Prophet, and is tied to a notion of the Prophet having a continuing spiritual presence of his own. In more recent times, the performance of *na't* has been associated with the South Asian Islamic traditions that place particular emphasis on devotion to the Prophet, foremost among them the Ahl-i Sunnat va Jama'at (hereafter Ahl-i Sunnat). The Ahl-i Sunnat is one of the movements of Islamic reform and revival that emerged in nineteenth-century colonial India. It is also known as the Barelwi tradition after the north Indian town of Bareilly, which was the residence and ancestral home of the movement's founder, the *'alim* Ahmad Riza Khan Barelwi (1856–1921), who is also known as an accomplished composer of *na't*. In marked contrast to other contemporary reform movements such as the school of Deoband and the Ahl-i Hadith, the Ahl-i Sunnat distinguishes itself by an emphasis on practices of intercession (*shafa'a*) and by an openness to Sufism. The Ahl-i Sunnat, for example, entertains a close relationship to the Sufi *tariqa* of the Qadriyya, and encourages the veneration of its founder, 'Abd al-Qadir Gilani. Most importantly, followers of this tradition often place the Prophet Mu-

hammad at the center of their devotional practices, informed by the doctrine of
hazir-o nazir (present and observant), according to which the Prophet continues
to have a spiritual presence of his own manifest as pure light (*nur-i muhammadi*)
and is capable of mediating between Muslims and God.

The recitation of *na't*, which eulogize the Prophet and ask for blessings to be bestowed on him, is one of the most important ways in which performers establish
such a special relationship to the Prophet and invoke his mediatory presence. *Na't*
is an immensely popular practice but nevertheless exists in a controversial context.
Its significance is one of the issues around which doctrinal differences among South
Asian Muslims on questions of intercession in Islamic tradition have often crystallized. *Na't* is often described as a "popular" Islamic practice, implying that it is part
of folk traditions largely untouched by modern waves of reformism in South Asian
Islam. But today, *na't* is often performed in contexts in which awareness of conflict
between followers of the Ahl-i Sunnat and the school of Deoband is widespread,
and in which an increasingly well-informed Islamic public in South Asia and its
diasporas debates and seeks justification for practices known to be controversial.
As a result, the performance of *na't* has often become a rather self-conscious affair,
in which its adherents are anxious to demonstrate its legitimacy with reference to
the Qur'an and the Sunna. As I will describe below, the use of contemporary electronic media has come to play a significant role in this process.

Most importantly, the performative aspects of *na't* deserve attention, as *na't* is
best understood as a transformative practice. Reciting *na't* not only establishes a
special relationship to the Prophet Muhammad by means of profuse praise and by
invoking his spiritual presence. It also imbues the performer with love and reverence for the Prophet and turns the reciter into a more pious person. While I was
doing fieldwork in Mauritius, my informants sometimes spoke about the transformative effects of *na't* in very personal and emotional terms. By opening one's heart
for the Prophet, they stressed, one builds a personal relationship and experiences
a kind of visceral closeness to him. *Na't* therefore attests to the performative power
of this devotional practice, which is not merely an enactment of pre-existing "beliefs" and orientations by participants, but crucially helps one to constitute and
produce pious dispositions, or in the words of two of my informants, "to become
a better person." This is the background against which adherents of the practice
of *na't* claim that reciting *na't* in proper ways and under proper circumstances results in the accumulation of spiritual merit (*sawab*).

Na't, Media and Transnational Contexts

Since the 1980s, audiocassette recordings of *na't* performances—and more recently audio CDs—have become increasingly popular both in South Asia and its
diasporas. Most recently, there are also a growing numbers of Web sites from
which *na't* sound files can be downloaded. Indeed, one could say that for many
Muslims in South Asia and its diasporas *na't* as a devotional activity is now firmly

grounded in electronic media practices. Listening to *na't* recordings in these media has extended this devotional practice to new contexts where it was previously absent. More importantly, it articulates in interesting ways with several aspects of *na't* practice, namely, questions of religious authority and the transnational contexts in which *na't* takes place.

As I have mentioned before, some Muslims criticize the strong focus on the Prophet Muhammad and the invocation of his powers of mediation, which are key dimensions of *na't* performances, seeing them as a dilution of the oneness of God. Some even go so far to brand these practices illegitimate additions to Islam. These differences build on contrasting perspectives about spiritual mediation in Islamic tradition and in the South Asian context, differences that constitute one of the main points of contention between Ahl-i Sunnat (Barelwi)-associated Muslims and those following representatives of the school of Deoband. In the face of Deobandi criticism of practices such as performing *na't*, those favoring *na't* have used electronic recordings of this genre to defend its legitimacy. During my research in Mauritius I found that participants in *na't* performances considered cassette and CD recordings authoritative models to emulate in their performances. Many stated that listening to recordings of accomplished *na't khwan* (*na't* performers) from South Asia, and more recently also from Mauritius, helped them to achieve a performative style they considered proper for reciting *na't*. They described this style as contrasting with those of popular musical entertainment genres, here especially Hindi film songs. Hindi films and their music are also extremely popular in Mauritius, and are frequently believed to heavily influence the way *na't* is performed locally. This is a point that critics of the practice frequently raise. But the use of audiocassette and CD recordings not only enhanced the legitimacy *na't* by highlighting the differences between this performative genre and the musical genres of popular entertainment. Mauritian Muslims of Indian origin I worked with also treated audiocassettes and CDs as enabling the reliable transmission of religious discourse and poetry by linking them to centers of Islamic authority in South Asia. Such recordings of well-known *na't khwan* from South Asia, and more recently also of Mauritians taught by Indian and Pakistani imams versed in *na't*, also reassured them that the poetry was authentic, in the sense of having been composed by learnèd figures of Islamic authority located in South Asia. That is, these electronic media were seen as both facilitating authentic textual transmission and as safeguarding a particular performative style. By helping local Muslims to perform *na't* in "proper" ways, the recordings would assist them in gaining spiritual merit. The use of cassettes or CD recordings of *na't* as sources of authenticity illustrates how electronic media have become part of the genealogy of Islamic authority, focused as it is on the transmission of authoritative discourse through long chains of reliable interlocutors.

In diasporic contexts, these uses of cassette and audio CD *na't* may become even more significant, since questions of religious authority frequently intersect with concerns about the authenticity of religious tradition in the diaspora. In Mauritius, for example, printed Urdu manuals and collections of *na't* have long been available, but since most Mauritian Muslims lack sufficient Urdu literacy skills, the wide circulation of *na't* via audiocassettes and CDs has brought about a new popularization of the genre. Also, the sense of being removed from a "homeland" from which ancestors migrated, together with the minority status of most South Asian Muslim diaspora communities, sometimes gives rise to fears about a "loss" of authentic Islamic tradition, as it certainly did among some of my interlocutors in Mauritius. In such diasporic contexts, easily circulated models of authoritative Islamic practice become enmeshed with questions of religious authority and legitimacy in particularly salient ways.

The following *na't* or excerpts of *na't* are from cassette and CD recordings produced in Mauritius. *Na't 1, Shah-i madinah,* is taken from my own recording of a local performance I attended in 2003, but recordings of this popular *na't* can also be found on locally produced audiocassettes and audio CDs. During my research in Mauritius I found that live performances of *na't* are now heavily influenced by these recordings and the booklets often sold with them; both are often consulted in preparing for *mahfil-i mawlud,* devotional gatherings held on festive occasions such as the birthday of the Prophet (*milad al-nabi*), anniversaries of the demise of revered saint-teachers (*'urs*), or auspicious occasions in the life of a family, such as weddings or moving into a new home. These devotional gatherings are a privileged setting for the recitation of *na't.* In the *mahfil-e mawlud* I attended, the events always began with a Qur'an recital. Very often the performers of *na't* begin the recital of a particular praise-poem by uttering *darud,* Arabic litanies in praise of the Prophet:

> May blessings be sent to the Prophet of God
> And greetings be sent to the beloved of God
> May blessings be sent to the Prophet of God
> And greetings be sent to the beloved of God

Following the *darud,* the performers turn to exuberant praising of the Prophet Muhammad's qualities, switching to Urdu, which also in Mauritius is the language most closely associated with the genre of *na't.* Nevertheless, in 2003 I attended a performance in which one very popular *na't* was recited in Mauritian Creole, a French-lexifier Creole, which is the predominant vernacular language of Mauritius. In Na't 1, as in many other *na't,* the performers directly address the Prophet. The closeness to the Prophet that the performers seek to establish by reciting the *na't* is also evoked by the use of the familiar in personal pronouns of address (*tu*) and in possessive pronouns (*tera/teri/tere*).

Other *na't* center on the faithfulness of the performers' devotion. In Na't 2, the reciting of *na't* enacts a promise of continued allegiance to the Prophet. Besides the direct addressing of the Prophet in uttering praises, *na't* performers also demonstrate devotion to him by humbling themselves. In Na't 3, the *na't khwan* does so by denying agency in the composition of the poems. The linguistic form *likhwayi* (from *likhna,* "to write") pluralizes the agency behind the writing of praises to the Prophet by using the grammatical form of the causative. While it is clear that someone devoted to the Prophet composed these poems which the actually present *na't khwan* claims to merely relay, the ultimate authorship is attributed to the Prophet himself: "I have not written it, but the Prophet has caused it to be written." (*Main ne likhi to nahin, sarkar ne likhwayi hai.* Here the Prophet is referred to with the honorific title *sarkar.*) Such multi-voiced authorship evokes the complexity of participants' roles in *na't* as a speech event, a factor that often plays a significant part in performances of this devotional genre.

Medina, the site of the Prophet Muhammad's tomb and, many believe, his favorite city, plays a central role in many *na't*. This is because *na't khwan* often express attachment to the Prophet through longing for Medina, as the reciters exuberantly describe the qualities of the city. In *Na't* 4, the delight the performer proclaims about being in Medina and obtaining a glance of its landmarks, is a metonym for the overwhelming joy of experiencing the Prophet's presence. In particular the green dome (*sabze gunbad, gunbad-i khazra*) of Muhammad's tomb is a conventional and frequently recurring motif in *na't*. Many also consider the focus on Medina a poetic strategy to deflect the criticism of those who charge that the praises of the Prophet voiced in *na't* are excessive because they in effect liken the Prophet to God.

Apart from the descriptions of Medina, another interesting point in *Na't* 4 is the use of the perfective participle of the verb *chalna* ("to walk, to move") in *main madine chala* ("Here I go to Medina," also translatable as "I will go to Medina right away") with reference to future time. This grammatical form is deployed to highlight an affective value in the willingness to immediately comply with a request. The form is also used in everyday contexts with this connotation, as in *main abhi aya* ("I will be back in just a moment"). Here, of course, the request is to go to Medina, which the reciter is happily willing to do, and the implication is that the one making the request is the Prophet himself. This particular phrasing of "Here I go to Medina" also underlines the performative power of *na't:* in the act of reciting the performer is, in a sense, visiting Medina.

In *Na't* 5, the *na't khwan* again directly addresses the Prophet Muhammad, but does so through attributes and features of the city of Medina, as in "you of the green dome" (*sabze gunbad wale*). He uses rather plain, everyday language and again employs the familiar in the imperative form of the verb in "accept my prayers" (*manzur du'a karna*), as also in "dwell in my eyes" (*ankhon men sama jana*), and "O, you hidden one, come hide in my heart" (*Ae pardah nashin dil ke, pardeh men raha karna*). The appellation "Light of God" (*nur-i khuda*) as one of the names of the Prophet also evokes the Sufist concept of *nur-i muhammadi*, according to which the Prophet enjoys an independent spiritual presence manifest as pure light (*nur*).

Other *na't*, such as *Na't* 6, center on a vivid description of the blessings derived from reciting *na't* and from the inner dispositions this act creates in pious persons, such as love for and remembrance of the Prophet. But it is not only those performing *na't*, but also those sponsoring a *mahfil-mawlud* who will be richly compensated, as is proclaimed in *Na't* 6. Again, this opens a perspective on the heteroglossic character of many *na't* performances, where the authorship of those known as accomplished composers of *na't* intersects with the performative creativity of *na't khwan*, while the speech event may unfold under the sponsorship of still other actors, such as a family celebrating a wedding. Finally, as we have seen above, the Prophet himself is sometimes invoked as the ultimate originator of the praise poetry.

Na't 7 addresses the key mediatory role of the Prophet Muhammad in the interactions of the performers with God. Again, the qualities of the Prophet are exalted, while he is also credited with the achievement of miracles, such as reversing the course of the sun. As the poet, whose pen name Anwar Bilal is mentioned in the last verse, proclaims, "every divine blessing is due to him" (*har ni'mat hai badawlat un ki*), while "he who has affection in his heart for him, also pleases the Supreme Lord." Such an exemplary believer enjoys divine favor; indeed "he belongs to God" (*wo hai Allah wala*).

Most *na't* are immediately addressed to the Prophet, but this is not always the case. *Na't khwan* often expand their devotion to include the members of the Prophet's family, the *Ahl-i Bayt*. To some it might come as a surprise that this devotional genre so heavily associated with a particular Sunni South Asian tradition also provides a frame for poetic lament and narration of the tragic events of the battle of Karbala, in which the Prophet's grandson Husayn and Husayn's followers were slain. In their mourning for Husayn and cursing of his killers (in particular Yazid), these performances strongly recall Shi'ite ritual traditions. Note also that in *Na't* 8 the poet, whose pen name Ehsan is mentioned in the last verse, calls Husayn his imam, which is consonant with Shi'ite practice, while the latter also receives the honorific pronoun of address (*ap*), as in *Hazrat Husayn, ap ko mera salam hai* ("Hazrat Husayn, my salutations to you").

Finally, there are *na't* performances that address figures other than the Prophet and his family. Among those South Asian Muslims close to the tradition of the *Ahl-i Sunnat va Jama'at*, the saint-teacher 'Abd al-Qadir Gilani, also known as Ghawth-i a'zam, is especially popular. In *Na't* 9, the *na't khwan* directly addresses this great Baghdadi mystic while praising him as a performer of amazing miracles, such as raising a ship that had sunk twelve years before from the bottom of the sea with everyone on board alive. Most importantly, the *na't khwan* celebrates Gilani's powers of intercession with the Prophet, and portrays him as the first among Sufis and other friends of God. His proclaimed leadership over other saints, as well as his special relationship to the Prophet points to nesting hierarchies of mediation reaching from minor mystics to greater saints, to the Prophet Muhammad, and finally to God himself. At the same time, both Gilani and the Prophet are cast as monarchical figures who preside over courtly assemblies (*darbar*).

1. Shah-i madina

Lord of Medina, Lord of Medina
Lord of Medina, Lord of Medina
All the other prophets come to beg for your favors at your door

Lord of Medina, Lord of Medina
Just for you the world was made, just for you the world was made
And draped with a blue sky, and draped with a blue sky
Without you, without you, the world would be empty and desolate
All the (other) prophets come to beg for your favors at your door
Lord of Medina, Lord of Medina
You have awakened the destiny of Halima [wet-nurse of the Prophet]
You have awakened the destiny of Halima
You have come into the world as a blessing
You have come into the world as a blessing
Supporter of the unfortunates
Supporter of the unfortunates
Friend of the orphans
All other prophets come to beg for your favors at your door
Lord of Medina, Lord of Medina
All splendors are just because of you, all splendors are just because of
    you
Our inhabited world is your work, our inhabited world is your work
All other beings, all other beings, are just imaginary
All other prophets beg at your door
Lord of Medina, Lord of Medina

2. *Lab peh na‘t-i pak ka naghmah*

Sweet and pure *na‘t* have adorned my lips in the past, and will also be
    manifest today
My relationship to my Prophet has been there in the past, and will also
    be manifest today
How can the one whom the Supreme Lord has elevated in rank be
    lowly?
His praises have been proclaimed in this world and the hereafter, and
    will also be proclaimed today
Sweet and pure *na‘t* have adorned my lips in the past, and will also be
    manifest today
My relationship to my Prophet has been there in the past, and will also
    be manifest today
Why turn anywhere else, why approach anybody else
Why turn anywhere else, why approach anybody else
If your source of favors has been there in Medina, and will also be there
    today
If your source of favors has been there in Medina, and will also be there
    today

Sweet and pure *na't* have adorned my lips in the past, and will also be
   manifest today
My relationship to my Prophet has been there in the past, and will also
   be manifest today

3. From *Na't-i mahbub*

The *na't* of the Beloved of God has come to my lips
I have not written it, but the Prophet has caused it to be written
If you want to have an idea of his greatness, ask the angels
Who have found their place at the side of the Prophet

4. *Phir karam ho gaya*

Yet another time he has favored me with a gift of Medina
Here I go to Medina, to Medina
How could I describe my heart's joy
When I heard the good news that I am to go to Medina
Yet another time he has favored me with a gift of Medina
Here I go to Medina, to Medina
The beloved of God from whom I will obtain pardon for my faults
I am ready to go to his home, I am to go to Medina
Yet another time he has favored me with a gift of Medina
Here I go to Medina, to Medina
When my glance falls on the green dome [of the resting place of the
   Prophet in Medina]
What joy this will bring to me, here I go to Medina
When my glance falls on its minaret [of the resting place of the Prophet
   in Medina]
What joy this will bring to me, here I go to Medina
Yet another time he has favored me with a gift of Medina
Here I go to Medina, to Medina

5. From *Ae sabze gunbad wale*

O you of the green dome, accept my prayers
When I breathe my last breath, give me the gift of your appearance
O Light of God, dwell in my eyes
Either invite me to your door or come into my dreams
O you hidden one, come hide in my heart

6. Na't-i mustafa (Sana khwan-i mustafa)

The one who hosts the reciters of Mustafa's [the Prophet's] praises
Will be guaranteed Mustafa's protection
The one whose words are full of praise for the Prophet
The one whose thoughts are perfumed with praises of him
The one whose tongue recites honorable salutations to the Prophet
A thousand welcomes to such a praise singer of Mustafa
The one who hosts the reciters of Mustafa's praises
Will be guaranteed Mustafa's protection
The one whose eyes shed tears having left the abode of the Prophet
Has inherited the treasures of this world and the hereafter
The one who has embellished his garments with this tear [lit. pearl]
The Almighty himself will declare him a faithful follower of Mustafa
The one who hosts the reciters of Mustafa's praises
Will be guaranteed Mustafa's protection
The one in whose breath the name of Muhammad lives continuously
Has lit for himself a light of guidance in the darkness
The one whose heart has turned his memory into its own beat
He is the beloved of Mustafa, the beloved of beloveds of Mustafa

7. Jin ka nam muhammad

Every believer is intoxicated with the one whose name is Muhammad
Love for him elevates one in this world and the hereafter
The prophet's mercy pervades both worlds, every divine blessing is due
  to him
He who has affection in his heart for him, also pleases the Supreme
  Lord
He belongs to God
Every believer is intoxicated with the one whose name is Muhammad
Love for him elevates one in this world and the hereafter
He is the basis of everything else, he is the guide on the path of God
He is the chief of all prophets and ranks right after God
He is the first among all creatures
Every believer is intoxicated with the one whose name is Muhammad
Love for him elevates one in this world and the hereafter
He cut the moon in half and the set sun rose again
If he wishes, seventy persons can be fed with a single cup of milk
Every believer is intoxicated with the one whose name is Muhammad
Love for him elevates one in this world and the hereafter

In all difficulties of life, at the moment of death, or in the tomb
He will protect us wherever we are, and also on the Day of Judgment
His grace supports us
Every believer is intoxicated with the one whose name is Muhammad
Love for him elevates one in this world and the hereafter
I ruined my whole life in sinful deeds, the only hope I have is his
    benevolent glance
God willing, Bilal Anwar will also receive the grace of his splendid
    appearance, which will illuminate his tomb
Every believer is intoxicated with the one whose name is Muhammad
Love for him elevates one in this world and the hereafter

8. *Bagh-i nabi ke phul (Salam-i karbala)*

In the garden of the Prophet, you are the most beautiful flower
O Husayn, my salutations to you
The one who is a martyr for divine truth never dies
These are not my words, but those of the Supreme Lord himself
In the garden of the Prophet, you are the most beautiful flower
O Husayn, my salutations to you
My friends, how beautiful is his last prayer
Prostrating himself before his creator even under the enemy's blade, this
    is my imam
In the garden of the Prophet, you are the most beautiful flower
O Husayn, my salutations to you
Every human being hates the accursed Yazid
For every heart is a servant of the child of the Lion of God ['Ali,
    Husayn's father and the Prophet's son-in law]
In the garden of the Prophet, you are the most beautiful flower
O Husayn, my salutations to you
For the sake of the progeny of Muhammad
O Ehsan, may their murderers be strictly banned from paradise
In the garden of the Prophet, you are the most beautiful flower
O Husayn, my salutations to you

9. *Allah, Allah kiya kehena (Ghaus-i a'zam ka darbar)*

The court of Ghaus-i a'zam, God, God! What can one say
In the illuminated bazaar of Baghdad, God, God! What can one say
You belong to us and we belong to you, you are the beloved of the
    Prophet
You support those in distress in the courtly assembly of the Prophet

You turn the desert into a garden, God, God! What can one say
The court of Ghaus -i a'zam, God, God! What can one say
In the illuminated bazaar of Baghdad, God, God! What can one say
You are the leader of the saints, mystics and Sufis, one higher than the
    other
All those friends of God salute you and come to your door
He is the chief of the friends of God, God, God! What can one say
The court of Ghaus -i a'zam, God, God! What can one say
In the illuminated bazaar of Baghdad, God, God! What can one say
He turns the thief into a friend of God in an instant and helps the
    afflicted
In an instant he brought a ship sunken for twelve years back to surface
The old mourning woman exclaimed over and over again, God, God!
    What can one say

Acknowledgments

I am indebted to the many Mauritians without whose help and friendship my research would have been impossible, and in this case my particular thanks go to Hossen Edun and his extended family and to the late Cassam Beebeejaum and his extended family. I also thank Nargis Virani for her help and excellent advice on several points of translation.

Sources

Na't 1: Author's recording, 1 August 2003. Na't 2: Shareef Chady, *Naaté-Rasool* (*SAW*) vol. 7, set of two audio CDs (Castel, Mauritius: Étoile Brilliant Sound, n.d.) Na't 3, 6, and 9: Shareef Chady, *Naaté-Rasool* (*SAW*) vol. 6, audiocassette (Castel, Mauritius: Étoile Brilliant Sound, 2000). Na't 4, 7, and 8: Shareef Chady, *Naaté-Rasool* (*SAW*) vol. 8, set of two audio CDs (Castel, Mauritius: Étoile Brilliant Sound, 2001). Na't 5: Shareef Chady, *Naaté-Rasool* (*SAW*) vol. 5, audiocassette (Castel, Mauritius: Étoile Brilliant Sound, 1998).

Further Reading

On *na't*, see Ali Asani, "In Praise of Muhammad: Sindhi and Urdu Poems"; and Marcia Hermansen, "Women's Celebration of Muhammad's Birth," in *Religions of India in Practice*, Donald S. Lopez, ed. (Princeton, NJ: Princeton University Press, 1995), pp. 159–186, 367–372, respectively. For an account of practicing *na't* in the diaspora, see Regula Burckhardt Qureshi, "Transcending Space: Recitation and Community among South Asian Muslims in Canada," in *Making Muslim Space in*

North America and Europe, Barbara Daly Metcalf, ed. (Berkeley, CA: University of California Press, 1996), pp. 46–64. On the Ahl-i Sunnat va Jama'at ("Barelwi") tradition, see Barbara D. Metcalf, *Islamic Revival in British India: Deoband 1860–1900* (Princeton, NJ: Princeton University Press, 1982); and in particular Usha Sanyal, *Devotional Islam and Politics in British India: Ahmad Riza Khan Barelwi and His Movement, 1870–1920* (Oxford: Oxford University Press, 1996). On the role of electronic media in the practice of *na't,* see Patrick Eisenlohr, "As Makkah Is Sweet and Beloved, So Is Madina: Islam, Devotional Genres and Electronic Mediation in Mauritius," *American Ethnologist* 33(2) (2006): 230–245.

Na't files can be downloaded from the following Web sites: *Islamicacademy.org* n.d. Naat Shareef. Urdu Panjabi Arabic Naats. Electronic document, http://www.islamicacademy.org/html/audio/Naat.htm, accessed March 5, 2006. *Naatsharif.com* n.d. Naat Sharif. A City of Ghulaman-e-Mustafa. Electronic document, http://www.naatsharif.com, accessed December 9, 2005. *Nooremadinah.net* n.d. Media Library. NooreMadinah Network. Electronic document, http://www.nooremadinah.net/MediaLibrary/MediaLSearch.asp?txtCategory=2, accessed December 9, 2005.

—7—

Shiʻi Mourning in Muhurram:
Nauha Laments for Children Killed at Karbala

Syed Akbar Hyder and Carla Petievich

The *nauha* is a distinctive poetic form chanted during the gatherings (*majalis*) of Muhurram, the primary annual observation of the Shiʻi community. In particular they are chanted during breaks from the more formal recitation of *marsiyas*, which recount the larger, communal tragedy of Karbala; both *marsiya* and *nauha* are accompanied by ritual chest-beating (*matam*). *Nauha* (laments), like the *marsiya*, kindle many forms of human mourning. The three compositions translated here, for example, which all focus on the deaths of children, bring to the forefront an immediacy of loss, of lives cut short by tyranny.

The texts in this chapter were collected in a single volume, but examples of the *nauha* genre tend to circulate orally. They are usually referred to by their refrain line.

Imam Husayn and Zaynab were the son and daughter of Hazrat ʻAli. Zaynab was mother to Aoun and Muhammad, whose deaths are lamented in the second *nauha* below. Zaynab was also godmother to Aliʼs son, Ali Akbar, whom she laments in the final *nauha* here, "The One Who Lived Only Eighteen Years."

Sakina's Lament: "Please, Don't Beat Me Anymore"

In this *nauha*, the narrator is Imam Husaynʼs young daughter, Sakina, who was cruelly beaten by the tyrant Shimr after the camp was overrun. The little girl cries out for her dead father to save her. She begs pitifully for mercy, trying to appease Shimr, trying to appeal to his better sense and sensibilities, for is he not himself a father?

Sakinaʼs Lament is usually performed during the final ten days of the month of Muharram, which are marked by commemoration of her suffering. The setting is the prison of Damascus, where the Prophetʼs family has been imprisoned. The same person who beheaded the imam is also accused of snatching away the earrings Husayn had given his daughter. Until his death she was known to have slept on his chest. Her very name indicates that she was "Husayn's Sukun" ("the one who brought Husayn repose"), though the name itself is never uttered here. Until the last couplet no proper name except for that of Shimr is invoked. This of course facilitates the community's identification with the story: the lament becomes that of the entire community, whose members are all, in some way, Sakina.

The poet is also demonstrating his own versatility, switching registers to intensify mood. The poem is composed in a mixture of two different dialects of Hindi-Urdu, and in three-verse sets. The first set is standard Urdu, the middle is Purabi (eastern vernacular), and the third, the four-line verse (*chaur-misra*) is a kind of baby-talk. The opening lines are longer, the Purabi lines a bit shorter, and the *chaur-misra* only half-lines and half refrain. Purabi is counterposed with standard Hindustani, intensifying the emotional impact, and making feminine the overall voice of lament; this is appropriate, as the poem's narrator is, after all, a child; and children and women are gender-equated insofar as they are both distinguished from men as having less *'aql* (intellect). Finally, the language switching catches the attention of the audience, ensuring that the long, drawn-out chant with its repeated refrain does not lull the mourners into an unconscious or semiconscious state. Their emotions are reengaged and made conscious as the diction changes, and this underlines how important a component of Shi'i piety is emotional engagement.

Sakina's Lament

[Standard Urdu]
In fear cried out the daughter
of the imam of both this world and that:
"Don't beat me, Shimr, I'll stop crying, 'O Father'!
But please, don't beat me anymore.

[Purabi]
"How can a tender heart
bear such brutal affliction?
How old can I be—
O why do you do this, you tyrant?

[*Chaur-misra*]
"I'm just a little girl, O please
don't beat me any more.
I'm still of tender years, O please,
entreating you with joined hands, please,
take pity on me, Oppressor, please
don't beat me anymore.

[Standard Urdu]
"Don't you have kids my age of your own,
Oppressor of terrible temperament?
Enough, O Shimr, your threats silence me,
don't beat me anymore.

[Purabi]
"Cherished by my father,
the one he made much of
(so people tell me),
My body is terribly tender, may
your hands be cut off for this!!

[*Chaur-misra*]
"Don't give me such sorrow, Shimr, please
don't beat me anymore.
Just see my tender innocence,
I'm so delicate of body,
my body's burning, stinging—
please don't beat me anymore.

[Standard Urdu]
"So dear was I to him, not even
a flowered switch would my father raise to me.
Have mercy on me, for my body's turned blue,
don't strike me anymore.

[Purabi]
"I'll speak to you in childlike words,
O Swordsman, please don't crush me,
I'm just a small child, how can you show
such terrible lack of pity?

[*Chaur-misra*]
"Behold the way I'm sighing, please
don't beat me anymore,
see how I'm pleading with you, please
don't beat me anymore.
Listen to how I'm sighing, please,
see how I pour out my heart to you,
behold my terror, please, O please
don't beat me anymore.

[Standard Urdu]
"Listen to my entreaties, please—
see how I tremble and babble like a babe,

see my diminutive height, won't you?
Think of my tender age, won't you, please
don't beat me anymore.

[Purabi]
"Cries burst and fly up from my torn heart,
I'm not used to beatings, my small heart it trembles.

[*Chaur-misra*]
"Shimr, I'm just a tiny child,
don't beat me anymore.
Raised delicately, with a silver spoon,
don't beat me anymore.
I'm the daughter of a king,
don't beat me anymore.
Shimr, I'm so afraid, O please
don't beat me anymore.

[Standard Urdu]
"I beg you, for your own kids' sake,
relentless one, don't strike,
my body's already black and blue.
See how I'm sobbing, Shimr, please,
don't beat me anymore.

[Purabi]
"My father's father, Aliji,
gives heart to everyone.
Tyrant, you keep on slapping me,
don't you want to be like him?

[*Chaur-misra*]
"I'm the Lion's granddaughter,
don't beat me anymore,
About to lose my life, O please
don't beat me any more.
Hear me crying, Shimr, please
don't beat me anymore.
Shimr, I'm about to swoon,
don't beat me anymore."
Terrified, the young child pled,
"Shimr, don't beat me anymore!"
Begged the daughter of the Both Worlds' Iman,
"Don't beat me anymore . . ."

Lament for Zaynab's Sons: *O Aoun, O Muhammad!*

Wept the mother over her dead sons,	"O Aoun, O Muhammad!
Alas, I offer myself to save you	O Aoun, O Muhammad!
You departed this world without wedding	
garlands	O Aoun, O Muhammad!
I longed to see you wed, then live in peace	O Aoun, O Muhammad!
But in the face of Fate my hands were tied	O Aoun, O Muhammad!
In place of two grooms [now] lie two corpses	
Let me be taken instead of you	
With what eyes can I look at you in this state	O Aoun, O Muhammad!
In front of me, a mother, lie your corpses	
How can I console my heart?	
Why not beat my head in lamentation	O Aoun, O Muhammad!
You lived up to your uncles' ideals	
But darlings, tell me this—	
Was your mother not worthy of your love,	
too,	O Aoun, O Muhammad!"
This was the mother's lament, Baqir,	
Over her sons' corpses—	
"Let me taken instead of you!	
You've both restored my honor,	O Aoun, O Muhammad!"
Wept the mother over her dead sons,	"O Aoun, O Muhammad!
Alas, I offer myself to save you	O Aoun, O Muhammad!
You departed this world without wedding	
garlands	O Aoun, O Muhammad!
I longed to see you wed, then live in peace	O Aoun, O Muhammad!
But in the face of Fate my hands were tied	O Aoun, O Muhammad!
In place of two grooms lie two corpses,	
let me be taken instead of you	
With what eyes can I look at you in this state	O Aoun, O Muhammad?
In front of me, a mother, lie your corpses—	
how can I console my heart?	
why not beat my head in lamentation	O Aoun, O Muhammad?
You lived up to your uncles' ideals	
but darlings, tell me this—	
was your mother not worthy of your love,	
too,	O Aoun, O Muhammad?"
This was the mother's lament, Baqir,	
over her sons' corpses—	
"Let me [be] taken instead of you!	
You've both restored my honor,	O Aoun, O Muhammad!"

Lament for Ali Akbar: The One Who Lived Only Eighteen Years

Lost was he in a foreign land,
  Zaynab,   the one who lived only eighteen
                                            years.
Muhammad's progeny shed   for the one who lived only eighteen
  tears   years.
Banu laments, her desires   over the corpse of him who lived
  unfulfilled   eighteen years.
"Where will this jail of a womb   the one who lived only eighteen
  find him   years.
with hope and care I nurtured
  him
but as his nuptials drew near
I lost him on the battlefield   he who lived only eighteen years.
To whom complain of my sad
  fate—
for all my services, this return,
to not even tie the bridal veil   on him who lived only eighteen
                                            years?

The King of Kerbala kept telling
  us
that this is what was fated;
now bear with patience,   the loss of the one who lived eighteen
  O daughter of Ali   years.
Shaukat, this is a mighty sorrow,
Shaukat, this is calamity,
the Prophet stands shedding tears by the head of the one who lived only
  eighteen years."

Sources

The *nauhas* cited in this text appear in Sayyid Turab Ali Rizvi, *Fughan-i Azadaran* (Hyderabad: Maktabah-e Turabiya, n.d.)

Further Reading

A thoroughly researched succinct analysis of South Asian Shi'i devotional litera-ture can be found in Regula Qureshi, "Islamic Music in an Indian Environment: The Shi'a Majlis," *Ethnomusicology* 25 (1981): 41–71. Two works that explore the devotion-gender nexus in Shi'i commemorative assemblies are Kamran Scot Aghaie, ed., *The Women of Karbala: Ritual Performance and Symbolic Discourses in*

Modern Shi'i Islam (Austin: University of Texas Press, 2005); and Amy Bard, "Value and Vitality in a Literary Tradition: Female Poets and the Urdu Marsiyah," in *The Annual of Urdu Studies* 15 (2000): 323–335. For a fine study of South Asian Shi'i rituals, see Vernon Schubel, *Religious Performance in Contemporary Islam: Shi'i Devotional Rituals in South Asia* (Columbia, SC: University of South Carolina Press, 1993).

8

Islam and the Devotional Image in Pakistan

Jamal J. Elias

Devotional objects play a central role in the popular piety of Muslims in South Asia, as they do in the lives of Muslims in many other parts of the world. These objects can either be relics, the shrines of dead saints, things belonging to or handled by living saints, or souvenirs and mementos of pilgrimages to religiously charged places or individuals. This chapter provides examples of two classes of objects that play a role in Muslim piety and practice in Pakistan: religious posters and truck decoration. Brightly colored posters, sometimes called calendar art or chromolithographs, are common in South Asia, across the Middle East, in Africa, and in other parts of the world as well. They are extremely common in Hindu piety and have been the subject of much study. The tradition of religious poster art in Pakistan is closely linked to the much larger phenomenon in India: production techniques and the visual aesthetic are often identical. Frequently even the symbolism of Muslim saint posters borrows heavily from that of Hindu imagery. The resemblance is all the more obvious when one compares posters of Sufi saints (pirs) to those of Sikh gurus.

Poster Art

The posters reproduced in this article fall into two categories, those representing Sufi saints and those of relics of the Prophet Muhammad. Posters are traditionally purchased as souvenirs of pilgrimages, with the expectation that some of the charisma or blessing (*barkat*) of the place or personage that is visited continues to reside in the poster representing it. This belief is stated quite clearly in the text written on the first poster.

Footprint of the Prophet (Figure 8.1)

This poster illustrates a holy relic of the Prophet's footprint housed in the reliquary of the Topkapi Palace in Istanbul. The text (in Urdu) provides a detailed list of miracles associated with possessing the image. The artist, M. Ishaq, has signed his work under the roses toward the left. It is printed by Malik Muhamad Shafique Art Publishers, Kashmiri Bazar, Lahore.

Title: *Image of the Blessed Foot of the Noble Messenger Prophet, may peace be upon him*

In the box on the right side: *The Blessings of the Image of the Blessed Foot*

- *Whoever keeps it with them is honored*
- *Whichever caravan carries it will not be robbed*
- *Whichever ship carries it will not sink*
- *Whatever goods contain it will not be stolen*
- *One will have the fortune of pilgrimage to the Holiest Tomb [i.e., that of the Prophet] or one will be honored by a dream pilgrimage to the Most Holy Presence of the Prophet, may peace be upon him*
- *When one reaches for it in any need, that need is fulfilled.*
- *Whoever is childless and says five Prayers of Benediction* (durud sharif) *and prays through the mediation of the Image of the Foot, God, May He be Exalted, will bless them with offspring.*

In the box on the left side: *Instructions of the Noble Messenger Prophet, may peace be upon him and upon his Family*

- *Whoever recites the Prayer of Benediction one time on me, God, May He be Exalted, sends them ten blessings.*
- *He forgives ten of their sins and raises them ten stations* (from the Noble Sahih Bukhari).

At middle left, source of image: *The Footstep of the Pure Messenger Prophet, may peace be upon him and upon his family. The imprint of the blessed right foot of the Prophet, may peace be upon him and upon his family, is set in fine stone. This image has been taken from the pamphlet "Tabarukkat-i Islam" [Sacred Relics of Islam] printed by the government of Turkey. The venerable stone is saved in the Topkapi Palace Museum in Turkey.*

Lower medallion: *They will never find the path to the Mi'raj's goal Who cannot even attain the image of your footprint.*

Sandalprint of the Prophet (Figure 8.2)

This poster depicts the Prophet's sandal according to a very traditional talismanic pattern.

The top of the diagram has the *Basmallah*: *In the name of God, the Compassionate, the Merciful.*

The four medallions in the corners name four archangels: *Hazrat Jibrail, on him be peace; Hazrat Mikail, on him be peace; Hazrat Izrail, on him be peace;* and *Hazrat Israfil, on him be peace.*

Fig. 8.1: Footprint of the Prophet. *Courtesy of the Museum of Ethnology, Munich, Germany.*

In Arabic on either side of the forefoot: *This is a representation of his sandal, blessings be upon him and upon his family.*

In Urdu on either side of the middle: *If I could find the pure sandal of the Prophet to place on my head, Then would I say, "Yes! I, too, wear a crown!" The Qur'an swore an oath by the dust of the path, "A million greetings to this print of the Sacred Foot!"* (Plac-

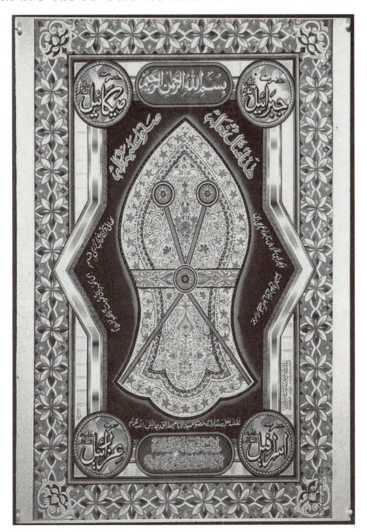

Fig. 8.2: Sandalprint of the Prophet. *Courtesy of the Museum of Ethnology,*
Munich, Germany.

ing a shoe on one's head symbolizes a high level of humility in South Asian Muslim culture. To place a shoe on one's own head is a potent gesture of subordina-
tion to the possessor of the shoe.)

In Persian in small print below the heel: *Illustration of the Blessed Sandal of His*
Presence, Master of all Creatures, according to the description of the Noble Imams.

A popular hadith in which God is the speaker appears in the lower rectangular
medallion, in Arabic; it refers to the Prophet's family, consisting of his daughter,
her husband, and their children. (These figures enjoy particular doctrinal impor-

tance in Shi'ism, although they are also venerated by many Sunnis in Pakistan. Muhammad's son-in-law, Ali, was also his paternal cousin and the first male convert to Islam. He is the first Shi'i Imam, but is also regarded as the first Sufi as well as the ideal man in Islamic chivalric writings: *I have five persons with whom I douse the crushing fires of pestilence—Muhammad, Ali, their sons [Hasan and Husayn], and Fatima.*)

Girl in Prayer (Figure 8.3)

This is a variation of a very common poster widely sold in religious stores in Pakistan as well as India. It follows a common tradition of depicting pious children in images that are then placed in the home to encourage younger members of the family to follow the poster's example of good behavior. The text reads: *In the Name of God, the Compassionate the Merciful* (in Arabic); *My Lord! Increase me in knowledge!* (in Arabic); *Oh my Lord! Please cause my knowledge to increase!* (in Urdu, translating the Arabic prayer).

Shahbaz Qalandar (Figure 8.4)

This poster is a souvenir from the shrine of one of the most popular Sufi saints of Pakistan, Lal Shahbaz Qalandar (d. 1252), who migrated to Sindh from northwestern Iran. He is famous for being drunk in his love for God and for his spiritual flight, both of which are represented in this poster by a dancer and an angel or bird-like figure, respectively. Some of the phrases on the poster are from well-known songs in his praise. The presence of God and the Prophet Muhammad are iconically represented by the Ka'ba in Mecca and the Prophet's Mosque in Medina; they are invoked textually between the two iconic representations as "Oh Allah!" and "Oh Muhammad!" The saint's name is centered across the top: " 'Ali Shahbaz Qalandar," and a popular Punjabi verse in his praise is written underneath. The term *qalandar* refers to Muslim religious figures who are antinomian in their appearance and emphasize love as the most important means of attaining religious goals. The verse also plays on the multiple identities Ali enjoys in popular Muslim piety: *The qalandar is drunk in every breath; Ali comes first.* At the top right Shahbaz Qalandar is depicted flying through the air; another popular Punjabi verse is written underneath him; this verse plays on his honorific title of "Falcon" (*Shahbaz*): *Shahbaz flies through the air, He knows secrets of the heart.*

Data Ganj Bakhsh and Khwaja Mu'inuddin (Figure 8.5)

Two august looking Sufi figures are represented in the foreground of the picture, recognizable as such by their turbans, robes, and shawls. Although their names are not written anywhere on the poster, the figure on the left is recognizable as Khwaja Mu'inuddin Chishti (d. 1236), the eponymous founder of the Chishti Sufi order whose shrine at Ajmer in India is the most important Muslim place of pilgrimage in all of South Asia (see chapter 3). On the right is the primary subject of the

Fig 8.3: Girl in prayer. *Courtesy of the Museum of Ethnology, Munich, Germany.*

poster, 'Ali Hujwiri (d. 1077), better known as Data Ganj Bakhsh (Generous Giver of Riches), the first important Sufi figure to settle in South Asia. The image in the background is a photograph of his tomb in Lahore, a place of resort for large numbers of the population as well as an object of patronage by political leaders seeking the aura of the saint's power. Although at first glance they appear as equals, the depiction of Khwaja Mu'inuddin as gazing intently at Data Ganj Bakhsh while the latter looks off into the distance subtly establishes the latter's superiority. Also, the open Qur'an placed close to Data Ganj Bakhsh contrasts with the prayer beads held by Khwaja Mu'inuddin to underline Data Ganj Bakhsh's greater scholarly cre-

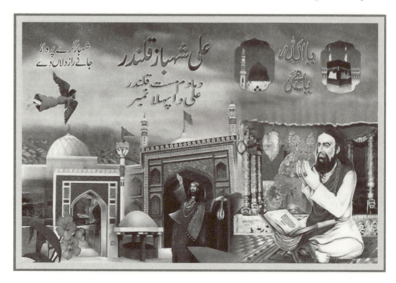

Fig. 8.4: Shahbaz Qalandar. *Courtesy of the Museum of Ethnology,*
Munich, Germany.

dentials. Other posters depict Khwaja Mu'inuddin sitting alone and praying in
front of Data Ganj Bakhsh's shrine. A Persian couplet in praise of Data Ganj Bakhsh
appears across the top of the poster. The same couplet is seen frequently on
posters depicting Data Ganj Bakhsh or his shrine in Lahore: *Ganj Bakhsh, bounty*
to the world, manifestation of the light of God. To the imperfect, a perfect master; to the
perfect, a saving guide. The Qur'an is open to a verse that speaks clearly about disbelief and idolatry, in all likelihood intended to remind the viewer of the important role played by Sufis in converting Hindus to Islam. In an attempt at realistic
representation, the writing ends mid-verse: *This is an immunity from Allah and His*
messenger to those idolaters with whom you made compacts. Travel, then, in the land
freely for four months, and know that you will never be able to thwart Allah, and that
Allah shall disgrace the unbelievers. This is a proclamation from Allah and His Messen-
ger to mankind on the day of the great pilgrimage, that Allah is absolved of the idolaters,
as is His Messenger. If you repent, it will be better for you; but if you turn away, know
that you shall never thwart Allah. Proclaim to those . . . (Qur'an 9:1–3)

Girl at Tomb of Data Ganj Bakhsh (Figure 8.6)

This poster gives 'Ali Hujwiri's status as the "Generous Giver of Riches," both visu-
ally and textually. (Malik Shafiq Art Publishers, Kashmiri Bazar, Lahore.) God and
the Prophet are represented iconically in the image, although the iconic representations also carry textual captions in the form of place names: *The House of Ka'ba*
and *Medina the Luminous.* The center top of the poster carries the Shahada, the

Fig. 8.5: Data Ganj Bakhsh and Khwaja Mu'inuddin. *Courtesy of the Museum of Ethnology, Munich, Germany.*

Fig. 8.6: Girl at tomb of Data Ganj. *Courtesy of the Museum of Ethnology, Munich, Germany*

Muslim profession of faith: *There is no god but Allah, and Muhammad is the messenger of Allah!* Lamps are commonly used to light tombs throughout South Asia during festivals. The multitude of lights emphasizes Data Ganj Bakhsh's status as well as his bounty. The same Persian couplet in praise of Data Ganj Bakhsh as appears in the previous illustration is printed underneath the images of the Ka'ba and the Prophet's Mosque: *Ganj Bakhsh, bounty to the world, manifestation of the light of God. To the imperfect, a perfect master; to the perfect, a saving guide.* In Punjabi at the bottom: *Whoever comes to the tomb of Data is granted any wish they utter.*

Sakhi Sarvar (Figure 8.7)

Sayyid Ahmad Sultan, better known as Sakhi Sarvar (Generous Master), is widely revered not just by Muslims but also by Hindus and especially Sikhs. His shrine at Dera Ghazi Khan in the Punjab consists of an impressive complex (as depicted in this poster) and was patronized by aristocrats of the Sikh dynasties that ruled Pakistan in the eighteenth and nineteenth centuries.

Unless otherwise noted, all text is in Urdu.

Title, at top: *The Court of the Honorable Sakhi Sarvar, also known as Lalan Vala, Dera Ghazi Khan.*

Slightly below: *To learn the complete story of the miracle of Sayyid Sakhi Sultan Ahmad, better known as Lalan Vala, involving the lame camel of the Merchant of Kandahar, Isa Khan, please consult the chain of spiritual lineage (shajra) of Sayyid Sakhi Sarvar.*

Directly above the drawing of his hilltop shrine complex is the Muslim profession of faith: *There is no god but Allah, and Muhammad is the messenger of Allah!* On the ramparts of the shrine is a Punjabi prayer: *Oh Lord! Accept Sakhi's Prayers!*

Below, in a mixture of Urdu and Punjabi: *Sakhi Sarvar is the benefactor of millions, his court is a treasury of mercy The world comes to kiss your feet!*

The Merchant of Kandahar, his white mare, and the lame camel—all figures from miracle stories—carry identifying captions in the poster. God and the Prophet are represented iconically in the top right-hand corner of the poster by the Ka'ba and the Prophet's Mosque. The situation of the Ka'ba directly behind the Prophet's mosque is significant in this image because it serves to symbolize God's authority as underlying that of the Prophet. A beam of light radiates from the Prophet's Mosque to the top of Sakhi Sarvar's head and is captioned: *The Vision of Grace (nigah-i karam)*, which historically refers to the Prophet. That saintly authority derives from the Prophet rather than directly from God is emphasized by the Urdu declaration to the left of this scene, directly above Sakhi Sarvar's head: *My Prophet is Greater!*

Shah 'Abdul Latif Bhitai (Figure 8.8)

Shah 'Abdul Latif Bhitai (d. 1752) is the most important Sufi poet of the Sindhi language, and enjoys immense popularity in contemporary Pakistan. He is famous for his asceticism and love for God, which he rendered in verses that are sung at

Fig. 8.7: Sakhi Sarvar. *Courtesy of the Museum of Ethnology, Munich, Germany.*

saints' festivals and other occasions to this day. His importance as a poet and an ascetic are clear from the way he is depicted in this poster.

In Urdu in the medallion to the side of the seated figure: *The blessed portrait of Shah 'Abdul Latif Bhitai, may God have mercy upon him.*

The top of the poster has the Muslim profession of faith (*shahada*).

Below it is a caption for the building depicted in the center: *The blessed tomb of the Honorable Shah 'Abdul Latif Bhitai.* The Ka'ba and the Prophet's Mosque appear on either side of this building, and both carry captions: *The House of Ka'ba* and *Medina the Luminous*, respectively.

There are Urdu verses below the images of the Ka'ba and the Prophet's Mosque: i) *If you seek your heart's desire then go and serve the begging Sufis. That pearl can never be found in the treasuries of kings;* ii) *The gusts of their breath can bring dead lamps back to life, Lord! What lies hidden in the breasts of divine lovers?*

Truck Art (Figure 8.9)

The overwhelming majority of privately owned Pakistani trucks are heavily decorated with a combination of carved wood, paint, hammered metal, and a kind of mosaic made from reflective tape. They carry a variety of images, calligraphy, and patterns, much of which is religious in nature and hence provides a great deal of

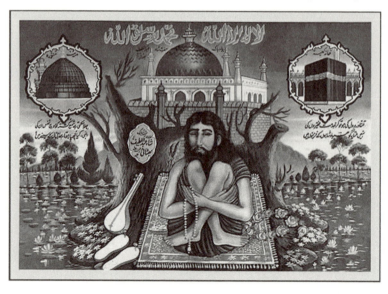

Fig. 8.8: Shah ʿAbdul Latif Bhitai. *Courtesy of the Museum of Ethnology,*
Munich, Germany.

information about the religious views of the owner of the truck as well as others
who are involved in the trucking industry.

The use of religious imagery and epigraphy is extensive in this example. The
Kaʿba and the Prophet's Mosque in Medina appear twice in pictorial form (on panels one and two). Accompanying their pictorial representations, God and Muhammad are invoked four times in writing as *Ya Allah! Ya Muhammad!* In each case the
inscription reads from right to left as one faces the truck: on the extreme ends of
panel one; on panel two just to the outside of the medallions with the Kaʿba and
Prophet's Mosque; toward the outside of panel three; and in very small writing on
the central medallion of panel two. To either side of this medallion is the phrase
sapurd-i khuda (in God's protection). Both central medallions invoke the names of
saints, the top one that of Shah Bilawal Nurani (Bilawal the Luminescent): *Lumi-*
nescent light, all afflictions stay away (*nurani nur har bala dur*), and the lower one of
Shahbaz Qalandar, a poster of whom appears earlier in the chapter.

There is extensive religious epigraphy on the upper section of the truck. Across
the very top is an Urdu couplet describing Muhammad's status as the primordial
human being: *In all God's creation Muhammad was made first, There was no Adam,*
there were no angels, God was not apparent.

At the bottom of panel one is the Persian inscription *tajdar-i haram hu nigah-i*
karam (crown-bearer of the sanctuary, he is, vision of grace), an honorific title
given to Muhammad by the classical Persian poet Saʿdi, but popularized in modern Pakistan in a qawwali song by the Sabri Brothers.

Fig. 8.9: Truck with Sufi and other religious motifs. *Photo: Jamal Elias.*

The medallions at the bottom of panel two have the names of the owners on either end (Anjum Khan and Nadim Khan) and the name of the truck in the middle (Lahuti Karvan [Divine Caravan]). The word *Fayzan* appears right above the windshield and is most likely another name for the truck.

The grill on either side of the central medallion on the main cowling (panel three) has two couplets, the first asserting that Muhammad, his daughter Fatima, her husband Ali, and their sons Hasan and Husayn are the best of human beings. The lower couplet in Urdu is very popular and appears on trucks in various parts of the country: *If you are faithful to Muhammad, then I am yours; What is this world after all, the pen and the tablet are yours.* This is the end of the top section of the truck's front.

At the bottom of the radiator (panel four), under the name "Bedford," there is a non-religious Urdu couplet: *Burn away in silence under the blazing sun, but never ask your relatives for the shade of a simple wall.* Below that is the registration number and two small panels on the ends of the bumper advertising the route. Directly under the oval registration plate is the name of the truck company (Pak China Goods, Gilgit). At the bottom is another non-religious Urdu couplet: *Who ever notices the tears of the morning dew, Everyone is busy looking at the smiling rosebud.*

Further Reading

For more information on religious posters in Pakistan, see Jürgen W. Frembgen, *The Friends of God: Sufi Saints in Islam—Popular Poster Art from Pakistan* (Karachi: Oxford University Press, 2006). For a detailed discussion of the role played by posters in the formation of religious and national identity in South Asia, see Christopher Pinney, *Photos of the Gods: The Printed Image and Political Struggle in India* (London: Reaktion Books, 2004). Several books deal with specific Sufi figures in Pakistan; for a discussion of the role of Sufism in Pakistani society, see Katherine P. Ewing, *Arguing Sainthood: Modernity, Psychoanalysis and Islam* (Durham, NC: Duke University Press, 1997). The best discussion of the role played by devotion to Sufi saints and shrines in the shared spirituality of Muslims, Hindus and Sikhs is in Harjot Oberoi, *The Construction of Religious Boundaries: Culture, Identity and Diversity in the Sikh Tradition* (Delhi: Oxford University Press, 1994). A Web site produced by Yousuf Saeed, "Popular Devotional Art of the Indian Muslims: Looking for Syncretic Symbols," includes reproductions of several Indian posters: http://www.alif-india.com/popart/gallery.html.

Holy and Exemplary Lives

HOLY AND EXEMPLARY LIVES

Introduction

Barbara D. Metcalf

The contributions that make up "Holy and Exemplary Lives" are closely linked to those in the section above. In this case they focus on specific living holy men from the fourteenth century to the twentieth. Elsewhere we will continue the theme of the roles and influence of saintly figures. An excerpt from a manual of meditation and ritual by Hajji Imdadullah, one of the most influential holy men of the late nineteenth century, exemplifies one dimension of the instruction imparted by a leading Sufi (Chapter 16). In Chapter 23, a tract offers advice on family relationships; it is written by Maulana Ashraf 'Ali Thanawi, one of the most revered scholars and influential Sufis of the twentieth century. Two other well-known twentieth-century Chishtis (Khwaja Hasan Nizami, a prolific writer in journals and other new media of his day; and Hazrat Inayat Khan, known for taking Sufism to Europe) are represented by examples of their writings on women (Chapter 25). We will also look at holy men in their roles in extending political influence; first, as part of forest clearing in pre-colonial Bengal (Chapter 28); and second, appealing to voters during the campaign for Pakistan (Chapter 31).

In this section, however, each chapter takes up a specific individual in order to show significant dimensions of his relationship to his followers and disciples. The authors contribute to our understanding of the differences between holy men in terms of their fidelity to formal practice, and they also suggest some of the many social roles these figures may play.

We will begin in Chapter 9 with an excerpt from the celebrated account of one of the greatest premodern travelers, the scholar of North African descent, Ibn Battuta, whose longest residence as he crossed Eurasia was in the Indian Subcontinent. The holy man of the chapter is not, however, the traveler himself, but Shah Jalal Mujarrad, in distant Sylhet, one of the many holy men the traveler sought out wherever he went. Timothy Macintosh-Smith, in his *Travels with a Tangerine: A Journey in the Footsteps of Ibn Battutah*, has commented that most readers of Ibn Battuta's famous travelogue have focused on the political and economic story that he conveyed. Macintosh-Smith suggests, however, that to neglect his veneration

of the Sufis, his visits to their lodges (*khanaqas*), and his own periodic quests for
the moral purification they espoused, is "to remove the soul of the book" (p. 145).
Ibn Battuta, moreover, not only sought out the wisdom and guidance of holy men
and devoted himself to spiritual disciplines, but he also, as this excerpt makes
clear, participated in the controversial and exhilarating Sufi ceremonies that we
have introduced in earlier chapters. The holy man of this chapter, Shah Jalal, re-
appears in Chapter 28 in legendary form under several guises: as a conqueror, an
agent of conversion, and a patron of agriculture. Ibn Battuta, however, focused on
the exemplary asceticism and the miraculous foreknowledge of the living saint.

In Chapter 10, Anna Bigelow translates material from the legendary account of
Shaykh Sadruddin (d. 1515), known as Haider Shaykh, who flourished in the Punjab area still under the control of Delhi at a time when central authority elsewhere
was devolving into regional states. Haider Shaykh is remembered as a person capable of powerful anger and as a force for miraculous interventions. The Afghan
Lodhi court of his day actively patronized Sufis and sought their blessings and
support. Haider Shaykh received a substantial land grant from the Lodhis, and he
accepted the sultan's daughter in marriage, a mark of the ruler's humility in relation to the saint. Like many Sufis of this era, he played an influential role in political life, shaping succession, directing alliances, and establishing border settlements. In the present, however, as Bigelow argues, most people care more about
him as an agent of miracles and a source of protection, a model of the superiority
of spiritual over worldly power, and a symbol of inter-religious pride.

To be the millennial messiah (see Chapter 29) is only the most extreme of the extraordinary claims to sanctity made by, and attributed to, living holy men, among
them, the Naqshbandi, Shaykh Ahmad Sirhindi (d. 1624). Sirhindi's arrest by Emperor Jahangir was on account of his self-aggrandizing claims. Many later writers
who have seen this period as a binary struggle between "liberal" and "orthodox"
Islam have understood opposition to Sirhindi as a lack of sympathy for his "orthodoxy." He did, to be sure, call on rulers to diminish the respect accorded "infidels."
But this was a minor theme in his writings. As for his arrest, once the emperor had
sufficiently chastened him, he was, in fact, permitted to return to court.

An excerpt from a biographical account of Ahmad Sirhindi's life by one of his
disciples is translated by Carl Ernst in Chapter 11. This selection does not deal at
all with the controversial issues surrounding Sirhindi, or with his influential scholarly writings, but rather purports to record how the great saint spent a typical day.
It demonstrates the extent to which a figure who aspired to holiness modeled his
every act on Prophetic *sunna*. In so doing, he reiterated the pattern of prayer,
Qur'anic reading, meditation, and bodily decorum that form a normative cycle of
Islamic practice.

The final two chapters focus on figures from the colonial period. In Chapter 12,
Usha Sanyal shows how a particular family of holy men nurtured a shrine containing the graves of great ancestors and preserved relics of the Prophet and others of
his lineage. They also guarded special prayers and sustained a distinctive cycle of
ritual observances. In an era without royal patronage, they sought popular sup-

port through publicity that elevated the legitimacy of their lineage and the sanctity of their shrine. The leaders of the Barelwi sectarian orientation among the 'ulama (explained in Chapter 17 and represented in Chapter 6) were disciples of the holy men of this shrine. As conduits of charisma themselves, the Barelwi 'ulama were typical of the scholarly leadership in this period.

The second figure from the colonial period, Banne Miyan (d. 1921), strikes a very different note from the others discussed above. He neither modeled ideal behavior nor had he inherited a great Sufi lineage. Banne Miyan was, in Nile Green's translation of the word *majzub*, "a holy fool." He was very much a product of the colonial culture, not only because he had served under British officers in the Nizam of Hyderabad's army, but also because he and his followers both faced the tension of his being categorized not as a recipient of divine favor but as "a madman" in the definition of the modern state. In the view of the colonialist and modernist criticism of this period, all of Sufism was suspect as superstition, and nowhere was this more true than in the case of a figure like Banne Miyan. His followers, however, credited him with foreknowledge and the ability to intervene miraculously in their lives. Islam, Green reminds us, is much more than "beliefs," entailing, as it does, diverse strategies, like the miracles of the fool, to navigate everyday life. Such conviction that at any point there are humans among us with special powers is evident in the careers of all the figures represented here.

9

Ibn Battuta Meets Shah Jalal al-Din Tabrizi in Bengal

Barbara D. Metcalf

Ibn Battuta (1304–1369), the great traveler and travel writer, had set out from his home in the Maghreb in 1325 with the intention of undertaking the pilgrimage to Mecca. It would be decades before he returned, having journeyed not only to Arabia, but into Central Asia, across western Asia, on to South Asia, where he would stay almost eight years, before traveling on to China. With the establishment of the Turko-Afghan dynasties of the early thirteenth century, India had become a central part of networks of trade and travel that reached into Central Asia and beyond, as well as a node in Arab-dominated sea routes across the Indian Ocean. Everywhere, even in China, Ibn Battuta found Muslims with whom he lodged and interacted.

A young man of modest attainments when he set out, Ibn Battuta nonetheless won a welcome everywhere thanks to his education, his command of Arabic, and, as he traveled, his stories of the travels themselves, replete as they were with horrors, shipwrecks, robberies, and other adventures. Returned home, he would then set out on yet another journey, this time south into Africa. Some thirty years after he began, he wrote an account of all these travels in his celebrated *Rihla*, the source of the excerpt below (as well as a second selection in Chapter 20 that describes on his role as a qadi in the Maldives). There had been no significant geographic writing about South Asia since al-Biruni's study written in the course of Ghaznavid conquests some 300 years earlier (see the Introduction to this volume). The *Rihla* provides detailed reminiscences not only of personal experiences but of the social, economic, cultural, political, and everyday life of the populations as well.

This selection from the *Rihla* is one of many that reflect the author's immersion in the world of holy men, piety, disciplinary practices, and dreams that permeated Muslim life in this period. Ibn Battuta was deeply devoted to saints even before his arrival in India. In 1326, less than a year into his travels, for example, he visited the most famous saint of Egypt, Shaykh Abu Abdallah al Murshidi, and, as he would write decades later, in that charisma-filled presence, he dreamed of himself mounted on an enormous bird, flying first to Mecca, thence to Yemen and onwards east and south toward a verdant land. The saint interpreted the dream as foretelling his travels to Mecca, to Medina and the tomb of the Prophet, on to Yemen, Iraq, and the lands of the Turks and the Indians: "In India you will stay for a long time, and you will meet there my brother Dilshad the Indian, who will rescue you from a great misfortune into which you will fall" (Macintosh-Smith 2005, 7–8). Ibn Battuta did indeed go to India, fall into difficulty, and interpret his rescue just as predicted.

In his travels, he invariably sought out the hospices and shrines of holy men. He himself at one point in Delhi, refusing to side with the sultan over a saint who had displeased him, was among many who were arrested. For five days, he wrote, he recited "Sufficient for us is God and excellent the Protector" 33,000 times, recited the entire Qur'an each day, and took only water. Released after the dissident *shaykh's* execution, Ibn Battuta withdrew from the court and, in the presence of yet another saint, "the learned and devout ascetic Kamal al-Din 'Abdallah al-Ghari [the Cave-Dweller]" whom he called "a man of great humility and godliness," he began himself to take up a life of asceticism, prayer, and disciplinary practices (Macintosh-Smith 2005, 86-93). He was only won away from this life five months later by the sultan's lavish inducements to him to undertake a grand diplomatic mission to China. It was in the course of that eventful trip, at the end of his sojourn in India, that he made his long stop in the Maldives as well as the pilgrimage to Bengal chronicled in this chapter.

Chronologically, the pilgrimage follows Ibn Battuta's stint in the Maldives as qadi. After some six weeks of travel by sea, he reached Bengal, and, like other travelers of the times, noted the remarkable abundance and cheapness of goods (in contrast to today's image of the area as one of unremitting poverty). He also recorded the Bengal sultan's partiality—one he shared—for "darwishes and Sufis." Even so, he made no effort to present himself at the royal court, then in rebellion against Delhi (worth noting lest anyone think of "Muslim rule" as monolithic). As someone identified with Muhammad Tughluq and the power in Delhi, Ibn Battuta opted for anonymity and set out directly on a month-long overland journey to seek out Shah Jalal, the holy man he had come to see, at his hospice in the Sylhet area of what is now Bangladesh.

In his account, Ibn Battuta provided abundant evidence of the saint's holiness, including stories of his foreknowledge, his ability to appear in Mecca, and occurrences of uncanny coincidence. Among the saint's miracles was his longevity, reported here in Mahdi Husayn's translation:

> He told me—may Allah have mercy on him!—that he had seen Caliph al-Musta'sim al-Abbasi at Baghdad, and that he was there at the time of his murder [1258 c.e.]. His companions told me subsequently [in China] that he died at the age of one hundred and fifty and that he observed fasts for about forty years during which he would break no fast of his until he had continued it for ten consecutive days (Ibn Battuta 1976, 238–239).

Later legends linked this saint to the defeat of the local raja by sultanate armies and the subsequent spread of Islam, symbolized by his overcoming the witches, for which the area is apparently known; this is the "magic" referred to in the selection below. Today a pond at the popular shrine contains catfish said to be the defeated black magicians. Shah Jalal may have been born in Konya or Yemen, but he is called by Ibn Battuta "Tabrizi," perhaps conflating him (as many do) with another celebrated saint who came to Bengal, Shaykh Jalal Tabrizi, who had died in 1244, and who is also linked to the early spread of Islam in the region.

This visit to Shah Jalal is of particular interest in the context of this volume since Chapter 28 takes up later legends about this saint in the conversion of Bengal to Islam. In that regard, the role of the Sufis in the spread of agriculture is symbolically reflected in the later legend that Shah Jalal had been entrusted with a handful of dirt by his uncle in Yemen and instructed to match that soil in Hindustan, settle there, and spread Islam.

FROM THE *RIHLA* OF IBN BATTUTA

TRANSLATED BY H.A.R. GIBB [HG]

I set out again, and we spent forty-three nights at sea, arriving eventually at the land of Bangala [Bengal—HG]. This is a vast country, abounding in rice, and nowhere in the world have I seen any land where prices are lower than there; on the other hand it is a gloomy place, and the people of Khurasan call it "A hell full of good things." I have seen fat fowls sold there at the rate of eight for a single dirham, young pigeons at fifteen to the dirham, and a fat ram sold for two dirhams. I saw too a piece of fine cotton cloth, of excellent quality, thirty cubits long, sold for two dinars, and a beautiful slave-girl for a single gold dinar, that is, two and a half gold dinars in Moroccan money. The first city in Bengal that we entered was Sudkawan [Satgaon or Chittagong?—HG], a large town on the coast of the great sea. Close by it the river Ganges, to which the Hindus go on pilgrimage, and the river Jun [according to Mahdi Husayn 1953 (hereafter MH), the Brahmaputra] unite and discharge together into the sea. They have a large fleet on the river, with which they make war on the inhabitants of the land of Laknawti [Gaur—HG].

The sultan of Bengal is Sultan Fakhr ad-Din, an excellent ruler with a partiality for strangers, especially darwishes and sufis. The kingship of this land belonged to Sultan Nasir ad-Din, whose grandson was taken prisoner by the sultan of Delhi, and released by Sultan Muhammad when he became king, on condition of sharing his sovereignty with him. He broke his promise and Sultan Muhammad went to war with him, put him to death, and appointed a relative by marriage of his own as governor of that country. This man was put to death by the troops and the kingdom was seized by Ali-Shah, who was then in Laknawti. When Fakhr ad-Din saw that the kingship had passed out of the hands of Nasir ad-Din's descendants (he was a client of theirs), he revolted in Sudkawan and Bengal and made himself an independent ruler. A violent strug-

gle took place between him and 'Ali-Shah. During the season of winter and
mud, Fakhr ad-Din used to make expeditions up the river against the land of
Laknawti, because of his naval superiority, but when the rainless season returned, 'Ali-Shah would make raids by land on Bengal, because of his superiority in land-forces. When I entered Sudkawan I did not visit the sultan, nor did
I meet him, as he is a rebel against the king of India, and I was afraid of the consequences which a visit to him might entail.

I set out from Sudkawan for the mountains of Kamaru [Karmpur in Assam—
MH], a month's journey from there. This is a vast range of mountains extending to China and also to the land of Thubbat [Tibet—HG], where the musk
deer are. The inhabitants of this range resemble the Turks; they possess great
endurance, and their value as slaves is many times greater than a slave of any
other nationality. They are famous for their magical practices. My purpose in
travelling to these mountains was to meet a notable saint who lives there,
namely, Shaykh Jalal ad-Din of Tabriz. At a distance of two days' journey from
his abode I was met by four of his disciples, who told me that the *shaykh* had
said to the darwishes who were with him, "The traveller from the West has
come to you; go out to welcome him." He had no knowledge whatever about
me, but this had been revealed to him. I went with them to the *shaykh* and arrived at his hermitage, situated outside the cave. There is no cultivated land
there, but the inhabitants of the country, both Muslim and infidel, come to visit
him, bringing gifts and presents, and the darwishes and travellers live on these
offerings. The *shaykh* however limits himself to a single cow, with whose milk
he breaks his fast every ten days. It was by his labours that the people of these
mountains became converted to Islam, and that was the reason for his settling
amongst them. When I came into his presence he rose to greet me and embraced me. He asked me about my native land and my travels, and when I had
given him an account of them he said to me, "You are the traveller of the Arabs."
Those of his disciples who were there said, "And the non-Arabs too, O our master." "And of the non-Arabs too," he repeated, " so show him honour." They
then took me to the hermitage and gave me hospitality for three days.

On the day when I visited the *shaykh* I saw that he was wearing a wide mantle of goat hair. It took my fancy and I said to myself, "I wish the *shaykh* could
have given it to me." When I visited him to bid him farewell, he went to the side
of the cave, took off the mantle and placed it upon me, together with a skull-
cap from his head, himself putting on a patched garment. The darwishes told
me that the *shaykh* was not in the habit of wearing this mantle and had put it
on only when I arrived, saying to them, "This mantle will be asked for by the
Moroccan, and it will be taken from him by an infidel sultan, who will give it
to our brother Burhan ad-Din of Sagharj, whose it is and for whom it was
made." When they told me this I said to them, "I have obtained the blessing of
the *shaykh* through his clothing me with his garments, and I for my part shall
not enter the presence of any sultan, infidel or Muslim, wearing this mantle."
With this I withdrew from the *shaykh's* presence. Now it came about a long time

afterwards that I visited China and eventually reached the city of Khansa [Hang-chow-fu—*HG*]. My party were separated from me by the pressure of the crowd and I was wearing this mantle. I happened to be in a certain street when the wazir came by with a large suite. His eye fell upon me, and summoning me he clasped my hand, asked me about my arrival, and continued talking to me until I came to the sultan's palace with him. At this point I wished to take leave of him, but he would not hear of it and introduced me into the sultan's presence. The latter questioned me about the Muhammadan sultans and when I replied to his questions, he looked at the mantle and took a liking to it. The wazir said to me, "Take it off," and I could not resist his order. So the sultan took it and ordered me to be given ten robes, a horse and harness, and a sum of money. The incident roused my anger, but afterwards I recalled the *shaykh's* saying that an infidel sultan would seize it and I was deeply amazed at the fulfillment of the prediction. The following year I entered the palace of the king of China at Khan-Baliq [Peking—*HG*], and sought out the convent of the Shaykh Burhan ad-Din of Sagharj. I found him reading and wearing that identical mantle. I was astonished and took it in my hand to examine it. He said to me, "Why examine it when you know it already?" "True," I replied, "it is the one that was taken from me by the sultan of Khansda." "This mantle," he went on "was made specially for me by my brother Jalal ad-Din, who wrote to me saying 'The mantle will reach you by the hand of so-and-so.'" Then he brought out the letter and I read it, marvelling at the *shaykh's* perfect foreknowledge. I told Burhan ad-Din the beginning of the story, and he said to me, "My brother Jalal ad-Din can do much more than all this, he has the powers of creation at his disposal, but he has now passed to the mercy of God. I have been told," he added, "that he prayed the dawn prayer every day at Mecca, and that he made the pilgrimage every year, for he used to disappear from sight on the days of 'Arafa and the festival, and no one knew where he went."

When I had bidden farewell to Shaykh Jalal ad-Din I journeyed to Habanq, an exceedingly large and beautiful city, traversed by the river which descends from the Kamaru mountains. This river is called the Blue River [Meghna—*HG*] and is used bv travellers to Bengal and Laknawti [Lakhnauti]. On its banks there are water wheels, orchards, and villages to right and to left, like the Nile in Egypt. Its people are infidels under Muslim rule [*zimma* "protected people"— *MH*], who are mulcted of half their crops and pay taxes over and above that. We travelled down the river for fifteen days between villages and orchards, just as if we were going through a bazaar. There are innumerable vessels on it and each vessel carries a drum; when two vessels meet, each of them beats its drum and they salute one another. Sultan Fakhr ad-Din gave orders that no passage-money should be taken on this river from darwishes, and that provisions were to be supplied to those of them who had none, and when a darwish comes to a town he is given half a dinar. After fifteen days' sailing down the river, as we have related, we reached the city of Sunurkawin [Sonargaon—*HG*] where we found a junk on the point of sailing for the land of Jawa [Sumatra], which is a journey of forty days from there, so we embarked on it.

Sources

The translation is excerpted from that of H.A.R. Gibb, *Ibn Battuta: Travels in Asia and Africa 1325–1354* (Delhi: Manohar, 2001), pp. 267–271. A second translation, *The Rehla of Ibn Battuta (India, Maldive Islands and Ceylon)*, trans. Madhi Husayn (Baroda: Oriental Institute, 1953) provides a fuller translation and additional informative notes.

Further Reading

A readable and scholarly retelling of the account is Ross E. Dunn's *The Adventures of Ibn Battuta: A Muslim Traveler of the 14th Century* (Berkeley, CA: University of California Press, 1986). See also Timothy Mackintosh-Smith's recent two-volume travelogue written as he retraced Ibn Battuta's steps, the *Rihla* in hand. The volume covering the India travels is *India: The Hall of a Thousand Columns: Hindustan to Malabar with Ibn Battutah* (London: John Murray, 2005). General historical background to the period is available in Catherine B. Asher and Cynthia Talbot, *India before Europe* (Cambridge: Cambridge University Press, 2006). For Bengal, see "Further Reading" at the end of Chapter 26.

—10—

Narratives of the Life of Haider Shaykh
in Punjab

Anna Bigelow

Hagiography is a well-established literary genre in South Asia in every religious tradition. *Tazkira* texts (biographies, memoirs) detail the lives of Muslim saints, generating and reflecting a stable core of historical data and legendary testimonies that often comprise a significant part of the saints' narrative legacy. However, the life stories of these pirs are also passed on in oral narratives that keep them alive for their devotees, integrating the teller into the world of the saint and the saint into the world of the teller. This chapter explores both written and oral narratives about a fifteenth-century saint in Punjab, Shaykh Sadruddin Sadr-i Jahan (d. 1515). Popularly known as Haider Shaykh, he is buried in the town of Maler Kotla where Sikhs and Hindus as well as Muslims visit his tomb. The stories included here represent a range of tellers, situations, and agendas, each story claiming a distinctive understanding of, or relationship with, Haider Shaykh.

The Story

It was a dark and stormy night. At least that is the scene at the beginning of nearly every account of Haider Shaykh's doings. This formula introduces, for example, the tale of the saint's encounter with the Afghan warlord Bahlol Lodhi, who was soon to become sultan at Delhi (r. 1451–1489). In the standard hagiography, Bahlol Lodhi camped near Haider Shaykh's retreat while en route to Delhi to challenge the weakening grip of the Sayyid Dynasty (1414–1451). Haider Shaykh, a Pathan Afghan, had come from Kabul via Multan, where he studied the spiritual path with a Suhrawardi Sufi guide. This *murshid* is variously identified as Baha al-Din Zakariyya (d. 1262) or his grandson, Rukn al-Din Abu al-Fath (d. 1335). Although historically impossible, this strategically links him to two renowned saints of the Suhrawardi order. At the behest of his *murshid*, whoever he may have been,

Haider Shaykh went east, eventually settling on the banks of a river. Bahlol Lodhi encountered him there and, impressed with his piety, married his daughter to the *shaykh* and gave a substantial land grant as dowry. After Haider Shaykh's death, his second son, 'Isa, inherited the land grant and his descendants became the ruling Nawabs. The eldest, Hassan, had fallen out of favor with his father and Hassan's descendants, the *khalifas* (or successors), became the caretakers of the saint's *dargah*, or tomb shrine.

Connecting with the Shaykh

Although residents of Maler Kotla who visit the shrine represent all faiths, most pilgrims from outside the town are non-Muslim. Unsurprisingly, these diverse narrators omit certain events, focus on others, or include variant elements in order to highlight their particular perspective on the saint's importance. For example, most non-resident devotees know very little about the historical saint. They are more concerned with what he does *now* than with who he was. These pilgrims consistently portray Haider Shaykh as a saint for *all* people. They describe him as *hamare sanjhe pir* (our common saint), and themselves as the *pirpanth* (the community of the saint), linking themselves to the wider world of the pirs. Additionally, pilgrims regardless of religious affiliation give testimonials of their personal experience of the *shaykh's* blessings, thereby authenticating his power and validating their own presence at the tomb. In one example, a Sikh living in Singapore came to the shrine and reported that his father and six uncles were all born after his grandparents had prayed at the tomb. He himself visits whenever he returns to Punjab. He and his wife, who grew up in Singapore, light lamps every Thursday and sing songs for Haider Shaykh. They believe their son and daughter were also born through the saint's blessings.

Through oral and written narratives, Haider Shaykh becomes a key symbol for both residents and pilgrims. He is credited with establishing the town and tomb cult, protecting and integrating their constituent populations, and modeling proper piety for everyone—Muslim, Hindu, and Sikh. Four kinds of accounts are given below, the first written and the others oral. They include a pamphlet written by the shrine manager, three stories told by his descendants, an account by a wandering *faqir*, and a version of the saint's significance related by a Hindu pilgrim.

A Written Hagiography by the Shrine's Manager

Anwar Ali Khan is the current *gaddi nishin* (head of the *dargah* or shrine) of Haider Shaykh, a role that in his case is less spiritual than managerial. In fact, Khan spends little time at the *dargah*. Some time ago he published a small chapbook (undated). In addition to giving a brief account of Haider Shaykh's life, the chapbook focuses on the saint's power and quick temper. It also describes the proper etiquette for pilgrims of all faiths who wish to avoid Haider Shaykh's anger. Most guidelines are directed towards a wide audience, but a few, regarding prayer, specifically target Muslim devotees. A broad audience is also indicated by the fact that the pamphlet raises no controversial issues of Sufism (such as the legitimacy of voiced *zikr* or the permissibility of the musical audition of *sama'*) and that it cites no specific sacred texts. Khan's description of his saintly ancestor emphasizes two themes in particular: Haider Shaykh's power and the inclusiveness of his cult.

Significantly, in the *gaddi nishin's* account, there is little reference to conversions, beyond a declaration that Haider Shaykh came for *tabligh karne*—to spread the faith. This may be because the audience for the pamphlet includes Sikhs and Hindus who need not convert in order to venerate the Muslim saint. The text's use of Punjabi script and a mixed Urdu, Hindi, and Punjabi vocabulary also indicates a wide audience. The text features none of the formulaic blessings, Qur'an quotations, or poetic couplets typical of *tazkiras*. Instead Khan stresses the saint's connection to worldly authority and his miraculous powers, the need to appease him, and the overwhelming importance of respecting and supporting (presumably financially) the company of the people of God.

THE COMPLETE LIFE OF HAZRAT SADR AL-DIN SADR-I JAHAN, (MAY THE MERCY OF GOD BE UPON HIM) KNOWN AS BABA HAZRAT SHAYKH JI, MALER KOTLA, BY KHALIFA ANWAR AHMAD KHAN, GADDI NISHIN

It is the pride of Punjab's holy ground that many great Sufi saints and pirs walked on this earth. There may not be even a single city or town in Punjab where some important Sufi saint or pir's *dargah* is not found. In Maler Kotla, the eminent Sufi saint and founder of the town is peacefully resting in a great *dargah*. To the Hindus, Sikhs, and Muslims of this region this pir is known by the name Baba Haider Shaykh. People come in hundreds of thousands at festival times. It is their belief that if Baba Haider Shaykh becomes angry then they will fall into trouble.

EKADASHI MELA

At the time of Ekadashi [the eleventh day of each month of the lunar calendar] the place is filled by a huge *mela* [festival]. This is done especially in the month of June, when deeply faithful people in great numbers arrive from all corners of India: Bombay, Calcutta, Punjab, Himachal Pradesh, Haryana. On this occasion there is a great crowd of people: children, men, women come in great waves like an ocean. Baba's devotees are seen in every direction. Around the bazaar and *dargah* in the alleys and neighborhoods there is absolutely no space, and moving through the bazaar becomes very difficult. Having harvested their crops, people are free and they have audiences with Babaji for two or three days.

Troupes playing drums and cymbals come to the *dargah*. They prostrate and having taken leave from the saint they go out. They believe that if they don't do this, when they make all their pious resolutions then Babaji will become angry with them, and their desires will not be fulfilled.

At this time many devotees become possessed. They say that Babaji's holy spirit enters them and that whatever is asked from them will be fulfilled. According to people of all conditions, Babaji's holy spirit has entered them, and the people possessed forget their own lives. Other devotees come and ask questions about the past and the future, and they place their heart's desires before those who are possessed.

BABA GIVES SONS

Although people with all kinds of desires come to this *mela* and their desires are fulfilled, the greatest number are couples whose marriage has been consummated but who have no children. They come and according to their ability to give they make vows saying, "Babaji, bless us with a son and we will come every time to your court, and some sort of *nazarana* (offering) will continue to be given." By the time they come again, a son has been born in their homes. Such people believe that no one who comes to Baba's door will be turned away empty-handed. Some are people who went to Ajmer Sharif [the famous shrine of Khwaja Mu'inuddin Chishti in Rajasthan] and were instructed to "go to Maler Kotla and there your desires will be fulfilled." Bringing their various desires they come and all are fulfilled at Babaji's *dargah*. They arrive and, as appropriate, a goat is offered, or a horse, or some sweets, or a cloth. At night they light up the *dargah* with candles.

Whatever information is available about Babaji's great life has been obtained from those sources and is here presented before you.

BIRTH

Babaji was born in 1434, in a place named Daraban of Sherwan. A writer Israr Afghani writes in his book that when Babaji was born then there was a strange light in the house. Also, before he was born, his mother had a dream of a lit candle. Then she sought understanding from wise people who gave the following explanation: a child will be born such that in other countries, lights will be lit in his name. This dream came true when Hazratji left his beloved country and came to Hindustan, and here it continues to be fulfilled.

STUDIES AND UPBRINGING

Hazrat Shaykh's early studies and upbringing occurred in the home. For higher studies, Maulana Jamaluddin Farasani's name has been mentioned. Even from his childhood he was a religious-minded person; thus he quickly achieved mastery of spiritual things. In all of Afghanistan his fame and notoriety spread with the publicity of his feats and miracles. He was brought to Hindustan and arrived with the army.

HIS HONORED PRESENCE IN HINDUSTAN

He may have come to Hindustan because even before his arrival his piety was known in Hindustan. In this way his connection with this country came about. But another cause is possible. In those days with the foreign Muslim rulers came a great number of pious people of the new religion. They kept coming and they spread the religion of Islam. It is recounted this way in the *Lives of the Lodhis* [by Israr Afghani, mentioned above]. Even in his childhood, Hazratji liked to read about the lives of travelers and wise people who had come to India. His teacher fed this desire. So in order to obtain more knowledge and to fulfill his longing he left his country of Sherwan by way of Daraban Kherba. There are two separate histories concerning Babaji's Indian travels. Major General Sir Henry White wrote in an article that the state of Patiala was founded in 1469 and Maler Kotla in 1467. *The Lives of the Lodhis* gives the date of 1449 for his coming to Hindustan. This is a more trustworthy date because in this book other facts about his life are recorded. So we can say that he arrived in Multan in 1449. In those days in Hindustan, Multan was the center of religious scholarship. He lived there for some time, then was given the order to go to his own place.

IN HAZRAT SHAYKH'S HUT LOCATED AT THE BHUMSI

Shaykh Sadri Jahan, a.k.a. Baba Haider Shaykhji, reached the river Sutlej and placed his hut on the bank of the ancient river in a place where no one was living. On the other side was a village called Bhumsi, which, it is said, Raja Bhim Sen had founded. Bhim Sen was Maharaja Yudishtira Pandava's brother [one of the five heroic brothers of the Indic epic, the *Mahabharata*]. While dwelling in the hut, the fame of the *shaykh's* wonders spread through all of Hindustan. From Hindustan's corners Baba's devotees visited him. Sirhind's governor also heard of Hazrat Shaykh's fame, and he came to take a glimpse of the *shaykh* and then expressed his belief in the *shaykh*.

SULTAN BAHLOL LODHI AND BABA'S MIRACLES

The connection between Hazrat Shaykh Sadri Jahan (may the mercy of God be upon him) and Bahlol Lodhi came about through a series of events. Among these the first occasion came when he was living in the hut and his fame had spread to all four directions. Having spread to all four directions, Bahlol Lodhi heard of the fame of his spiritual achievements. Having heard of the fame of his spiritual achievements, Bahlol Lodhi came to perform his service and to make a special devotional prayer. The second incident that is often related is that Bahlol Lodhi had stopped to camp in Maler when suddenly a great flood came in the river. The sultan's possessions were washed away and a lot of damage was done. Then Bahlol Lodhi was very surprised when he saw that Hazrat's hut was standing totally peacefully. From this event the faith in Bahlol Lodhi's heart grew. The next day he presented himself at the *shaykh*'s place and entreated his prayer for victory in war. Hazrat assured him of victory, God permitting. The third amazing occurrence was that Hazratji was in a poor state when Bahlol Lodhi offered him out of devotion a great horse and some money. But Hazratji sacrificed the horse to feed the fakirs and divided the money among the needy poor. The ruler sent a messenger demanding the horse back, but the messenger saw that in that place hundreds of horses were present. He could not determine which was the Shah's horse. He admitted his failure. At this Hazratji ordered the Shah's horse to present itself and that horse came to Hazratji. And so one more reason was given for believing in Hazratji.

One time Babaji was doing his ablutions before prayer at the side of the river and his shoe fell in. His disciple was upset, but Babaji said, "There is no need to be distressed. The water itself will give back our shoe." The man saw that a little while afterwards the shoe was on the bank.

One time he was sitting with his disciples when an army officer arrived bringing some money as an offering. Hazratji refused to take it and threw it into a tub of water. After some time passed, what did he see? In place of the currency, spots of blood were floating in the water and bubbles were being made. He gave the judgment that these earnings were from forbidden sources.

HAZRAT SHAYKHJI'S WEDDING AND LAND GRANT

Clearly from the above-mentioned incidents a deep faith in Shaykh Sadruddin Sadri Jahan arose in Sultan Lodhi and so the Sultan asked the *shaykh* to take his daughter in marriage. In 1454 the Sultan went from Multan towards Lahore, but then out of devotion went to Hazrat Shaykh's place. While meeting with the *shaykh* he asked a second time that he take his daughter in marriage because he was a greatly pious and religious [person] and no one equal to the *shaykh* could be found. Bahlol Lodhi married his daughter Taj Murassa Begum to Hazratji and gave twelve villages and fifty-six plots of land in a grant and 300,000 rupees were made an annual grant from the Lodhi government. Bahlol Lodhi gave his seal and signature with this land grant. The original copy was among the state records of Maler Kotla, but during a military campaign all our government records were burned, and in that event this historic document was also destroyed.

Hazratji's second marriage in 1458 was with the daughter of Kapurthala's Raja, Bahiram Bhatti. Because Hazratji's position in Punjab was understood to be so close to the Delhi Court, the rulers of Punjab's other states revered him limitlessly.

MALER KOTLA'S LAND

From those villages which Hazratji obtained, grew the state of Maler Kotla. Among these was probably a village called Maler. According to legend, one Raja Maler Singh had built a fort (*kotla*) named Maler Kotla near the Bhumsi [River]. The town of Maler was near this fort and because of this when Hazratji began the work of settling the new place then he kept the name Maler and his heirs followed his lead.

According to one legend, Sahib Singh Bedi [a descendant of the Sikh Guru Nanak from the late eighteenth–early nineteenth C.] destroyed the region of Maler.

Hazrat Shaykh's sixth generation descendant was Nawab Saifulmulk Bazid Khan. He established the population in Maler and laid the foundation of the government. The lineage of Hazrat Shaykh Sadr-i Jahan also had limitless faith and devotion, and because of this Nawab Bazid had the *shaykh*'s tomb built.

It is also commonly heard that the four walls of the *dargah* were built and the very large stone slab floor was placed in a single night.

HAZRAT SHAYKH'S TEACHINGS AND ADVICE

1. Remaining in the company of the people of God is an excellent practice for improving the mind.
2. With every breath remember God. No one knows when the breath will stop and only with constant repentance will you be able to remember God.
3. At two times give total attention to yourself, while speaking and while eating.
4. Let such prayers come constantly from your tongue such that you will not commit sins and thus your prayers will be accepted.
5. For every Muslim it is a duty that they must seek knowledge: knowledge, faith, prayer, fasting, the Hajj, service of mother, father and neighbors, the knowledge of buying and selling, what is forbidden and what is accepted. Without knowledge of these, humanity becomes corrupt.
6. Advise your women that along with these duties there are five good qualities of character:
    1. Remain pious and chaste,
    2. Be frugal,
    3. Look to your husband with respect,
    4. Obtaining your husband's approval will preserve you from discord,
    5. Proclaim the Lord's goodness with joy.
7. Hazratji recommends that pious women be loving and affectionate like a mother and patient and subservient like a maidservant.
8. He was asked, "What path should be followed to be accepted by the people?" He recommended that from generosity and justice you will be popular with the people and will arrive near to the Lord.

9. Do not make friends with ignorant people. They will lead to your downfall.

10. It was asked of Hazrat, who is an improving influence? He replied that there is only Hazrat Mohammad Mustafa (May the blessings of Allah be upon him) and who else could there be?

11. In every single, tiny thing of this world the Lord's enormous generosity and the influence of his presence are found. Those who do not understand this are blind and deaf.

12. He recommended that the dervishes and God-fearing people be given more attention even than one's own brother and that supporting those of religious learning is the duty of every Muslim. I direct you to support the people of knowledge.

CONCLUSION

Hazrat Shaykh Sadr-i Jahan, a.k.a. Haider Shaykh, awoke for morning *namaz* (prayer) on 13 Ramadan, 915 Hijri/1510 C.E. and performed *wuzu* (ablutions). After *namaz*, he was sitting as usual when his health suddenly became bad. He was taken to his residential cell and his condition grew worse and finally he left completely from this mortal world and went to heaven.

His *'urs* (death day observation) is celebrated every Ramadan. After him, *khalifahs* have come and nowadays Khalifa Anwar Ahmad Khan is the *gaddi nishin*.

The Emperor and the *Shaykh*: Oral Accounts by the Saint's Descendants

The descendants of the saint remain closely connected to the shrine and stress the saint's relationship to worldly power, along with the popular miracle stories given in Khan's chapbook: the candle in the storm and the gift of the horse. For them, as for the *gaddi nishin*, these stories both highlight their own royal lineage and make clear the superiority of spiritual power over worldly authority. Of course this simultaneously asserts the authority of the *khalifah* side of the family over the Nawabs who ruled Maler Kotla until independence in 1947. Both branches of the family remain politically and socially influential today. The second story below is particularly interesting for suggesting a link between the coming of a Sufi saint and the domestication of a wilderness area (in the manner described for Bengal in Chapter 27), even though the *khalifas* themselves do not make that explicit. The third draws on the familiar trope (studied by Simon Digby, 2000) of a contest between a Sufi and a yogi, which the Sufi always wins. Although such stories have a long history, they are unusual at this shrine today, where most stories seek to integrate the Muslim and non-Muslim communities linked to the saint. The stories are oral narratives collected in Maler Kotla in 2000 and 2001.

THE FIRST *KHALIFA'S* TALE

The eldest son of the *gaddi nishin*, responds to a question about pilgrims' desires:

> *Khalifah*: People ask about his history. He came from Kabul, and he was a Sufi saint, a big *buzurg* [saint, *literally* pious elder]. He came from Kabul to Punjab. One night Babaji was inside his hut. From another direction Bahlol Lodhi Badshah was traveling on a military campaign, and he also put his tents there. Suddenly a storm came and [Bahlol Lodhi's] tents were destroyed, but in Babaji's hut a lamp was still burning. The rest of the people were really surprised that in spite of such a great storm his lamp was still burning. So they were impressed by him. The king asked Babaji to pray for him so that he should be victorious in the war. Babaji prayed for him and he won the battle. The Badshah out of happiness presented Babaji with a horse. But Babaji was a Sufi, what was he to do with the horse? Babaji gave the horse to somebody else. Then somebody complained to the Badshah that Babaji did not accept his gift. When the Badshah asked [what happened to the horse], Babaji with his miraculous powers lined up a thousand horses just like that one in front of the Badshah. Then the sultan married his daughter to Babaji.
>
> *Anna Bigelow*: Have you heard of any such miracles these days?
>
> *Khalifah*: If somebody does not keep his dress properly, then Babaji gets annoyed. My grandfather saw Babaji's miracles in the night. Otherwise he is a gentle-natured *buzurg*. But if somebody makes a mistake, then he shows his power, he gets annoyed. My grandfather saw his miracles. He saw the vehicle in which he travels and it was full of light.

THE SECOND *KHALIFAH'S* TALE: THE SAINT AS WARRIOR

> *Khalifah*: Baba Haider Shaykh Sadruddin Sadri Jahan (may the mercy of God be upon him) is his full name. He was a general in the army first, but he was also a *faqir*. Once, the king asked him to go somewhere as there was a revolt going on there. But when the orders came to him he took them and threw them on one side, because he was doing *zikr* at that time, in God's name. So some of his followers who were *jinn* they picked it up. Those *jinn* were under his command—they picked it up. And so they understood that *they* were given this command. They went to that place and conquered it. And they got the booty from the people there. Then the king asked, "If my army didn't go there, how were they conquered?" He inquired, "My general was here and my army was also here, so who went to conquer that place?" [Haider Shaykh] said, "Your command came, but I was praying so I threw it to one side. My followers thought the command

was for them, so they went there and conquered the place." So the king ordered that [Haider Shaykh] should not be given any work, he should only rest. So Haider Shaykh left his post [with the army] because his secret was revealed in front of everyone, which isn't good. So his pir [the Sufi master who was his teacher] ordered him to go to Maler Kotla and to spread Islam there and pray to God. At that time, on all sides there was water here, except the place where the *dargah* is now, which was dry. So he sat there.

AB: There was water here?

Khalifah: This place near the *dargah* was dry. The Sutlej [one of the major rivers of Punjab] used to flow here.

Hafizji (an elderly Islamic teacher who was also present): Now it is in Ludhiana, [it went] in one night.

AB: In one night it went?

Khalifah: What happened was that one day when he was doing *wuzu* (ablutions before prayer) in that river, one of his shoes fell into the river. So he ordered the river to go away from that place, [saying] "Otherwise I will not spare you!" So in one night it dried up and began flowing near Ludhiana [about 60 kilometers away].

AB: That far!

Khalifah: It went near to Ludhiana, and afterwards water never came here. After that the Lodhi came to Maler Kotla, and he saw that a light was here, and he asked, "Who is there?" Someone told him that there is a *dervish* (a renunciant Sufi).

AB: What was the light?

Khalifah: A lamp was burning, and he asked whose lamp is burning. They said that a dervish is sitting there. So he went to him. And Babaji told him, "You will be one day the king of Delhi. Your law will be observed." Hearing this, in his heart Bahlol Lodhi declared, "If this happens I will marry my daughter with him. He is Pathan, he is from our community, he is from that same place where I am from." And he gave a horse to him as *nazarana* (offering), an Arab horse. But when he went back [after the battle] somebody told him, "The horse that you gave Babaji, he ate him by cutting him into pieces." Such a good horse! That dervish! How? And he [Bahlol Lodhi] ordered him to give back the horse. So his servants went and asked, "The king has asked us to bring back his horse." So Babaji said that the horse was in a nearby house. When they went there the whole stable was full of horses of the same kind. . "Take back your horse!" [laughs] That was his miracle. The same color horse as the one that was given to him was standing in great numbers, about twenty-five! The servants who came told the whole story of the miracle to the Badshah. Then the king and his wife came and married Babaji with their daughter Taj Murassa Begum. And in dowry gave many possessions to him and among them were fifty-six villages.

AB: Did he give up the *faqiri* life?

Khalifah: No he was still living the *faqiri* life, but the king had earlier sworn, "I want to marry my daughter to him." And he is also a Pathan. We are from his family.

THE THIRD *KHALIFAH'S* TALE: THE WONDER-WORKING *SHAYKH*

Yes, it is commonly known. Once there was a competition between Babaji [Haider Shaykh] and a yogi. He [the yogi] said, "Bring Babaji to me." He sent two men to bring Babaji, but they did not return. Then he sent more, and they also did not return. When the fourth time men were sent he asked them not to sit there but to bring the others back. But they were not able to stand [i.e., they were incapacitated], so the yogi himself went there. He said, "I am flying. If you have some power, pull me back down." And he flew with his magic. Babaji put off his slippers, they went up and banged on the yogi's head and he came down. Then he [the yogi] felt sorry and said, "Do not send me away from here. Please keep me here." And Babaji said, "You can stand outside this gate." Then he used to stand here and later his children would stand.

THE TALE OF A WANDERING *FAQIR*: THE *SHAYKH* AS AN APOSTLE OF PEACE

A visiting *faqir* from Uttar Pradesh portrayed Haider Shaykh as a peaceful apostle of the faith. This *faqir* travels continuously from one *dargah* to another, and the tomb shrine in Maler Kotla is among his regular haunts. He was one of the rare non-locals with a large repertoire of tales about Haider Shaykh. The *faqir* depicted Haider Shaykh as a warrior, but in his version, the saint's military career becomes a classic conversion story as he forsakes his past ungodly life and takes up a life dedicated to Allah. The audience for the *faqir's* story is clearly wide as he referred to God by multiple names, several common to Hindus, indicating that these are merely various names for the same deity. The *faqir* closed by asserting that people were drawn to pray *through* the *shaykh*, not *to* him. This is a response to Muslim critics of pilgrimage who fear that pilgrims partner saints with God as givers of blessings. Whereas Sikhs and Hindus have few reservations in this regard, some even referring to the saint as *bhagvan*, or god, most Muslims who attend the shrines today are extremely careful to explain that their prayers are dedicated to God alone through the pir.

Faqir: Sherwan, he was a resident of Sherwan [in Afghanistan]. At that time he was a major in the military, and he came to see that the world's law was *jutha* [untrue] and that the Lord's law was true. To adopt the rules of Allah he did whatever Allah, Ishvar, Prabhu, Bhagwan, Paramatma, he did whatever pleased Allah Most High. When Allah was happy, then he was Allah and Allah was his. And because of this, he resigned from the army and came to Maler Kotla, which is a princely state, and this was a region where a lot of other saints were preaching. And when he stopped in this region, after seeing his personality, the people were drawn to pray through him to Allah.

THE HINDU CARPENTER'S TALE: HINDUS AND THE *SHAYKH*

Hindu and Sikh stories about Haider Shaykh often establish a direct link between the saint and non-Muslims, a minority living in the only substantial Muslim community in Indian Punjab. An elderly, low-caste Hindu recounted the story below. Rather than focusing on the saint's lineage as the *khalifahs* and many Muslim residents did, this Hindu narrator emphasized the superiority of spiritual over temporal authority. He also integrated popular Hindu stories into his account of the *shaykh*. In this way he used the story of Haider Shaykh's arrival to criticize autocratic and imperious rulers who insist on having their own way, thereby embedding in his tale an assessment of the political situation in Maler Kotla, where Muslims have dominated for five hundred years. He told the story in the presence of several Hindus and Jains, beginning in a standard fashion with the saint's encounter with Sultan Bahlol Lodhi:

When Bahlol Lodhi's army came [i.e., to Maler Kotla], they were on the march. Suddenly a storm came and all the tents blew up. The King saw that the tents had blown away, except one a long distance away, and in it a light was burning. He stopped and went to him [Haider Shaykh] and said, "Give me a blessing that I should conquer Delhi." As the saint's work is to give blessings, he gave it, but the King put him in a fix as he gave him a horse. Baba said, "I am a saint, I do not need a horse." But he [i.e., Lodhi] said, "I have come to a saint, so I should give something," and he forced the horse on him.

We [meaning people in general] have three kinds of stubbornness or rigidity. One is the king's stubbornness or rigidity, one is the woman's stubbornness, and the third is the child's stubbornness, and in front of these even God has to bow. No one can speak in front of the king's stubbornness. We have a lot of examples of the stubbornness of women. Ram Chandra went into exile because of his mother's stubbornness [a reference to Ram's stepmother in the epic *Ramayana*]. The example of a child's rigidity occurs [in a tale] from Babur [actually, Emperor Akbar] and Birbal [a Hindu courtier whose tales are legendary] who were sitting together, and Babur said, "I have seen the king's and the woman's stubbornness. The king's example is me, the woman's is in the *Ramayana*, but what is the stubbornness of a child?" Birbal said, "I will show you just now." He brought a child from somewhere and soon the child started crying. The king asked, "What do you want?" The child said, "A small pot." He was given it. He became quiet, but again started crying. The king asked again,

"What do you want?" He said, "An elephant." He was given it, but then again he started crying and said, "I want to put this elephant into the pot." But this was impossible, so the king had to acknowledge his point.

So the king [Bahlol Lodhi] because of that [stubborn] nature tied the horse there and left. He won in Delhi. In the meantime Haider Shaykh gave the horse to one of his disciples. Somebody complained to the king saying, "He did not accept your offer and gave it to somebody." So the king came and asked, "Where is the horse?" Then he said, "I told you before that I do not need it, so I gave it to somebody." So Haider Shaykh made [i.e., miraculously] a horse and gave it to the king, but the king said, "I want *my* horse." So Haider Shaykh said, "You are arrogant, but I will give you your horse. You just close your eyes." Bahlol Lodhi blinked his eyes and saw there were thousands of horses more beautiful than his horse standing there, and his horse was standing behind them all and was eating the [excrement] of all the other horses. He saw the miracle and cooled down. He apologized and said, "I will marry my daughter to you." His daughter was thirty-five years old. She gave birth to two children. [Lodhi] gave them fifty-five villages in dowry. Faith in [Haider Shaykh] was endless.

Sources

The first excerpt above is from Khalifah Anwar Ahmad Khan's *Hazrat Sadruddin Sadar-i Jahan (Rehmat) Urf Baba Hazrat Shaykh Ji Malerkotla Di Puri Jivani* (Maler Kotla: Jivan Glass House, n.d.). Iftikhar Ali Khan's *History of the Ruling Family of Shaykh Sadruddin Sadar-i-Jahan of Maler Kotla, A.D. 1449 to 1948*, R. K. Ghai, ed. (Patiala: Punjabi University Press, 2000 [1948]) provides a genealogical history of Maler Kotla written by the last Nawab of the kingdom.

Further Reading

For other stories of Sufi saints, see Simon Digby, "Medieval Sufi Tales of Jogis & Tales from the Afghan Sultanates in India" in *Wonder Tales of South Asia* (New Delhi: Manohar, 2000), pp. 221–240. On the role of Sufis in the dissemination of Islam, see Richard Eaton's "Sufi Folk Literature and the Expansion of Indian Islam," *History of Religions* 14, no. 2, (1974): 115–127; and *The Rise of Islam and the Bengal Frontier* (Berkeley, CA: University of California Press, 1993). On the *tazkira*, see Marcia Hermansen, "Religious Literature and the Inscription of Identity: The Sufi Tazkira Tradition in Muslim South Asia," *The Muslim World* 87, no. 3–4, (1997): 315–329. For a more formal guidebook on the etiquette of pilgrimage, see Carl Ernst, "An Indo-Persian Guide to Sufi Shrine Pilgrimage" in *Manifestations of Sainthood in Islam*, Grace Martin and Carl W. Ernst Smith, eds. (Istanbul: The Isis Press, 1993). An interesting theoretical contribution to the study of shared religious traditions is Tony K. Stewart's "In Search of Equivalence: Conceiving the Muslim-Hindu Encounter through Translation Theory," *History of Religions* 40, no. 3 (2001): 260–287. For a contemporary example of a Sufi's role in taming the wilderness, see Pnina Werbner, *Pilgrims of Love: The Anthropology of a Global Sufi Cult* (Bloomington: Indiana University Press, 2003), pp. 30–60.

——11——

The Daily Life of a Saint, Ahmad Sirhindi,
by Badr al-Din Sirhindi

Carl Ernst

One of the most prominent features of Islam in South Asia is the Sufi tradition, especially as embodied in the major Sufi orders. Among these, the Naqshbandi order is distinctive for its rigorous practices and well known for its charismatic leaders. Originating in Central Asia, the Naqshbandi lineage had a history of strong involvement in politics. In terms of Sufi practice, the Naqshbandis were known for insisting on the silent recollection (*zikr*) of the names of God and for a resolute avoidance of music.

Of all the leaders of the Naqshbandi order, one of the most important was Shaykh Ahmad Sirhindi (1574–1624), whose metaphysical and mystical teachings are preserved in his large collection of letters, the *Maktubat*. Sirhindi became controversial for certain claims that he made regarding his spiritual status, which according to some came close to disrespect for the Prophet Muhammad. The emperor Jahangir briefly imprisoned him, and his letters were proscribed by Aurangzeb. Nevertheless, his followers regarded him as the "renewer of the second millennium," and they granted him near-messianic status as he reasserted the centrality of Islamic law and ritual practice in the lives of Muslims. In recent times, Sirhindi has been viewed as a reformer whose ideas prefigure modern notions of religious identity, such as the formation of Pakistan as an Islamic state; these interpretations considerably exaggerate the importance of a few political remarks by Sirhindi (such as his antipathy for Shi'i and for non-Muslims), which were rather peripheral to his central religious concerns.

The passage translated here is taken from a contemporary hagiography dedicated to Sirhindi and his successors, composed and completed around 1643 by Sirhindi's disciple Badr al-Din Sirhindi. It comprises the fifth section of the book, on the spiritual practices of Sirhindi. It is preceded by sections on his mystical genealogy, predictions of his advent, and his unique characteristics, and it is followed by chapters defending him against his critics, recording his sayings and his miracles, and offering short accounts of his descendants and successors.

The emphasis throughout this selection is on Sirhindi as the epitome and embodiment of the authentic practice of the example (*sunna*) of the Prophet Muhammad in every possible detail. His daily routine is nothing less than an exhaustive account of the performance of the five obligatory ritual prayers of Islam, along with the supererogatory ("extra credit") prayers that were so commonly observed in Sufi circles. Minute details are provided about his behavior with respect to ritual ablutions before prayer, sleep, eating, the toilet, etc., extending to such details as the toothbrush (*miswak*) recommended in pious Muslim practice as an emulation of a habit of the Prophet. The Qur'an is present throughout, frequently recited during ritual prayer, and continually invoked in additional meditations. Sirhindi acts as imam and leads his followers in ritual prayer. He also is presented as rejecting certain customary practices that he views as incompatible with the strict teachings of the Hanafi school of law, which was dominant in Central Asia and South Asia. This rhetorical insistence on Sirhindi as the defining figure of correct Islamic practice was also integral to the later Naqshbandi defense of Sirhindi against his critics.

Sufi practices are invoked throughout this hagiographical portrait, although in an unobtrusive fashion. Sirhindi is depicted as leading a circle of recollection (*zikr*), where disciples would chant the names of God or Arabic formulas such as the Muslim profession of faith. Although he is shown as experiencing extraordinary spiritual states, his strength of character is such that he makes no physical display or reaction whatever. He is naturally ascetic, and only indulges in food in order to comply with the example of the Prophet. His recitation of the Qur'an and his performance of prayer are awe-inspiring to his disciples, but he makes no attempt to embellish his recitation of the Qur'an with musical emphasis. He is surrounded by disciples, both novices and adepts, whom he counsels on the basis of his profound mystical insights; he can also act directly on their inner states through his power of concentration (*tawajjuh*), a faculty particularly cultivated by Naqshbandi masters. He is regarded as the personification of correct behavior.

Taken as a whole, this excerpt is a good example of a hagiographical presentation that aims at enhancing the sanctity of its saintly subject in terms of the core ritual practices of Islam.

FROM BADR AL-DIN SIRHINDI'S *HAZARAT AL-QUDS* [SACRED PRESENCES]

MIDNIGHT PURIFICATIONS

His practice in both cold and hot weather, both away and at home, was that after midnight he awakened and recited the prescribed invocations of that hour. After that he went to the toilet, first putting his left foot in the toilet area, and after that the right foot, and then reciting the prescribed prayer of that hour.

After he was done with the toilet, he stood on his left foot and then cleaned himself with earth and water according to prophetic custom. Then he performed ablutions, sat facing the direction of prayer, asking someone's assistance in ablutions. With a ewer in his left hand, he first poured water on the right hand and then on the left. After that he washed both hands together and the spaces between the fingers from the palm of the hand outward. While rinsing he employed a toothbrush, brushing three times on the right, three times on the left, and three times on the top; if he did more than that, it was to care for the gums, beginning from the upper teeth of the right side, then the lower teeth of the same side, then the upper teeth on the left side, and after that the lower teeth of that side. In every ablution, he employed the toothbrush, and when he was finished, as this writer has witnessed, he placed the toothbrush above his ear, and frequently also entrusted it to the attendant. His companions kept their toothbrushes in a fold of their turbans. He then spat out the rinse water and three times rinsed his mouth and nostrils with fresh water. He slowly poured water on his blessed face with perfect gentleness from the top of his forehead. He gave a slight precedence to passing his right hand over his right cheek before passing the left hand over the left cheek, so that he could begin with the right. When washing his blessed face, he pushed his turban to one side so that part of his head would be exposed, and he washed it from that side. The amount of water that he poured on his blessed face was such that the drops never splashed on his robe or his body. Every time he let all the drops fall from his hand to his face, so that none of it dripped on his robe.

After that he washed the arms up to the elbow three times, each time repeatedly wiping his right hand upward so that not a drop remained, and likewise with the left hand. He poured water on the fingers, and the water for wiping that he took in his right hand he conveyed to the left hand, scattering it far away so the drops would not splash on the ground and reach his robe. He wiped his whole head from the front to the back, and he wiped the top of the head with the inside of his right-hand fingers, and the sides of the head with the palms of both hands, bringing them from the back to the front. Then with the same water he wiped the inside of the ear with the index finger and the outside with the thumb. Then with the back of the hand he wiped the neck. He repeated the washing of the right and left feet three times, washing the ankle part of the leg, rubbing the hand upward every time so that it nearly became dry. He observed the customary prayers prescribed for the time of performing a full body ablution.

LATE NIGHT PRAYERS (SUPEREROGATORY)

After completing ablutions, he also recited customary prayers, but he did not clean the body with a robe after ablutions. Then he put on a fine clean robe, and with a splendid and dignified bearing he headed to ritual prayer. He performed two minimum cycles of ritual prayer, and he did the rest of the late night prayer with lengthy recitations from the Qur'an. Usually he recited two or three portions of the thirty equal portions of the Qur'an. Sometimes he went from midnight to dawn in a single cycle of prayer. When the attendant called, saying that dawn had arrived, he performed a second cycle of ritual prayer in the minimum fashion and said the peace. Most of the time he performed up to twelve cycles of ritual prayer, more or less, according to the needs of the hour. After every double prayer, in submission and humility, he became absorbed in meditation, and when he was done, he prayed for forgiveness and performed other prayers and blessings a hundred times. He meditated until dawn, or else recited the profession of faith, and a little before dawn, in accordance with the traditional example of the Prophet (prayers, blessings, and salutations upon its source), he would go to sleep, thus realizing the saying, "Keep late night vigil between two times of sleep."

DAWN PRAYER (OBLIGATORY)

Before dawn he would awaken and, after performing a new ablution, would follow custom in his house. After that he would stretch out facing the direction of prayer with his right hand propped under the right side of his chin, but later he would stop stretching out. After that, he performed the obligatory dawn prayer in the mosque with a large crowd, at the first light and the last twilight. He himself acted as imam, reciting the Qur'an at length and in detail. After completing ritual prayer, he recited some customary prayers, and then turning to the people, or the left, or the right, lifted up his hands in voluntary prayer.

MORNING PRAYER (SUPEREROGATORY)

After the voluntary prayer, he drew both hands across his face, and he then sat in the circle of recollection with his companions and performed this internal practice, until the sun rose up a spear's length. Within the circle they sometimes also listened to the Qur'an from one who had memorized it. Then he performed two cycles of the morning prayer with lengthy recitations. Then he performed two minimum cycles of prayer, after which he recited the prayer of seeking guidance and the completion of the customary appointed prayers.

ADVISING DISCIPLES

Then he went into seclusion, and according to the requirements of his spiritual state, was absorbed in recitation of the holy Qur'an, or sometimes the recitation of the profession of faith. Sometimes he summoned his disciples separately, asking each one questions about his spiritual state, and in accordance with that state gave guidance to each. There were many whose hidden spiritual states he explained, regarding both present and future, and he clarified them in detail. He trained them, and he made them aware of the divine names, the spiritual stations, the ecstasies, and the visitations.

Sometimes he summoned his advanced disciples, explained his own chosen secrets, and unveiled to them divine knowledge. He ordinarily tried to conceal those secrets with all his heart, but when he did explain divine knowledge, it was perceptible that he was in the spiritual state of encountering and receiving that knowledge. There were many who, when they heard this sublime divine knowledge from his pearl-scattering tongue, in gazing upon him at that very instant themselves experienced that divine knowledge. Most of the time that this revered one spent with his companions and others was in silence. His companions, from their extreme awe and wonder at him, did not even have the power to breathe. His control was at such a level that, in spite of the onslaught and frequency of numerous kinds of enrapturing visitations, no external sign of the rapture of that revered one ever appeared. He was never seen to be agitated, to exclaim, to shout, or to cry out, except on very rare occasions. Occasionally he wiped away a tear or was close to weeping, and sometimes in the midst of explaining divine realities his face became flushed.

MEALTIME

To return to the topic of discussion, when the morning became advanced, he performed two cycles of the morning prayer, though at times from necessity he performed four. He then took food, and while eating he could be seen most of the time to be dividing food for the dervishes, his family, the attendants, and guests. During this time he would sometimes pick up a morsel with three fingers, and sometimes reaching to a plate he would put some food in his mouth and taste it. At that time it was well known that he scarcely needed any food, and he only ate because eating is the prophetic tradition; prophets have not dispensed with that. At the time of eating, his manner of sitting was by the path of the prophetic tradition: sometimes he pulled up both knees, and sometimes he put the right foot on the left foot and the right knee on the left knee. After finishing with food, he recited the customary prayers of that hour, but he did not, according to popular practice, recite the Opening [fatiha, the first chapter of the Qur'an] after eating, for that is not in accordance with the prophetic example.

FORENOON PRAYER (SUPEREROGATORY) AND NOON PRAYER (OBLIGATORY)

After eating, for an hour he took a siesta, in accordance with the prophetic example. Then when shadows disappeared at noon, and the muezzin gave the call to prayer, the muezzin's words, "God is most great," and the awakening of that revered saint took place simultaneously. Immediately, with firmness and dispatch, he stood up on the ground; he never varied from this routine. While listening to the call to prayer, he repeated every word, except that during the two invitations ("Come to prayer" and "Come to salvation") he recited the prayer, "There is no might or power save in God." After he was done listening to the call to prayer, he recited a voluntary prayer, and when that was done, he got up, performed ablutions, put on a clean robe, and came to the mosque. First he performed two cycles of ritual prayer in salutation of the mosque, and after that he performed the four prescribed cycles of the forenoon ritual prayer with lengthy recitations from the Qur'an. After that, he performed the four prescribed cycles of ritual prayer set for noontime. Then he recited the standing glorification of God, led prayers as imam, and recited from the Qur'an at length and in detail. After the completion of the required duties, he arose, performing no other prayers except, "God! You are peace, and peace is from you. You have blessed us, glorious and generous one." He performed the two other prescribed ritual prayers set for that time. Then he performed the four cycles of ritual prayer that are in addition to the prescribed ones, and he recited the invocations that are customary after the obligatory ones. Then he sat down facing the people and had his companions form a circle. One who had memorized the Qur'an recited it, while he with his disciples sat attentively in meditation.

AFTERNOON PRAYER (OBLIGATORY)

When that was completed, he completed one or two elementary lessons until the time of mid-afternoon arrived. He arose to perform fresh ablutions. After the return of two-thirds of the original shadow, at the beginning of the time of afternoon prayer, he came to the mosque and performed two cycles of the prayer of salutation to the mosque and four cycles of prescribed ritual prayer. Then he led prayer as imam and performed the obligatory afternoon prayer with a large crowd. After that he recited the invocations that are customary after the obligatory ones. Then he sat down facing the people and had his companions form a circle. One who had memorized the Qur'an recited it, and that revered one and his companions were absorbed in it. During this time, he was internally concentrating on their spiritual states, and he exerted his concentration for their advancement. Sometimes he performed other virtuous actions.

SUNSET PRAYER (OBLIGATORY)

After that, he first performed the ritual prayer of sunset. After the obligatory rituals, he performed the two cycles of prescribed ritual prayer set for that time, with neither delay nor haste. Then he recited six cycles of ritual prayer, with three repetitions of the peace, and lengthy readings from the Qur'an. Most of the readings that had been read during the prayer of the penitents, or mid-morning prayer, i.e., the book of the Event [Qur'an 56] and the book of Sincerity [Qur'an 112] as well as others, were read now also.

EVENING PRAYER (OBLIGATORY)

He then came to the mosque for the evening prayer after "the departure of the whitening of the horizon," (which, according to "the greatest imam," Abu Hanifa, is an expression for twilight, and an agreed-upon time). First he recited two cycles of ritual prayer or of salutation of the mosque, and after that he per-

formed four cycles of prescribed ritual prayer. After that he performed four cycles of obligatory ritual prayer in congregation, performing no other prayers except, "God! You are peace. . . ." Then he arose and performed two cycles of prescribed ritual prayer set for that time and four additional recommended cycles
of ritual prayer. Then he offered special voluntary prayers. After that, he recited
the book of Prostration [Qur'an 32], and sometimes in the four cycles of ritual
prayer after the obligatory ones, he recited the book of Prostration, the book of
the Blessed [Qur'an 67], the book of the Unbelievers [Qur'an 109], and the
book of Sincerity. Sometimes in the four cycles of ritual prayer he recited all
four books that begin with "Say," and in the special voluntary prayers he recited
praise of the divine name, the book of the Unbelievers, and the book of Sincerity. He then combined the two standing prayers of the Hanafi and Shafi'i schools
of law, which the Hanafis combine and consider good. After the special voluntary prayer, he recited the beginning of two cycles of ritual prayer, reciting from
the book of the Earthquake [Qur'an 99] and the book of the Unbelievers. But
at the end, he left off the two cycles of ritual prayer, saying that there is disagreement about them. The prostration that is usually observed after the special voluntary prayer was not performed by that revered one, for the legal scholars have
agreed that it is objectionable. Sometimes he performed the special voluntary
prayer at the beginning of the evening, and sometimes at the end. After the late-
night prayer, he repeated it, for according to the saying of the Prophet (peace
be upon him), a single night does not have two special voluntary prayers. After
that, at the time of sleeping, having recited books, verses, praises, and prescribed prayers, he stretched himself out in a long arbor, so that he faced the direction of prayer and his right hand was beneath his face. And the righteous
sleep of that revered one was completely in the presence of meditation, union,
and witnessing the divine beauty.

> How wonderful are the degrees of the sleep that is better than
> wakefulness!

When reciting the Qur'an, during prayer or at other times, he had a way of
reciting that you would swear actually conveyed the meaning within each
word. On listening to his recitation, it would suddenly become apparent to listeners that the secrets of the Qur'an were pouring forth upon that one who was
brought near to the glorious God. Most of the people who had not entered the
circle of his disciples said that this revered one recited the Qur'an in such a
manner that one would say that the words came forth from his heart. But he
never attempted to recite in a musical style. During the long prayers of Ramadan, we saw few listeners who did not succumb to sleep, but when they
heard that revered one recite the Qur'an, most of them were standing up, and
they were never affected by sleep.

That revered one had disciples, masters of spiritual states, whom he had
guided as students in his presence. Before they reached the level of perfection
and the capacity to perfect others, he gave them permission to teach the spiri-

tual path, so that by saving people from the whirlpool of error, they could guide them towards God (glory be to Him). But because of their lack of perfection, he repeatedly and emphatically explained to them that they should never imagine themselves to be perfect, for they would fall into consternation and the path of their advancement would be blocked. Of all the paths of the masters, he considered the lofty path of the Naqshbandis to be the best, for he said that this path is identical with the path of the holy companions of the Prophet, so he held this lineage to be superior to other lineages.

This lowly one [i.e., Badr al-Din Sirhindi], prior to entry into the group of servants of that imam who is the source of concentration, several times went to his mosque, and I saw him performing prayer. Involuntarily I left my place, for I knew that he was talking face to face with the Leader of Creation (i.e., Muhammad, may God bless him and grant him peace), and that he saw that revered Prophet (may God bless him and grant him peace) performing prayer; he himself was performing prayer according to that example. Otherwise, this lowly one has seen religious scholars and masters, but I have never seen this kind of prayer from anyone.

He had perfect morals, humility, compassion for God's creatures, acceptance, and submission. His relatives suffered much from corrupt rulers, but with submission and acceptance he paid them no attention. Whenever an important person came to see him, he arose respectfully and gave a place to the visitor at the head of the assembly, speaking to him according to the man's measure. He never showed respect to infidels, even if they were politically powerful and prominent. It was his custom that he was first to greet anyone, and it is not known if anyone ever succeeded in being first to greet him. He exerted himself with extreme compassion in protection of the rights of the people, and whenever the news of someone's death reached him, he took it as a warning and expressed his regret. He said words of consolation and attended funeral prayers, reciting prayers for assistance.

Sources

The selections translated here are from the Persian work compiled by Badr al-Din Sirhindi (d. 1648), *Hazarat al-quds* [Sacred Presences] (Lahore: Mahkama-i Awqaf, 1971), pp. 80–92.

Further Reading

A good biographical study is available in Yohanan Friedmann's *Shaykh Ahmad Sirhindi, An Outline of His Thought and a Study of His Image in the Eyes of Posterity* (Montreal and London: McGill-Queens University Press, 1971).

— 12 —

Sufi Ritual Practice among the Barkatiyya Sayyids of U.P.: Nuri Miyan's Life and 'Urs, Late Nineteenth–Early Twentieth Centuries

Usha Sanyal

The Barkatiyya Sayyids are a Sufi family based in Marehrah, a small town about 120 miles southeast of Delhi in the Etah District, in the western part of Uttar Pradesh. Their settlement was founded in the late seventeenth century by their ancestor Shah Barkatullah (d. 1729), after whom they name themselves "Barkatiyya." Prior to this the family had been based in Bilgram, in the eastern part of the state, where a branch of the family (the "eastern" branch) still lives.

The events described in this chapter took place in the context of the slow dissolution of the late Mughal empire in the eighteenth century, when regional states (particularly the Shi'i nawabs of Awadh and Bengal) became prominent in north India and elsewhere, and the British East India Company vied with other European trading companies, particularly the French, for control over trading rights in a number of port cities. In the contest for power, the Mughal emperor Aurangzeb (d. 1707) and some of his successors gave Sufi families such as the Barkatiyya Sayyids revenue-free land grants in small country towns throughout north India in a bid to legitimize their rule with the local population. In so doing, they reversed the policy of previous emperors not to make permanent gifts of land to other sectors of society, for fear that this could threaten their own power down the road. As for the Barkatiyya Sayyids, such patronage was crucial to their ability to survive the political and economic disruption and insecurity of the eighteenth century.

The Barkatiyya Sayyids, as Sufis, were Qadiris, though they were also affiliated with the Naqshbandi, Suhrawardi, and Chishti orders. Over the centuries, one of the things that had greatly added to their prestige in the eyes of followers (both the peasantry amongst whom they lived and the 'ulama, erudite Muslim families with scholarly credentials) was their collection of relics (*tabarrukat*). Preeminent among these was a hair of the Prophet acquired during Shah Barkatullah's time, which was kept in a pewter needlecase and viewed by pilgrims during the death anniversaries ('urs) of eminent Sufi masters of the family. Other relics included a robe of 'Ali, the fourth Sunni caliph (and first Shi'i Imam), and hairs of Hasan and Husayn, 'Ali's two sons (and the second and third Shi'i Imams, respectively). Each of these holy objects had its own history prior to its acquisition by the Barkatiyya Sayyid family, which history reflects the spiritual genealogy of the family from the Prophet Muhammad to his cousin and son-in-law 'Ali, 'Ali's sons Hasan and Husayn, Shaykh 'Abd al-Qadir Gilani (the twelfth-century founder of the Qadiri order in Iraq), and the Chishti Sufi masters Shaykh Mu'inuddin Chishti of Ajmer (d. 1236) and his successors, finally reaching Shah Barkatullah in Marehrah.

These relics were part of the inheritance passed down from one generation to another. So were special prayers (du'a), which were known only to those to whom they were entrusted. For example, Nuri Miyan (the nineteenth-century Sufi whose biography is sketched below) received special permission from one of his teachers to recite the Hirz-i Yamani, a name given to certain verses of the Qur'an. These special prayers were so highly prized that the date on which a disciple acquired permission to recite or use them was recorded, and was considered part of his progress along the Sufi path.

Possession of the relics, the prayers, and the annual cycle of rituals—particularly the 'urs—were some of the important means by which the Barkatiyya family expressed its corporate unity. This unity was also preserved by carefully regulating marriages to other Sayyids (sometimes with members of a different branch of the family). The author of the Barkatiyya family history, Khandan-i Barakat, notes the exact location of each of his ancestors' graves: men in one part of the shrine complex (dargah), women in another.

Family unity also appears to have been preserved by the practice of choosing a Sufi successor (sajjada-nishin) from within the family rather than outside. In the absence of a son (and sometimes even when there was a son), incumbents chose a close relative such as a brother or grandson. The case of Nuri Miyan, whose biography is given below, is illustrative. He himself (together with another family member) succeeded his grandfather Shah Al-i Rasul (d. 1879), even though the latter had sons of his own. And when Nuri Miyan died, because he left no heirs he was succeeded by a cousin.

These few examples of the importance of family unity point (albeit obliquely) to another facet of the issue, namely, that the succession of a Sufi master and his spiritual and worldly legacy were often disputed by rival members of the family. After Shah Al-i Rasul died, Nuri Miyan initially served as deputy for one of his uncles; later the two of them shared the sajjada-nishini jointly. Family histories such as the one used here (Khandan-i Barakat) to reconstruct these events are themselves often written to further a claim, and thus tell their tale with a particular purpose in mind.

The 'urs of a Sufi master is, as mentioned, the most important annual event in the ritual calendar. Nuri Miyan's 'urs, reported in the Dabdaba-i Sikandari, an Urdu newspaper published in Rampur, an independent Muslim princely state during

British rule, lasted between four and six days every year. In 1912, a year for which we have accounts, the five-day 'urs consisted of recital of the entire Qur'an (khatma) for the first two days, recital of na't poetry in praise of the Prophet, and sermons by the 'ulama. On the third day, there was a khirqa-poshi (robe wearing) ritual in which the sajjada-nishin ceremonially wore 'Ali's robe (khirqa) and performed the Fatiha ceremony at Nuri Miyan's gravesite. There was also a qul, a ceremony marking the exact time of his death. The fourth day included a pilgrimage to the holy relics of the Prophet, Hasan, Husayn, and Shaykh 'Abd al-Qadir. Finally, on the fifth day, there was a ghusl or ceremonial washing of the tomb. The Barkatiyya Sufis took great pride in their self-conscious observance of the shari'a at all times, because of which, they believed, participation at the 'urs was a source of religious merit (sawab) to all its attendees.

However, as we compare accounts of Nuri Miyan's 'urs from different years, it is evident that there were variations on the general pattern from year to year. Sometimes unforeseen circumstances forced a change in the original plan, as in the 1921'urs. Sometimes there were controversial features, such as sama' and qawwali, that were not included in other years.

A BIOGRAPHY OF NURI MIYAN

From his father's side, Nuri Miyan was a Husayni Zaidi sayyid. On his mother's side, he was amongst the twentieth generation of Sayyid Muhammad Sughra Bilgrami's descendants. In every generation, his ancestors had been leaders who had been followed. In 1217–18 c.e., this family conquered Bilgram and settled there [though the precise date is a matter of debate]. . . . In 1608/09, Nuri Miyan's ancestor was chosen as the ghawth [a saintly title meaning "provider of aid and succor"] and qutb ["spiritual axis" or "pole"] of Marehrah, and settled there (Tazkira-i Nuri, p. 53).

NURI MIYAN'S CHILDHOOD AND RELATIONSHIP WITH HIS GRANDFATHER

Nuri Miyan was born on 19 Shawwal 1255 [26 December 1839] in Marehrah. . . . He was brought up by [his grandfather] Shah Al-i Rasul, and for forty-one years he enjoyed his company and served him. When he was two-and-a-half, his mother died. The responsibility for his upbringing was assumed by his grandparents. His grandfather was very fond of him and taught him the prayers (waza'if) and recital of the Qur'an (tilawat).

The boy accompanied his grandfather at his prayers and would go with him to the dargah. He would rest next to him. He was with him day and night, learning from him as the day passed. When it was time for him to join the maktab, Shah Al-i Rasul made a group of elders responsible for him. Even then, however, Shah Al-i Rasul watched over him constantly. On the surface, he said this was necessary because the boy had been orphaned at such a young age. But in fact he wanted to make him his successor (*ja-nishin*) and heir, and to honor him with his blessings. Nuri Miyan studied the Qur'an, grammar, Islamic law and principles of Islamic law, logic, hadith, and exegesis of the Qur'an from learned 'ulama. Side by side, he was also studying contemplation (*tasawwuf*) and the Sufi way (*suluk*) from wise elders ('urafa).

Nuri Miyan was eleven when his father died.

His first wife was Raqiya Begum, the daughter of his father's elder brother (*cha-cha*). And his second wife was Ulfat Fatima, the daughter of his father's younger sister (*phuphi*). But he had no children from either marriage (*Khandan-i Barakat*, p. 30).

NURI MIYAN'S RELATIONS WITH THE SUFI PIRS OF BADAYUN, AND WITH AHMAD RIZA KHAN BARELWI

During the time of Acche Miyan (Shah Al-i Ahmad, 1747–1819), the fame of the Barkatiyya family spread far and wide. The town of Badayun was especially favored by his blessings. From this time on, the famous Usmani family of Bada-yun joined his circle of discipleship (*halqa-i iradat*). When Shah 'Abd al-Majid [Badayuni] became Acche Miyan's disciple, the ties between the two families became really close. After 'Abd al-Majid's death, his son Shah Fazl-i Rasul Badayuni became his *sajjada-nishin*. He wrote many books and had many students. Nuri Miyan was one of the most notable of these (*Tazkira-i Nuri*, pp. 4–10).

Nuri Miyan also enjoyed a close relationship with Shah Fazl-i Rasul's son Shah 'Abd al-Qadir Badayuni [d. 1901], as also with Maulana Ahmad Riza Khan Barelwi [d. 1921]. Together Shah 'Abd al-Qadir and Maulana Ahmad Riza Khan created grave difficulties for the Nadwa movement. They consulted with one another over fine points of Islamic law, and stayed with one another from time to time.

Ahmad Riza Khan was a Sufi disciple of Nuri Miyan's grandfather, Shah Al-i Rasul, and after Shah Al-i Rasul's death, he regarded Nuri Miyan [who was technically his *pir-bhai*, or "Sufi brother," as they were both disciples of the same master] as his pir.

NURI MIYAN'S LIFESTYLE AND DEVOTION TO SHAH AL-I RASUL

When not reading the *namaz*, praying, or meditating, [Nuri Miyan] would enquire into the affairs of his helpers (*khuddam*) and those who came to him with petitions, reply to letters received, visit the sick, write amulets, take a break and get some rest, then spend some time with his books, reading or writing. . . . He also paid his respects to Shah Al-i Rasul, presenting himself at his court (*dar-bar*), learning of various affairs and receiving advice. [In addition] he was responsible for the well-being of hundreds of thousands of helpers. Every day a variety of problems presented themselves before him, and he would deal with them. Never did he put off dealing with something till the next day on the plea that he was too busy or fail to do something at its proper time. In everything he did, the spirit of the law (*shari'a*) and the rules of the mystic way (*tariqa*) reigned (*Tazkira-i Nuri*, pp. 59–60, 91).

[Nuri Miyan] loved and respected his Sufi master (*shaykh*); indeed he loved everyone who was associated with him and all the members of his family. He followed his master['s commands]; presented himself before him at his court; sought his company; and was completely absorbed in him. His face had the same radiance as his master's; his personality had the same stamp (*hal*); he walked with the same gait; when he spoke, it was in the same tone. His clothes had the same appearance; he dealt with others in the same way. In his devotions and strivings, he followed the same path (*maslak*). The times set apart for rest in the afternoon and sleep at night were times when he went to his master particularly, receiving from him guidance in every matter and warning of every danger.

Nuri Miyan died in 1906. Thereafter, every year his death anniversary was commemorated—as was customary for all the male heads of Sufi lineages in the family—in an annual celebration, or *'urs*, in the month of Rajab, the seventh month of the Islamic calendar, which was when he had died.

'URS AT MAREHRAH FOR NURI MIYAN, JUNE 1915

An *'urs* was celebrated at Marehrah in honor of Nuri Miyan, from 10th Rajab to 15th Rajab. People had come from several parts of India, such as Bombay, Calcutta, Bhopal, Gwalior, Ajmer, Pakpattan, Bankipur, Bahraich, Rampur, Bareilly . . . Badayun, etc. Maulana Shah Mehdi Hussain [Hasan?] Qadiri Nuri, heir to the Barkatiyya throne (*masnad*), looked after all the guests without distinction, and made arrangements for their food. Ahmad Riza Khan had come together with his close followers and disciples. The sermons of the 'ulama, and the verses in praise of the Prophet Muhammad (*na't*) of the reciters (*milad-khwan*) added to the splendor (*raunaq*) of the *'urs*. The entrance to the shrine (*astana*) was sparkling with its ornamentation of mirrors. Gas-lights were strung out all the way from the station to the tomb. The police made sure that despite the large crowd of people nothing untoward happened. The local authorities extended their help to the *sajjada-nishin* in making the arrangements. There were many more guests [this year] than last year. In this *'urs*, a poetry recital (*musha'ira*) was also held. The host for this was Sahib Iftikhar Husayn "Muztarr" Khairabadi. It was managed by a notable (*ra'is*) of Marehrah. The elegance and wit of the poets were a source of great enjoyment. . . . At the end, there was a *majlis-i sama.'* The qawwals were given prizes. And then the *'urs* came to an end (*Dabdaba-i Sikandari*, 7 June 1915, vol. 51, no. 29, pp.6–7).

NURI MIYAN'S 'URS, 1921

There was an *'urs* for Nuri Qadiri Barkati this year, as usual, on 21–23 March 1921, at the Dargah 'Aliya Barkatiyya. On the first day, the "sandal ritual" was performed from 8 o'clock until 2 o'clock at night. This ceremony was held in the Bari Dargah, accompanied by *na't khwani*. On the second day, the *khirqa-poshi* ceremony was performed at night. On this occasion, an impressive verse by Maulvi Ansar Husayn "Zalali," an attorney (*wakil*) at Badayun, was read. In the morning, there was the *qul ki fatiha*. Right through, on each day, day and night, there was Qur'an reading and *na't* and *manqabat-khwani* [poetry in praise of the Prophet]. A week before the '*urs*, a young daughter of the *dargah* had a "female" tragedy at Lucknow and died. [The only surviving child of Mehdi Hasan, a daughter, Fatima al-Zuhra, died soon after delivering a daughter. The daughter also died shortly before her mother did.] Her body was brought to Marehrah, and she was buried in the *dargah* there. Because of this grave accident, it appeared that this year the '*urs* would have to be postponed and notices to this effect were in fact put in the newspapers. But eventually it was decided to hold it on the dates originally planned. Because of this, and because there was insufficient time to put in a fresh notice about the non-postponement of the '*urs*, this year there weren't as many people as usual. Whereas usually there are about twenty thousand people, this time there were only four or five thousand. Guests were looked after very well. Each guest, without distinction, was given a sleeping mat (*chattai*), water (in an earthenware jug, or *ghara*), small metal pots (*lotas*), food and drink (*nosh*), betel (*pan, chhali*), tobacco, etc., at designated times during the day. Twice a day food would be brought to each one at his lodgings, from the Dargah 'Aliya. The entire arrangements were made by Ahmad Riza Khan's nephew (*hamshirazada*). Due to his fine arrangements, none of the pilgrims experienced any difficulty of any sort whatsoever. On the occasion of the *qul*, Shah Tufail Ahmad Badayuni . . . read verses [about the Prophet?] with such feeling that he had the whole audience in tears (*Dabdaba-i Sikandari*, 4 April 1921, vol. 57, no. 29, p. 4).

Sources

Dabdaba-i Sikandari, Rampur. Weekly newspaper 1915, 1921. Raza Library, Rampur, U.P. India. Ghulam Shabar Qadiri Nuri Badayuni, *Tazkira-i Nuri: mufassal halat o sawanih-i Abu'l Hussain Nuri Miyan Marharwi* (La'ilpur, 1968). "Muhammad Miyan" Qadiri, *Khandan-i Barakat* (c. 1927).

Further Reading

For a study of the Ahl-i Sunnat or "Barelwi" movement in British India, with which Nuri Miyan was affiliated, see Usha Sanyal's *Devotional Islam and Politics in British India: Ahmad Riza Khan Barelwi and His Movement, 1870–1920* (Delhi: Oxford University Press, 1999). To understand the broader context of Islamic revivalism and its other major trends, see Barbara D. Metcalf's *Islamic Revival in British India: Deoband 1860–1900* (Princeton, NJ: Princeton University Press, 1982). For an overview of South Asian Sufism and its most important order, the Chishti brotherhood, see Christian W. Troll, ed. *Muslim Shrines in India: Their Character, History and Significance* (Delhi: Oxford University Press, 1989); Carl W. Ernst and Bruce B. Lawrence, *Sufi Martyrs of Love: The Chishti Order in South Asia and Beyond* (New York: Palgrave Macmillan, 2002); and P. M. Currie, *The Shrine and Cult of Mu'in al-din Chishti of Ajmer* (Delhi: Oxford University Press, 1989).

—13—

Transgressions of a Holy Fool:
A *Majzub* in Colonial India

Nile Green

Although neglected by modernist Muslims and academics alike, the holy fool is one of the most interesting and significant figures in the social and religious history of Islamic South Asia. Stories of such ecstatics—or *majzubs*—can still be heard all over South Asia, demonstrating an approach to the social dilemma of deviant behavior that is based on very different principles from the modern pathology of mental illness. In precolonial India "madness," that is, actions and states of mind that demonstrably and persistently clashed with established norms, could be interpreted as a sign of divine grace and favor that set certain individuals apart from ordinary folk. When given meaning through religious interpretation, such aberrance was conceived as *jazb* or "attraction" to the divine that resulted in a state of absorption or ecstasy that took on the appearance of madness. By drawing upon the typology and terminology of Islamic and particularly Sufi tradition, this approach to psychosocial deviance could explain and indeed legitimize the behavior of persons who did not conform to the norms of wider society but who, through the concept of *jazb*, were nonetheless allowed to find a place within it. From a sociological point of view, the category of the *majzub* was in this sense a means of incorporating insanity into public life.

Regarded as channels through which the power of God could be transmitted to the world and rendered accessible, such holy fools remind us that much of the character of Muslim religious practice in South Asia was concerned less with matters of belief than with more mundane issues of survival in an environment plagued by manifold insecurities. In this sense Islam has served not only as a "belief system" in line with essentially Protestant formulations of religion, but also as a set of strategies with which to navigate the day-to-day perils of life in the world. Holy fools were not viewed as teachers or preceptors, and unlike many other figures associated with the idiom of Sufism their behavior was rarely if ever seen as exemplary. Instead, by reading the symptoms of their "madness" as signs of divine favor, the communities that surrounded these holy fools were able to provide themselves with a source from which to access the power of God. For in their vivid social alterity holy fools were vivid signifiers of the otherness of God, who like his unruly friends was also expected to disrupt the mundane order through miraculous intervention.

Of course, the models of mental and social normality constructed by any society require constant adjustment when faced with the intransigent mutability of the world, and the problem of distinguishing madness that was divinely inspired from more humdrum forms of madness was one that permanently surrounded holy fools. Among their supporters, the *majzubs* stood above the concern for propriety (*adab*) that governed the life of ordinary South Asian Muslims. For both in terms of their own behavior and that of their followers, they presented a stark contrast with what was regarded as acceptable in other spheres of life in South Asia. The *majzub* could break the rules that governed the life of ordinary Muslims because of his special dispensation from God. As a result, the stories that surround such figures are often celebrations of the transgressive and forbidden. Yet at the same time, the *majzub* and his (or sometimes her) supporters always occupied a position of tension within the wider social world. For the legitimacy of the fool's behavior and others' devotion to him rested entirely on the claim that his raving was inspired *jazb* and as such the result of a special divine dispensation. The coming of colonial rule and the evolution of modern psychiatric classifications of "sick" and "healthy" minds during the nineteenth century brought a new template for interpreting the behavior of such individuals that was reinforced by the discursive weight of empire. For this reason, the activities of holy fools occupied a position of precarious legitimacy. During the period of British rule in India, we find accounts of such figures condemned by the British as insane in accordance with developing European models of psychiatric disorder, but defended by their Indian supporters as God's representatives on earth. These competing claims were further complicated by the evolution of a new colonial institution, the asylum, pitting the claims of the partisans of the *majzub* against an entire colonial apparatus of incarceration and pathology; tales of miraculous escapes from colonial asylums are associated with a number of such contested madmen. In these circumstances, British rule offered new possibilities for both transgression and its punishment, such that the heyday of colonial rule in India saw holy madness at the center of a nexus of wider struggles, political and discursive, for control of Indian society and its meanings.

The underlying social and political tensions made manifest in the transgressions of the fools of God are well exemplified in the career of Banne Miyan, a *majzub* who lived in Aurangabad in the "independent" princely state of Hyderabad and died in 1921. Although the sources on the early life of this holy fool are contradictory, before his turn towards ecstasy it seems that Banne Miyan served as a soldier in the Hyderabad Contingent. Commanded by a British officer class, the Contingent was the principal instrument of British power in the Nizam's State of Hyderabad and, through its presence in a series of cantonments across the state in which the Nizam had no jurisdiction, it formed the main point of encounter between the people of Hyderabad and the political reality of colonization. It was after Banne Miyan's dismissal from the Contingent and his incarceration (possibly in one of the new asylums administered by the British in Hyderabad) that he was recognized as a *majzub* and began the career of miracles and disorder that made him famous. However, he seems to have maintained his connections with the army, for many of his followers were Indian soldiers serving in the Contingent, while like other holy fools of the colonial period one of his specialties seems to have been miraculously outwitting the representatives of empire. Yet despite his military background and the historical connection between colonial soldiering and insanity that saw the emergence of military, and later civilian asylums in India, there is also a more tender dimension to this Lord of Misrule. It is this aspect of Banne Miyan's cultic persona that is expressed in his nickname of *banne*, the term for a bridegroom that is also widely used in Urdu as a term of endearment for boisterous young boys. Free of the constraints of work and marriage, Banne Miyan was in this sense the embodiment of a certain cultural formulation of youth. Able to break social taboos like a child, Banne Miyan's transgressive practices were an expression of the playfulness and freedom of youth transposed into the political contexts of provincial princely India at the turn of the twentieth century.

Translated in the following pages are a series of anecdotes from the life of Banne Miyan recorded by his nephew Muhammad Isma'il Khan (d. 1956) in the Urdu biography *A'zam al-karamat*, either shortly before or after Banne Miyan's death in 1921. Many of the stories are richly detailed, providing a vivid impression of the practices of both Banne Miyan and the devotees he attracted through his errant ways. The text also makes oblique references to historical events, such as the major drought and plague outbreaks that affected western India during the 1910s, so testing religious custom in the furnace of history. But in the stories below we also see the connection of the holy fool to a wider cultural repertoire of food customs, the paying of respectful visits, and the singing performances of courtesans or *tawa'if*.

While Banne Miyan seems to have already been condemned by the British as a madman, his and his followers' practices were also under attack from a new generation of Muslim reformists. For this reason, the *A'zam al-karamat* takes especial care to establish Banne Miyan as a *majzub* and not merely a bazaar hooligan. While illustrating the lifestyle of this holy fool, the text also attempts to imbue disreputable practices with God's grace: in one vivid example translated below Banne Miyan's cannabis pipe becomes a miraculous remedy for snake poison. Other objects connected with the saint and mentioned in the text, such as his tin bucket and the blanket that was his sole (and even then only occasional) item of clothing, were later preserved as relics by his family. These relics were originally kept at the shrine constructed around Banne Miyan's tomb in the years after this death. Aptly, the shrine later gained a reputation for bringing relief to those suffering from mental trauma and possession, so providing a space to socialize and lend meaning to madness.

ANECDOTE 1

His Holiness (*hazrat aqdas*) Banne Miyan's pious ancestors came from the town of Shaykhupura in Punjab. Their kinship group (*qawm*) is *shaykh*, and they used to be readers of learned Friday sermons. His Holiness's respected name is Muhammad A'zam Khan; his father's name was Muhammad Nur Khan; and his grandfather's name was Muhammad Bahadur Khan. It was he who left Punjab to come to the Deccan. His Holiness's father was serving in the Third Regiment [of the Hyderabad Contingent] in the Cantonment of Hyderabad when the spiritual guide and elder Sayyid Shah Afzal Biyabani Qadiri al-Rifa'i al-Chishti [d.1273/1856] (on whom be the mercy of God), radiant with the sun of sainthood, was uniting people with God through the power of his glance. Thousands received the honour of pledging allegiance to Sayyid Shah Afzal. It was at that time that His Holiness's father, His Holiness Banne Miyan himself, and this humble writer were honored to take the pledge of allegiance to Sayyid Shah Afzal. Even at an early age, Banne Miyan showed signs of spiritual greatness and on pledging allegiance came to understand hidden blessings, and so eventually that child became Banne Miyan. The story is that one day as a child His Holiness came before Shaykh Afzal Biyabani, who called to him, saying, "Come, my young groom (*banne*)." From that day he became famous as Banne Miyan. Even since Afzal Biyabani's time, he has been famous as a master of ecstasy and spiritual unveilings. Through his spiritual guide and elder, he entered into both the ways of the Qadiriyya and the Chishtiyya. He has the documentation of this spiritual ancestry in his possession. But to reach Eternal Riches is a divine gift and not something that can be merely inherited, and it was from this that he became famous for his countless miracles. These are still going on, too. Whether it is the humble and great from among the Hindus, Muslims, Parsis, or British passing through Aurangabad, all are acquainted with him and so his fame has spread far and wide. One of his special miracles is to give guidance in different languages. If a local Hyderabadi person comes to him, then he speaks the local language; if someone from Afghanistan comes to him, then he speaks to them in the Afghan language, Pashto; and if an Arab comes to him, then he holds forth in Arabic. Inspired knowledge is laid open before him. Thus there is one of the spiritual Great Ones (*buzurg*) in Hyderabad by the name of Sayyid Ahmad before whom an Arab brought his wishes, but that Great One instead told the Arab to take his faith to Banne Miyan and so sent the Arab off into Banne Miyan's service. When he came before His Holiness, he gave his answers to that Arab in purest Arabic. (*A'zam al-Karamat*, pp. 11–12)

ANECDOTE 2

His Holiness spent twelve years in the jungle busy in spiritual exercises and strivings. After that he came to the step-well near to the Regimental Cantonment in Aurangabad, which is known as Nanbatdari's step-well. Near the step-well is a stream and in that stream there is a small mound, and on leaving the jungle Banne Miyan came to that mound. For twelve years he made inverted prayers (*namaz-i-ma'kus*) suspended upside down inside that well. Even when the stream was flooded, he refused to leave his place to go elsewhere. One time a bug went into his ear and grew really large inside it such that there were soon many more bugs in there, but Banne Miyan felt pity for them and left them alone in his ear. His followers debated over what they should do, but he still wanted to stay in the same condition. Eventually though they called a doctor, who poured medicine into His Holiness's ear and shortly afterwards hundreds of bugs came running out of his ear. But Banne Miyan felt great sadness and pity for all of the bugs [an allusion to popular legends of the prophet Ayub (Job), who similarly suffered patiently from sores filled with maggots and on seeing one of the maggots fall on the ground praised God for having created them]. His state is still like this today, going for a week without food or water, wandering in the heat of the sun, calling out to this and that. (*A'zam al-Karamat*, p. 17)

ANECDOTE 3

One day Mamun Sahib took His Holiness to the wedding of one of his devotees. But while he was there, Banne Miyan went into one of his states of holy rage (*jalal*), so Mamun Sahib decided to put him into a shed and close the door, locking it behind him. Right up to the end of the wedding, no one heard anything of Banne Miyan, so the thought came to Mamun Sahib that he would go and open the shed. So off he went and saw that His Holiness was not in the shed after all. Only his clothes were there. So Mamun Sahib set off to search for His Holiness and looked everywhere but was unable to find him. It was only several months later that he heard that Banne Miyan was back in his old place, sitting on the mound in the middle of the stream. (*A'zam al-Karamat*, p. 18)

ANECDOTE 4

A strange thing happened when Mufti Nur al-Ziya al-Din [who is a descendant of Mawlana Qamar al-din Naqshbandi (d. 1193 [1779]), an important Sufi scholar and theoretician, famous for his learning and spiritual bounties] came from Hyderabad to Aurangabad. Sayyid Ahmad Khan Rizwi went with him to meet with Shahbaz Khan Afghan, a pashmina merchant from Ghazni in Afghanistan, in order to see his merchandise. Mufti Nur al-Ziya suggested to Sayyid Ahmad Khan that they should go to kiss the foot of His Holiness and Shahbaz Khan also agreed to go. The mufti suggested that they buy some sweets to give to His Holiness, so they gave some money to Shahbaz Khan to buy them and off he set. Mufti Nur al-Ziya and Sayyid Ahmad proceeded to Banne Miyan's compound and found His Holiness sitting there in a white blanket leaning with his blessed back against the wall.

Turning towards Mufti Nur al-Ziya and Sayyid Ahmad, Banne Miyan exclaimed, "Ah, Mecca and Medina have arrived!" He then said to Sayyid Ahmad, "Humble yourself and tremble!" and then said, "Submit yourself more, tremble more!" He gave this advice, "Pride in one's ancestry and past riches is pointless and foolish," and "Ruling is not empty of disbelief!" After that Shahbaz Khan arrived and came and stood before Mufti Nur al-Ziya and Sayyid Ahmad. His Holiness threw a bone in the direction of Sayyid Ahmad, but Shahbaz Khan picked it up. Banne Miyan then got up and took Shahbaz Khan with both hands and led him out of his compound and into the gully outside. The meaning of this was that Shahbaz Khan was avaricious in taking the bone, for if he had taken a mere bone what would he take next?

Shahbaz Khan looked as though he was about to faint and then seemed to take on a different state of being, and in the end his conscience was pricked. He started dancing round and stamping his feet, and he lost his desire for the goods he had sold or for gaining any of the money he was owed by his debtors. People gathered in amazement. The square, used as a camping ground, turned into a place of great commotion. Shahbaz Khan had gone out of himself and wasn't even aware of his head or feet. He refused to eat or drink and just went on dancing around in ecstasy. His business companions were dismissed to return without him to Ghazni with his remaining goods. Shahbaz Khan had such a terrible pain in his heart that he knew that either he would have to say farewell to this world in order to turn his heart away from worldly love towards divine love, or else die of that pain. And then, when his heart was in this terrible dilemma and he could bear it no longer, God helped him to fulfill his wish. And all this happened through the blessing of His Holiness Banne Miyan. (A'zam al-Karamat, pp. 20–22)

ANECDOTE 5

Sayyid Muhammad Nami is an Arab resident of Medina who came to Aurangabad and is famous there by the name of Madani Sahib. For a long time he has been residing in the Big Mosque in Juna Bazaar in Aurangabad. He is a great ascetic, reclusive and of good morals. He related one of the strange events that happened to him. Once there was an orphan girl who was being brought up under the guidance of a servant girl. However, at that point, although the girl was still under the age of maturity and Madani Sahib was older, he decided that they should become engaged to marry, and they did so. But after the marriage, the servant girl tried to persuade her mistress that it would be easy to annul the marriage since the husband was a weak foreign traveler without any friends. It entered the servant girl's mind to cause trouble in this marriage so that her mistress could marry someone else. Poor Madani Sahib couldn't even understand

Urdu properly either, because Arabic was his mother tongue rather than Urdu. Nevertheless, Madani Sahib learned of the plan for his wife to marry someone else and started to plead and fight with the servant girl. But in the end she went and hid Madani Sahib's wife so that he couldn't find her.

Being an honorable man, Madani Sahib became very concerned and worried and could see no way out of his situation and had no idea what he should do as he was so completely helpless. And then it entered Madani Sahib's mind that since His Holiness was so famous in Aurangabad for helping people, he could flee to his residence. Once he was in that place of holiness, he saw Banne Miyan climbing up the wall, and he opened his heart to him and explained that he was a helpless Arab *sayyid* with no money and poor Urdu and that this terrible situation had occurred and that he now sought help and justice. Banne Miyan, still climbing his wall, told him it was nothing to worry about. Still worried, Madani Sahib stood there quietly and politely, worrying where his loved one was. But as the famous [Persian] saying goes,

> Who heeds the pleas of the pauper,
> Especially when they come from the pauper's own tongue?

And so Madani Sahib waited quietly at Banne Miyan's residence for a while. Then what did he see but the local police accompanying a boy with a turban wrapped tightly round his head entering Banne Miyan's compound. The boy was none other than Madani Sahib's wife but in disguise. Banne Miyan pointed to Madani Sahib telling him to call out. Madani Sahib then felt absolutely certain in his heart that this was his wife, even though he hadn't recognized that it was her. So Madani Sahib then grabbed the boy's hands, but the police pushed him away and started struggling with him and beating him with their hands and feet. But Madani Sahib would not give in, for now with Banne Miyan's help he was convinced this was his wife and so attacked the young policemen fearlessly and managed to fight them off. More policemen were called and soon the whole place was filled with them. Madani Sahib was really worried about where he should go, because it was now so hard for him to find a way out to reach home. But Banne Miyan showed him the direction in which to escape, pointing towards the direction of Chihlapura, and from there he headed towards the Luta Karanjar quarter and so was able to reach his home with his wife.

From his house he could see the police running everywhere looking for him, wanting to arrest him, but they had been unable to see him anywhere. One would say it was as though a curtain had fallen, even though it was a very broad and public street. And so Madani Sahib was able to escape arrest, all the way from the compound of Banne Miyan back to his house, with his wife alongside him. Wherever the police looked, trying to arrest him, they were unable to see him anywhere. This is what we call power and authority (*qudrat aur ikhtiyar*), which is given to his special servants from Allah the Pure through their relationship with his chosen Prophet (may peace be upon him, his family, and his companions). (*A'zam al-Karamat*, pp. 23–25)

ANECDOTE 6

One day, with the help of the Bazaar Master, the Cantonment Magistrate of Aurangabad had Banne Miyan taken to the asylum by bullock cart by some soldiers of the regiment. They took him to the house of the superintendent of the
asylum and left him there. But after sunset a number of people saw Banne Miyan
entering the shop of an opium dealer in the regimental cantonment bazaar in
Aurangabad. The police immediately informed the Bazaar Master what had happened. In the morning the Bazaar Master came and asked the soldiers why they
hadn't deposited their priest (*padri*) with the superintendent. "But sir," they
replied, "we did take him to the superintendent's house!" The Bazaar Master
then ordered them to take Banne Miyan by cart and deliver him into the care of
the superintendent and bring back a receipt. The soldiers then saw Banne
Miyan just in front of the cart and so carried him away in it to the asylum where
they delivered him again to the superintendent's house in Jalna and handed him
over and took a receipt. Yet in the morning again all the people saw Banne
Miyan back in the same bazaar in the same opium shop, and so once again they
informed the Bazaar Master. He was amazed because he had the receipt of
Banne Miyan's arrival at the asylum. So he set off to see the truth of the matter
and saw Banne Miyan there in the bazaar with his own eyes. He exclaimed,
"Undoubtedly, you are a great Sufi padre (*pir padri*)," then lifted his hat in respect to salaam Banne Miyan. After that he would sometimes go to Banne
Miyan to pay his respects. (*A'zam al-Karamat,* pp. 25–26)

ANECDOTE 7

There is an Arab, who now works in Aurangabad in the treasury department of
the Nizam's administration, who had a great desire to memorize the Holy
Qur'an. So he went to Banne Miyan and took the Qur'an along with him and
explained that he wished to memorize the Qur'an. So he sat facing His Holiness
and began reading from the Qur'an, and he carried on with this practice every
day, reading two or three sections of the scripture under the supervision of
Banne Miyan. And when he made any mistake in his recitation, His Holiness
would correct him. And by the grace of God, that Arab has now memorized the
entire Qur'an. (*A'zam al-Karamat,* pp. 26–27)

ANECDOTE 8

Muhammad Isma'il Khan, the nephew of His Holiness, gave a cannabis pipe
(*chillam*) to Banne Miyan, who then sat smoking it. Banne Miyan then said,

"Take this pipe to the gentleman and make him smoke it to ward off the snake."
So Muhammad Isma'il Khan took the pipe and ran off down the street. In the
street a crowd of people had gathered, and they were shouting that Munawwar
Khan had been bitten by a snake in his garden. So Muhammad Isma'il Khan ran
alongside them to that person's garden. What did he see when he arrived but
that the poison of that snake had already started to take effect on Munawwar
Khan's body. Muhammad Isma'il Khan told him to take the pipe and smoke it,
because this was what His Holiness had commanded. Munawwar Khan smoked
the pipe and the poison immediately ceased to take effect and he came back to
good health. After that Munawwar Khan came to kiss the feet of Banne Miyan.
(*A'zam al-Karamat,* pp. 28–29)

ANECDOTE 9

It is said that one day a large group of people came to Banne Miyan, because
there was a drought. Having paid their respects to him, they asked if he would
say some prayers for rain. His Holiness got up and walked out onto the town
square. Covering himself with his blanket, he lay down to sleep. A few minutes,
later by the grace of the Almighty, it started to rain heavily. For the rest of that
year there was no shortage of rain. (*A'zam al-Karamat,* p. 29)

ANECDOTE 10

Muhammad Asad al-Din Khan is one of the important landowners and the
grandson of Nawwab Hafiz Yar Jang Bahadur. When he made the pledge of allegiance to Banne Miyan, His Holiness ordered him to bring an old tin jug of
water. Banne Miyan drank a little of it and then gave the rest to Asad al-Din and
then accepted his pledge of allegiance. Later Asad al-Din said that he had never
tasted anything like that drink in his whole life and that he could not describe
its flavor. It gave off a fragrance like the essence of rosewater and the kiora
flower. The children and the whole household of Asad al-Din also came to
pledge allegiance to His Holiness. (*A'zam al-Karamat,* p. 29)

ANECDOTE 11

Sayyid Risan Khan was always in the service of His Holiness. One day he asked
Banne Miyan to feed him. His Holiness told Risan Khan to come with him, and
they set off together to the mansion of Nawwab Muqtadir al-Dawla Bahadur.
Banne Miyan walked into the kitchens where around two or three pounds of
red chili peppers had been weighed. He took the big bowl of chili peppers and

fed them to Risan Khan with his own blessed hand. Risan Khan later said that he had never eaten anything so sweet and tasty in his whole life. (A'zam al-Karamat, p. 31)

ANECDOTE 12

Mir Munawwar 'Ali is an aristocrat and a disciple of Shah Sarwar Biyabani [d. 1331 (1912), the successor of Banne Miyan's spiritual master, Afzal Shah]. He recounted that one day he came to visit Banne Miyan, and that while he was on his way he thought to himself in his heart that he had heard it said that every day there is music played in the presence of Banne Miyan. But when he arrived he found that the praise singers (qawwals) had already come to kiss the master's feet, but that there was no singing. At that moment His Holiness commanded, "Now the sky (asman) will play the tabla!" About an hour later a courtesan singer (tawa'if) arrived wearing a sky-blue (asmani) mantle and carrying her lute and other instruments. She started to sing. (A'zam al-Karamat, pp. 28–29)

ANECDOTE 13

One day a courtesan singer came to sing to His Holiness and sat for a long time waiting to be given permission to sing. But because His Holiness didn't say anything, the courtesan became very depressed. The other people present told her to wait until His Holiness had gone off to his room to attend to his affairs and then she should begin singing. So the courtesan waited, and when His Holiness went into his room after sunset she began to sing a thumri. The courtesan scarcely repeated a song line four times, when His Holiness got up and took a tin bucket that was brimful with four or five liters of water. Then he lifted it up with his hands and repeated the same verse back to her. He poured that bucket of water onto a lamp that was on the ground, about nine or ten feet below the roof. But the roof was made from straw, and when he poured the water on the lamp the flame spread from it and caught fire with the roof, his hand, and everything. Everyone could see that the flame had spread from the lamp and was burning the roof, and the water that he had poured over the lamp then caught fire as though it were oil. The lamp, Banne Miyan's hand, and the whole roof were all completely burned. When the water had all finished, His Holiness put down the bucket and went back into his room. And then the lamp began to give out light just as it did before and burned as normal. One could see by the lamplight that there was no sign of any of the water on the ground, and neither was there any trace of burning on His Holiness's hand nor on his roof. (A'zam al-Karamat, pp. 51–52)

ANECDOTE 14

Another disciple of His Holiness is Amir al-Din "the Teacher" [who recounted this event]. "One day I set off to visit the district of Vaizapur on business. On the same day I was coming back to my house, when I was stopped at the railway station in Aurangabad by a British doctor who was on Plague Duty. The doctor came onto the platform and started rounding up all of the passengers from the train compartments and told them that they would be kept in quarantine until the next day. I became really worried, so I cried out to His Holiness, 'Oh blessed elder and guide.' And at that very moment he helped me. Suddenly mercy came into the heart of the Doctor Sahib, and he gave the order that I, and the other passengers seated in my compartment, did not need to be put in quarantine because we were all perfectly healthy. Through the grace of God I was able to return home safely." (A'zam al-Karamat, pp. 69–70)

ANECDOTE 15

Ghulam Husayn Khan was a private in the 1st Cavalry of the Hyderabad Contingent, stationed in the cantonment. One day he was in the cavalry bazaar in Aurangabad and His Holiness passed in front of him and called out, "Hey officer (daf'adar), where are you going?" Ghulam Husayn turned and respectfully said to him, "I am only a sepoy and not an officer." But His Holiness replied, "No, you are an officer." Later that day Ghulam Husayn Khan rode his new horse before Major Colonel Ross [1869–1938; Colonel Harry Ross was the most senior British officer based nearby at Ahmadnagar in British India]. Major Colonel Ross saw Ghulam Husayn and said, "Who is that sepoy?" and the cavalry officer replied, "Oh, just a sepoy, sir." But Major Colonel Ross said, "That person has the qualifications to be an officer, and so I am going to appoint him as one." And so on that day Ghulam Husayn Khan was promoted to the rank of officer. Later he went before His Holiness to pay the respect of kissing his feet. (A'zam al-Karamat, p. 70)

ANECDOTE 16

Sayyid Muhammad Husam al-Din 'Ali is a resident of Qazipeth [to the northeast of Hyderabad] and the son-in-law of Sayyid Shah Sarwar Biyabani. He recounted this story: "In the year 1304 [1886], I was in Qazipeth in the company of about twenty or twenty-five sepoys serving in the 3rd Cavalry Regiment at the Hyderabad Cantonment. They were in Qazipeth to fulfill a vow of offering [at the shrine of Afzal Shah Biyabani], and when I inquired why they told me this story. "We were making the hajj to the House of God, when our ship was hit by a storm and the sea became extremely rough, such that our ship started to sink. Even the ship's captain said that there was no hope and told us all to call on God to save the ship. So when we heard that we all called on Banne Miyan. Five minutes later, what did we see but Banne Miyan in the sea bearing up the ship on his shoulder. The upper part of his body could be seen, and all of the passengers on the ship saw him with their own eyes. Even the captain saw him and shouted, 'Some fool has jumped from the ship into the water!' We all explained that this was our Sufi padre (*pir padri*), to whom we had called and who had now come to help us. Through the grace of God, with Banne Miyan's help our ship was saved from sinking. When we came back from our hajj, we went to Banne Miyan and told him what had happened, but he said that it was not him but his own master Afzal Biyabani, the saint of Qazipeth, to whom we should go and make an offering. And so we have come here to Qazipeth to make an offering in accordance with Banne Miyan's command." (*A'zam al-Karamat,* pp. 72–73)

Sources

The above anecdotes are taken from Banne Miyan's Urdu hagiography: Muhammad Isma'il Shah Qadiri, *A'zam al-Karamat* (Aurangabad: Mu'in Prēs, n.d.)

Further Reading

On Banne Miyan, his contemporary holy fools, and his hagiography, see Nile Green, "Making a 'Muslim' Saint: Writing Customary Religion in an Indian Princely State," *Comparative Studies of South Asia, Africa and the Middle East* 25, 3 (2005): 617–633; and Nile Green, *Islam and the Army in Colonial India: Sepoy Religion in the Service of Empire* (Cambridge: Cambridge University Press, 2009). On the Deccan's Sufis more generally, see Carl W. Ernst, *Eternal Garden: Mysticism, History, and Politics at a South Asian Sufi Center,* 2nd ed. (Delhi: Oxford University Press, 2004); Richard M. Eaton, *Sufis of Bijapur: Social Roles of Sufis in Medieval India* (Princeton, NJ: Princeton University Press, 1978), especially Chapter 9 on earlier *majzubs*; and Nile Green, *Indian Sufism since the Seventeenth Century: Saints, Books and Empires in the Muslim Deccan* (London and New York: Routledge, 2006).

The Transmission of Learning

THE TRANSMISSION OF LEARNING

Introduction

Barbara D. Metcalf

The following chapters look at a variety of ways by which knowledge of Islamic doctrine, ritual practices, sacred texts, and spiritual disciplines have been communicated. At some level, virtually every entry in the volume entails the communication of Islamic teachings in some way or another: through music; bodily practices of vision, movement, and enactment; models of fidelity, holiness, and intercession; and judicial and political guidance. In this section, however, we will look specifically at communication through the production of pedagogic texts and through three modern institutions—the formally organized madrasa; a mass-based *da'wa* or preaching movement; and a local cell loosely affiliated with the most important Islamist movement of the subcontinent, the Jama'at-i Islami.

The earliest text included here is an excerpt from a sixteenth-century Tamil work translated by Ronit Ricci in Chapter 14. It serves as an example of the long tradition of Muslim Tamil literature that shares content and genre with Tamil literature as a whole, drawing on common vocabulary, tropes, and depictions of the local terrain. This work, *The Book of One Thousand Questions,* began as an Arabic text of the tenth century or earlier. It was subsequently translated into Tamil, as it has been into many other languages across a broad swath of land from the Middle East through Southeast Asia. Like the Malabar text translated in Chapter 30, it was composed in the context of Portuguese expansion and may have been intended to fortify Islamic beliefs at a time of great challenge. Like the author of that text, the Tamil author shows himself embedded in a rich regional culture.

Though the Tamil text seems to have been stimulated by the aggressive threats of the Portuguese, texts setting out correct beliefs and teachings have been perhaps more typically written in the context of intra-Muslim challenges. This point needs to be underlined, especially for the modern period when so much interpretation assumes that monolithic "Muslim" and "Hindu" protagonists alone fill the stage. An excerpt from one of the founding documents of modern Sunni reform is included in Chapter 15. Written in the 1820s, the *Taqwiyyat al-Iman* addressed itself above all to what were deemed false practices derived from deviant Sufi and Shi'i practices. The text was produced as part of a movement by reformers who hoped to establish a polity of their own guided by Islamic norms.

In subsequent decades, militant strategies had little scope as the British East India Company effectively established their control over the entire subcontinent. This was especially the case in the period that followed an army mutiny and civilian insurrection in 1857–1858. In the harsh aftermath of the mutiny, Islamic scholars, like other Indians for the most part, accepted the reality of colonial rule. A significant response looked inward and focused on cultural renewal and the practical goal of preserving Muslim teachings and family interests when so much had been put at risk. For some, this renewal entailed the foundation of popularly supported madrasas. In Chapter 17, Muhammad Qasim Zaman translates part of a first-hand account of the experiences of a student, Manazir Ahsan Gilani, at the Deoband madrasa in the early twentieth century. It provides a remarkable example of a student's penetrating engagement with his studies and with other intellectual currents of the time, and it demonstrates the close link between what is erroneously imagined as incompatible scholarly (outer) and spiritual (inner) learning.

Maulana Mahmudul Hasan, Manazar Ahsan's revered teacher, was himself a disciple of Hajji Imdadullah (d. 1899), *shaykh* to many of the early generation of Deobandi teachers who had taken up residence in Mecca after 1857. Although concerned that Sufi practices not stray in directions that could be considered deviant, the Deobandis cherished the loyalties, devotion to their *shaykh* or pir, and the meditational and disciplinary practices of the Sufism embodied in Chishti, Naqshbandi, and other historic traditions. In Chapter 16, Scott Kugle translates a selection from Imdadullah's most famous book, which teaches methods of bodily control, concentration, and visualization integral to the *zikr*, or remembrance of God, that is a basic practice of Sufis, both individually and communally. Imdadullah's cosmological vision of the body as a microcosm of the universe recalls Aditya Behl's proposal that the hero's quest in the *Padmavat* mirrors a similar understanding. This entry stands as an example, like the earlier *Taqwiyyat al-Iman* discussed above, of the newly available, reasonably priced, vernacular Islamic publications that transformed religious life from the late nineteenth century on.

At the same time as a new class of professionally trained 'ulama were emerging from schools like Deoband, many others without traditionalist scholarly learning (or the standing as holy men that such scholars typically also held) took up roles as interpreters and teachers of Islamic knowledge. Best known are the modernists, products of the now bifurcated educational world in which western-style curricula offers an alternative to training in the classic Islamic disciplines. But others outside the elites also took on roles as teachers, some in fact in close relationship to the 'ulama.

Of these one of the most important began under Deobandi influence in the 1920s. This period saw the introduction of mass politics and a colonial structure that emphasized religious "community" as a fundamental building block of society and politics. A range of Muslim movements in this period sought to shore up Muslim identity through popular education. The movements were known as *ta-*

bligh (delivering or preaching a message). Of the many movements of the day, one that became known as Tablighi Jama'at proved long-lived and extensive. In a classic distinction of moral obligation, it argued that teaching was not only the duty of the 'ulama to carry out on behalf of all Muslims (*farz al kifaya*) but one that was incumbent on all Muslims (*farz al 'ain*), even those who lacked education or respectable social status. Uprooted from their home environments on preaching tours, participants would relate to each other on an egalitarian basis and fulfill their ritual obligations in a way that would influence them and those who saw them. Upon returning from a tour, the group would provide an account, like the one excerpted in Chapter 18. This is certainly not a typical example as it emerged from the horrendous conditions that ensued with the partition of the subcontinent in 1947.

The Jama'at-i Islami, organized by its founder Abu'l A'la Maududi in 1941, also encouraged leadership on the part of participants not trained in traditionalist seminaries. As illustrated in Chapter 34 on the Jama'at in independent India, the organization has evolved in different ways in each of the independent South Asian states. Moreover, the various affiliated organizations in each setting may well have different strategies and even different visions of their desired outcomes. In Chapter 19, Maimuna Huq introduces a Qur'anic lesson given by a Bangladeshi college girl affiliated with a girls' organization that takes its inspiration from Maulana Maududi and the Jama'at. This young woman exemplifies in practice the new roles given to non-specialists in disseminating Islamic knowledge and norms of correct practice. Huq's excerpt also illustrates the way reformist efforts may socialize followers to what could loosely be called middle-class norms of behavior, a theme also evidenced in the twentieth-century ladies' magazines presented in Chapter 26. It makes clear as well the social and ethical dimensions of an Islamic movement too readily reduced to "militancy." In all these cases, much more than the words on the page or the words spoken is communicated. It is in the social and cultural practices surrounding each text that larger messages—a kind of informal curriculum—also needs to be understood.

— 14 —

Saving Tamil Muslims from the Torments of Hell:

Vannapparimalappulavar's Book of

One Thousand Questions

Ronit Ricci

The *Ayira Macala*—"[Book of] One Thousand Questions"—is a Tamil rendering of a story well known across the Muslim world. Originally composed in Arabic, it harks back to the tenth century at the latest, with its broadest contours appearing already in early hadith collections. Translated into many languages, among them Persian, Turkish, Urdu, Latin, French, Malay, and Javanese, it was transmitted across great geographical and cultural distances.

Although the story is retold with local touches and emphases in the different languages, a common frame and many of the details remain constant: a Jewish leader by the name of Abdullah Ibn Salam meets with the Prophet Muhammad in seventh-century Arabia; the Jew challenges the Prophet with many questions on various topics pertaining to Islam's beliefs, history, and rituals; convinced by the Prophet's replies, Abdullah, along with his people, eagerly embrace Islam.

The *Ayira Macala* is widely considered the earliest complete Muslim Tamil text that is extant today, and the first of its genre (*macala*, from Arabic *masa'il* "question and answer debates") in Tamil. Its most recent edition was published in Madras in 1984. The Tamil text, composed by Vannapparimalappulavar, who is known also by his Muslim name Ceyku Mutali Icukakku, was first read aloud in the traditional ceremony of *arankerram* (formal introduction, public dedication of a new work) in the Madurai court in the Hijri year of 980 (1572).

The *Ayira Macala* was composed in the final years of Portuguese rule in the Tamil region. The Portuguese political and economic expansion in South India was accompanied by an anti-Muslim campaign that imposed severe limitations on trade, property confiscation, and possibly forced conversions to Catholicism. However, Muslim life was not entirely stifled during this period. A recent writer, Shu'ayb 'Alim, has noted the resistance against Portuguese presence and policies that was exercised by Muslim military leaders in Kerala, Tamil Nadu, and Sri

Lanka, as well as by religious and spiritual figures. Most noteworthy among the latter was the great "saint" Shahul Hamid of Nagore (1504–1570), whose life coincided almost exactly with the Portuguese threat.

Under the difficult circumstances of Portuguese dominance—which resulted in severe cultural losses for Muslim communities—a comprehensive work that included Islamic doctrine, descriptions and rationales for many rituals, stories of the prophets, important religious genealogies and, very prominently, highlighted the unique features of God's Messenger, was most probably perceived as an important necessity for Tamil Muslims. Through the question and answer dialogue presented in the *Ayira Macala* and through Abdullah's subsequent conversion, sharper focus was brought to bear not only on the above-mentioned elements, but also on the wider questions of what it meant to be a Muslim and why—despite potential threats and obstacles—one should chose to remain a believer.

The *Ayira Macala* is based on a Persian source, a fact that is not surprising when we consider that Persian was widely used in South India as a religious, literary, and court language at the time when the text was written. The text mentions that its author received assistance from another scholar in the form of a Tamil commentary on, or translation of, the Persian source, which he then used to create his own version of the story. This form of "indirect translation" was common to many Tamil Muslim works that were based on Arabic and Persian sources. The *Ayira Macala* contains a large number of Arabic terms and probably served as a model in this regard for subsequent generations of Muslim writers.

The *Ayira Macala:* Themes and Structure

The Tamil text, as already mentioned, retains many motifs common to the story as told in other languages, such as a description of a letter sent to the Jews by Muhammad and mention of the seven hundred followers who accompanied Abdullah on his journey. The Tamil work employs poetic language throughout and is written in metrical verse meant to be recited. It includes many descriptive passages, sound play, and allusions to contemporary practices, from childbirth to fortune-telling. The language is difficult and at times obscure, due to errors introduced as the text was copied and recopied over time, to the use of concepts no longer readily understood, and to condensed references to events or textual sources that are part of a larger sphere of cultural literacy.

The work is divided into many parts, including four introductory sections followed by twenty-seven thematic "chapters." They vary in length from a few to several dozen verses. The major topics covered include God's throne, the skies, paradise, hell, women's sins, Adam's story, the netherworlds, depictions of Kopukka (the mountain range which, according to popular Islamic cosmology, is made of emerald and surrounds the earth), the Day of Judgment, matters of eschatology, sections on Jesus, the children of infidels, death, and the scene of Ibn Salam's conversion. The text is made up of a total of 1,095 verses.

We have noted the work's author as well as its time and place of composition. More difficult to ascertain is whether it represents a particular viewpoint within the Muslim community, one which stands in opposition to rival ideologies, or whether it is primarily intended to emphasize lines dividing Muslims and non-Muslims in their everyday practices and their beliefs. This latter intention may have been especially significant at a time when the Muslim community was threatened from without and needed to regroup around common ideals. Evidence of the work's contemporary status is found in the writings of the German missionary Ziegenbalg, who lived in the Danish colony of Tranquebar in the early eighteenth century. When discussing the *Ayromuschala* (no doubt a corruption of *Ayira Macala*), he remarks that the Muslims of the region held the text in such high regard that children were supposed to memorize it.

A Tamil Hell

Descriptions of the afterlife—both the pleasures of paradise and the torments of hell—are prominent in many Muslim works. Such scenes allow for a mapping of what is permitted and what is forbidden according to mainstream Muslim tradition, while also underscoring specific boundaries espoused by an author in a particular society at a given time and place. In the *Ayira Macala* the depictions of hell open a window both to the way in which the text accords with broader Muslim agendas and to the particularities of its Tamil context.

The text includes two rather long and detailed sections devoted to descriptions of hell (*narakam*): the "Hell Chapter" (*Narakattin Varalaru*), followed by "The Faults of Women" (*Pilai Matar*), comprising together a total of 135 verses. Opening with mention of the seven burning hells and a depiction of great raging fires, the text continues with Abdullah expressing fear and anxiety as he asks the Prophet who will be sent to suffer their heat. The Prophet enumerates many categories of people, including some expected on any Islamic list: those who neglect to pray, who take interest, who lie, who do not give alms to the poor, and who harm orphans; those who speak ill of others, steal and cheat, deny the Prophet's role, and find fault in the Qur'an. An additional category that is expected—and found here—is that of women disobeying their husbands' commands, speaking words of love to another man, or dressing in an improper way.

Side by side with those categorized as hell-deserving sinners for the above-mentioned—and similar—reasons, we find mention of people who commit sins of a different kind. These include, for example, bereavement customs deemed illegitimate: weeping loudly, beating the chest, and falling down to the ground with little regard for one's hair or dress. Other prominent local customs alluded to include various modes of fortune-telling, omen-reading, and predictions, which are identified by particular Tamil terms. These point to shades of meaning in a shadowy world—considered wrong and dangerous by the text—in which human beings attempt to influence future events. For example, *innakurram* refers to covering the palm with dark powder, then blowing it off and "reading" the solution to a problem; *tunnimittam* is trusting in bad omens; a *cuni* is an expert versed in powerful spells to whom one should not turn for help, and *maikkalavu*—literally "black love"—refers to plotting someone else's future.

In the second chapter, which is dedicated to the question of who is destined for hell, Abdullah focuses his interest on women and the punishments they will encounter for specific sins. In this section we again encounter ways in which the text delineates what is socially permissible or forbidden—this time for Muslim women—with the underlying message that women have more opportunities, in part because of their assumed nature and tendencies, to take the wrong path and later to regret it deeply. Once again we encounter the more general feminine sins and their appropriate punishments, ones that fit the crime: women who lied to their husbands will have their tongues pulled out; those who bear children in *haram* (through immoral relationships) will have their bellies rise like mountains; the tongues of those who gossip and speak ill of others will be crushed like gravel, causing them great pain whenever food is served; and those who take interest will have their bodies squeezed like the *punnai* fruit, just as they had figuratively squeezed their clients into difficulty by imposing the forbidden interest. Repeating superstitions—a sin to which women are more susceptible then men—will accrue scorpion bites on their tongues; those who adorn themselves with anklets, tiny bells, and tinkling ankle rings that attract the eye and ear will have their bodies "adorned" with chains as they melt and burn.

In a later section of this chapter, as the Prophet goes on enumerating more and more examples, he no longer restricts himself to women. A particularly interesting point is made in his reference to homosexual relationships, which are depicted as shameless, deserving of terrible punishment. Employing the powerful word *cana* [A. *zina*, fornication, a term usually referring to adulterous male-female relationships] the author clearly places homosexuality beyond the pale of legitimacy.

One set of injunctions explicitly targets Hindu practices. Care is taken to stress the great sin of idol worship, which is how Muslims perceived the daily rituals in homes and temples of the surrounding communities. Statues of the Hindu deities were highly visible, and, the author reminds his audience, Muslims must never slip into adopting their neighbors' view that these images are anything but lumps of copper and stone. We see in these examples how the text addresses specific concerns of Muslims living among a non-Muslim majority. For example, women are forbidden to listen to music, a crime for which hot lead will be poured into their ears. This prohibition is repeated and in a second mention expanded to include different kinds of songs and even lullabies. This is in part a reaction to the wide prevalence of music in Tamil culture, including in most temple rituals. Accepting superstitions and adorning the body in an attractive way are similarly viewed as vile imitation and a threat to the "good" Muslim woman.

A category that Abdullah inquires about specifically in a follow-up question is the *munapik*, the hypocrites. Some of the Prophet's worst enemies during the early years of his preaching belonged to this category. Residents of Medina who ostensibly converted to Islam but did not devote themselves to the Prophet and the new religion, the *munapik* were officially Muslim but in fact ridiculed and disobeyed the Prophet, posing a threat and a nuisance to him that only gradually disappeared. The reply to Abdullah concerning this group is instructive.

Stressing the inner realms of faith as opposed to the outer piety, religious knowledge, and practice displayed by the hypocrites, the text again points, however subtly, to a distinction between good Muslims and the surrounding culture with its abundance of colorful and sensuous rituals. At the same time, these stresses correspond to classic concerns of Sufism, widely cultivated in this period, that emphasize purity of intention and sincerity in all external acts. This approach does not mean to relegate Islamic rituals of prayer and fasting to the margins, but it does imply that external expressions are insufficient. Whether a Muslim is a true believer or is only pretending—and perhaps still adheres to infidel convictions—will be clearly known to God, who will then condemn the hypocrite to hell.

It has been suggested that Indian Muslims and Hindus shared many customs, rituals, and attitudes in the past, and that their consolidation into distinct—and often opposing—communities took place in large part during British colonial rule, introducing as it did censuses and other bureaucratic impositions that forced people to identify themselves with a specific, narrow, and religiously defined category. This is true only in part. It is also the case, even today, that Muslims and Hindus in South India share customs and sacred sites, especially in regard to pilgrimage to the tombs of holy men. We might also notice that the category "Hindus" (or "Siva worshippers," "Goddess worshippers," or other local sectarian names) appears nowhere in the *Ayira Macala's* descriptions, thus denying us the ability of pointing to a concrete and unified identity—symbolized by a name—for the non-Muslims (the only such designation, employed very broadly, is *kapir* [*kafir*], infidel). And yet an examination of the topics presented—a list of acts and attitudes that sharply separate Muslim from non-Muslim—as well as the use of *Islam* and *din* to refer to the Muslims' allegiance, point to a strong sense of a distinct religious community. Moreover, some customs that today are associated with reformist Islam were already a part—at least ideally—of Tamil Muslims' culture in the sixteenth century.

Opposing music and physical adornment; rejecting superstitions, fortune-telling, and "folk magic"; embracing the covering of women's hair and their housebound etiquette; as well as a prohibition on homosexuality are presented as pillars of a strong community of the faithful which must continuously struggle to differentiate itself from the majority culture. The fact that those who practiced the forbidden customs were threatened with such terrifying consequences suggests that precisely these customs were at the nexus of common temptation in this particular locale and therefore needed to be rejected most urgently.

Two categories of hell-goers stand out in their absence from the Tamil text: Jews and Christians. In, for example, Malay and Javanese versions of the story these two categories consistently appear, always listed by their Arabic names, *Yahudi* (Jews) and *Nasrani* (Christians). This absence provides further indication that the Tamil text is more focused on negating the practices and beliefs of its audience's immediate neighbors than those of religious groups that had a relatively marginal local following, or no following at all in the Tamil region at the time. That Christians, as a group, are not mentioned in the text as destined for hell is especially noteworthy given the strong affiliation of the Portuguese with Christianity and the fact that their religious convictions were a major source of anti-Muslim sentiment. This absence of Christians may raise questions as to whether the link, proposed above, between the Portuguese assault and the translation of the *Ayira Macala* into Tamil at this particular time was indeed significant. It may also be that it was risky to explicitly denounce Christianity in a literary work of the period, or that the sources used by the poet failed to mention the Christians and Jews. The most persuasive rationale remains, however, that the Tamil author was most preoccupied with denouncing the surrounding culture in an attempt to remind Muslims of their faith and practices and to revitalize the community following a period of decline.

A characteristic element of the hell scenes—and indeed of the text as a whole—is its stress on sensuality and emotion, a trait common to many Tamil works. Colors, flavors, sounds, scents, and feelings appear repeatedly and add a "Tamil touch" to the narrative throughout. One can readily picture the Tamil woman, adorned with ankle bells and her beautiful eyes recalling those of the Madurai goddess Meenakshi (meaning "fish-eyed"). The scent of musk, the image of the dark rain cloud, and the sweetness of nectar and honey pervade the text. An example of an emotional tone appearing in the hell scenes can be found in the Prophet's reply to the question about sins and sinners, in which the author portrays in detail the personal, and very human, suffering voices of hell's inhabitants. Abdullah—and the readers—are not only told what actions and attitudes should be avoided but also get a glimpse of how the most powerful and confident on earth will fare if they do not follow the right path. This is not so much about why people go to hell and what awaits them there, as it is about how *anyone* at all could find themselves in a similar situation (including, implicitly, Abdullah, if he doesn't convert).

The translated verses below present the more "conventional" Muslim sins to be punished in hell, as well as several examples of sins that are specific to the Tamil rendering of the story. These are all described to Ibn Salam by the Prophet Muhammad. Verses containing the sinners' voices are also included. For the sake of clarity brief notes on context are presented in brackets.

TRANSLATIONS FROM THE *AYIRA MACALA*

A GENERAL DEPICTION OF HELL

> Many rooms, many fires,
> A sea of light, everywhere fire.
> Not even a needle-sized space is fire-free.
> Decaying, dissolving in fire,

Fettered,
The sinners of the earth
Can be seen. (530)

When the scorpions and snakes bite,
Fire rises.
That's what it's like in hell.
Those who argue, don't pray five times
Or destroy religion
Will be bitten.
The angels will capture them,
With God's grace. (560)

ON FORBIDDEN FUNERAL CUSTOMS

Weeping, slapping themselves, falling down.
Letting loose their long hair, beating their bodies
They stand,
Calling God and scolding Him.
These sinners will go to hell. (538)
Ladies join, collapsing on the body, weeping,
Clasping hands, they cry.
Those surrounding the corpse, those watching,
Along with the dead
Will assemble in hell. (539)

ON IDOL WORSHIP

The sinners
Have no escape.
Everyday, always
Roasting, melting, sinking.
Praising as God idols of copper and stone,
In vain infidelity,
Perished those kapirs,
He said. (555)

ON HOMOSEXUAL RELATIONS

Man with man embrace in lust
Committing cana.
Shameless,
Like dogs.
They are tossed into the water then,

Their bodies bloated,
Blood and pus flow
As they cry. (611)

ON THE HYPOCRITES

Seemingly a Muslim,
Knowing all about religion,
Fasting and prayer.
But in his heart a kapir,
Wholly opposed to din.
Such is the hypocrite. (627)

SINNERS TO BE PUNISHED IN HELL

Those who harm orphans,
Who don't give alms
Who watch kuttu dramas,
Who listen to music, (540)

Drunkards, angry men,
Sun worshippers,
Those forsaking knowledge and customs,
Committers of even minor offences,
Gather in hell. (541)

Those who cause pain to their parents,
Believe in the devils,
Embrace haram,
Fight their families,
Speak ill of others:
Like dogs and pigs,
Assemble in burning hell. (542)

Women who go without permission to another's home,
Sleep with other men, speak words of love,
Who appear before others with bare shoulders and head,
Charming with fish-like eyes:
They too will sink low. (545)

Made up, beautifully dressed, sitting at home,
Behaving like a scorned kapir:
Imitating their paths,
Slapping daily with their tongues,
Abusing, arguing,

Speaking ill of the deceased:
They are hell-bound. (546)

Women adorned with anklets,
Small and beautiful bells,
The sound of their feet
Delicately tinkling,
Attracting eyes and ears.
Bitten by snakes
Their bodies shall be adorned with chains
Expanding and melting in fire. (595)

THE SINNERS' VOICES

Those who did not worship the King,
Old people crowd together in the fire of hell.
Their bodies bent, their hair all white.
Aiyo!
They cry. (566)

Aiyo! We didn't know.
We are alone.
Aiyo! We are old,
Lowly, weeping.
Aiyo! we suffer great hunger.
Aiyo! What thirst!
We are lost. (567)

Oh God we refused your orders.
Your forgiveness we neglected to beg.
We didn't expect death to be like this.
Oho! Ayo!
They weep for their sins. (568)

Aiyo! we did not worship,
Aiyo! we ignored all we were told,
Aiyo! we lied,
Aiyo! we did evil,
Aiyo! we acted falsely,
They list their faults. (569)

An old man then tells his suffering to God
And begs forgiveness:
Our youth in flames,
Our bodies melting,
Admitting all faults,

We suffer now.
Our bodies suffer this heat,
Please help with your grace,
They beg of God. (570)

We sinned, we did not know.
Oh our youth! Oh our beauty!
Our strong arms! Victorious bodies!
Aiyo! Aiyo! Our desires, our virility!
So they weep. (571)

Oh our greatness! Oh our courage!
Our words! Our bodies!
All I wished for was mine,
Thus did I live.
Father! Son! Aiyo!
I was a fool.
God grant me love,
Alarmed, they weep. (572)

The body is food for snakes, all over
Beaten, in pain.
See? All feared me in the past.
See? I used to be important.
But here there's no pity.
The beauty of youth has turned ugly,
All scorched,
Because of our sins. (574)

Sources

The verses translated above are from the two "hell chapters" of Vannapparimalap-pulavar's *Ayira Macala*, M. Cayitu Muhammad "Hasan," ed. (Madras: M. Itris Ma-raikkayar/Millat Publishers, 1984).

Further Reading

Introductions to Tamil Islamic literature can be found in M. M. Uwise, *Muslim Contributions to Tamil Literature* (Kilakarai: Fifth International Islamic Tamil Liter-ary Conference, 1990), and Tayka Shu'ayb Alim, *Arabic, Arwi and Persian in Saran-dib and Tamil Nadu: A Study of the Contribution of Sri Lanka and Tamil Nadu to Ara-bic, Arwi, Persian, and Urdu Languages, Literature and Education* (Madras: Imamul 'Arus Trust for the Ministry of State for Muslim Religious and Cultural Affairs,

Colombo, Sri Lanka, 1993). For examples of particular Tamil-Islamic literary works and their analysis, see David Shulman, "Muslim Popular Literature in Tamil: The *Tamimancari Malai*" in Yohanan Friedmann, ed., *Islam in Asia* (Jerusalem: Magnes, 1984), pp. 174–207; and Paula Richman, "Veneration of the Prophet Muhammad in an Islamic Pillaittamil," *Journal of the American Oriental Society* 113, no.1 (1993): 57–74. For a study of Islamization in Tamil Nadu, see Susan Bayly, *Saints, Goddesses and Kings: Muslims and Christians in South Indian Society 1700–1900* (Cambridge: Cambridge University Press, 1989).

—15—

The *Taqwiyyat al-Iman* (Support of the Faith)
by Shah Isma'il Shahid

Barbara D. Metcalf

In the first half of the nineteenth century, Muslim reformist movements in upper India and Bengal introduced enduring themes and forms of organization into Islamic faith, practice, and organization. One of the most important centers of intellectual vitality was the beleaguered capital city of Delhi where the great scholar of the eighteenth century, Shah Waliullah (d. 1762), and others in his circle, were primarily concerned with establishing proper understanding of prophetic hadith. In part this entailed a critique of customs deemed to violate the doctrine of Unity (*tauhid*) by unduly honoring holy men and the imams of the Shi'a in a way that compromised the honor due to Allah alone. Shah Waliullah's successors embraced this scholarly and teaching goal in a movement known as the Tariqa-i Muhammadiyya, "the path of the Prophet." In the first sentences of the reformist tract *Taqwiyyat al-Iman*, the subject of this chapter, its author, Shah Waliullah's grandson Shah Isma'il Shahid (d. 1831), made clear the importance of the Prophet as human model rather than as a source of miracles or a mere conduit of revelation. This focus, stimulating a proliferation of biographical writings on the Prophet, was a fundamental characteristic of reformist thought beginning in the nineteenth century.

In political terms, Shah Waliullah, as his letters to potential rulers indicate, had placed his hopes, in vain, on the advent of a new leader who could create stability and a context in which Islamic scholarly and moral life could flourish. The strategies of his successors were not the same. In the hands of Shah Ismai'il Shahid and his fellow reformers, efforts turned from influencing court politics to efforts to secure extensive popular influence. In the 1820s Shah Isma'il and others of his circle became disciples of a charismatic figure, deemed the recipient of dreams and visions, Sayyid Ahmad Barelvi (d. 1831), who himself was a disciple of Shah Waliullah's son, Shah 'Abdul 'Aziz (d. 1832). Sayyid Ahmad was not a scholar but a military figure who had participated in the successful attempt to establish the small north Indian state of Tonk.

Now he turned to a new militant project, launched by a slow journey to Calcutta devoted to teaching and recruitment as prelude to the hajj. In 1826, having returned from their pilgrimage, the reformers traveled to the northwest to launch what proved to be an unsuccessful jihad to defeat the Sikh regime centered in the Punjab, which they condemned as repressive of Islamic practice. Both Sayyid Ahmad and Isma'il Shahid died in the mountains of Balakot in 1831. Although the British long feared Muslim conspiracy and the lingering embers of this jihad across north India, in fact its influence was brief and limited. It would be the teaching of the reformers that would prove enduring. From Isma'il and other reformers flowed a new style of reformist writing, produced in the vernacular language of Urdu and printed for wide distribution on the newly available lithographic presses of the day. Translations of the Qur'an were also available in Urdu by the second decade of the nineteenth century, and religious classics generally were increasingly available in print. The spread of familiarity with Islamic teachings, and the debates over correct interpretation that fueled this spread, could not have happened to anything like the extent they did without these printed texts.

The message of religious books reached an audience far larger than the relatively limited number of those who were literate. A collection of anecdotes later compiled about followers of this reformed tradition provides an example of this text "in practice":

> In the town of Uldhan [in contemporary Uttar Pradesh] there lived a very old man who was the disciple of Shah 'Abdul 'Aziz. He was barely able to see or hear. When the *Taqwiyyat al-Iman* was first published, copies came to his town. People engaged in extensive debates and discussions, some being for the book, some against. Finally the old man, Tabarukullah, said, "I see you young men flourishing sheaves of pages around and talking incessantly. What is going on?" They explained that a new book had been published. At his request, they proceeded to read him the entire work aloud, from the first page to the last. When he had heard it, he asked them to assemble the entire town to hear his opinion. He then declared that heretofore he had despaired of the world, for no one cared about anything and all were on the wrong path. Now he had found someone who had separated the chaff from the grain and shown them the right path. Now they, he continued, had the power to choose to follow it. (Zuhurul Hasan Kasoli, *Arwah-i Thalathah*, pp. 82–83)

Key issues raised by the reformers were discussed not only in village and town squares, but riveted intellectual circles in Delhi as well. A rival printed literature emerged almost immediately. An article published in the *Journal of the Asiatic Society* in 1832, only a year after the defeat of the mujahideen, set out to summarize the history and the doctrine of the movement, identifying its key issues in part by summarizing the points of disputation in a published rejoinder by one "Fazil-i madrasi," a learned man from the far-off southeastern coastal presidency of Madras (J.R.C., pp. 478–498).

The most influential reformist text was the *Taqwiyyat al-Iman*. A reformer at the end of the nineteenth century estimated that 200,000 or 250,000 people had been "set aright" in Shah Isma'il's own lifetime and that numbers beyond counting had been influenced since (Zuhurul Hasan Kasoli, p. 82). The contemporary publisher of an online translation of the text ventures a count: the book, he writes, "proved to be so much popular among the peoples that it has so far been published in millions and has enlightened trillions of delinquent and strayed people and has guided them to the Right Path" (http://islambasics.com/view.php?bkID=162& chapter=1). As even the brief passages included here suggest, the implications of the movement's message were far-reaching.

Some of those implications, perhaps surprisingly, resemble those of the best-known reformist movement of the 1820s in South Asia, that associated with the Calcutta-based activist, Ram Mohun Roy (1772–1833). A Brahmin who learned the classical languages of Persian, Arabic, and Sanskrit at an early age, he was employed by the East India Company, interacted with officials and missionaries, and ultimately traveled to England where he died. Joined by like-minded people in a voluntary association known as the Brahmo Samaj, he was committed to what he saw as a true revival of a monotheism that he found in sacred Sanskrit texts. He was a proponent of an end of social customs, like *sati* (the practice of a widow being burned on her husband's funeral pyre) and other brahmanic rituals that he deemed deviant. He translated sacred texts into the vernacular language of Bengali and challenged priestly authority to interpret the Sanskritic tradition. Ram Mohun Roy helped shape the emerging institutions of a "public sphere" of new-style voluntary organizations, petitions to government, public meetings, and newspapers, and he deployed the language of good government and the rights of subjects that was shared, in principle, with the British rulers. He supported English-language-based education.

The Delhi movement was far less a product of interaction with European and colonial institutions than the Bengali movement whose leadership knew English and were in Company service. Nonetheless the leading Delhi Islamic scholars interacted with colonial officials, experienced a missionary critique of their social customs and doctrinal beliefs, and welcomed access to the newly available technology of print. Both the Brahmo-style reformers and the Delhi movement championed a return to sacred scriptures and the translation of those scriptures into the vernacular. Both also published writings that distilled those teachings into simple language for an audience beyond the traditionally learnèd. As the *Taqwiyyat* insists, not only the learnèd but also ordinary people should read these texts and know what is correct. Both movements challenged the authority of ritual and scholarly specialists, in the Brahmo case, those associated with Hindu temples and pilgrimage sites. The Muslim reformers similarly opposed those who led and organized the Muharram observation (with effigies and processions) that was of particular importance to the Shi'a as well as those Sufis whom they regarded as mired in false customs. The movements also challenged many customs that sustained family and community life. The Brahmos sought to end child marriage; the Muslim reformers, like the Bengalis, encouraged widows to remarry. A Brahmo son would absent himself from the death ceremony for his father; the follower of the

Tariqa-i Muhammadiyya would not participate in the customary *fatiha* ceremony of prayers and food offerings, variously understood to honor or propitiate the dead. Both reformist traditions discouraged extravagant ceremonies at marriage and other life cycle events.

In both reform traditions there was a strong emphasis on individual choice and an individual's own responsibility for his actions: no intermediary, no priest, no relative could secure the rewards for someone else's actions. Both focused on a single, theistic Being as the focus of cosmology and worship. In the Brahmo case, Ram Mohun Roy interpreted philosophical Upanishadic texts as monotheistic, and he challenged the prevailing practices of worshiping multiple divinities and of devotion to icons. In the Muslim case, reformers challenged the de facto divinity accorded various intermediaries and the proliferation of rituals and specialists that sustained them. In both cases, the reformist teachings were ones that fostered independence from local customs that tied participants to specific places and times. They thus served well individuals participating in what would be a society of increasing social and geographic mobility.

The terms that would form the core of debate among Muslims over sectarian issues in subsequent decades are evident in the pioneering text translated here, above all: *tauhid* (Unity), and its opposite, *shirk* (assigning partners to God); *sunna* (obedience to Prophetic example), and its opposite, *bid'a* (deviant innovation). What those terms precisely meant was the problem. Arguments would rage, for example, over the meaning of *tauhid*. Was it extolling Allah's singularity to say that he could do anything, even create a Prophet equivalent to Muhammad—an issue raised here—or even tell a lie, as the reformers said? Or did such statements denigrate the matchlessness of the Prophet in the first case or the character of Allah in the second? Did denying the Prophet's ability to know what was hidden, or to be spiritually present in all places, preserve Allah's uniqueness or did it fail to respect the greatness of the Prophet? These issues engaged intellectuals, but they also legitimated or undermined such widespread customs as the celebration of the Prophet's birthday, the expectation that he could be one's intercessor, or even practices of naming that elevated the Prophet (or the saints or imams) by identifying a child as his "servant" (e.g., 'Abdun Nabi), or his "gift" (Nabi Bakhsh), honors, the reformers argued, that rightly belonged to Allah alone. That the reformers' influence was always limited is made clear by the fact that the issue of *bid'ati* naming was still a problem almost two hundred years later (Chapter 26).

Most of the translation below focuses on the exuberant devotion and ceremonies associated with the holy men whose burial sites were important places of pilgrimage and resort. Shah Isma'il routinely lists with the holy men other figures who are excessively venerated for their presumed power—prophets, imams, martyrs, angels, fairies, and ghosts—thus including not only the prophets, imams, and angels known from sacred texts, but also other figures in many cases of only local provenance, namely saints, martyrs, fairies, and ghosts. It is in fact the saints and the ceremonies at their shrines that are particularly denounced in the tract. As observers of Islam on the Indian Subcontinent then and now unfailingly note, such practices have been central to Muslim traditions of devotion, intercession, and community for centuries, and they continue to the present. Even though what were seen as the abuses of Sufism served as the reformers' target, it is important to underline that the organization and concepts of the Tariqa-i Muhammadiyya, and the overriding goal of spiritual progress and proximity to the Divine, all derive from the practices and institutions of Sufism.

To make clear how inappropriate shrine-focused behavior is, Shah Isma'il in the selection below describes its practices as those that properly belong to canonical prayer (like *sijda, ruku'*) and the requisite hajj pilgrimage to Mecca (like circum-ambulation [*tawaf*], making supplication, touching or kissing the black stone, cherishing the water of the Meccan shrine's well, and so forth). Elevation of other beings by the ceremonies and beliefs owed only to Allah is a violation whose ana-logue, he argues, is elevation of an official or even an untouchable by according them the honor of the king. Just as a good king would not forgive that offense, so Allah cannot forgive such an offense to his honor.

A great deal in shrine-oriented worship is, of course, shared across religious tra-ditions on the Indian Subcontinent. The argument to eliminate these customs, however, is made here not on the grounds of drawing community boundaries, but on the grounds of Islamic fidelity. This is an important distinction because at a later period, as community identity became a larger part of public life, customs would indeed be given an archaeology of origin as "Hindu" or "Muslim" that was not important here. The critical line in this period is intra-Muslim, and the offend-ers are those holy men, scholars, and others who foster deviance. That the argu-mentation underlying reform shares significant elements in theological under-standing with the contemporaneous reforms of Bengalis is also notable, sharing in something it would seem of a common Zeitgeist.

The Tariqa-i Muhammadiyya and the jihad, when placed into the nationalist histories that came to shape public life in the twentieth century, are typically taken either as a step toward Muslim separatism or as signs of an early nationalist strug-gle by freedom fighters (whose real opponent was the British, not the Sikhs). The British labeled the movement "Wahhabi," a term of opprobrium given the violence of that movement in Arabia. It was also a term that missed, for example, the en-during (reformed) Sufi dimension of the movement. As for the shape that the early reformist movements would subsequently take, they cannot be predicted from their origins but only as they evolve in the context of many historically contingent events, including colonial policies, in the decades that followed.

FROM THE *TAQWIYYAT AL-IMAN* (SUPPORT OF THE FAITH) BY SHAH ISMA'IL SHAHID

Thousand upon thousands of thanks to your Pure Being, O Allah, that you have given us thousands of blessings, taught us your true faith, led us on a straight path, taught us true Unity (*tauhid*), and made us part of the community of your beloved Muhammad, the Messenger of Allah (on whom be Allah's peace and blessings!). You inspired us to learn his way and the way of his deputies who showed us his way (*tariqa*), led us in it, and gave us love for him. Oh, our Creator, bestow thousand upon thousands of blessings and greetings on your Beloved and on his family, his Companions, and all his deputies. Have mercy on all who follow him, and include us among them, and keep us on his path, whether alive or dead. Count us among those obedient to him. Amen, O Lord of the Worlds.

All must hear that they are Allah's servants. What a servant does is service. Not to render service means you are not a servant. Rectification of one's faith is the essence of service. Allah rejects the service of anyone whose faith is defective, whereas he counts as immense even some minor service on the part of someone whose faith is true. Everyone should strive to rectify his faith as a priority above all else.

Nowadays people follow many paths in matters of faith. Some hold on to the customs of ancestors, some look to the tales of holy men (*buzurg*), and some follow the *maulavis'* words that they have cleverly devised out of their own minds. Some let their own reasoning interfere. Yet the best path is holding the word of Allah and the Messenger to be authentic, making it one's charter, and giving no entry at all to one's own opinion. Certainly, accept the stories of holy men or the words of *maulavis* if they accord with that word, but reject the rest. Give up any custom that is not in accord.

Ordinary people often hold that it is very hard to understand the word of Allah and the Messenger. They say: "For this, one needs great knowledge. What power have we to understand their word? Following this course is the job of the great holy men. What power have we to do so? Their sayings are enough for us." This is a great error. The lord Allah declared that the words of the Noble Qur'an are very clear and not difficult to understand. Thus, in *Surah Baqara* [v. 99] he declared:

> We have sent down to thee manifest signs (*ayat*); and none reject them but those who are perverse.

To understand these passages is not difficult, but to act on them is hard because one's willful self (*nafs*) dislikes submitting to another's order. . . . It is one of the great blessing of Allah that he sent us such a Messenger who has made the careless, careful; the impure, pure; the ignorant, learnèd; the foolish, wise. . . . It is for everyone, learnèd and not (*khas o 'am*) to investigate the word of Allah, understand it, act on it, and rectify one's faith in accord with it.

There are two parts to faith: to know the Lord as the Lord (*khuda*) and the Messenger as the Messenger. To understand the Lord as the Lord means to join no one to him, and to know the Messenger as the Messenger is to hold to no path other than his. The first point is Unity (*tauhid*) and its opposite is association (*shirk*). The second point is obedience to the Messenger's practice (*sunna*) and its opposite is deviation (*bid‘a*). . . . It is necessary that you should take as your master (*pir*) and teacher (*ustad*) someone who is perfect in Unity and obedience to the *sunna* and far from *shirk* and *bid‘a*. He should be a person in whose company others are influenced as well. . . .

Often in a time of difficulty people call on their masters (*pir*), apostles, imams, martyrs, angels, and fairies. They beseech them for their wishes and make vows to them. On account of their needs, they make gifts and offerings to them. They dedicate their children to them in order to forestall evil. One will name a child ‘Abdun Nabi [“Servant of the Prophet”]; another, ‘Ali Bakhsh [“Given by ‘Ali” (the Prophet’s son-in-law and the first Shi‘a Imam)]; yet another, Hasan Bakhsh or Husayn Bakhsh [“Given by Hasan/Husayn” (‘Ali’s sons),] Pir Bakhsh or Madar Baksh [“Given by Badi’uddin Zinda Shah Madar” (a north Indian saint)], or Salar Bakhsh [“Given by Salar Mas’ud Ghazi” (the legendary north Indian warrior saint)], [and so forth]. . . . To ensure the child’s life, one keeps a tuft of hair in someone’s name, another puts on some chain or string in someone’s honor, or perhaps clothing [blessed] in that name. . . . In times of trouble, one person cries out for help to someone; another takes an oath in their affairs in someone’s name. In short, as the Hindus act with their gods, these false Muslims act with their prophets, saints, imams, martyrs, angels, and fairies, yet they claim to be Muslims! . . .

[They defend themselves as follows:] “We are not engaged in *shirk* but only manifest our belief in the honor of the apostles and saints. If we held [them] equal to Allah, then it would be *shirk*, but we don’t. We know that they are servants of Allah, his creation, and he bestowed on them their power. They exert power in the world through his wish. To call on them is to really call on Allah, to ask them for help is to ask Him. Those who are beloved of Allah can do whatever they want. They are our intercessors and mediators with him . . . the more we know them, the closer we come to Allah.”

And this is the kind of nonsense they speak. This is because they forsake the word of the Lord and the Messenger and give room to their own reason; they fall in behind false tales and make wrong customs their charter. . . . They forsake the truth, namely, that Allah is closer to his servant than anyone else is. They make false statements and attach themselves to others as their helpers. They fail to recognize and fail to offer thanks for what was Allah’s blessing, that only by *his* grace and without any mediation, *he* fulfills all desires and prevails against all ills. . . .

Now it is necessary to investigate which things are special to the lord Allah alone and in which no one else should be associated. These are many. But by identifying some, and proving them from Qur’an and hadith, one can extrapolate to the others.

The first distinction is to be omnipresent (*hazir o nazir rahna*) and omniscient at every point, far and near, hidden or open, in darkness or in light, in the heavens or on earth, on mountain peaks or the depth of the sea—this is Allah’s glory alone and the glory of no one else. . . .

The second distinction is to have power over all the earth, to enforce orders, to cause death or life at will, to contract or expand anyone's means, to produce sickness or heath, to give victory or defeat, to effect prosperity or adversity, to fulfill all desires, to grant all needs, to forestall all ills, to succor anyone in difficulty—these are all the glory of Allah alone. This glory belongs to no prophet or saint, pir or martyr, ghost or fairy. . . .

The third distinction is that Allah has specified many acts of veneration for himself, known as worship ('ibadat), for example prostration (sijda), bowing (ruku'), and standing with hands folded. Likewise, to spend money in his name or fast in his name. [Wrong acts include] undertaking a distant trip to a shrine in such a manner that everyone knows that one is going on pilgrimage (ziyarat)—for example, calling out a master's name along the way and other such absurdities, or abstaining from killing animals, requiring circumambulation (tawaf), prostrating at the shrine, taking an animal there, spreading a covering (ghilaf) to fulfill a vow, making a supplication while standing at the threshold, making entreaty and supplications for worldly and religious matters, kissing some stone, rubbing one's face or chest against the wall, making supplication while holding on to the shrine's covering, circling it with light, becoming a servant (mujawir) of the shrine and rendering service like sweeping, supplying illumination, cleaning the floor, providing water for ablution (wazu', ghusl), or righting people's encumbrances. It is also wrong to drink the well water as a relic (tabarruk), to sprinkle it on one's body, to share it with others, and to take some along for those absent; to leave the shrine walking backwards, to honor the undeveloped nearby land by not killing animals or cutting down trees or grass and by feeding cattle. Allah has assigned to his servants all this worship for himself alone. . . .

The fourth distinction is that the lord Allah has had his servants taught that they should recall *his* name in their worldly acts and glorify *him*. Thus their faith stands firm and their deeds yield blessing (barkat). For example, one ought to make an offering to Allah in return for a vow, call on him in the time of trouble, and invoke him at the beginning of any undertaking. If there are offspring, in thanks to him, sacrifice an animal in his name and name the child "Servant of Allah" ('Abdullah), "Servant of the Compassionate" ('Abdurrahman), or "Gift of the Lord" (Khudabakhsh) . . . and set aside something in his name from the field and garden as well as from the flocks. Any animal being taken to his house should be treated with respect, neither ridden nor laden down. One ought to proceed in dress, food, and clothing according to his order. . . . Whatever good or ill may happen in the world, like famine and abundance, health and sickness, victory and defeat, prosperity and poverty, joy and sadness, know all to be in his power and by his will. In speaking of any future work, first acknowledge him, saying, "If Allah wills, we shall do such and such a thing. . . ."

Here is an analogue [to the evil of *shirk*]. The subjects of a king may commit any number of offenses—theft, robbery, sleeping on watch, lateness in coming to his court, fleeing from the battlefield, reneging on taxes. Although each merits a punishment fixed by the king, the king can choose either to seize the culprit or to pardon him. But there are crimes that are tantamount to treason, like addressing someone else as king, whether that person be a prince, minister, headman or accountant (*amir, wazir, chaudhuri, qanungo*), on the one hand, or an [untouchable] sweeper or leatherworker (*chuhra, chamar*) on the other. Similarly wrong is preparing a throne or crown for such a person, addressing him as "Shadow of Allah," making obeisance to him as a king, setting a day for celebration and making offerings to him, all as to a king. Such crimes are greater than any others and the fixed punishment is set. A king who was neglectful, and who failed to render punishment, would be failing in kingship. Therefore, intelligent people speak of such a king as shameless. Hence, one must surely fear the King of Kings, the Emperor jealous of his honor, who holds the highest order of power and has such a sense of honor. How can *he* neglect to punish those who associate others with him (*mushrikin*)? Oh Allah, have mercy on all Muslims and save them from the calamity of *shirk*!

The Mighty Allah in *Surah Luqman* [v. 13] said:

Behold, Luqman said to his son by way of instruction: "Oh my son! Join not in worship [of] (Others) with Allah: for false worship is indeed the highest wrongdoing."

In the chapter of the *Mishkat* [a compilation of hadith] "al-Kaba'ir,"

It is written that according to Bukhari and Muslim [two of the "authentic" Sunni books of hadith on which the Mishkat is based], Ibn Mas'ud (on whom be peace and blessings) says a person asked the Messenger of Allah (on whom be peace and blessings!): "O Messenger of Allah, which is the greatest of all crimes before Allah?" He answered, "That you call on any other than Allah who created you.

Since Allah is our Creator, and he made us, we must call on him alone in all our works. What has anyone else to do with us? It is as if one became the slave of a King and rendered every work for him, not to another king, let alone to some sweeper or leatherworker (*chuhre, chamar*)! In the chapter of *Mishkat*, "al-Istighfar,"

It is written that Tirmizi [another "authentic" compilation of hadith] said that Anas (on whom be peace and blessings!) heard the Messenger observe, "Allah said, 'Oh children of Adam! If you come before me with faults equal to the whole earth, yet come before me without *shirk*, I will come before you with the full earth of pardon and will pardon any sins you have committed.

What this means is that in this world all commit sins, and present even now are Pharaoh and Hamam [tyrants mentioned in the Qur'an], even Satan as well. So you must understand that if one person commits as many sins as those of all these sinners, but is free of *shirk*, the lord Allah will forgive him. From this hadith it is clear that *tauhid* is such a blessing that from it all sins are forgiven, just as from the disaster of *shirk*, all good deeds effect nothing. . . .

[It is a great error to look to intercession with the expectation that a wish would be granted out of respect for the intercessor.] Anyone who considers some prophet, imam, martyr, angel, or pir to be an intercessor of this sort with Allah, is truly associating others with him and is very ignorant. He understands nothing at all of the Lord's essence, nor of the power of this king of kings. In an instant, with the order of "Be!" he can, if he like, create scores of prophets, saints, *jinn*, and angels, the equal of Gabriel and Muhammad (on whom be Allah's peace and blessings!). And he can subvert all the earth, from the firmament to the ground, and fix another earth in its place. Only with his will does all come into being, and he has no need to gather any materials. . . .

[A different kind of intercession is illustrated by the case of a repentant thief who had somehow been led astray and knows himself deserving of punishment.] This criminal does not flee from the king to seek refuge with some *amir* or *wazir*, and he seeks no one's protection against him, but night and day looks to the king alone to await the order against him. Seeing his state, the king feels compassion for him but respects the norms of kingship and does not readily set them aside lest people devalue them in their hearts. But some official, seeing the king's inclination, commends the criminal. The king, to raise the official's honor, pardons the criminal, ostensibly on the grounds of the commendation. The official did not make the commendation on account of some relationship with the criminal, or because he was acquainted with him or was his protector, but only because he sensed the king's own preference. He is the king's official, not the thief's. . . . Any intercession of a prophet or saint mentioned in the Qur'an or hadith is of this sort. Each person should call on Allah alone and fear him, make supplication to him, and acknowledge his sins before him, and know him as his master and protector. . . .

Allah is very benevolent and merciful. There is no need of intercession. He himself remembers anyone who remembers him, whether there be intercession or not. . . . His court is not like that of kings where ordinary subjects cannot approach. There officials enact orders on the people, who then have to obey them and honor them. Allah is very close to his servants. The humblest servant who attends to him with his heart will find Allah before him. Other than his own forgetfulness, there is no curtain that distances him from Allah. . . . So anyone who calls on a pir or a prophet to attain closeness to Allah has not understood that the pir and prophet are in fact far away, yet Allah is close. It is as if a subject was sitting alone with the king, who was attentive to hearing his wishes. But the subject called on an official who was far off, asking him to present his plea for him to his majesty! Such a subject is either blind or mad. . . .

There are people who are related to a holy man and put their trust in his protection. Proud of him, they have little fear of Allah. For this reason the lord Allah said to his Prophet to warn his own relatives. So he told even his daughter clearly that a person can only fulfill the obligation of kinship in relation to what is in his power. Thus, he explained that in relation to his own property, he was not stingy about it, but any matters related to Allah were outside his power. For that he could offer protection to no one nor make himself an agent on their behalf. Everyone had to settle matters himself and make plans to save himself from hell. This hadith makes clear that a relationship with a holy man is of no use with Allah. . . .

Sources

The excerpts are from Hazrat Maulana Shah Isma'il Shahid, *Taqwiyyat al-Iman* (Deoband: Rashid Kampani, n.d.). Translations of the Qur'anic verses cited are from *The Holy Qur'an: Text, Translation, and Commentary by A. Yusuf Ali* (Lahore: Shaykh Muhammad Ashraf, 1975). The secondary sources cited in the introduction are J. R.C. [sic], "Notice of the Peculiar Tenets Held by the Followers of Syed Ahmad. Taken chiefly from the Sirat ul Mustaqim," *Journal of the Asiatic Society of Bengal* 1 (1832): 478–498; Zuhurul Hasan Kasoli, ed., *Arwah-i Thalathah* (Saharanpur: Kutubkhana isha'atul 'ulum, 1950).

Further Reading

The best introduction to the history of Muslims in British India is Peter Hardy's *The Muslims of British India* (Cambridge: Cambridge University Press, 1972). On this reform movement, see Harlan O. Pearson, *Islamic Reform and Revival in Nineteenth-century India: The Tariqah-i Muhammadiyah*, with a Foreword by David Lelyveld (New Delhi: Yoda Press, 2008).

— 16 —

The Brilliance of Hearts: Hajji Imdadullah
Teaches Meditation and Ritual

Scott Kugle

Hajji Imdadullah (1817–1899) was a Chishti Sufi master who engaged the body through his imaginative use of ritual and meditation. Born in Thanah Bhavan in the United Provinces, he became a respected spiritual teacher and ethical exemplar as well as a politically conscious opponent of British colonial forces in the 1857 uprising. The full extent of his participation is uncertain; the British alleged that he led members of his Sufi community in combat and fired on British forces. They closed down his devotional center and arrested many of his disciples. Imdadullah eventually made the pilgrimage to Mecca, from where he continued to guide and train disciples. Among those disciples were the founders of the Deoband Academy (see Chapter 17), who resorted to educational and juridical activism to found and revive Islamic law and learning in the new colonial context. Central to their teaching was the importance of devotion to a holy and learnèd guide; as Hajji Imdadullah writes below, only "in service to a complete Master" can the devout reach their spiritual goal.

Hajji Imdadullah wrote several books in Persian and Urdu, including *Jihad-i Akbar* (The Greater Struggle), an allegorical poem about spiritual warfare over the human soul. In it, the Sultan of Spirit and his Vizier of Reason send out the Army of Morality and Awareness to counter the offensives of the Despot of Satan, his Commander of Selfishness, and their Horde of Corruption and Perversity. He also wrote a commentary on Mawlana Rumi's famous Sufi poem, *Masnavi-yi Ma'navi* (The Allegorical Ode). However, his most famous book is *Zia al-Qulub* (The Brilliance of Hearts), from which excerpts are translated here.

Imdadullah presents a combination of bodily control, concentration through repeated vocalizations, and intense visualization of words and phrases from the Qur'an, the most basic of which is reciting the profession of faith: *la ilaha ila allah*.

The bodily vehicle for this profession of faith is retaining the breath, drawn in from the navel, and directing it toward the heart. This combination will lead ultimately to a holistic transformation of the self. Repeating this phrase is called *zikr*, or "remembrance of God," and it is the basic practice of all Sufi communities whether in isolation or in a communal group, whether pronounced silently in each breath or chanted aloud to a rhythm or music.

Zikr could also be practiced using phrases drawn from the Qur'an, or various names of God (*asma'-i husna*) as revealed in the Qur'an, or single sounds that condense the name of God into a syllable. Any word, object of imaginative contemplation, or action that brings God's presence to mind is a means of *zikr*. The word has many valences of meaning, and is translated variously throughout. It can mean an act of recalling to mind, and thus is "remembering," but *zikr* is also a systematic practice of remembering, not just a mental function, and is thus translated as "recollection." This is systematized through repeatedly vocalizing certain phrases or litanies, and thus is translated commonly as "recitation." Imdadullah offers many such examples and variations, some simple and some highly complex.

The imaginative dimension of this exercise depends upon envisioning the appearance of the Arabic letters *alif* and *lam*, which are essential to the grammar and rhyme of *la ilaha illa allah* or "No god but God." Together, the *alif* (letter "a") and the *lam* (letter "l") make up the negation of "no" and the exception of "but." When written together in Arabic script, they appear like a pair of scissors held upright, or like a double-bladed saber like the famed *Dhu'l-Fiqar*, the sword of 'Ali. 'Ali was the cousin and son-in-law of the Prophet Muhammad, and the Chishti Sufis claim that to 'Ali the Prophet Muhammad first taught the method of *zikr* in repeating "No god but God" with rhythmic concentration.

The Chishti Sufi order, whose founder's shrine in Ajmer is discussed in Chapter 3, blossomed in Delhi and its environs. The next in this lineage of great masters is the rigorously ascetic Shaykh Farid al-Din (d. 1265). Farid al-Din had two great disciples of high stature and opposite dispositions: 'Ala' al-Din 'Ali Sabir, who was fiercely ascetic and fiery, and Nizamuddin Awliya, gentle and poetic. From the former developed a sub-group of this Sufi community, called the Chishti-Sabiri lineage; it is to this sub-group that Hajji Imdadullah belonged. They preserved yogic traditions and focused on body control in a more intense way than Chishti-Nizamis. These distinct features of the lineage are apparent in Imdadullah's ritual manual, *The Brilliance of Hearts*, in its profound focus upon the body and the breath.

This text is based specifically on the text of a prior Chishti master, Shaykh Nizamuddin Awrangabadi (d. 1729), the *Nizam al-Qulub* (The Harmonic Order of Hearts), the first Chishti work to record the meditative and bodily techniques that had previously been passed on orally. The world as represented in Imdadullah's devotional manual may seem strange to modern readers. In general, he relies on very ancient understandings of the world, in which the outer being of the cosmos mirrors the internal being of the human person, a belief well attested in both Greek philosophy (Stoicism and Neo-Platonism), which Muslims inherited and expanded, and in the Vedic foundations of yogic discipline. These two dimensions of the world, the macrocosmic and the microcosmic, meet in the human body. The cosmos is imagined to consist of several layers, each one more lofty, more subtle, and more luminous than the last, stretching from this material earthly plane up to God's divine presence. Imdadullah uses the Islamic theological terms *nasut*, *malakut*, *jabarut*, and *lahut*, to refer to four realms of the cosmos (the realm of humanity, the realm of the angelical, the realm of archetypal might, and the realm of transcendent divinity) that rise above the everyday level of sensory and selfish existence, increasing in illumination, power, and intimacy from the realm of selfhood to the ultimate level of the realm of the Creator's identity. Above these realms expands the Footstool and the Throne of God, mentioned in the famous "throne verse" (Qur'an 2:255).

In Sufi symbolism, the Throne of God is the heavenly manifestation of God's presence, while the Ka'ba in Mecca is the earthly manifestation of God's presence, and the inner heart is the real, intimate and bodily manifestation of God's presence. The body, like the cosmos, is imagined to have layers that are less material and more spiritual as one moves from the surface into the center. These are the internal and external "veils" that, as Imdadullah teaches, will be rent asunder as one engages in *zikr* and meditation with sincere concentration, for the breath is what connects the evident, material world with the hidden, subtle reality within the body.

Imdadullah also frames his discussion of the body in ritual in terms of the medical theories current in his time. These medical theories were based on *Unani* (Greek) medicine, the Islamic traditional medicine, which is based on Galenic ideas that health results from the harmonic balance of the four humors within the body, the balance of which mirrors the harmonic order of the material world based upon the four elements (earth, air, fire, and water) with their four qualities (moist, dry, cold, and hot). Many doctors in South Asia today practice *Unani* medicine, and this can be seen to be in seamless harmony with Sufism, which advocates *Ruhani* medicine, or spiritual healing for the soul, based on a rhyming word derived from *ruh* ("spirit" in Arabic, Persian, and Urdu). Yet Imdadullah's discussion of fatty deposits blocking the arteries, which he pictures as analogous to selfish and evil thoughts that block spiritual light, sounds surprisingly modern and relevant to our consumer-driven prosperity.

The Brilliance of Hearts was written in Persian in 1865–1866 but was quickly translated into Urdu for more popular consumption and remains the most widely used Sufi ritual manual among South Asian Muslims. It was a huge success and spread through the new printing media in Arabic and Turkish, though it has never previously been translated into English. Words in curved brackets are from the editor of the Urdu text; insertions in brackets are those of the translator; "he" and "she" are used interchangeably to refer to the disciple, since Imdadullah is known to have had women as well as men as disciples. The excerpt below gives only a sample of the text's concerns and its richly detailed discussion of ritual practice.

The Brilliance of Hearts

BENEDICTION

In the name of God, the compassionate One, the One who cares.

May all praise be to that singular essence, the One who is the universal object of worshipful adoration and the absolutely pure existence, exalted beyond description. May all dimensions of benediction be upon the noble messenger of God, Muhammad, who is the manifestation of the universe and the deputy of the real One—may blessings and peace be upon him, and upon his family and all his companions.

This most lowly and insignificant person, who is from head to toe error and sin, namely the author, Imdadullah, presents this book. He is of the Faruqi family, in the Chishti spiritual community and from Thanah by birth, who is surely the most menial of servants and least of disciples and humble sweeper of the dust of the doorstep of his saintly guide . . . his honor and holiness, Nur Muhammad Jhanjhanvi. This book was commissioned by some friends in my spiritual community, especially my dear Hafiz Muhammad Yusuf. They petitioned me, "Please write down with the pen all the meditations, exercises, and contemplations that we practice in the Chishti-Sabiri Sufi community, for the distance between us is so great as you have chosen to serve the two holy sanctuaries [in Arabia] while we are staying so far away on the soil of Hindustan [India]! Whatever you have written is the correct practice, we shall surely emulate your example and follow your direction."

As this hopeless and hapless man received such a commission, a challenge for which he is surely not equipped, I turned to beseech the holiest presence, the true One. Then my heart was inspired with the directive "Write!" For it is the custom of God that, from the tongue and pen of one in whom others believe and have trust, words may proceed that have a beneficial influence. Even if such words already exist in other books, I might take care to write down what I have learned from my own spiritual guide, about those meditations and spiritual exercises which reached you from the great masters in the past in the Chishti, Qadiri and Naqshbandi communities. Perhaps, with the prayer of those who asked for it and by the force of their high spiritual aspiration, I might be granted success to arrange an answer that might lead them to felicity, as the verse describes: *For God guides whomever God wills to a straight path* (Qur'an 2:213).

INTRODUCTION

May God the exalted One aid you to travel the path leading to true reality. You should know that God, if God wills to give spiritual seekers success in traveling the path to the true One, casts into their hearts a light from the brilliant illumination of guidance, *for God guides by divine light whomever God wills* (Qur'an 24:35). With this, God removes the rust of misguidance and heedlessness from their breasts. Then desire for the glittering mirror of worldly trinkets becomes cool and their breasts warm toward seeking the next life. They extend their hands to grasp the reins of repentance and raise their feet to the stirrups of regret—they mount the swift steed of begging forgiveness. Making firm their resolve and turning their backs to previous sinful rebellion, they face the prayer-niche of obedience and worship of the true One alone. Then they open their eyes to find a spiritual guide of complete mastery. . . .

Since the spiritual Masters are the delegated assistants of the messenger of God, their service is indispensable. On account of this, people who spend all of their time in service to a complete Master and who devote their entire self-will to the Master may hope to surely reach the goal. An advisory: at this time, I will give a brief and abridged discourse about behavior on the Sufi path. Since every disease has its own distinct cure, the skillful doctor pronounces the cure for each disease of the inner heart one by one. . . . All the time spent in this Way is devoted to constantly realizing the recommendation [in a hadith report], "Understand yourself to have died before your death."

In this Way, there are ten means toward achieving success. First: repentance, such that you should seek no aim other than God, as if the time of death is constantly present. Second: renunciation, such that you keep no dependent relation to the world (and all that is in it), as if the time of death is constantly present. Third: complete trust, such that you take leave of all apparent causes, as you will leave at the time of death. Fourth: contentment, such that you leave all selfish and passionate stirring and tumult, as they will depart from you at the time of death. Fifth: detachment, such that you withdraw from other people and keep in isolation, just as the time of death severs you from them. Sixth: concentration, that you keep all your attention focused on God and turn all your aims in that single orientation, as you will be turned in the time of death. Seventh: patience, that you leave aside all your selfish enjoyments and pleasures, just as the time of death leaves them aside. Eighth: consent, such that you refuse to follow your own selfish will and stay consenting to God's contentment, staying within the limits and becoming tied to the Eternal Decrees, as you will be subject to them at the time of your death. Ninth: recollection, such that you leave off remembering anything other than the recollection of God, as you will recollect in the time of death. Tenth: contemplation, that you desert all your own assertive power and will, as you will in the time of death.

Finally, seekers should safeguard themselves through obedience to the Master from all damaging moral behavior that is the very foundation and necessary ingredient for substantial materiality. Seekers should build for themselves a mosque in the heart for the gathering of virtues and perfections. Do not allow any space in the heart for imagining anything other than God. . . .

In Exposition of the Detailed Conditions of Recitation of the Chishti Masters

From the beginning of the book until this moment, the word recitation (*zikr*) has been used in many levels of meaning. Yet up until now, it has not been explained what recitation actually is. In the terminology of the Sufis, recitation is that process through which humans manage to recall the memory of God by forgetting everything other than God. This is the process through which humans collect the intimate nearness of God and fellowship with God within the presence of the inner heart. . . . It should be known that there are many varieties of recitation, but the intended goal of each is the same, to gain the ultimate goal. So whatever works to gain this beneficial result can be "recitation," whether that be canonical prayer and fasting, or the noble *durud* of calling down blessings and peace upon the Prophet Muhammad, or the two prayers. However this aim cannot be reached until the reciter effaces the self. The seeker after God should become so absorbed that he forgets the self along with everything other than God.

When the seeker reaches this level of absorption then virtuous qualities will exist and subsist in and of themselves: qualities like renunciation, trust, retirement from social interaction, contentment, patience, quietude and consent to the will of God. At this point, both the recollection and the one who recollects, both the recitation and the one who recites will be effaced, obliterated and wiped clean; only the one recollected, namely God alone, will remain. God witnessed there is no deity but God, as has been told in a hadith when the Prophet said, "Reciting *No God but God* is the best of all recitations." Because of this, most Sufi masters also give instruction with this recitation. Now I will turn to writing down several varieties of recitation. . . .

Section in Exposition of Pronounced Recitation by Exhaling and
Inhaling and Recitation by the Essential Name, in Addition
to the Twelve Praises of the Chishti Masters

This is the Way of performing the recitation of the Twelve Praises. The twelve prostrations of the nightly prayer vigil should be completed six times. In each prostration, recite *Surat al-Ikhlas* three times. Say: *That is God, just One, God the One eternal, never begetting and not begotten, God to whom none other is similar* (Qur'an 112). At the end, raise your hands and with humility and lowliness pronounce this prayer of petition three, five or six times: "O God, purify my heart from any other than you and illumine my heart with the knowledge of you." After repenting sincerely and asking forgiveness, repeat the following twenty-one times: "I seek forgiveness from God, *the One besides whom there is no god, the Living One, the One everlasting* (Qur'an 2:225), and I seek repentance with God"

Then say the *durud* three times while rising and descending: "May praise and peace be with you, O messenger of God, may praise and peace be with you, O beloved of God, may praise and peace be with you, O prophet of God."

Then sit down, taking your right foot's big toe and those toes that are near it, and with these toes firmly compress the artery *kimas* [behind the left knee]. Keep both hands on your knees while facing in the direction of Mecca. At the time of saying "No god," raise your finger, and at the time of saying "but God," lower your finger. And keep yourself tranquil and quiescent. And with sincere intention and with beautiful intonation, recite the verse, *I seek refuge with God from the accursed tempter—In the name of God, the compassionate One, the One who cares* (Qur'an 1:1). This should be followed by three repetitions of "There is no god but God, and Muhammad is the messenger of God" and one repetition of the words of witnessing.

After this, bow your head so that your forehead comes very near your left knee. Then say, "No God" while moving your forehead very near your right knee. Then in taking a single breath, imagine three rhythmic beats. Bowing your head toward your center near the belly, imagine that "I have ignored and left behind me everything other than God." In releasing the breath, direct the rhythm of "but God" onto the heart with all your might, imagining that "my heart is overflowing with the passion and love of God." When inhaling, open the eyes, and when exhaling, close them. In this manner, recite this two hundred times, and each time direct four rhythmic beats onto the heart. After completing every ten cycles, say, "Muhammad is the messenger of God." However in the beginning, at the time of saying "No god," you should imagine, "there is no other object of worship (*la ma'bud*)," and in the middle imagine "there is no other object of desire (*la maqsud*)," while at the end of completing the cycle, imagine "there is no other existence—One is all (*la mawjud—hame ust*)." After this, for a short time imagine through contemplation that in the faithful person's heart, divinity keeps pouring in bounteously at every moment.

It should be understood in performing this sequence of actions that evil thoughts reside in the left knee, and selfish thoughts reside in the right knee, while angelic thoughts reside in the right shoulder and finally, divinely compassionate thoughts dwell in the heart nearer to the left shoulder. Thus, saying "No god" drives back evil temptations of the left knee. Taking this phrase to the right knee repulses selfishness. Drawing this phrase up to the right shoulder inhales angelic thoughts. Finally, with "but God," you exhale divinely compassionate thoughts toward the heart.

The disciple should be taught these recitations and benedictions in a non-Arabic version as well as the Arabic given in this text, so that the pupil might understand them. . . .

Other Ways of Performing Recitation During Inhaling and Exhaling, Other than This Way

There are seven subtle substances related to the heart. These levels are implied in the tradition (hadith *qudsi*) in which God says, "In the body of Adam is a small knot of flesh, and in this knot is the inner heart, and in this heart is a moral core, and in this core is a spirit, and in this spirit is a secret, and in this secret there is a light, and in this light there I am." Since there are seven such layers to the heart, the recitation of inhaling and exhaling has been designed with seven levels as well. In each level, there is inhaling and exhaling with its corresponding negation and affirmation. Therefore the disciple should become immersed in the vocalized recitation, which is in relation to material, solid bodies, the lowest level of the cosmos, as if there were no other levels besides this level of recitation. Do not draw in a single breath without reciting in the manner appropriate to this level.

When the seeker has become accustomed to this level and has mastered its experiences, a subtle level will have been reached above the realm of materiality. The disciple ought to be fully occupied with this level of recitation and cognition, the level of "No god," such that all things will be negated except for the affirmation of "but God." Once the seeker attains this level, he has transcended the level of the self and has arrived at the level of the heart. And since the recitation of the heart is "but God," the seeker should hold the image of "but God" in the presence of the inner heart and her own individual essence and attributes should become bound up with the essence and attributes of the sustaining lord of the universe, such that everything becomes negated with the exception of "but God." When the seeker attains a new level by leaving the designated level of the heart, he will have arrived at the level of the spirit. Since the recitation of the spirit is the recitation of the God's essential name, *allahu*, the seeker should concentrate only on the recitation of the essential name, such that the "al-" which precedes the name *allahu* no longer remains. Only the pronominal syllable -*hu* is allowed to persist.

Upon entering this level, the seeker will become recitation and recollection from head to toe. By progressing through the level of the spirit, the seeker will arrive at the level of the secret. After this, the seeker should become absorbed to the furthest possible extent in the recitation of *hu hu*, such that the One recollected, I mean God, becomes the very self. This is the meaning of obliteration within obliteration (*fana' dar fana'*). Upon reaching this level, the seeker will actually become transformed from head to toe into light.

The Way of Retaining the Breath

All human beings should be mindful and watchful with each breath. Without the helpful practice of retaining the breath, no person could ever be purified of perturbing murk and blinding obscurity. In the technical terminology of the Sufis, retention of the breath is this action: taking in breath and pushing it out while at the same time performing recitation in either an audible voice or a concealed voice, by saying "No god" at the time of taking breath, and saying "but God" at the time of breathing out. However in concealed recitation, recite only through breathing without vocalizing the words. While inhaling and exhaling, keep your gaze on your navel, keep your mouth completely shut, and move the tongue in the common manner of speaking. As far as possible, stay constrained and steadfast until your breath begins to recite by its own will.

Another way is this. While exhaling, express the syllable *allah-*, and while inhaling express the syllable *-hu*. Imagine that inside you and outside you, every place is an epiphany of God, a place of God's manifestation. Increase your recitation beyond the customary intensity so that your breath becomes accustomed to the recitation and you remain reciting whether in a state of wakefulness or heedlessness, enjoying the beneficial profits of retention of breath and purifying the inner heart of all that is other than God. Since this recitation purifies the heart completely and clears all obscurities, it builds a pure foundation upon which the divine illuminations can alight. For this reason it is known as "the heart's sweeper" in the terminology of the Sufis. . . . There are two inlets into the heart. One is in the lower side of the heart, which is connected to the spirit, while the other is in the upper side of the heart, which is connected to the body. When the reciter is reciting in an audible voice, the heart becomes intensively preoccupied both above and below; then the upper aperture opens. However, the lower aperture opens only through means of concealed and silent recitation, which is retaining the breath (*habs-i dam*). This very retention of breath is the original root of all forms of recitation.

The masters of the Chishti and Qadiri lineages have recommended the performance of these recitations. Naqshbandi masters have not recommended it, but neither have they disapproved of its preeminence.

The Way of Breath Retention through Inhaling in Negation and Exhaling in Affirmation

Some people call this exercise "inhaling and exhaling," and its method is as follows. Having shut their eyes and cleft the tongue to the palate, draw in breath [as if] through the navel, and hold it in the heart. Begin the phrase "No god" with your left thigh, and bring "No god" to your right thigh, and complete the circle through your right shoulder to your chest and apply the beat of "but God" with your fullest force upon your heart. On the first day of conducting this exercise, draw in and hold ten breaths, and in each breath perform these three steps of completing the circle with each phrase.

After this, day by day, step by step, gradually keep increasing the number of beats retained by one. And keep in mind the phrase, "God is the unique One and loves uniqueness," until an interior heat arises in the heart and the fatty oils melt and the thoughts of the Tempter are averted and the Tempter is overcome. When drawing in the breath becomes habitual, then a state of absorption and effacement will become evident in the heart and the heat will spread throughout the entire body, and every limb, by its own volition, will become a reciter, while the fire of divine passion will illumine the heart. However, in the midst of averting tempting thoughts and drawing in breaths, it is necessary to keep the stomach empty of food. This is especially necessary in the beginning stages of learning this exercise.

Beneficial moral results: In enacting breath retention, one should avoid contact with cold things, for instance cold drafts or cold water. These should be avoided because the heart's interior heat could be cooled off. Out of fear of disease and sickness caused by imbalance, hot things should also be avoided. Walk about as seldom as possible, or you will become fatigued. Eat as little as possible, or you will become weakened.

Another Way of Retaining the Breath through Inhaling and Exhaling

It is preferable that you sit on a stool or bench all alone. Shut your eyes. Take hold of the great toe of your right foot and its surrounding toes and compress the flesh of the artery *kimas* firmly. Keeping your hands in your lap, draw in breath [as if] through the navel, as previously described. Then take the breath and move it toward the heart and lodge it in the place called "the source of the mind" (*umm al-dimagh*). {Editor's note: There is a secret point about this mysterious organ, the "source of the mind." Just as the navel is in the center of the human being on the surface of the body, there is a small knot of flesh like an embryo inside the body just behind the heart, and this is the region of the body where the self resides. If one begins inhaling from this point and conveys the breath up to the source of the mind (*umm al-dimagh*), then certain things will happen internally that will exert influence on the heart, and veils of obscurity will be lifted from it.} Without vocalization, begin the motion of moving "No god but God" in a circle through the body. With deep concentration and intense thought, take hold of the syllable "No," and move toward the spirit. With the syllables "God" (*Allah*), arrive at the mind. Take the phrase further and strike on the heart with the climax "but God." In this way, each breath has five or six stages. Then slowly exhale. In the time of exhaling, fill your imagination with the image of "Muhammad is the messenger of God—may blessings and peace be upon him." In opening the eyes, imagine "There is no other object of love except God." In drawing another breath, close the eyes, imagining "There is no real existence except for God." Gradually generate this cycle in your breathing, and take ten such breaths each day. Every day, keep increasing the number of cycles by one, until in a single breath one hundred and twenty-one recitations are strung together. At that time, the doorway of the inner-heart will open and the heart will glow from the light of witnessing. . . .

The Way of the Exercise "The Assisting Authority" (Sultan Nasir)

There is a tradition narrated from Khwaja Mu'in ad-Din Chishti that this exercise has many virtues, especially its marvelous effects in averting tempting thoughts. The method of this exercise is recorded here. In the morning and evening, kneel facing the direction of Mecca. With tranquil thoughts, gaze at your nostrils with both eyes or close one eye and gaze at your nostril with the other eye, without lowering the eyelids, as if you were gazing at the light of a lamp or a star. Imagine an imperceptibly subtle light beyond luminosity. Become so absorbed in this foundation that you become fully effaced, as if intoxicated. In the initial performance of this exercise, you will surely encounter difficulty with your eyes, and they may tear up. However, after a few days' practice, once you have become accustomed to these efforts, then the difficulty eases. Your eyes will begin to see your own form, as if you were looking in a mirror, and it will begin radiating with divine light. You will accrue an accordingly subtle and delightful personal condition in harmony with this luminous effulgence.

The Exercise Called "The Dominating Power of Recitations" (Sultan al-Adhkar)

The seeker should enter into seclusion, alone and without belongings, in a place untouched by the voices of tumult and disturbance. Then recite the word of peace and benediction upon the Prophet, the phrases of seeking forgiveness from God, the two verses of seeking protection with God, and invoke the name of God. [The two verses of seeking protection are Qur'an 113: *Say: I seek refuge in the lord of the dawn, from the harm of what is created, from the harm of the dark-ness when it deepens, from the harm of those who blow on knots tied, and from the harm of the envious one who is jealous*; and Qur'an 114: *Say: I seek refuge in the lord of humankind, the master of humankind, the God of humankind, from the harm of the whisperings of the cowering slinker who whispers in the breasts of human-kind, from among the disembodied beings and from humankind.*] Then repeat three times the expression "God give me light, bestow upon me light, increase for me the light, and make me myself light." Repeat this expression with the inner-heart fully present as you imagine its full meaning.

After this, either lying, sitting or standing, allow your body to lighten and feel at ease. Imagine that you have died, and gather all your attention from head to foot, and become high-mindedly bold. And as you inhale, then it is God's breath. As you exhale imagine the syllable -*hu*, "that One is." As you inhale and exhale, imagine that every hair of your body keeps expressing the syllable -*hu*. You should become so engrossed in such a recollection that your own imagina-tive faculty will pass away and each moment will be stabilized by *the living One, the One everlasting* (Qur'an 2:255). After a few days of this, the following result will accrue: every single hair on the body, even the slightest down, will begin to recite God's unique existence, and the lights of God's luminous manifestation will begin to glow.

Stop the five senses with cotton or with the fingertips. {Editor's note: It is an even more effective means of closing the senses if the seeker performs this ex-ercise while swimming in a pond or reservoir.} Draw in the breath from beneath the navel, retain it in the source of the mind (*umm al-dimagh*), and convey the breath into the circulations of the heart. While reciting the essential name of God (*allahu*) and listening to the speaking voice, convey it from the inner heart into the kernel of the inner heart that is like a lucid point in the imagination. It is the point of the heart revolving, which is within the source of the mind. Some people call this point the most concealed subtle center. Keep this up until this point has become wide and spacious to the greatest degree, such that the whole body becomes luminous. After this, from the highest level of heaven to the foundation of the earth, light and only light is visible. In this encompassing light, the features of angels and the archetypes of truth become visible. When the seeker acquires this level of devotional experience, then the seeker's own truth-reality begins to appear more profuse than the existing, created world. In this spiritual stage, seekers should understand their own qualities to be the divine qualities of the creator, *for God sustains with life whomever God wills* (Qur'an 42:19).

Sources

This translation is from the Urdu text: Hajji Imdadullah Muhajir Makki, *Zia al-Qulub*, Shahid, ed. and trans. (Deoband: Rashid Publishing Company, n.d.) The text was prepared with close reference to the original Persian lithographic printing (*Kulliyat-i Imdadiyya* [Lucknow: Fakhr al-Matabi', n.d.])

Further Reading

For Hajji Imdadullah's life and works, see Scott Kugle, "The Heart of Ritual Is the Body: Anatomy of an Islamic Devotional Manual of the Nineteenth Century, Hajji Imdadullah's *Zia al-Qulub*," *Journal of Ritual Studies* 17/1 (2003), pp. 42–60; and chapter 5 of Scott Kugle's *Sufis and Saints' Bodies: Mysticism, Corporeality and Sacred Power in Islamic Culture* (Chapel Hill: University of North Carolina, 2007). Background to the Deoband school is provided in Barbara D. Metcalf, *Islamic Revival in British India: Deoband, 1860–1900*, 2nd ed (New Delhi: Oxford University Press, 2002). For background to the Chishtis, see Carl Ernst and Bruce Lawrence, *Sufi Martyrs of Love: The Chishti Order in South Asia and Beyond* (New York: Palgrave Macmillan, 2002). For the defense of such Chishti Sufi practices as qawwali (discussed in Chapter 4), in which Imdadullah participated, see Robert Rozehnal, "Debating Orthodoxy, Contesting Tradition: Islam in Contemporary South Asia," in Michael Feener, ed., *Islam in World Cultures: Comparative Perspectives* (Santa Barbara: ABC-CLIO, 2004). Other important books on the Chishtis include Bruce Lawrence, *Notes from a Distant Flute: The Existent Literature of Pre-Mughal Indian Sufism* (Tehran: Imperial Iranian Academy of Philosophy, 1978); Simon Digby, "Tabarrukat and Succession among the Great Chishti Shaykhs," in R. E. Frykenberg, ed., *Delhi Through the Ages: Essay in Urban History, Culture and Society* (Delhi: Oxford University Press, 1986); Khaliq Ahmad Nizami, *The Life and Times of Shaykh*

Nizam al-Din Auliya (Delhi: Idarah-i Adabyat-i Delli, 1991); Bruce Lawrence, trans., *Nizam al-Din Awliya: Morals for the Heart* (New York: Paulist Press "Classics of Western Spirituality" Series 74, 1992); and Carl Ernst, *Eternal Garden: Mysticism, History, and Politics at a South Asian Sufi Center* (Albany: State University of New York Press, 1992).

—17—

Studying Hadith in a Madrasa in
the Early Twentieth Century

Muhammad Qasim Zaman

The study of hadith, the reported statements and teachings of the Prophet Muhammad, occupies a position of central importance in the scholarly culture of traditionally educated Muslim religious scholars, the 'ulama. Since the thirteenth century, the Sunnis have recognized six early collections of hadith, compiled by scholars of the late ninth and tenth centuries, as containing the most authentic statements attributable to the Prophet and therefore as the most authoritative. There were major developments in hadith scholarship in north India during the seventeenth and eighteenth centuries, and the study of hadith has continued to receive serious scholarly attention in the nineteenth and twentieth centuries. Indeed, since the late nineteenth century, all six of the "canonical" Sunni collections of hadith have come to serve as the "capstone" of advanced learning in the South Asian institutions of traditional Islamic learning, the madrasas, even as many new commentaries on classical collections of hadith were produced by the leading 'ulama.

The prominence of hadith in the culture of the South Asian 'ulama has had much to do, of course, with these scholars' sense of belonging to, and wishing to continue, a scholarly tradition that links them to scholars across the Muslim world, a tradition to which they see earlier Indian 'ulama as having made distinguished contributions. This sense of continuity with the past, and of scholarly ties with Muslims elsewhere, seemed especially important at a time of great anxiety brought about by the demise of Muslim political authority and the onset of British colonial rule in India. But the renewed importance of the study of hadith in this late nineteenth century context also had to do with efforts, on the part of many 'ulama, to "reform" local Muslim practices in light of what they saw as the proper understanding of the Islamic foundational texts—the Qur'an and the hadith—and of the legal and other religious norms anchored in them.

Not everyone was convinced that there was much to criticize about how Muslims had lived their lives all along, how they commemorated their saints or celebrated the memory of the Prophet. Those belonging to the "Deobandi" orientation came to insist, however, that there was a considerable distance between textually grounded Islamic legal and ethical norms and the customary devotional practices of ordinary believers, and that people needed to reform their ways if they were to live as "good" Muslims ought. The Deobandis—so called by association with a madrasa, the Dar al-'Ulum, founded in the north Indian town of Deoband in 1867 and regarded as a parent institution by thousands of other madrasas subsequently established throughout South Asia—were not alone in this orientation. One of their many sectarian rivals, the Ahl-i Hadith (the Adherents of Hadith), also argued that the Islamic foundational texts ought to guide all facets of Muslim life. But where the Ahl-i Hadith rejected the authority of the medieval schools of law and sought to base their norms on an unmediated access to the foundational texts, the Deobandis were firmly committed to the Hanafi school of law and devoted great energy towards showing, against Ahl-i Hadith critiques, that the Hanafi legal norms were clearly in consonance with the foundational texts. Indeed, at least some of the vast hadith scholarship produced by Deobandi 'ulama is directly attributable to their awareness of the challenge posed by the Ahl-i Hadith. Sufi piety was, furthermore, no less important to the Deobandis than it was to some of their most vociferous sectarian rivals, notably the "Barelawis." But here, too, the Deobandi concern was to show Sufi doctrine and practice as being altogether in concord with juristic norms, which meant, among other things, self-consciously distancing themselves from the popular devotional practices, often centered on saints and their shrines, that were characteristic of the Barelawis.

The Deobandi emphasis on hadith also stood in marked contrast to the importance the "rational sciences"—notably logic and philosophy—had long enjoyed in the scholarly tradition of the 'ulama, in India and elsewhere. There was some disagreement among the founders of the Dar al-'Ulum at Deoband over the place the rational sciences ought to have in the curriculum of the new madrasa, not unlike disagreements among 'ulama, especially of a later age, on the degree to which their institutions should be open to modern, Western forms of knowledge. Unlike the modern Western sciences, the Islamic rational sciences permeated the study of not a few "transmitted" sciences, notably Islamic law. Even so, it was not always easy to reconcile their competing claims. And though the "doubts" that sometimes beset madrasa students (and teachers) have a colorful history and diverse expressions, some of them arose precisely from these competing claims, as we will briefly observe in the selections translated here.

The author of this work is Manazir Ahsan Gilani, one of the most distinguished Muslim intellectual historians of twentieth-century South Asia. Gilani was born in Bihar, in eastern India and, after a preliminary education, studied for seven years in Tonk, in Rajasthan, with a noted scholar in the Islamic rationalist tradition. He arrived at the Dar al-'Ulum of Deoband in 1912 as an advanced student, and spent the next two years or so studying hadith at the madrasa. Following his graduation, he briefly taught at this madrasa, though it was in the theology department of Osmania University in Hyderabad that he was to spend much of his academic career.

He maintained lifelong ties with Deoband and Deobandi 'ulama, however. From 1930 to 1948, he was a member of the Dar al-'Ulum's consultative committee. And among his last major works is a detailed biography of Muhammad Qasim Nanotawi (d. 1877), one of the founders of the Deoband madrasa. Gilani also wrote many other books, including a biography of Abu Hanifa (d. 767), the eponymous founder of the Hanafi school of Sunni law; a study of the eighteenth-century Indian thinker Shah Wali Allah (d. 1762); one of the earliest modern works in the genre of "Islamic economics"; and a wide-ranging history of Islamic education in South Asia. He died in his native village in Bihar in 1956.

Gilani's *Ihata-yi Dar al-'Ulum main bite huwe din* (The days spent in the arena of the Dar al-'Ulum [i.e., the Deoband Madrasa]), from which selections are translated here, is his memoir of the time he spent studying hadith at Deoband. This account was written for, and first serialized (1951–1955) in, a monthly magazine published by the Deoband madrasa. Nearly four decades had passed since the time Gilani had been a student at Deoband, and some allowance must obviously be made for lapses of memory—which he frequently acknowledges himself— and also for particular ways in which he may have chosen to characterize life at the madrasa. For the most part, the account appears to be reasonably credible, however, and it may be taken to illustrate several important features of the scholarly culture of the Deobandi 'ulama in the early twentieth century. Some of these features are worth noting here.

First, Gilani provides us with a vivid sense not only of the depth of Deobandi intellectual engagement with the canonical collections of hadith, but also of how the modern 'ulama have continued to think of their work as constituting a scholarly *tradition*. Second, and within this traditional framework, Gilani illustrates the considerable diversity in how the leading scholars at the madrasa approached the study of hadith: as will be observed, the manner in which Anwarshah Kashmiri (d. 1933), a distinguished scholar then teaching at Deoband, discoursed on hadith was clearly very different from that of "the master-scholar of India" (*Shaykh al-Hind*), Mahmud Hasan (d. 1920). Third, discourses on hadith—some of which, including Kashmiri's, were recorded in writing in the classroom and subsequently further elaborated and published—were not merely a matter of repeating themes and questions discussed by earlier generations of scholars, although there was that, too. They were also occasions for critiquing particular facets of the scholarly tradition, particular views held by earlier generations of scholars and by contemporaries, and for exploring new directions. As Gilani describes it, Anwarshah Kashmiri's effort to remedy some of the opprobrium commonly associated with "exegesis according to opinion" is precisely an effort to allow greater exegetical scope in approaching the foundational texts than many medieval and modern commentators allowed. Conversely, Kashmiri's critique of those who would want to see all forms of knowledge as already contained in the Qur'an is directed, at least in part, against apologists eager to affirm Islam's compatibility with modernity by showing how the Qur'an anticipates modern scientific knowledge.

Finally, Gilani's account shows how political concerns and controversies were making their way into early twentieth-century Deobandi study circles and beginning to cause what turned out to be some major rifts among the 'ulama. Unlike many of his colleagues at Deoband, Mahmud Hasan had come to believe that the 'ulama ought to actively engage in efforts to challenge and subvert British colonial rule in India. When an abortive effort towards this end came to light during World War I, Mahmud Hasan was exiled by the British to the island of Malta. There he remained, together with one of his former students, Husayn Ahmad Madani (d. 1957), until shortly after the end of World War I. The portion of Gilani's account translated here concludes by describing some of the nervousness among the administrators of the Deoband madrasa regarding Mahmud Hasan's political orientations and those of his devotees. Many more controversies lay in Deoband's future. And the debates to come would continue to be waged through discourses on hadith.

STUDYING HADITH IN A MADRASA IN THE EARLY TWENTIETH CENTURY

THE HADITH LECTURES OF ANWARSHAH AL-KASHMIRI

I don't remember the exact number of students with whom I participated in [Anwarshah Kashmiri's] hadith study circle [in 1913], but they were probably between seventy and eighty in number. For someone who had never had more than ten or fifteen classmates, this was an altogether new experience, of being part of a veritable student fair. The students here were from the United Provinces [now Uttar Pradesh], Bihar, Bengal, Punjab, the [northwest] Frontier, Kabul, Qandahar, Bukhara, and probably also Chinese Turkestan and Kashgar. . . .

I had assumed that, as is customary in our madrasas, students would read the text of the book aloud [in this case, the hadith collection compiled by Muslim b. al-Hajjaj, d. 875] and Shah Sahib [i.e., Anwar Shah Kashmiri] would explain the meaning of the passage being read. But now I experienced something new: even before the reading of the text had formally begun with "In the name of God," I felt as if an ocean of knowledge had begun to overwhelm my heart and mind. I had studied with teachers who, in beginning the teaching of a book, would discuss such needless questions as why the author had commenced his book with the praise of God, and they would then repeat, with but little modification, all the standard answers given in the standard textbooks. . . . Questions and answers generated by an author's prefatory remarks and the traditional stock of disputation long transmitted in commentaries and glosses would be presented to the hapless student as proof of the professor's breadth of learning. Imam [Anwarshah] al-Kashmiri, by contrast, captivated us with his discourse well before the study of the book had formally begun. It is not easy to recall all the topics broached in his lectures, for it has been forty years [since I attended those lectures]. But my memory still preserves traces of their transformative impact. . . .

From the very first lesson, it was clear that I had begun understanding things it normally took years to learn. For instance, until then, I had thought that, apart from the Qur'an, there were few hadith reports whose provenance could be attributed with full confidence and complete certainty to the Prophet. Put differently, much about the [foundations of] religion was a matter of "probability" rather than of "certainty." We now understood that commonly encountered assertions about the severely limited stock of what constituted the most authentic of hadith reports was really only a discussion about particular kinds of *isnad*—the chains through which a hadith report had been transmitted. [There were other ways of arriving at certitude as well, and these included:] the sense of continuity from one generation to the next; the continuity of lived practice; and the continuous transmission of the content of particular hadith reports [i.e., irrespective of the actual words or of their precise chains of transmission]. In fact, a great deal of other religious knowledge had *also* been transmitted from generation to generation through varied forms of continuous, multiple transmission (*tawatur*), and these modes of transmission carried the same logical and psychological ability to inspire certitude as did the scarce hadith reports endowed with multiple chains of transmission. This was the first day that, in addition to the Qur'an, the fundamental system of religion became, in its entirety, a matter of absolute certainty for me . . .

Shah Sahib was a natural litterateur. Urdu was not his mother tongue, though he could have distinguished himself as an outstanding writer and speaker in that language. As a consequence of his continuous study of Arabic works and of Arabic literature, words from the Arabic language tended to dominate his speech; his style of discourse was likewise shaped by Arabic modes of expression. A result was that, though Urdu was the language in which he taught, he found himself constantly using Arabic terms not commonly used in Urdu. . . . [When I decided to start writing down his lectures in order to better remember their contents,] I found, in view of the peculiarities of his style of discourse, that it was easier to commit it to writing in Arabic than it was in Urdu. . . . Writing down lectures on hadith was nothing new at the Deoband madrasa. Some people had in their possession the written record of Mawlana [Rashid Ahmad] Gangohi's [d. 1905] discourses on hadith. Students also had the Shaykh al-Hind's [i.e., Mahmud Hasan's] discourse on the hadith collection of al-Tirmidhi [d. 892] available to them. But as far as I know, I was the first to think of committing Imam al-Kashmiri's words to writing. Nor am I aware of anyone before me who had recorded the [Deoband professors'] lectures in the *Arabic* language. I thank God that, after me, students more capable and energetic than myself gathered around Shah Sahib and made it their life's purpose to commit the ocean of his learning to writing. . . .

It was not only matters of hadith, but also the fundamental principles of other religious sciences, that were illuminated in the course of [Kashmiri's] lectures . . . In the field of the principles of jurisprudence (*usul-i fiqh*), he had practically memorized the work of Ibn Humam [d. 1459]. In positive law (*fiqh*), he was much influenced by the work of Abu Bakr Kasani [d. 1191, the author of *Badayi'*], al-Sarakhsi [d. ca. 1096], and Ibn Nujaym [d. 1563, the author of *Bahr al-ra'iq*]. He seemed to have little faith in the juridical acumen of "the Syrian" [i.e., Ibn 'Abidin of Damascus, d. 1836]. But he was very fond of the author of the *Hidaya* [al-Marghinani, d. 1196-97]. He used to say that, if he wished, he could write a book like Ibn Humam's *Fath al-qadir*; but that he was altogether incapable of writing anything like the *Hidaya*. . . .

If, however, there was one book in whose great awe Shah Sahib stood, indeed excessively so, it was the book of God, the Qur'an. The sort of liberties people take these days with the interpretation of the Qur'an now help me understand the secret behind Shah Sahib's reticence in matters of scriptural exegesis . . . Nonetheless, in the course of his lectures on hadith, he did often turn to the other religious sciences [and, in doing so, elucidated matters relating to the Qur'an as well]. . . .

For instance, he would occasionally caution his students against the view, common among self-professed but foolish "friends" of the Qur'an, that it encompasses all forms of knowledge, that because God is all-knowing, His book, too, should be all-encompassing. In support of their contention, such people adduced verses like "There is nothing, fresh or withered, that is not contained in a clear book" [Qur'an 6.59]. . . . Yet, [according to Shah Sahib] if we assume that God has revealed the Qur'an in order to give expression to His own knowledge, then clearly such knowledge could not be properly expressed even if the entire universe were to be turned into paper [on which to write it down]. . . . The Qur'an has been revealed only to inform people about the universal principles governing the system [of human life], and this alone is its basic subject. To look for anything else in the Qur'an is not only proof of the foolishness of those engaging in such a search; it is also to attribute the sort of deficiency towards the Revealer of the Qur'an that any intelligent [human] author would not allow in his own book. After all, who would doubt the foolishness of someone who looks for juridical problems of the sort discussed in *Sharh al-Wiqayah* [a fourteenth-century work of Hanafi law] in a *medical* handbook, or matters discussed by poets like Amir [Khusraw, d. 1325] and Dagh [d. 1905] in a *juridical* work like the *Sharh al-Wiqayah*. . . .

Another principle I recall from Shah Sahib as regards the Qur'an concerns the question of "exegesis according to opinion" (*tafsir bi'l-ra'y*). Some statements [attributed to the Prophet] forbid interpretation on the basis of opinion, characterize it as an act of insolence, and threaten those engaging in it with hell. On the basis of such reports, the view has taken hold that no one might properly explain the meaning of the Qur'anic verses unless that meaning is supported by an explicit statement [of the Prophet or of the Companions]. As a result, it is exegetical works basing themselves on such transmitted statements that have had the greatest standing. The commentary of Ibn Jarir al-Tabari [d. 923], for instance, has gathered an unusually large stock of such transmitted statements [in following this method]. After him, the great esteem enjoyed by al-Suyuti's [d. 1505] *al-Durr al-manthur* owes itself to the same method. Conversely, a common saying about the exegetical work of [the rationalist theologian Fakhr al-din] al-Razi [d. 1210] is that "it has everything in it *except* exegesis." . . .

May God reward Shah Sahib for correcting the wrong understanding of what was meant by "exegesis according to opinion." God is to be thanked for the blessing that the correct understanding [as elucidated by Kashmiri] has now also been preserved in the written version of his discourses on the hadith collection of Bukhari. As he used to say—and as [also] reported in the written version of his lectures—"What stops the 'ulama from bringing forth the meanings of the texts after careful consideration of the context, an examination of the connotations of the relevant terms, and in accordance with the beliefs known to have been held by the pious forbears." . . . He went on, again as reported in the written record of his lectures, "Indeed, to do so is their rightful share from the Book, for they are the people who look into its remarkable features, bring out facets of its subtleties and its concealed truths. This sort of 'exegesis by opinion' is the right of the people of knowledge and of the accomplished scholars." Yet . . . he also had this to say as an admonition: "As for the person who speaks about these matters while lacking the necessary tools—i.e., one ignorant of the statements of the pious forbears and of the later scholars, a person who has no sense of the Arabic language and is one of those low-ranking people whose impudence and ignorance leads them to embark on [mis]interpreting the Book of God—then woe to him! It is the likes of *him* who deserve hell."

THE HADITH LECTURES OF SHAYKH AL-HIND MAHMUD HASAN

The Shaykh al-Hind's style in the teaching of hadith was very different from that of Shah Sahib. . . . The student would proceed with reading hadith reports aloud, and the Shaykh al-Hind would listen. At this stage [of hadith study], it was no longer a matter of translating [hadith reports] into Urdu. For in studying the *Mishkat* [a widely used collection of hadith], the students had already studied the text of the hadith [together with its translation] so that, as is commonly known, students at this advanced stage no longer had any need for texts to be translated. One hadith report now followed another in quick succession and, other than an occasional "Let's proceed," the Shaykh al-Hind would barely say a word. This was a veritable *silent* lesson. When the students came upon a hadith report that seemed to contradict the norms of the Hanafi school of law, and the person reading it, or someone else, paused to remark on this dissonance, the Shaykh al-Hind would smile and say, "Well, yes, it is opposed [to the Hanafi norms]. But what can I do about it! Let's proceed." "But sir, has this difficulty not been addressed by or on behalf of the Imam [Abu Hanifa]?" the student would ask. "Your texts would have something in them about this; you should look it up there," he would respond . . . When the student insisted further, he would say, "There are glosses by leading scholars available in your texts, read them there." When students continued to demand an answer, he would offer a few further suggestions. At the time, I did not realize the importance of these brief comments. But I can say without exaggeration, at least for myself, that a lifetime of teaching and writing has only increased my estimation for such comments. On numerous matters of juridical disagreement [as preserved in the scholarly tradition], the most authoritative position proved, indeed, to be the one to which the Shaykh al-Hind had already alluded.

Such comments initially did not have much of an impact on intellectually immature students. They would go on raising questions. In response, the Shaykh al-Hind would go a bit deeper, and so things would proceed. In this manner, he would gradually teach students how to probe more deeply into questions, how to think for themselves. A casual observer would not have been much impressed by this [seemingly simplistic] style of teaching . . . , and the truth is that, without great humility, ordinary teachers would not dare to attempt this [self-effacing] style of teaching. This dialectical mode of instruction ultimately convinced me, however, of the great acumen of this revered old man. I continued to experience his brilliance [during the course of his teaching], though I had yet to personally introduce myself to him . . .

During this time, I began to experience a strange condition. As far as I can remember, I would experience it with especial intensity during the Shaykh al-Hind's hadith sessions. . . . As soon as the study of hadith began, I would be afflicted with a storm of anxieties, doubts of various kinds on every single hadith report. These were not the kind of doubts common among madrasa students and 'ulama [i.e., objections of the sort mentioned earlier]. The trouble was that—and with God is the refuge!—these evil ideas often related to none other than the person of the Prophet himself. A veritable fire of bad thoughts would blaze inside me: the study of Tirmidhi's [hadith collection] would continue for two hours, and this wretched fellow would keep burning in fires of doubt this entire time. Every hadith report was, for me, the cause of wicked thoughts. . . . Admittedly, together with ancient philosophy, I had become acquainted, through newspapers and magazines, with wayward intellectual trends of the present day. But as far as I can recall, never before had I experienced any doubts about the prophethood of Muhammad—the final foundation of religion. It is this belief [in the Prophet] that, despite my other failings, had kept me within the bounds of faith. Now it seemed that I had slipped off the very bedrock of religion. . . . It appeared that the Creator had destined me for hell. As my condition deteriorated, I began to contemplate leaving the madrasa. . . .

Around this time, a form of divine help presented itself. Amir Shah—may God have mercy on him—who was a famous member of the Deobandi circles though not a scholar himself, came on a visit to Deoband. . . . Within a few days [of my becoming acquainted with him], he began to treat me with special affection. . . . As this affection grew, I told him of what troubled me. He listened to me carefully, and then said, "Why don't you talk to your teacher, Mahmud Hasan?" "It is my misfortune that I can no longer go into his presence," I said.

"I have long been in Deoband, yet never did I go to pay my respects to him; and I am too embarrassed to go now." [Amir Shah] Khan Sahib consoled me, however, and said that I should, indeed, go [to Mahmud Hasan] and that he would himself take me there.

[On visiting Mahmud Hasan a few days later] I tearfully told him all that I had been experiencing. He listened silently . . . and then said, "Mawlawi Sahib, why are you so worried? If this condition of yours really feels so intolerable to you, then that already is a sign of your faith rather than of a loss of faith. . . ." Then he asked me what I had studied previously, and where. I told him about my studies, and the fact that much of my time so far had been spent studying logic and ancient philosophy. "The 'raw' and the 'cooked' that you have been indiscriminately swallowing is what is causing trouble now," he said. "But don't be alarmed." I cried, "Whatever their provenance, I can no longer bear these doubts, these wicked thoughts. My life itself is in danger because of them!" He responded, "Mawlawi Sahib, go now, and never again will you experience doubts of any kind," or something to that effect. Irrespective of whether or not anyone wants to believe this, my heart and my mind bear witness: In the forty years since then, I have—praise be to God!—never again experienced a doubt regarding any Qur'anic verse or any hadith report. Even if I encounter something [seemingly problematic], many possible solutions immediately suggest themselves to my mind. . . . I now consider myself, my mind, and my intellectual inclinations to be the very embodiment of the miracle performed by the Shaykh al-Hind [with his words]. . . . The next day, I went as usual to his study circle, but it was all different now. My attendance now had a new dimension to it, which was only strengthened with every passing day. Everything he said [in the course of the hadith study] now seemed to make its way straight into my heart. . . . I experienced his sagacity especially in the course of his teaching of Bukhari's [collection of hadith].

As those who know such matters are well aware, one of the major issues pertaining to Bukhari's collection is the question of how he has organized his chapters. Just as the question of how particular Qur'anic verses relate to one another is a matter of the Qur'an's great [but elusive] wisdom, so too is the case with how the titles of Bukhari's chapters relate to the chapters' contents: the secret of their consonance lies in the very appearance of their dissonance. Precisely what is the relationship between the particular hadith reports and the chapter in which they have been gathered together? Perhaps from the day Bukhari's work was introduced into scholarly circles, people have been busy trying to solve this puzzle. What they have thought about over the course of a thousand years is preserved in their books, though the more discerning have always recognized that the scholarly community owes it to Bukhari to provide a better solution to this problem than has been offered so far. For all the other achievements of Ibn Hajar's [d. 1449] comprehensive commentary on Bukhari, this aspect has remained in need of further discussion. Shah Wali Allah also devoted

a treatise to this puzzle. Indeed, with this treatise, Wali Allah opened new avenues towards the understanding of this problem. And the Shaykh al-Hind was
the legatee of this new approach.

The fact of the matter is that, once a discussion of Bukhari's chapters began
in the Shaykh al-Hind's circle, a particular state would overcome him. The listeners, too, seemed to be in awe. It was as if the entire group was in ecstasy. . . .
New information, new knowledge—things that had not been heard or read
elsewhere—seemed to be in the process of being unveiled . . . Bukhari's practice is to incorporate relevant Qur'anic verses into his chapter headings, wherever he deemed it necessary to do so. Consequently [in Mahmud Hasan's study
circle], opportunities were created not only for coming to know new facets relating to particular Qur'anic verses, but also new avenues for an understanding
of the Qur'an in general. Once the study of Bukhari had begun [with the
Shaykh al-Hind], following the study of Tirmidhi, both the heart and the mind
thrived on this nourishment—one not found in any work of logic, philosophy,
belles-lettres, or any other discipline. I can't speak for others but, so far as I am
concerned, I felt that I was being transformed both outwardly and inwardly.

These changes were taking place very rapidly. Within a few days, I realized
that whatever I had previously imbibed—the distinctive features with which I
had entered the Dar al-'Ulum—had left me. . . . As it happened, some students
of the Dar al-'Ulum began insisting that I teach them the *Risala* of Mir Zahid [d.
1689], a famous textbook of the rational sciences. This was a treatise that I had
studied for over a year with Mawlana Sayyid Barakat Ahmad in Tonk. Although
he had taught me all rationalist texts with unusual care, his style of teaching
Mir Zahid's *Risala* was novel and probably peculiar to him. He would begin
with passages from the base text—Qutbuddin Razi's *Qutbiyya* [on which Mir
Zahid's *Risala* is the commentary]—and then have me read Mir Zahid's commentary on the relevant portions. Then we would study Mir Zahid's notes [sic]
on his own commentary, which are often referred to in madrasa circles as the
"Manhiyya." I would then be taught the glosses written on the Manhiyya by
Ghulam Yahya Bihari, followed by a study of the published glosses by 'Abd al-
Haqq Khayrabadi on the glosses of Ghulam Yahya [Bihari]. Then, I would have
to read whatever Hakim Sahib [i.e., Gilani's teacher Sayyid Barakat Ahmad] had
himself written on Khayrabadi's glosses. This is how I had read this book, and
with all the effort that I could muster; in doing so, I had also recorded my
teacher's lectures on it in the Urdu language. Obviously, I would have had no
difficulty teaching a work I had studied so thoroughly.

After some initial excuses about being too busy, I agreed to teach [Mir Zahid's
Risala], and promised to begin the following day. I went to the library and got
the *Risala* together with 'Abd al-Haqq Khayrabadi's glosses on it. Once finished
with my own studies [for the day], I thought I would look over the glosses. It
is then that I had a strange experience. People might refuse to believe it, yet
what happened was this: Each time I tried opening the book, my hands would

begin to shake and my heartbeat accelerated. "O God," I thought, ". . . only a few days ago, reading this book was a matter of great satisfaction for me. What has changed?" I continued to shiver. Yet, despite this condition, I was determined to prepare for the next day's lesson. My peers thought highly of the expertise in logic and the rational sciences I had acquired in Tonk, and I didn't wish to embarrass myself. The fear of embarrassment overcame my agitated state, and I studied—but in a way that I had control neither over my heart nor over my mind . . . Uncharacteristically, I then dozed off.

I saw myself in a vast plain where I was being attacked by wild boars. I tried to run, but they continued to pursue me. I saw a tree, climbed it, and seated myself on a high branch. The boars encircled the tree, gazing at me relentlessly. I did not know how to get rid of them. Just then, I saw a man with a gun in his hand. He began shooting at the boars, injuring and killing some and forcing them all to flee. Still perched on the tree, it occurred to me that the man with the gun was none other than Mawlana Husayn Ahmad Madani. That is the point at which I woke up. The interesting thing is that, while I was acquainted with the name of Mawlana Madani [who lived in Medina at that time], I had never actually seen him before. I had just supposed that God's grace had embodied itself for me [in this dream] in the guise of [Madani's] name. A few days later, however, Madani returned from Medina to Deoband, and I realized that he was exactly as I had seen him in the dream. . . . I still recall the mixed feelings of great surprise and relief [that this dream had left in me]. Obviously, after this dream, my mind was made up . . . When the students came to me the following day, I didn't narrate my dream to them, but I did tell them that I was no longer capable of teaching them the book I had promised I would. There was nothing they could do about this, except to turn away in disappointment.

As I have mentioned, Shaykh Madani returned to Deoband while the Shaykh al-Hind's lectures on Bukhari were still in progress. I had the great fortune not only to study with a teacher like the Shaykh al-Hind, but also to witness the Shaykh of Medina [i.e., Madani]—who had had his own study circle of hadith in the Prophet's Mosque in Medina—join the Shaykh al-Hind's study circle as a student. Shaykh Madani was now the person reciting the text of Bukhari [as other students had previously done] in the presence of the Shaykh al-Hind. In this sort of a study circle, other, ordinary participants could not be much more than mere listeners. . . . Those who did not witness these remarkable occasions can only imagine the questions a mature scholar-turned-student would have asked his benevolent teacher, and the answers he would have received. . . . The Shaykh al-Hind and the Shaykh of Medina would discuss each and every issue [related to the hadith texts before them] at great length. This was a remarkable spectacle, with two experienced "players" bringing all their skills to bear [on their discussion]. I consider it a matter of great good fortune to have been one of those in attendance. . . .

THEOLOGICAL AND POLITICAL CONTROVERSIES

I cannot count the blessings of having been a student of the Shaykh al-Hind and of adopting him as my Sufi master. But I should also acknowledge that I was never among those who occupied a position of any great proximity or significance in relation to him. . . . Even so, there are two important matters concerning him of which I know; and though others closer to him have better right to report them, it does not seem proper for me to keep them to myself simply because of the lowly position I had occupied in his company.

The first of these concerns the late ʿUbayd Allah Sindhi [d. 1944, a prominent but controversial student and devotee of Mahmud Hasan]. When I entered the Dar al-ʿUlum, the tensions between the administrators of Deoband and Mawlana Sindhi had reached a point where he had withdrawn from Deoband to settle in Delhi. There he had established the Nizarat al-Maʿarif al-Qurʾaniyya, an institution at which he was teaching the Qurʾan to select students according to his own peculiar points of view. His students there included some who had graduated from the Dar al-ʿUlum and others who had had an English education. In those days, Mawlana Sindhi would sometimes come to Deoband. His real purpose in doing so would be to meet with the Shaykh al-Hind, though, if possible, he would sometimes also visit the Dar al-ʿUlum. As a young man newly arrived at the Dar al-ʿUlum, I shared the general mindset of the students. The circle of students in which I moved believed that, because the Deoband administrators were unhappy with Mawlana Sindhi, any students meeting with him were also monitored. These might have been mere youthful fantasies. In any case, I was acquainted not only with his name but also with some of his work. I admired him and had heard much about his learning. Whenever I saw him at the Dar al-ʿUlum, I wanted to meet him, but then I would resist the temptation for fear that the madrasa administrators might come to hear about this. . . . One day, however, I did manage to secretly go to him. I don't quite remember everything that we discussed, but I do recall one portion of the conversation. I asked him what he was trying to accomplish, what his activity amounted to. Mawlana Sindhi responded that the ʿulama were in a state of severe degeneration, while those with [a modern] education had gone far ahead. He wanted to bring the ʿulama and the modern-educated closer to one another . . . This initial meeting ended in a few minutes, and he soon returned to Delhi.

It was not long before he was back in Deoband. There were rumors that Mawlana Sindhi's case was being discussed by the madrasa's consultative committee and that the professors were debating with him on a particular matter. All I had heard was that there was some dispute on the question of the preaching of Islam (*tabligh*). The next thing I saw was that all the major figures of the madrasa—everyone except the Shaykh al-Hind—had gathered in the Dar al-ʿUlum's mosque, together with a good number of students who had come to watch. Though I don't recall the precise sequence, several speakers, including Mawlana Shabbir Ahmad ʿUthmani [d. 1949], Mawlana Sindhi, and Mawlawi Ghulam Rasul, the professor of logic and philosophy, stood up to deliver their speeches. As I remember, Mawlana 'Ubayd Allah said that his understanding of the Qur'anic verse, ". . . this Qur'an was revealed so that I might warn you and whoever it reaches . . . [Qur'an 6:19]," was that people who had not received the message of the Qur'an would not [on the Day of Judgment] be deemed liable for failing to accept Islam. I don't remember the entire speech, though I recall his acknowledgement that this was not the view commonly held by the 'ulama. They commonly believed, rather, that everyone had, in fact, received the message so that no individual or community was now excusable for failing to accept Islam. . . . I also vaguely recall the late Mawlana Shabbir Ahmad 'Uthmani angrily refuting [Sindhi's position]. And I cannot forget the statement made by Mawlawi Ghulam Rasul that, though Sindhi had been a member of our group, he has now been expelled from it, for when a limb becomes diseased, it must be severed . . .

The session ended, but I remained much affected by the proceedings. Perhaps a day or so later, in the course of the Shaykh al-Hind's lectures on Tirmidhi, I gathered enough courage to ask him his view of the disagreement on the question of proselytism . . . It appeared that he had been apprised of the proceedings of the meeting as well, and was troubled by them. Contrary to his custom, he suddenly became very attentive and then spoke on the matter in a way that has come to constitute for me the final word on it. The following is the gist of what he had said.

The overall status of bringing the message (*tabligh*) to people and the question of their being accountable [to God, for their acceptance or refusal of it (*mu'akhadha*)] are among ambiguous matters. The manner in which the Prophet had introduced Abu Bakr [one of his earliest followers and later his first successor as the caliph] to Islam is not comparable to that in which *we* might introduce someone to Islam. Abu Bakr was the confidant of the Prophet's innermost thoughts; the closeness he enjoyed to the Prophet is obviously not the lot of today's ordinary Muslims. Likewise, God's making people accountable for their deeds is also not of the same order in every instance. After all, the way in which Abu Jahl [a contemporary and arch enemy of the Prophet] would be held accountable [for his rejection of Islam] cannot match the manner in which those others are accountable who did not see the proofs [of the Prophet's truth] with the same clarity as Abu Jahl had done. The view to take on this question, then, is that one's liability is tied to the character and quality of what has reached him about this faith. It is quite possible that one might be living in India or Arabia but, because of one's peculiar circumstances, may not have adequately received the summons to the truth faith. Conversely, someone living in Europe or America might have formally studied Islam, its teachings, and its books [and thus be more fully acquainted with it than the Arab or the Indian]. In short, so far as individual cases are concerned, God alone knows how much of the message one has received, and He alone will judge everyone according to what He knows about that person. For us, it is sufficient to under-

stand that one's accountability broadly depends on the degree of one's expo-
sure to the message . . .

The [Shaykh al-Hind's] lecture that day had turned out to be an emotionally
charged affair. Members of the madrasa's consultative committee had also been
apprised that a certain student had raised this question in the Shaykh al-Hind's
study circle and that the latter had responded to it in a certain way. There was
much talk about this. Even a special gathering was convoked to clarify that,
while some might construe what the Shaykh al-Hind had said as supporting the
viewpoint of Mawlana 'Ubayd Allah Sindhi, the two views were, in fact, not the
same . . .

The second matter [that I remember as regards the Shaykh al-Hind] is related
to the first. The tensions between 'Ubayd Allah Sindhi and the Deoband establishment had continued [even after his removal from Deoband]. It was clear
that the viewpoints of the Shaykh al-Hind and 'Ubayd Allah Sindhi, on the one
hand, and those of the Deoband administrators, on the other, were becoming
increasingly divergent. The question of the preaching of Islam was an academic
issue. The real disagreement between the two groups concerned politics. As I
recall, one day Mawlana Habib al-Rahman, the vice principal of the madrasa,
summoned me and asked that I inquire from the Shaykh al-Hind about his true
political stance. I wonder why Mawlana Habib al-Rahman had entrusted this
crucially important task to me. In any case, it was the Shaykh al-Hind's practice
to work after midday prayers on his Urdu translation of the Qur'an—[which
turned out to be] the last of his academic ventures—in a room that was then
called the Writing Center . . . I went to him there, and I addressed to him the
question I had been instructed to ask. He listened. . . . Then, referring to his
teacher, Muhammad Qasim [Nanotawi], the founder of the Dar al-'Ulum, he
said: "Did the exalted teacher"—as he typically referred to Muhammad Qasim—
"establish the madrasa [merely] for teaching and learning? The madrasa was
established before my own eyes. As far as I know, it was decided in the aftermath of the failure of the 1857 revolt to establish an institution which would
train the sort of people who could remedy [the effects of] the defeat of 1857."

This conversation took place forty years ago, and it is futile to expect a ver-
batim account of all that he said. What I had understood from him then is what
I am describing now—the gist of the long response he had given me on that occasion. At the end, he had said, "I do not wish to obstruct the path of those who
want to be concerned [exclusively] with teaching and learning. But as for myself, I have chosen the very same path for which, as I see it, the exalted teacher
[Nanotawi] had established the Dar al-'Ulum in the first place." The two paths
became distinct from then on: one was the path of teaching, scholarship, and
publishing; and the other was the path [of political activism] that the Shaykh
al-Hind came to adopt and which he pursued until the end of his life . . . Whatever I had heard from him on this occasion I transmitted to those who had sent
me to him as their emissary.

Sources

The selections above are translated from Manazir Ahsan Gilani's *Ihata-yi Dar al-'Ulum main bite huwe din* (Deoband: Maktaba-yi tayyiba, n.d.), pp. 77–171. The text has been abridged in translation, and the paragraph division does not necessarily reflect that of the Urdu original. Ellipses within a sentence are indicated by three dots, and those of a full sentence or more are shown by four. The parentheses are retained from the Urdu original; all words in square brackets, including the subtitles, have been added by the translator. Commonly occurring non-English words, such as hadith, madrasa, and 'ulama, are not italicized.

Apart from Manazir Ahsan Gilani's memoirs used here, the most detailed account of Gilani's life is to be found in the biography by Muhammad Zafir al-din Miftahi, *Hayat-i Mawlana Gilani* (Banaras: Muhammad Yusuf Academy, 1989). A collection of Gilani's letters also illuminates much about his thought and career: *Makatib-i Gilani*, Minnat Allah Rahmani, ed. (Mongir: Dar al-isha'at-i Rahmani, 1972). The hadith lectures of Anwarshah Kashmiri, to which Gilani refers in the text translated here, were first published in Cairo in 1938. For a more recent edition, see Anwarshah Kashmiri, *Fayd al-bari 'ala Sahih al-Bukhari*, compiled by Muhammad Badr-i 'Alam Mirathi, 4 vols. (Deoband: al-Maktaba al-ashrafiyya, 2000).

Further Reading

The most comprehensive account of the early history of the Deoband madrasa and its social and cultural milieu is Barbara D. Metcalf, *Islamic Revival in British India: Deoband, 1860–1900* (Princeton, NJ: Princeton University Press, 1982). For an analysis of some of the later transformations that are to be observed in the thought and politics of the Deobandi 'ulama, see Muhammad Qasim Zaman, *The Ulama in Contemporary Islam: Custodians of Change* (Princeton, NJ: Princeton University Press, 2002). Other studies of the 'ulama, their scholarly culture, and their institutions of learning include Francis Robinson, *The 'Ulama of Farangi Mahall and Islamic Culture in South Asia* (London: Hurst, 2001); and Robert W. Hefner and Muhammad Qasim Zaman, eds., *Schooling Islam: The Culture and Politics of Muslim Education* (Princeton, NJ: Princeton University Press, 2007).

— 18 —

Jihad in the Way of God:
A Tablighi Jama'at Account
of a Mission in India

Barbara D. Metcalf

The Muslim movement popularly known as Tablighi Jama'at (the "preaching" or "inviting" society) is one of many movements of the colonial period that sought to return to original teachings and that, simultaneously, sought to expand responsibility for religious guidance from specialists to all believers. This movement is notable, however, in that it stands apart from another far-reaching change of the period, namely the momentous emergence of politicized religious communities in public life. Tabligh certainly enhanced individuals' identity as Muslims, but it did not express explicit concerns about public life or engage in any competition to secure communal interests in the larger society. It is a movement of piety and self-improvement.

The Tablighi Jama'at traces its origins to north India in the 1920s. It was one of many Muslim movements stimulated to action by aggressive Hindu attempts to "reconvert" those seen as nominal Muslims to Islam. The movement took on new energy after the partition of the subcontinent in 1947, for example in the Mewat area southeast of Delhi, where Hindus had engaged in ruthless "ethnic cleansing." Tablighi Jama'at subsequently began a worldwide program, particularly from the 1960s, with the spread of immigrant populations to America and Europe and beyond. It now engages non-Indo-Pakistani populations as well, virtually across the globe, and it may well be the largest "movement," if one can call it that given its shifting participation and lack of bureaucracy, among Muslims today. In this regard, it is conventional today to point to either of the Tablighi Jama'at's annual international three-day congregations held in Raiwind in Pakistan or Tungi in Bangladesh and describe the turnout at each—of some two million-odd—as the largest annual congregations of Muslims outside those who gather each year to perform the hajj at Mecca. Even in India, where there has been a preference for security reasons for regional meetings rather than a single national meeting, early twenty-first-century meetings could draw a million people.

Those who began this movement were themselves 'ulama linked to the reformist seminary at Deoband discussed in Chapter 17. Among them were two influential figures taken as the movement's founders, Maulana Muhammad Ilyas (d. 1944) and Maulana Muhammad Zakariyya Kandhlawi (d. 1982), the latter the author of the movement's *vade mecum*, the *Tablighi Nisab* compendium of hadith-based guidance (referred to in the translation below).

Maulana Ilyas responded to the Hindu-Muslim riots and intense missionary activities of the Arya Samajis not, as many in the 1920s did, by political action, but rather by intensifying the original Deobandi program of inner-looking grassroots reform of individual lives as a solution to the same problem of defending Islam. He argued that what had been seen as the responsibility (*farz al-kifaya*) of the 'ulama, namely teaching fidelity to correct behavior, was in fact the obligation of all Muslims (*farz al-'ain*), a radical example of the trend toward "lay" leadership. The key to his program was to get Muslims to move out of their normal everyday enmeshments and pressures and instead to go out in small groups to call other Muslims to this correct practice. He felt that schools were not the way to reach people. Lived experience was. Group interactions while on a mission, coupled with the powerful impact on the teacher himself or herself of teaching others, were the keys to his program.

There is no formal bureaucratic structure to this highly decentralized, voluntary movement; there are no offices, no paid staff, no (known) archives. There are centers, mosque-based *markaz* in countries, regions, and cities with locally chosen leaders, or *amirs*. The primary center adjoins the shrine of Hazrat Nizamuddin Chishti (d. 1325) in Delhi, where Maulana Ilyas had based himself; successive leaders, including his son (the Maulana Yusuf [d. 1966] or "Hazratji" of the account below) and other descendants, have been based there as well. Groups (*jama'at*) form at this center, as they do at other centers throughout the world, through a process of assembly (*tashkil*) in response to the *amir's* call, each typically comprised of about a dozen individuals. Women only travel in *jama'ats* in the company of their menfolk, but they have done so from the movement's earliest days. Their primary *tablighi* role is understood to be within the family and among local women.

A group typically volunteers for three days, forty days, or one hundred twenty days. It is meant to operate through egalitarian consultation (*mashwara*) in order to assign tasks and to choose an itinerary (*rukh*) for its program. Its project is hard work (*mihnat*) in the way of God (*fi sabil allah*). A *jama'at* is meant to be self-supporting, stay in mosques, prepare humble and basic food for itself, and spend time in prayer and mutual instruction (*ta'lim*) when not actively inviting others to join in. In due course, members return to the center and offer an account (*karguzari*), such as the one translated below, in this case a dictated account, as we learn in the course of it that all the members of the group were illiterate.

Although it was usual to produce an account of each mission, the example presented here is profoundly atypical. To begin with, according to a full-time Tabligh worker who resides in Raiwind, written accounts of tours once read are not kept. Some few have been available, even occasionally posted on the Web. For example, one site in the late 1990s posted *karguzari* characterized as "true stories in the path of Allah" (www.al-madina.com), but the site disappeared, perhaps because in the United States after 9/11 the movement was alleged to be involved with terrorism. Several highly publicized "terrorists" had participated in Tablighi activities, but, arguably, this is simply because the movement exists virtually everywhere.

The record that follows, produced immediately after Partition and published in 1950, has, presumably, been preserved and informally reprinted because it is such a powerful and dramatic account of Tabligh at a time of considerable danger and difficulty. It is readily available, whether as a copy that can be purchased for a few pennies, lithographed on eight folded sheets with no publication information (as I first found it at an outdoor book table) or reprinted in more conventional pamphlet format. Its substance is as atypical as its availability because it tells the story of an attempt to bring back to Islam Muslims who, in the brutal and violent post-Partition context, had apostatized to save their lives. This extraordinary account is organized in terms of a dynamic: four successive severe tests, each met with divine aid, each followed by new resolve and, ultimately, success.

The account not only exemplifies Tablighi Jama'at procedures, as briefly outlined above, but also the two shaping discourses through which Tablighi activities are understood, that of jihad, and, implicitly, that of Sufism. The term *jihad* as used here does not pertain to warfare or violence but instead to peaceful preaching, with its attendant efforts at self-control and self-improvement. The rhetoric of jihad in all its meanings is the same. Fundamental to the concept in recent times is the belief that this is again a time of *jahiliyya*, a time of ignorance classically understood as the pre-Muhammadan age in Arabia, an understanding shared with twentieth-century Islamist thinkers like Maulana Abul A'la Maududi (1903–1979), whose movement is discussed in Chapter 34.

Tablighi jama'ats, like political undertakings, are led by an *amir* and guided by consultation (*shura, mashwara*). Tablighi preaching tours are described as *gasht* (patrols) and *khuruj* (sorties). Anyone who dies in the course of a *tabligh* tour is a *shahid* (martyr), just as much as someone who dies in a militant jihad. Tablighis' efforts, like those of an armed *mujahid*, are understood to be *fi sabil allah* (in the path of God) and, as a prophetic hadith quoted below indicates, the motivation to both forms of jihad is generosity on the part of the jihadi, modeled on God's own gracious bounty to humankind. In both forms of jihad, the participant will receive exponentially increased reward for all acts performed. In each, the believer is enjoined to effective action in a world that needs to be changed.

Tablighi ideology also draws on the idiom of Sufism. Tablighis believe themselves able to receive, through divine blessings granted on account of their work, the high spiritual state and charisma accorded to Sufis. The Sufis gain their blessings through lives devoted to ritual disciplines, meditation, and moral purification, coupled with the powerful charisma of succession transmitted through the elder to whom they pledge allegiance. These states can now to be gained directly by participation in the charismatic community of the *jama'at*. Thus, the participant gains through his experiential states in this life the assurance that what he is doing is receiving divine blessing. The account below speaks of being granted the light of insight (*nur-i basirat*) and of the cognition (*ma'arifat*) and disclosures (*inkishaf*) accorded those who participated. Story after story, like the one below, illustrate how a *jama'at* becomes a vehicle for what are essentially the *karamat,* or miracles, gained in classic Sufi accounts by a particular holy man who enjoys God's favor.

Some observers assume that participation in the peaceful jihad of Tablighi Jama'at is a first stage toward militant jihad, or at least toward more active political forms of organization. That assumption, like the more extreme position that the Tablighi Jama'at serves as a cover for terrorists, remains to be demonstrated. It is, in contrast, clear that for millions of participants the injunction to disseminate individual moral reform is the movement's only mission. If pressed to talk about political issues, some Tablighis, in fact, will emphasize Muslim failure to live morally as a cause of Muslim suffering in recent years, particularly in the swath of land that swings from Chechnya through Kashmir, to Afghanistan, Iraq, Bosnia, and Palestine, in contrast to those more public Muslim voices who explicitly condemn Christian, Zionist, and other oppression. One of the foundational texts of the movement (1945) uses as its English title "Muslim Degeneracy" to target its primary concern.

Yet, despite these crucial differences, Tablighis do share fundamental attitudes with the militants, not least their belief that Islam must be defended. They also are shaped by a commitment to individual action as effective in shaping the larger world, and they share the conviction that the faithful few, who act "in the way of Allah," can achieve far-reaching transformations. They also cultivate a cultural encapsulation that divides them starkly from a larger, evil, and threatening world. Tablighis thus become, as a Qur'an verse in the text suggests, the Prophet's *ansar* (the term used for the his "helpers" in Medina) and *khulafa* (his very successors), to which the text adds, even though they have no political power.

Karguzari (An accounting)

In the name of God, the merciful, the compassionate: ". . . we will guide in their way those servants who exert themselves in our way and for our faith. Surely Almighty God is with the righteous and supports them." (Surah Ankabut 69)

COMMENTARY

Almighty God will bestow upon those who undertake hardships, endure difficulties, and are zealous in their many efforts for His sake, a special light of insight (*nur-i basirat*). He will show them His nearness and pleasure and the paths of heaven. The more they progress in discipline and exertions, the more their level of cognition (*ma'rifat*) and disclosures (*inkishaf*) will rise, and this will be manifest in such a way that it is wholly imperceptible to others. Almighty God's protection and generosity is with the righteous.

The honorable Maulana Mufti Muhammad Shafi' writes that in this verse is the true meaning of jihad, namely, removal of the obstacles in faith, whether in the jihad that is with the unbelievers, or the jihad with the lower self and Satan. In this verse is the promise for both kinds of jihad: "that Almighty God guides in their path those undertaking jihad." (*Ma'rifatu'l Qur'an* VI, 704).

Those who struggle in service to the faith and exert themselves in its way are the Helpers (*ansar*) of God and the Successors (*khulafa*) of the Prophet (peace be upon him).

The honorable Maulana Muhammad Manzur No'mani (may the mercy of God be upon him) writes in his pamphlet, "Service to the Faith," that throughout the entire history of this community (*umma*), any righteous servant who has exerted himself only for the sake of guidance and help for God's servants, and for the pleasure of Almighty God—whether through preaching (*da'wat o tabligh*) or teaching, sermons or writing, or by any other means—all of them, without doubt, are counted among the Helpers of God (*ansar*) and the Party of God (*hizbu'llah*). Although they may have no connection to governance or state, they are among the Successors (*khulafa*) of the Prophet (peace be upon him).

That said, I confirm that for those people who invite others (*da'wat*) to Almighty God and have affirmed that they are among those who follow his order (*farmanbardar*)—and if God has affirmed that through them even one person has found guidance—this is better for them than [extremely costly] red camels. In another declaration: Any servant of God who guides another to good deeds receives the same reward as the one who did the good deed. (Muslim [d. 831, a compiler of hadith].) The Prophet asked if anyone knew who was greatest in bounty and generosity (*jud o sakha*). The Companions demurred from answering, saying that God and his Prophet know better. He answered that the highest rank is that of Almighty God, then my own, then that of the person who has acquired knowledge of the guidance of Almighty God and conveys it to others and in this conveying exerts great effort. Such a person on the Day of Judgment becomes a lord (*sardar*). And this: A single person will make a community (Behaqi).

This is the account of such a struggling (*mujahid*) *jama'at* (party) that set out to save Muslims from the crisis (*fitna*) of apostasy. Maulana Muhammad Yusuf sent out two *jama'ats* of which the *amir* of one was Miyanji Muhammad Ishaq. That *jama'at* achieved arduous stages (*manzil*), sustained great ordeals, and emerged as pure gold. At the direction of Hazratji, after working for five and one-half months, they returned safely to Basti Nizamuddin Sharif, Delhi's Tablighi center (*markaz*). My revered elder and friend al Haj Lad Khan, after long entreaty, heard and wrote down this account from the words of the late Janab Miyanji Muhammad Ishaq [since, as we learn later, all in the *jama'at* were illiterate].

May Almighty God accept all us Muslims for the struggle for the faith like this struggling *jama'at* and make us worthy of the merits recorded in hadith. Amen.

In the name of God, the Compassionate, the Merciful.

DEPARTURE

After the partition of India in August 1947, Muslims of the eastern districts of Punjab apostatized. This was a great blow to Hazratji Maulana Muhammad Yusuf when he learned of this situation. In March of 1950, in the Tablighi center of Nizamuddin, he discoursed (*bayan farmaya*) on this subject for some eight days. He encouraged people to give him not forty days (*chilla*) or one hundred twenty days [i.e., as mission volunteers], but to see the necessity of being willing to either die (i.e., give their life in the way of God) or bring the apostates of eastern Punjab back into Islam. There could be no limit on the amount of time it would take. At this request, twenty-two people put forward their names and accepted his request, promising that God willing, as he had ordered, they would either give their lives or at least exert themselves (*mehnat karna*) to bring the apostates of eastern Punjab back again into Islam.

INCIVILITY ON ACCOUNT OF FEAR

Thus these twenty-two dear ones (*ahbab*) were assembled (*tashkil*) into two *jama'ats* consisting of eleven people each. Muhammad Iqbal Sahib was made the *amir* of one, and Hajji Kamal al-Din Saharanpurwaala of the other. Maulana Muhammad Yusuf, weeping, came out of the mosque barefoot, made supplication, entrusted both *jama'ats* to God, and long stood there, watching and praying. While dismissing them, he also told them to seek advice (*mashwara*) from Maulana Baqa'ullah Sahib [at their destination] and then to begin their work.

When both *jama'ats* reached Maulana Baqa'ullah Sahib, at their sight he immediately asked what they were doing for fear that they would put the lives [of local Muslims] at risk. He denounced the dear ones of the *jama'at* and expelled them from the mosque, refusing to let them stay there. The *jama'ats* had no choice but to go outside the city and stay for some time in a mosque known as the Mosque of Imam Sahib. They consulted among themselves (*mushwara*) and agreed on a program: each *jama'at* would go in a different direction (*rukh*) and work for a week, then reunite in Chilapur. Thus, in accordance with this plan, they worked and met at the appointed time.

THE CONDITION OF THE REGION

There were five mosques and twelve households of Muslims, all of whom had apostatized. They had taken down the minaret of one of the mosques and in its place put an idol, which they now worshipped. We talked to them and encouraged them with the invitation (da'wat) to again enter into Islam. One among them agreed and led us to other villages. In one ten to twelve people secretly said their prayer (namaz), though the rest had apostatized. We secretly encouraged them to return to Islam. Two among them were imams who had shaved their beards and now kept a tuft of hair [a Hindu practice].

THE FIRST TRIAL

We worked in this area for a week, and from there our jama'at continued to District Jind. Here were ten mosques and a good number of Muslims, most of whom had apostatized. The rest secretly prayed, and of them five joined us. We worked there for five days. We gave the call to prayer, and many friends began to pray. It began to be known in the area that people of our sort had come, who are bringing the apostates back into Islam. The police also heard about us, whereupon twenty of them arrived in a truck and entered the mosque where we were staying. They used their staffs and rifle butts to beat those who had joined the jama'at, three or four on top of one of them, beating and cursing. All our companions soiled themselves and fell unconscious. These tyrants picked us all up in this condition and threw us in the truck to take us to the jail in Ambala. They locked us into a narrow and dark cell. In the morning they got us out and forced us to remove the night soil of the other prisoners. We spent three days thus, and they did not even give us water to drink.

THE FIRST OCCASION OF AID FROM BEYOND (GHAYBI MADAD)

On the fourth day we were busy with our teachings (ta'lim) when an officer came and asked what we were reading. We explained the goal of our teaching, but he failed to understand. He took our Ta'limi Nisab, read it for a while, and then said, "When I was in Multan before the upheaval [1947], whenever our children had any problem we would take them to Muslims just like you who were called "Tablighi Jama'at Wale," and you seem just like them. They would recite the word of God and breathe on them, and then our children would be better. They were good people and we loved them. If you have any kind of difficulty, I'm ready to help you." We said, "We are closed up in a small room and required to remove the prisoners' excrement with the result that our clothes are impure. We also have had no food for three days." He summoned the responsible officers and told them to provide a larger room, stop requiring us to clean up the excrement, start providing us with rations, and from now on cause us no further discomfort. That said, he shook hands with us and departed.

Almighty God gave us aid, and after this it was easy. We said the call to prayer and prayed. We searched and found out that there were about two hundred fifty Muslims in the jail who began to pray with us and often joined our teaching. Thus we spent eighteen days inside the jail before being released.

After this, half of the members turned back, but the rest continued to face further trials.

In the second trial, refugee Sikhs arrived "with guns and rifles ready to kill." The Tablighis besought them for permission to pray, but soon "the floor was red with blood." Through divine aid, however, the guns of the Sikhs jammed, so frightening the Sikhs that they brought a doctor to nurse the Tablighis, and one even stayed on to help guide them on the next stage of their journey.

Again the Tablighis set out, and again they faced a dramatic trial. First, they were imprisoned (after settling at a mosque being used by the government for border control) in an old *haveli* (a courtyard residence) where the well still reeked from the bodies of Muslims killed during Partition and left to die. Found alive a week later, they were ordered to the mountains where yet again the police seized, beat, robbed, and threw them into the Ganges in flood. Divine aid this time came in the form of the roots of a tree, which saved them. They took refuge in a mosque, but when the police arrived, the other Muslims lamented the trouble the Tablighis had brought on them. Then a Sikh police officer, knowing what had happened, declared that the police had been cruel in trying to kill them, and that there clearly was some extraordinary power (*zabardast taaqat*) with them. He expressed his wish to convert to Islam.

We said to him that we were illiterate and had ourselves come out in order to learn our faith. In this gathering there were scholars and pious people, including the Imam of the Panipat mosque and the [Tablighi] head (*zimmedar*) of the district, Muhammad Taqi Sahib. They then had him do the major ablution (*ghusl*) and recite the attestation of faith and fully enter Islam. He said to us, "You are completely free, today there is no further restriction on you."

DISPLAYING A DIVINE VICTORY

After our freedom and the Sikh's acceptance of Islam they got clothes for us and a good provision of milk, sweets, food, etc. It was past 6:00 when we sat down to eat, with the Pure God providing for us after some thirty hours during which, by His power, He kept us in his care. We spent this *'ashara* [first ten days of the month of Muhurram, commemorating the suffering of the Prophet's grandson and companions at Karbala] in a situation of esteem, with Muslims and non-Muslims coming in pilgrimage (*ziyarat*) from afar and asking our prayers. Many apostates on their own re-entered Islam.

THE RETURN TO NIZAMUDDIN AT THE WORD OF HAZRATJI

From here we dispatched our *karguzari* to the Tablighi *markaz*. Hazratji sent money, etc., to us through Miyanji Din Muhammad Marchuni [?], telling us to return with him to Nizamuddin. Thus, after some five and one-half months, we arrived with him at the *markaz* at Nizamuddin and the service of Hazrat

Maulana Muhamad Yusuf (may the mercy of God be upon him). Hazratji heard our whole account in detail and blessed us greatly.

THE WORK OF DA'WAT

Oh estimable Elders! Friends, the Pure God is happy with those servants of his who, for the work of the faith, venture their lives. The High True One will bestow on them rewards in this life and the next—on whomever holds complete belief that He is the bearer of the most exalted qualities, and belief in the divinity, greatness, power, and lordship of the exalted being of the Pure God, and in the sum of his qualities; and those who, as well, have made known the intention of pleasing this Being, their neck bowed in obedience and servanthood; and whoever also holds beloved the traditions (*sunnat*) and treasured being of the Bountiful Messenger (*hazrat akram rasul*) (peace be upon him)—whose hearts are absorbed in prayer, teaching, learning, recitation of the Pure Qur'an, and remembering (*zikr*) God.

Whoever discharges their duties to others, whose prized habits are: what has been taught by superiors, kindness to inferiors, mutual affection, and honesty in interactions; those who hold in their heart sorrow and grief at the effacing of religion; those for whom it is a matter of pleasure to endure troubles on this path, to hear both self-reproach and the reproach of kin, and to take up what is against their own nature; those who want the reward for these sacrifices in the Afterlife and who have ripped out from their hearts this contemptible world— they indeed are those who will receive very high rank in the Afterlife.

Peace.

Sources

The text is from *Ek tablighi jama'at ki karguzari ma' akabir-i tabligh ki cheh baten* (Delhi: Sartaj Kampani, n.d). The selection itself refers to the Qur'an, as well as to two other well-known texts. Maulana Muhammad Zakariyya's *Tablighi Nisab* is a compendium of several works on *faza'il* (the merits of acts of worship), written beginning in the 1930s; these are also available separately and as a compendium issued under the (more common nowadays) alternate title *Faza'il-i A'mal*, not only in their original Urdu but in languages that include English, Arabic, French, and Hindi. Mufti Muhammad Shafi'i's *Ma'arif al-Qur'an* is a multi-volume, late twentieth-century Qur'an commentary by a prominent Deobandi who migrated to Pakistan.

Further Reading

An excellent overview including general articles and case studies from around the world is Muhammad Khalid Masud, ed., *Travellers in Faith: Studies of the Tablighi*

Jama'at as a Transnational Islamic Movement for Faith Renewal (Leiden: E. J. Brill, 2000). See also Yoginder Sikand's *The Origins and Development of the Tablighi Jama'at (1920–2000): A Cross-Country Comparative Study* (New Delhi: Orient Longman, 2002), based on fieldwork in India, Bangladesh, and Britain. Barbara D. Metcalf's "Living Hadith in the Tablighi Jama'at" in *The Journal of Asian Studies* (52, 3 [1993]: 584–608) is a study of a key *tablighi* text, the *Faza'il-i A'mal*.

—19—

A College Girl Gives a Qur'an
Lesson in Bangladesh

Maimuna Huq

For various Islamic activist organizations in Bangladesh and elsewhere, Qur'anic lessons (*dars al-Qur'an,* or simply *dars*)—exegetical talks on Qur'anic themes—are a fundamental tool for the moral and practical training of activists. In large organizations seeking to recruit new members, such lessons are meant not only to assist individual self-cultivation but also to equip each activist to disseminate the group's call for Islamic sociopolitical transformation through the broader medium of "Qur'an classes" or "*tafsir* classes," less-intensive teaching events offered by activists to the public. Qur'anic exegetical talks are also used by less tightly organized movements and by unaffiliated individuals (both those who have trained in traditional religious schools, and, as is increasingly the case, graduates of modern non-religious schools who are nonetheless well versed in Islamic knowledge as a result of personal study) to restore the morality of the surrounding social terrain and promote individual religiosity in local neighborhoods.

The text below is a *dars* delivered by a member of an Islamic activist organization of women students, the *Bangladesh Islami Chatri Sangstha* (Bangladesh Female Students' Islamic Association, BICSA), an informal branch of the Jama'at-i Islami Bangladesh (whose Indian organization is discussed in Chapter 34). This particular *dars* was part of a neighborhood-based BICSA organizational meeting conducted in a lower-middle-class residential area in Dhaka, Bangladesh, on May 28, 2003. The subject text of this *dars,* verses 284–286 of *Surah Baqarah* of the Qur'an, had been announced at the previous meeting (about a week and a half before) so that members would have time to prepare. BICSA *dars* meetings, intended for relatively new and inexperienced members, usually take place three times a month. Group size is typically from four to ten. The leader or chairwoman of the group selects a member at random to deliver the *dars*. Hence all members must prepare for it. Following the delivery of the *dars*, which includes first reciting the Arabic verses concerned, members must critique the performance of the deliverer by remarking on the quality of the recitation, the contents of the *dars* delivered, and the style of delivery. Comments are sometimes interspersed with questions. If the deliverer is unable to answer, then either the chairwoman or somebody else may attempt to do so. A kind of discussion follows the delivery of a *dars*, and this seems to serve three purposes. First, through questions and comments, it allows for clarification of details and of any murky areas for both the speaker and listeners, and it trains activists in the art of posing questions. Second, the deliverer gets direct feedback on her performance and can use these comments to improve future performances. Third, the listeners are tested for their attentiveness during the *dars* and are also able to hone their ability to provide "constructive criticism," a skill they will use frequently throughout their activist careers as leaders, colleagues, and administrators.

The Physical Setting

On a hot, humid, sunny afternoon in the lower-middle-class neighborhood of Modhubag within the city of Dhaka, six workers comprising an organizational cell or unit of BICSA gather in the home of Polly, the unit's chairwoman and a first-year college student, for the second "worker meeting" of the month.

The home consists of only two small rooms. Polly's parents occupy one and she and her sister the other. Since her parents' room is even smaller, barely large enough to hold a twin bed, a cupboard for clothing and for storing light winter blankets, and a valet stand, the room she shares with her sister houses the "kitchen" with a kerosene stove and a small bamboo mattress that is spread out on the floor at mealtimes as a makeshift dining area. The few pots and pans the family owns are kept under the bed. Stashed against the bed is an old wooden sideboard containing some melamine plates and bowls and a few glasses used for guests. On the other side of the bed stands a small, rickety chair and table at which Polly and her sister study school texts together for a few hours each evening. Stacked on the table are two neat piles of books and notebooks, one belonging to Polly and the other to her sister.

We sit in a tight circle on the bed Polly shares with her younger sister. The house has a mud floor and walls and ceiling made out of tin, which, being a good conductor of heat, turns the inside of the room into a veritable furnace. The old ceiling fan suspended over the bed rotates sluggishly, but the air inside the room is so hot that the fan seems to have little effect and within minutes, the participants begin to perspire visibly, beads of perspiration appearing on the foreheads of most of the women and then trickling down the faces of some from the edges of the headcoverings that frame their faces so closely that every single strand of hair is tucked well in and cannot escape. Each worker uncovers her face upon entering the room, but despite the intense heat and humidity, not a single woman relaxes her tightly worn headcovering or removes the long-sleeved, ankle-length loose overcoat that she wears over her customary clothing of a *salwar kamiz*, a tunic worn over a pair of loose pants and a light, matching wrap worn loosely across the chest with an end thrown over each shoulder. Motivated largely (but not exclusively) by piety and by the concomitant desire to discipline their emotions and enhance their capacity for embodied devotion to God, BICSA workers strive to dress modestly not only in public, where rigorous veiling (including veiling of most of the face leaving only the eyes open) is compulsory in BICSA, but even indoors, at women-only meetings, where veiling is in theory not obligatory. The room seems to grow warmer as one woman after another drifts in, greeting those present softly with the traditional Islamic greeting of "Peace" (*assalamu alaykum*). Polly places the materials she needs for the meeting before her: her copy of *Tafhim al-Qur'an*, the Qur'anic commentary by the South Asian Islamist Abul A'la Mawdudi (1903–1979), whose writings are basic to Jama'at-i Islami's and hence BICSA's, Islamist ideology; a pen; a personal notebook in which she had recorded points concerning the assigned Qur'anic verses; and an organizational notebook where the unit's secretary usually records the meeting proceedings quite meticulously, since these are periodically reviewed by "auditors" and senior activists from BICSA's central or larger city offices.

A *dars* is central to a typical "worker meeting." In BICSA, medium-level cadres are referred to as "workers," a term possibly picked up from rival Marxist organizations. The meeting had been scheduled to start at 3:00 PM. However, as is quite typical, most members arrive late. Since they must rush home after school ends around 1:30 PM, undress and grab a bite to eat, and then get dressed and walk or travel by rickshaw (a manually driven three-wheeled contraption) to the site of the neighborhood meeting, BICSA workers rarely arrive on time. As always, Polly gently reprimands the latecomers, urging them to be more punctual in the future, and then kicks off the meeting at 3:30 PM. She asks Seema, a twelfth-grade (senior) high-school student, to present the designated *dars*.

The *Dars* Format

Seema first recites the verses in the original Arabic from the first volume of *Tafhim al-Qur'an*. Next she reads out Mawdudi's Bangla translation of the verses and proceeds to elaborate on their meaning. Throughout much of her presentation she adheres closely to Mawdudi's exegesis; however, a proper *dars* includes as many Qur'anic verses (whether from other surahs [chapters of the Qur'an] or other parts of the assigned surah), hadith (teachings traditionally attributed to the Prophet Muhammad), and *bastob udahoron* ("practical examples," real-life applications) as possible to clarify its points. Thus, while BICSA activists are expected to treat Mawdudi's *Tafhim al-Qur'an* as their primary source, they are also encouraged to consult other Islamic literature, especially the passages on the assigned Qur'anic verses that are included the organizational syllabus (authored by Mawdudi and his followers), as these might mention relevant Qur'anic verses, hadith, and examples of real-life applications. Besides *Tafhim al-Qur'an* and other Islamic texts, "training sessions," "teaching camps," and "group meetings" constitute other important sources of information on verses, hadith, and relevant illustrations. Certain surahs, verses, and topics are considered so crucial that these are not only integral to the organizational syllabus and mastered through *dars* at worker meetings, but are studied repeatedly, under the guidance of different leaders, through different training programs, and in greater depth than that possible within the basic structure of a single worker meeting.

Seema's *dars*, extracted below, provides us with some sense of the structure, scope, and content of the Qur'anic lessons typically delivered at BICSA worker meetings. Following Mawdudi's style of exegesis—a relatively simple, methodical form derived from traditional exegesis—Seema works her way through a series of sub-topics: Naming, Period of Revelation, Historical Context, Summary of Verses, and Explanation of Verses. Up to this point, she more or less paraphrases Mawdudi, hopefully making his ideas more accessible and attractive to a modern, educated Bangladeshi audience by transposing them into contemporary Bangla. As she moves into the explication of the particular verses under discussion, she begins to improvise content as well as form.

Seema discusses each of the assigned (last three) verses of *Surah Baqarah*, verses 284–286, in order. Each verse is explained in parts that center on the successive points the verse is understood as making. Following Mawdudi, Seema explains verse 284 in three parts. The translation of the first part states, *All that is in the heavens and the earth belongs to Allah.* In elaborating, she offers a "practical example" linking this verse directly to daily life and to BICSA's central project of transforming all of social, political, cultural, and economic life in keeping with Islamic guidance. Seema next speaks of the second part of verse 284, which states that Allah knows all that a person thinks, whether they express or conceal it, and that they must account to Allah in the Hereafter. Seema adds to Mawdudi's explanation (*Tafhim al-Qur'an*, vol. 1, 253–254) by linking this part of the verse to Islamic organizational life in BICSA. The third and last part of the verse states that Allah, in his omnipotence, forgives whom He pleases and punishes whom He pleases. Seema complements Mawdudi's explanation with a cautionary note concerning arrogance. She explains this part of the verse in a manner similar to that in which she had explained the earlier two.

At every point, Seema paraphrases Mawdudi but supplements his general points with points drawn from her own experiences and training as a BICSA activist. Verse 286 is relatively clear and self-explanatory. It is divided by Mawdudi (and so by Seema) into five parts, of which she focuses on two. The first part of the verse states that Allah does not burden anybody with responsibilities beyond their capacity. In explaining this verse, Mawdudi says that "it is important to remember in this context that one cannot decide whether one is capable of conducting a particular task or not. Only Allah can know this" (*Tafhim al-Qur'an*, vol. 1, 256). The latter point is of great importance within BICSA's discourse. Sometimes activists are very reluctant to assume certain responsibilities, such as that of a chairwoman of a unit or of a larger administrative division. Such positions are characterized by more and harder duties requiring more time, effort, conviction, and personal sacrifice in terms of school performance, health, career, and familial relationships and expectations. However, while BICSA activists may balk in the beginning at being assigned greater responsibilities by superiors, in most cases they ultimately comply.

Seema concludes her *dars* with a call to action combined with prayers. Ideally, prior to the call, the speaker must summarize the "teachings" of the verses concerned. However, sometimes, in order to stick to the twenty to thirty minutes normally allowed for a *dars*, the speaker skips reviewing the teachings. This time limit is set so that the rest of the agenda of the meeting can be attended to in a timely fashion. A worker meeting usually lasts from one and a half to two hours, not including the offering of the afternoon prayers. The participants must reach home before sunset so that their families do not worry. Upon Seema's completion of her presentation, her peers critique her performance.

While Seema adheres closely to the form and content of Mawdudi's exegesis of *Surah Baqarah*, her presentation is more than an extended paraphrase of Mawdudi and differs from Mawdudi's narrative in two ways. First, in Seema's efforts to transform Mawdudi's commentary (translated from Urdu into Bangla) into an oral presentation sufficiently engaging for an audience largely educated in contemporary Bangla-medium state schools, the language changes significantly and is rendered more accessible to the average modern-educated person in present-day Bangladesh. Even though Bangla translations of Mawdudi's Urdu texts (both his Qur'anic commentary and many other booklets) grow crisper and adhere more closely to modern standard Bangla with each edition, BICSA women sometimes complain that they still find the sentences too tortuous and dry and many of the words too archaic.

Second, Seema improvises occasionally, especially later in her presentation, by linking the Qur'anic verses in question to BICSA activists' lived experience in her offering of "practical examples." She and her peer reviewers also seek to insert additional references to hadith and other surahs in their narratives to lend greater authority to their *Tafhim*-based discussions of the Qur'anic verses. The frequency and quality of such improvisations depend on the extent of a speaker's expertise and preparation. More experienced or advanced workers often quote some of the additional references to Qur'anic verses accurately in Arabic, especially the shorter verses or parts of a verse, and then quote the translation in Bangla. Quoting a verse in Arabic followed by translation carries much more weight and lends greater authority to the point being made than vaguely referring to a surah or a verse and generalizing its content, as workers sometimes do owing either to the limited amount of time they can spare for the preparation of a *dars*, or to a lack of resources (not having easy access to the texts needed, for example), or to the time constraints of the delivery itself—or possibly to some combination of these factors.

Upon Seema's conclusion of her *dars*, the chairwoman, Polly, opens up the floor for comments, asking each member in turn, beginning with the member on Polly's right, to comment on Seema's *dars*. The first commentator begins by commending Seema on her performance. This is typical of the style of "constructive criticism" BICSA encourages. Three other participants then comment on Seema's performance. The chairwoman, Polly, wraps up the *dars* session with comments of her own. Interestingly, as we will see, she begins not with the first theme that has been discussed, the might of Allah, but with the later theme: that Allah does not burden anybody with a responsibility exceeding her capacity.

Seema, her peers, and Polly all seek to understand the assigned verses of *Surah Baqarah* primarily within the context of present-day Islamic movements. They believe that these verses contain guidance particularly crucial and relevant for Islamic activists in Bangladesh today. This is in accord with BICSA's strong emphasis on the following four basic themes: (1) hypocrisy, interpreted in BICSA circles as a privileging of this-worldly desires over otherworldly success that results in lack of commitment to the Islamic movement; (2) emotional discipline, including cultivation of inner zeal toward any movement (Islam-related) work; (3) enthusiastic submission to divinely-ordained "burdens," especially (in BICSA's interpretation) duties assigned by the organization; and (4) accountability not only for one's own actions but also others' actions that have been shaped by one's own. Here, the actions in question are defined as explicit responsibilities entailed by embodying and representing "true Islam" (as understood by BICSA).

Through socially shaped interpretation of the Qur'anic verses discussed above, BICSA women come to see themselves in the image of the early band of besieged Muslims led by the Prophet, thus establishing a strong connection with the Islamic tradition of "striving in the path of Allah" (*jihad fi sabilillah*) against dominant, oppressive foes. A continuity is established with the Prophetic mission to preach and establish Islam. The present day in Bangladesh is imagined as *ayaam-i-jaheliyat*, the alleged period of darkness and ignorance in pre-Islamic Arabia. The truly faithful are those who *wholeheartedly* obey instructions issued from Islamic organizations such as BICSA. Stressed members of those organizations are expected to find emotional relief in the fact that their hardships are far less than those faced by the Prophet and his companions.

However, the standard of moral conduct and the "work methodology" (*kormopodhyoti*) or blueprint for (re)fashioning the self that is derived from Qur'anic verses such as those discussed below is at least as important in the daily lives of BICSA activists as any strategic guidance or emotional support. As the following transcribed presentation and comments reveal, the struggle to transform the self into an ideal Muslim activist is arduous and ongoing for most of BICSA's young women. These are not polished, obedient products of an ideological machine but inchoate human beings, however well trained and committed to submission to an Islamic way of life. These Islamic activist women strive daily to attain a difficult ideal in the midst of a complex—sometimes harmonious and sometimes conflicting—web of desires, motivations, pressures, and influences.

SEEMA'S DARS

I begin with the naming of the *Surah Baqarah*. As is the case with most surahs, there is no significant reasoning behind the naming of this surah. Since all long

Qur'anic surahs treat a wide variety of topics, it is not possible to find a truly appropriate title given the limits of human languages. Thus the Prophet, inspired by Allah, chose merely symbolic names for most surahs; the naming of *Surah Baqarah* was based on nothing more than a mere mention of "cow" somewhere within the body of the surah.

Next I want to say a few words about the period of revelation for this surah. What were the historical circumstances of its revelation? As we know, some surahs, revealed entirely in Mecca prior to the *hijrah*, are simply known as *Makki* surahs. Others, revealed entirely in Medina, are categorized as *Madani* surahs. But this is not true of *Surah Baqarah* and many other such surahs. Much of *Surah Baqarah* was revealed immediately following the Prophet's *hijrah* to Medina, and some smaller parts, such as the verses forbidding interest, were revealed towards the very end of the Prophet's life. The last verses of the surah, that is the verses to be discussed today, however, were revealed in Mecca, prior to the *hijrah*. As is the case with many surahs, the overall arrangement of the verses in *Surah Baqarah* is not synchronic but in keeping with topics being discussed. Thus verses concerning a particular topic have been grouped together in a certain part of the surah even though these verses may have been revealed at different times during the Prophet's lifetime.

Since much of *Surah Baqarah* was revealed towards the very beginning of the Prophet's new life in Medina, marking the beginning of a critical phase in his and his companions' struggle to establish Islam, the historical context is especially significant. A good grasp of this context is thus crucial to the understanding of the surah as a whole. There are four points in this historical context that we should pay attention to.

First, the foremost verses are directed towards the Jewish community in Medina. Until the *hijrah*, revealed Qur'anic verses revealed addressed the pagan Arabs in Mecca, who were unfamiliar with the message of Islam. Thus many *Makki* surahs tried to explain the basic principles of Islam to them, to persuade. These verses also sought to morally train the new Muslims. But after the *hijrah*, the Prophet and his small but growing band of Muslims encountered the Jewish communities adjacent to Medina, who already believed in Allah but had distorted the original message of Islam conveyed to them through the Prophet Moses and the scripture Torah. Thus upon the Prophet's arrival in Medina, Allah instructed him to invite the Jewish community towards the true religion. The 15th and 16th sections of *Surah Baqarah* critique the contemporary Jewish community for having strayed from their true religion, from what had originally been revealed in the Torah.

Second, with the Prophet's arrival in Medina, the call toward Islam reached a new phase. A small Islamic state began to develop. The last twenty-three sections of *Surah Baqarah* thus delineate the guidelines for conducting various aspects of life under this new state—the moral, economic, social, and political.

Third, in this particular surah Allah guides the nascent Muslim community in Medina towards certain measures crucial for its survival at that juncture. Until then, the Prophet and his followers had been scattered in Mecca, preaching largely within their individual homes, neighborhoods, and tribes, and facing persecution there. But upon the *hijrah*, a small Muslim community found itself besieged on all sides by the entire Arab world bent on its destruction. In order to survive and succeed, first, the Muslims were to preach vigorously, persuading as many people as they possibly could to embrace Islam. Second, through intelligent argumentation, the Muslims must prove the falseness of the opposition's ideologies beyond any doubt. Third, despite destitution, resulting from the flight to Medina, and a profound lack of security, owing to besiegement, the Muslims must be steadfast. Fourth, the Muslims must not allow themselves to be cowed by the sheer superior numbers and strength of the non-believers. Fifth, should the pagan Arabs continue to be hostile to the Muslims, the latter must be prepared for armed resistance to ensure the survival and success of Islam.

My last point concerning the historical and sociopolitical context of *Surah Baqarah's* revelation is that this surah discusses different kinds of hypocrisy. In Mecca, prior to the *hijrah*, only one kind of hypocrisy was found. From the description of hypocrites in the Makki period that we find in *Surah Ankabut*, we learn that these individuals recognized Allah but were afraid to declare themselves Muslim in public out of fear of persecution. Their hypocrisy basically lay in the weakness of their faith. They believed but were not willing to take any risks on account of their faith. However, in Medina, and thus in a later stage of the struggle to uphold Islam, additional types of hypocrites emerged. One group embraced Islam in public, but with the intention of creating chaos (*fitna*) from within. Another group joined Islam only because of its predominance in Medina. But these individuals continued to befriend the non-believers as well. This way, they felt their interests would be best protected regardless of whether the Muslims or the non-believers prevailed at any particular time. Yet a third group of hypocrites embraced Islam because most members of their families or tribes had become Muslims, and they wanted to fit in. But since these individuals did not embrace Islam out of sincere conviction, they felt constantly torn between Islam and paganism. A final group of hypocrites was characterized by a lack of sincerity. These people believed in Islam but were not sufficiently committed to practice Islam conscientiously in every aspect of life.

What then is the gist (*mool boktobyo*) of these verses? In these verses, Allah outlines the key teachings of Islam, those beliefs fundamental to Islam, such as the belief in Allah's Unity, in the books Allah revealed, in the prophets and messengers He sent, etc. These constitute the eternal work methodology (*kormopodhyoti*) for a worker of Islam.

What does Allah say in verse 284? He says: "All that is in the heavens and the earth belongs to Allah. Whether you disclose whatever is in your heart or conceal it, Allah will call you to account for it, and then will forgive whomever He wills, and will chastise whomever He wills. Allah has power over everything."

The key message of Islam is that we must obey Allah because we, and everything else in this and any other world, belong to Him. And yet, we habitually say things like MY home, MY car, MY wealth, MY talents, etc. And when we think like this, we also become arrogant and prone to using these things as though these truly belonged to us. But if we realize the truth, that we are merely trustees where all that we enjoy and all our possessions and gifts are concerned, we will feel bound to use these only in the way Allah prescribes. And what is this way? We must use all that we possess, every resource, every skill, to realize Islam both in our own daily individual lives and in every other aspect of life—social, political, cultural, economic. We must thank Allah constantly for His numerous blessings—such as the very air we breathe and the very food we eat.

Sometimes those of us involved in the Islamic movement perform duties halfheartedly; we may appear enthusiastic externally but may grumble internally. Since Allah knows not only what we express but what we hide as well, we must strive to harmonize our internal state with our external performances. In other words, we must try to purify our souls and discipline our emotions, for intention is as crucial in Islam as the performance itself, if not more so.

Sometimes we think that by joining the Islamic movement we have become superior to others, that Allah is more likely to forgive our sins. We tend to judge others on the basis of little evidence, confident that Allah will surely punish certain individuals. But this is not so. Only Allah knows whom He will pardon and whom He will punish in the end.

What does Allah say in verse 285? He says: "The Messenger believes, and so do the believers, in the guidance sent down upon him from his Lord: each one believes in Allah, and in His angels, and in His Books, and in His Messengers. They say: 'We make no distinction between any of His messengers. We hear and obey. Our Lord! Grant us Your forgiveness; to You we are destined to return.'"

This verse articulates the fundamental Islamic beliefs and "work methodology" (kormopodhyoti). The beliefs are those in Allah, in His angels, books, and prophets, and in the Last Day of Judgment. The only right course of action open to a believer is complete obedience to Allah's commands. Muslims must not brag about their good deeds but must constantly, as in the verse, seek Allah's forgiveness. The issues of obedience and of vigilance against complacency and vanity are very important. First, I want to talk a little about obedience, which seems especially important for our purposes as workers of Islam. Allah is stating the defining characteristic of the believers here: *they hear and obey*. We know from the hadith that the verse forbidding alcohol was revealed at a time when alcohol was widely consumed in Arab society. As soon as Muslims heard the new verse, bottles of alcohol were thrown out of the house and glasses cast to the floor; it was as though Arabia was flooded with discarded alcohol. Then we know of another companion who had been drinking alcohol but induced vomiting as soon as he heard the new command. This is the way Muslims at that time responded to Allah's command. How do we compare with that? For instance, we know that each of the five daily prayers must be observed with great care and that observing *porda* [veiling for women] is obligatory (*foroz*), but do we observe these things adequately? We know that every task we perform for the Islamic organization is obligatory, but we are often reluctant to perform the duties the organization assigns to us. The other thing we should pay attention to in this verse is that we must never fail to thank Allah for enabling us to do some good.

In addition to obeying each and every one of Allah's commands eagerly, we must also guard constantly against arrogance. The Islamic prescription for responding to success contrasts sharply with the manner in which victory is celebrated in current Bangladeshi political culture: What happens in our country when a political leader is victorious? We see processions of glee and triumph (*anondo michil, bijoy michil*) with people singing, dancing, and chanting arrogant slogans glorifying the leader. But what are we told in *Surah Nasr*? We see that when Prophet Muhammad (peace be upon him) finally succeeded in establishing Islam in Arabia following a long, hard, perilous struggle of twenty-three years, a lot of persecution, and many sacrifices, Allah instructed him that when you see people embracing Islam in groups and large numbers, express your gratitude to Allah and seek His forgiveness. Thus, whenever our work for the cause of Allah results in any measure of success, we must never feel that we have done enough, but we must always thank Allah instead in remembrance that it is Allah who has facilitated our success. We know from the hadith that a person, no matter how pious in every other way, will not be able to enter paradise as long as an iota of vanity remains within them. Today, the need for humility, perseverance, self-critique, and greater sacrifice in emulation of the Prophet and his companions is greater than ever before.

What does Allah say in verse 286? He says: "Allah does not lay a responsibility on anyone beyond his capacity. In his favor shall be whatever good each one does, and against him whatever evil he does. (Believers! Pray thus to your Lord): O Lord! Take us not to task if we forget or commit mistakes. Our Lord! Lay not on us a burden such as You laid on those gone before us. Our Lord! Lay not on us burdens which we do not have the power to bear. And overlook our faults, and forgive us, and have mercy upon us. You are our Guardian; grant us victory, then, against the unbelieving folk."

We must not mistakenly use this verse as an excuse for not practicing this or that command of Allah, because all Islamic requirements, such as veiling, struggling to establish Islam, praying, etc., have always been well within human ability to follow. Additionally, we must remember that any responsibility we encounter, in fact, comes from Allah. Thus, we must do our very best to attend to any responsibility that comes our way.

The last part of this verse is essentially a prayer that is particularly useful for Islamic workers such as ourselves. In this verse, Allah Himself teaches us how to implore Him for mercy, forgiveness, and help in encounters with the infidels. Since the Giver Himself shows the way to beseech Him, there is no doubt such a prayer would be heard. This very certainty was meant to effectively comfort the new band of severely persecuted Muslims in Mecca, for this verse [*Our Lord! Lay not on us a burden such as You laid on those gone before us. Our Lord!*

Lay not on us burdens which we do not have the power to bear] was revealed during that very difficult period just prior to the *hijrah*, around the time of the *mi'raaj*. This prayer is therefore particularly relevant for us. We become flustered even though, thanks to Allah, the opposition we encounter is far less harsh than the kind of persecution the Prophet's companions faced in Mecca. Thus, even though we know that the course of an Islamic movement is necessarily characterized by numerous difficulties, we must constantly pray to Allah that the hardships He tests us with do not exceed our capacities for endurance.

A second thing to note about Verse 286 is that it ends with "Help us in our encounter with the unbelievers." This is important for the moral training of Islamic movement workers. Here Muslims are being told not to channel their emotions in an erroneous manner, but to cultivate these in accordance with this prayer. Even though the unbelievers persecuted the Muslims in Mecca severely at that time, Allah taught the Muslims not to curse the enemy out of frustration or to seek revenge. Thus we, too, must not lose patience in the face of harassment, but must persevere, as contentedly and successfully as possible, in our preaching and other efforts to establish Islam. We must not express any arrogance or irritation or anger towards our opponents, but must pray for their guidance and must try to respond to them in an intelligent manner.

I close my *dars* with the prayer that Allah enable us to sincerely realize in our practical lives every teaching we have garnered from the verses discussed today. May He enable us to remain steadfast on His path. Amen.

Seema's *dars* is followed by some brief encouraging comments from her peers, who praise her performance, but also suggest various kinds of improvement. One worker, for instance, advises that Seema consider reciting the Qur'an regularly following the dawn prayer in order to attain greater fluency and that, more importantly, such a practice also helps cultivate intimacy with Allah. Another worker points out that Seema might have used more citations from the Qur'an and hadith in her talk.

POLLY, THE CHAIRWOMAN, OFFERS A FEW WORDS IN CLOSING

Alhamdulillah (praise be to God). Seema has recited well and, Allah willing, she will benefit from the other sisters' important comments on pronunciation and practice. Seema has presented the *dars* beautifully. Training ourselves to prepare *dars* well and to present it well is vital for our organization, but often we are not willing to spend the time and energy required for such a task. Oftentimes we are negligent towards our organizational responsibilities. And yet, as we learned today and have heard many times before today, our responsibilities are ultimately assigned from above and Allah never delegates responsibilities in excess of our abilities. We cannot know whether we can successfully carry out our duties in the end or not, only Allah can know that. All we are charged with is doing our very best and doing so not reluctantly but with eagerness and deter-mination, for our sole purpose is to please Allah.

We have been reminded today of the greatness of Allah's power. He created and owns everything. Despite how wealthy or talented or courageous we might be, none of these has any real merit till invested in the way pleasing to Allah. This theme of Allah's might reverberates throughout *Surah Baqarah* and through-out the Qur'an for that matter. The last three verses of *Surah Hashr*, for instance, state some of Allah's powers.

Secondly, we discussed Islam's basic rules and regulations and the need for us to cohere our emotions with these fundamentals. Since as verse 284 states, Allah knows both what we reveal and what we don't, and we must account to Him for both. It's essential that not only our words and actions but also our very thoughts and feelings be aligned with the principles of Islam. We know from a hadith how concerned the Prophet's companions became upon the revelation of this verse, since undesirable thoughts sometimes entered even *their* minds despite their outstanding discipline and devotion to Allah and His Prophet. The Prophet responded, in resonance with the Qur'an, that the very characteristic of a believer is that he hears and obeys, and that with sufficient practice, this becomes habitual, and that should one err despite one's most sincere efforts, then one must ask for forgiveness, and surely, Allah is most merciful, most com-passionate. Allah then revealed the verse stating that Allah's commands are al-ways within our ability to follow. Thus whenever an instruction is in accord with the Qur'an and hadith, we must obey promptly and as happily as possible.

Since Allah is just, everybody will be accountable only for his deeds alone, never for the deeds of another. However, we know from a hadith that should a person's bad influence lead others astray, then he will be held accountable for all those bad deeds committed as a result of his influence, not only during his lifetime but even after his death. Similarly, should a person inspire others to do good deeds, then he will be rewarded for those good deeds committed as a re-sult of his influence during his life and after. This is very important for us, since to many we represent true Islam, we are role models. People see that we observe *porda* properly, that we are affiliated with an Islamic organization, and that we seem to know more about Islam than others. So they are likely to observe us closely, to follow us, and to learn from us. This means Allah would hold us re-sponsible should anything in our behavior or deeds misguide anybody in any way and lead that person and others towards bad deeds. We must therefore con-stantly strive to better ourselves as Muslims, to acquire greater knowledge, to practice Islam more closely. We must constantly practice vigilance, especially in purifying our moral state to cohere with our appearance and words as war-riors of Islam.

Note: In transliterating Bangla words, I have preferred to go by the modern, standard pronunciation rather than following the conventional system, which treats Bangla words as though they were Sanskrit.

Further Reading

While much has been written about the resurgence of Islamic movements over the past three decades, the concomitant proliferation of religious study circles has so far drawn little attention. A pioneering essay in this area is Hakan Yavuz's "Nur Study Circles (Dershanes) and the Formation of New Religious Consciousness in Turkey," in Ibrahim M. Abu-Rab, ed., *Islam at the Crossroads: On the Life and Thought of Bediuzzaman Said Nursi* (Albany: State University of New York Press, 2003), 297–316. For a rich description of specific texts read by participants in the transnational Islamic pietist group Tabligh Jama'at, see Barbara D. Metcalf, "Living Hadith in the Tablighi Jama'at," *The Journal of Asian Studies* 52, no. 3 (1993): 584–608. Illuminating glimpses into the pedagogical world of women in the mosque movement in Cairo are found in the groundbreaking study by Saba Mahmood, *Politics of Piety: The Islamic Revival and the Feminist Subject* (Princeton, NJ: Princeton University Press, 2005), pp. 79–117. For another instructive treatment of women's religious lesson practices, see the essay on present-day Oman by Mandana E. Limbert, "Gender, Religious Knowledge and Education in Oman," in Paul Dresch and James Piscatori, eds., *Monarchies and Nations: Globalisation and Identity in the Arab States of the Gulf* (London: I. B. Tauris, 2005), pp. 182–201. The pioneering article by Dale Eickelman, "The Art of Memory: Islamic Education and Its Social Reproduction," *Comparative Studies in Society and History* 20, no. 4 (1978): 485-516, remains a classic in the broader field of traditional Islamic education; it identifies and analyzes informal study practices in early to mid twentieth-century Morocco. A similar kind of informal Islamic peer learning is investigated in the shifting contexts of late twentieth-century Yemen through the educational practices in the life of a modern Yemeni student in the seminal essay by Brinkley Messick, "Genealogies of Reading," in S. C. Humphreys, ed., *Cultures of Scholarship* (Ann Arbor, MI: University of Michigan Press, 1997), pp. 387–412.

Guidance, Sharia, and Law

GUIDANCE, SHARIA, AND LAW

Introduction

Barbara D. Metcalf

In the last section, "The Transmission of Learning," we focused on texts demonstrating the transmission of doctrine, hadith, spiritual disciplines, basic rituals, and Qur'anic lessons in manuals, popular texts, school teaching, preaching missions, and study circles. We turn now to institutions that seek to provide guidance, or to adjudicate correct Islamic behavior, in light of the ethical parameters of *shari'a* that, ideally, are informed by this transmitted knowledge. These institutions include the precolonial qadi or *qazi* (judge), official colonial and postcolonial secular courts, informal courts, fatwas, and a new style of popular leaders who establish themselves through public appearances, publications, and other media. The Arabic term *shari'a* points to the proper "path" for ethical conduct in all dimensions of life. As such, it is far more encompassing and far less codified than a translation like "law" (as in "*shari'a* means Islamic law") would suggest.

Muslim rulers did indeed establish courts to deal with crimes and civil conflicts, but a great deal was beyond court jurisdiction—matters related to piety or traits of character, for example, like the fatwas discussed below in Chapter 26 advising questioners about choosing proper names. Thus, to underline the point made above, *shari'a* entails far *more* in terms of ethical behavior than is legally enforceable. Conversely, *shari'a* may in actual practice involve *less* than one might expect. State interests, not sacred texts, have typically informed administrative or revenue regulations. Similarly, Muslim rulers themselves might well be guided by ethical norms conducive to larger issues of political stability and social well-being that take precedence over specific *shari'a* guidance, the subject of Chapter 21. Finally, court officials facing local customary practices might in actual practice be limited in their ability to influence what they deemed correct behavior. This was the situation of a fourteenth-century *qazi*, for example, confronting regional patterns of dress in the selection in Chapter 20.

The *qazi* in question is the North African, Ibn Battuta (1304–1377), introduced in Chapter 9 in relation to his devotion to Sufis. The sultans of the era founded and supported madrasas for the training of 'ulama, whom they consulted and appointed as teachers, prayer leaders, preachers, guardians of pious endowments (*waqf*, pl. *auqaf*), and *qazis* to uphold justice in urban settings. But they also welcomed an outsider like Ibn Battuta, in part as a tool to curb any local power base, in part to bring honor to the court by patronizing a scholar from afar. As a *qazi* in the Maldives, Ibn Battuta encountered cultural practices completely unlike his own. He intervened in some cases, gave up on others, but overall recognized the piety of Muslims whose everyday practices diverged dramatically from his.

In Chapter 21, Muzaffar Alam argues that the Mughal rulers, in power from the sixteenth through the eighteenth century, opted for pragmatism, justice, and their subjects' well-being over any religious code. The Mughals in many ways adhered to their Timurid heritage, he suggests, by their creation of a culturally plural elite, their characteristic openness to sectarian variety, and their lack of any narrow ideological program. All of this, Alam argues, was evident in the pride of place they gave to a thirteenth-century Persian treatise on political ethics, the *Akhlaq-i Nasiri*, composed by Khwaja Nasir al-Din Tusi, a text widely taught in madrasas in Mughal India. It was regularly read aloud to the illiterate Akbar (r. 1556–1605). As Alam's translation of the perhaps surprising dialogue between a sultan and a *qazi* suggests, rulers were more pragmatic than ideological in actual practice.

As the British established territorial power in the late eighteenth century, they staked their legitimacy on the grounds that theirs was to be a "rule of law." This was what defined them in contrast to the "despotism" they imagined to sum up the "East." Under Warren Hastings, Governor-General of Bengal from 1772–1785, they moved quickly to take into their own hands criminal law, seen as key to securing stability, and began a process that would culminate in a codified criminal law such as Britain itself did not possess. Most important of the changes in relation to Islamic precedents was the move to make many crimes, of which murder was the most important, a crime against the state and not against a family, which could negotiate forms of settlement.

As for non-criminal matters, Hastings and others operated under the assumption that India had law codes which had, over time, become corrupted, and that they, the new rulers, would now restore codes to deal with matters of "personal law": marriage, divorce, inheritance, adoption, and the like. There were, to their way of thinking, distinct and separate codes for "Hindus" and "Muslims." Thus they not only drew a line between these two groups but also posited a single set of "laws" as the norm for populations that in fact varied internally by sect, caste, and regional culture, to say nothing of familiarity with any kind of textual practice at all. As a result, colonial courts would play a significant and perhaps surprising role in "Islam in practice."

The new system of law inaugurated the practice of making "religion," in this reified sense, fundamental to British administration as colonial rule progressed. The result was a "homogenization" of law. In the case of the Hindu code, this entailed a Brahmanization of norms and gave an unprecedented role to Brahman scholars. Until 1864, Hindu *pandits* and Muslim *maulavis* were attached to the courts as advisors. But the goal now was to make texts the guide. "Anglo-Mohammedan law," as it was called, turned to a few late medieval Central Asian texts, like al-Marghi-nani's *Hidaya*, as the basis for legal decisions.

Alan Guenther (in Chapter 22) provides an example of a decision rendered under Anglo-Mohammedan law at the end of the nineteenth century in the High Court for upper India at Allahabad. As Guenther points out, the judge in this case was a Muslim, son of the leading modernist thinker and activist of the late nine-teenth century and the first Muslim to be appointed to any high court in India. It was thus by chance that a Muslim jurist participated in a case entailing Islamic be-liefs and practices; more typically, as exemplified in Chapter 27, non-Muslim ju-rists would play that role. Educated at Cambridge, the judge's legal reasoning was that of the British legal traditions of procedures and precedents, not the tradition of the madrasa (which is represented in Chapters 20, 24, and 26). His background would be typical of Muslim judges throughout the colonial system.

Yet the case entailed nothing less than the anomaly of a colonial court defining the parameters of legitimate participation in ritual practice! Such delineating of re-ligious boundaries was not uncommon in the colonial courts; in fact there were cases that adjudicated matters of doctrine, not only, as in the case here, of prac-tice. These decisions are the more striking in light of the Queen's Proclamation of 1858 assuring non-interference in religion on the part of the government. The court's initial point of entry into this nineteenth-century case, as in the later Shah Bano case (Chapter 27), was an issue of criminal law, thus reinforcing a governing perspective that often linked "religion" to issues of law and order.

Anglo-Mohammedan law is not some unmediated "Islamic law," as Hastings imagined it. The Muslim jurist and scholar, A.A.A. Fyzee (1899–1981), argued that neither Anglo-Mohammedan law nor its successor in independent India, Muslim Personal Law, was *shari'a* as such, but rather, as he put it, a compound of the *shari'a*, case law, and the influence of English procedures and such English legal principles as "justice, equity, and good conscience" that judges were called upon to employ. Apart from the abolition of Islamic criminal law in favor of the Indian Penal Code, gone were provisions for apostasy and legal slavery; new was criminalization of such practices as child marriage; new, as well, rules of equity that shaped some property decisions. British usage defined laws of evidence and procedure, and case law constrained judges in new ways.

Public debates about law in the colonial period impacted Hindu law—and community identity—differently from Muslim law. At key moments, controversy over what were seen primarily as matters of Hindu practice, all of them in relation to women, dominated an emerging public sphere and culminated in the passage of positive laws. These laws included the abolition of *sati* (1829), the legalization of Hindu widow remarriage (1856), specification of the legal age of marital cohab-itation (1891), and legal penalties for child marriage (1929). Mobilization in rela-tion to these acts, whether defensive or reformist, implicitly contributed to mak-ing Hinduism central to Indian nationalism.

Key colonial laws codifying issues of Mohammedan law came later, and they were never subject to as much public debate. The driving force behind these laws was arguably less a concern to reform than to preserve the practical interests of Muslim families and communities. Thus the Musalman Waqf Validating Act (1913) fostered the preservation of family wealth in inheritance; the Dissolution of Muslim Marriages Act (1939) protected erosion of Muslim numbers by allowing divorce without women's resorting to conversion; and the Muslim Personal Law (*Shari'at*) Application Act (1937), was, above all, intended as a symbol of unity as the Muslim League competed for votes at the end of the colonial period. This last Act in principle challenged "customary law" that had protected family lands and the dominance of "tribal" chiefs in places like Punjab through non-Islamic inheritance customs that in particular prohibited female inheritance.

A leading scholarly figure in encouraging the Dissolution of Muslim Marriages Act was the Deobandi Maulana Ashraf 'Ali Thanawi (1863–1943), a prolific writer and spiritual guide to large numbers of disciples. Thanawi, faced with the reality that desperate Muslim women were resorting to apostasy to escape unwanted marriages, demonstrated that resources for engaging with contemporary problems were available within the historic tradition. To this end, he wrote *Al Hilatun Najiza*, a document of great importance in providing alternatives to apostasy for wives seeking divorce. Although firmly committed to preserving Hanafi law, in this instance he allowed as one strategy teachings of a different law school, the Maliki.

In Chapter 23, Fareeha Khan translates a section of another treatise by Thanawi, in this case one on family obligations. This was a document, Khan argues, intended for both a scholarly and a general audience. In relation to this document, she asks whether the specific teachings of the traditionalist 'ulama represented only rigid regurgitation of old teachings, or did they offer fresh engagement with individual and social issues of the day. In answer to this important question, Khan suggests that a scholar like Thanawi did indeed respond to new social issues, but that he did so, as the treatise shows, from within the historic learnèd tradition transmitted through madrasa education.

A younger contemporary of Thanawi's serves as a reminder that others besides the 'ulama now sought to speak authoritatively on matters of personal behavior and morality. Hazrat Inayat Khan (1882—1927) began his career as a musician at the princely court of Baroda. He subsequently found his way to a role, largely in Europe, as a kind of modern self-made holy man, a pattern in some ways pioneered by the Hindu Swami Vivekananda (1863–1902), who first captivated audiences at the World Parliament of Religions in Chicago in 1893. What Inayat Khan offered was presented as universal truth. He, and teachers like him, thus provided a presumed solution to the twentieth-century dilemma of religious traditions with competing truth claims coming into new interactions with one another. Inayat Khan, as Marcia Hermansen writes in Chapter 25, offered Sufism without Islam. These teachings provided moral instruction, including, as in the excerpt presented here, guidance on issues related to the behavior of women. Inayat Khan's audience in the end was substantially European, and his elegant modern tomb in the shadow of the old tomb of Hazrat Nizam al-Din Auliya (d. 1325) attracts many international visitors. (The tomb is shown in Figure I.12 in the Introduction.)

Another contemporary was the prolific writer, traveler, gifted Urdu stylist, and activist, Khwaja Hasan Nizami (1878–1955), a descendant of the great saint of Delhi, Nizam al-Din Auliya. Hasan Nizami launched one of many *tabligh* movements of the era (like the more enduring one described in Chapter 18). He also, Marcia Hermansen tells us in Chapter 25, wrote introductions to other religious traditions with the hope of fostering mutual understanding. Nizami even ventured into the new genre of "ladies'" magazines in his effort to disseminate correct behavior. Such teachings on proper behavior for Muslims, although often interpreted as separatist, were in part fueled by a quest for social mobility and respectability, as Nizami's injunction to act like "English women and well-educated Indian ladies" suggests. This was a common motive of women's reform across religious traditions.

In the interwar period when all three of these figures were active, many Muslim political leaders saw their position enhanced by transnational ties. Indian support to Muslims in the Ottoman lands was evident as early as the Russo-Turkish war of 1878 and took organizational form in associations to defend Muslim interests in the Hejaz during the pre–World War I Balkan Wars. The end of the Great War brought acute disappointment to Indians generally at Britain's failure to fulfill what had seemed a promise of self-determination, made the worse by heavy-handed post-war security laws and repression. For Muslims especially, however, there was also outrage at British treatment of the Ottoman Empire, expressed in the formation of the Khilafat Movement to defend the spiritual authority of the sultan as caliph. Muslim leaders of this movement found sympathetic supporters in Gandhi and others in the Indian National Congress, and they eagerly joined in Gandhi's nationalist movement of non-cooperation.

In Chapter 24, Ebrahim Moosa presents a speech from the 1920s favoring the creation of separate Muslim courts outside the colonial state, an idea launched as part of the non-cooperation movement that used boycott of government institutions as a powerful form of protest. The speaker, Abul Mahasin Muhammad Sajjad (d. 1940), was an active member of the Jamiat-e-Ulama Hind (Organization of Ulama of India), founded in 1918 in the course of defending the Khilafat. Sajjad saw the independence movement and his Islamic activism as complementary. The text in this chapter is a speech he delivered to the Bihar provincial Jamiat-e-Ulama. Addresses at the annual meetings of political organizations were important occasions for articulating a platform for action. Reported in the newspapers and often subsequently published, as was the case here, such texts reached an extensive audience. Sajjad's goal of establishing Islamic courts apart from the state achieved some success, in Bihar in particular. Such courts continue to exist in Bihar and elsewhere in limited numbers, and are meant to serve as an alternative, both quicker and more Islamic, to government courts.

Throughout, the 'ulama continued to provide guidance by issuing advisory opinions or fatwas. Fatwas now are found on the Web, and interactive sites invite questions from those seeking guidance. In Chapter 26, Khalid Masud translates several fatwas offering guidance on the proper name to give a child, echoing one of Ismaiʿil Shahidʾs reformist points presented in Chapter 15, where he discouraged names that gave undue honor to prophets, saints, and imams. The earlier fatwas are translated from printed books; the last, taken from a Web site. This last scholarʾs weekly talks (*bayan*) can similarly be heard through the Web worldwide. Fatwas and guidance now circulate at great speed internationally.

Although informal courts and individual scholars give advice in India, where Muslims live as a minority, the preservation of Muslim Personal Law in the official courts has been a primary concern of the leadership. The issue came to head in the mid-1980s in a legal case concerning the question of long-term maintenance for an elderly woman, Shah Bano, following her divorce. The case exemplified the tension between sympathy for a minority seeking to preserve a distinctive culture, on the one hand, and, on the other, a commitment to "gender justice," in this case that a woman be compensated more fully than the modest support seemingly endorsed by Muslim law. In Chapter 27, Sylvia Vatuk provides texts from this debate that reveal the climate of anti-Muslim sentiments and the politicization in which the debate proceeded and an aftermath in which courts argued on *Islamic* grounds for greater latitude than the newly passed positive law seemed to allow.

Although no texts are included on this subject, the efforts within Pakistan to create state-mandated "Islamic law" are a significant development for Islamic practice in the subcontinent. The most important steps in this direction were taken by General Ziaul Haq, who remained in power for eleven years after a military coup in 1977. "Islamization" represented one side of a persistent tension within the country over whether it was a secular state for Muslims, as founders like Jinnah had imagined, or an Islamic state with its institutions in principle derived from Islamic precedents. The key documents for his Islamic program, the *Hudud* Ordinances, provided punishment for criminal offenses like theft and illegal sexual intercourse conflated with rape. Whatever its moral appeal, "Islamization" served to enhance the power of an autocratic ruler who was supported by Saudis and Americans as a surrogate for fighting the Soviets in Afghanistan.

Critics judged the Islamic regulations put in place to be largely cosmetic, and some argued that policies based on true Islamic values would have focused on issues of social justice. The most controversial of these laws were those related to rape and blasphemy. As developments in Pakistan make clear, the sites and institutions engaged with Islamic moral and legal guidance have varied greatly. That continues to be the case today throughout the subcontinent. Even in Pakistan, the sources of Islamic guidance and law continue to be diverse: individual conscience coexists with the authority of holy men and learnèd scholars (in person or electronically present), informal *shariʿa* courts, television personalities, and both secular and Islamic courts.

—20—

Ibn Battuta as a Qadi in the Maldives

Barbara D. Metcalf

The extraordinary journey and travel account of Ibn Battuta have been described above in the Introduction and in Chapter 9. When Ibn Battuta arrived in Delhi, after elaborate preparations of gifts and protocol for his meeting with the sultan, Muhammad Shah Tuqhluq (r. 1325–51), he was warmly welcomed and, at the age of only thirty, appointed as qadi of Delhi. His legal training was modest (and that, too, in the Maliki tradition of jurisprudence, while the Muslim population of north India, with its Central Asian roots, would have been primarily Hanafi). He knew no Persian, the language of the court (for which he was promised an interpreter). His job has every appearance of a sinecure with the everyday work carried out by others. He seems however to have worked hard in a second appointment; namely, superintendence of the mausoleum of Sultan Qutbuddin, the then sultan's predecessor two removes back, in whose service Muhammad Shah had served and whose dignity he saw as associated with his own. Ibn Battuta oversaw several hundred functionaries at the site, including Qur'an reciters, teachers and students, Sufis, and a wide range of maintenance staff. He won approval from the sultan by using the shrine's endowment (*waqf*) to feed the hungry during a period of famine. Ibn Battuta's life in Delhi was not quiet. After many adventures, including falling out of favor with the sultan and retreating to a Sufi hospice, Ibn Battuta was enticed out of seclusion by the sultan to serve as his ambassador to the Mongol king of China.

Ibn Battuta set out with a vast array of retainers, animals, and gifts. Plunder, shipwreck, and other adventures ensued, and he ultimately wound up on the Maldive Islands, off the southwest coast of the subcontinent, where he was inveigled into staying on and becoming the qadi of the island's Maliki population. He was surely right to say, as he did, that he owed his immediate acclaim to the favor he was presumed to enjoy of the powerful sultan in Delhi. But possibly he had also gained credibility simply by dint of being from the Maghreb. In the Maldives, Ibn Battuta heard the legend of a Maghrebi traveler who long ago had defeated a demon who demanded regular female sacrifice. The traveler's weapon was continuous Qur'anic recitation that kept the demon at bay so successfully that he soon disappeared. This story, retold and actually reenacted by the local people on a monthly basis, was remembered as nothing less than the occasion of the islands' conversion to Islam.

Ibn Battuta soon entangled himself in the rivalries and ambitions of the local nobility. He married a noble woman and seems to have taken on the role of *qazi* with energy. Of his domestic life on the Maldives, Ibn Battuta writes, in Mahdi Hussain's translation, "From [their diet, especially fish and coconut products], the inhabitants acquire a remarkable and incomparable sexual vigour, and the islanders are astounding in this respect. I myself had in this country four wives besides slave girls. . . . I have found nowhere in the world women whose society was more pleasant." There seems to have been an ease to marriage and divorce, at least in this geographic area, which would be unheard of in much of Muslim society in later centuries. The practice of "temporary" marriage, with its limited obligations, was current; this was *muta'*, a word Ibn Battuta uses to describe the arrangement made by seamen who came to the Maldives for short stays.

Multiple relationships, marital and political, were not easy to manage. Eight months after his arrival, Ibn Battuta left the islands ensnared in a cloud of divorces, confusion, disagreements, and a certain degree of bad feeling on many sides. In the end, he infuriated the grand wazir, husband of the sultana, over a case involving a slave and a royal concubine, and this was the immediate cause of his decision to depart.

The excerpt below, taken from the translation by H.A.R. Gibb, provides information on several issues relevant to "Islam in practice" in fourteenth-century South Asia. There is clearly great diversity regionally, and even within a single region, in what is regarded as legitimate in relation to such matters as gender roles, family norms (which in the Maldives were both patrilocal and matrilocal, as they were for the Mapilla Muslims of the southwest Indian coast), dress, and taxation. On all these matters, Ibn Battuta notes differences with north India and with what he takes to be Islamic ideals. He tried by persuasion, but with no success, to change women's dress; he had more success in modifying the estate tax. He noted the "strangeness" of there being a woman ruler, with the Friday sermon read in her name, but seemed to accept it. If in these matters there was a generous tolerance on Ibn Battuta's part, on other issues he describes himself as draconian: beating those men who allowed women to stay in their homes after divorce, enforcing male attendance at Friday prayer, and sending out reminders of their duties to imams and muezzins.

As for non-Muslims, here and throughout the account Ibn Battuta evinces complete indifference: their religious behavior, in a sense, was none of his concern. In this regard, the behavior he describes at the shrine of Adam's footprint in Ceylon, a trip he subsequently made, is striking. Hindus, Buddhists, and Muslims alike frequented the place, and he, like the others, seemed to recognize the multiple facets of the site's holiness, variously linked to Adam, the Buddha, and Lord Siva. This is a notable contrast to today's nationalist/"fundamentalist" monolithic claims to single truths and single rights over heretofore shared holy places in India and elsewhere, linked as they are to modern nationalism.

In relation to the Islamic practices of the Maldives, Ibn Battuta found much, in fact, to admire. As he wrote (in Mahdi Husain's translation):

> The inhabitants of these islands are upright and religious and are men of right beliefs and good intentions. Their diet is consistent with the Islamic law (shari'at) and their prayers are accepted by the Almighty God. When one man meets another he says to the latter, "God is my Lord, Muhammad my Prophet and I am a poor ignoramus."

Ibn Battuta wrote approvingly of the many wooden mosques of the islands. He also, no doubt, was impressed with the respect shown to him. When anyone met a *qazi* or preacher, he would, apparently, remove his upper garment as a mark of humility and accompany the Islamic scholar to his destination. The islanders also shared his respect for holy men. When a group of darwishes arrived, coming from a visit to the shrine of Adam's footprint in Ceylon, for example, many of the notables contributed to a feast he organized in their honor. At the feast, ecstatic song and dance allowed them to enter unharmed a fire, prepared by the *qazi* Ibn Battuta, whose Islamic practice, like that of the populations he lived among, had many strands.

FROM THE *RIHLA* OF IBN BATTUTA

TRANSLATED BY H.A.R. GIBB [HG]

The people of the Maldive Islands are upright and pious, sound in belief and sincere in thought; their bodies are weak, they are unused to fighting, and their armour is prayer. Once when I ordered a thief's hand to be cut off, a number of those in the room fainted. . . . Their womenfolk do not cover their heads, not even their queen does so, and they comb their hair and gather it at one side. Most of them wear only an apron from their waist to the ground, the rest of their bodies being uncovered. When I held the qadiship there, I tried to put an end to this practice and ordered them to wear clothes, but I met with no success. No woman was admitted to my presence in a lawsuit unless her body was covered, but apart from that I was unable to affect anything. I had some slave-girls who wore garments like those worn at Delhi and who covered their heads, but it was more of a disfigurement than an ornament in their case, since they were not accustomed to it. A custom among them is to hire themselves out as servants in houses at a fixed wage of five dinars or less, their employer being responsible for their upkeep; they do not look upon this as dishonourable, and most of their girls do so. You will find ten or twenty of them in a rich man's house. Every utensil that a girl breaks is charged up against her. When she wishes to transfer from one house to another, her new employers give her the sum which she owes to her former employers; she pays this to the latter and remains so much in debt to her new employers. The chief occupation of these hired women is spinning *qanbar* [coconut fiber]. It is easy to get married in these islands on account of the smallness of the dowries and the pleasure of their women's society. When ships arrive, the crew marry wives, and when they are about to sail they divorce them. It is really a sort of temporary marriage. The women never leave their country.

It is a strange thing about these islands that their ruler is a woman, Khadija. The sovereignty belonged to her grandfather, then to her father, and after his death to her brother Shihab ad-Din, who was a minor. When he was deposed and put to death some years later, none of the royal house remained but Khadija and her two younger sisters, so they raised Khadija to the throne. She was married to their preacher, Jamal ad-Din, who became Wazir and the real holder of authority, but orders are issued in her name only. They write the orders on palm leaves with a curved iron instrument resembling a knife; they write nothing on paper but copies of the Koran [Qur'an] and works on theology. When a stranger comes to the islands and visits the audience-hall, custom demands that he take two pieces of cloth with him. He makes obeisance towards the Sultana and throws down one of these cloths, then to her Wazir, who is her husband Jamil ad-Din, and throws down the other. Her army comprises about a thousand men, recruited from abroad, though some are natives. They come to the palace every day, make obeisance, and retire, and they are paid in rice monthly. At the end of each month they come to the palace, make obeisance, and say to the Wazir, "Transmit our homage and make it known that we have come for our pay," whereupon orders are given for it to be issued to them. The qadi and the officials, whom they call Wazirs, also present their homage daily at the palace, and after the eunuchs have transmitted it they withdraw. The qadi is held in greater respect among the people than all the other functionaries; his orders are obeyed as implicitly as those of the ruler or even more so. He sits on a carpet in the palace, and enjoys the entire revenue of three islands, according to ancient custom. There is no prison in these islands; criminals are confined in wooden chambers intended for merchandise. Each of them is secured by a piece of wood, as is done among us [in Morocco] with Christian prisoners. . . .

The custom of the country is that no one may go ashore without permission. When permission was given to us I wished to repair to one of the mosques, but the attendants on shore prevented me, saying that it was imperative that I should visit the Wazir. I had previously enjoined the captain of the ship to say, if he were asked about me, "I do not know him," fearing that I should be detained by them, and ignorant of the fact that some busybody had written to them telling them about me and that I had been qadi at Delhi. On reaching the palace we halted in some porticoes by the third gateway. The qadi 'Isa of Yemen came up and greeted me and I greeted the Wazir. The captain brought ten pieces of cloth and made obeisance towards the Sultana, throwing down one piece, then to the Wazir, throwing down another in the same way. When he had thrown them all down he was asked about me and answered, "I do not know him." Afterwards they brought out betel and rose-water to us, this being their mark of honour, and lodged us in a house, where they sent us food, consisting of a large platter of rice surrounded by plates containing salted meat, chickens, ghee, and fish. Two days later the Wazir sent me a robe, with a hospitality-gift of food and a hundred thousand cowries for my expenses.

When ten days had passed a ship arrived from Ceylon bringing some darwishes, Arabs and Persians, who recognized me and told the Wazir's attendants who I was. This made him all the more delighted to have me, and at the beginning of Ramadan he sent for me to join in a banquet attended by the amirs and ministers. Later on I asked his permission to give a banquet to the darwishes who had come from visiting the Foot [of Adam, in Ceylon—HG]. He gave permission, and sent me five sheep, which are rarities among them because they are imported from Ma'bar, Mulaybir, and Maqdashaw, together with rice, chickens, ghee, and spices. I sent all this to the house of the Wazir Sulaymin, who had it excellently cooked for me, and added to it besides, sending carpets and brass utensils. I asked the Wazir's permission for some of the ministers to attend my banquet, and he said to me, "And I shall come too." So I thanked him and on returning home to my house found him already there with the ministers and high officials. The Wazir sat in an elevated wooden pavilion, and all the amirs and ministers who came greeted him and threw down an unsewn cloth, so that there were collected about a hundred cloths, which were taken by the darwishes. The food was then served, and when the guests had eaten, the Koran-readers chanted in beautiful voices. The darwishes then began their ritual chants and dances. I had made ready a fire and they went into it, treading it with their feet, and some of them ate it as one eats sweetmeats, until it was extinguished. When the night came to an end, the Wazir withdrew and I went with him. As we passed by an orchard belonging to the treasury he said to me, "This orchard is yours, and I shall build a house in it for you to live in." I thanked him and prayed for his happiness. Afterwards he sent me two slave-girls, some pieces of silk, and a casket of jewels.

The attitude of the Wazir afterwards became hostile to me [after complex arrangements over marriages, objections to his departure unless he refunded the gifts given to him, and negotiation that he would be provided a horse—BDM]. Immediately after the Ramadan fast I made an agreement with the Wazir Sulayman to marry his daughter, so I sent to the Wazir Jamil ad-Din requesting that the ceremony might be held in his presence at the palace. He gave his consent, and sent the customary betel and sandalwood. The guests arrived but the Wazir Sulayman delayed. He was sent for but still did not come, and on being summoned a second time excused himself on the ground of his daughter's illness. The Wazir then said to me privately, "His daughter has refused, and she is her own mistress. The people have assembled, so what do you say to marrying the Sultana's mother-in-law?" (It was her daughter to whom the Wazir's son was married.) I said, "Very well," so the qadi and notaries were summoned, and the profession of faith recited. She was the best of women.

After this marriage the Wazir forced me to take the office of qadi. The reason for this was that I had reproached the qadi for his practice of taking a tenth of all estates when he divided them amongst the heirs, saying to him "You should have nothing but a fee agreed upon between you and the heirs." Besides he never did anything properly. When I was appointed, I strove my utmost to establish the prescriptions of the Sacred Law. There are not lawsuits there like those in our land. The first bad custom I changed was the practice of divorced wives of staying in the houses of their former husbands, for they all do so till they marry another husband. I soon put that to rights. About twenty-five men who had acted thus were brought before me; I had them beaten and paraded in the bazaars, and the women put away from them. Afterwards I gave strict injunctions that the prayers were to be observed, and ordered men to go swiftly to the streets and bazaars after the Friday service; anyone whom they found not having prayed I had beaten and paraded. I compelled the salaried prayer-leaders and muezzins to be assiduous in their duties and sent letters to all the islands to the same effect. I tried also to make the women wear clothes, but I could not manage that. . . .

Now it happened that a slave belonging to the sultan Shihab ad-Din was brought before me on a charge of adultery, and I had him beaten and put in prison. The Wazir sent some of his principal attendants to me to ask me to set him at liberty. I said to them, "Are you going to intercede for a Negro slave who has violated his master's honour, when you yourselves but yesterday deposed Shihab ad-Din and put him to death because he had entered the house of one of his slaves?" Thereupon I sent for the slave and had him beaten with bamboo rods, which give heavier blows than whips, and paraded through the island with a rope round his neck. When the Wazir heard of this he fell into a violent rage, assembled the ministers and army commanders and sent for me. I came to him, and though I usually made obeisance to him, I did not make obeisance but simply said *Salam 'aleykum*. Then I said to those present, "Be my witnesses that I resign the office of qadi because of my inability to carry out its duties." . . . The respect in which I was held amongst them was due solely to the sultan of India, for they were aware of the regard in which he held me, and even though they are far distant from him yet the fear of him is in their hearts. . . . [The Wazir] sent [the former qadi to me] to say "you are aiming only at leaving us; give back your wives' dowries and pay your debts and go, if you will."

After travel to Malabar, Sri Lanka, and back to Malabar, where he fell ill, Ibn Battuta heard news of changes in the Maldives as well as of the birth of his son, and he decided to risk a return visit. In terms of Islam "in practice," note his use of a Qur'anic omen (*istikhara*) below, a common method for seeking divine guidance to an action or decision. The wazir in fact welcomed him, but, perhaps moved by the mother's pleas, Ibn Battuta abandoned the idea of recovering his son. After only five days, Ibn Battuta resolved "to hasten [his] departure" and left for Bengal (as described in Chapter 9).

At Calicut, I learned of the marriage of the Sultana Khadija [of the Maldive islands—HG] with the Wazir 'Abdallah after the death of the Wazir Jamal ad-Din, and that my wife, whom I had left there pregnant, had given birth to a son. I thought therefore of making a journey to the islands, but remembering the hostility of the Wazir 'Abdallah towards me I [sought an omen from the Koran and—trans.] opened the volume at these words: *The angels shall descend upon them saying, "Fear not, neither be sad."* So I commended myself to God, and set sail. Ten days later I disembarked at Kannalus, where the governor received me with honour, made me his guest, and fitted out a boat for me. Some of the islanders went to the Wazir 'Abdallah and informed him of my arrival. He asked about me and who had come with me, and was told that the purpose of my visit was to fetch my son, who was about two years old. His mother came to the Wazir to lay a complaint against this, but he replied to her, "I for my part will not hinder him from taking away his son." He pressed me to visit the island [of Mahal—trans.], and lodged me in a house facing the tower of his palace, that he might observe my movements. My son was brought to me, but I thought it better that he should stay with them so I gave him back to them. After a stay of five days, it appeared to me that the best plan was to hasten my departure, and I asked permission to leave. The Wazir summoned me, and when I entered his presence he seated me at his side and asked how I fared. I ate a meal in his company and washed my hands in the same basin with him, a thing which he does with no one. Betel was brought in and I took my leave. He sent me robes and hundreds of thousands of cowries, and was most generous in his treatment of me.

Sources

The translation is excerpted from that of H.A.R. Gibb, *Ibn Battuta: Travels in Asia and Africa 1325–1354* (Delhi: Manohar, 2001), pp. 242–267. Madhi Husain, trans., *The Rehla of Ibn Battuta (India, Maldive Islands and Ceylon)* (Baroda: Oriental Institute, 1953) provides a fuller translation and additional informative notes.

Further Reading

A readable and scholarly retelling of the account is Ross E. Dunn, *The Adventures of Ibn Battuta: A Muslim Traveler of the 14th Century* (Berkeley, CA: University of California Press, 1986). See also Timothy Mackintosh-Smith's recent two-volume travelogue written as he retraced Ibn Battuta's steps, the *Rehla* in hand. The volume covering the India travels is Timothy Mackintosh-Smith, *India: The Hall of a Thousand Columns: Hindustan to Malabar with Ibn Battutah* (London: John Murray, 2005). General historical background to the period is available in Catherine B.

Asher and Cynthia Talbot, *India before Europe* (Cambridge: Cambridge University Press, 2006). For a discussion of *qazi* decisions in Gujarat in the Mughal period, based on primary documents, see Farhat Hasan, *State and Locality in Mughal India: Power Relations in Western India, c. 1572–1730* (Cambridge: Cambridge University Press, 2004).

—21—

Guiding the Ruler and Prince

Muzaffar Alam

The three passages excerpted in this section all deal, in one way or another, with the various efforts of three early Perso-Turkic sultans of Delhi to reconcile the practical realities of exercising Islamic state power in India with the idealized, *shari'a*-based political Islam advocated by the 'ulama. By the thirteenth century, when the Delhi Sultanate was established in northern India, the sultans already had several hundred years of both pre-Islamic and post-Islamic Persian courtly traditions and political philosophy to draw on in organizing their state. This pre-existing body of thought grappled especially with trying to understand the worldly nature and necessity of kingship, especially given Islam's emphasis on social equality. Thus, right from the early centuries, Islamic political and ethical theorists recognized the need to give serious consideration to adjusting the ideals of the *shari'a* to the realities of state formation and social order, and in the process developed an idiom that gave legitimacy to the ordinary duties of the king on the grounds of political expediency.

We see this tension between ruler and religious elite as early as the reign of Sultan Shams al-Din Iltutmish, the first sovereign Delhi sultan, whose wazir was said to have readily dismissed the demand of theologians that the infidel Hindus should either be forced to accept Islam or face death, given that the Muslims in Hindustan were so few, like salt in a dish. Iltutmish continued to show little regard for conservative interpretations of the *shari'a* in other matters, as for instance when, despite having eligible sons, he nominated his daughter Raziya as his successor. Iltutmish also set the pattern for his successors in turning more towards the Sufis than the 'ulama in a bid to seek legitimacy.

This approach to the exercise of state power, regard for local practices and cultivation of relationships with Sufis as a counterbalance to the 'ulama, continued under Ghiyas al-Din Balban, the second major Delhi sultan, who elaborates on these principles in his *wasaya* (advice) to his son Bughra Khan, in the first selection below.

The author of this section, and of the one that follows, is the courtier and historian Zia al-Din Barani (d. c. 1360), writing in the century after the events he purports to record. Barani is no ordinary writer. First, one must consider the circumstances under which he wrote the text; namely, that he wrote not only from jail, but also (as a result) from memory as well, without sources at his disposal. Second, Barani had a very enigmatic personality. On the one hand, he was a devotee of Nizam al-Din Auliya (d. 1325), the celebrated Sufi saint who was a paragon of tolerance and liberal interpretation of Islam; and on the other hand, his writings often reflect an extremely reactionary perspective. He was also very closely associated with the administration, and indeed held a very high position in the court of Muhammad bin Tughlaq (r. 1325–1351), but because of an impolitic step following this sultan's death, he fell from grace and was imprisoned. It is thus all the more necessary to be alert to Barani's potential prejudices, biases, and even inconsistencies. Nevertheless, Barani is clearly aware of the role of the historian and the regard that a historian must have for the truth. That said, he has no concern for literal accuracy. He creates dialogues, for example, for which there are no records, in order to articulate what he holds to be the morals and lessons on the past that he seeks to further in the present.

In the first selection, Barani reports Sultan Balban trying to explain the practices and virtues on which true kingship rests. In a letter (not excerpted here) to his elder son, Sultan Muhammad, he had divided the general principles of governance into two main categories. First, those principles inherited from tradition, according to which the true kings of the early Islamic past had to act in order to establish and defend the Prophet's religion. In this category would fall such aggressive policies as rooting out infidelity, humiliating idol-worshippers, waging incessant religious war, and creating conditions for all the subcommunities of the Muslims to act in full accordance with the shari'a, and so on. But Balban also made clear that such policies were the ideals of the superior time of the first caliphs, and thus are ideals to which kings in his own time cannot aspire.

He then elaborates a second category of principles, which are translated here, addressed to his younger son, Bughra Khan. According to this latter category, the king's main concerns should be with ensuring security, justice, and social stability, making sure to give access to state employment only to those who are worthy, and striving to improve *himself* spiritually that he might be more tolerant and just. In other words, this category of precepts speaks mostly to the routine, mundane aspects of rulership and governance, whereas religion comes into the picture only as an aspect of the ruler's personal life and duty to refine his moral character. Note his revealing anecdote about Caliph Harun al-Rashid, the purpose of which seems twofold. On the one hand, he is cautioning Bughra Khan to seek out divines of true enlightenment, piety, and detachment from this world, rather than those who boast about their piety while seeking the wealth of this world (*Tarikh-i Firoz Shahi*, 154–155). But the story implies, equally strongly, that the true man of religion is the one who refrains from interfering in affairs of the state—in effect a direct rebuke to those religious leaders who would interfere with the sultan's policies.

The fraught relationship between the shari'a and the state comes out more clearly in the second passage presented here, the conversations between Sultan Ala al-Din Khalji (r. 1296–1316) and a representative of the theologians, one Qazi Mughis. By the time of Ala al-Din's reign, the power of the Muslim rulers in India had extended far and wide. Nevertheless, even here the sultan does want to understand what the *shari'a* demands of him as a ruler—for therein lay a path to legitimacy—though not so much that it interferes with what he believes is in the best interests of his power.

It is not possible to read off historical fact directly from Barani's report of Ala al-Din's conversation with Qazi Mugis. For instance, when Barani cites the hadith to the effect that "the Hindus should accept Islam or be killed," he is taking certain interpretive liberties, since there is no evidence that the Prophet used the term "Hindu" anywhere. Similarly, statements that Hindu women and children were reduced to begging in Ala al-Din's reign, or that every Hindu house turned into a mint during the reign of Muhammad bin Tughluq, does not, in either case, mean *all* Hindus. Nor does it mean all Muslims when he writes:

> In their [Capital] Muslim kings not only allow but are pleased with the fact that infidels, polytheists, idol-worshippers and cow-dung (*sargin*) worshippers build houses like palaces, wear clothes of brocade and ride Arab horses caparisoned with gold and silver ornaments. . . . *They take Musalmans into their service and make them run before their horses; the poor Musalmans beg of them at their doors.* (Quoted in Mohammad Habib and Afsar Umar Salim Khan, *Political Theory of the Delhi Sultanate*, p. 48, emphasis added.)

Barani's main problem seems to be that he is somewhat uncomfortable with the results that followed from the policies of the sultans of his own time. Disgraced, imprisoned, and at the end of his life, he lamented the obvious fact in front of him: that political considerations had led the Delhi sultans to seek rapprochement with Hindus, while a person like himself was excluded. Barani consoles himself by describing with exaggerated emphasis aspects of earlier times that accord with his own conservative views. Contrary to his wishes, however, the conditions had already emerged for the Muslims to appropriate various features of the lives of the Hindus, and the Hindus were already quite accepting of and comfortable with the political reality of living under Perso-Turkish rulers.

In the final selection, from another fourteenth-century historian, Shams Siraj Afif (d. ca. 1400), we see this strategy of appropriation and accommodation in practice. We might pause to consider the historical background of the incident below, taken from the time of Sultan Firuz Shah Tughlaq (r. 1351–1388). The rise of Tughlaq rule had coincided with a response to Ala al-Din's harsh policies designed to reduce the strength of the erstwhile ruling chiefs and princes. With his death, the rural land magnates began a process of reconsolidating and unifying their various clans under the banner of Rajput identity, and they succeeded in creating a greater sense of unity among village magnates and the peasantry. Ghiyas al-Din Tughlaq (r. 1320–1324), in response, modified the Khalji sultans' policies by exempting the village headmen from paying taxes on their cattle and cultivation. Later, Muhammad bin Tughlaq, after an initial false start, extended services such as *taqavi* loans to the peasants. Firuz Tughlaq extended further conciliatory gestures toward them: the building of irrigation canals, the writing off of debt from previous imperial loans, and so on. Moreover, around the same time, Rajputs and other Hindu groups also began to figure more heavily in the imperial power structure as members of the state service. In the cultural realm, Muhammad Tughlaq was in the habit of holding regular meetings and dialogues with Jain scholars and saints, while Firuz Tughlaq showed a keen interest in Indian religions and heritage, and even commissioned Persian translations of some important Sanskrit texts.

The selection quoted here describes another of Firuz Shah's massive politico-cultural projects—in this case, to ingeniously excavate two ancient pillars from the reign of Ashoka (273–232 B.C.E.)—of whose history there was no living memory at the time. His installation of the pillars at his court in Delhi as monuments to his own power fits squarely within this historical trajectory. Firuz Shah clearly accepted the (spurious) significance of the pillars, namely that they were said to have served as the walking sticks of the ancient Hindu hero Bhima, and he sought to incorporate them into a projection of his own legitimate authority. With the help of a clever reading of the pillars' inscriptions by some local Brahmans, he attempted simultaneously to insert himself into a conceptual lineage of Indian rulership.

Thus, as these three selections make clear, despite the very real presence of occasional tensions, from the very earliest stages of Perso-Turkic rule in India we see a particularly South Asian vision of political Islam emerging, whereby, if need be, the sultan could supplement (indeed supersede) inherited traditions and *shari'a* by framing state regulations (*zawabit*) in accord with local exigencies and political necessity.

KINGSHIP AND GOVERNANCE: IDEALS AND REALITIES

BALBAN'S ADVICE (*WASAYA*) TO HIS YOUNGEST SON, BUGHRA KHAN, BY BARANI

The first admonition that can ensure the stability of this worldly power of yours is this, that in matters of governance (*iqlim-dari*) you should not exceed the limits of those established precedents which have guaranteed the stability and strength [of the regime], and which have provided tranquility to the people in [times of] difficulty, and comfort (*asuda-hal*) to the indigent. You should not unreasonably increase your demands upon those who are [already] obedient, and you should continue implementing only those regulations that were followed by earlier rulers. Don't keep issuing new orders based on your own whims, and in your dealings with the people (*ri'aya*), you should adopt a method that will be neither totally dependent on their submissiveness, nor unnecessarily harsh. Similarly, in the extraction of revenue (*kharaj*), you should follow a middle path (*miyana-ravi*). Neither should you take so much from them that they are rendered completely indigent, nor should you take so little that they become rebellious and headstrong. Overabundance of possessions and wealth results in great excess, which creates a kind of vertigo in the people, on account of which they lose their balance. Drunk with wealth, the intoxication of wealth will stupefy them, and the ripple of rebellion will start to swell like a wave in their breasts. It's the duty of the ruler to keep both the army and the people in a state of balance [e.g., in terms of income] so that, year after year, the former receive their salaries and the latter can pursue the business of tillage contentedly and without fear. They should not be lacking anything; otherwise they will turn to rebellion.

The above-mentioned principles (*usul*) for managing the people and the army—the implementation of which require a great deal of deliberation (*mashwara*) and attention—are not simply significant and critical matters of statecraft and governance (*hukumat o jahandari*), but are in fact amongst the most precious ideals of Kings Solomon and Alexander. . . .

The second admonition for you, Mahmud, is to instruct your advisors to prepare consistent regulations for administering state matters, and in managing those affairs you should not transgress these regulations. Do not, on your own initiative and your own whims, give one order in the morning, and then a different one in the evening, at night one order, then the next day some other which contradicts it, because the affairs of state get ruined if the regulations are unstable and the kings and ministers are capricious. It should never happen that Satan overpowers you, Mahmud, and instills in your heart the idea that "I am the King, and I am ruler over all, therefore I can do whatever comes into my head and whatever suits my mood." This is precisely the satanic delusion that has deposited so many great pharaohs and tyrants (*jabir*) down in the dust, and caused them to suffer punishment in hell for all time.

The third advice for Mahmud is this, that a day should not go by when he does not review the conditions/status of the army. The ruler's needs and business vis-à-vis the peasants arise but a few times a year, whereas he is in constant need of the army. No ruler can succeed if he is oblivious to the needs of the army.

The fourth advice is that the well-being of your realm and power lies in understanding that kingship is the opposite of submission, and thus constitutes the epitome of success and triumph, while submission (*mussalmani*) is the opposite of success and triumph. If I tell you that, in gratitude for the privilege of kingship, you should keep on prostrating and genuflecting, and try all manner of thanking God for the favor, even then you cannot possibly do justice to the gift that you have been given. Indeed, even amongst the [great] kings only those with a special gift [for expressing thanks and devotion] were able to express the sufficient gratitude. Thus, regard yourself as a slave and creation of God, and no matter what happens adhere to the five daily prayers, and do so in public (*ba jama'at*)—this is amongst the most important of the Prophet's precepts (*sunnat-i mu'akkadah*). Also, remember these traditions (*hadis*) of the

Prophet: "To say prayer in public is amongst the traditions of the guided (*huda*); he who gives it up is a hypocrite (*munafiq*)"; "He who skips the *jama'at* is damned"; and "The first *takbir* with the imam is better than the world and whatever is in it." If you miss a prayer, you should perform it later, without much delay, whether it is day or night. In this way it is hoped that you will be rewarded in the life hereafter.

After these suggestions, Sultan Balban told Bughra Khan: "O Mahmud, the advice that I have given you is according to the reality of our times. And if I give you the kind of advice which might be appropriate for [ideally] religious and faithful kings—i.e., tell you to devote your entire effort to uprooting infidelity and idolatry, to humiliate or incapacitate the idol-worshipers so that you have a place in the company of the Prophets, to completely annihilate the Brahmans so that all traces of infidelity disappear [from this world], to be always alert in obeying the Prophet's commands and following his traditions, to consider kingly pomp and [ostentatious] éclat to be at variance with those traditions, to seek permission for your power from the Abbasid Caliphs, to make your capitol the seat of 'ulama, saints, Sayyids, traditionalists, exegetists, memorizers of the Qur'an, sermonizers, and other learned people, and to establish the Friday prayer with the permission of the Caliph—doling out such advice is not appropriate for me, nor does it deserve to be given to you who are so overpowered with lust and worldly desires.

My last advice to you is this, which ensures deliverance in the life hereafter for lusty people like you, provided you act upon it. That last advice is as follows: if it is at all possible, try in all humility to beseech and seek the refuge and protection of a person who has turned his face against this world, in appearance and also in reality, one who has devoted himself totally to the worship of God [i.e., a mystical preceptor]. Never go to the company of one who accepts anything from you, and who in any manner has an inclination for this world or worldly things. Regard such a one as a this-world-seeker, and never count him amongst the people of God.

I, Balban, the slave of Shams al-Din [Iltutmish], have heard from Qazi Jalal 'Arus, a prominent Qazi who had traveled from Baghdad [to Delhi] as an ambassador, that he had brought a parable which was indicative of Harun Rashid's exemplary lifestyle as a gift for the Sultan [Iltutmish]. The Sultan was so elated simply on hearing this parable that he wished to grant half of his kingdom to the Qazi in return. . . . Harun Rashid, in spite of his pomp and glory, had in his personality the inclination to visit the house of Da'ud Ta'i and Muhammad Samak, who were amongst the ascetics (*zahid*) of Baghdad. He used to go there on foot, with only a few servants, and would sit waiting on the bare ground, even for more than three hours at a time—yet these dervishes would not open the door of their house to let him in. Time and again he would visit them [unsuccessfully], and yet not feel humiliated by it. Rather, he held them in even higher esteem, and his faith in them only increased. He desired to have someone [formally] introduce him to them, even if he must promise to give him [i.e., the intermediary] some money.

[Here Mamun adds that] he and the Caliph's other courtiers resented not only the fact that the Caliph would go to the door of these dervishes in this [unseemly] manner, but worse still that they treated him with such indifference. For they would allow entry even to ordinary people [beggars and the poor], and yet they would not invite the Amir al-Muminin (Commander of the Faithful).

One day, he [Mamun] was sitting with the Caliph when Qazi Abu Yusuf visited. The Amir al-Muminin said to him: "Can you arrange a meeting between me and Da'ud Ta'i? I have heard that you and he were tutored together by Abu Hanifa." Qazi Abu Yusuf replied: "When I was a poor man, he would let me in, but since the time I was appointed Qazi, I have gone to the door of his house twenty times, and have not been allowed to enter." The Caliph proclaimed: "From what you say his stature in my eyes grows even higher." To this Abu Yusuf protested: "From all over the world, the 'ulama, saints, and scholars who have respect for the faith of Muhammad visit your court and consider meeting with you as auspicious, because you are the Commander of the Faithful (amir al-muminin), not to mention a descendant of the Prophet's own uncle, 'Abbas. If these two beggars residing in Baghdad itself do not recognize your authority and relationship to the Prophet of Allah, and if they thus ignore/disregard your privileges, then why do you go to them? Already the news that this evening you, the Caliph, went to their door and were refused entry, is known to the entire city." The Caliph replied: "This is precisely the reason that I have such faith in them, and exactly why I hold them in such high regard. Having observed their lives, I am convinced that they have turned their faces against this world, in reality as well as in appearance. It is solely due to their love for God that they are hostile to this world. Today, I represent only this world. I have acquired this-worldly glory, and since they are sincere enemies of this world then how could they not also consider me their enemy, and how could they accept my presence? And this is exactly why I love and cherish such people, who take the world as their enemy and God as their friend. By befriending them, I will earn rewards in the life hereafter, whereas they deserve such reward precisely for regarding me as their enemy. I therefore constantly endeavor to support such renunciants, that they may thereby gain deliverance from all the suffering accruing from worldliness. . . ."

Having explained this ethos, the Amir al-Muminin began to weep. He cried: "I find all my thoughts and actions, commissions and omissions, to be contrary to the tradition of the Prophet. I don't know how I will face the Prophet tomorrow on the Day of Judgment (qayamat), and I don't know whose shelter (himayat) I can go to for deliverance from the troubles (shada'id) of the Day of Judgment." And on hearing this ethos, Qazi Abu Yusuf kissed the knees of the Caliph and exclaimed: "I have obtained so much knowledge ('ilm), but today I have learned the gnosis (ma'rifat) of God from the Caliph."

Balban's purpose in relating this anecdote to Mahmud was that he was constrained by his fatherly affection to implore Mahmud to speak and act in such a way that he gets deliverance from punishment in the life hereafter.

Sultan Balban explained these precepts and suggestions to Bughra Khan verbally, and also asked his *dabir* (secretary) to record them, after which he presented him a robe of honor, kissed his cheek and eyes, and wept for a while. After that, he gave Bughra leave to depart and return to Lakhnauti.

SHARI'A AND THE KINGSHIP IN PRACTICE

SULTAN 'ALA AL-DIN'S CONVERSATION WITH QAZI MUGHIS, BY BARANI

Sultan 'Ala al-Din [r. 1296–1316] was a king who had no idea of what learning is. He had never associated with the 'ulama, and when he acquired kingship he considered governance and state administration to be a separate matter from the traditions and commands of *shari'a*; that is, the *qazis* and muftis had responsibility for the *shari'a* injunctions, whereas matters of kingship pertained to the king [alone]. Because of this understanding on his part, he conducted the business of governance based on whatever he believed to be for the good of the state (*salah-i mulk*), without any consideration for whether it was lawful or unlawful (*mashru', na-mashru'*). He never asked about *shari'a* injunctions that might pertain to state matters, and had little interaction with the learnèd. There were, however, [learnèd men like] Qazi Ziya al-Din Bayana, Maulana Zahir Lang, and Maulana Mushayyad Kuhrami, who were regularly invited to dine with him at the royal banquet, but they would normally sit at the outer table with the *amir*s [and therefore did not get to converse much with the king]. Often, Qazi Mughis of Bayana would also meet with Sultan 'Ala al-Din and sit with the *amir*s in their private assemblies. And in those very same days when the large scale revenue collection efforts were going on, he met the Qazi [Mughis] and told him: "Today I want to ask you about a few matters (*mas'ala*). In response, you tell me whatever is correct (*haqq*). The Qazi responded by saying: "It appears my death has come close."

'Ala al-Din asked: "How do you know that?" And the Qazi replied, "His Majesty has enquired about the religious matters, and since I will tell the truth, His Majesty will then become angry and execute me." 'Ala al-Din insisted, "I would not kill you! Whatever I ask you, just tell me what is right and correct."

The Qazi said, "Whatever His Majesty might ask, I will respond in accord with what is there in the books."

The first issue that the Sultan asked the Qazi about was this: "In the *shari'a*, what is the legal designation of Hindus who pay the *kharaj*?" The Qazi answered: "In legal terms, a Hindu *kharaj*-payer is one who should, when the collector from the *divan*'s office demands silver from him, offer gold instead, and do so in all humility, without any hesitation; even if the collector wants to spit in his mouth, he should offer it without any resistance, and in such manner demonstrate his subservience to the collector. The significance of the Hindu showing such humility, and the collector's spitting into his mouth, is to emphasize the extreme servility and obedience [required] of a *zimmi*, to mark the glory of the true religion of Islam, and to insult the untrue faith. In connection with their humiliation God has said: 'They pay from their hand and should be humble.' In particular, to disgrace the Hindus is one of the tasks of maintaining the faith, because they are the worst enemies of the Prophet. It is for this reason that the Prophet ordered that either Hindus must accept Islam, or else be killed, made into spoils of war, or enslaved. They should be imprisoned, and their possessions and country be made into booty. Except Imam-i 'Azam [i.e., Abu Hanifa], whose school [of jurisprudence] we follow; no other authority on jurisprudence allows the taking of *jizya* from the Hindus. According to these other 'ulama, the choice for the Hindu is either Islam or death."

'Ala al-Din laughed at Qazi Mughis's reply, and said: "I don't know about all that, but I receive lots of reports that *khots* and *muqaddams* ride on good horses, wear fine garments, and use Persian bows and arrows [high quality weapons]. They fight amongst themselves and even go for hunting expeditions. They do not pay even a single *jital* in *kharaaj*, *jizya*, or other taxes, such as property taxes (*ghari*) and grazing fees (*chara'i*). On top of that, they also collect the *khoti* share from the villages, and they hold parties, drink wine, and some of them, whether they are summoned or not, don't even bother to present themselves at the *divan*'s office, much less pay any attention to the collectors. [Of course,] I am very angry about this. Here I was thinking of the desire to conquer the countries of others, while in my own country within a range of 100 *kos* people do not follow the rules I have set. Thus how could I make the other lands obedient to me? I have issued numerous regulations designed to make the people obedient, to the extent that by now they have all scurried into holes like rats—and now here you are telling me that according to *shari'a*, too, the Hindus should be made completely servile?! [In other words, I've already done it, even without any knowledge of *shari'a*.] O Maulana Mughis, you are a wise and learned person, but you have no [worldly] experience. I am an illiterate, but have much experience. You must know that a Hindu can never be obedient to a Muslim until he is denuded of whatever possessions he has. And I thus issued an order that the people be left with only enough grain, milk, and yogurt to live through the year, and there should not be any hoarding beyond their needs."

The second issue that 'Ala al-Din enquired about from Qazi Mughis concerned the [regulation of] state officials. He asked: "Is there any injunction of the *shari'a* regarding state officials who indulge in theft and bribery, or perform accounting mischief and trickery with their pens?" The Qazi replied, "There is no injunction anywhere regarding them, at least in the texts that I have read. But, if the 'ummals (officials) are paid inadequately, and thus steal something from the treasury where the tax revenue is kept, or take bribes, or embezzle funds from the amount collected in revenues, then the ruler can punish them in whatever way he sees fit—either by imposing fines, or imprisonment, or torture and beating. But regarding thievery specifically from the treasury, there is no particular command for cutting off the hands."

'Ala al-Din added: "If the officials' reported accounts fall short of revenue expectations, then they are kicked, beaten with wooden sticks, chained, and squeezed. And ever since these stringent measures have been applied to revenue collection, it is now reported to me that thefts and bribery have declined. I have thus ordered that salaries of officials should be such that they can live respectably (*ba abru*), but if in spite of this they commit theft, or there is a shortfall in the collected revenues, then they will be beaten and the money extracted from them. Now you see how harshly these officials are treated."

The third issue about which Sultan 'Ala al-Din questioned the Qazi was whether the wealth that he had acquired [during the conquest of] Deogir, while still a prince, belonged to him or to the State treasury (*bait al-mal*). Qazi Mughis answered: "I have no other option but to tell you truth, which is that the wealth that His Majesty brought from Deogir was all acquired due to the strength of the army of Islam, and whatever is acquired through the strength of the army of Islam thus belongs to the Treasury of the Muslim community. If His Majesty would have brought wealth on his own, and its acquisition had been lawful, then it would certainly have been [considered] a personal possession of His Majesty." Sultan 'Ala al-Din became angry with the Qazi and said: "What are you talking about? Do you have any idea what you are saying? The wealth that I have acquired by staking my own life and the lives of my servants, which I obtained from the Hindus in the days when I was just a mere noble—this wealth, of which the people in Delhi did not even have a clue, which I never deposited with the royal treasury and have used for my own self, how can all this be considered property of the royal treasury?

The Qazi replied: "His majesty has asked me a legal question. If I did not say what I have read in the books, and if in order to placate His Majesty I were to prevaricate, and then His Majesty enquired about this same issue from some other learnèd person and discovered the difference of opinion—then what will His Majesty think about me, and how could he then ask me anything relating to *shari'a* [ever again]?"

The fourth question that Sultan 'Ala al-Din put forth was this: "Over what portion of the state treasury do I and my children (*farzandan*) have a claim?" The Qazi replied: "Now the time of my death has arrived." 'Ala al-Din asked: "What do you mean the time of your death has arrived?" The Qazi said: "If I give the correct answer to His Majesty's question, it will infuriate you and you will kill me. But if I answer dishonestly, I will go to hell in the life hereafter [*lit.*, tomorrow]." The Sultan assured him: "Just tell me what the *shari'a* injunction is, I will not kill you."

The Qazi explained: "If Your Majesty were to follow [the example of] the Pious Caliphs, and desire high position in the life hereafter, then you should keep for your and your wife's expenses the same 234 *tankas* that you have fixed for the soldiers of jihad. If Your Majesty prefers to follow a middle path, and thinks that the soldiers' salary is insufficient to maintain the dignity of a ruler, then take the amount that you give to the high nobles of your court such as Malik Qiran, Malik Qir Beg, Malik Naib Vakil-i Dar, and Malik Hajib-i Khass. Or, if Your Majesty prefers to do [the maximum of] what the 'ulama have permitted, then take more for yourself and your wife than the nobles, only to the extent necessary to maintain a position distinct from the others, such that the dignity of rulership is not lowered. If Your Majesty transgresses these three options that I have mentioned, and [for instance] bestows lakhs and crores [of tankas] and gold jewels on the *harem*, then you will account for it on the Day of Judgment."

The Sultan was furious, and told the Qazi: "Don't you fear my sword? You [dare] say that all of the money spent on my family (*haram*) is unlawful?" The Qazi replied: "I do fear Your Majesty's sword, and [indeed] always keep my funeral shroud with me, tied as this turban [over my head]. [But] Your Majesty has asked me a question pertaining to *shari'a*, and I can only answer according to what I know. If Your Majesty had asked me what was politically appropriate, then of course I would say that there should be a thousand times more spent on the *haram*, since it would enhance the dignity of the king in the eyes of the people, and any increase in the glory of the king is politically prudent."

Following the discussion of these matters, Sultan 'Ala al-Din said to the Qazi: "In this way you could characterize all my works as unlawful (*na-mashru'*). I have ordered that three years' salary be withheld from any soldier who does not present himself for review at muster; I put wine sellers and drinkers into prison cells; I cut off the offending organ of those who commit adultery with another's wife, and have the woman put to death; and I put all insurgents to death, [whether] good or bad, poor or rich, make their women and children destitute, and thus destroy them. I use harsh methods of beating and clubbing the people in extracting the revenues due to the state (*mal-i mutalaba*), and I put them into prison until even a single [underpaid] *jital* is recovered. I torture state prisoners and keep them in prison forever. You will say that all this is unlawful."

The Qazi then left his seat, moved to the place where shoes were taken off, bent his head to the ground and said in a loud voice: "O King of the world, whether you allow this *faqir* to live or order me to be killed this very moment, [I insist that] all of this is unlawful (*na-mashru'*). Nowhere in the traditions (*hadis*) of the Prophet, peace be upon him, and the traditions of the 'ulama is there precedent for the ruler to do whatever he chooses in enforcing his policies."

Sultan Ala al-Din heard this, remained silent, put on his shoes and retired to the private apartments (*andarun-i haram*). Qazi Mughis also went back home.

Next day, he [the Qazi] bade farewell to his family, dispensed alms, had a bath, tied a sword around his waist and came to the court [ready to die]. But Sultan Ala al-Din summoned him to his presence, favored him by bestowing the robe that he himself was wearing [on the Qazi], along with a thousand *tankas*, and said: "O Qazi Mughis, even though I am illiterate, and have not read any books, I am a Muslim, and have been born in a family which has been Muslim for many generations. I issue orders for the good of the country and people, in order to stop discord, which causes death to thousands. When the people in the countryside turn headstrong and refuse to obey my orders, it becomes necessary for me to issue strict regulations to keep them in check. I do not know if these orders are sanctioned by *shari'a* or not, [but] I order whatever is good for the land and is expedient at the time."

APPROPRIATING THE NON-ISLAMIC

FIRUZ SHAH TUGHLAQ AND THE ASHOKAN PILLARS, BY SHAMS SIRAJ AFIF (D. CA.1400).

In the vicinity of Delhi, there were two stone columns from earlier times: one in the district of Salora and Khizrabad in the village of Topra, toward the foothills of the mountains; and the other at a distance, in *qasba* Meratta/Meerut. Both had stood there since the time of the Pandavas, and no ruler had ever tried to move them to the city. Firuz Shah [Tughlaq], however, was fortunate to make indefatigable efforts to install them in the city—one, which was known as the Golden Tower (*manara-i zarrin*), inside of the Firuzabad palace (*kushak*) adjacent to the grand mosque, while the other was relocated to the hunting palace (*kushak-i shikar*).

This humble historian, Shams Siraj Afif, was told by several respectable (*sharif*) persons that these columns had been the walking sticks of the accursed Bhim, who was very tall and was matchless in physical strength. He was a brave warrior who wrestled triumphantly with all the wrestlers of his time. According to the histories of the infidels, his daily consumption of food measured a thousand maunds, and none could dare compete with him in strength. If he hoisted an elephant on the point of his spear, he could fling it from east to west, and back again from west to east. In those days, all of Hind was inhabited by the infidels, who often fought amongst themselves. The damned Bhim was the youngest of five brothers, and had the responsibility of grazing their cattle stock. He used these columns as the staffs with which he tended and herded the cattle. With the permission of God even the cattle of those years, like human beings, were of unusually large stature. They all lived in and around Delhi, and Bhim left these columns as his memorials after his death. The infidels then unanimously decided to keep them safe and intact as a token of fortune. . . . When Firuz Shah visited the sites of these columns, he was filled with astonishment and admiration at these wonders. And that is when, divinely inspired, he resolved to move them to Delhi, which he did with unsparing efforts, relocating them to the city of Firuzabad (Delhi) and the hunting palace. . . .

After the palace was erected, a few additional tiers of black and white stone were then added to its spire, capped with a gold-polished copper cupola, of the type known in Hindavi as *kalas*. The pillar is thirty-two yards high, eight of which are under the base structure, while the remaining twenty-four are visible above the base. It could not be ascertained who erected it in the village Topra, but there were a few lines in Hindavi characters inscribed over the lower parts of the pillar. Sultan Firuz Shah summoned many Brahmans and Hindu devotees (*sevagan*), but none could read the inscription. Yet there are those who say that some Hindus were indeed able to read that Hindavi inscription, and that it said the following: that nobody could move this pillar from its original location, neither amongst the Muslim sultans nor the Hindu rajas. But in later times, there would be a powerful monarch (*badshah*) who will be known as Sultan Firuz, who will transfer the pillar from this place. Since all this is with the blessing of God, whatever Sultan Firuz planned, he achieved it. . . .

Sources

The original source for the first and second selections, "Kingship and Governance," is Zia al-Din Barani, *Tarikh-i Firuz Shahi*, Sayyid Ahmad Khan, ed. (Calcutta: Bilbiotheca Indica, 1862 (reprint Aligarh: Sir Syed Academy, Aligarh Muslim University, 2005), pp. 100–106, 289–299. A (partial and selective) English translation of the text is available in Sir H. M. Elliot and John Dowson, *History of India as Told by Its Own Historians*, 8 vols. (New York: AMS Press, 1966) vol. 3, pp. 93–268. Another partial English translation of the section in *Tarikh-i Firuz Shahi* dealing with the Khaljis is available in A. R. Fuller and A. Khallaque, *The Reign of Alauddin Khilji: Translated from Zia-ud-Din Barani's Tarikh-i-Firuz Shahi* (Calcutta: Pilgrim Publishers, 1967).

The third selection, "Appropriating the Non-Islamic," is taken from Shams Siraj Afif, *Tarikh-i Firuz Shahi*, Maulavi Wilayat Husain, ed. (Calcutta: Bibliotheca Indica, 1890), pp. 305–307, 308, 312. For a partial English translation of this text, see again Sir H. M. Elliot and John Dowson, *History of India as Told by Its Own Historians*, 8 vols. (New York: AMS Press, 1966) vol. 3, 269–374. There is also a complete translation of the text by R. C. Jauhri, but it remains unedited due to his death. This version has been published as *Medieval India in Transition: Tarikh-i Firuz Shahi, A Firsthand Account* (New Delhi: Sundeep Prakashan, 2001).

Further Reading

The most comprehensive account of Zia al-Din Barani, along with an analysis of his biography, his social and intellectual milieu, and his writings, is to be found in Mohammad Habib, "Life and Thought of Ziauddin Barani," in *Politics and Society during the Early Medieval Period: Collected Works of Professor Mohammad Habib 2*, K. A. Nizami, ed. (New Delhi: People's Publishing House, 1981), pp. 286–366.

For further analysis of Barani's *Tarikh* and its political implications, see Peter

Hardy, *Historians of Medieval India: Studies in Indo-Muslim Historical Writing* (London: Luzac, 1960); and S. Moinul Haq, *Barani's History of the Tughluqs (Being a Critical Study of the Relevant Chapters of Tarikh-i Firuz Shahi)* (Karachi: Pakistan Historical Society, 1959).

There are also good general discussions of the history of the time, the nature of politics, as well as commentary on Barani and other relevant sources, in the following: Khaliq Ahmad Nizami, *Some Aspects of Religion and Politics in India during the Thirteenth Century* (Delhi: Idarah-i Adabiyat-i Delli, 1974); Peter Jackson, *The Delhi Sultanate: A Political and Military History* (Cambridge: Cambridge University Press, 1999).

—22—

A Colonial Court Defines a Muslim

Alan M. Guenther

The printing of the Indian Law Reports by the various high courts in British India created a new source of Muslim law for the Muslims in South Asia, thereby becoming another factor in the complete transformation of Muslim law in India in the nineteenth century. The administration of Muslim law had been undergoing a significant transformation under British rule, since the late eighteenth century. The East India Company had increasingly altered the content of the Muslim law by issuing "Regulations" that conformed the law to a British sense of justice. In the 1860s, the British colonial government introduced law codes that replaced entire sections of the existing law, particularly criminal law and procedural law. Civil law was to retain more of its traditional content; but here, too, there were significant changes, most notably in its administration and application.

Throughout the nineteenth century, the British officials in India increasingly marginalized the participation of Muslim legal scholars, as they did Hindu pandits, in the administration of religion-based law. Initially, muftis and maulvis were attached to the courts as "court officers" to provide authoritative rulings which the British judges, who were largely ignorant of Muslim law, were bound to administer. But from the beginning, British officials expressed their dissatisfaction with this arrangement. They desired to be free from such a direct reliance on Muslim legal experts and their fatwas, citing a lack of consistency and integrity on the part of the court officers and their rulings. To this end they effectively replaced the Muslim legal scholar with a legal text by means of the parallel processes of translation, legislation, and adjudication. Through the process of translation, the number of texts on which a judge relied in forming his judgment on matters pertaining to Muslim law were reduced to portions of two or three key texts, which were frequently republished in their English translations. Through the process of legislation, the regulations and codes mentioned earlier narrowed the application of those Muslim laws that were still in force. Through the process of adjudication, judges built up a body of precedents that became increasingly authoritative in determining applicable law.

The official Law Reports were a record of this body of precedents, and functioned to preserve select judgments made by the various high courts in India. When dealing with judgments involving Muslim law, these Reports had regularly cited the fatwas issued by the Muslim court officers until the abolition of the office in 1864, even though their effectiveness and authority had considerably eroded by that time. Therefore, their direct contribution to Muslim law as it was being officially administered by the British colonial regime in India came to an end. The Law Reports Act of 1875 brought the publication of high court decisions under direct government control and, at the same time, further established the authority of the judgments made by high court judges. The bill declared that every judgment delivered by any high court and reported in the Government Reports would be binding on all subordinate courts throughout British India, and that no court would be bound to hear reports of cases not published under the authority of the government.

With the appointment of Syed Mahmood to the position of an officiating judge of the high court at Allahabad in 1882 and as a full puisne judge in 1887, the Muslim community once again had a voice in the content and administration of Muslim law at the highest level of the British legal system in India. Syed Mahmood (1850–1903) was the son of Sir Syed Ahmad Khan, and had assisted his father in the founding of the college that eventually became Aligarh Muslim University. He was one of the first Indian Muslims to study law in England and the first non-European member of the Allahabad Bar, in addition to becoming the first Indian Muslim appointed as a judge to any high court in British India. He was not a traditionally trained Islamic scholar, as the earlier muftis had been; his heritage was primarily that of an Islamic modernist committed to individual interpretation of sacred texts with limited attention to the historical traditions of commentaries.

Mahmood's pioneering contributions to the genre of law reports during the ten years that he served as a judge were remarkable. The Law Reports contain approximately three hundred of his written decisions, ranging from brief judgments of one or two pages, to several on Muslim law that were forty to fifty pages in length. His recorded judgments dominate the volumes of the Allahabad Law Reports from 1882 to 1992, completely overshadowing the contributions of his fellow judges.

Syed Mahmood broke with the legal fashion of his day of recording terse decisions, and devoted much time to research and to writing extensive judgments on the cases that appeared before him. His prolixity became legendary and led to the complaint from his fellow judges that he unnecessarily delayed the workings of the court by spending too much time in the preparation of these judgments. He responded by arguing that he was not prepared to sacrifice the quality of his judgments in order to dispose of a greater number of cases.

Another reason for Mahmood's protracted rulings was that they were often dissentient rulings in which he took great pains to explain the grounds for his dissent. The judgment presented below was a separate ruling that Syed Mahmood wrote to express the points of his dissent from a full bench ruling on a case involving the behavior of worshippers in a mosque. He objected to the case in question being treated under criminal law, insisting that it rightly belonged to the jurisdiction of civil law, and that the relevant law was thus Muslim law. In his judgment he is also sharply critical of his fellow judges for not waiting for him to complete a thorough review of the Muslim legal works relevant to the case before presenting their opinion. He was vindicated in the decades that followed, as his minority ruling became the precedent most frequently quoted in matters involving disputes over the use of mosques.

Syed Mahmood's contributions to the Indian Law Reports are conspicuous for more than just their length and careful argument. What immediately stand out are the frequent passages in Arabic script contained in extended footnotes. Whereas previous efforts at translating Muslim legal works into English had reduced the number of such works used by the judges, Mahmood now brought many more sources into the legal discourse by quoting and translating relevant passages in his submissions to the official law reports. As the only Muslim on the bench, Mahmood took a special interest in cases involving Muslim law, considering it his duty to provide thorough answers to questions raised by the cases. In his opinion, poor translations of a limited number of Muslim legal sources had resulted in the inferior administration of Muslim law in India. By his inclusion of a multitude of quotations from original sources, he sought to rectify the situation.

Syed Mahmood seems to have fully embraced the British legal idiom as a means to express Muslim law. Although highly critical of certain aspects of its administration, Mahmood does not appear to question the right of the British legal system in India to adjudicate matters of Muslim law. His contemporary, Syed Ameer Ali, who was appointed to the Calcutta High Court in 1890, likewise contributed to the trend of rethinking Muslim law within British legal discourse. Unlike Mahmood's, however, Ameer Ali's contribution was not primarily in the Law Reports but in two volumes on Muslim law in which he systematically outlined, in a British framework, those elements of Muslim law still enforced by the government. Subsequently, other judges of Muslim background, including Muhammad Yusuf Khan Bahadur, A.F.M. Abdur Rahman, Syed Karamat Husein, Abdur Rahim, Faiz Hassan Badruddin Tyabji, S. Khuda Bakhsh, and Syed H. R. Abdul Majid, followed the trail blazed by Mahmood and Ameer Ali in their participation in the Anglo-Indian legal system and in developing the amalgam that came to be known as Anglo-Muhammadan law. But Anglo-Muhammadan Law, like the Muslim Personal Law that continued in the Republic of India, was also shaped by non-Muslim judges of Christian, Hindu, or other background, as exemplified in the decisions in the celebrated Shah Bano case (Chapter 27).

To claim that the Law Reports became a new source of Muslim law is perhaps startling at first glance. Yet, the legal history of India adequately bears that out. So prominent a Muslim jurist as Tahir Mahmood has stated in a recent publication that, because the English doctrine of judicial precedent has become part of the Indian legal system, "Judicial decisions on Islamic law as recorded in the Law Reports are, thus, an important 'source' of Islamic law in India." The case containing the ruling by Syed Mahmood on the matter of Muslim identity, below, thus carries considerable weight.

THE CASE: QUEEN EMPRESS V. RAMZAN (7 MARCH 1885)

This was an application to the High Court for the exercise of its powers of revision [i.e., appeal] under s. 439 of the Criminal Procedure Code. It appeared that the applicants, Ramzan, Muhammad Husain, and Abdul Rahman, were convicted by the Cantonment Magistrate of Benares, Major R. Annesley, by an order dated the 25th September 1884, of an offence under s. 296, Indian Penal Code. The judgment of the Cantonment Magistrate was as follows:

> The particulars of this case are as follow: In muhalla Madanpura, City Benares, a large *masjid* exists, generally called Allu's *masjid*, after the builder. Abdulla, the complainant, was left in charge of this *masjid* after Allu's death, some years ago, and Ramzan, accused, is a grand-nephew of Allu's, and also his son-in-law. During the month of August 1884, Ramzan, who it seems had not frequented this *masjid* for many years, suddenly returned to it. He was accompanied by Muhammad Husain, accused, and Abdul Rahman, accused, and these three men at once began a series of annoyances to the assembly engaged in prayer in the *masjid*. The men who use the *masjid* nearly all belong to a sect called Hanifis, and Ramzan also formerly belonged to it, but has lately become a Wahhabi. It appears the Wahhabis use the word 'amen' at the top of their voices, and by doing so in the Allu *masjid* the three accused naturally disturbed the Hanifis engaged in prayer. The evidence for the prosecution is perfectly clear; first, as to the fact of the three accused having entered the *masjid* on four successive Fridays during August and September 1884; secondly, as to having by their behaviour disturbed the assembly at prayers; and thirdly, as to police intervention being necessary, on the 22nd August 1884, to quell a disturbance occasioned by the accused, and which threatened to become serious. The witnesses are respectable persons, and most moderate in the views they express when giving evidence. They consider the presence of Ramzan and his companions not desirable in the *masjid*, but raise no objection to their joining the worshippers as long as they cause no disturbance. Ramzan states that there is enmity between him and Abdulla on account of the *masjid* accounts, and that therefore he was turned out of it on pretence of his saying 'amen' loudly, which is not objectionable to the Hanafis, the real reason being that Abdulla will not give him a statement of the *masjid's* income, also that he has always prayed at that *masjid*. The other two accused say that on 22nd August 1884, they saw Ramzan being beaten and interfered with; on which Abdulla and his party have included them in the charge brought against Ramzan. The witnesses for the defence merely state that they consider that calling out 'amen' loudly does not disturb an assembly at prayers, and yet they all state they only speak the word very low themselves. They also speak to the quarrel having originated in money matters about repairs to the *masjid*, and further, that the three accused have fre-

quented this *masjid* for years. I note, however, that the only independent witness, a Hindu named Harpal, who keeps a shop under the *masjid*, states that
he has been there for five years, and that only within the last month has
Ramzan come to the *masjid*,—never before. Be that as it may, Ramzan and
his companions, the two other accused, had not a shadow of an excuse for
disturbing the people of the *masjid*. It is useless to inquire whether it is lawful or not to use the word '*amen.*' As long as by doing so the accused disturbed the assembly, they rendered themselves liable to punishment under s.
296, Indian Penal Code. If it be true that the enmity between Ramzan and
Abdulla originated in a quarrel about the income of the *masjid*, his conduct
is all the more reprehensible, for he has disturbed a large number of persons
engaged in prayer, merely to gratify his spite against an individual. The
Courts of law are the proper places to settle money quarrels in, and not places
of religious worship, and it is intolerable that men like the accused should be
allowed to cause annoyance to a whole community.

The Court is of opinion that Ramzan, son of Maddar, Muhammad Husain,
son of Allahdin, and Abdul Rahman, son of Abdul Karim, are guilty of the
charge preferred against them, *viz*., that they voluntarily disturbed an assembly engaged in religious worship, thereby committing an offence punishable
under s. 296, Indian Penal Code; and the Court directs that the said Ramzan,
Muhammad Husain, and Abdul Rahman, pay a fine of twenty-five rupees
each, or, in default, be rigorously imprisoned for one month. The ground of
this application for revision was that "to pronounce the word '*amin*' (amen)
in a loud tone during the prayers is not an offence punishable under s. 296
of the Indian Penal Code."

————

On the 14th March the following opinion was delivered by Mahmood, J., on
the question referred to the full bench:

MAHMOOD, J.—This case originally came on for hearing in the Single
Bench before my brother Brodhurst, and, in view of the peculiarities of the
question with regard to the right of worshipping in mosques possessed by
Muhammadans, my learned brother referred the case to a Division Bench, of
which, at his suggestion, and with the approval of the learned Chief Justice,
I was to be a member. The case was accordingly heard by a Bench consisting
of my brother Oldfield and myself; and, in consideration that the main object of the application for revision obviously was to obtain an authoritative
ruling upon the question, and also because the applicant's counsel informed
us that the applicants, having paid the fines inflicted upon them, were not
undergoing the alternative sentence of imprisonment, we referred the case to
the Full Bench, before which the case was re-argued by Mr. Amir-ud-din on
behalf of the applicants, and the learned Public Prosecutor on behalf of the
Crown. Upon that occasion, after having fully heard the arguments on either

side, I was unable to form any opinion such as could be made the basis of any order in the case, and being desirous of consulting the original authorities of Muhammadan Law, I wished to reserve my order to enable me to prepare a judgment in writing, as the question raised by the reference seemed to be far from simple, specially as, in my opinion, it turned upon a very minute point of the Muhammadan Ecclesiastical Law. The learned Chief Justice and my learned brethren, however, were able on that occasion to form an opinion in the case, and made an order remanding the case for re-trial on certain issues. My brother Straight, whilst consenting to the order of re-trial, was inclined to the opinion that the evidence on the record was sufficient to justify the conviction. I was, however, unfortunately not able to concur in, or dissent from, the order for the simple reason that I had formed no definite opinion in the absence of the authorities of Muhammadan Law, which had not been cited on either side.

Under these circumstances, it has devolved upon me now to deliver my judgment in the case, and I regret that the conclusion at which I have arrived is different from that at which the learned Chief Justice and the rest of the Court have done. In view of this circumstance, and also because facts similar to those that exist in this case have before now been made the subject of criminal prosecutions in cases which have ultimately come up to this Court in revision, I wish to explain my reasons fully.

The facts of the case itself are very simple. The mosque in question in this case is situated in muhalla Maddanpura, in the city of Benares, and it was built by one Ali Muhammad *alias* Allu, who is stated by the prosecution to have followed the doctrines of Imam Abu Hanifa, and was therefore a Hanafi. The prosecutor, Abdulla, is a brother-in-law of the founder of the mosque, his sister having been married to Allu, and the principal accused, Ramzan, is the son-in-law of Allu, and also otherwise related to him. The other two accused, Muhammad Husain and Abdul Rahman, are persons holding religious views similar to those held by Ramzan.

It appears that on the 22nd of August 1884, the three accused joined the congregation in the mosque, and during the prayer said the word "*ámín*" aloud. This appears to have led to a discussion as to whether it was right to say the word aloud in prayers, and a heated argument took place, resulting in the accused being turned out of the mosque with the help of the police, and the prosecutor prohibiting them from coming to the mosque again unless they renounced the rite of saying "*ámín*" aloud in prayers.

On the 1st of September, 1884, Abdulla, and some other persons presented an application to the Magistrate, describing the occurrence of the 22nd August, and asking for the interference of the Magisterial authorities, on the ground that breach of the peace was likely to take place by reason of the accused insisting upon saying the word "*ámín*" aloud in prayers. No definite action appears to have been taken by the Magisterial authorities on that application beyond sending it for inquiry to the City Inspector of Police, and matters seemed to have stood thus, when, on the 20th of September, 1884, Abdulla by himself filed another petition, complaining of the accused, and charging them with "the offence of insulting the religion of Hanafia Musalmans" under ss. 297, 298, and 351 of the Indian Penal Code. The Magistrate, after having examined the prosecutor and the witnesses for the prosecution, framed charges against the accused under s. 296 of the Indian Penal Code, and after having taken the evidence on behalf of the defence, convicted them under that section, and sentenced them to pay a fine of Rs. 25 each, and in default to undergo rigorous imprisonment for one month. The accused have applied for revision to this Court under s. 439 of the Criminal Procedure Code, on the ground that "to pronounce the word '*ámín*' in a loud tone during the prayers is not an offence punishable under s. 296 of the Indian Penal Code."

The question so raised seems to me to involve mixed considerations of the meaning of the Indian Penal Code and the Muhammadan Ecclesiastical Law; for, according to my view, the application of the former depends upon the interpretation of the latter in connection with this case. But before discussing this question, I wish to express my views with reference to the observation which was made in the course of the argument, that this Court is not bound to consider the Muhammadan Ecclesiastical Law in such cases without having the rules of that law proved by specific evidence like any other fact in a litigation. I am unable to accept this view, because, if it is conceded that the decision of this case depends (as I shall presently endeavour to show it does depend) upon the interpretation of the Muhammadan Ecclesiastical Law, it is to my mind the duty of this Court, and of all Courts subordinate to it, to take judicial notice of such law. I hold that cl. (1) of s. 57 of the Evidence Act (I of 1872) fully covers the Muhammadan Ecclesiastical Law in such cases, because, whenever a question of civil right or the lawfulness of an act arises in a judicial proceeding, even a Criminal Court is bound, *ex necessitate*, to resort to the civil branch of the law; and, in a case like the present, the question being the right of a Muhammadan to pray in a mosque according to his tenets, the question of legality or illegality would fall under the purview of the express guarantee given by the Legislature in s. 24 of the Bengal Civil Courts Act (VI of 1871), that the Muhammadan Law shall be administered with reference to all questions regarding "any religious usage or institution." That the application of some of the sections of the Indian Penal Code depends almost entirely upon the correct interpretation of the rules of civil law, cannot, in my opinion, be doubted; and if it be so, the present case is only another illustration of this principle. Indeed, I am prepared to go the length of saying that, but for this principle, the rules of the Penal Code would in many cases operate as a great injustice, and acts fully justified by the civil law would constitute offences under that Code. I hold therefore that in a case like the present, the provisions of s. 56 of the Evidence Act fully relieve the parties from the necessity of proving the Muhammadan Ecclesiastical Law upon the subject, that that law is not to be placed upon the same footing with reference to this matter as any foreign law of which judicial notice cannot be taken by the Courts in British India; and it follows that I can refer to the Muhammadan Ecclesiastical Law for the purposes of this case, notwithstanding the absence of any specific evidence on the record regarding its rules.

———

In order to understand the exact difficulty which has arisen in this case with reference to the word *amín*, it is necessary to bear in mind that Muhammadanism, like other religions, is divided into various sects or schools of doctrine, differing from each other either in matters of principle or in matters of detail as to the minor points of ritual. "The Musalmans who assume to themselves the distinction of orthodox, are such as maintain the most obvious interpretation of the Kuran and the obligatory force of the traditions in opposition to the innovations of the sectaries, whence they are termed *Sunnis* or traditionists . . . and it is their opinion alone which is admitted to have any weight in the determinations of jurisprudence." These four schools or sects, of which this concise account has been given by Mr. Hamilton in the Preliminary Discourse of his translation of the Hedaya, were founded by the four *orthodox* Imams, namely, Abu Hanifa, Malik, Shafai, and Hanbal, all of whom flourished within the first two centuries of the Muhammadan era, or the eighth century of the Christian era. To use the language of Mr. Hamilton again: "The word *orthodox* as here used is confined purely to a justness of thinking in spiritual matters, concerning which the opinions of those four sects perfectly coincide, the differences among them relating solely to their expositions of the temporal law."

I have mentioned all this in order to render intelligible what I am going to say presently regarding the Muhammadan Ecclesiastical Law with reference to pronouncing the word *amín* in prayers. All parties concerned in this case admittedly belong to the *Sunni* persuasion, and the mosque in question belongs also to the *Sunni* section of the Muhammadan population. It is an indisputable matter of the Muhammadan Ecclesiastical Law that the word *amín* should be pronounced in prayers after the *Sura-i-Fateha*, or the first chapter of the Kuran, and that the only difference of opinion among the four Imams is, whether it should be pronounced aloud or in a low voice. The Hedaya, which is the most celebrated text-book of the Hanafi school of law, lays down the rule in the following terms: "When the imam (leader in prayers) has said 'nor of those who go astray,' he should say *amín*, and so should those who are following him in the prayers; because the Prophet has said that 'when the imam says *amín*, you must say *amín* too, . . . and it must be said in a low voice, because such is the tradition stated by Ibu-i-Masud, and also because the word is the prayer, and should therefore be pronounced in a low voice." That this doctrine is the result of weighing the authority of conflicting traditions is apparent from the commentary on the above passage of the Hedaya by Ibu-i-Humam, a celebrated author of the Hanafi school. These traditions are collected in the celebrated collections of traditions (*Sahi*) of Bukhari and Muslim, both equally acknowledged as accurate traditionists by all the schools of the Sunni Muhammadans. From the same traditions the followers of Imam Shafai have evolved the doctrine that *amín* should be pronounced aloud, and the views of that school are best stated by Nawawi, a commentator on *Sahi Muslim*. The followers of the other two Imams, namely, Malik and Hanbal, also maintain that the word *amín* should be pronounced aloud. But it is not necessary to cite authorities for this proposition, because their followers do not exist in British India. From what I have already said, it is clear that the doctrines of all the four Imams are regarded by Sunni Muhammadans as orthodox, and that the differences of opinion which exist between them are pure matters of detail. Indeed, in the greatest mosque in the world, namely, the *Kaaba* itself, the followers of all the four Imams are at full liberty to pray according to their own tenets. The Shafais, as is apparent from the texts which I have already quoted, pronounce the word *amín* aloud in prayers, and to this no objection is or can be made on the ground that the practice is heterodox from a Sunni point of view. Indeed, the prosecutor in this very case, in his petition of the 20th September, 1884, after stating that the orthodox Muhammadans are the followers of the four Imams, goes on to say that "if the defendants had been the followers of any one of the four Imams, the complainant, who is a Hanafi, and other Muhammadans, would not have shrunk from associating with them," and the ground of the complaint is stated in the petition to be that the defendants "are not the followers of any of the four Imams," that "they intend to set up a new form of worship for themselves;" that "they are therefore no longer Muhammadans;" and by saying the word *amín* aloud they "have been guilty of the offence of insulting the religion of the Hanafia Musalmans." Now unless these allegations are substantiated, I am of the opinion that there can be no case against the accused under s. 296 of the Indian Penal Code. The prosecutor states himself and the founder of the mosque to be a Hanafi, that is, the follower of Imam Abu Hanifa's doctrines. One of the highest authorities of that school is the *Durr-i-Mukhtar*, in which the strongest text is to be found against saying *amín* aloud; but the text itself falls far short of substantiating the rule of Ecclesiastical Law, upon establishing which the case for the prosecution in my opinion depends. The text is as follows: "It is in accord with the practice of the Prophet to say *amín* in a low voice, but the departure from such practice does not necessitate invalidity (of the prayer), nor a mistake, but it is only a detriment." Even this passage only relates to the efficacy or validity of the prayer of the person who says *amín* aloud or in a low tone. There is absolutely no authority in the Hanafia or any other of the three orthodox schools of Muhammadan Ecclesiastical Law which goes to maintain the proposition that if any person in the congregation says the word *amín* aloud at the end of the "*Sura-i-Fateha*," the utterance of the word causes the small-

est injury, in the religious sense, to the prayers of any other person in the congregation, who, according to his tenets, does not say that word aloud. It is a
matter of notoriety that in all the Muhammadan countries like Turkey, Egypt,
and Arabia itself, Hanafis and Shafais go to the same mosque, and form members of the same congregation, and, whilst the Hanafis say the word *amín* in
a low voice, the Shafias pronounce it aloud. To say that the utterance of the
word *amín* aloud, after the imam has recited the "*Sura-i-Fateha*" causes a disturbance in the prayers of a congregation, some or many of whom say the
word in a low tone, is to contradict the express provisions of the Muhammadan Ecclesiastical Law as explained by all the four orthodox Imams. I now
pass to the next step in the case, namely, whether the accused in this case had
the legal right to enter into and worship in the mosque with the congregation according to their own tenets. There is absolutely no evidence in the
case to substantiate the accusation brought by the prosecutor against them
that they are "no longer Muhammadans." They call themselves "Muhammadi," which is the Arabic for "Muhammadan," and although the prosecutor brands them as Wahhabis, there is nothing to prove that they belong to
any heterodox sect. Indeed, the only tangible ground upon which the prosecutor objects to their worshipping in the mosque and calls them Wahhabis
is their saying the *amín* aloud—a practice which, as I said before, is commended by three out of the four orthodox Imams of the Sunni persuasion,
and which, according to the doctrine of Imam Abu Hanifa himself, does not
vitiate the prayers. Now, it is a fundamental principle of the Muhammadan
Law of *wakf*, too well known to require the citation of authorities, that when
a mosque is built and consecrated by public worship, it ceases to be the property of the builder and vests in God (to use the language of the Hedaya) "in
such a manner as subjects it to the rules of Divine property, whence the ap-
propriator's right in it is extinguished, and it becomes a property of God by
the advantage of it resulting to his creatures." A mosque once so consecrated
cannot in any case revert to the founder, and every Muhammadan has the
legal right to enter it, and perform devotions according to his own tenets so
long as the form of worship is in accord with the recognized rules of Muhammadan Ecclesiastical Law. The defendants therefore were fully justified by
law in entering the mosque in question and in joining the congregation, and
they were strictly within their legal rights, according to the orthodox rule of
the Muhammadan Ecclesiastical Law, in saying the word *amín* aloud.

———

At the hearing of the case before the Full Bench, the learned Public Prosecutor laid considerable stress upon the argument that to justify a conviction
under s. 296, Indian Penal Code, it is of no consequence whether the act
which causes the disturbance is in itself lawful or unlawful, that the mere fact
of the disturbance being caused to the religious assembly is sufficient to constitute the offence, specially as the accused in this case had reason to believe

that saying the word *ámín* might be objectionable to the prosecutor and his party, and might cause breach of the peace. I am unable to accept this view of the law, for to use the words of Field, J., in *Beatty* v. *Gillbanks* (L. R. 9 Q. B. D. 303), "it amounts to this, that a man may be convicted for doing a lawful act if he knows that his doing it may cause another to do an unlawful act. There is no authority for such a proposition." Not only do I hold that s. 79 of the Code furnishes a full answer to the argument; but that such a principle would place the minority at the mercy of the majority, and would, in a case like this, deprive them of the right of worship which the law distinctly confers upon them. Indeed if such a view were adopted, it would open the door for wrongful prosecution of innocent persons, who in the exercise of their lawful rights of worship resort to mosques for devotion. Such indeed may be the case here, because there is enough in the evidence for the defence to raise a suspicion that the saying of *ámín* aloud has been made a pretext for the prosecution with the object of preventing the accused from resorting to the mosque for worship, and thus to debar them from asking the prosecutor to render accounts of the disbursement of the income of the property belonging to the mosque, of which he states himself to be the *mutawalli* or superintendent. The witnesses for the defence, who are themselves Hanafis, have solemnly deposed that they do not object to *ámín* being pronounced aloud in prayers, and their statements deserve weight, being in perfect accord with the doctrines of Imam Abu Hanifa himself.

Having taken this view of the case, I regret I am unable to concur in the order of re-trial passed by the learned Chief Justice and my learned brethren, and I would return the case to the referring Bench with a negative answer to the question referred.

Sources

The case presented here is from *The Indian Law Reports: Allahabad series. Containing cases determined by the High Court at Allahabad and by the Supreme Court of India on appeal therefrom* (Allahabad: Superintendent, Printing and Stationery, 1885), pp. 461–477. The quote in the final paragraph of the introduction is from Tahir Mamood, *Islamic Law in Indian Courts since Independence: Fifty Years of Judicial Interpretation*. IOS Readings in Islamic Law (New Delhi: Institute of Objective Studies, 1997), pp. 4–5.

Further Reading

For other writings of early Muslim judges, see Syed Ameer Ali, *The Personal Law of the Mahommedans, according to All the Schools, together with a Comparative Sketch of the Law of Inheritance among the Sunnis and the Shiahs* (London: W. H. Allen,

1880); and Abdur Rahim, *The Principles of Muhammadan Jurisprudence according to the Hanafi, Maliki, Shafi'i and Hanbali Schools* (London: Luzac & Company, 1911). For further information on the British handling of the Muslim law of *waqf* (trust or endowment), see Gregory C. Kozlowski, *Muslim Endowments and Society in British India* (Cambridge: Cambridge University Press, 1985). For further information on the early period of British law in India, see Radhika Singha, *A Despotism of Law: Crime and Justice in Early Colonial India* (New Delhi: Oxford University Press, 1998).

23

Maulana Thanawi's Fatwa on the Limits of Parental Rights over Children

Fareeha Khan

A common theme in Islamic thought on family relations has been the obligation to take care of, and to obey, one's parents, an aspect of religiously oriented social practice that can in no way be rightly ignored. Indeed, disobedience to one's parents is considered to be one of the most serious of enormities. Muslims from the subcontinent, like South Asians generally, give shape to filial piety by a cultural preference for the extended family over the nuclear. Given this context, a religious scholar discussing parental rights might be expected to encourage adult children's obedience and responsibility toward their parents, even at the expense of the interests of the son's wife or children.

For this reason, Maulana Ashraf 'Ali Thanawi's treatise on "Balancing Parental Rights" (*Ta'dil Huquq al-Walidayn*), the source of the translation below, may come as a surprise to many pious Muslims. In this treatise, Thanawi places spousal rights as well as one's own individual rights at the same level as the rights owed parents, and recognizes the possibility that the former could take precedence over the latter under some circumstances.

Ashraf 'Ali Thanawi (d. 1943) was one of the key figures affiliated with the influential Deoband madrasa (discussed in Chapter 18), a seminary known for its emphasis on hadith and a reformist ideology that emphasized religious learning and opposed many popular Muslim beliefs and practices of the day. One of the most prominent of all the leading Deobandis, Thanawi was both an accomplished jurist (*faqih*) and an influential Sufi and spiritual guide. Thanawi's reformist advice on how Muslim men and women could improve their religious practice is evident throughout his many published writings, whether his fatwa collections, his dense works on Sufi thought, or his popular manual of religious conduct, the *Bihishti Zewar* (Heavenly Ornaments), a text initially directed to women.

Thanawi's sense of urgency in wanting to bring about reform is partly a consequence of the immense societal changes taking place at the time. With the loss of Muslim political control and the competition of alternate Western models of education, the 'ulama became intensely aware that their role as definers and maintainers of right practice and belief was ever more critical. Through the legal work of the jurist (*faqih*, pl. *fuqaha*) grounded in traditional learning, scholars like Thanawi claimed authority to guide the lay Muslim on how to implement Islam in daily life. Such determinations stand in contrast to the new articulations of the modernists. The reformist 'ulama of Deoband were not calling for a reform that would "modernize" Islamic law. Rather, they based their arguments about current social practice on traditional legal texts.

In relation to the text on "parental rights" below, it is important to note at the start that the notion of "rights" within Islamic legal discourse is very different from the concept of rights in Western intellectual and legal thought. The word *haqq* (pl. *huquq*) in the Arabic language translates as "right" or "what one is due," but this is more in the sense of duties and responsibilities that others owe one than of intrinsic rights that each individual possesses. So, for example, we read in Islamic legal manuals that prayer is a *haqq* of Allah, a duty that one owes God. Similarly, we hear that a good name is the *haqq* of a child, so that it is the duty of parents to bestow upon their children names that are dignified and of virtuous meaning (as discussed in the fatwas of Chapter 26). In Islamic sources, a "right" is what is befitting or due to one.

"Balancing Parental Rights" is an interesting example of reform-minded legal literature, since it attempted to correct the practice of *already religiously minded* Muslims. Other fatwas and legal tracts reprimand individuals who neglect the needs of their parents: Thanawi's text addresses those on the opposite end of the spectrum who take parental obedience to an extreme, thereby neglecting their families and their own selves. By questioning the notion of absolute obedience to parents, Thanawi is critiquing deeply engrained cultural mores that had come to be accepted as not only socially, but also religiously, mandated modes of behavior.

Thanawi writes as a traditional scholar by engaging well-established religious texts and pre-existing commentaries. He writes with both the lay Muslim and the religious scholar in mind. Thanawi divides the treatise into three sections: the first is a discussion on the need for his treatise; the second comprises all the legal evidences and commentary with which he will back up his arguments; and the third lays out in clear terms the legal rulings relating to parental rights. The first and third sections are written in easy-to-understand Urdu, and so are accessible to even the average literate South Asian Muslim. The second section, however, the one that contains the legal "proofs," is completely in Arabic and immensely dense and complex. It is intended for trained 'ulama familiar with the sources from which he is quoting.

Many times in this final section Thanawi does not even provide a full citation; he will mention just the first few words of a hadith, or even just a phrase from a legal commentary, and the reader is expected to know exactly which hadith or fatwa is being referred to, or, at the very least, know how to find it. The Arabic section also mentions a host of important figures from across Muslim intellectual history, only some of whom the average reader may recognize. A number of the prominent Companions (*Sahabah*) of the Prophet Muhammad are cited as transmitters of hadith, among them Abu Bakr and 'Umar (the first two caliphs), Mu'adh ibn Jabal, and 'Abdullah ibn 'Abbas. Others are mostly hadith scholars (*muhaddithun*) and prominent jurists, on whom Thanawi relies for his argument.

Thanawi cites hadith compilers from as early as the third century of Islam, such as Imam Tirmidhi (d. 279 A.H./892 C.E.) and Imam Abu Dawud (d. 276/889), as well as hadith specialists from as late as the seventeenth century. In fact, the hadith texts he relies on most heavily are from the later period: the *Mishkat al-Masabih* was compiled by at-Tibrizi, who died in 741 (1340). Its famous commentary, *Mirqat al-Mafatih*, which is heavily cited by Thanawi, was written some centuries later by Mulla 'Ali al-Qari (d. 1014/1605).

Thanawi cites a number of legal scholars as well, the earliest being Imam Abu Hanifa (d. 150/767), the eponymous founder of his own Hanafi *madhhab*, as well as Abu Hanifa's student, Muhammad al-Shaybani (d. 189/804). Thanawi frequently cites *al-Durr al-Mukhtar*, which was written by al-Haskafi in 462 (1070), as well as the renowned commentary on this text, *ar-Radd al-Muhtar*, by Muhammad Amin ibn 'Abidin (d. 1252/1836), the most celebrated Hanafi jurist of the modern period.

There are five major categories in Islamic law that describe the legal status of any given action. Obedience to one's parents, though often wrongly assumed to be unquestionably *wajib* (legally incumbent), is described by Thanawi as fitting into every one of these categories, depending on the situation. Thus, at times it can be *wajib*, at times *mustahabb* (preferred), at times *mubah* (a neutral category that can be translated as "permissible"), at times *makruh* (offensive), and sometimes even *haram* (unlawful). The ascription of parental obedience to these various categories is not simply based on what the parents are commanding. It is obvious, for instance, to even the most devoutly obedient son that if his parents command him to drink wine or murder another individual, he is not obliged to obey them. Instead, Thanawi stresses that one must gauge the requirement to honor one's parents' wishes on the basis of whether or not their desires will come into conflict with the rights of others.

Thanawi lays out three separate parties whose rights must all be somehow balanced: 1) one's parents, 2) one's spouse and children, and 3) one's own self. Thanawi says that each of these three parties has certain *wajib* or religiously incumbent rights, and that one must be careful when trying to fulfill the incumbent rights of one party, not to neglect those of another.

The most striking feature of the treatise is likely Thanawi's treatment of the rights of the wife. Thanawi is very aware that his equating of parental and spousal rights is the most controversial aspect of his tract; it is probably for this reason that he deliberately discusses the famous hadith of 'Umar right at the start of his commentary section. In the hadith, the famous companion of the Prophet, 'Umar ibn al-Khattab, commands his son to divorce his wife. The son is reluctant to do so, but the Prophet backs up the opinion of 'Umar and requires the son to obey his father. It is easy to draw the conclusion from this hadith that one must unconditionally prefer one's father over one's wife. In fact, most of the primary texts Thanawi cites seem to indicate that parental rights always take precedence. However, he firmly insists that this is not the case; rather he shows that obedience to one's parents is in fact a highly nuanced aspect of Islamic law.

Thanawi's willingness to revisit the rights of women may stem from the changing conception of family in the nineteenth century, particularly on the part of Indian reformers, both Muslim and non-Muslim, who emphasized the mother's role in the foundation of a solid community. He is also grappling with how to rearticulate men's roles as caretakers of the family (extended and nuclear), given evolving ideas on obligations owed to non-nuclear family members. Thanawi's ideas on spousal rights are certainly not revolutionary: his call for the provision of a woman's own separate residence and his insistence that the wife's rights not be neglected, draw on premodern sources that he himself quotes. The 'ulama had always discussed spousal rights, just as they discussed parental ones. What is distinctive about Thanawi's treatise is that he seeks to reconcile the two issues within one tract. As a religious advisor to many thousands of spiritual disciples, he may well have seen conflicts between parental and spousal obligations first hand.

Perhaps the most subtle yet most significant aspect of the treatise, however, is Thanawi's emphasis on the rights of one's own self, or soul (*nafs*). Thanawi warns that even one's own self has rights over one, and that to expend too much effort in trying to please one's parents may not only be mentally and spiritually daunting, but also damaging to one's religious faith. Thanawi here writes as a spiritual guide concerned with inner attitudes. Thus he encourages a person to acquire sufficient learning to know what is required and what is not. If, after doing so, a person decides to carry out duties that are not religiously required, that then becomes a matter of conscious choice and the action will be performed with a positive, not negative, mindset, thereby taking much less toll on the individual's emotional and psychological well-being. Thanawi thus bolsters the importance of Islamic guidance by demonstrating its this-worldly benefit as well as its next-worldly benefit for those who wish to follow its guidance.

Just as with the issue of spousal rights, Thanawi's championing of "individual rights" finds precedent, not least in a tradition of the Prophet: "Your self has rights over you!" His instruction to avoid overburdening one's soul with doing too much good resonates with what is found in sacred texts and premodern commentaries (and particularly with what is found in Sufi works). At the same time, Thanawi's tract is relevant and new, addressing contemporary formulations of the tension between individual and communal responsibility. His real accomplishment, then, is that he has successfully translated the tradition of the past into a fully authentic present.

FROM THANAWI'S IMDAD AL-FATAWA: BALANCING PARENTAL RIGHTS

In the Name of God, the Compassionate, the Most Merciful.

PART ONE [URDU]

We send praise upon Him and seek blessings for His Ennobled Messenger. God the Exalted says in a verse of the Qur'an, "Verily, God commands that you fulfill your trusts to whom they are due, and when you must judge between people, do so with justice" [4:58]. Two legal rulings can be understood from the general meaning of this verse: the first is that it is incumbent upon those who have obligatory rights to fulfill these rights. The second is that when fulfilling the rights of one person, the rights of another must not be violated.

The aim of this treatise is to discuss two specific cases that can be derived from the two general rulings mentioned above. The first of these specific cases is an enunciation of the obligatory and non-obligatory rights of parents. The second is a discussion of how to balance the rights of one's parents, particularly when the fulfillment of these rights comes in conflict with the fulfillment of the rights of one's wife or children.

The reason for this study is that after having faced innumerable such incidents, we know that there are some people who commit gross negligence in fulfilling the rights of their parents, who ignore the sacred texts that state that the fulfillment of these rights is a religious obligation, and thereby bring upon themselves the divine wrath that results from disobedience to one's parents. [Conversely,] there are also certain pious folk who are excessive in the fulfillment of their parents' rights, such that the rights of another, such as the wife or the children, are thereby neglected. These people ignore yet another set of sacred texts, those that necessitate care and protection (of one's wife and children), and so bring upon themselves the divine wrath that results from the violation of another's rights.

And then there is a third group. They do not neglect any other individual's rights, but they believe that certain non-obligatory rights are in fact obligatory, and they go about attempting to fulfill these rights with such a mindset. But since at times they cannot bear all of this responsibility, they soon become distressed. They begin experiencing religious misgivings such as, "The *shari'a* has some rulings that are simply unbearable and too strict!" In this way these poor souls harm their own religious faith. In this last category of people there is [in actuality] still one whose obligatory rights are being neglected, and that is the man's own self, since the self also has certain obligatory rights. The Prophet, peace and blessings of God be upon him, said: "Your self has rights over you!" And of the obligatory rights [which your self/soul possesses], the most important is the protection of religious belief. Thus, having the mindset that the non-obligatory rights of one's parents are in fact obligatory leads one toward the sin mentioned above [that of becoming overwhelmed and experiencing religious misgivings]. For this reason, the knowledge of which rights are obligatory is in itself obligatory. Once one understands the distinction between obligatory and non-obligatory rights, then if one decides to still fulfill the non-obligatory ones, knowing that they are not obligatory, the danger mentioned above will not occur. He will interpret any difficulty entailed as something he has brought upon himself and however long he will tolerate it, it will be because of his own high intentions. In fact, by perceiving the situation in this way, he will in fact derive some pleasure from it. Such a person will think to himself, "Despite the fact that I am not responsible for this, I am still taking on this [important] task." And he will know that he can fulfill this task according to his own will. From this we see that in possessing the knowledge of the religious rulings there is only great benefit, while in being ignorant of them there is only compounded harm. Thus I write these few lines with the goal of conveying a specific kind of discernment. Following this introduction, I will gather together the important hadith (prophetic narrations or traditions), as well as legal rulings that are relevant to this topic. I will then expound on the legal rulings that can be derived from the gathered citations. My intention in writing this short treatise is that an accurate perception of parental rights may be gained. . . . In this light, it would not be inappropriate for me to name this treatise "Balancing Parental Rights." And God is the One from whom aid is sought, and to whom we entrust our affairs.

PART TWO [ARABIC]

In the *Mishkat* it is related on the authority of Ibn 'Umar, who narrates: "I was married to a woman whom I loved, and 'Umar [Ibn 'Umar's father] disliked her. So he said to me, 'Divorce her,' but I refused to do so. Then he went to the Messenger of God, may God bless him and grant him peace, and mentioned this to him as well. Thereupon the Messenger of God said to me, 'Divorce her.'" (Originally cited by Imam Tirmidhi.)

In the *Mirqat*, a commentary on the *Mishkat*, the command "Divorce her" is legally preferred (*mandub*), or else incumbent (*wajib*), but only incumbent if there is some other extenuating circumstance. Imam Ghazali in his *Ihya 'Ulum al-Din* (vol. 2, p. 26, Kishwary edition) comments as follows: "This hadith indicates that the right of the father takes precedence [over the right of the wife], but this is only if the father does not dislike the wife due to some corrupt reason. 'Umar is an example of such a one [who would not express his dislike due to some evil intention]."

In the *Mishkat* there is a narration related on the authority of Mu'adh in which he says, "The Messenger of God counseled me." He transmitted the hadith and in it we find, "Do not disobey your parents, even if they command you to leave your wife or your wealth." In the *Mirqat* it is explained that the condition ["even if they command you to leave your wife or your wealth"] is an exaggeration [for emphasis] and indicates the extreme limit [of obedience to one's parents].

"As far as the actual legal [obligation] is concerned, he would not be required to divorce his wife," even if his remaining married to her would cause them great trouble. This is because the man himself would suffer harm by [such a divorce], and so he would not be required to do this for their sake. Had the parents realized that such harm would come to their son, out of natural compassion they would not have commanded him to divorce in the first place. Now if they insisted [on the divorce] despite the harm it would cause their son, this would be foolishness on their part, and the son would not be required to pay heed to their instruction. This same reasoning applies as well to abandoning one's wealth.

In summary, the evidence that [the Prophet was] exaggerating [for emphasis] can be seen [in his use of a similar rhetorical device] in the following hadith: "Do not associate partners with God, even if you are slaughtered or burnt alive." This is most definitely exaggeration. Permissibility for pronouncing words of unbelief under duress is in fact established by the statement of God, "Those who repudiate God after having had faith, not one who is compelled while his heart rests securely in faith, rather only those who open their breasts to disbelief, wrath from God is upon them, and for them there is tremendous torment." (16:106)

In the *Mishkat* there is another hadith, this one related by Ibn 'Abbas, who said that the Prophet, peace and blessings of God be upon him, said: "Whoever awakens in the morning obedient to God by way of his parents, two doors of Heaven are opened for him, and one door will be opened if only one [parent is alive]. And if he disobeys them, then two doors of Hell will be opened for him, and one door if only one [parent is alive.]" A man said, "Even if his parents are unjust in their treatment towards him?" And the Prophet replied, "Even if they are unjust, even if they are unjust, even if they are unjust!" (Related by al-Bayhaqi in *Shu'ab al-iman.*)

In the *Mirqat* the phrase "by way of his parents" is explained to mean, "by fulfilling their rights." It is also explained that obedience to parents is not an independent form of obedience, but rather it is [directly tied] to obedience to God Himself, i.e., the command of God [calling for obedience to parents] has reached such an extent that [it is as if] obedience to them *is* obedience to God. This is supported by the Prophetic tradition: "There is no obedience of creation which entails disobedience of the Creator."

With regard to the statement "Even if they are unjust," the commentator al-Tibi explains that what is meant by injustice here is only in terms of worldly matters, not matters which relate to [one's standing] in the Hereafter. Also, this statement, "Even if they are unjust," is like the statement of the Prophet, peace be upon him, about pleasing the *zakat* (alms-tax) collectors: "Please them, even if they are unjust." (Related by Abu Dawud) In the *Lama'at* it is explained that this statement "even if they are unjust" is meant for emphasis [to encourage the fulfillment of the tax-collectors' claim toward what is obligatory on the individual]. For if the tax-collectors were truly unjust and oppressive in their work [exacting more alms-tax than what is actually religiously required], how could one be compelled to please them?

In the *Mishkat* a story told by the Prophet, may God send peace and blessings upon him, is related on the authority of Ibn 'Umar. Three men were traveling when they were overcome by rain. They took refuge in a cave when suddenly a boulder descended and blocked the mouth of the cave, trapping them inside. [The three of them decided to implore God for help on the basis of a past righteous act which they felt was done sincerely for His sake.] One of them recounted that he [used to take care of] his parents, who were quite old, and he hated to begin serving his children before serving them, even while the children were crying about his feet. This hadith is agreed upon [to be authentic by the hadith transmitters Bukhari and Muslim].

In the *Mirqat* [it is explained that his] preference to attend to the needs of his parents over the needs of his children is due to the age-difference between his children and his parents. [And it is also because] even though he may be a grown man, [the son] will remain as a young child [in the eyes of his parents, thus explaining his automatic deference to them]. The crying of the children in the above incident is like that of the children in the incident of Abu Talhah [one of the Companions of the Prophet]. When guests arrived at Abu Talhah's home, he asked his wife, "Do you have anything for them?" To which she replied, "Only the children's food." It was necessary that [the guests] be given something, so he [asked her to put the children to bed]. In the *Lama'at* the author explains that the children here were not in need of the food. Their crying was simply the usual noise that children make, crying that has nothing to do with hunger. Had it truly been out of hunger, it would have been incumbent that they be presented with the food before others. [How could someone of the rank of Abu Talhah and his wife] neglect an incumbent religious duty, when God Himself has praised them? This explanation of the incident, that in fact the right of one's child takes precedence over the right of one's father, is supported by the following text in *al-Durr al-Mukhtar*, in the chapter on expenditure: "If a man has both father and son living, the son has more right over him [than the father]. According to a weaker opinion it is stated that he must divide between the two."

In the *Kitab al-Athar* of Imam Muhammad [there is a hadith] related on the authority of Aisha, where she said: "The best of what you eat is from your own earnings [as opposed to something gained from begging or as charity], and your children's [earnings] are part of your earnings." Based on this statement, Imam Muhammad said, "There is no harm if one, out of necessity, takes from the wealth of his child in a reasonable manner. However, if the father is without need and takes from the child's wealth, then this would become a debt which he would owe to his son." This is also the opinion of Imam Abu Hanifa.

Imam Muhammad narrates from Imam Abu Hanifa who narrates from Hammad who narrates from Ibrahim who said: "A man is not entitled to any of his son's wealth except that which he requires for food, drink, or clothing." And this was the opinion of Imam Abu Hanifa.

In *Kanz al-'Ummal* it is narrated on the authority of Hakim and others: "Your children are surely a gift God the Exalted bestows upon you. He gifts whomever

He wishes with female children, and he gifts whomever He wishes with male children. They and their wealth are for you, if you are in need." This statement of the Prophet, upon him be peace, where he says, "if you are in need," supports Imam Muhammad's qualification to Aisha's statement "your children's [earnings] are from your earnings" [since Imam Muhammad says that one can only take "out of necessity" from one's children's wealth]. Also, this restriction necessitates that the wealth taken become a debt on the father if it is taken from the child without need.

Abu Bakr, may God be pleased with him, has a similar explanation for the following statement of the Prophet: "You and your wealth belong to your father." Abu Bakr said that here "the Prophet meant only to the extent of necessary daily expenditure." (This was narrated by al-Bayhaqi in *Tarikh al-Khulafa*, p. 65.)

It is mentioned in *al-Durr al-Mukhtar*: "It is not obligatory for a boy or an adult to go out in battle when either both or one of his parents are in need of his care, because obedience to parents is a *fard 'ayn* (a personal obligation) [as opposed to fighting in battle, which is often simply a *fard kifayah* (communal obligation, or an obligation required of the community as a whole)]. . . . And it is not permissible to go out on a journey in which there is some danger except with the permission of one's parents. As for the journey which entails no risk, it can be undertaken without the permission of one's parents, and this includes a journey undertaken with the intention of seeking sacred knowledge."

From *Radd al-Muhtar*: "Parents have the right to prevent their child from traveling if his travel will bring them great difficulty, and this applies even if the parents are unbelievers [non-Muslims]. If however the parents are preventing the son to travel because he will be going out to fight members of their own religion, then he is not obliged to obey them, as long as there is no fear that they will suffer harm [by his leaving]. Of course if the parents are poor and in need of the son's care, then the son will be obliged to [stay back from fighting and] take care of his parents, even though they be unbelievers. This is because it is not right that one leaves a personal obligation in order to fulfill a communal obligation.

A dangerous journey is one that is undertaken for the sake of battle or a sea voyage. As for "journeys which entail no risk," these include journeys undertaken for trade or for the hajj or the lesser pilgrimage, as long as there is no fear that the parents will suffer harm (as cited in Sarakhsi). Travel for the sake of sacred knowledge falls into this latter category as well, since it takes precedence over travel for trade purposes, as long as the journey is a safe one and no harm to the parents is feared (Sarakhsi). Similar statements can be found in *al-Bahr al-Ra'iq* and the *Fatawa Hindiyya*.

In *al-Durr al-Mukhtar* it is recorded that "it is necessary (*wajib*) for a man to provide a place of residence for his wife in which none of his relatives or her relatives reside." In the *Radd al-Muhtar*, after various statements on this issue are quoted, it states that "legally a wealthy wife must be provided for with a moderate room of her own. It would be sufficient that she have a room [or section] of her own in a larger abode. . . . The people of our city Damascus do not live in homes in which strangers reside, and this I mean with respect to the middle-class folk, so obviously it applies to a greater degree to the noble and wealthy. An exception to this rule would be if brothers for example were to inherit and share a house, but each would reside [with his immediate family] in a separate section of the house, with the general amenities [such as kitchen, bathroom, etc.] being shared among all of them.

"Of course, the customary practice of people changes with time and place, so it is upon the jurist (mufti) that he take into account the state of the people of his own time and place. Without such consideration, a balanced society will not be attainable."

PART THREE [URDU]

From these narrations, a few different legal rulings can be derived:

1. If parents forbid one from carrying out a religiously incumbent (wajib) duty, it would not be permissible for one to follow their order, let alone it being incumbent to follow their command. The following few specific rulings fall under this more general one:
   a. If a man has very limited material resources, such that if he were to help his parents, he would cause hardship to his wife and children, it would be impermissible for this man to harm his wife and children and spend instead on his parents.
   b. It is the wife's right to ask for a place of residence separate from that of her in-laws. So if she were to ask to live separate from her husband's parents, but his parents want her to live with them, then it would not be permissible for the husband to require his wife to live with his parents. In fact, it would be religiously incumbent upon him that he arrange a separate residence for his wife.
   c. If the son wishes to go on hajj or the lesser pilgrimage, or to travel for the sake of seeking essential knowledge of the religion, then in this case as well it would not be permissible to obey one's parents.
2. If parents command one to do something that is religiously prohibited, then in this case it would also be impermissible to obey them. Some examples of this are: if they ask one to take on a profession that is not religiously sanctioned, or if they ask one to partake in unlawful rituals and ceremonies.
3. In the case of an act that is neither incumbent nor prohibited, say it is simply something permissible (mubah) or even preferred (mustahabb) in the sacred law, for such a case it is necessary that further details be examined.
   a. It could be that the individual is in severe need of carrying out this action, such that if he did not, he would suffer harm. An example of this would be if there is a poor man who has no money and no opportuni-

ties for work in his village, but his parents refuse to let him leave. If he
really were in serious need of leaving the village in order to support
himself, it would not be necessary for him to obey his parents.

b. If however his need for work outside the village was not really so great,
[then it must be seen if either he or else his parents would be harmed
due to his departure]. One must determine whether the work he intends to take on has any inherent danger or poses any threat to his life
or health. It must also be seen whether, when taking on this particular
job, he would be unable to make arrangements for his parents' care
were he to leave (by way of a servant and/or the provision of their daily
necessities). If his job poses any danger to him, or if by his disappear-
ance the parents will be harmed due to lack of care and provision, then
going against their wishes would be impermissible.

Further examples [of the above-mentioned situation]: he is going
off to fight in a battle that he is not religiously required to participate
in; he wishes to embark on a sea-voyage; he leaves them with no one
to ask about their needs, and he does not have enough money to make
arrangements for their care and provision before his departure; and in
all of these cases, the work or the journey is not necessary. For these
situations, obeying their wishes would be incumbent.

c. Now if neither of these two factors is present—i.e., neither the work
nor the journey pose any harm, nor is there any fear that the parents
will suffer difficulty or harm—then in these cases, despite the fact that
he is not in real need of the work or the journey, it would be permissible for him to undertake this task, even though [his parents] forbid
him from it. Still, even in this case it would be legally preferred that he
honor his parents' wishes.

The following specific cases serve to further highlight the rules described
above [where parents forbid a permissible or preferred action]:

If the parents, without any reason, demand that the son give his wife a divorce, it would not be incumbent for him to obey them. [In Arabic:] *The hadith
of Ibn 'Umar is interpreted as indicating the recommended action [i.e., to obey the
parents when they make such a demand], or else that 'Umar had some real grounds
that justified his request.*

If the parents demand that the son hand over all his earnings to them, then
in this case as well it would not be incumbent for him to obey them. And if they
were to coerce him to do so, they would be sinful. [In Arabic:] *The hadith "Your
person and your wealth belong to your parents" applies to situations of need on the
part of the parents. How can it be otherwise when the Prophet, peace be upon him,
has [also] said, "The wealth of a man may not be lawfully taken by another except
with his whole-hearted consent."*

And if they take without permission from their son's wealth more than their
basic requirements, this wealth would be a debt that they owe him. The son

may demand repayment in this world, and if he is not repaid, they will have to suffer its payment in the Hereafter [i.e., by having to face the anger and possibly punishment of God]. The unambiguous statements of the jurists suffice to prove this. The jurists are fully qualified and competent in their understanding of the meanings of the hadith, particularly when the condition "if you are in need" included in the hadith of Hakim [mentioned above in the second part of the treatise] is clear in its meaning. And God knows best.

Sources

Thanawi's treatise *Ta'dil huquq al-walidayn* is included in *Imdad al-Fatawa*, a major collection of his legal opinions. I took the treatise from the following edition: *Imdad al-Fatawa*, vol.4 (Karachi: Maktaba Darul Uloom, Muharram 1422 [2001]), pp.480–485.

Further Reading

For further reading on Islamic law and reform in South Asia, see Barbara D. Metcalf, *Islamic Revival in British India: Deoband, 1860–1900* (Princeton, NJ: Princeton University Press, 1982), pp. 138–197; Francis Robinson, *Islam and Muslim History in South Asia* (Delhi: Oxford University Press, 2000); Fareeha Khan, "Traditionalist Approaches to Shari'ah Reform: Mawlana Ashraf 'Ali Thanawi's Fatwa on Women's Right to Divorce," PhD diss., Department of Near Eastern Languages, University of Michigan, 2008. For an insightful treatment of the particular role of the 'ulama with respect to reform in the modern period, see Muhammad Qasim Zaman, *The Ulama in Contemporary Islam: Custodians of Change* (Princeton, NJ: Princeton University Press, 2002). For a more thorough account of the life and work of Thanawi, see Muhammad Qasim Zaman, *Ashraf 'Ali Thanawi: Islam in Modern South Asia* (Oxford: Oneworld, 2008). On sources of Islamic law and its application, see Muhammad Hashim Kamali, *Shari'ah Law: An Introduction* (Oxford: Oneworld, 2008); Muhammad Khalid Masud, Brinkley Messick, and David S. Powers, eds., *Islamic Legal Interpretation: Muftis and Their Fatwas* (Cambridge, MA: Harvard University Press, 1996); and Judith Tucker, *In the House of the Law: Gender and Islamic Law in Ottoman Syria and Palestine* (Berkeley, CA: University of California Press, 1998). On the changing role of women within the family in the modern period, see Lila Abu-Lughod, ed., *Remaking Women: Feminism and Modernity in the Middle East* (Princeton, NJ: Princeton University Press, 1998); and Barbara D. Metcalf, *Perfecting Women: Maulana Ashraf 'Ali Thanawi's Bihishti Zewar* (Berkeley, CA: University of California Press, 1990). For a sample of Thanawi's own writings on Sufism, see Masihullah Khan, *The Path to Perfection: An Edited Anthology of the Spiritual Teachings of Hakim ul-Umma Mawlana Ashraf 'Ali Thanawi* (Santa Barbara, CA: White Thread Press, 2005).

—24—

Shari'at Governance in Colonial
and Postcolonial India

Ebrahim Moosa

In contemporary India, especially in the states of Bihar, Orissa, and Madhya Pradesh, as well as in a few others, a network of informal tribunals known as the Imarat-i Shari'at (juridical-ethical councils adjudicating cases dealing with marriage, divorce and inheritance issues in terms of Islamic law) continue to flourish in rural as well as urban areas. This network of institutions of civil society dispensing *shari'at*-based ethical and moral governance is also loosely tied to the authoritative All India Muslim Personal Law Board (AIMPLB). The latter is a non-governmental body that emerged in 1973 to represent and defend the family law interests of a cross section of Muslim branches and sects in post-independence India. In recent years several breakaway boards have been formed on sectarian and gender grounds, but the AIMPLB still seeks both to mediate intra-Muslim interests in matters of family law and to serve as a negotiating forum with the government on political and juridical matters of a religious order.

The Imarat-i Shari'at movement in India, an informal Muslim juridical network, was led by a little-known traditional Muslim figure, Abul Mahasin Muhammad Sajjad (1301–1359 A.H./1883–1940 C.E.). Sajjad was born in the village of Panhasa near the Bihar provincial capital of Patna. After early studies in his village, he moved successively to madrasas in Bihar, Kanpur, and, briefly, the famous Dar al-'Ulum in Deoband (discussed in Chapters 17 and 18). He completed his education in the Madrasa Subhaniyya in Allahabad, from which he graduated after five years. Sajjad made a lasting impression on his peers. In Allahabad one of his students, Zahid Khan Daryabadi, provided him with a translated digest of the daily English newspapers. National and international events forcefully brought home to Sajjad the importance of mobilizing Indian Muslims to function as a cohesive social unit and, more importantly for him, in an organized fashion. Failing to do so, he feared, could have catastrophic consequences for Muslim society in a multi-religious India.

After a teaching career culminating in sixteen years at his alma mater in Allahabad, he decided to give attention on a full-time basis to social, political, and cultural concerns that affected the Muslims of Bihar. Between 1917 and his death in
1940, Sajjad worked closely with the major political players as well as the traditional Muslim leaders who represented Muslims in the political life of the Indian
National Congress and their rivals, the Muslim League. He was active in the *Jami'at
'Ulama-i Hind* (JUH), a national 'ulama council dominated by Deobandis, which
was founded in 1918 and was an ally of the Indian National Congress.

Like them, Sajjad firmly supported the Gandhian non-cooperation movement
and as late as 1938 tried to convince Muhammad Ali Jinnah, leader of the Muslim
League, of the need to join in support: "To get rid of tyrants and despots and to replace their governance with divinely approved justice and equity, the oppressed
must be prepared to make sacrifices in terms of life and property. From the very
beginning there were two ways of executing this principle: one was recourse to
armed resistance (*jihad bi al-sayf*); the second way, without renouncing jihad, was
to proclaim the truth and verbally and practically combat falsehood. This is also
called a pacifist war (*harb-i silmi*) and, in general parlance, it is nonviolent civil disobedience ('*adm tashaddud ke sath siwil na farmani*)." He even reminded Jinnah that
acts of civil disobedience were spearheaded in 1907 by two Muslim peasants in
the Champaran District, even before Gandhi used nonviolence as a tactic. Sajjad
was deeply skeptical of the Muslim League, which he suspected of rank oppor-
tunism and loyalty to the British.

Sajjad was instrumental in the formation of the Muslim Independent Party
(MIP) in Bihar, which cooperated with the Congress Party. In 1936 the MIP won
the second largest number of votes in the state. Every member belonging to the
MIP had to commit to the idea of furthering *shari'at*-based governance. The MIP
for a time formed the state government and addressed issues related to Muslims,
including recognition of the Urdu language as the official language of Bihar.

Sajjad's primary loyalty was to the poor, especially the rural poor with whom he
closely identified given his own rural background. During the devastating Bihar
earthquake of 1934, Sajjad personally proposed a mutual help scheme in the
Champaran District in which groups of peasants helped to re-build each others'
homes. Sajjad himself spent time living among the peasants and labored alongside
them making roofing implements of jute for use in the construction of homes.

Sajjad's distinctive focus was his tireless work on behalf of the institutionaliza-
tion of *shari'at* courts. Disillusioned by the continuous erosion of Islamic law
within the colonial state structure, which was also a direct attack and affront to the
authority of the 'ulama as interpreters of the law, Sajjad called the 'ulama to action:
"When infidels usurp the land of Muslims and dominate it, then it is obligatory for
them to establish and safeguard their legal order (*nizam-i shar'i*) by appointing a
Muslim guardian (*wali*)—the head of the *shari'at* court (*amir-i mahakmat-i shar'
iat*)." However, the *raison d'etre* for *shari'at* governance is closely wedded to his
fundamental premise; namely, the prevalence of a fallen condition of humanity, a
state of *jahiliyyat* ("barbarity" or "ignorance") resembling the pre-Islamic period of

Arabia, from which Muslims should be rescued through a normative order. (The term *jahiliyyat* was also used by the Jama'at-i Islami ideologue Mawlana Abul Ala Mawdudi, and it was later popularized and developed into a fully-fledged political and sociological category by Sayyid Qutb, the Egyptian Muslim Brotherhood ideologue.)

Sounding the jeremiads, Sajjad announces: "Do not the Muslims of India today live a non-shar'i existence and in an overwhelming state of *jahiliyyat*?" Lamenting the fact that even the 'ulama had ignored their duty to promote *shari'at* regulations affecting individual and social conduct, he stated: "We have acquiesced to a [flawed] belief that by fulfilling individual obligations (*fara'id*) without the aid of a *shari'at* order (*tanzim-i shar'i*), we have attained the greatest happiness and consider that our salvation. In one sense this is a form of monasticism (*rahbaniyyat*) and can be categorized as a form of *jahiliyyat*." By charging its religious leadership with dereliction of its duty to apply the *shari'at*, this must possibly go down as one of the most trenchant indictments of Indian Muslim society.

In 1921 Sajjad initiated the *dar al-qada*, an informal legal tribunal system, in Bihar at Phulwari Sharif, near Patna, which later blossomed into branches in Orissa. The first *amir* of Bihar was Mawlana Shah Badruddin, with Sajjad as his deputy. In *Divine Governance*, published posthumously in 1941 as a prologue to a larger unfinished work, Sajjad outlined an elaborate political philosophy explaining why it was imperative for Muslims to have an Islamic government and an order based on *shari'at*. He deployed the now familiar argument made by the twelfth-century Muslim thinker Abu Hamid al-Ghazali (d. 1111), and later masterfully elaborated by the fourteenth-century Andalusian thinker Abu Ishaq al-Shatibi (d. 1388) about the five objectives of the *shari'at*; namely, to preserve religion, life, reason, property, and honor. While he was not opposed to democratic governance neither was he an advocate: he remained skeptical as to whether a democratic order could meet the legitimate expectations of humans. The flaw in democracy, Sajjad argued, was that its normative and legal order was utterly subject to human molestation. Only a situation where the Lawgiver is intimately related to the subjectivity of the ethical subject, in his view, could ensure that the objectives of governance be executed and fulfilled. So, if the political order contradicted the primary religious subjectivity of the individual and community, Sajjad argued, it was bound to fail in realizing its objectives. To his mind, most European democracies were failing in the pre–World War II period, an observation that was vindicated by the rise of European fascism.

Sajjad in many ways saw the creation of *shari'at*-centered governance within a nation-state polity as in some way fulfilling the theological requirements of a caliphate. The caliphate is reified and reduced to its essential function: the application of a law and moral code, even though the template and format of the classical model of a caliphate is absent. In the late twentieth century the fourth *amir* of the *shari'at* in India, Mawlana Minnatullah Rahmani, as head of the Shari'at Governance Council, Imarat-i Shari'at, spelled out the trajectory of Sajjad's 1941 vision. Once the Imarat-i Shari'at had developed further, Rahmani argued, it would require only a few more steps before it could become an Islamic caliphate (*khilafat-i Islamiyya*) with some minimum alterations to the concept to make it workable. In fact, the very infrastructure of the *shari'at* governance in India, Rahmani continued, was of such a nature that once it was enforced it would be possible to argue that it was "nothing else but an Islamic caliphate." In other words, the implementation of *shari'at* was figuratively as effective as a caliphate in Rahmani's view.

Thus there was a new set of dynamics: a religious law complete with tribunals functioning within a secular nation-state. Over the years the movement known as the "governance of the *shari'at*" (*imarat-i shari'at*), would make new advances and become a symbol of Muslim juridical autonomy in post-Partition India. The movement makes for a fascinating case study of the elective affinity of Islamic law to modern legal systems, and it serves as a splendid example of what sociologists would call the "antagonistic acculturation" of Muslim law. By offering simpler and often more expedient resolution of problems, one might add, the courts also better serve the poor, the goal that Sajjad always sought.

The translation below, of one of Sajjad's speeches delivered to a special session of the Bihar branch of the 'ulama association, the Jami'at-i 'Ulama, recapitulates several of the themes for which he had gained renown and also reflects his passion and commitment to the idea of governance by the dictates of the *shari'at* within a nation-state paradigm. The exact date of this speech cannot be established with certainty, but it was most probably delivered a few years before 1921, when the first tribunal was established.

ABUL MAHASIN MUHAMMAD SAJJAD'S LETTER ADDRESSED TO THE NOBLE 'ULAMA AND HONORED SPIRITUAL LEADERS OF BIHAR

I offer my heartfelt thanks for inviting me to this extraordinary session of the Jami'at-i 'Ulama of Bihar, bearing in mind the reason for convening this event. I think it appropriate to express my thoughts from the perspective of Islamic law (*shari'at*) so that no misunderstanding remains. Furthermore, it will also eliminate whatever doubts and falsehoods prevail with regard to this matter [the appointment of a leader (*amir*) of the *shari'at*].

Respected sirs, surely you are all well aware of the paramount importance of the following matter: that when non-Muslims conquer (*istila*) and dominate over Muslim lands, then under such circumstance it becomes obligatory upon Muslims to appoint a superior authority (*wali*) as leader of the *shari'at* court (*amir-i mahkamat-i shari'at*) who will oversee the establishment and viability of an order based on the *shari'at*.

For more than 150 years it has been a responsibility placed on Indian Muslims to establish such an order. In other words, since the decline of Islamic rule in India this has been incumbent. But due to negligence and carelessness, or due to hostile reasons or due to a lack of cooperation, Indian Muslims have not give attention to this obligation. The consequences that followed were inevitable.

Are Indian Muslims not following a lifestyle that is non-compliant to the *shari'at* and indulging in a lifestyle resembling that of the "age of ignorance" (*jahili*)? Living a confused life without a leader is a life of general ignorance (*jahiliyyat-i 'am*). We never gave attention to legal and moral requirements (*ahkam*) and the way they applied to individual and social life; we ignored its importance. We only considered the fulfillment of personal obligations that could be fulfilled without the need for religious organization (*shar'i tanzim*), seeing this as the highest desideratum and as a means of salvation: in one sense this is monasticism (*rahbaniyyat*), which could also be explained as a "state of ignorance" (*jahiliyyat*).

There is no excuse for neglecting this all-important obligation till today. Our shortcomings are no grounds to proclaim innocence in the eyes of God. Internecine strife and conflict, disagreements over secondary issues or claims that our time lacks men of caliber, the likes of Imam Abu Hanifa, Imam Bukhari, Hazrat Umar ibn al-Khattab, may God be pleased with them, is an unacceptable excuse; these arguments do not repeal the obligation. It is no secret that the first excuse [of internal differences] is one of choice. The second excuse [of the age lacking great men of piety] is rendered invalid by the very example of the pious ancestors who even in a matter as serious as the requirements for "supreme moral governance" (*imarat-i 'uzma*) were prepared to make compromises to the extent necessary. Hence, one can no longer adopt the excuse that, since the cumulative requirements [for *shari'at* governance] are absent, therefore the original obligation to establish political leadership (*imamat*) also falls away. Today we have made people aware of this responsibility. And divine guidance has also been of assistance, making it a heinous crime to show negligence in fulfilling this obligation. It is especially important in the light of current and anticipated conditions that *shari'at* governance be adopted. Failing to do so will only reveal the consequences of such gross negligence. Now there is no question of delaying this matter any further; rather, it is imperative that we immediately and speedily implement it. The distance of years will have to be traversed in months, the work of months be accomplished in days, and that of days in moments.

Remember: God forbid that competition and pride among us become an obstacle and secondary differences turn into barriers, for then our future in India will be worse than what it is today. And more importantly, the scholars and leaders would have practically demonstrated to the world that they were unable to act in unison. This group of leaders and scholars will then have no other option but to relinquish claims to being reformers of the Muslim community (*ummat*) and being heirs to the legacy of prophets. For then we should have the courage and honesty to announce that we do not have the capacity to guide the Muslim community. Then the Muslim community can choose others as their leadership.

Honorable sirs, do you know which group is primarily responsible in the eyes of God for guiding the community and caring for its welfare? It falls on the honorable religious scholars ('ulama) and those knowledgeable spiritual leaders; only they are responsible. These are the only people who are providentially appointed by God as the leaders of Muslims. Leadership and all the associated responsibilities fall on their shoulders. They are, in religious terms (shar'an), firstly the people who "bind and unbind" [moral and legal authority]. Therefore, the proper execution of this important task falls to them. This is another reason why one has to meet the challenges by courageously making sacrifices; and, in my view this goal is easily attainable. To do so requires one to sacrifice one's self-interest and ego, as well as to restrain suspicion and doubt. Thereafter, there will be unanimity in thought and action for the sake of God and the religion of Islam.

What turns into a mountain of objections that makes our 'ulama and spiritual leaders doubt and prevents them from making progress—despite their acknowledgement of the necessity—is a misconception that the leader of shari'at governance will have unfettered powers with absolute authority. Of greater concern by some is that the intellectual orientation and shade of opinion adopted by the leader will color his judgments, which he will foist on all others. The further concern is that disobedience to the leader will constitute a violation of the oath of loyalty, a heinous sin. Another concern is that if people follow authority unconfirmed by their personal research and beliefs, then it would be antithetical to religiosity. These are objections that no doubt cross the minds of many.

Surely, if the leader wields unfettered authority then every knowledgeable and religious person will be justified in harboring doubts. But the reality is this: the leader's powers will be limited.

1. It is expected that the leader will be highly thoughtful and aware of the objectives (masalih) of the shari'at: in short, the amir (leader) will only implement unanimous verdicts supported by incontrovertible textual authority.

2. The leader will always keep in mind the objectives and means of "elevating the word of God" [i'la kalimat allah, a Qur'anic phrase used to describe the obligation of Muslims to announce the Muhammadan proclamation to the world] and will implement certain rules accordingly.

3. The leader will implement such rules that do not discriminate against any sect, and will strive to advance the success and happiness of the confessional community (ummat).

4. The leader will have no truck with secondary and controversial matters nor implement them, especially when they have no relevance to social life.

5. He will not oppose investigations into controversial matters, provided such investigations do not further internecine conflict, fuel polemics, or prove to be disruptive.

6. The leader's actions and ideas will not be binding on all Islamic sects. If an individual scholar's investigation proves to be contrary to the views of the leader, then in such a specific issue there will be no harm if the scholar

does not follow the *amir*; neither will such a person be criticized, nor will his allegiance be put into question. You know well that in many issues the companion Abd Allah bin Umar opposed Umar [ibn al-Khattab], may God be pleased with both. Did Abdullah Ibn Masud not disagree with Uthman, may God be pleased with both of them, in a number of secondary issues? So, did anyone till today consider this a violation of the oath of allegiance or criticize such disagreement? Do you think that differences in secondary matters made these revered figures disloyal to the *amir* in following the social rules? Not at all!

We know all these issues, but it is our misfortune that we show a lack of faith purely on suspicion and thus procrastinate in the most important obligation.

Honorable sirs, if the following creed represents our faith: "Indeed my prayer, my sacrifices, my life and death is only for God, sustainer of the worlds," and if we are responsible for the reform and prosperity of the *ummat*, then we should not procrastinate in implementing that supreme obligation. With self-confidence, faith, and trust in God we should give effect to this task.

Honorable sirs, with regard to this matter, two questions naturally arise and deserve a reply. The first question is this: why did the state of Bihar, among all of India's states, take the initiative, and why is there no resolution as to who should be the religious leader of India (*amir al-Hind*)? The second question is, what are the preconditions for an *amir* at present in this region, and according to which principles will he be elected and what will be his function?

The reply to the first question is that ideally it would have been most appropriate to first appoint an all-India leader (*amir al-Hind*) after which a leader (*amir*) for each state could be appointed. Unfortunately, what can one say of the misfortune that has befallen Indian Muslims, that they are as yet not prepared to establish a central authority? Under these circumstances there is no other option but to elect leaders (*amirs*) for each state. India's negligence cannot become an alibi for us, and India's sinfulness cannot become a reason why we also must remain in sin.

As you know, *shari'at* governance becomes obligatory on every inhabited area (*balad*). The jurists have not restricted governance to the level of a polity (*mulk*). Most of you know the goals and purposes for which the Jami'at-i 'Ulama Bihar was established, the first association of its kind on Indian soil. At that time the 'ulama were very anxious: even in our state the most prominent 'ulama were hesitant about its formation. But you have witnessed the results of this courageous initiative; within three years many 'ulama associations with similar goals to the one in Bihar were established in all other states. And the mountain of objections posing as a stumbling block vanished. Similarly, it is eminently possible, if not overwhelmingly probable, that after implementing this project in the state of Bihar, God the Almighty willing, the appointment of *amirs* in all other states will very soon be implemented. In the same way that the Jami'at-i 'Ulama of India came into existence, similarly the "religious leader of India" (*amir al-Hind*) will also be appointed just as easily.

The reply to the second question goes like this: since this project has to be implemented from both religious (*shar'i*) and political (*siyasi*) perspectives, it is necessary to consider all aspects of the debate. At a time when there is a dearth of men of integrity, the terms according to which an amir must be appointed—keeping in mind the goals and objectives of the *shari'at*—are as follows, and I trust you will approve of them.

1. Be an observant, knowledgeable person who is capable of issuing juridical responsa (fatwas) of commanding intellectual rigor and of gaining the respect of fellow 'ulama who will accept his authority. He should be a person with a vision, who is mindful of the fact that one should also have a strategy for the implementation of the rules of the *shari'at*.
2. Be someone who enjoys the respect of the leaders of the spiritual orders (*masha'ikh-i tariqat*), whose ability to mobilize Muslims into a reliable organization can be harnessed so that the commoners and elites both recognize his authority and he can establish a religious and social organization as soon as possible.
3. Always bear witness to the truth and not be made vulnerable and be seduced by material interests and influences.
4. Have insight into contemporary issues and then give efficient and speedy effect to the project.
5. Abstain from negligence and avoid the disease of self-importance.

Considering the rules of the *shari'at* under current circumstances, in my view these are sufficient conditions. In fact, measured by this standard, only one or two persons will qualify for the post as *amir* on a state-wide basis. As you know, for some time now the precondition that a political leader (imam) and jurisconsult (mufti) be qualified in order to do independent juridical and moral reasoning (*ijtihad*) has been rescinded on the grounds of necessity.

As to the principles involving the election of an *amir*, it is evident that this is a task assigned to those who qualify as the "people who bind and unbind" [namely, have executive functions in moral decision-making]. They are the revered 'ulama and knowledgeable spiritual leaders who are duty bound by the *shari'at* to undertake this task. And the public is obliged to follow leadership.

It is also clear that at the time of the election of an *amir* in each state, it is not necessary for every learnèd scholar (*alim*), spiritual leader, and person qualified to undertake executive functions to attend the election, nor are they required to reach unanimous agreement. The election of the first caliph [Abu Bakr] is an example. His election took place without the entire qualified executive (*arbab-i hall o 'aqd*) being in attendance, but the emergence of a consensus was an endorsement of the soundness of the procedure. In fact, the election itself was not even announced in the entire city of Medina or other Islamic lands. (My purpose is to draw attention to the legal precedent, not to suggest that the *amir* of the state of Bihar will become the caliph of all Muslims, as some people misunderstood it.)

As for the date, in terms of *shari'at* it will be a sound procedure for the scholars and the spiritual leaders (and other significant people of expertise) to first fix a date, then make a general announcement, and then issue special invitations to the electoral council. All other people will be required to adhere to the decision. The *amir's modus operandi* will be to identify a few scholars (as well as experts) to be part of an advisory council (*majlis-i shura*) whose counsel he will seek (in serious matters). In accordance with the principles of the *shari'at*, the *amir* will take the final decisions and implement rules just as was the practice in the early centuries of Islam.

Honorable sirs, let me invite you once again to carefully study the proposals I have presented. If you agree to the requirements and standards, then I would urge you to solicit whomsoever you deem worthy and fit in our state to assume the leadership as *amir*. And if, in your view there are other better standards in view of the circumstances and the principles of the *shari'at*, then I would appreciate being informed about these.

And my success is only granted by Allah, on Whom I rely and to Whom I turn.

With greetings of peace.

Your servant, Abul Mahasin Muhammad Sajjad

Sources

The source of this translation is Abul Mahasin Muhammad Sajjad, *Makatib-i Sajjad*, Muhammad Zamanullah Nadim and Mujahidulislam Qasimi, eds. (Patnah: Imarat Shar'iyah Bihar wa Orissa, 1999), pp. 7–16. The quotations from his letters in this volume (in the order quoted) are at pages 27–28, 29, 60, 41, 7, 8, and 8. The quotations from Minnatullah Rahmani are from Minnatullah Rahmani, "Ard-i Nashir," in *Hukumat-i Ilahi*, Abul Mahasin Muhammad Sajjad and Mujahidulislam Qasimi, eds. (Patna: Imarat Shar'iyya Bihar wa Orissa, 1999), p. 14.

Further Reading

For background on the Deoband school and on Azad, see Barbara D. Metcalf, *Islamic Revival in British India: Deoband, 1860–1900* (Princeton, NJ: Princeton University Press, 1982); and Ian Henderson Douglas, *Abul Kalam Azad, An Intellectual and Religious Biography*, Gail Minault and Christian W. Troll, eds. (Delhi: Oxford University Press, 1988). For an intricate interpretation of the views of Indian scholars on the status of the various territorial jurisdictions in Islamic constitutional jurisprudence, see

Muhammad Khalid Masud, "The World of Shah 'Abd al-Aziz (1746–1824)," in *Perspectives of Mutual Encounters in South Asian History 1760–1860*, Jamal Malik, ed. (Leiden: E. J. Brill, 2000), pp. 307–313.

— 25 —

Two Sufis on Molding the New Muslim Woman:
Khwaja Hasan Nizami (1878–1955) and
Hazrat Inayat Khan (1882–1927)

Marcia Hermansen

Khwaja Hasan Nizami and Hazrat Inayat Khan were South Asian Muslim Sufis who, as part of their role as spiritual guides, struggled with the social and religious issues of their day. The passages translated here, representative of their respective writings and teachings of the 1920s, demonstrate each author's preoccupations with the issue of women, who were becoming more visible, educated, and active on a global scale. Both dealt also with the pressing question of religious pluralism.

We find in both Sufis the need to compare and contrast "East" and "West." Each defends correct Indian Muslim mores and traditions against the encroachments of what are seen as the modern West while striving to identify flawed Eastern customs and attitudes in the light of positive elements of Western practices. Each addressed a new breed of Muslim woman whom they hoped to engage in a reformist project of educational and spiritual work.

In relation to other religions, Inayat Khan's teachings recall the spirit of Swami Vivekananda (d. 1902), the Indian Vedantist who carried his teachings of Eastern spirituality to the West. Like him, Inayat Khan proposed a solution to religious pluralism through teachings that, he claimed, transcended any single religious tradition. Thus his was a universal movement that did not privilege the acceptance of Islam but did require initiation in reorganized Sufism. Inayat Khan was not a writer, but his speeches, given in English to his European followers, were later compiled and edited. Various branches of the Inayat Khan Sufi Movement continue to attract small numbers of disciples worldwide, but his approach is widely disseminated. His speeches are available on CD and in full-text versions on the Internet.

Nizami, whose focus continued to be India itself, addressed issues of religious pluralism in a very different way. In the complex context of colonial India, where communal identities were accentuated in the wake of the beginnings of mass politics in the 1920s, he participated in intra-Muslim missionary (*tabligh*) movements that emphasized the distinctiveness of Muslims within a national framework. At the same time, he wrote to acquaint Muslims with the basics of other religions. His treatises on aspects of Sikhism, Hinduism, and even Christianity, stressed commonalities and could be viewed as efforts to maintain intercommunal harmony in an increasingly fragile situation. In contrast to Inayat Khan, Nizami was known as a master of Urdu prose. His literary fame as the "depicter of nature" (*musawwir-i fitrat*) and his vast output of popular tracts, edifying discourses, and, best known of all, his diary (the *Roznamcha*), ultimately eclipsed the legacy of his role as a spiritual guide and political activist during the 1920s.

Inayat Khan

Hazrat Inayat Khan was born in the princely state of Baroda into a family of prominent classical Indian musicians in 1882. As a young man he frequented courtly society and became a Sufi disciple of the Hyderabadi Chishti *murshid*, Abu Hashim Madani (d. 1907). His teacher instructed him that his mission lay far to the West, and Inayat Khan first embarked on a career bringing classical Hindustani music to America in 1910. In the aftermath of the World Parliament of Religions in Chicago in 1893, and through the activities of individuals like Vivekananda and groups such as the Theosophical Society, the West was ready to receive Eastern spirituality of a certain type. Inayat Khan is said to have realized that his Western audiences in many cases needed spiritual enlightenment from him more than musical edification. He therefore reoriented his activities and to a great extent sacrificed his music in order to serve what he perceived as the spiritual needs of the West.

Inayat Khan traveled throughout the United States, western Europe, and Russia, giving lectures and musical performances, after which he would often hold informal talks with potential disciples, conferring formal initiation into the Sufi Order upon all those who requested it. Circles of disciples, or "mureeds" (from *murid*) as they were called, were established in England, France, Switzerland, and the United States. In 1915 the Sufi Order of the West was registered in London under the "Rules and Regulations of the Sufi Order," and in 1923 the International Headquarters of the Sufi Movement was legally instituted in Geneva.

In the United States, Inayat Khan's first disciple, and later head of the American branch of the Sufi Order, was a woman, Ada (Rabia) Martin (d. 1945). Another early American disciple, Samuel Lewis (d. 1971), was to become a seminal figure in the development of American Sufism in the 1960s. In 1914 Inayat Khan married an American, Ora Ray Baker, who had initially been his student in music.

Inayat Khan's career as a Sufi master was cut short by his death during a return visit to India at the age of forty-four. By this time he had initiated a number of European and American disciples into Sufism and had given copious teachings and lectures. His teachings explored the common spiritual themes of various world re-

ligions, and he did not require his followers to formally accept Islam or to practice the Islamic *shari'a.*

Khwaja Hasan Nizami

Nizami was born in 1878 into the tight inner circle of families who were hereditary
custodians of the shrine of Nizam al-Din Auliya (d. 1325) in Delhi. His parents and
two sisters died before he was twelve, after which he was brought up by his older
brother. He received a traditional Islamic education in the Nizamuddin area and
later studied for one and a half years at the feet of one of the founders of the
madrasa at Deoband (see Chapter 17), Maulana Rashid Ahmad Gangohi (d. 1905).
Nizami primarily pursued literary and journalistic activities. He frequented intellectual and Muslim political circles and had disciples numbering in the thousands.
In the latter years of his life, he was afflicted with weakening health and loss of eye-
sight. He lived through the difficult times of the Partition and in his old age seems
to have felt embattled by the political and ideological conflicts raging around him.

The 1920s were the most active political stage of his life. The selections included
here date from that period. At this time Nizami started his own version of a *tabligh*
movement, distinct from the Tablighi Jama'at movement of Muhammad Ilyas (see
Chapter 18). Both movements responded to the efforts of the Hindu Arya Samaj
to convert what were regarded as religiously marginal groups to Hinduism. Nizami's strategies to counter this included providing simple and basic education
about Islam to such Muslims, in addition to uplifting and reforming (*islah*) Muslims morally and economically. Topics that he addressed therefore included such
subjects as basic Islamic principles, social practices and customs, the need for a
strong work ethic, and so on. In terms of institution building, he did attempt to
set up a school in Delhi, but this project seems to have been less successful.

Khwaja Hasan Nizami composed a series of three treatises on women, including *The Education of the Wife,* a collection of religious, family, and economic instructions. In later editions sections were appended that dealt with topics of contemporary political urgency, such as British colonialism and the Indian home rule
movement. In terms of his respect for women, Nizami modestly claimed in his
preface that what he had learned in twenty years, his wife Laila Banu (d. 1985),
could learn in twenty days. After each of his lessons, his wife replies within the
text, commenting on his opinions. Later she was listed as the publisher of his magazine, *Tabligh-i Niswan* (Tabligh for Women).

This work was ultimately joined by two others, *Bivi ki Tarbiyyat* (Training of the
Wife) and *Aulad ki Shadi* (Marriage of the Offspring). In the 1920s and 1930s he
also published several women's magazines, including *Ustani* (Female Teacher),
Niswani Dunya (Women's World), and *Tabligh-i Niswan* (Tabligh for Women), from
which several selections will be translated below. Some of the concerns regarding
women evidenced by Nizami are shared by his well-known contemporary, Maulana Ashraf Ali Thanavi (d. 1943), the author of *Bihishti Zewar.* Examples are piety,

obligations and social skills conducive to respectability (the *sharafat* of the new middle class), and marriage arrangements (for Thanavi, see Chapter 23). At other points Nizami supports the popular practices associated with the Barelvi (Ahl-i Sunnat wa al-Jama'at) practice of Islam, such as honoring the lives of departed saints and commemorating the Prophet's birthday (*milad*) (see Chapter 12).

Hazrat Inayat Khan went even further in recognizing women as spiritual leaders, giving female disciples the highest initiations and leadership roles in his organization. In fact, all four persons initiated by Inayat Khan to the level of *murshid* (spiritual guide), were Western women: Murshida Rabia Martin, Murshida Sophia Green, Murshida Sharifa Goodenough, and Murshida Fazal Mai Egeling. In this regard, the fact that Inayat Khan worked in the West is no doubt significant, but recall that even in Europe and America at that time women were restricted from assuming many public roles, especially those of religious leadership, as well as in many expressions of religion. Despite this, Inayat Khan presents rather essentialist views of distinct gender roles as evident in the two passages presented here, on veiling and child rearing.

FROM KHWAJA HASAN NIZAMI'S *TABLIGH-I NISWAN* (TABLIGH FOR WOMEN) MAGAZINE (1926)

"WHAT WILL BE FOUND IN THIS MAGAZINE?"

1. No article will be longer than a page (except in special circumstances).
2. It will present whatever is suitable for publication regarding the household situations of every lady and girl.
3. There will be articles aimed at increasing women's religious and historical knowledge.
4. Women will be taught how to spread Islam and prevent apostasy.
5. Women will be instructed how to hone their skills in writing and speaking.
6. Women will be told principles of maintaining health.
7. Women will be saved from the useless and superfluous practices associated with occasions of joy and sorrow.
8. Women will be instructed about the way to teach and train children.
9. Women will be encouraged to serve Islam, the community and the nation.
10. Men and women will be taught how to live together in sincerity and love, as well as informed about the respective (Islamic) rights of men regarding women and women regarding men.

"THE FIRST RESPONSIBILITY OF MUSLIM WOMEN"

For those Muslim women upon whom Allah has bestowed children, the first task after completing the morning prayer should be to sit all the children down in front of them and verbally instruct them for ten minutes, so as to have them commit the following principles to memory:

We are Muslims, and a Muslim is a person who believes that Allah is one and that Muhammad is the messenger of Allah. A Muslim is one who prays five times a day and fasts during the month of Ramadan, who pays the alms assessment (zakat) if possessing the necessary resources, who performs the pilgrimage to the Kaaba if he is financially able, who accepts the Qur'an as the true divine book, and who acknowledges all of God's books, prophets and the day of resurrection as true.

In summary, every Muslim woman's children should be aware of these necessary pillars of Islam, and when anyone asks the child, "What is your religion?" he will say "Islam, and in Islam all of these things are required."

"RICH LADIES, PERFORM YOUR PRAYERS"

The influence of those women whom God has made affluent consumers is very great on poor women. If such an affluent and wealthy woman begins to perform her prayers regularly, then those who observe her in the home, such as servants, cooks, and all the poor ladies, will start offering prayers regularly.

My wife, Khwaja Banu, and my daughter, Hur Banu, in addition to the five required prayers, also perform the extra night prayer (tahajjud) on a regular basis. As a result, all the women in the household perform prayers regularly, especially those women who come to stay as guests, who also develop a desire to perform the tahajjud prayer.

Rich women, like affluent men, are not known for performing prayers. [The poet] Akbar Allahabadi spoke correctly when he said:

In every official council there are a lot of upper class men (sayyids)
While in the mosque there are a lot of poor people.

He meant that in the official councils and government jobs we find a preponderance of the upper echelons of society, but only the poor attend the communal prayers; rich people don't come to the mosques.

If wealthy women would become devoted to performing the prayers, then men would be shamed into praying on a regular basis. At times I feel laziness at the time of the tahajjud prayer and I don't want to get up from my mattress; then I am shamed by the tahajjud of my good wife; that she, a woman, is performing the tahajjud, while I, a man, am in bed asleep.

Listen, Ladies: Now it has become incumbent upon you to make the community religious and active, because the men are becoming negligent concerning religious matters. If you make efforts, in a short time all Muslim men will begin to perform the prayers regularly, and the strength of Islam in India will become firm. Otherwise the influence of the Arya Samaj will quickly impact unobservant Muslims and, God forbid, some will leave Islam altogether!

"DON'T MAKE YOUR CHILDREN INTO COWARDS"

In India we have the harmful practice that when a child is mischievous, cries, or refuses to go to sleep, the mother quiets the child by the terrifying mention of ghosts, jinns, witches, and so on.

Fright takes root in the child's heart and engenders fear and cowardice. Even when older, this fear will not dissipate. Such people are handicapped from rendering any service to their nation and community.

Study of those great and famous people of the past whose deeds are still a source of pride to their countrymen, shows that the secret of their success lies hidden in their early formation. For example, Napoleon's mother was always recounting to him tales of the military feats of the heroes of the past. The famous Islamic conquerors have the same stature. Therefore Muslim women, instead of frightening their children with tales of jinns, ghosts, evil spirits, and sprites, should tell them about the magnificent achievements of Muslim kings and conquerors such as Hazrat Umar, Hazrat Ali, Khalid ibn Walid, Timur, Mahmud of Ghazna, Muhammad Ghauri, Ala al-Din Khilji, Akbar, Tipu Sultan, and their like. Then they should say to them, "You too should aspire to become great like them."

The outcome of this will be that once again the glory and splendor of Islam will emerge among Muslims, along with the effects of renewed religious fervor.

"WOMEN DON'T KNOW HOW TO MAKE CONVERSATION"

Imagine ladies have come to see Khwaja Banu [his wife]. She wants to make conversation with them to make them feel relaxed and properly treated. She thinks, "What shall I talk to them about?" The usual practice is that first one asks about the household, then the number of children, the mother-in-law, and the husband's sisters. Then, once everyone is comfortable, she might ask about the health of her husband and how he treats her.

Khwaja Banu is thinking that in addition to asking the usual questions, she could, like the English, comment on the weather, "Today it's very hot," or "Today it's very cold," or discuss some important matter relating to Muslims. Alternatively, she could say something with regard to improving the status of women. However, no appropriate topic comes to mind.

Therefore she sits in silence and the visitors sit in silence, and each one looks at the other's face. This problem arises from ignorance and a lack of conversational skills. English women and well-educated Indian ladies are able to discuss all sorts of topics due to their being well informed. . . .

I used the name of Khwaja Banu just as an example. None of the ladies from "respectable" (sharif) families know how to make conversation. They do, however, know how to quarrel really well. Polite and refined conversation eludes them.

When someone comes to visit them, or when they go to visit other women, instead of taking about personal matters, they should also discuss Islamic and reformist issues. Gradually they will become accustomed to good conversation. They should smile while they are speaking and talk cheerfully, so that the ladies they are talking to will not wonder if they are uneasy about meeting them.

FROM KHWAJA HASAN NIZAMI'S *AULAD KI SHADI* (MARRIAGE OF THE OFFSPRING) (1921)

"MARRIAGE ADVERTISEMENTS"

Ever since British rule began in this country all sorts of things have become part of our custom, including people putting ads in the newspapers to find matches for their sons and daughters. In some instances marriages are contracted based solely on these ads.

My experience is that this is extremely troubling and worrisome. There is only one benefit, which is providing the addresses of those seeking a proposal. Otherwise, there may be all kinds of negative elements and no useful ones. Certainly, if after learning the address of the boy or girl, a person goes to the location on his own to verify the information, spends some time there, and gains additional details, he may well be reassured about all the points raised in the present book.

However, negotiating a marriage simply through advertisements and exchanges of correspondence is not safe. No matter how trustworthy the middleman may be, relying on his correspondence is a very mistaken practice.

I have personal experience of matches based on marriage ads that have not worked out. Many people placed ads through me, and I wrote up all of my investigations. Even then, after the marriage had taken place, unimaginable secrets came to light that the marriage seekers had cleverly concealed.

People who place marriage ads generally are those who, due to some disgrace or negative factor, are unable to find a match or who, despite already having one or more wives, still are driven to contract another marriage.

Several times it turned out that I had assisted men who were placing marriage ads and got them married within my circle of acquaintances after having made a proper investigation to ascertain that the man had no other wife. However, later it turned out that one had three other wives, another two, and some one. Others had the bad habit of divorcing after six months of marriage and constantly remarrying.

Some corrupt men have a habit of placing ads without any intent of marriage; rather they want to get personal information about secluded women from good households, because they take a prurient interest in these details. Therefore, in response to letters regarding these ads, it is not advisable for the girl's family to discuss many details about her. When these sorts of situations arise, one must go to the actual place where the man resides, since merely communicating in writing inevitably leads to unfortunate results.

"WHY INDIAN MEN SHOULD NOT MARRY EUROPEAN WOMEN"

It is an interesting coincidence that the previous section on Sunni-Shi'a marriage was the twelfth and Shi'a consider the number twelve to be very auspicious. The number thirteen, according to the belief of European men and women, is very unlucky and by chance thirteen is the number of this section about European women. Not only on the basis of number, but also on the basis of social experience, it is not good for Indians, especially Muslims, to marry European women.

Indeed, Islam had given Muslim males permission to marry Christian or Jewish women. However, in today's times getting married to European women is unadvisable from several aspects. One is the problem that European women cannot maintain parda because they are not accustomed to observing it. The second difficulty is that between their customs and those of Indians there is a world of difference. The third difficulty is that European women really spend a lot of money. The fourth difficulty is that European women are used to moving about in society, and, after marrying Indians, the problem will arise that their husbands will not approve of them mixing with unrelated males. Indian women are not able to converse and interact with European women. They will view such a wife with distaste and fear, while the European woman will view them with contempt and dislike since they seem to be completely alien to her culture. The fifth difficulty is that the European woman will regard her husband as one ruled and subjugated by her nation, and therefore in her regard the husband will not receive the respect he deserves. The biggest source of conflict occurs when European women marry Indians while in their own culture at a time when the man is completely immersed in European society. When she comes to India with her husband, then the wife experiences her cultural difference from her husband and finds him to be opposed to her customs, and she cannot tolerate this.

Muslim men can marry multiple wives and are used to this, while in Europe this is a shame and a crime. For this reason, if the husband of a European should have the intention of contracting another marriage, then it will be time for a trip to the court.

As long as a person is not cognizant of all of the customs and practices of Europe and does not know the way to keep a European women happy, and as long as he does not have an abundance of extra funds on hand, he should never even think of marrying a European.

Despite the innumerable dangers of marrying a European woman, there are still a few positive elements. A Christian woman enters the sphere of influence of Islam. Even if she does not become a Muslim, still she will be under the control of a Muslim, and there may be some hope that eventually she will convert to Islam. Secondly, the husband will feel good that a woman from the ruling nation is under his command (on the condition that he is able to control her!) Third, coming from an educated and civilized people, she will be able to assist her husband greatly, and he will experience some of the real joy of life.

In summary, my advice is that it is better not to think of marrying a European woman, since it has been proven by the outcomes that only very rarely will European women remain happy with Indian men. There will generally be constant quarrels and problems between them.

FROM *THE SUFI MESSAGE OF HAZRAT INAYAT KHAN*

"THE ORIGIN OF THE CUSTOM OF THE SECLUSION OF WOMEN" (EARLY 1920S)

The custom of the seclusion of women has its source in mystical thought. There used to be mystical orders of people in the East who contemplated in solitude and lived in seclusion. The magnetism and power of influence that they developed by seclusion was in itself a marvel. This gave power to their gaze, power in their word, and influence in their atmosphere. This custom of seclusion was then imitated by the kings and people of high rank.

They had two ways of veiling themselves when away from home. One was to put a covering over the back of the head, which was made to hang down in front, so that the eyes could be half-covered; and the other was to put a veil over the face. It was a sort of mantle that they put on their head. Every prophet of Beni Israel had this. In the ancient pictures of the prophets of the Semitic race one will always see the head covered with a mantle. In the Hindu race also many orders of Buddhists and yogis wore a mantle over the head. The veil which the kings used, which was called *Makna*, later became customary in the East, and ladies of high rank wore what is called in Turkish the *Yashmak*. For thousands of years it has been the custom among Parsis that during their religious services the priest covers his head with a turban together with a mantle, and Parsi women have kept the custom of covering the head with a white cloth, though it is less observed at the present time. In India, among Hindus as well as among Muslims, there is a custom at weddings of veiling the faces of bride and bridegroom with jasmine flowers.

Behind all these different customs of veiling the head and face lies mystical significance. Man's form is considered by Sufis as consisting of two parts: the head and the body; the body for action and the head for thought. Since the head is for thought its radiance is incomparably greater than that of the body, and the hairs are as rays of that radiance in a physical form. It is a constant outpouring of light that one observes in man's life. Every action of looking, or breathing, or speaking, steals much of the radiance out of man's life. By preserving this radiance the mystic develops within himself the influence, power, and magnetism that, in the average person, are wasted. For instance, closing the eyes, which is a custom among mystics, not only helps in concentration and repose of mind, but during the moment when the eyes are closed, it preserves the radiance from flowing out. These customs were helpful to kings and commanders for developing their power and influence, and they were valued by ladies of rank as a means of preserving their beauty and charm. We learn from this that a life but little exposed to the outer world, whether through seclusion, or silence, or a perfect state of repose with closed eyes, clasped hands and crossed legs, has a great influence.

The custom of the seclusion of mystics remains only in the mystical orders, but one finds the seclusion of women prevalent in the East. When a custom takes root in a section of society certainly it can be used and abused as people may choose. No doubt jealousy, which is in human nature, is a proof of love, but jealousy can be the source of a great many crimes. Man has always guarded the treasures that he values under all sorts of coverings, and since that which man can love most is woman, he has often ignorantly tried to guard her in the same way as he guards all things of value and importance. And the custom of seclusion has been in his hand a means that has enabled him to control his household in the manner he likes.

However, it is not true that this custom was the outcome of the teaching of the Prophet. There are only two places in the records where an utterance of the Prophet on the subject is to be found. In one place it is told that when some coarse dances were going on among the peasants of his land, he said that women must be clad properly. In the other place [it is said] that when the ladies of the Prophet's household were returning home after taking care of the Prophet and his army during a battle, they were disinclined to look at the battlefield and to show themselves to their enemies, and the only thing that could be advised by the Prophet was that now that peace had been made, if they did not like to show themselves, they might veil their faces.

In India one sees the custom that an aged woman covers her face, a widow covers her face, and a bride veils her face. There is some little psychological meaning in it. It is in the nature of every soul to wish to hide its sorrow, and by veiling her face the widow veils her sorrow from others. The veil that one sees on the face of an aged woman is there for the reason that in age the emotions become more visible and one has little control so as to hide them from others, and when the heart has become softened at every little touch, however gentle, it is easily moved, and the covering is as a shield over it. On the face of a bride the veil is for the preservation of her charm, of her magnetism; at the same time the finest beauty in human nature is modesty, in whatever form it appears.

From the physical as well as the occult point of view, woman is more impressionable than man. The task of woman as a mother is of a greater importance than that of a man in any position. Woman with her thought and feeling molds the character of her child, and as she is susceptible to outward impressions, her impressions always have their influence on the child. During the period before motherhood very great care must be taken, for any word spoken to her reaches the depth of her being, and it re-echoes in the soul of the child. If a word made her bitter at the time or cross at a moment, it can create bitterness or crossness in the child. Especially during that period woman is more sensitive and susceptible to all impressions, beautiful or ugly. Anything striking impresses her soul deeply. A color, lightning, thunder, storm, all make impressions upon her. Conditions of life, misery or joy, all tell upon her more than on another person. Having this in consideration, the custom of seclusion has been kept in the East, and still exists among certain communities.

No doubt there is another side to consider: that home and state are not two separate things. Home is the miniature of the state; and if woman performs a part equally important at home, why must she not perform an equally important part in the outward life? No doubt these ancient customs, even with their psychological importance, often make an iron bar before the progress of the generality. In the East, for maid and mistress both, there are days set apart for rest in every month—and this in all the different religions: among Hindus, Parsis, and Muslims. Life in the world is a constant battle, and a hard battle if one has any delicacy of feeling, any refinement of manner. The position of woman in this battle is worse than that of man. She is there robbed of her womanly grace and fine sentiments. Man is more dependent upon woman than woman on man. From the first moment any child, whether boy or girl, opens his eyes in the world, he seeks the protection of woman. Woman, as his mother, sister, daughter, friend, or wife, in every form, is the source of his happiness, comfort, and peace. However he may undertake to do it—whether by means of a crude custom such seclusion in the East or by some other means— to guard a woman against the hard knocks that fall on every soul living in this world of selfishness is the first duty of a thoughtful man.

"THE EDUCATION OF THE CHILD"

The time between the ages of ten and twelve years is the period that finishes a cycle, the first cycle in the life of every soul. Mystics consider each cycle as twelve years. Therefore these last three years of the first cycle are of very great importance in the life of the child. During this particular period at the ages of ten, eleven and twelve, what is taught is like the finishing touch given by an artist after having painted a picture. And after this another cycle begins.

The time of preparing children for the next cycle is a most important period. If the child by this time has not been taught, has not been corrected, has not been given that direction which it ought to have taken, then later on it will be difficult; for the most important period has passed. The more guardians understand of their responsibility, the more they will realize that if things were not taught which should have been taught at that time they can never be taught later.

The appropriate direction must be given to the girls and to the boys. One cannot drive both with the same whip. For instance, a word of displeasure will touch the boy on the surface and the girl to the depth. And it is the same with a word of appreciation; often with the boy it will go in one ear and out the other, whereas the girl will keep it with her perhaps for her whole life. Those who think that boys and girls can both be directed in the same way will find in the end that they have made a great mistake. The psychology of the boy is quite different from the girl's, and for each a special method must be used in order to bring them up.

If the girl or the boy receives a word of admiration or of blame, it must be given in different terms and in different words. And one should be most lenient towards the girl, whereas it does not matter so much with the boy. Often the boy takes a punishment and after half an hour, or even before half an hour, he forgets it. And often a girl remembers it for months and months. It affects her most deeply. Besides there are certain characteristics to be developed in the boy and certain characteristics to be developed in the girl. And you cannot call them virtues for both. For instance, courage in the boy, modesty in the girl. Common sense in the boy, idealism in the girl. Responsibility in the boy, duty in the girl. God-ideal in the boy, religion in the girl. Also, thought in the boy, consideration in the girl.

One may ask why it is necessary to develop the inherent qualities of boys and girls. Why not pay attention first to their opposites? The reason is this: that any quality that is an inherent quality is born in a person because that quality will lead to the purpose of his life. For instance, the lion is given the quality of the lion. That is his purpose, that is his destiny. And the deer is given the quality needed for the purpose of its life. But if the lion had the deer quality or the deer had the lion quality, neither would be properly equipped for living in the world. What the deer is shows in its own quality, what the lion is shows in its own quality. One must not think it is not necessary for the other quality to come to the boy or girl. But what should be developed is the particular quality, and the other quality will come by itself. It does not mean that a boy must not have those qualities which have been said to belong to a girl. For instance, if the boy is without any ideal he is useless. But the ideal will come. In the girl, however, it must be planted, it must be developed.

It is the psychology of the boy and the girl that makes it necessary to give certain things to the boy and certain things to the girl. But as they develop they take each other's qualities. With development it comes naturally. Balance is best, whether in the boy or in the girl. And balance comes through opposite qualities. The work of the teacher is not to teach balance, the work of the teacher is to teach qualities. Life will bring about balance by itself, as long as boys and girls are taught that particular quality which belongs to them.

Sources

The following selections are from Khwaja Hasan Nizami, ed., *Tabligh-i Niswan*, (Tabligh for Women) 1, no. 2 (May 17, 1926): "What Will Be Found in this Magazine?" (frontispiece); "The First Responsibility of Muslim Women," p. 2; "Rich

Ladies, Perform your Prayers," p. 10; "Don't Make Your Children into Cowards" (A letter to the editor signed Dhu al-Nun Ahmad [Meerut], p. 24); and "Women Don't Know how to Make Conversation," p. 24. The following selections are from Khwaja Hasan Nizami, *Aulad ki Shadi (Marriage of the Offspring)* (Delhi: Karkun-i Khwaja Depot, 1921): "Marriage Advertisements," pp. 23–24; "Why Indian Men Should Not Marry European Women," pp. 30–31. Inayat Khan's "The Origin of the Custom of the Seclusion of Women," written in the early 1920s, is from *The Sufi Message of Hazrat Inayat Khan*, vol. XIII, available online at http://wahiduddin .net/mv2/XIII/XIII_1.htm. "The Education of the Child" is from *The Sufi Message of Hazrat Inayat Khan*, vol. III, available online at http://wahiduddin.net/mv2/III/ III_I_3.htm.

The selections from *The Sufi Message of Hazrat Inayat Khan* are from a part of Inayat Khan's legacy known as the "Gathas." These consisted of teachings given privately to his disciples, which were long read only within limited circles of higher initiates.

Further Reading

For an extended comparison of the two Sufis, see Marcia Hermansen, "Common Themes, Uncommon Contexts: The Sufi Movements of Khwaja Hasan Nizami (1878–1955) and Hazrat Inayat Khan (1882–1927)" in Zia Inayat Khan, ed., *A Pearl in Wine: Essays on the Life, Music and Sufism of Hazrat Inayat Khan* (New Lebanon, NY: Omega, 2001), pp. 323–353. For an interpretive translation of a contemporary manual for Muslim women's formation, see Barbara D. Metcalf's *Perfecting Women: Maulana Ashraf 'Ali Thanawi's Bihishti Zewar* (Berkeley, CA: University of California Press, 1990). Other works that explore the changing roles available to Muslim women as the end of colonial rule in South Asia approached are: Gail Minault, *Voices of Silence: English Translation of Khwaja Altaf Hussain Hali's Majalis Un-Nissa and Chup Ki Dad* (Delhi: Chanakya, 1986); Gail Minault, *Secluded Scholars: Women's Education and Muslim Social Reform in Colonial India* (Delhi: Oxford University Press, 1999); Rokeya Sakhawat Hossein, *Sultana's Dream and Selections from The Secluded Ones* (New York: Feminist Press, 1988); Sonia Nishat Amin, *World of Muslim Women in Colonial Bengal, 1876–1939* (Leiden: E. J. Brill, 1996).

—26—

Fatwa Advice on Proper Muslim Names

Muhammad Khalid Masud

The fatwa (expert opinion about a moral or legal question) has been the most enduring form of guidance in Muslim society. There are other popular forms of moral guidance, such as stories about the life of the Prophet, the sayings of the Prophet, stories of prophets and pious people, stories about miracles, poems about battles between the pious and the evil, Sufi writings, and legal literature itself. None of them, however, has been able to gain the authority of a fatwa, for the simple reason that the fatwa provides direct guidance on specific issues. It also encompasses a wider range of subjects, especially in modern times. This chapter focuses on how fatwas provide guidance about Muslim names. Translated below are modern fatwas on this issue by scholars of different schools of Muslim thought in South Asia.

The Fatwa

Fatwas began quite early in Islam in the simple oral form of question and answer. There are several verses in the Qur'an that provide moral guidance in this form: "They ask thee what they should spend (on charity). Say: *Whatever ye spend that is good for parents and kindred and orphans and those in want and for wayfarers. And whatever ye do that is good, Allah knoweth it well*" (Qur'an 2:215). In another verse, the Qur'an uses the word *yastaftunak* (they ask you) for the question and *uftikum* (He directs/replies to you) for the answer (Qur'an 4:176). The word "fatwa" and the question and answer form probably have their origins in these verses. Consequently, the question is called *istifta*, the person who poses the question is called *mustafti*, and the expert who issues a fatwa is called a mufti.

Fatwas not only answer questions about law and morals but also about the meaning of difficult passages in the Qur'an and the hadith, and they can provide information about history and other such matters as well. A fatwa defines the boundaries between heresy and belief. More importantly, it provides specific guidance on rituals and social practices. It determines whether certain practices conform to or deviate from the teachings of Islam. As a form of legal guidance, the fatwa played a crucial role in the history of Islamic law. Muslim judges frequently sought guidance from earlier fatwas, which have been preserved and collected more regularly than the judgments of the qadis. Compared to the judgments of qadis, which were very specific and whose application was limited to particular cases, fatwas were general. Accordingly, while a qadi's judgment was binding on the litigants, a fatwa was not legally binding and a questioner could seek another opinion. A fatwa has moral weight because the inquirer seeks the opinion of an expert in view of that expert's good reputation. In some countries, a mufti is appointed officially and thus has official authority, but this has not been the practice in South Asia.

The role of the fatwa increased during the colonial period in the absence of qadis. Disputes relating to marriage, divorce, inheritance, and other personal causes were often settled by fatwas. In this period, moreover, Muslim societies encountered a wide range of new political, educational, economic, technological, and social challenges, and fatwas offered moral and legal guidance on new subjects about which the law books and manuals were silent. The fatwa, as an institution, was also quick to benefit from modern developments in communication, including printed books, newspapers, radio, television, and now the Internet. Fatwas today do not create a central religious authority but rather generate discourse on specific issues. Each fatwa argues for a definitive conclusion, often explaining the reasons and sources from which it is drawn. It also uses rhetorical strategies like appeal to sectarian loyalty or to reason.

The Structure of a Fatwa Text

Istifta

In general, a formally written *istifta* (the question that a fatwa is written to answer) has the following structure:

1. Preliminaries of formulaic phrases that confirm the inquirer's belief in the religion and law of Islam.
2. Context of the query or facts of the case. This is essentially the inquirer's side of the story. The mufti can respond only to these facts.
3. The question.
4. Closing formulaic phrases asking the mufti to answer according to the divine law, requesting him to explain his answer clearly with evidence from the revealed sources, reminding him of his duty to answer the query and of the promise of divine reward.
5. The name of the questioner and the date of the query. Since ideally the mufti does not answer anonymous queries, the inquirer must give his name. The name may be omitted in published versions.

Fatwa

The following elements are commonly present in an elaborate fatwa:

1. Opening: A fatwa opens with general comments on the facts of the case and comments about Islamic law.

2. Answer: Most often, a mufti will say that if this is so as the inquirer says, then the answer is such and such. Manuals for fatwa writing advise a mufti to answer on the back of the paper on which the query was written so that the fatwa cannot be misused.

3. Evidence: Often the evidence is limited to the texts of a particular law school, most commonly, the school to which the mufti belongs. Theoretically, in the Sunni tradition there are four sources to which a mufti may refer: Qur'an, hadith, *ijma'* (consensus or the agreed views of the jurists), and *qiyas* (analogy based on a precedent or text from the aforementioned three sources). Sometimes, extra evidence from history, science, and medical sources is also provided.

4. Argument and Citations: If the point of law is controversial in the mufti's view—i.e., where there can be more than one opinion—the mufti develops his argument providing additional citations.

5. Concluding Remarks: After reiterating his answer, the mufti may comment on other matters beyond the query. Sometimes the mufti does not give a clear answer but cautiously resists saying that something is valid or legal, and uses phrases like, "It is better . . . ," "Care should be taken . . . ," "One should better avoid . . . ," and "It is advisable . . . ."

6. Closing: Often muftis close fatwas with a formulaic phrase, such as "And God knows the best," "Only God knows what is right," or "God supports the truth." This formula affirms that the real authority belongs to God, and the mufti admits the possibility that his opinion may be wrong, even though he has done his best to state the true position of law on the point in question. These phrases are followed by the name of the mufti, the date of the fatwa, and the signature and seal of the mufti with his affiliation to an institution, if any.

Names and Identity

Names in any culture may entail links to social, political, economic, and religious institutions. One of the most critical issues of modernity has been a heightened concern with questions of identity, as evident in the scientific passion for classification and exactness in such practices as the census, and political contexts such as nationalism and elections. Islamic modernity, articulated through revival and reform movements, insisted on Arabic names and names that would avoid implication of association with God (*shirk*) or, in India, resemblance to the names of Hindus.

The naming ceremony is performed in a variety of ways among Muslims in South Asia. The *'aqiqa*, as it is generally called, includes elements from pre-Islamic

Arab society, from the *Sunna* of the Prophet, and from some local South Asian practices. The ceremony historically included a feast, for which an animal was sacrificed, and the shaving of the the the child's head, two components borrowed from the rituals of the hajj. The great eighteenth-century hadith scholar, Shah Waliullah, explains that the whole ceremony marks initiation into the community, especially through the uttering of the call to prayer (*adhan*) in the ears of the newborn. The child is also given a Muslim name at this ceremony, if she or he has not received one already.

The following fatwas represent several different sectarian orientations in modern South Asia. They are organized chronologically. The first is by Mawlana Abu'l Hasanat 'Abd al-Hayy (1848–1888), a member of the celebrated Lucknow family of 'ulama known by the name of their seminary at Farangi Mahall. He himself was close to the reformist orientation of Deoband. Educated by his father, Mawlana Abdul Halim, he wrote on almost every subject, but is most famous for his multivolume biographical dictionary of Indian Hanafi scholars and for his contribution to Islamic jurisprudence. He debated with Nawwab Siddiq Hasan Khan of Bhopal (1832–1890), a well-known Ahl-i Hadith scholar.

The second fatwa is by Mawlana Ahmad Rada Khan (1856–1921), the founder of the sectarian orientation Ahl-i Sunnat wa Jama'at, known to outsiders as "Barelvis" after the north Indian town of Bareilly where the founder was born. Mawlana Rada Khan completed his religious education with his father, Naqi 'Ali Khan, mastering rational sciences like geometry, mathematics, logic, and philosophy. He also studied hadith with Arab scholars in the Hijaz when he performed the hajj in 1878. He wrote more than one thousand books and treatises. His collected fatwas, *Fatawa Ridwiyya*, comprise several volumes, hardly surprising given his typical style of extensive hadith citation, evident in the fatwa here (even though it is heavily abbreviated in translation). Mawlana Ahmad Rada Khan agrees with the reformers that names that clearly suggest association with God should be avoided. But, challenging in particular the fatwa of Mawlana Abu'l Hasanat 'Abd al-Hayy of Farangi Mahall, he argues that other names, like "Hidayat 'Ali," which Lakhnawi finds ambiguous and suggestive of association, are in fact permissible. By 'Abd al-Hayy's logic, Ahmad Rada argues, his own name "'Abd al-Hayy" could imply association. Their debate is characteristic of differences between Deobandis and Barelvis in which both argue within the Hanafi tradition, but the latter defend a wide range of popular practices. Note that Ahmad Rada labels his opponents "Wahhabi," a sensitive term in colonial India, since it associated them with a violent and extremist Arabian sect.

The third fatwa, by 'Abdullah Muhaddith Ropari (ca. 1885–1964), questions the validity of such Muslim names as Ghulam 'Ali (the Slave of 'Ali) which, he argues, is grammatically incorrect in Arabic and also suggests association with God by elevating the status of the first Imam of the Shi'as (the Prophet's son-in-law and nephew). Mawlana Ropari was associated with the Ahl-i Hadith, a reformist orientation that rejected the historic schools of law and was, generally speaking, even more stringent in regard to customary practices than the Deobandis. He studied at various madrasas in India, and, after completing his education in 1914, began teaching in his birthplace, the Punjabi town of Ropar. In 1947, when most of his family was killed by Sikhs, he moved to Lahore in Pakistan, where he died in 1964. A prolific writer, he composed some thirty-six books and in 1933 founded a weekly, *Tanzim Ahl-i Hadith,* which he edited until his death.

The final fatwa is by Mufti Taqi 'Usmani, born in Deoband in 1942 and long a teacher at the Darul Uloom in Karachi. He is one of the foremost Deobandi scholars in Pakistan. With both seminary training and a modern law education, he has served as a judge in the Shari'at Court established in Pakistan in the 1980s. His stature is also enhanced by his role as a spiritual guide in the lineage of Mawlana Ashraf 'Ali Thanawi. In his fatwa he favors the use of an Arabic name, grammatically correct and preferably taken from the Qur'an, after the names of the first generation Muslims. He argues that a name marks a religious identity, and, invoking modern psychology, he suggests that it is also a source of influence on one's life. Like Chapter 6 on the ties of Mauritian Muslims to Pakistani scholars, this fatwa illustrates the vibrant networks among populations of South Asian descent worldwide.

A FATWA BY MAWLANA ABD AL-HAYY LAKHNAWI (D. 1888)

Question: A person was named Hidayat al-'Ali. He came to suspect that this was one of the names suggesting association with God, so he changed his name to Hidayat 'Ali. Someone raised an objection that the word Hidayat, guidance, is equivocal; that is, it has two meanings: "showing the path" and "reaching the destination." Similarly, the word " 'Ali" without the prefix "al" is equivocal, referring both to the names of God ("The Exalted") and of 'Ali, May God ennoble his face ['Ali Murtada, the Prophet's son-in-law and the first Imam of the Shi'as]. Hidayat 'Ali responded that he (i.e., the one who objected), in fact, concurred with the name change. Since the words Hidayat and 'Ali each have two possible meanings, together they suggest four interpretations: (1) God shows the path; (2) God reaches the destination; (3) 'Ali shows the path; (4) 'Ali reaches the destination. The first three interpretations entail nothing prohibited. The fourth, however, implies a human dimension to God and associates 'Ali with God's attributes. One should avoid names that imply such association. As an analogy to the use of a disputed name, is it correct to forbid calling "*Ya 'Ali*" (Oh, 'Ali!)? Please clarify and be rewarded.

Answer: 'Ali is one of the names of God, the prefix "al" is added to it for respect, as in al-Fadl and al-Nu'man. [Here the mufti cites *Sharh Kafiya* and *Hawashi Mir Zahid Mulla Jala,* arguing that (except for Ilah) prefix al- can be added to all the names of God and that Muhammad and 'Ali are proper names to which the prefix al- cannot be added when they are used as names.] . . . Therefore Hidayat al-'Ali is preferable to Hidayat 'Ali, because the former does not imply that guidance is being attributed to 'Ali Murtada. In the latter form, however, forbidden implications exist because of the equivocal meanings of the words Hidayat and ʿAli. One must avoid names whose ambiguity suggests something unlawful. It is for this reason that the scholars forbid having names like ʿAbd al-Nabi (Slave of the Prophet). As to the name ʿAbd Allah, there is no ambiguity. Similarly, to call "Ya ʿAli" is not controversial as long as it is meant as a call to God. Written by Abuʾl Hasanat.

A FATWA BY MAWLANA AHMAD RADA KHAN (D. 1921)

A certain Shaykh Shawkat ʿAli Faruqi asked Mawlana Ahmad Raza Khan about names on 6 Jumada al-Ula 1320 [10 August 1902].

Question: What do the scholars of religion and the experts in the divine law say concerning names such as the following: ʿAli Jan (dear, loved one), Nabi (prophet) Jan, Muhammad Jan, Muhammad Nabi, Ahmad Nabi, Nabi Ahmad, Muhammad Yasin, Muhammad Taha, Ghafurud Din, Ghulam ʿAli, Ghulam Husayn [the name of the third Shiʿa Imam], Ghulam Ghauth and Ghulam Jilani [both referring to the great Sufi ʿAbd al-Qadir Gilani], and Hidayat ʿAli. Are such names permissible or not? Mawlawi ʿAbd al-Hayy Lakhnawi in his Fatwa has ruled that names like Hidayat ʿAli are impermissible. What is the true position? Please explain and be rewarded [by God]. Shawkat ʿAli, May he be forgiven.

Answer: Numerous salutations. The names Muhammad Nabi, Ahmad Nabi and Nabi Ahmad, May God's blessings be on him, are specific to the Prophet Muhammad, and only he deserves them, May God's best salutations be on him. It is prohibited to name others with these names. It is true that they do not connote any claim to Prophethood, or they would amount to pure denial of Islam, but a semblance of such claim still exists, and that is also forbidden.

It is not correct, neither in law nor in custom, to presume that proper names do not denote their primary meanings. It is true that one may not intend the primary meanings, but it is wrong to say that they are totally ignored.

A large number of authentic sayings of the Prophet establish the fact that the Prophet, peace be on him, frequently changed names whose primary meaning denoted evil. [Here follow, in the original, chains of narrators for each hadith, taken from the collections whose brief titles are given in the translation.] "The Prophet, peace be on him, used to change bad names" (*Tirmadhi*). The Prophet changed the names ʿAsi (sinner), ʿAziz (the mighty), Utla (destitute), Shaytan (devil), Hakam (arbiter), Ghurab (crow), Hubab (bubble), and Shihab (shooting star). He substituted the name Zurʿa (seed) for Asram (destitute) and Jamila (beautiful) for Asiba (a palm branch stripped of its leaves) (*Sunan Abu Daʾud*). The Prophet changed the name Birra to Zaynab (sweet smelling beautiful tree), saying, "Do not claim to be righteous yourselves; God knows who are the righteous among you" (*Muslim*). *Birra*, meaning a pious woman, implied egotism. The Prophet, peace be on Him, says, "On the Judgment day you will be called by your name and by the names of your parents, hence choose good names for yourselves" (*Ahmad* and *Dawud*).

Now, if it is possible to ignore the primary meanings of names, what is the meaning of calling one name bad and another good and changing the former? What about the egotism of using a name for someone who may not have the quality it denotes? Furthermore, just ask people if they would like to name their children Shaytan (devil), Mal'un (accursed), Rafidi (deserter), Khabith (evil), Khuk (pig), and so on? Certainly not. Then it is clear that primary meanings are significant. Then how can you approve of calling yourself or your children Nabi? Would a Muslim allow someone to name himself or his child Rasul Allah (Messenger of God), Khatam al-Nabiyyin (Seal of the Prophets) or Sayyid al-Mursilin (Chief of the Apostles)? Never! Then how are the names Muhammad Nabi, Ahmad Nabi, or Nabi Ahmad permissible?

People who come up with arguments to justify such names will wind up using names like Allah Azza wa Jalla or Ilah al-Alamin [i.e., names for God himself], on the grounds that the primary meaning is not denoted in a proper name! God forbid! Someone named for the Prophet feels constrained to justify it. But the same argument that they advance regarding a name like Muhammad Nabi also applies to a name like Allah Azza wa Jalla. Their name was given without regard to the implication of doing so, purely for good luck because there is a blessing in the name of the Prophet.

The name Nabi Jan (Dear Prophet) is improper. If we regard the word Jan as an addition, appended to show love, as it commonly is, then it is obviously a reference to the Prophet. If we regard the name as a reverse compound phrase; i.e., Jan-i Nabi (Beloved of the Prophet), then the name is a thousand times more egoistic than Birra. The Prophet did not like the latter, so how can he like a name like this?

Similarly, the names Yasin and Taha are prohibited because they are names of God or the Prophet whose meaning is not known to us. It would not be surprising if they contain meanings that cannot apply to other than God and the Prophet. They must therefore be avoided, just as mantras and charms of unknown meanings are not allowed lest they contain association with God (*shirk*) or deviation (*bid'a*).

Imam Abu Bakr Ibn al-'Arabi comments in *Ahkam al-Qur'an*, "Ashhab narrates Malik saying: 'No one should have the name Yasin because it is God's name.'" That is a very original statement. Using this name is forbidden because this is one of those names whose meanings we do not know. It may have a unique meaning that belongs only to God. One must not present to God something whose danger is unknown. That is why reason forbids it.

Shahab al-Din Khaffaji Hanafi Misri admiringly cites the above statement in *Nasim al-Riyad,* a commentary on Qadi Iyad's *Shifa,* and says, "This is a very fine statement." I noted on the margin that the prohibition is clear on the basis of this interpretation, but it is clearer in view of the fact that this is the name of the Prophet, peace be on him. Perhaps this is a better explanation than saying that it may imply some meaning unique to God. God knows the best. The same is true about Taha. . . . The name Ghafur al-Din is also extremely ugly and abominable. Ghafur means "the one who erases and conceals something." God conceals sins; that is, in His mercy, He conceals the sins of His servants. Thus Ghafur al-Din would mean "the one who erases religion." It is like calling someone Shaytan (Devil); such names were changed by the Prophet. Or, it could mean, "the one who conceals his religion" as taqiyya (strategic dissimulation). It is like naming someone Rafidi (deserter). In short, this name is quite repulsive. The name Asiya (sinner), which the Prophet changed, is less repulsive because sins generally denote action, but concealing religion refers to faith and beliefs. I seek refuge in God. . . .

I have witnessed myself the dire influence of bad names on people's lives. I have seen some Sunnis of sound nature reduced to concealing religion and striving for unlawful things at the end of their lives.

One appalling problem is that customarily people add to such abominable names the name Pak (pure) Muhammad. The truth is that adding such a sacred name to this deviant name is by itself an insult to this honorable name.

That is why I never consent to adding the sacred name to names like Kalb-i-'Ali ('Ali's dog), Banda-i-Hasan (slave of Hasan), Nithar Husayn (one who is ready to self-sacrifice for Husayn), Ghulam 'Ali (the servant of 'Ali), Qurban Hasan (a sacrifice to Hasan), and Fida Husayn (an offering to Husayn). May God bestow upon us the best of refinement and keep us away from the causes of His anger. Amen.

Out of the fourteen names about which the inquirer asked, seven are forbidden; there is no harm in the other seven. Quite obviously, 'Ali Jan and Muhammad Jan are justified, because the real name is 'Ali and Muhammad. Jan is added to show devotion. It is established in hadith that naming someone after the favorites of God—i.e., the Prophets and saints—is recommended in so far as these names are not specific to them. The Prophet said, "Name after the names of the Prophets." (Bukhari, Abu Daud, and al-Nisa'i). [Fifteen hadith on this subject follow.] Names like Ghulam 'Ali, Ghulam Husayn, Ghulam Ghauth, Ghulam Jilani, which add the word Ghulam in a genitive construction with the names of those who love God, are clearly permissible. May God forgive me; I have written a detailed fatwa on such names and have provided justification from the Qur'an, hadith and even from the statements of the leaders of the Wahhabiyya. God says, "Round about them will serve young male servants (ghilman) as if they are well-guarded pearls [52:24]." The Messenger of God, may peace be on him, said, "None of you should call them 'my slave.' All of you are slaves of God. But one should say, 'my lad (ghulam).'" (Muslim)

The Wahhabiyya claims about association with God are always like this example. The Qur'an and hadith are replete with statements [they deny]. The Wahhabiyya do not spare even God and the Prophet from the accusation of association. I take refuge with God the sustainer of the world.

Mawlawi 'Abd al-Hayy Lakhnawi raised objections against the name [Hidayat 'Ali] in Majmu'a Fatawa (vol. 1, p. 464). In the beginning of his fatwa he judged it simply as not preferable, but he concluded by calling it sin and impermissible. In fact, he is totally incorrect. [A summary of this fatwa, translated above, follows.]

My comment [on the fatwa of Mawlawi 'Abd al-Hayy Lakhnawi]:

This answer is the wonder of wonders. It looks like a joke or is rather a joke. First, the very foundation of this incoherent statement is pure fantasy. Something is forbidden if its meaning is equivocal with association with God, not if the meaning is implicit. There is a huge difference between equivocalness and implication. Equivocalness indicates immediate understanding; i.e., the forbidden meaning jumps to mind immediately. It is different from identifying one of the possible implications as denoting a forbidden meaning. The *Talkhis [al-Ma'ani]* explains: "Equivocation occurs when a word that has two meanings, one immediate and one remote, is used in the remote meaning without any indication." Sayyid Sharif, may his noble secret be venerated, writes in his book *Ta'rifat,* "Equivocalness, also called 'equivocation,' means that one uses a word that has two meanings, one immediate and the other remote. While the immediate meaning comes to the listener's mind, the speaker intends the remote meaning. Most of the obscure [passages in the Qur'an] belong to this type. God says, 'And the heavens will be rolled up in his right hand' [39:67]."

If mere implication were the basis of prohibition of a statement, there would be few statements free from prohibition or censure. All the statements about voluntary acts, like "Zayd came," "Zayd went," "Zayd got up," "Zayd sat," and "'Amr ate, drank, and spoke," and "Mujib studied the question and replied," attribute an act to a person. This attribution implies two meanings. One is that Zayd, 'Amr, and Mujib performed these acts in their personal, complete, and permanent capacity. The second is that they did so by the capacity that is bestowed on them and is thus incomplete and limited. The first sense is certainly association with God. Therefore, such unqualified statements must be avoided. The learned mufti would also have used such equivocations of association in his daily speech all his life. His books must be filled with thousands of such allusions of association. That aside, you must recite in your prayer the phrase "*wa ta'ala jadduka*" (may Your esteem grow higher). The word *jadd* has two meanings (one meaning grandfather). If we take this second meaning, which is the more familiar one, would it not be clear and emphatic infidelity? One wonders why allusion to such enormous infidelity is not forbidden. In sum, in equivocation what matters is the meanings that come to mind immediately, and that warrant prohibition—not mere implication.

Second, if you favor such hair splitting, then why pick on only the name Hidayat 'Ali? Why do you not find fault with 'Ali, the pure name of Master 'Ali, May God ennoble his face? In other names you found only one of the four aspects implying association with God. Here in this name one of the two aspects implies association. The word 'Ali has two meanings: first, essential sublimity, which is exclusive to the essence and beyond any additions; second, relative sublimity as an attribute of creation. If affirmation of the first meaning is definitely association with God, then the name 'Ali has twice the equivocation of association of Hidayat 'Ali. Not to speak of a learnèd person, even an ignorant one would not make such a statement.

Third, it is not only 'Ali, all those names that are common for both the creator and the creation, for instance Rashid, Hamid, Jamil, Jalil, Karim, 'Alim, Rahim, and Halim, when applied to humans will denote the same equivocation of association. The fact is that God Himself gave some of his beautiful names to the prophets, may salutations and peace be on them. Scholars have provided details on this point in al-Mawahib and other books. The Prophet himself mentioned Hashir as his blessed name. Numerous elders among the companions, successors, and religious leaders had the name Malik. What would you say about the equivocation of these names? The authentic books like Durr Mukhtar have clearly stated that such names are permissible. The meaning in the case of humans will be different from the meaning intended for God. "Naming someone with the names common to God and His creation, such as 'Ali and Rashid and so on, is permissible; the meaning in our case will not be the same as they are in reference to God."

Fourth, the name 'Abd al-Hayy has two parts, and both parts have double meanings. 'Abd has two meanings, one vis à vis God, and the other vis à vis master. Similarly, Hayy in one sense is a name of God, which describes His life, which is essential, eternal, and necessary; and, in another sense, Hayy applies to me, you, Zayd, and Amr. If you take 'Abd in the first sense and Hayy in the second meaning, it is definitely association with God. Thus there are the same four possible forms [as in Hidayat 'Ali], and similarly one of these forms denotes association. If so, then how is the name 'Abd al-Hayy secure from the equivocation of association? One should have avoided this name as well.

Fifth, regarding ya 'Ali, he says if one intends to call on God, then the usage is not disputable. But here also the second implication exists. Equivocation and implication is not removable by the intention of the speaker. Equivocation occurs exactly where the speaker does not intend those possible meanings. If one relies on the intention of the speaker, then there should be no debate on the name Hidayat 'Ali because no association is intended.

Sixth, adding the prefix al- cannot secure the name from such a universal equivocation of association. Also, al- may not be added to a proper noun, but it can be added to an adjectival noun. 'Ali as an adjective is certainly a common attribute. Thus implication still exists and therefore it must be avoided. It is clear in Sirajiyya, Tatar Khaniyya, and Minh al-Ghaffar that having a name al-'Ali, with the prefix, is permissible. Radd al-Muhtar notes, "Tatar Khaniyya cites the following from al-Sirajiyya: 'Naming someone with a name found in the book of God, like al-'Ali, al-Kabir, al-Rashid, and al-Badi' is allowed. . . .' A similar view is found in Minh. It is clearly permissible, even as a proper noun with the prefix al-." [The Fatwa goes on enumerating other arguments on the same pattern.]

A FATWA BY 'ABD ALLAH MUHADDITH ROPARI (D.1964)

Question: Is it permissible to have names like Ghulam Rasul, Ghulam Ilahi, Mawla Bakhsh (Given by the Master), given that names like Ghulam Rasul and Ghulam Ilahi are understood to mean Servant of the Apostle, or Servant of God? If such names are not permissible, is it necessary to change existing names?

Answer: Some people find justification for the permissibility of names like Ghulam Rasul in the following hadith: Abu Hurayra reported the Prophet saying, "None of you should say 'my slave' ['*abd*] or 'my slave girl'; all of you are slaves of God and all of your women are slave girls of God. But you should say 'my boy' (*ghulam*), 'my girl,' or 'my daughter'." (*Mishkat*, Bab al-asami).

This hadith, however, does not provide a sufficient explanation, because it refers to a temporary relationship. In a name the relationship is permanent. Therefore, one needs to exercise care in avoiding such names. Further, those who give such names do in fact believe in the powers of the elders. They cherish their relationship with them and take pride in this relationship, as the name itself shows. Even those who do not believe in such powers look like those who do if they use these names. That is also a reason to avoid them. In the hadith above, the acceptable names are invoked to distinguish ownership, that one is a slave of Zayd, not of 'Amr. It does not indicate any reverence implying association with God. Care requires therefore avoiding such names.

Regarding the matter of names already registered in certificates and other documents, they may stay as they are in those documents, since there is no way to change them. It is best, however, to change the name for everyday communication.

A FATWA BY MUFTI TAQI 'USMANI (B.1943-)

Question: Is it mandatory in Islam to name our children with Arabic names? Please answer in the light of Qur'an and *Sunna*, thank you. [Murad]

Answer: Psychologists now acknowledge the effect a person's name has on his life. But Muhammad, Peace be upon him, had revealed this fact to his followers already 1400 years ago. His teaching to his followers was that children should be given good names, and that meaningless names and those having unsavory connotations should be avoided. Subsequently, we find many incidents mentioned in the hadith where Rasulullah, Peace be upon him, changed the names of people with this object.

Another aspect of a person's name is that it bespeaks a person's religion. Hence, the name of a Muslim is usually of such a nature that by the mere mention of it, the listener understands that the person so addressed is a Muslim. It is for this reason that our elders laid great emphasis on keeping good and pleasant names. But since the spread of Western culture throughout the world, it has become customary amongst Muslims not to take into cognizance the meaning of the name when naming a child. Many do not even bother to ascertain whether it is permissible for one to keep such a name or not. Often, even if the name is correct and suitable, then by abbreviating it, its Islamic connotation is distorted. In fact, at times it even becomes unlawful to address one by such a name. For example, Abdurrahman is called Rahman; Abdur-Razzaaq, Razaaq; Abdul-Wahhab, Wahhab—whereas Rahman, Razaaq, and Wahhab are the exclusive epithets of Allah Ta'ala. To address any creation by such a name is therefore unlawful.

While this disease is rampant in the entire Muslim world, it is especially in vogue in some countries like South Africa: Suleiman is called Solly; Yoosuf is called Joosub, Essop or Joe; Uthman is called Ossy, etc. In this way the blessed names of the prophets, Peace be upon them, and companions, May Allah be pleased with them, are distorted and needlessly rendered meaningless. Moreover, one may never know whether the one so addressed is a Muslim or not.

Hence, with regards to naming children, there has been a need for compiling a book wherein all misconceptions could be eradicated and guidance could be given as to the importance of giving correct and meaningful names. Praise be to Allah, our respected Brother, Moulana Qaree Muhammad Rafeeq, a teacher at the Madrasah Islamia, Lenasia, has fulfilled this need proficiently. The respected compiler has in his introduction explained most ably the Islamic teachings regarding a newborn child. The issues pertaining to Tahneek [the softened date placed in the newborn's mouth], the call to prayer, supplications, circumcision, naming a child, and many more, have been explained in detail. In addition to compiling Muslim names in an alphabetical order, he has also provided their meanings and historical dimensions. During my tour of South Africa, I have had a cursory perusal of various portions of the book and found it to be most invaluable. In my opinion, it should find a place in the home of every Muslim. No family should be without it. May Allah Ta'ala grant the compiler the best of rewards in both worlds for the services rendered by him, grant him the guidance to render more and greater service of this nature and may He also grant this book wide acceptance. Amen.

Sources

The fatwa by 'Abd al-Hayy Lakhnawi was translated from Abu al-Hasanat Muhammad 'Abd al-Hayy, *Majmu'a Fatawa Mawlana Abd al-Hayy* (Karachi: Qur'an Mahal, 1964) 1, pp. 544–545. The fatwa by Ahmad Rada Khan was translated from *Fatawa Ridwiyya* (Karachi: Dar al-'Ulum Amjadiyya, 1992) 10, pp. 200–207. The fatwa by 'Abd Allah Muhaddith Ropari was translated from *Fatawa Ahl-i Hadith* (Sargodha: Idara Ihya al-Sunna al-nabawiyya, n.d.) 2, p. 550. The fatwa by Mufti Taqi 'Usmani given in English is from Mufti Taqi Usmani, "Q & A: Children's Names," in *Albalagh, an Islamic E-Journal*, http://www.albalagh.net/qa/children_names.shtml (last accessed 25 November 2006).

Further Reading

For a history of the institution of fatwa and its development in Muslim societies, see Muhammad Khalid Masud, Brinkley Messick, and David Powers, eds., *Islamic Legal Interpretation: The Muftis and their Fatwas* (Cambridge, MA: Harvard University Press, 1996).

27

A Rallying Cry for Muslim Personal Law:
The Shah Bano Case and Its Aftermath

Sylvia Vatuk

In the Indian legal system, marriage, divorce, inheritance, and related matters are regulated principally by legislation enacted at the central government level. There are several distinct bodies of "family" or "personal" law that are applied—by the civil judges who hear all matrimonial and related cases—according to the litigant's religious affiliation: Hindu (a category that includes Sikhs, Jains, and Buddhists), Muslim, Christian, Parsi, or Jewish. Couples professing different religions—or preferring not to marry in a religious ceremony—have the option of contracting a civil union under the Special Marriage Act (first enacted in 1954 and amended most recently in 1976). Any subsequent marital dispute will be dealt with under that Act's provisions, rather than by the laws applicable to others of their religious background.

The persistence of this system of multiple bodies of personal law has long been the subject of controversy in India and continues to be so in the context of public debates over the rights of religious minorities within a majority "Hindu" nation. These debates have a significant gender component. Thus the principal argument put forward by those who favor abolishing the existing system and enacting a so-called Uniform Civil Code (UCC) applicable to all citizens regardless of religion, (a "Directive Principle" of India's Constitution) is that Muslim Personal Law (MPL) is particularly detrimental to women's well-being, denying them legal protections that are available to women of other religious communities. These critics of MPL call special attention to three provisions of MPL: (1) a Muslim man may marry up to four wives at one time, whereas polygamy is illegal for men of other religions; (2) he can divorce his wife extra-judicially and unilaterally, whereas other men must file for divorce in a court of law and prove either mutual consent or one or more specified grounds under which the marriage may be dissolved; and (3) he need not support his former wife beyond a religiously prescribed three months after the divorce, whereas a court may order a man of any other religion to maintain his former wife indefinitely, if she has no other means of supporting herself. However, it should be noted that, whereas this characterization of MPL conforms to widely held popular understandings of the law, a recent Supreme Court decision has placed important restrictions on unilateral divorce by the so-called "triple talaq" (in *Shamim Ara v. State of U.P.,* AIR 2002 SCW 4162) and, in a follow-up to the case discussed in this essay, that court has interpreted the Muslim law of maintenance in such a way as to make it incumbent upon a man who divorces his wife to make some additional financial provision for her future (in *Danial Latifi v. Union of India,* AIR 2001 [7] SCC 740, excerpted below).

For feminist proponents of a UCC, gender bias in MPL is a fundamental women's rights issue. For others it is closely linked to an explicitly anti-Muslim political agenda. Thus, Hindu chauvinist politicians and their followers regularly cite the fact that MPL allows Muslim men legal "privileges" not available to men of other faiths as evidence of flawed government policies of "appeasement" of a "backward-looking" and "misogynous" Muslim religious leadership. That such rhetoric has come to dominate the campaign for a UCC has placed women's rights activists in an uncomfortable position. Not wanting to be associated with "communalist" sentiments of this sort, many have chosen to back off from actively promoting the notion of a UCC and now advocate instead encouraging the improvement of Muslim women's legal position through "internal changes" in MPL, brought about by reform-minded members of their own community.

In these debates over whether MPL should be retained, reformed, or replaced by a UCC, Muslim women, regarded—by their own community as well as by outsiders—as the principal repositories of Muslim religious identity, occupy a key symbolic place. They often find themselves obliged to put their identity as Muslims before their interests as women, if they are to avoid being accused of betraying their own community and damaging its ability to present a united front in the struggle against majority domination. They cannot easily speak out in favor of a UCC or even publicly criticize those provisions of MPL that militate against their interests as women. This is not to say that Muslim women's rights activists do not exist. But they are relatively few in number and tread a perilous path in striving to balance a desire for legal change with their religious commitments and their need for community acceptance.

After Independence, the issue of reform of personal law was high on the agenda of the builders of the new nation. A principal motive was to rectify the gender inequities that pervaded every one of the codes. But rather than attempt to develop a comprehensive set of new laws that would apply to all citizens, they began by drafting new laws of marriage, divorce, succession, inheritance, and child guardianship for Hindus and adherents of related religions, who together constituted at that time approximately 87 percent of the country's population. Despite opposition from the orthodox Hindu religious leadership, a secularized and relatively gender-equitable Hindu Marriage Act was passed in 1955. The Hindu Succession Act and Hindu Adoption and Maintenance Act followed in 1956. No serious attempt was ever made to undertake a similarly comprehensive reform of the personal laws of any of the minority communities. The government's particular reluctance to touch MPL reflected the unsettled situation of Hindu-Muslim relations following the religious violence that had accompanied the partition of British India into independent India and Pakistan in 1947. It was felt to be especially important that those Muslims who had remained in India (then approximately 10.4 percent of the population) become well integrated into the new, unified nation. Fears that any attempt to alter existing Muslim Personal Law would arouse strong opposition and create suspicion within that community made it politically risky to press forward with a legal reform agenda.

In April 1978, a case was filed in the magistrate's court of Indore, Madhya Pradesh, that eventually became a rallying point for the defense of Muslim Personal Law as a central symbol of Muslim minority rights in India. The background of this case goes back to 1898, when a revision of the Criminal Procedure Code (CrPC) was undertaken by the government of British India. Chapter XXVI, Section 488 of the revised code dealt with orders of maintenance for destitute women and children. This section was intended to address what was perceived to be a growing social problem at the time, that of "vagrancy." Rather than allow persons with no income or assets to become burdens on the state, the new law placed responsibility for the support of indigent wives and children squarely upon their husbands and fathers, respectively.

Twenty-six years after Independence, in 1973, the CrPC was again revised, and in the course of that revision an important change was made in the section dealing with maintenance orders (now Chapter IX, Sections 125–127): the meaning of "wife" was expanded to include not only a *currently married* woman, but also "a woman *who has been divorced by, or has obtained a divorce from, her husband* and has not remarried [italics mine]." When Muslim religious leaders became aware of this change they strongly objected. They demanded that men of their community be exempted from the requirement to maintain a *divorced* wife (under the new Section 125), on the grounds that this was in conflict with MPL. Citing numerous religio-legal authorities, they contended that a Muslim man who has divorced his wife need only hand over the wedding gift (*mahr*) he promised her in their marriage contract—if it has not already been paid in full. He must then maintain her for a religiously prescribed '*iddat* period of three months (or three complete menstrual courses) or, should she happen to be pregnant, until she gives birth. At that point his financial responsibility for her is at an end.

The government refused to accede to the demand for a special exemption, but it responded to Muslim complaints by adding to the chapter a special clause providing for the cancellation of an order of maintenance in the event that the divorced woman had received "the whole of the sum which, under any customary or personal law applicable to the parties, was payable" to her (Section 127[3] [b]). While the amendment does not specifically mention religion, the reference is clearly to the Muslim woman's *mahr* and living expenses during '*iddat*. Notwithstanding its intent, however, in subsequent years Muslim divorcées continued to file suits for maintenance, and in many cases the courts saw fit to comply with their petitions.

The 1978 suit in question was filed by a married woman in her 60s named Shah Bano, who was estranged and living apart from her husband, Mohommed Ahmed Khan. She sought a maintenance order for Rs. 500 per month, the maximum allowable under the law at that time (this limit has recently been lifted). Khan was a successful lawyer who—according to his wife's petition—was earning approximately Rs. 5,000 per month. The couple, who were first cousins, had been married for forty-six years and had five adult offspring. Khan had also fathered another seven children by his second wife, also a cousin. The whole family had lived together in one house for many years. However, three years prior to this, for reasons that are unknown, Khan had forced Shah Bano out of their home, and since then they had been living apart. For the first two years of their separation he had been giving her Rs. 200 a month, but for the past year he had made no further contribution to her living expenses. At this point, she decided to resort to the law.

It is not surprising that Shah Bano and her husband were cousins as well as husband and wife. Muslim parents often prefer to have their child marry a close relative rather than someone whose family's antecedents are less well known and whose customs and ways of life may differ from theirs. Shah Bano's situation was unusual in some other respects, however. Contrary to prevalent stereotypes, polygamy, although permitted under MPL, is not a common practice among Indian Muslims. And in the event that a married man does decide to take another wife, he is much more likely to divorce or abandon the first than to bring the second into the existing household. Furthermore, even if he should be both so inclined and in a financial position to keep two wives, he will typically arrange separate accommodations for each, rather than deal with the jealousies and tensions that invariably arise when co-wives and their respective sets of children share living quarters. It is probably safe to assume that intra-familial conflicts of some sort lay behind Shah Bano's expulsion from her husband's house in 1975. But it is less clear why the separation should have occurred after so many years, when she and her husband were both so advanced in age. Most instances of marital breakdown in this society occur in the very early years of marriage. What's more, Shah Bano had several grown sons. There is a strong social obligation in Indian society for sons to maintain and care for their aging parents. Someone in Shah Bano's position would normally expect to be taken in by one or more of her sons when she was forced to leave their father's home. But the evidence presented to the Supreme Court of India, where this case eventually wound up, does not enlighten us as to with whom she was living when she filed the maintenance suit or what roles her children may have played, either in her life more generally or in relation to the legal case that brought her such notoriety. In this, as in some other respects, there is a great deal more to Shah Bano's story than meets the eye.

In November 1978, before the Indore magistrate had reached his verdict in the case, Khan appeared to inform the court that he had just divorced his wife and to defend himself against her suit on the grounds that under MPL a man need not maintain his former wife beyond the 'iddat period. He stated that he now intended to discharge his remaining financial obligations to her by paying her *mahr* and depositing Rs. 3000 with the court to cover her 'iddat expenses. But the magistrate disagreed with Khan's understanding of the law and ordered him to begin making maintenance payments, though only in the meager amount of Rs. 25 per month. Not surprisingly, Shah Bano's lawyer soon applied to the High Court of Madhya Pradesh for an enhancement of this stipend, and in July 1980 that court ordered it raised to Rs. 179.20. At this point Khan decided to turn to the Supreme Court of India for relief. His appeal progressed slowly over the next four-and-a-half years until on April 23, 1985, it was finally dismissed by a five-judge bench that upheld the high court's decision and in addition assessed the petitioner Rs. 10,000 toward his wife's legal costs. This is the Supreme Court judgment excerpted below.

In the judgment, Justice Y. V. Chandrachud disputed the petitioner's contention that under Muslim law the husband is not obligated to support a divorced wife who is otherwise unable to maintain herself. As the colonial courts had done, the secular court — here in the person of a judge of Hindu background — based its arguments in part on an interpretation of sacred Islamic texts. The decision specifically referred to certain passages in the Qur'an (2:241–242) that, in the judge's view, "leave no doubt" that, upon divorce, the Muslim husband must make a "reasonable provision" for his former wife, over and above her 'iddat expenses. In closing, the court also chose to express its regret that no action had ever been taken toward implementing Article 44 of the Constitution by drafting a Uniform Civil Code (UCC) of personal law.

Since 1973 several earlier high court judgments and two Supreme Court decisions (*Bai Tahira v. Ali Hussain Fideali Chotthea*, AIR 1979 SC 362 and *Fuzlunbi v. K. Khader Vali and another*, 1980[4] SCC 125) had similarly affirmed the right of a divorced Muslim woman to claim maintenance, if the amounts she had received in *mahr* and 'iddat maintenance were insufficient to meet her survival needs. These judgments had not aroused any particular public controversy. But the decision in the Shah Bano case unleashed a storm of protest from various segments of the Muslim community. The orthodox leadership was particularly indignant that a (Hindu) judge had taken it upon himself to interpret the Holy Qur'an and had also essentially called for doing away altogether with MPL. A range of Muslim spokesmen and groups, including the All-India Muslim Personal Law Board, demanded that the issue be settled once and for all by enacting a law specifically barring divorced Muslim women from availing themselves of Section 125 of the CrPC. Though Muslim community opinion was hardly unanimous on the issue, the ruling Congress Party government soon bowed to pressure from the clerical leadership and introduced the Muslim Women (Protection of Rights on Divorce) Bill into Parliament. Women's organizations, various progressive, secular political groups, and some specifically Muslim organizations vehemently opposed this attempt to exclude Muslim women from the purview of this part of the CrPC and reiterated the demand for passage of the long-promised UCC. The issue became extremely heated and divisive, the fires stoked by media attention that framed it as a battle between "fundamentalist, orthodox, obscurantist male chauvinists" and "modern, secular, pro-women rationalists." Before long, Shah Bano herself was issuing an open letter to the people of her community, rejecting and disassociating herself from the Supreme Court judgment and apologizing for having unknowingly transgressed her own religious law (*shari'a*) when she asked that her former husband be ordered to provide for her.

Ultimately the critics of the judgment prevailed, and in May of 1986 the Muslim Women (Protection of Rights on Divorce) Act (MWA) was passed. It outlines the entitlements of a divorced woman as "a reasonable and fair provision and maintenance made and paid to her within the '*iddat* period," provision for the children of the marriage up to two years of age, payment of her *mahr* as well as handing over any goods she had been given by her relatives and friends or by those of her husband either before, at, or after the wedding. If, after this, she is still not able to maintain herself and has not remarried, she may apply to a magistrate for an order directing her adult children and/or any natal relatives—specifically, those who "would be entitled to inherit her property on her death"—to provide for her. In their absence or inability to pay, her local Wakf Board (the state agency charged with regulating and managing Muslim endowments) may be ordered to assist her financially.

In a decade of mounting anti-Muslim sentiment, under the aegis of Hindu nationalist organizations like the VHP and others, Shah Bano's case became, in the public mind and discourse, emblematic of Muslim male misogyny. For many Muslims, however, it was precisely this critique that made them cling even more to MPL as a symbol of their cultural rights and identity in India. Many activists, Muslim and non-Muslim both, who were troubled by decisions that compromised women's interests drew back from criticism in order to avoid alignment with "the Hindu right." At first it was taken for granted by all who had opposed passage of MWA that it would have an extremely negative impact on the ability of poor Muslim women to survive after divorce. It was predicted that its effects would be both direct (reducing the length of time during which divorced women could expect to be supported by their ex-husbands) and indirect (increasing men's motivation to resort to unilateral divorce rather than remain married to their estranged wives). This is still the received wisdom within the non-Muslim public at large, for politicians promoting the desirability of enacting a UCC, and for many feminist legal activists and scholars. The limited data that are available do confirm that the MWA provides a convenient out for Muslim men threatened by maintenance suits. Advocates routinely inform male clients that they can avoid a maintenance order by simply pronouncing divorce (*talaq*). Some lower court judges have a similar understanding of the Act's intent; they not infrequently throw out a woman's case immediately upon learning that she has been divorced.

But high court cases from different states of India have begun to accumulate that indicate some judges are interpreting the law quite differently from the way its clerical authors intended. Most such cases were filed by men, in appeal of judgements ordering them to pay maintenance to their wives or ex-wives under Section

125 of the CrPC. Typically the appellants argued, citing the MWA, that they had already divorced their wives and paid the *mahr* and *'iddat*-period support and hence were no longer legally bound to pay maintenance. But in many of these cases, the high courts have decided for the respondents, ordering the men to make additional, longer-term financial provisions for their former wives, usually in the form of lump-sum paymens. The amounts ordered vary widely, according to the judges' assessment of the men's income and assets and the wives' needs, taking into account the standard of living to which they were accustomed before the divorce.

The key concept at issue in these cases is the "reasonable and fair provision" that the MWA directs the husband to make for his ex-wife during the *'iddat* period. The question is, should this "provision" be interpreted as one coterminous with the "maintenance" that it is generally agreed a man must pay during his ex-wife's *'iddat*, or as something to which she is entitled above and beyond that? In at least fifteen of the reported cases decided under the Act between 1987 and 2000, the divorced woman's right to an additional amount as "reasonable and fair provision" was upheld on appeal. Women who had been married to men of means were sometimes awarded substantial sums. In 2001 such an interpretation of the law was definitively confirmed in a Supreme Court decision on a Writ Petition that had been filed in 1986, shortly after the MWA was enacted. This petition challenged the Act's constitutionality, on the grounds that it violated the fundamental rights of Muslim divorced women by excluding them from the protection of Section 125 of the CrPC (*Danial Latifi v. Union of India*, AIR 2001 (7) SCC 740, excerpted briefly below). While the Supreme Court did uphold the constitutionality of the Act, it nevertheless decreed that the most crucial passage of the MWA is to be read as meaning not that the woman must be maintained only during the *'iddat* period, but that *during* the *'iddat* period the husband is liable *to make "reasonable and fair" provision for her future* (italics mine).

As the news of the various high court decisions began to spread, some within the Muslim clerical leadership became concerned that the original intent of the law was being subverted through judicial activism, and these concerns became more acute with the announcement of the outcome of the Latifi case. Scholarly assessments of the impact of the MWA have likewise begun to change with growing awareness of these trends in recent case law on the issue of the maintenance of divorced Muslim women. Some observers have even begun to regard the Act as "a blessing in disguise" for divorced Muslim women, who are now in a position to obtain large, one-time lump-sum payments rather than the small monthly stipends awarded under Section 125 that—among their other shortcomings—are often difficult or impossible to collect on a regular basis as the months and years go by. But such a positive outcome can be achieved only if the man against whom the divorcée is filing earns a comfortable income or has substantial assets. A woman divorced from a low-wage laborer or from a man who is only irregularly employed is not likely to find that the MWA, even under the new interpretative guidelines, provides much practical succor.

EXCERPTS FROM *MOHD. AHMED KHAN V. SHAH BANO BEGUM,* AIR 1985 SC 945

HON'BLE JUSTICE Y. V. CHANDRACHUD (CJI)

CHANDRACHUD, C.J. This appeal does not involve any question of constitutional importance, but that is not to say that it does not involve any question of importance. Some questions which arise under the ordinary civil and criminal law are of a far-reaching significance to large segments of society which have been traditionally subjected to unjust treatment. Women are one such segment. "*Na stree swatantramarhati,*" said Manu, the lawgiver: The woman does not deserve independence. And, it is alleged that the "fatal point in law is the degradation of woman" (*Selections from Kuran,* Edward William Lane 1843, Reprint 1982, page xc). To the Prophet is ascribed the statement, hopefully wrongly, that "Woman was made from a crooked rib, and if you try to bend it straight, it will break; therefore treat your wives kindly." . . .

Does the Muslim Personal Law impose no obligation upon the husband to provide for the maintenance of his divorced wife? Undoubtedly, the Muslim husband enjoys the privilege of being able to discard his wife whenever he chooses to do so, for reasons good, bad or indifferent. Indeed, for no reason at all. But, is the only price of that privilege the dole of a pittance during the period of *'iddat*? And, is the law so ruthless in its inequality that, no matter how much the husband pays for the maintenance of his divorced wife during the period of *'iddat*, the mere fact that he has paid something, no matter how little, absolves him for ever from the duty of paying adequately so as to enable her to keep her body and soul together? Then again, is there any provision in the Muslim Personal Law under which a sum is payable to the wife "on divorce"? These are some of the important, though agonising, questions which arise for our decision. . . .

Under section 125(1)(a), a person who, having sufficient means, neglects or refuses to maintain his wife who is unable to maintain herself, can be asked by the court to pay a monthly maintenance to her at a rate not exceeding Five Hundred rupees. By clause (b) of the Explanation to section 125(1), "wife" includes a divorced woman who has not remarried. These provisions are too clear and precise to admit of any doubt or refinement. The religion professed by a spouse or by the spouses has no place in the scheme of these provisions. Whether the spouses are Hindus or Muslims, Christians or Parsis, pagans or heathens, is wholly irrelevant in the application of these provisions. The reason for this is axiomatic, in the sense that section 125 is a part of the Code of Criminal Procedure, not of the Civil Laws which define and govern the rights and obligations of the parties belonging to particular religions, like the Hindu Adoption and Maintenance Act, the *shari'at*, or the Parsi Matrimonial Act. Section 125 was enacted in order to provide a quick and summary remedy to a class of persons who are unable to maintain themselves. What difference would it then make as to what is the religion professed by the neglected wife, child or parent? Neglect by a person of sufficient means to maintain these and the inability of these persons to maintain themselves are the objective criteria which determine the applicability of section 125. Such provisions, which are essentially of a prophylactic nature, cut across the barriers of religion. True, that they do not supplant the personal law of the parties but, equally, the religion professed by the parties or the state of the personal law by which they are governed, cannot have any repercussion on the applicability of such laws unless, within the framework of the Constitution, their application is restricted to a defined category of religious groups or classes. The liability imposed by section 125 to maintain close relatives who are indigent is founded upon the individual's obligation to the society to prevent vagrancy and destitution. That is the moral edict of the law and morality cannot be clubbed with religion. Clause (b) of the Explanation to section 125(1), which defines "wife" as including a divorced wife, contains no words of limitation to justify the exclusion of Muslim women from its scope. Section 125 is truly secular in character. . . . The whole of this discussion as to whether the right conferred by section 125 prevails over the personal law of the parties, has proceeded on the assumption that there is a conflict between the provisions of that section and those of the Muslim Personal Law. The argument that by reason of section 2 of the Shari'at Act, XXVI of 1937, the rule of decision in matters relating, *inter alia*, to maintenance "shall be the Muslim Personal Law" also proceeds upon a similar assumption. We embarked upon the decision of the question of priority between the Code and the Muslim Personal Law on the assumption that there was a conflict between the two because, in so far as it lies in our power, we wanted to set at rest, once for all, the question whether section 125 would prevail over the personal law of the parties, in cases where they are in conflict. . . .

The next logical step to take is to examine the question, on which considerable argument has been advanced before us, whether there is any conflict between the provisions of section 125 and those of the Muslim Personal Law on the liability of the Muslim husband to provide for the maintenance of his divorced wife.

The contention of the husband and of the interveners who support him is that, under the Muslim Personal Law, the liability of the husband to maintain a divorced wife is limited to the period of *'iddat*. In support of this proposition, they rely upon the statement of law on the point contained in certain text books. In *Mulla's Mahomedan Law* (18th Edition, para 279, page 301), there is a statement to the effect that after divorce, the wife is entitled to maintenance during the period of *'iddat*. At page 302, the learned author says:

> Where an order is made for the maintenance of a wife under section 488 of Criminal Procedure Code and the wife is afterwards divorced, the order ceases to operate on the expiration of the period of *'iddat*. The result is that a Mahomedan may defeat an order made against him under section 488 by di-

vorcing his wife immediately after the order is made. His obligation to maintain his wife will cease in that case on the completion of her *'iddat.*

Tyabji's Muslim law (4th Edition, para 304, pages 268–269), contains the
statement that:

On the expiration of the *'iddat* after talaq, the wife's right to maintenance
ceases, whether based on the Muslim Law, or on an order under the Criminal Procedure Code.

According to Dr. Paras Diwan:

When a marriage is dissolved by divorce the wife is entitled to maintenance
during the period of *'iddat.* . . . On the expiration of the period of *'iddat,* the
wife is not entitled to any maintenance under any circumstances. Muslim law
does not recognise any obligation on the part of a man to maintain a wife
whom he had divorced. (*Muslim Law in Modern India,* 1982 Edition, page 130)

These statements in the text book are inadequate to establish the proposition
that the Muslim husband is not under an obligation to provide for the maintenance of his divorced wife, who is unable to maintain herself. One must have
regard to the entire conspectus of the Muslim Personal Law in order to determine the extent, both in quantum and in duration, of the husband's liability to
provide for the maintenance of an indigent wife who has been divorced by him.
Under that law, the husband is bound to pay *Mahr* to the wife as a mark of respect to her. True, that he may settle any amount he likes by way of dower upon
his wife, which cannot be less than 10 Dirhams, which is equivalent to three or
four rupees (*Mulla's Mahomedan Law,* 18th Edition, para 286, page 308). But,
one must have regard to the realities of life. *Mahr* is a mark of respect to the
wife. The sum settled by way of *Mahr* is generally expected to take care of the
ordinary requirements of the wife, during the marriage and after. But these provisions of the Muslim Personal Law do not countenance cases in which the wife
is unable to maintain herself after the divorce. We consider it not only incorrect
but unjust, to extend the scope of the statements extracted above to cases in
which a divorced wife is unable to maintain herself. We are of the opinion that
the application of those statements of law must be restricted to that class of
cases, in which there is no possibility of vagrancy or destitution arising out of
the indigence of the divorced wife. We are not concerned here with the broad
and general question whether a husband is liable to maintain his wife, which
includes a divorced wife, in all circumstances and at all events. That is not the
subject matter of section 125.

There can be no greater authority on this question than the Holy Qur'an. The
Qur'an, the Sacred Book of Islam, comprises in its 114 *Suras* or chapters the
total of revelations believed to have been communicated to Prophet Muhammed, as a final expression of God's will." (*The Qur'an—Interpreted* by Arthur J.
Arberry). Verses (Aiyats) 241 and 242 of the Qur'an show that there is an obli-

gation on Muslim husbands to provide for their divorced wives. The Arabic version of those Aiyats and their English translation are reproduced below. . . . The correctness of the translation of these Aiyats is not in dispute except that, the contention of the appellant is that the word "Mata" in Aiyat No. 241 means "provision" and not "maintenance." That is a distinction without a difference. Nor are we impressed by the shuffling plea of the All India Muslim Personal Law Board that, in Aiyat 241, the exhortation is to the "*muttaqin*" that is, to the more pious and the more God-fearing, not to the general run of the Muslims, the "*muslimin*." In Aiyat 242, the Qur'an says: "It is expected that you will use your commonsense."

The English version of the two Aiyats in Mukammed Zafrullah Khan's *The Qur'an* (page 38) reads thus:

For divorced women also there shall be provision according to what is fair. This is an obligation binding on the righteous. Thus does Allah make His commandments clear to you that you may understand.

The translation of Aiyats 240 to 242 in *The Meaning of the Qur'an* (Vol. 1, published by the Board of Islamic Publications, Delhi) reads thus:

240–241: Those of you, who shall die and leave wives behind them, should make a will to the effect that they should be provided with a year's maintenance and should not be turned out of their homes. But if they leave their homes of their own accord, you shall not be answerable for whatever they choose for themselves in a fair way; Allah is All-Powerful, All-Wise. Likewise, the divorced women should also be given something in accordance with the known fair standard. This is an obligation upon the God-fearing people.

242: Thus Allah makes clear His commandments for you: It is expected that you will use your commonsense.

In *The Running Commentary of The Holy Qur'an* (1964 Edition) by Dr. Allamah Khadim Rahmani Nuri, Aiyat No. 241 is translated thus:

241: And for the divorced woman (also) a provision (should be made) with fairness (in addition to her dower); (This is) a duty (incumbent) on the reverent.

In *The Meaning of the Glorious Qur'an. Text and Explanatory Translation* by Marmaduke Pickthall, (Taj Company Ltd., Karachi), Aiyat 241 is translated thus:

241: For divorced women a provision in kindness: A duty for those who ward off (evil).

Finally, in *The Qur'an Interpreted* by Arthur J. Arberry, Aiyat 241 is translated thus:

241: There shall be for divorced women provision honourable—an obligation on the godfearing. So God makes clear His signs for you. Happily you will understand.

Dr. K. R. Nuri in his book quoted above *The Running Commentary of The Holy Qur'an* says in the preface:

> Belief in Islam does not mean mere confession of the existence of something. It really means the translation of the faith into action. Words without deeds carry no meaning in Islam. Therefore the term "believe and do good" has been used like a phrase all over the Qur'an. Belief in something means that man should inculcate the qualities or carry out the promptings or guidance of that thing in his action. Belief in Allah means that besides acknowledging the existence of the Author of the Universe, we are to show obedience to His commandments. . . .

These Aiyats leave no doubt that the Qur'an imposes an obligation on the Muslim husband to make provision for or to provide maintenance to the divorced wife. The contrary argument does less than justice to the teachings of the Qur'an. As observed by Mr. Hidayatullah in his introduction to *Mulla's Mahomedan Law*, the Qur'an is Al-farqan, that is, one showing truth from falsehood and right from wrong. . . .

If *Mahr* is an amount which the wife is entitled to receive from the husband in consideration of the marriage, that is the very opposite of the amount being payable in consideration of divorce. Divorce dissolves the marriage. Therefore, no amount which is payable in consideration of the marriage can possibly be described as an amount payable in consideration of divorce. The alternative premise that *Mahr* is an obligation imposed upon the husband as a mark of respect for the wife, is wholly detrimental to the stance that it is an amount payable to the wife on divorce. A man may marry a woman for love, looks, learning or nothing at all. And, he may settle a sum upon her as a mark of respect for her. But he does not divorce her as a mark of respect. Therefore, a sum payable to the wife out of respect cannot be a sum payable "on divorce." . . .

It is also a matter of regret that Article 44 of our Constitution has remained a dead letter. It provides that:

> That State shall endeavour to secure for the citizens a uniform civil code throughout the territory of India.

There is no evidence of any official activity for framing a common civil code for the country. A belief seems to have gained ground that it is for the Muslim community to take a lead in the matter of reforms of their personal law. A common Civil Code will help the cause of national integration by removing disparate loyalties to laws which have conflicting ideologies. No community is likely to bell the cat by making gratuitous concessions on this issue. It is the State which is charged with the duty of securing a uniform civil code for the cit-

izens of the country and, unquestionably, it has the legislative competence to
do so. A counsel in the case whispered, somewhat audibly, that legislative competence is one thing, the political courage to use that competence is quite another. We understand the difficulties involved in bringing persons of different
faiths and persuasions on a common platform. But, a beginning has to be made
if the Constitution is to have any meaning. Inevitably, the role of the reformer
has to be assumed by the courts because, it is beyond the endurance of sensitive minds to allow injustice to be suffered when it is so palpable. But piecemeal
attempts of courts to bridge the gap between personal laws cannot take the
place of a common Civil Code. Justice to all is a far more satisfactory way of dispensing justice than justice from case to case. Appeal dismissed.

EXCERPTS FROM *DANIAL LATIFI V. UNION OF INDIA*, AIR 2001 (7) SCC 740

DECIDED-DATE-1: 28 SEPTEMBER 2001
GB PATTANAIK, S RAJENDRA BABU, DP MOHAPATRA, DORAISWAMY
RAJU AND SHIVARAJ V PATIL JJ
JUDGMENT BY: S Rajendra Babu J
The constitutional validity of the Muslim Women (Protection of Rights on
Divorce) Act 1986 (hereinafter referred to as "the Act") is in challenge before
us in these cases. . . .

In interpreting the provisions [of the Act] where matrimonial relationship is
involved, we have to consider the social conditions prevalent in our society. In
our society, whether they belong to the majority or the minority group, what is
apparent is that there exists a great disparity in the matter of economic re-
sourcefulness between a man and a woman. Our society is male dominated
both economically and socially and women are assigned, invariably, a dependent role, irrespective of the class of society to which she belongs. A woman on
her marriage very often, though highly educated, gives up all other avocations
and entirely devotes herself to the welfare of the family, in particular she shares
with her husband her emotions, sentiments, mind, and body, and her investment in the marriage is her entire life—a sacramental sacrifice of her individual self that is far too enormous to be measured in terms of money. When a relationship of this nature breaks up, in what manner we could compensate her
so far as emotional fracture or loss of investment is concerned, there can be no
answer. It is a small solace to say that such a woman should be compensated in
terms of money towards her livelihood and such a relief which partakes basic
human rights to secure gender and social justice is universally recognised by
persons belonging to all religions and it is difficult to perceive that Muslim law
intends to provide a different kind of responsibility by passing on the same to
those unconnected with the matrimonial life such as the heirs who were likely
to inherit the property from her or the wakf boards. Such an approach appears

to us to be a kind of distortion of the social facts. Solutions to such societal problems of universal magnitude pertaining to horizons of basic human rights, culture, dignity and decency of life and dictates of necessity in the pursuit of social justice should be invariably left to be decided on considerations other than religion or religious faith or beliefs or national, sectarian, racial or communal constraints. Bearing this aspect in mind, we have to interpret the provisions of the Act in question. . . .

A careful reading of the provisions of the Act would indicate that a divorced woman is entitled to a reasonable and fair provision for maintenance. It was stated that Parliament seems to intend that the divorced woman gets sufficient means of livelihood, after the divorce and, therefore, the word "provision" indicates that something is provided in advance for meeting some needs. In other words, at the time of divorce the Muslim husband is required to contemplate the future needs and make preparatory arrangements in advance for meeting those needs. Reasonable and fair provision may include provision for her residence, her food, her clothes, and other articles.

The important section in the Act is s. 3 which provides that the divorced woman is entitled to obtain from her former husband "maintenance," "provision" and "mahr," and to recover from his possession her wedding presents and dowry and authorizes the magistrate to order payment or restoration of these sums or properties. The crux of the matter is that the divorced woman shall be entitled to a reasonable and fair provision and maintenance to be made and paid to her within the *'iddat* period by her former husband. The wordings of s. 3 of the Act appear to indicate that the husband has two separate and distinct obligations: (1) to make a "reasonable and fair provision" for his divorced wife; and (2) to provide "maintenance" for her. The emphasis of this section is not on the nature or duration of any such "provision" or "maintenance," but on the time by which an arrangement for payment of provision and maintenance should be concluded, namely, "within the *'iddat* period.". . . Precisely, the point that arose for consideration in Shah Bano's case was that the husband has not made a "reasonable and fair provision" for his divorced wife even if he had paid the amount agreed as *mahr* half a century earlier and provided *'iddat* maintenance and he was, therefore, ordered to pay a specified sum monthly to her under s. 125 Cr PC. This position was available to Parliament on the date it enacted the law but even so, the provisions enacted under the Act are "a reasonable and fair provision and maintenance to be made and paid" as provided under s. 3(1)(a) of the Act and these expressions cover different things, firstly, by the use of two different verbs — "to be made and paid to her within the *'iddat* period" — it is clear that a fair and reasonable provision is to be made while maintenance is to be paid. . . .

In Shah Bano's case this court has clearly explained as to the rationale behind s. 125 Cr PC to make provision for maintenance to be paid to a divorced Muslim wife and this is clearly to avoid vagrancy or destitution on the part of a Muslim woman. . . . Before the Act, a Muslim woman who was divorced by her husband was granted a right to maintenance from her husband under the provisions of s.125 Cr PC until she may re-marry and such a right, if deprived, would not be reasonable, just and fair. Thus the provisions of the Act depriving the divorced Muslim women of such a right to maintenance from her husband and providing for her maintenance to be paid by the former husband only for the period of 'iddat and thereafter to make her run from pillar to post in search of her relatives one after the other and ultimately to knock at the doors of the Wakf Board does not appear to be reasonable and fair substitute of the provisions of s. 125 Cr PC. Such deprivation of the divorced Muslim women of their right to maintenance from their former husbands under the beneficial provisions of the Code of Criminal Procedure which are otherwise available to all other women in India cannot be stated to have been effected by a reasonable, right, just and fair law and, if these provisions are less beneficial than the provisions of chapter IX of the Code of Criminal Procedure, a divorced Muslim woman has obviously been unreasonably discriminated and got out of the protection of the provisions of the general law as indicated under the Code which are available to Hindu, Buddhist, Jain, Parsi, or Christian women, or women belonging to any other community. The provisions prima facie, therefore, appear to be violative of art. 14 of the Constitution mandating equality and equal protection of law to all persons otherwise similarly circumstanced and also violative of art. 15 of the Constitution which prohibits any discrimination on the ground of religion as the Act would obviously apply to Muslim divorced women only and solely on the ground of their belonging to the Muslim religion. . . . It is well settled that when by appropriate reading of an enactment the validity of the act can be upheld, such interpretation is accepted by courts and not the other way. . . .

While upholding the validity of the Act, we may sum up our conclusions:

1. A Muslim husband is liable to make reasonable and fair provision for the future of the divorced wife which obviously includes her maintenance as well. Such a reasonable and fair provision extending beyond the 'iddat period must be made by the husband within the 'iddat period in terms of s. 3(1)(a) of the Act.
2. Liability of Muslim husband to his divorced wife arising under s. 3(1)(a) of the Act to pay maintenance is not confined to 'iddat period. . . .
4. The provisions of the Act do not offend arts. 14, 15 and 21 of the Constitution of India.

Sources

A full record of *Mohd. Ahmed Khan v. Shah Bano Begum*, AIR 1985 SC 945 is available at http://www.cscsarchive.org/dataarchive/textfiles/textfile.2008-07-22.2150472 804/file; and http://www.cscsarchive.org/dataarchive/textfiles/textfile.2008-07-22.21 50472804/file.

For *Danial Latifi v. Union of India*, see http://supremecourtcaselaw.com/. Twenty cases adjudicated by various courts under the 1986 Act are available at http://www.rishabhdara.com/sc/search.php?cx=006286370844832724840%3Ac8g8ep wgfsa&filter=0&cof=FORID%3A9&q=%22Muslim+women%22&sa=Case+Law+Search#938.

Paragraph numbers in the original have been omitted for ease in reading.

Further Reading

The Shah Bano case has generated a very large body of literature. Archana Parashar's *Women and Family Law Reform in India: Uniform Civil Code and Gender Equality* (New Delhi: Sage Publications, 1992), pp. 173–189, is a good place to start. See also Kavita R. Khory, "The Shah Bano Case: Some Political Implications," in Robert D. Baird, ed. *Religion and Law in Independent India* (Delhi: Manohar Publishers, 2005), 149–165. For some of the issues raised by the case and the public response to it, see the article by Zakia Pathak and Rajeshwari Sunder Rajan, "Shahbano," *Signs* 14, no. 3 (1989), pp. 558–582. Asghar Ali Engineer provides a valuable collection of primary source materials in his book, *The Shah Bano Controversy* (Bombay: Sangam Books, 1987). Some more recent developments in the debate over the MWA are addressed by Lucy Carroll, ed., *Shah Bano and the Muslim Women Act a Decade On: The Right of the Divorced Muslim Woman to* Mataa (Bombay: Women's Research Action Group, 1998); and by Flavia Agnes, *Judgement Call: An Insight into Muslim Women's Right to Maintenance* (Mumbai: Majlis, 2001). One of the more insightful of the many published discussions of the broader manifestations and implications of the politics of gender, law, and Muslim minority identity is to be found in Zoya Hasan, "Gender Politics, Legal Reform, and the Muslim Community in India," *Resisting the Sacred and the Secular: Women's Activism and Politicized Religion in South Asia,* Patricia Jeffery and Amrita Basu, eds. (New Delhi: Kali for Women, 1999).

Belonging

BELONGING

Introduction

Barbara D. Metcalf

As has been true throughout the volume, the following chapters typically illustrate more than one of the five themes that structure the sections of the book. Thus in these chapters there are holy men who are the focus of devotion, learnèd scholars instructing their followers, debates over the role of the state in Islamic law and guidance, and controversy over the basis of Islamic traditionalist authority. The theme of this section, however, "Belonging," is meant to point to "belonging" in the sense of authorities and arguments that define the basis of community.

The nature of the ties of followers to their Sufi leaders varies widely at any given time, as do the bonds among those linked to the same saintly person. In Chapter 28, Richard Eaton presents texts that show the pivotal place of Sufi figures in organizing the social and economic foundations of local Muslims societies in Mughal India. They are, he argues, key to the very fact that in the far northeast and northwest areas of the subcontinent there are majority Muslim populations at all. That this is the case in the northeast, given the relative remoteness of the area from centers of Muslim dynastic rule, is particularly notable. The gradual identification of the two northern populations with Islam is specifically linked to the expanding frontier of settled agriculture. In this process, Sufis oversaw the clearing of forested land and served as mediators to both worldly and divine powers. In areas of the subcontinent ruled by non-Muslims, Brahmins and others performed much the same role. The chapter includes two praise poems, one focused on a legendary miracle-working Muslim saint, to whom the Durga-worshipping king entrusts land; the second, which is dedicated to the goddess Chandi, describing a Muslim and his followers as the agents of forest-clearing. Eaton also translates a section of a nineteenth-century text recounting the life of Shah Jalal Mujarrad, the same miracle-working saint encountered by Ibn Battuta in the fourteenth century (Chapter 9). His story underwent periodic reshaping until it acquired the form encountered here, where the saint is presented as having been drawn to the region by its very soil, symbol of the agricultural base then well established as the livelihood of the Muslim population. In this period, as sketched in the Introduction, Bengali Muslims were increasingly conscious of their religious and social identity as a largely peasant population—for whom such a symbol was particularly meaningful—with interests that diverged from those of the primarily Hindu landlords.

A very different kind of loyalty is evident in Chapter 29, where Azfar Moin presents a text by the sixteenth-century courtier, 'Abd al-Qadir Badayuni. Badayuni, he shows, participated in the pervasive quest at the turn of the first Islamic millennium to find the exalted personage who would usher in a new era. For Badayuni, it was in fact this issue that lay at the base of his opposition to the legitimacy of the Emperor Akbar, whom, even as he openly served, he secretly opposed—a fact revealed in his hidden chronicles. Later historians have interpreted these chronicles as evidence that Akbar was an example of "syncretic" or even deviant Islam and that he represented "liberal" Islam in opposition to the "orthodox" Islam of someone like Badayuni. According to Moin, however, other complaints were incidental to his rejection of Akbar's millennial preeminence. Such a preoccupation suggests the complexity of religious thought in this period and its defiance of any simple category like "orthodox." It also introduces the importance of millenarianism and its potential for creating communities loyal to imagined messiahs, from the sixteenth-century Mahdi of Jaunpur to the nineteenth-century Mirza Ghulam Ahmad of the Ahmadiyya movement, to others as well.

A third chapter that focuses primarily on the Mughal era introduces an Arabic text from sixteenth-century Malabar. In Chapter 30, Engseng Ho translates excerpts of a tract written in the domains of the Hindu ruler of Calicut by a jurist of Yemeni Arab descent whose family had arrived a century earlier. Arabs had long been welcomed by the rajas of this area, but they now were at risk, thanks to an alliance of the Portuguese with one of these rulers, the raja of Cochin. Seeking to arouse Muslims against the Portuguese, the author makes clear at once the rootedness of Islam in Malabar society along with its simultaneous transregional networks. The selection suggests, Ho argues, how Islam "in a process of mutual moral adjustment" became entrenched in the area, which thus ought to be defended against the Portuguese marauders. As Ho argues, the problematic interpretations of Muslim history that posit either conflict, at one extreme, or porous "syncretism" on the other, miss the more characteristic reality of Muslims who articulate a Muslim identity that *belongs* in a specific place.

By the end of the colonial period, for most of those involved in politics it was axiomatic that Muslims constituted a census-based "minority," whose members required their own representation and state protection. In 1940, the Muslim League declared itself in favor of a separate state for Muslims, and, in the 1945–1946 election, the small proportion of the population that enjoyed voting rights was essentially called on to vote in favor either of separation or of a united India.

The leading Muslim political figure in the Indian National Congress, Maulana Abu'l Kalam Azad, who would emerge as independent India's first Minister of Education, essentially put forward a secular argument that Muslim Indians shared such profound cultural and historical links with their fellow Indians that there was no basis for separation. The Deobandi, Maulana Husayn Ahmad Madani, president of the Association of Indian Ulama, relentlessly opposed partition on specific Islamic grounds, namely that Prophetic example supported Muslims participating jointly in a polity with non-Muslims. He also adduced the practical argument that Muslims were too scattered to form a state and too divided into sects to form an "Islamic" state in any case. He also provided a mythic argument, in the spirit of modern nationalism, arguing that Adam's expulsion from paradise onto the island of Sri Lanka (where a mountain is known as "Adam's Peak"), along with his subsequent travels through India, shows that Muslims were the first inhabitants of the land (given Muslim understanding that Adam was the first Islamic prophet).

None of these arguments was persuasive for those who favored the creation of a separate Muslim state. In Chapter 31, David Gilmartin translates a range of Muslim League posters dating from the final election in British India. "Islam" in the League campaign did not require the normative behavior that nineteenth-century Bengali reformers, Deobandis, the *tabligh* movement, and others had been promoting. That program would have been difficult, not least because leaders like Jinnah were not themselves known for formal religious practices. "Islam" for the League had primarily meant a commitment to the Muslim community as an overriding identity and a source of the values of democracy and justice. Yet, as the posters make clear, the new participation of 'ulama and Sufis in Muslim League politics in the 1940s introduced into the election a new level of argumentation based on religious symbols and sanctions that defined correct Islam as loyalty to a Muslim state.

The formation of the separate state of Pakistan did not solve the question of what kind of state would emerge. For Bengalis in 1971, the ties of shared religion proved insufficient to bind them to the Pakistani state. Meanwhile, the vexed debate over whether Pakistan was to be a homeland for Muslims or a state that would legislate Islamic principles continued. Already in the early 1950s the question had crystallized after riots against the Ahmadiyya sect, followers of Mirza Ghulam Ahmad, who was accused of claiming to supplant the Prophet Muhammad's status as the final prophet. The Ahmadis were notable for their high level of education, international connections, and success in government and the professions; opposition to them was at least in part an opportunity to assert one's own nationalist and Islamic credentials. Religious figures, including members of the Islamist Jama'at-i Islami led the opposition to them—and some twenty years later, in 1974, under the presumably secular Prime Minister Zulfiqar Ali Bhutto, the state in fact legislated that Ahmadis were not Muslim, thus restricting their full participation in both the religious and political life of the country. This legislation is an example of attempts to make Pakistan not only a state for Muslims, Jinnah's vision, but, in some sense, an Islamic state.

The Munir Report, the official report on the initial anti-Ahmadi disturbance in 1953, insisted on the vacuity of any vision of state-sponsored Islamic doctrine or institutions, largely on the grounds that religious scholars themselves were unable to agree on what an Islamic state should be. The Munir Report soon assumed its status as a touchstone for those convinced that Pakistan's future as a modern state rested in secular liberalism. In Asad Ahmed's subtle reading of the Report in Chapter 32, however, the ambiguities of the document are laid clear. Even while rejecting the claims of those favoring the Islamic state, the Report essentially accepted the Islamist understanding that Islam is "a complete way of life," thus giving new circulation to the undeveloped notion of "the Islamic state."

Subsequent attempts to define Islam at a state level in Pakistan have produced substantial intra-Muslim dissent that has only grown since the anti-Ahmadi crisis when sectarianism first came into public view. The writings of Maulana Yusuf Ludhianvi (1932–2000), a traditionalist scholar, introduced by Naveeda Khan in Chapter 33, reflect the growth of this sectarianism. Although Ludhianvi insists on the mutual legitimacy of sects, in fact he places many beyond the pale and thus, himself, implicitly contributes to the very conflict he deplores. Again, a text ostensibly avowing one position, implicitly supports its opposite, and, as in the Munir Report, demonstrates the contradictions and ambiguities advanced in Pakistan in the quest for religious and political legitimacy.

The final entry in this section, Chapter 34, turns to the subject of Islamic organizations and activism in the Republic of India on the part of the Jama'at-i Islami Hind. In an extraordinary transition from Maududi's founding vision of a vanguard party aloof from political life until a full Islamist order could be created, the organization after independence evolved toward encouraging its members to participate actively in secular electoral politics. The party now seeks to build bonds with the non-Muslim community and operates as an educational and social service organization. As Irfan Ahmad argues in his analysis, these texts demonstrate the ability of an "Islamist" party to reinvent itself under appropriate conditions. The distinctive patterns of the Jama'at-i Islami in the different countries of South Asia, given its political activism and even militance elsewere, are a fascinating example of the importance of the larger political context in shaping Islamic political behavior and ideology. This chapter thus seems an ideal conclusion to a volume that argues the importance of studying Islam "in practice"—in specific times and places and contexts—and not from any hermetic notion that "Islam" can be reduced to transparent and undeviating sacred texts or common mindsets.

—28—

Forest Clearing and the Growth
of Islam in Bengal

Richard Eaton

Bengalis comprise the world's largest Muslim ethnic population, after the Arabs. This fact seems all the more remarkable in view of Bengal's geographic position. With the Himalayan mountains lying to the north, the Indian Ocean to the south, Buddhist Burma to the east, and the mainly Hindu Upper Gangetic valley to the west, the delta occupies something of a geocultural cul-de-sac, quite isolated from the rest of the Muslim world.

To explain the growth of Bengal's large Muslim population, especially in the eastern delta where the density of Muslims is highest, one must look for historical processes that can be correlated with it. One of these is geographic in nature. In the early thirteenth century, at the dawn of Muslim rule in the delta, a Brahmanic social order, organized into hierarchically arranged castes and presided over by Brahmins, was already entrenched in largely agrarian western Bengal. In 1349 a Chinese merchant, Wang Ta-yuan, who had spent several decades visiting overseas localities for the purpose of trade, described the densely populated and agrarian western delta of Bengal, where he found a flourishing textile industry, intensive farming, regular taxation, and the circulation of silver currency. He also alluded to the process of forest-clearing and land reclamation, evidently referring activities already undertaken in western Bengal by Hindu pioneers.

In Bengal's sparsely populated and more thickly forested eastern tracts, by contrast, Brahmanic religious and social institutions had by that time barely begun to appear. Gradually, however, a slow but steady eastward shift of the region's major river systems caused agrarian civilization, and with it the delta's demographic epicenter, to migrate from west to east. As this happened, the great forests of the central and eastern delta were cut and the land prepared for regular cultivation, while local inhabitants were transformed from shifting (swidden, or *jhum*) cultivators to settled wet-rice farmers. This means that the growth of Islam in Bengal's eastern tracts, which occurred after this ecological shift had begun, did not entail the "conversion" of Hindus to Islam. Rather, an Islamic identity gradually grew among non-Hindu forest-dwellers as they adopted an agrarian life. The growth of Islam in Bengal, in short, was closely tied to wet-rice agriculture.

Although armies of the Delhi Sultanate conquered and annexed the western delta in 1204, the emergence of substantial Bengali Muslim peasant communities did not begin until the late sixteenth century. That was when the main channel of the Ganges River abandoned its former path leading straight down to the Bay of Bengal and shifted eastward, opening up the eastern delta for rapid and extensive agricultural development. That was also when the whole delta fell under the political control of the imperial Mughals. Ruling from capitals in north India, Mughal emperors planted their provincial capital in the heart of the delta's most ecologically active and rapidly developing sector—in the newly established city of Dhaka, in eastern Bengal.

In the medieval and early modern periods, then, one sees three overlapping frontiers moving together from west to east across the delta. One was political, as first the sultans of Delhi, then local sultans who had already rebelled (in 1342) against their overlords in Delhi, and finally the imperial Mughals pushed eastward, annexing ever more territory to their expanding domains. One was economic, as lands formerly forested fell under the plow. And one was religious, as communities formerly saturated with cults focused on forest divinities gradually acquired an Islamic identity.

The selections that follow have been chosen with a view to illustrating how these three frontiers were interrelated, and especially how, for the delta's indigenous peoples, Islamic conceptions of prophethood, divinity, and cosmology were connected to processes of geographic, political, and economic change. Arranged in rough chronological order, the selections fall into three categories. The first is a genre of medieval Bengali literature known as *mangala-kavya*, poems written in praise of a local hero or divinity. The second consists of narratives of the life of Shah Jalal of Sylhet, Bengal's most popular Muslim saint. And the third category consists of revenue documents dating to the Mughal period. Although such documents stand in stark contrast to the other categories of primary material, they too shed light on the convergence of Bengal's economic, political, and religious frontiers, which formed such a remarkable feature of the region's medieval socio-religious evolution.

A *Mangala-kavya* Honoring Shaykh Jalal al-Din Tabrizi

Our first category of source materials includes several narrative poems called *mangala-kavyas*. Oral forms of this literature doubtless circulated in very early times; the first written versions, however, were composed no earlier than the fifteenth century. *Mangala-kavyas* promote the spiritual powers and the miraculous deeds of indigenous Bengali deities such as Chandi, Manasa, Dharma, Sasthi, etc., or less commonly, of mythologized heroes. Typically, the hearer or reader is assured of the blessings, boons, or good fortune that would surely result from giving devotion to the figure honored in the poem.

Although most *mangala-kavyas* honor deities, the present text, the *Sekasubhodaya*, focuses on an historical figure, Shaykh Jalal al-Din Tabrizi (d. 1244/45). Composed in Sanskrit mixed with early Middle Bengali, and recorded in Bengali script, the text as we have it dates to the second half of the sixteenth century. However, oral traditions concerning its hero appear to have crystallized within a century or so of his lifetime, since the work draws on popular legends datable to the fourteenth or fifteenth century. Jalal al-Din Tabrizi's known biographical facts are spare. Around 1228 he left his native Tabriz in Iran for Baghdad, where he studied Sufism with Shaykh Shihab al-Din Suhrawardi. Sometime after 1235, when his master died, he journeyed to Delhi, capital of the newly established and rapidly expanding Delhi Sultanate. Not feeling welcome there, the *shaykh* continued on to Lakhnauti, in the sultanate's easternmost province of Bengal. There he remained until his death in 1244/45.

Mainly because the *shaykh* reached Bengal at a critical juncture in the delta's political and cultural history, folk memory considerably elaborated on his life and career. In 1204, not long before his arrival, armies of the Delhi Sultanate had invaded eastern India and overthrown Lakshmana Sena, ruler of Bengal under its last Hindu dynasty, the Senas. After driving the king into the remote swamps of the eastern delta, the conquerors annexed western Bengal to the Delhi Sultanate, establishing their provincial base in Lakhnauti, a former capital of the deposed raja. Seeking to explain the region's abrupt political upheaval, subsequent generations of Bengalis appear to have seized upon an evolving memory of Jalal al-Din Tabrizi, whose career coincided approximately in place and time with that upheaval. Although the *shaykh* reached the delta several decades after the Turkish conquest, the narrative has him arriving while Lakshmana Sena was still reigning. And even though the conquering Turks had forcibly imposed their rule on Bengal, the narrative makes no mention of the conquest.

By a process of "creative remembering," then, Jalal al-Din's career as reworked in the *Sekasubhodaya* eases the transition from an older to a newer political order. Recalling that the written version we have dates to the later sixteenth century, it also serves to connect the delta's Hindu past with a Muslim "present." The text does this not only by narrating the story of how the *shaykh* built Bengal's first mosque, symbolizing the establishment of Islam in the delta, but also by drawing attention to Lakshmana Sena's assistance in the project. For it is the raja who transfers to Jalal al-Din uncultivated forest land to which the *shaykh* recruits laborers, and on which he establishes new settlements.

The narrative thus encapsulates complex socio-religious processes that had already begun by the late sixteenth century, when the text achieved its written form. The text depicts a state handing over forestlands to a charismatic Muslim pioneer, who in turn organizes and finances local labor in order to found agrarian settlements and establish markets, thereby bringing formerly forested areas into productive use. Crucially, the whole enterprise revolves around a single institution—

a mosque. In this way, the story of Jalal al-Din Tabrizi served as a mirror onto which Bengalis of later generations back-projected socio-religious processes that were occurring in their own day.

EXCERPTS FROM HALAYUDHYA MISRA, *SEKASUBHODAYA* (CA. 1550–1600)

On the bank of the Ganga [Ganges River] Laksmana, the high-souled ornament of a great king, a ruler of the earth . . . a conqueror whose greatness is proclaimed in inscriptions, was looking toward the river. The ruler saw [a man] coming into his view from the western quarter and asked him, "Who are you? Where from are you?" . . .

Then the king thought within himself. Bowing low his head to the [river] goddess after muttering "Ganga, Ganga," the king saw him in the west, [walking] over water.

He, wearing black clothes, stalwart, engaged in putting on a turban and looking about, was approaching the king quicker and quicker. . . . The king said, "I have indeed seen a wondrous act: a man rising up from the stream and walking on water. His person appears shining with the glow of penance." . . .

The *shaykh*, his face smiling, raised his hand, slowly came up and spoke to the king, . . . "A scion of the house of the Senas! as has been said by you to us, you, famous on earth [by the name] Laksmana, are sung as king by men. . . . But you dare claim [to be] ruler of the earth."

At this time there appears a heron holding a *gaci* fish in its beak. The *shaykh* pointed it out to the king and said: "Listen, O king. You indeed claim to be ruler of the earth. Ask the heron; let it give up the fish." Then the king replied: "The heron is a bird indeed and has no human sense. How can it give up the fish by our order? If you have power, speak. Let it give up by your order."

Then the *shaykh* said: "See, O king, my power." At a look from the *shaykh* the heron dropped the fish and flew away. Then the king became thoughtful. He appealed mentally to his tutelary deity Durga: "Supreme Lady, save me. The *shaykh* has come before me as if assuming the form of my fate. I am afraid I shall not survive this day."

Then the minister spoke to the king, "You have done wrongly, O king, as you are walking in this fellow's company. He wears a black garment and he looks like a Mussalman."

Then the king said to the minister, "What rubbish are you talking, you fool, not knowing the secret of the master. Wearing the robes of a dervish, Indra has come here in person."

. . . .

If the *shaykh's* life-story is heard in a gathering of men, harms do not visit there, nor do fears from thieves.

.   .   .   .

Whoever hears the narrative of the *shaykh* or makes others hear his auspicious advent, no harm comes to him and his prosperity increases.

Then the *shaykh* began speaking:

"Listen, king. I have come from the west. My birth was in the kingdom of Attava. My father is named Kafur.

.   .   .   .

"On one day I said to the Great Person [*pradhanpurusa*, i.e., God], 'Master, why don't I see you face to face?' Then the Master replied to me, 'You shall see me with your eyes, but the time is not come. Now listen to my advice. Go you to the eastern country. There is a great king named Laksmanasena. He kills any Mussalman who goes there. There is none that can vanquish him. You can speak the Indian tongue [i.e., Bengali] . . . After raising a mosque [*devasadana*, "house of God"] and wandering through the fourteen regions, you would come again here.' . . .

"Then the Master said to me, 'Take the amulet kept in my turban,' and saying this he detached it and gave it to me. Then the Master gave a pot filled with water. He said, 'This pot never becomes empty of water. If its water is drunk there is no more suffering from hunger and thirst.' Then an *asa* [Arabic "staff"] was given. He said, 'On seeing this staff no one could approach you out of fear.' Then a pair of shoes was given. He added, 'Riding on this you can walk freely on water or fire. It can go anywhere.' . . .

"Wearing the shoes, taking the water pot and the staff in my hands and saluting the Master, I started walking over the sea. As I was walking I saw a crystal palace. There I went. A king by the name of Candasimha was living with the wife. Seeing me, he said, 'O fool, where are you going?' I replied, 'To the eastern quarter, in the land of Gauda [i.e., western Bengal] there is a king named Laksmanasena, victorious in battles and favored by God. He does not fear anybody.' The king said to me, 'You are indeed a Mussalman; so he would certainly kill you. Who would save you? If life is dear to you, do stop and stay here.' I replied, 'He is a king and you also are a king; there is no difference.'"

.   .   .   .

To king Laksmanasena the *shaykh* said, "As long as I am here, you have nothing to fear. Do not be afraid. Be assured."

.   .   .   .

Then the *shaykh* told [the king's senior councilors], "You listen, I have come here as sent by the Supreme Being. You fear me not. . . . If you are all agreed, then I shall build a house of God, known as *Masjid*. At first, in the region of

Pandu [ancient Pandua, in northern Bengal] . . . " Then they all, except the minister, said, "Very well." . . .

To the king, who was looking for a suitable place, the *shaykh* said, "I shall put on a disguise and move about. Wherever I would find a good spot I shall raise a house of God." The *shaykh* came to Pandu city and sat down in the front terrace of a cowherd's home.

Then the *shaykh* said, " . . . within this area I will build a house of God." Now after a few days the king heard and came there. . . .

Then the *shaykh* requested the king, "Listen, king,
    "In the midst [of the ocean] there is the house of the Pirs; above it stands the sanctuary of the Supreme Being.
    "Three cupped-handfuls [of water] are offered in his name.
    "In the east the hill is called the Sunrise Mount; the sun rises from there at dawning of the morn. A Kirata [a mountain or forest dweller] will know and pay respect to my abode. The fourth cupped-handful is offered in his name.

"In the north is the Himalayas, the abode of the gods. There I shall go. When I arrive there they would honor me. The fifth cupped-handful is offered in their name.

"My parents are offsprings of poor people; they suffered a great deal on my score. Let them be freshened by water from me. The sixth cupped-handful is offered in their name.

"The people of the world know my name. Some call me good, some heap insults on me. The seventh cupped-handful is offered in their name.

"Who being a king would do honor to me and would give food in my name to a person coming for the first time, in his name is offered the eighth cupped-handful.

"Who would stay in my village, and if in spite of suffering, he does no harm but pays respect afterwards, in his name the ninth cupped-handful is offered.

"Many men would, out of their own accord, bow down at my abode. Some (of them) desire for money and children, and the boon of recovery. I will save them. The tenth cupped-handful is offered in their name."

Saying this, he dug a pond and worshipping it with flower and sandal-paste set a pillar in it. Everyone heard a spontaneous shout of cheers. . . .

Then on the other day the king called all the masons together. When they were assembled, the *shaykh* said to them, "O masons, you all work together and build up a house of God, famous in the world as *Masjid*." The masons replied to the *shaykh*, "O great one, we have never seen or heard what a *Masjid* is. How can we build it?". . .

Then the king ordered the collection of materials. Then the artisans spoke, "How shall we get our wages? You are a beggar." Then the *shaykh* smiled and said to the artisans, "Take a Bakul leaf and by my order write. . . ." Into it he placed his gracious hand and told the artisans, "You go to the market-place and opening the bundle, give it to a merchant. You will get your respective wages."

Then the king said to the *shaykh* . . . "As the first thing I offer this forest land to you. For the rest, what pleases you to command, do you command. This forest is granted to you." . . . So the *shaykh* himself first started the name of the place as Devatala. . . . Then he invited people from the country and had them settled in that land. . . .

Thus a few days were passed as the house of God was being built. When the building of the house of God was completed, the *shaykh* told the king, "King, I wish to make a daily charity of fifty coins from the house of God to [persons], whether kings or beggars. And you give it to me as to borrowers." Then the king replied, "I will give it daily at your command."

The *shaykh* knew all the land and territory. . . . Devatala was established as the chief [of the *shaykh's*] villages. He then made [the village of] Nandauvetipura fine and prosperous in Varendri [northern Bengal].

At first Devatala was acquired. [Then he acquired] Nandauva, after that Asamana-hatta, and in the northern region, villages worth six thousand, (namely) Lahu-cari, Bahaba, Rajadina. . . .

Where there is the city of Ramavati renowned in the world, beyond that Purva-hatta (eastern market), Uttarahatta (northern market), and Madaihatta (central market). He acquired all of them and had them surveyed. Documents were made for [a revenue of] twenty-two thousand [coins].

After the *shaykh* had taken possession of the village and the king was informed, the good king issued a writ written by his own hand. He submitted to the *shaykh*, "Do what is to be done." Then the *shaykh* brought all men together and issued documents of settlement.

The *shaykh* divided the money and distributed a [permanent gift] that would never be discontinued to all indebted persons and to travelers. To all these the *shaykh* made his charity, including the very low-born bearers. . . . No one should be found very much needy; doles should be obtained daily; there should be no need to hoard money, and the daily bread should be available [to all].

. . . .

[The *shaykh* said,] "The house of God, *Masjid*, was made ready and named after myself, and the territory was named Seka-jalala-tabreji [Shaykh Jalal Tabrizi] and settled."

This story of the glorious Shah Jalal Tabrez, popular among men (has been written) very carefully for the use of Sri-Jagannatha Ray. In the month of Bhadra, in the fifth day of the dark fortnight on a Friday, the book was carefully written [i.e., copied] by Sri Ramabhadra Sarma.

. . . Salutation to Sri Krsna. Salutation to Sri Ramacandra. In the Mussalman year 604, in the Vikramaditya Saka year 1134 [in the month of] Kartika, the glorious Shah Jalal came to the hermitage (*asrama*).

In the Mussalman year 610 in the Vikramaditya Saka year 1136 on the dark third day in [the month of] Caitra, in the lunar [month of] Rajjab, the glorious Shah Jalal's departure from this country happened. . . .

A *Mangala-kavya* Honoring the Goddess Chandi

The theme of forest-clearing, agrarian expansion, and the growth of communities of Muslim settlers is also seen, albeit from a very different angle, in another *mangala-kavya* commonly known as the *Chandi-mangala*, composed by the Bengali poet Mukundaram in western Bengal around 1590.

In this poem, the forest goddess Chandi, hearing complaints from her animal subjects about violence committed by the mighty hunter Kalaketu, offers to give the latter a kingdom if he would renounce the hunt and promote her cult. Kalaketu agrees. The goddess Chandi now undertakes to protect the kingdom, in return for which Kalaketu and all his subjects, both animal and human, will render devotion to her. As Chandi's earthly agent, Kalaketu agrees to cut a tract of dense forest and build a great city and a lofty temple in honor of the goddess. For this purpose Chandi gives Kalaketu a valuable ring, which he sells in order to advance cash to landlords. The latter then advance rice, seed, and salary to the thousands of laborers who would come and settle on the newly claimed lands.

The *Chandi-mangala* can thus be read as a grand epic dramatizing the process of civilization-building in Bengal, and more precisely, the advance of an agrarian economy into formerly forested lands. While the model of royal authority in this epic is unambiguously Hindu, the principal pioneers responsible for actually clearing the forest were Muslims. Led by a chieftain or organizer named "Zafar Mian," the twenty-two thousand Muslims put to work on this operation comprise by far the largest number of forest-clearing pioneers mentioned in the poem. Even if one cannot read this *mangala-kavya* as an eyewitness account, it nonetheless suggests a larger process that in the late sixteenth century was already well under way—the clearing of forests and the settling of new lands by Muslim pioneers.

EXCERPTS FROM MUKUNDARAM, *KAVIKANKANA CANDI* (CA. 1590)

The Great Hero [Kalaketu] is clearing the forest,
   Hearing the news, outsiders came from various lands.

The Hero then bought and distributed among them
   Heavy knives, axes, battle-axes, and pikes.
From the north came the Das (people),
   One hundred of them advanced.

They were struck with wonder on seeing the Hero,
   Who distributed betel nut to each of them.
From the south came the harvesters,
   Five hundred of them under one organizer.

From the west came Zafar Mian,
   Together with twenty-two thousand men.
Sulaimani beads in their hands,
   They chanted the names of their pir (spiritual guide) and the
      Prophet.

Having cleared the forest,
   They established markets.

Hundreds and hundreds of foreigners
   Ate and entered the forest.

Hearing the sound of the ax,
   Tigers became apprehensive and ran away, roaring.

Hagiographical Narratives of Shah Jalal

Hagiographies, the recorded lives of saints, comprise another source for the history of Islam in Bengal. Like the *mangala-kavya*s examined above, these are also socially constructed texts. Though purporting to describe another person's life story, they often reflect the culture, the social class, and the worldview of the communities that produce them. As a result, hagiographies of one and the same saint can vary enormously, depending on the context of their composition. A case in point is the career of Bengal's most renowned saint, Shah Jalal Mujarrad (d. 1346) of Sylhet, a town on the far eastern edge of the Bengal delta.

The earliest notice of Shah Jalal was made by the famous Moroccan traveler Ibn Battuta (d. 1377), who met the *shaykh* in 1345 in his mountain cave near Sylhet. The Moroccan described Shah Jalal as a man of hoary age, locally renowned for his miraculous powers. A 1512–1513 inscription describes him simply as a revered ascetic. The earliest hagiographical record of Shah Jalal appeared a century later in a collection of notices on Indian Sufis, the *Gulzar-i Abrar*, compiled in 1613 by Muhammad Ghauthi. By this time Mughal imperialists had consolidated their control over most of north India, including Bengal, while a sizeable Muslim peasant society had already begun to appear in the eastern delta. Endeavoring to account for these new realities, Indo-Persian hagiographers of this period often conflated military conquest with religious conversion. They accomplished this by back-projecting onto the lives of earlier holy men the persona of the warrior-saint, a fearsome ascetic who with one hand defeats infidel warriors and with the other "brings Islam" to the general population. Accordingly, the *Gulzar-i Abrar* portrays Shah Jalal as a Central Asian Sufi who, burning with desire to wage the "lesser jihad" against infidels, persuades his teacher to send him to India. Reaching Sylhet, Shah Jalal and his several hundred warrior-companions (*ghazis*) engage and defeat an army of one hundred thousand soldiers commanded by the local raja, Gur Govind, who is killed in battle. Shah Jalal then distributes the raja's land to his followers to govern.

In contrast to this militant portrayal of Shah Jalal, we may consider the hagiography that appears below, the *Suhail-i Yaman*, which was compiled at a much later date, in 1859. Its compiler, Maulvi Muhammad Nasir al-Din Haidar, wrote that his work was based on two earlier manuscripts, both now lost: the *Rauzat al-Salihin*, said to have been compiled in the reign of Aurangzeb (1658–1707), and the *Risala-yi Mu'in al-Din Khadim*, composed between 1716 and 1727. The *Suhail-i Yaman* may thus be understood as a composite reconstruction based on traditions stretching across several hundred years, from the mid-seventeenth to the mid-nineteenth centuries. During this period Islam in Bengal had become an over-whelmingly agrarian phenomenon, with most Muslims farming the earth as rice cultivators. Not surprisingly, the text views Shah Jalal through the lens of agrarian piety. The reason the *shaykh* chooses to settle in Sylhet is not because he is looking for infidels to slay or convert, but because Sylhet's soil is right: its smell, taste, and color exactly match the clump of soil that his spiritual teacher had given him before he, Shah Jalal, departed for India. Even today Muslim cultivators in north-central Bangladesh relate the story of Shah Jalal and his clump of soil as the explanation for how their ancestors became Muslims.

The *Suhail-i Yaman* differs from earlier accounts of Shah Jalal in still other ways. Reflecting the cultural orientation of the Mughals, whose founders had migrated to India from Central Asia, the 1613 *Gulzar-i Abrar* identifies Shah Jalal as having come to Bengal from Turkestan. It further identifies the *shaykh's* spiritual guide as Ahmad Yesevi (d. 1166), the founder of the Central Asian Sufi tradition. The *Suhail-i Yaman*, by contrast, reflected a later moment in the history of South Asian Islam, by which time Muslims had begun to place emphasis on their spiritual roots in the Middle East, rather than their genealogical roots in Central Asia. Hence in this text Shah Jalal's origins are no longer held to be in Turkestan but rather in Yemen; the work's title, *Suhail-i Yaman*, means "the Canopus (star) of Yemen." And finally, the Hindu raja of Sylhet, Gur Govind, is not crushed by Shah Jalal as he was in the earlier, 1613, hagiography, rather, he assists the newcomer in building the region's first mosque, thereby involving himself in establishing Islam in Bengal. In this respect, his role resembles that of Lakshmana Sena in the *Sekasubho-daya*: because a former raja assists in building the first mosque, a prior Hindu cultural world is construed as connected to a subsequent Muslim world, and not annihilated by that world.

EXCERPTS FROM MAULVI MUHAMMAD NASIR AL-DIN HAIDAR, *SUHAIL-I YAMAN*

He was born in Yemen, the son of Shaykh Mahmud bin Muhammad Ibrahim, a member of the Quraish clan of Yemen. His mother was a Saiyida. . . . His maternal uncle, Ahmad Kabir Suhrawardi, nourished him on the milk of cattle. When the boy attained maturity, his uncle gave him training in the Suhrawardi school of mystical knowledge, which was transmitted to him by the following chain of authority: from [the school's founder] Shaykh Shihab al-Din Suhrawardi, to Shaykh Makhdum Baha al-Din, to Abu'l-fazl Sadr al-Din, to Shaykh Abu'l-fatah Rukn al-Din, to Jalal al-Din Bukhari, to Saiyid Ahmad Kabir Suhrawardi, to Shah Jalal.

Being very pleased with Jalal's spiritual growth, his uncle said to him, "Jalal, you have attained the utmost; your heart and mine have become one. But I do not wish to keep you imprisoned." Then taking a clump of soil that he had earlier picked up from the ground underneath his own spiritual retreat, he placed that clump in the hand of his disciple, saying, "Now you must go to India, and when you find soil with the same color, smell, and taste as this soil, you should stop and settle in that land, after driving out the infidels." . . .

In short, that "soil of [the prophet] Khizr" traveled, as that holy man [Shaykh Jalal], together with twelve dependents, including Haji Yusuf and Haji Khalil, turned their faces toward India. . . .

Together with Prince Sikandar [of the Delhi Sultanate] and other servitors, [Shah Jalal] traveled east with the intention of liberating Sylhet from the hands of its oppressor. Finding no boat when he reached the banks of the Brahmaputra River, he spread out his prayer carpet so that he and the other fighters (*muhajidin*) might cross it.

[When he reached Sylhet] he shouted out to its reigning monarch, "Oh, Gur Govind, how is your health?" When Govind heard the *shaykh's* soothing voice, he jumped out of his sandals and lowered his head to the ground in a gesture of servitude. Then he said, "I have handed over the rule of this kingdom to Sikandar. What further service is there I might do for you?" Shah Jalal replied, "If you can, get enough stone and brick for building a pleasing mosque.". . .

Gur Govind went to the mountains and with the supervision of his chief minister found the requisite stones and bricks, which he sent to Shah Jalal. From these materials, the *shaykh* then built a mosque having one hundred and twenty domes. . . .

While [Shah Jalal] was in the city [of Sylhet], he noticed that one particular mound of earth—the one where his shrine is now located—possessed a soil of the same smell, taste, and color as that given him by his own *shaykh*. So he settled there. . . . He then assigned the administration of Sylhet's towns and *parganas* [revenue circles] to his 360 companions, keeping his closest associates—the Prince of Yemen, Haji Yusuf, and Haji Khalil, and his most advanced disciples—near his hospice.

Revenue Documents from Mughal Bengal (1574–1765)

Whereas the preceding extracts are all in some sense literary, the next three readings are routine, internal documents that circulated within the vast revenue bureaucracy of the imperial Mughals, who governed Bengal between 1574 and 1765.
The two centuries of Mughal rule witnessed Bengal's most rapid economic growth,
especially in the relatively undeveloped eastern delta, where the frontier of arable
land steadily pushed into tracts previously covered by dense forests. As these documents show, this dynamic process was spearheaded mainly by Muslim pioneers,
who established institutions that would serve as nuclei for new communities of
rice cultivators.

Written by clerks for other clerks, the records translated below are illustrative
of the thousands of Mughal documents that pertained to land—locating it, mea-
suring it, assessing its productive capacity, identifying who had rights to its produce. References to Muslims and to Islamic institutions, when they appear in these
documents at all, are very concrete. People are mentioned by name and occupation, some are given genealogies; institutions are identified and located; all documents are dated. Such precise information enables one to plot the growth and spa-
tial distribution of any institution that generated or consumed revenue, and which
was therefore of interest to the state—mosques, temples, shrines, irrigation tanks,
caravanserais, Sufi *dargah*s, markets, etc.

The first document, though dating from the mid-eighteenth century, summa-
rizes the revenue history of the Mughal province of Bihar, adjacent to Bengal, highlighting Emperor Shah Jahan's practice of using military expeditions as a vehicle
for reclaiming arable land from forests. As the document makes clear, cutting the
forests, expanding the area under the plow, and attracting cultivators were all
strategic Mughal objectives.

HAQIQAT-I SUBA BIHAR (CA. 1765)

From the time of Shah Jahan [1627–1658], it was customary that woodcutters
and ploughmen used to accompany his troops, so that forests might be cleared
and land cultivated. Ploughs used to be donated by the government. Short-term
*patta*s [documents stating revenue demand] were given, [and these] fixed government demand at the rate of 1 anna per bigha during the first year. *Chaudhuri*s (intermediaries) were appointed to keep the *ri'aya* (peasants) happy with
their considerate behavior and to populate the country. They were to ensure
that the *patta*s were issued in accordance with Imperial orders and the pledged
word was kept.

There was a general order that whosoever cleared a forest and brought land
under cultivation, such land would be his *zamindari* [land over which he had
rights]. . . .

Ploughs should also be given on behalf of the State. The price of these ploughs should be realized from the *zamindar*s in two to three years. Each *hal mir* [one who has four or five ploughs] should be found out and given a *dastar* [sash or turban; i.e., mark of honor] so that he may clear the forests and bring land into cultivation. In this manner, the people and the *ri'aya* would be attracted by good treatment to come from other regions and *suba*s (provinces) to bring under cultivation wasteland and land under forests.

If the above record provides a general statement on Mughal land management policies, the following document, a *sanad* (order) issued early in Aurangzeb's reign, is very narrowly focused. In granting tax-free status to a mosque and its affiliates on the condition that the latter bring some 166 acres of jungle into cultivation, the document links Islamic piety with agrarian policy. Hundreds of such land grants had the combined effect of transferring management of large tracts of former jungle to tiny mosques, whose managers took the lead in supervising the cutting of forests and introducing cultivation.

A MUGHAL IMPERIAL *SANAD* FROM CHITTAGONG
(2 SEPTEMBER 1666)

Clerks, assessors past and present, headmen, accounts, and peasants of the revenue circles of Sarkar Islamabad [i.e., Chittagong], know that:

Shah Zain al-'Abidin has made it known that he has many dependents and has built a mosque, where a great many *faqirs* and inhabitants come and go. But, as he has no means of maintaining the mosque, he is hopeful that the government will bestow some land on him.

Having investigated the matter, the revenue department has fixed the sum of six *shahi dun* and eight *kani* [i.e., 166.4 acres] of jungle land, lying outside the revenue rolls, and located in villages Nayapara and others of *pargana* Havili Chittagong, as a charity for the expenses of the mosque as well as a charity for the person mentioned above. Once the land is brought under cultivation, the produce of the land must be used for the expenses of the mosque as well as the needs of himself, his descendants, and his dependents. And he must assiduously pray for the survival of the powerful State.

He and his descendants are not required to pay any land revenue or non-land revenue, highway taxes, bridge taxes, special cesses, or any other assessments issuing from either the administrative or the revenue branches of government. Nor is he bound to seek a fresh *sanad* each year. Take great care to execute this order. Dated 2 Rabi I 1077 [A.H.]

In the following order, the Mughal government issues 250 *qulbas* [975 acres] of jungle, lying outside the revenue rolls but capable of being cultivated, to the "organization"—actually, a labor force—of one Maulavi Muhammad Rabi'. This is one of four land grants that the provincial officials issued to this individual. Since the combined area granted to Muhammad Rabi' in these grants came to 15,717 acres, or over twenty-four square miles, his work force would have been of considerable size.

Revenue documents like this confirm what the *mangala-kavya* and hagiographic literature hint at, namely, that states rewarded Muslim pioneers who agreed to settle former jungle lands by recruiting local labor to cut forests and farm new arable lands. The fact that the beneficiaries of the grants were Islamic institutions—in the present instance, a madrasa and a mosque—meant that non-Muslim laborers recruited to work on these units would become gradually absorbed into communities informed by Islamic ideas and values.

A MUGHAL IMPERIAL *SANAD* FROM SYLHET (11 MARCH 1756)

Present and former clerks of public affairs, landholders (*chaudhuris*), accountants, recorders, peasants, and cultivators of [such and such] revenue circle, in the district of Sylhet, attached to the province of Bengal, know that:

In the second regnal year the amount of two hundred and fifty *qulba*s [975 acres] of jungle land that lies outside of the revenue register but is capable of cultivation, and which is located in the above-mentioned revenue circle, was established to meet the expenses of a mosque, a house, a Qur'an school (*madrasa*), the dependents, those who come and go, the *faqir*s, and the welfare (*madad-i ma'ash*) of the laborers and the deeds of the organization (*dastgah*) of Maulavi Muhammad Rabi', together with his children and dependents.

It is agreed that once the above-mentioned land is brought into cultivation, its produce should be used to support the expenses of the mosque, the Qur'an school, those who come and go, the *faqir*s, and his own needs, together with those of his children and his dependents, and that he shall busy himself in prayers for the long life of the State.

You are ordered to make over the above-mentioned land to him, his children, and his dependents, that it be in their possession.

Sources

Sekasubhodaya: Sukumar Sen, ed. and trans., *Sekasubhodaya of Halayudha Misra* (Calcutta: Asiatic Society, 1963), pp. 135–255. *Kavikankana Candi*: Mukundaram, *Kavikankana Candi*, Srikumar Bandyopadhyay and Visvapati Chaudhuri, eds. (Calcutta: University of Calcutta, 1974), pp. 299–300. *Suhail-i Yaman*: *Suhail-i Yemen, ya Tarikh-i Jalali*, comp. Maulvi Muhammad Nasir al-Din Haidar, 1277 A.H. Persian MS in the Muslim Sahitya Samsad, Sylhet, 4–27. *Haqiqat-I Suba Bihar*: Cataloged under the title *Kaifiyat-i Suba Bihar* in Wilhelm Pertsch, *Handschriften-Verzeichniss der Königlichen Bibliothek zu Berlin* (Berlin: A. Asher, 1888), *Persische Handschriften* no. 500, 4:484. Summarized and partially translated by S. Nurul

Hasan, "Three Studies of Zamindari System," in *Medieval India—A Miscellany*, vol. 1 (Bombay: Asia Publishing House, 1969), pp. 237–238. Imperial edict from Chittagong: Chittagong District Collectorate Record Room, "Kanun Daimer Nathi," Bundle 59, Case no. 3863. Imperial edict from Sylhet: "Register of Sanads," Sylhet District Collectorate Record Room, vol. 21, no. 609.

Further Reading

On the history of medieval Bengal's rivers, which patterned so much of Bengal's sociocultural destiny, see R. K. Mukerjee, *The Changing Face of Bengal: A Study of Riverine Economy* (Calcutta: University of Calcutta, 1938). For early medieval society and politics, see A. Akhtarazzaman, "The Muslim Rulers and their Non-Muslim Subjects in Thirteenth- and Fourteenth-Century Eastern India," in Perween Hasan and Mufakharul Islam, eds., *Essays in Memory of Momtazur Rahman Tarafdar* (Dhaka: Dhaka University, 1999), pp 132–148.

For studies focused on medieval Bengali literature, see William L. Smith, *The One-eyed Goddess: A Study of the Manasa-Mangal* (Stockholm: Almquist & Wiksell, 1980); David Cashin, *The Ocean of Love: Middle Bengali Sufi Literature and the Fakirs of Bengal* (Stockholm: Association of Oriental Studies, 1995); and T. W. Clark, "Evolution of Hinduism in Medieval Bengali Literature: Siva, Candi, Manasa," *Bulletin of the School of Oriental and African Studies* 17, no. 3 (1955), pp. 503–518.

For broad surveys of the Islamization of medieval Bengal, see Asim Roy, *Islamic Syncretistic Tradition in Bengal* (Princeton, NJ: Princeton University Press, 1983); and Richard M. Eaton, *The Rise of Islam and the Bengal Frontier, 1204–1760* (Berkeley, CA: University of California Press, 1993).

29

Challenging the Mughal Emperor: The Islamic Millennium according to 'Abd al-Qadir Badayuni

Ahmed Azfar Moin

The end of the sixteenth century was an exciting time in Mughal India. It co-incided with the end of the first millennium of Islam. There was widespread expectation of a great change in the political and religious order of things. Either Islam would be renewed and revivified, or it would wither away and be replaced. Thus, the great Mughal emperor Jalal al-Din Akbar (r. 1556–1605) declared the end of Islam and the beginning of a new dispensation with himself as its harbinger. That is, if we are to believe his courtier and historian 'Abd al-Qadir Badayuni (d. ca. 1615).

A man of broad learning, Badayuni was an authority on the religious sciences, adept at mysticism, and skilled in astronomy and astrology. His duties at court included the translation from Sanskrit into Persian of *Mahabharata* and *Ramayana*, the two great epic poems of India. He remains most famous, however, for clandestinely composing a set of chronicles called *Muntakhab al-Tawarikh* (Selected Histories) that challenge the royal history composed by the emperor's favorite courtier, Abu al-Fazl. It is Badayuni who reports that in the year 990 A.H. (1582 C.E.), Akbar made a grand millennial claim.

Modern scholars have treated Badayuni as the epitome of Islamic orthodoxy—a majoritarian, scriptural, and unchanging standard against which the deviance of the emperor can easily be measured. In this view, Badayuni, along with the Naqsh-bandi Sufi leader Shaykh Ahmad Sirhindi (d. 1624) and the theologian Shaykh 'Abd al-Haqq Dihlawi (d. 1642), led the intellectual struggle against the emperor's religious waywardness, and preserved Sunni Islam in India. Such an image of Islamic orthodoxy in India, needless to say, is a sanitized and ahistorical one. This perspective, moreover, is a result of reading Badayuni's history while ignoring his other writings, including the text excerpted here, the *Najat al-Rashid* (Salvation of the Rightly Guided). This work reveals that Badayuni and Akbar shared one of their era's most widespread discourses, one that imagined the imminent advent of a new moral and political order marking the close of the first millennium of the Islamic revelation.

Akbar's new order, usually known as *Din-i ilahi* (Divine Faith) can aptly be called millennial for it was announced at the end of the first millennium of Islam and under a major cosmological sign, the greatest conjunction of Saturn and Jupiter, which signaled great religio-political change. What is less well known is that Badayuni did not merely reject his master's claim but did so from within a distinctly millenarian worldview. To call Badayuni "orthodox" misses the extent to which he shared with Akbar an understanding of the world based on the idea of the millennium, an understanding supported by sophisticated conceptions of astronomy, astrology, cyclical time, and the reincarnation of the human soul. This disagreement between king and courtier, moreover, was not merely spiritual or metaphysical, but also had a deeply political aspect.

The ancient tenet that each community founded by a great religio-political figure—a prophet or king—lasted at most a thousand years enjoyed widespread currency at the time. It informed imperial practice and discourse in the Mughal, Safavid, and Ottoman realms, the three great Muslim empires of the early modern period. Moreover, it was not only the rulers who deployed millennial symbolism. Strong competition came from numerous messianic groups, each of whose leaders claimed to be the divinely promised savior—or even the Divine reincarnated—who would establish justice on earth by ushering in the next millennial order. A variety of Islamic eschatological and apocalyptic traditions were used to support such claims. These traditions were based not only on religious texts such as the Qur'an and prophetic sayings, but also on elaborate systems of divination among which, arguably, the most important one was astrology. Together these forms of knowledge made up the science of the millennium used to predict the rise and fall of a "nation" (*ummat*), the appearance of a savior, and the fall of a dynasty. Millennial theory was, in other words, an eminently practical political science.

Akbar had for several years shown a keen interest in the doctrines of other sects and religions. For this reason, a special venue called the *'Ibadat khana* or "House of Worship" was built on the palace premises. Here, in the presence of the emperor, the learnèd authorities—Muslims, Hindus, Christians, Zoroastrians, and others—debated religion and defended their beliefs. Badayuni, who had witnessed these debates, describes with much anguish what he saw as insults heaped on Islam. Today, the ahistorical understanding of Badayuni as "orthodox" finds a parallel in the treatment of Akbar's religious endeavors as those of a "liberal" attempting to establish a multicultural and inclusive realm. In both these modern emplotments, the competition for the millennium between the courtier and his royal patron is ignored.

Fortunately, we have a detailed exposition of Badayuni's own millennial ideas in *Najat al-rashid*, commonly described as a work of Sufi ethics. A chronogram, the name of the text gives the date of its completion as 999 A.H. Unlike Badayuni's secret chronicles, this was a publicly written work that did not mention the emperor or his religious efforts. Badayuni says that he wrote *Najat al-Rashid* while traveling, implying that he composed it mainly from memory. With a broad audience in mind, he translated Arabic quotations into Persian and explained obscure and technical terms with examples from everyday life. From the arrangement of material as answers to questions, it is plausible to see the work as Badayuni's record of and response to the religious discussions at court. At first glance, the work appears to have little political or historical relevance. Poor in empirical data, it seems to offer little to the historian. Using a tedious and rambling didactic style, Badayuni outlines in it the rules of proper conduct for lay Muslims and explains the mysteries of the cosmos for the uninitiated. The greatest of these mysteries, however, pertains to a question of immense religious and political import: Who will usher in the new millennium?

The sections of the *Najat al-Rashid* translated here reveal that despite his contempt for Akbar's millennial claim, Badayuni accepted the basic premise that the era of Islam was drawing to a close. He maintained that religions like Islam or Christianity, having been ushered in by a great prophet, come to an end after a certain period of time, usually a thousand years. It was commonly accepted in Jewish, Christian, and Islamic traditions that the age of the world is predetermined to be seven thousand years. Specifically, one Islamic version of this tradition held that the Prophet Muhammad ushered in Islam at the beginning of the last millennium, at the end of which the world would be destroyed. Going beyond this traditional view of the millennium, however, Badayuni argued that the age of the world could be much greater than seven thousand years. His evidence was based on astronomical knowledge as well as mystical lore. He even quoted the great Andalusian mystic Ibn al-'Arabi to suggest that cosmological time was cyclical: that after every seven thousand years the world is regenerated, and Adam is born anew.

The idea of cosmic regeneration, antithetical to the biblical idea of a fixed age of the Earth but pervasive in Indian and pre-Islamic Iranian intellectual traditions, had also seeped into Islamic cosmological teachings. The notion that the Flood recurred in every cycle of time was propagated by the most famous astrologer of medieval times, Abu Ma'shar (d. 886, known as Albumazar in Europe), who subscribed to Indic cosmological concepts. This was a radical assertion that could be used—as al-Biruni, the famous eleventh-century polymath and the first Muslim scholar to write in detail about Indian society and religion, pointed out—to deny fundamental tenets of Islam, such as the belief in the Day of Judgment.

Cyclical time was considered a dangerous concept, not only because of its deviance from mainstream Islamic tradition, but also because of its links to politically subversive messianic movements. Such groups were often given the pejorative rubric of "exaggerators" (*ghulat*) for denying traditional Islamic eschatology. They asserted that paradise was simply a millennial utopia on earth, and that the messiah was continually reincarnated at the dawn of every millennial era, a claim threatening to those in power. Reincarnation, another tenet of Indic religions, was a key concept in such theories. It was believed to occur through the mechanisms of transmigration of the soul (*tanasukh*) and infusion or inhabitation of the divine spirit in the human body (*hulul*). The dawn of the millennium and coming of the messiah, moreover, could be foretold by various divinatory techniques, chief among them astrology.

In his chronicles Badayuni disparaged the Nuqtavi order, a messianic *ghulat* movement whose members had found refuge at Akbar's court after being brutally suppressed in Safavid Iran. He reported that the Nuqtavis were among those who had influenced the emperor's millennial claim. Indeed, Badayuni began his description of the millennial year at court by accusing the emperor of upholding the heretical doctrine of transmigration. But in his ethical treatise, he argued for a cosmology and a messianic theory that comes surprisingly close to that held by the millenarian Nuqtavis.

In *Najat al-Rashid*, Badayuni provided unambiguous support for the messianic claims of two fifteenth-century Sufis: Sayyid Muhammad Jaunpuri (d. 1505), the founder of the Mahdawiyya movement in India, and Sayyid Muhammad Nurbakhsh (d. 1464), the founder of the Nurbakhshiyya Sufi order in Timurid Balkh. Both these movements had enjoyed a substantial following, and many of their leaders were persecuted and killed by political authorities. As a child, Badayuni had heard about the execution of a Mahdawiyya leader and even composed a chronogram to commemorate his death. By the time of the writing of *Najat al-Rashid*, however, both orders had become quietist and blended with mainstream Sunni and Sufi trends.

How was it possible for two holy men to be the promised messiah in the same age? Badayuni solved this conundrum with the spiritual mechanism of *buruz* or "projection of the soul," which he proposed as a doctrinally acceptable alternative to the heretical concept of transmigration. The messiah of the age comes into being, according to Badayuni, when a perfecting soul projects itself into the body of a spiritually accomplished man. In projection, unlike transmigration, there was no need for the projector to die in order for the cycle of messianic reincarnation to continue. Without explicitly stating it, he followed the theory of *buruz* as originally conceived and outlined by the Central Asian messianic claimant Nurbakhsh himself.

What conclusion can we draw from the similarities between the millennial stance of the "orthodox" Badayuni and that of his "heterodox" antagonists? I submit that Badayuni's millennial conceptions were indicative of a larger cultural pattern at work. The millennium was an important religious and political symbol of this period. There was intense competition over its meaning, and the prize was not mere intellectual or spiritual gratification but political power and imperial legitimacy. Moreover, forms of knowledge such as astrology, divination, and gnosis were, among other things, millenarian techniques of power. Badayuni may not have been able to openly denounce the emperor's millennial claims, but he could still repudiate them by arguing for a competing interpretation of the millennium. In doing so, however, he used the same conceptual bases—astronomy, astrology, cyclical time, and the reincarnation of the soul—as the "deviant" emperor. Thus, the millennial competition between the Mughal monarch and his courtier should make us reconsider how Islam was imagined, lived, and practiced by the powerful and the learnèd of an earlier age.

FROM BADAYUNI'S *NAJAT AL-RASHID*

THE RISE AND FALL OF A COMMUNITY (*UMMAT*)

The affairs of religion rise and fall every few centuries and years, and therefore the community of a prophet exists for a thousand years. Thus it is found in some commentaries (*tafasir*). Due to proliferation, change, and errors in copying the gospel (*injil*), the religion and law of Jesus, may peace be upon him, became corrupt and lost its essence. Other religions suffered similarly.

Although in the time close to the era of the Prophet, may peace be upon him, there was a unique peace and prosperity, in this age when a thousand years from that time have passed, necessarily, religion must come to suffer. Things are what they are because of the conflict amongst the 'ulama, their debates and denunciations, and the profusion of tricks and chicaneries of those in power. So we have seen what must be seen. This trend exists everywhere, in every land and country. Piety and self-improvement are, as it were, rare novelties or fanciful and mysterious notions. It is for this reason that the Messenger, peace be upon him, said that the religion was revealed when, in the beginning, conditions were deplorable, and that at the end of time they will once again become deplorable. Thus, may there be happiness for the unfortunate ones:

> It is God's mercy, Oh hosts of the past
> That he submitted the world to the care of a man
> Who cared for the stranger's welfare, with utmost compassion
> As if it was the good of his own
> Since those people will not live again,
> One hopes, these worthless ones may die

It is said that a person formally sought the opinion of the eminent authorities of the two holy sites [in Mecca and Medina]. Its subject was the validity of the tradition of the Prophet that "I will not remain in the ground for more than a thousand years," and of another tradition that "the span of man's existence is seven thousand years and Adam, may peace be upon him, was born at the beginning of the first millennium and the Messenger of God, may peace be upon him, was appointed at the beginning of the seventh millennium."

Shaykh Jalal Suyuti [d. 1505, a famous Egyptian theologian and Qur'anic scholar], after much deliberation upon what was acceptable and not with regards to these prophetic traditions, which he showed to be of moderate and even weak authority, proved with various arguments that the lifespan of this religious community was to be one thousand and three hundred years. After this, he said that when the major signs of the end times, for example the coming of Jesus and the Messiah (*mahdi*) and the rising of the sun from the west, have become manifest, then the first trumpet shall sound. Exactly five hundred years from this moment, the second trumpet will blow and the resurrection and the gathering take place. He has written a treatise in this regard. God knows best.

The writer of these lines, going further than him and those who came before and after him, found in a treatise attributed to the model of the masters of *wujud* [ontological monism] and of the masters of *shuhud* [phenomenological monism], Shaykh Muhyi al-Din Ibn-i ʿArabi [d. 1240, a famous Andalusian mystic and thinker known for expounding a monistic metaphysics], may God bless his soul, a few lines in Arabic which are translated into Persian here. The *shaykh*, may God be pleased with him, said, "I observed in some visions of mine, when one day I was circumambulating the House of Kaʿba, I saw a group circumambulating whom I did not recognize. They were singing two couplets. Of these, I forgot one but still remember the other, which is:

[In Arabic]
We have circled around, just as you do, annually
Circling this Abode, around and around, in unity.
[Persian translation:] We have also performed many circumambulations
 of this House for years just as you do now.

"Then one among that group looked towards me and said, 'I am from your forefathers.' I asked, 'How long ago was it that you passed away from this world?' He said, 'Forty and some thousand years ago.' I said again, 'The creation of Adam himself, may peace be upon him, was not this long ago, for not even seven thousand years have passed since his birth.' He said, 'You are talking about this Adam who passed close to you and was born at the beginning of these seven thousand years.'" The *shaykh*, may God bless him, said, "At that moment I remembered that statement of the Prophet of God, may peace be upon him, who said, 'God Almighty has created a hundred thousand Adams and despite this fact this world is a created entity and there is no escaping its destruction.'" The words of the *shaykh*, may God be pleased with him, end here.

It is mentioned in another place that at the top of the Pyramid, which is a high building in Egypt, this statement is written [in Arabic]: "The construction of the Pyramid concluded when the Flying Eagle (*al-nasr al-taʾir* [the constellation of Aquila]) was in Cancer." That is [in Persian]: "The Pyramid was built at the time when the Flying Eagle was in Cancer." The Flying Eagle is presently in Capricorn. Therefore, based on this estimate, the age of its construction is twelve thousand and three hundred, if I consider it to be the first cycle. This figure could be multiplied indefinitely if one assumes multiple cycles, for the constellation of Eagle remains in each mansion of the zodiac for approximately one thousand and six hundred years. Regarding this matter, there are other mysteries that dare not be related and explained here. [In Arabic:] I believe in

God as He is with his Names and Properties and I accept all his orders; there is no divinity but God and Muhammad is His Prophet [a standard formula used to reaffirm one's faith, often recited when one has heard or said something that may be taken for blasphemy]. By the author [Bayuni]:

> The astrologer says the ascendant of the world is Aries, I do not know
> Which Libra balanced the sky across from Aries at the time of its birth.
> You will get your heart's desire by the way of the Prophet, not through
>   logic or philosophy.
> Now that the Arab has risen in Arabia, do not look for treasure
>   elsewhere.

The discussion had begun with Muslims of the earliest era. The Prophet, may peace be upon him, said that the best among the centuries is my century, then the century that comes after it, and then the next century; after these three centuries a corrupt order (*durugh*) will spread. The "first century" means the Companions of the Prophet, the "second century," the Followers of the Companions; and the "third century" the Followers of the Followers.

Question: In another tradition the Prophet, may peace be upon him, has said that the condition of my nation is like rain, and it is not known whether the beginning of rain is better or the end. Therefore, great wars and calamities occurred in the time of the Companions and their Followers, and in other centuries. Yazid the Schismatic [Yazid ibn Mu'awiyya (d. 683), of the Umayyad dynasty and arch-villain of early Islamic history] and Hajjaj the Tyrant [Hajjaj ibn Yusuf, (d. 718), an Umayyad governor of Iraq famous for his cruelty] existed in the first two centuries in which no tyrant or great misfortune may occur. Also, at the end of time, the hope of the coming of the messiah and the descent of Jesus and the manifestation of justice is to be realized. Thus, taking into account all these aspects, why do people of the earlier period enjoy greater merit (*fazl*) [over people of the latter ages]?

Answer: I say that the Prophet, may peace be upon him, and the Companions and the Followers and the Followers of the Followers enjoy, in this order, a noble rank that people of later centuries do not because of their proximity to the era of revelation, the strength of Islam, and the descent of the Qur'an. For, after this period, truth was swept aside as opposition, innovation, and fancy reigned supreme, and corrupt religions and flimsy and worthless beliefs arose. And due to extreme partisanship, the affairs of the community were ruined by mutual boasting and confrontation—as I now see around me.

On the other hand, the wars involving the Companions, may God be pleased with them, were pregnant with signs and omens, and their battles and confrontations did not hinder the spread of Islam and the light of religion. The world was filled and sated with competent 'ulama, distinguished ascetics, and masters of ecstasies, mysticism, and miracles. Indeed, it is clear proof and sincere evidence for the greater merit of the first centuries that there was not the least need for the coming of the messiah and Jesus in order to lead and guide the people. For it is only near the time of resurrection, when extreme cruelty and tyranny will have ensnared the earth, that the road will be clear for these two guides of religion and establishers of the law of the best of the Prophets, may peace be upon him. May praise be to God and his bounty that the later Muslims enjoy the great fortune and complete felicity of still believing in the unseen and of being resolute in religion and true to the beliefs of Islam, despite the fact that this age is far from the time of prophecy, and miracles, marvels, and daily wonders have ceased to occur. This is a source of grace (*fazl*), but the maxim regarding consummate grace (*fazl-i kulli*) is well known and enduring; that is, "The wild beasts of the Muslims of yore are better than the pious of the successive ages." (*Najat al-Rashid*, pp. 327–332)

REINCARNATION OF THE MESSIAH

There is another class of unbelievers who believe in the transmigration of the soul (*tanasukh*) and say that the soul of each who dies attaches itself to another body. According to them, every birth is another death and every death another birth. These people are of several types. A faction says that on leaving the body, if the soul inhabits (*hulul*) another noble (*sharif*) body and lives in carefree luxury in the world, this very place is its heaven; and if it descends into an unclean body and suffers toil and hardship, it is condemned to hell. A group holds that transmigration has four degrees: first is *naskh*, the immanence of the human soul in a noble human body; second is *raskh*, its infusion into an unclean human body; third is *maskh*, its transformation into animal form; fourth is *faskh*, its transference into inanimate form. Some say that man's soul always moves from body to body and for several cycles it enters and leaves this world until it reaches, according to its ability, the stage of perfection. When it reaches this stage, it breaks from the cycle completely and joins the Absolute realm (*'alam-i itlaq*). From hereon there is freedom from all hardships and, for this group, this indeed is true heaven. Verse:

The face of the beloved is our paradise and to be distant from it, hell.

This belief is associated with Hindus (*hinduvan*). On this matter I have, on different occasions, debated at length with their learnèd authorities and, with divine blessing, made them see their errors, such that some of them turned away from their own religion. However space does not permit further discussion on this matter.

Shakamuni [the Buddha], whom the transmigrationists (*tanasukhiyya*) hold to be a prophet, said, "I have seen myself in one thousand and seven hundred forms." Near the time of writing, I heard that a member of this community was close to death. An agent (*da'i*) of their leader sent him a message that "His Excellency sits waiting (*hazrat jalisand*) and has sent a god—who [we Muslims know] has no beginning and no end, and no visible and no invisible—in your presence. Apparently you seem to want to leave this dominion (*mulk*). Go, for you have leave." This dying man replied, "We depart as circumstances dictate (*ba hasb-i surat*) in order that we may serve again in good form (*ba husn-i surat*), and the site of manifestation (*matla'*) will be in Iraq." [In Arabic:] May God protect us from the manipulation of His signs. The holy Qur'an informs us about this group:

> [In Arabic:] And they say there is nothing but our life in this world, we die and we live and nothing destroys us but time. [Qur'an 45:24]

[Persian Translation of the Qur'anic verse:] "The unbelievers say that there is no life except the life of this world; that we die and become alive," meaning that some of us die and others are born so that when we die again, we are born again in this world in another form. They say that nothing destroys us but the passage of time and old age and decrepitude, which results from the revolution of the heavenly spheres; the spheres are of one nature and one movement and while they last, they are and will be so.

I wish that someone would inform them about the arguments for the eternity (*qidam*) of the world, and ask them why it could not have been that there existed another sphere before these spheres, as the learned authorities of this group have maintained: "There is nothing beyond the count of nine spheres; this is the limit necessary for maintaining the order of the world, and our experience has confirmed that this number is sufficient." It is possible for there to be even a greater number than this. This statement regarding the heavenly spheres is generally accepted, but if one takes into account the dissenting opinion, it is said that up to twenty-five is possible. For certain, if ancientness (*qadim*) means, as they say, that the elements are eternal, then it is correct. But this neither supports nor contradicts their assertions. In this matter sophisticated scholars have conducted excellent inquiries. Alas, a little presence of mind is required to appreciate them:

> My intellect is clouded by the turbulence of life
> Wonder of wonders, then, if the pearl of lucidity is found.

Question: At this juncture, one may wonder about the statement of some of the leaders of the mystics (*ahl-i 'irfan*) who, much like Shakamuni had asserted, have said that:

> If I relate the account of the state of life
> I have seen nine hundred and seventy forms (*qalib*).

What is the difference between these two statements [of the Sufis and the Buddha]? And here one can ask whether there is any religion in which the tenet of transmigration of the soul (*tanasukh*) does not have a firm foothold?

We reply that the leaders of the community of mysticism and gnosis subscribe to the projection of the soul (*buruz*), not to transmigration. There is a difference between projection and transmigration. It is evident that transmigration is that in which a soul is separated from a dead body and immediately enters into the body of a species that has become capable of life, and the former body becomes wasted and worthless. This process takes no longer than an instant, according to the transmigrationists.

On the other hand, projection is that in which the perfecting (*mukammil*) soul manifests (*tajalli*) itself in the accomplished (*kamil*) soul, just as the owner, occupier, and governor at the gate of the city. The existence of the accomplished soul is thus brought to perfection (*mukammal*), without requiring the soul of that accomplished one to leave the body.

The unsettled question here is whether the perfecting one has to be in this world or not. Apparently, it is more common that it be so, for many among the saints have projected in their own lifetimes onto some accomplished ones. This is akin to how the light of a weak lamp is subdued by the rays of a strong lamp without, however, being extinguished. When you accept the notion that *jinn* have the ability to dominate and subdue some imperfect human souls, as it is has been witnessed many times, I imagine that you will not oppose the notion of spiritual projection. For how could the ability of the prophets and the pure ones be less than that of *jinn*?

For this reason, of many of the saints of God who reached this stage, some made the claim of being Jesus and some made other claims, and these claims brought disasters upon their heads and upon everyone. Examples of such men include Mir Sayyid Mahmud Nurbaksh Badakhshi and Amir Sayyid Mahmud Jaunpuri, may God bless their souls. It is known, however, that in truth Jesus and the messiah promised to us, may peace be upon him, are not more than one, and anyone who made this claim is in the right and justified. The details of these matters must be seen in the book *Sharh-i Gulshan-i Raz* [a famous Sufi text by Muhammad Lahiji (d. 1506), a disciple of Nurbakhsh] and other places. On this basis, you must remain compassionate towards all and erase the words of partisanship and prejudice from the slate of your heart and not tear at anyone's breast with the thorn of denunciation. For if you do, it does them no harm; however you should worry about your own inner condition.

> [A couplet by Hafiz]
> If you see a head at the threshold of the tavern
> Kick it not, for unknown is its intent.

Regarding this science and knowledge (*'ilm-o danish*), since you accept the legitimacy of the guild (*muhtarifa*) who pursue it day and night, and since you brook no disagreement with them in this matter, why do you denounce the men of God who struggled to obtain the ultimate goal, who spent their entire life in pursuit of truth and divine knowledge, and who thought nothing of sacrificing their possessions and life in this cause? They attained a place in this world and the next with great determination and gave up everything except God. It would only be just that as they do not interfere with you in the realm of positive and technical sciences (*'ulum-i waz'iyya wa istilahiyya*) and accept your competence, you should also find them to be competent in these rational

and divine sciences (*'ulum-i 'aqliyya wa ilahiyya*) which are beyond your understanding.

> [In Arabic:]
> Above every knowledgeable one is the all-knowing one. [Qur'an 12:76])
> [A couplet by Hafiz]
> That which must be said, I say to you.
> Take counsel from my words, or vexation.

As the discussion has led us here, it is necessary to relate something of the
lives of those two great ones. (*Najat al-Rashid,* pp. 70–74)

In the pages that follow, which have not been included here, Badayuni gives extensive details about the lives and miracles of the two "messiahs," Sayyid Muhammad Nurbaksh and Sayyid Muhammad Jaunpuri. He writes hagiographically and
includes the mystical, scriptural, and astrological proofs of the messianic claims of
these two men. Then he continues below.

A story (*hikayat*): The writer of these pages had a friend named Mustafa Beg
Rumi ["from the land of Rum or Byzantium," meaning an Ottoman Turk], who
was among the notables of that country and had done well for himself. One day
when we were sitting together and I had some time, he heard from me the difference between projection and transmigration of the soul.

In response he related, "When I was a youth in Egypt, a master of mysticism
and miracles, whose dear name was Shaykh Sayas Misri, looked upon me with
love and kindness, and under the influence of his companionship, day by day I
found in myself an amazing *baraka* and a most complete knowledge. And so
time passed until I had the chance to travel to Aleppo.

"That dear one, because of the affection he possessed, also decided to accompany me, and we stayed for some time in that city. One day when I went to the
market, he said, 'Buy for me some beads, corals, necklaces, and such pretty little
trinkets that women use.' I asked him, 'For what?' He said, 'For my children and
yours, so you can take these back to them.'

"When we got back to our house, he asked me to stay a while because the
time of his departure from this world was near, and said that we should bid each
other farewell. I asked him if he was suffering from a disease or bodily pain. He
said 'No, but I have knowledge of my departure.'

"Upon hearing this I broke down in tears and despite all efforts I was unable
to control myself. He asked me, 'Why do you show such weakness, for I will always be there to look after your affairs.' He took the name of an ascetic and said,
'For your sake I will come back to the world and take on his shape and form.
You will hear from him sign-laden words which we will exchange.'

"Then he advised me to name my future son after him, and gave me his will
for his family and children, and departed from this world. From that day on, the
worrying thought often gnawed at my heart that how could that beloved one,

who was undoubtedly a man of God and spiritually accomplished, make a claim of transmigration (*tanasukh*)? However, when I heard from you this difference [between transmigration and projection] my suspicion of many years ended, and I became happy." May God be praised for this.

A poem:
Since the philosopher's two eyes were cross-eyed
He was unable to see the unity of truth.
From blindness came the opinion of divine anthropomorphism (*tashbih*)
From squinting, the realization of absolute transcendence (*tanzih*),
Transmigration, for this reason, became a blasphemous lie,
Which, in truth, springs from lack of vision.
(*Najat al-Rashid*, pp. 82–83)

Sources

The source for this translation is a critical edition of Abd al-Qadir ibn Muluk Shah Bada'uni's *Najat al-Rashid*, with an introduction and footnotes in Urdu by Sayyid Mu'in al-Haqq (Lahore: Idarah-i Tahqiqat-i Pakistan, Danishgah-i Panjab, 1972).

Further Reading

For a general account of the religious climate at the Mughal court, see Khaliq Ahmad Nizami, *Akbar and Religion* (Delhi: Idarah-i-Adabiyat-i-Delli, 1989); and Saiyid Athar Abbas Rizvi, *Religious and Intellectual History of the Muslims in Akbar's Reign, with Special Reference to Abul Fazl, 1556–1605* (New Delhi: Munshiram Manoharlal Publishers, 1975). The English translation of Badayuni's chronicles is also a valuable source of history of the period: see Abd al-Qadir ibn Muluk Shah Bada'uni, *Muntakhabut-tawarikh: by 'Abdul Qadir bin-Muluk Shah known as al-Badaoni*, George Spiers, Alexander Ranking, and W. H. Lowe, trans., 3 vols., 1st Pakistani ed. (Karachi: Karimsons, 1976).

Detailed treatment of the two messianic movements mentioned by Badayuni, the Mahdawiyya and the Nurbakhshiyya, can be found, respectively, in Saiyid Athar Abbas Rizvi, *Muslim Revivalist Movements in Northern India in the Sixteenth and Seventeenth Centuries* (Agra: Agra University, 1965); and Shahzad Bashir, *Messianic Hopes and Mystical Visions: The Nurbakhshiya between Medieval and Modern Islam* (Columbia, SC: University of South Carolina Press, 2003). An in-depth analysis of how millennial ideas shaped imperial policies and politics in general in Safavid Iran is available in Kathryn Babayan, *Mystics, Monarchs, and Messiahs: Cultural Landscapes of Early Modern Iran* (Cambridge, MA: Harvard University Press, 2002). For a similar but shorter overview of millennial practices in the Ottoman court, see Cornell Fleischer, "The Lawgiver as Messiah: The Making of the Imperial Image in the Reign of Suleyman," in *Suleyman the Magnificent and His Time: Acts of the Parisian Conference, Galeries Nationales du Grand Palais, 7–10 March 1990*, Gilles Veinstein, ed. (Paris: École de hautes études en sciences sociales, 1990), pp. 159–177.

For an introduction to the intertwined theories of the age of the world, astrology, and astronomy in Islamic intellectual traditions and their overlap with ancient Indian and Iranian cosmology, see the chapter "On the Nature of Eras," in Muhammad ibn Ahmad Biruni and Eduard Sachau, *The Chronology of Ancient Nations: An English Version of the Arabic Text of the Athar-ul-Bakiya of Albiruni* (London: Published for the Oriental Translations Fund of Great Britain & Ireland by W. H. Allen, 1879); J. M. Millas, "Abu Ma'shar," in *The Encyclopaedia of Islam, CD-ROM ed.* (Leiden: E. J. Brill, 1999); and D. Pingree, "Kiran," in *The Encyclopaedia of Islam, CD-ROM ed.* (Leiden: E. J. Brill, 1999).

30

Custom and Conversion in Malabar:
Zayn al-Din al-Malibari's *Gift of the Mujahidin:*
Some Accounts of the Portuguese

Engseng Ho

Muslim society and culture in the Indian Subcontinent cannot be understood in isolation, separated from other socio-religious traditions and communities. While many scholarly studies accept this challenge, to look at Islam and Muslims in South Asia in their interaction with others, such responses have been subjected to a strong polarizing tendency, between mutually exclusivist conflict on the one hand, and happy syncretism on the other. It is against this backdrop that the virtues of the following extract emerge. Zayn al-Din al-Malibari's *Gift of the Mujahidin: Some Accounts of the Portuguese*, is very clear on what separates Muslims from others, but also on what brings them together. Al-Malibari was a Muslim jurist in Malabar, of Yemeni Arab descent, born probably in Ponnan in 1532. He wrote his *Gift* in 1583 to mobilize resistance against Portuguese depredations.

Muslims from Arabia and elsewhere had been trading on the Malabar coast for centuries. Ponnan, known as the "Mecca of Malabar," was famed for its old Arab connections; al-Malibari's family had arrived there in the fifteenth century. In the port cities of Malabar and the Coromandel coast, communities of Muslims had developed out of a history of international trade, conversion, marriage, migration, and population growth. Muslims maintained formal differences from non-Muslims, even as they engaged in broad social exchanges with them; they flourished under the patronage of non-Muslim rulers. The ruler of Calicut, known as the Samudri Raja, or Ruler of the Sea, was one such Hindu ruler who particularly valued his Muslim subjects and foreign Muslim traders, and benefited from fostering their international commerce. The Portuguese, intent on supplanting Muslims (and their Venetian associates) as carriers of valuable Indian products like pepper to Europe, made alliances of their own, such as with the rulers of Cochin, and attacked Muslims and their local patrons and allies in port cities such as Calicut.

Al-Malibari's *Gift* was an explicit response to the Portuguese. In it, he sets out the case against them, detailing Portuguese military actions across the Indian Ocean, in particular those that targeted Muslims. He also presents arguments from Islamic law to oblige Muslims to fight the Portuguese. But the country of Malabar was not originally Muslim, and Muslims remained a small proportion of its population. So on what basis could al-Malibari claim that they were defending their own country against interlopers? Part of Al-Malibari's answer to this question is given in the third chapter of the *Gift*, translated below. Here, in the middle of this historical, military, and legal treatise, we are surprisingly confronted with a detailed ethnography of Malabar customs. Al-Malibari approaches this subject with the eye of a lawyer, making divisions and subdivisions among and within categories of Malabar society. His description of local customs, in jural terms of rules and their transgression, provides a clear understanding of how separation is maintained between social categories. At the same time, however, his lawyerly account also traces how the rules governing behavior within a group also push individuals to move outside of their group, to consort with others for an evening, and even to convert to a different religion for good. The intricate account of cross-cultural interaction that emerges from his ethnography thus provides an analytical basis for understanding how Islam became entrenched in the country of Malabar. Because this entrenchment was gradual, took place in a process of mutual moral adjustment, and was a consequence of the nature of Malabar society itself, Islam became a genuine part of Malabar society, even as Muslims continued trading and consorting with foreign lands and peoples. Al-Malibari himself was from an eminent Malabar family of Muslim scholars who originated in Yemen, and his writing reflects the double perspective of being both insider and outsider, and of having both local and transregional concerns. As al-Malibari's text shows, the ability to hold together multiple perspectives was part of the experience of being Muslim in South Asia in the sixteenth century.

FROM AL-MALIBARI'S *TUHFAT AL-MUJAHIDIN*, CHAPTER 3: AN ACCOUNT OF THE STRANGE CUSTOMS OF THE MALABAR UNBELIEVERS

Know that among the infidels of Malabar are strange customs unknown in other regions. Among these is that if their leader is killed in battle, his soldiers will fall upon his adversary and his adversary's town until they themselves are all killed; or they destroy the whole kingdom of his adversary. Because of this, Malabaris greatly dread killing leaders. This is an old custom, even if they hold less to it in this age.

Among these customs is that the people of Malabar are of two divisions: those allied with the Samuri [King of Calicut] and those allied with the leader of Cochin. This division remains unless an attack or disturbance occurs, and when that disappears, they return to their initial division.

Among these customs is that they do not employ deception in warfare. They designate a known day for the hostilities, and do not deviate from it. They view treachery in this matter a disgrace.

Among these customs is that if an elder among them dies, such as a father, a mother or an elder brother among the Brahmins, the carpenters, and the like; and such as the mother or the mother's brother or elder brother among the Nayar and their relatives, they avoid for a full year sleeping with women, consuming animals, betel nut, and tobacco, cutting their hair and clipping their nails. They do not violate these customs, and in this way consider themselves close to the departed.

Of these customs is that among the Nayar and those related to them, inheritance goes to the mother's brothers, or to the children of their sisters or their mothers' sisters or relatives on the mother's side. The children inherit neither money nor property. This custom—I mean the non-inheritance of the children—has spread to the Muslims of Cannanore and their followers nearby, even though among them are those who read and memorize the Qur'an, who read it well, are knowledgeable in religion and are active in the rituals of worship. As for the Brahmins and the gold and silversmiths, the carpenters and ironsmiths, the coconut pickers, the fishermen and others, inheritance among them goes to the children, and they marry. As for the Nayar, they do not marry, but rather tie a string around the neck of the woman at the first encounter. After that, the matter depends on the situation, there being no difference between one who makes a marriage contract and one who does not. As for the Brahmins, if there are brothers, only the eldest marries, so long as it has not been confirmed that he cannot beget. The others do not marry, in order that the inheritors do not multiply and give rise to conflict. Instead, they go to the Nayar women out of wedlock. If any of them begets with any of the Nayar women a child, they do not pass inheritance on to him. If it is confirmed that the eldest cannot beget, however, then another brother marries.

Among their customs is that two or four or more men agree upon one woman of the Nayar group or those close to them, each one spending a night with her in turn, just as the Muslim husband is divided amongst his wives. Little enmity or rancor arises among them in this. The carpenters, the ironsmiths, the gold and silversmiths, and the like, follow the Brahmins in having more than one man agreeing upon one woman, except that here the men are brothers or relatives in order that the inheritance not be fragmented, and in order to minimize disputes over inheritance.

Among these customs is that they expose their bodies and do not cover them except for the private parts and what adjoins them. The rest of the body is exposed. In this the men and the women are alike, as are the kings and the nobles. Their women are not veiled to anybody, except for the women of the Brahmins, for they are veiled. As for the Nayar, their women are adorned with jewelry and precious clothes. They parade them abroad during their large gatherings, that the men may see and appreciate them.

And among their customs is that no one becomes king except for him who is the eldest in age, even by a shade, be he a simpleton, or blind, weak, or from the offspring of the mother's sisters. It is unheard of for any of the brothers or sons of the mother's sisters to kill one older in order to become king in a hurry.

Among their customs is that if there are few heirs, or none, they adopt an outsider, even if he is grown, and make him heir in the place of a son or brother or sister's son. Thereupon they make no distinction between him and a genuine legatee in inheritance and possession. This custom prevails among all the unbelievers of Malabar, the kings and the commoners alike, the highest and the lowest, in order that their legacy be not interrupted.

And among these customs is that they are subject to many burdensome ceremonies which they do not deviate from, because they are divided into many sorts: among them the highest and the lowest, and those in between. If contact occurs between the highest and the lowest, or in a similar way proximity to a known degree between them and one of the lowly agriculturalists, the higher status one has to undergo a ritual washing. They do not permit him to eat food before washing. If he does eat before washing, he is demoted and no longer included with them in their high station. There is no salvation for him but in fleeing to a place where no one knows his circumstances. Otherwise, the chief of the town takes him and sells him to one below him in rank, in the event that he is a youth or a woman. Or else he comes to us and converts to Islam, or becomes a Yogi or a Christian. In this way, they do not permit the superior to consume food cooked by the inferior, for eating outside of his rank entails the above-mentioned consequences.

The people of the thread, i.e., those who are required to wear the string across their shoulders, are the most eminent of all the unbelievers of Malabar. And among them are subdivisions: the highest, the lowest, and those in between. The Brahmins are the highest of the people of the thread, and they are composed of classes. Apart from the people of the thread, there are the Nayar: they are the soldiers of the people of Malabar, and the mightiest and most numerous of them. They are also composed of different classes, the highest and the lowest among them, and those in between. Apart from these are the coconut pickers. They are the ones who climb the coconut trees in order to throw their coconuts down to the ground to extract their water, which becomes an intoxicant or is cooked and made into sugar.

And apart from them are the carpenters, and the ironsmiths, and the gold and silversmiths, and the fishermen, and others. There are yet others, the lowliest, who are involved in ploughing and planting, and related activities; they are also composed of different sorts. And if a pebble is cast by one of the low-status males at a woman of higher status on one of the nights of the year known amongst them, she is dropped from her station if she is not accompanied by a male, even if she is pregnant. The governor will either take and sell her, or bring her to us whereupon she converts to Islam; or she becomes a Christian or a Yogi. And this transpires if intercourse occurs between a high-status woman and a low-status man, or the reverse; the superior is dropped from his or her rank. Thus he has no recourse but to one of the above, unless he is one of the people of the string who have intercourse with the Nayar women: they are not ejected from their station. They made this a custom among them, when it became such that no one but the eldest brother among the Brahmins married, while the others went to the Nayar women.

How many are the burdensome customs they impose upon themselves, in their ignorance and their foolishness. God most high and praised has made this the principal reason for their entry into the religion of Islam, by His bounty.

This talk however is a digression, for words lead to more words. Let us return to our purpose in these pages. Thus when Sharaf bin Malik—and Malik bin Dinar, and Habib bin Malik, and others mentioned earlier—entered Malabar and built mosques in the aforementioned port towns and spread in them the religion of Islam, its folk entered Islam little by little. And merchants came to Malabar from many regions, and they built up other towns, such as Calicut, Veliyankode, and Tirurangadi; then Tanur, Ponnani and Parappanangadi, then Paravanna, in the vicinity of Shaliyat port; and towns such as Kakkad and Trikodi and others, from around Fundreah; and towns such as Cannanore and Adkad and Tiruvangad and Mahe and Chimnya near Darmaftun, and south of it Valapattanam and Nadapuram; and south of Kadnagalore such as Shay and Bit, and Palapuram and other ports. Their populations increased and prospered with Muslims and their commerce, on account of the little injustice found among their chiefs, even though they and their soldiers were unbelievers, and even though their subjects hold to their aforementioned customs and rarely transgress them. The Muslims in Malabar were subjects, small in number—not exceeding one-tenth of the society.

The greatest of the Malabar ports from ancient times and the most famous of them by reputation was the port of Calicut. But it became weak and fell into disrepair after the Portuguese arrived and disrupted the travels of its people. In all of the Malabar lands, the Muslims had no mighty prince ruling over them. Their rulers were unbelievers who governed them by supervising their affairs and by imposing fines upon those who deserved them under prevailing custom. Nonetheless, the Muslims enjoyed respect and standing, because most of the buildings in the towns were theirs, and they were able to hold Friday congregational prayers and festivals. They appointed judges and muezzins for the call to prayer, and carried out Islamic law amongst the Muslims. They did not permit disruption of the Friday prayers, and anyone who did so was accosted and fined in most towns. And if a Muslim commits a crime deserving among them of execution, they execute him with the permission of the leading Muslims. Then the Muslims take him and wash and prepare him, say the funeral prayer for him, and bury him in the Muslim cemetery. And if an unbeliever commits a crime deserving of execution, they kill him, crucify him, and leave him where he was slain, until the dogs and the jackals eat him. They do not take other than the one-tenth tax on trade, except for fines, if actions are committed which among them require penalty. And they do not take land taxes from the farmers and gardeners, even if they be many. They do not enter the houses of the Muslims without their permission if a Muslim commits a crime, even if it be an unjust murder. Rather, they get the Muslims themselves to eject him from the house by perseverance, starvation, or like methods. They do not subject to harm anyone of them who converts to Islam; instead, they respect him as they do other Muslims, even if he is from one of their lowliest groups. The Muslim traders in the olden days took up collections for the convert.

Sources

This translation is based on two very similar Arabic recensions of al-Malibari's text: Hamza Chelakodan, ed., *Tuhfat al-Mujahidin fi-ba'd akhbar al-Burtughaliyyin* (Calicut, India: Maktabat al-Huda, 1996); and Amin Tawfiq al-Tayyibi, ed., *Tuhfat al-Mujahidin fi-ba'd akhbar al-Burtughaliyyin* (Tripoli, Libya: Kuliyyat al-Da'wa al-Islamiyya, 1987). An early English translation of al-Malibari's text was published soon after the establishment of British rule over Malabar by Lieut. M. J. Rowlandson, ed., *Tohfut-ul-Mujahideen, An Historical Work in the Arabic Language* (London: The Oriental Translations Fund of Great Britain and Ireland, 1833).

Further Reading

Genevieve Bouchon provides a view of Calicut in al-Malibari's time, in "A Microcosm: Calicut in the Sixteenth Century," in *Asian Merchants and Businessmen in the Indian Ocean and the China Sea*, Denys Lombard and Jean Aubin, eds. (Oxford: Oxford University Press, 2000), pp. 40–49. For long-term historical studies of Muslim society in Malabar, see Stephen Frederic Dale, *Islamic Society on the South Asian Frontier: The Mappilas of Malabar, 1498–1922* (Oxford: Clarendon Press, 1980); V. Kunhali, *Sufism in Kerala.* (Calicut: Calicut University Press, 2004); Roland E. Miller, *Mappila Muslims of Kerala: A Study in Islamic Trends* (London: Sangam Books, 1992). For an anthropological history that treats both Muslim and Christian society in South India and their relations with Hindu traditions, see Susan Bayly, *Saints, Goddesses and Kings: Muslims and Christians in South Indian Society* (Cambridge: Cambridge University Press, 1989). For a study that places al-Malibari's anti-imperial project in relation to subsequent Muslim anti-imperial movements in the Indian Ocean, see Engseng Ho, "Empire through Diasporic Eyes: A View from the Other Boat," in *Comparative Studies in Society and History* 46, no. 2 (2004): 210–246.

— 31 —

Muslim League Appeals to the Voters of Punjab
for Support of Pakistan

David Gilmartin

At no point did ideas about Islam and their relationship to the constitution of the state enter into greater practical currency in South Asia than in the elections of 1946. The Muslim League fought these elections largely on the demand for the creation in India of a separate Muslim state, Pakistan. The high-level constitutional negotiation that led to the partition plan of 1947 and to the emergence of Pakistan as an independent nation is well known. But the Muslim League's electoral appeals from 1945–1946 suggest the frameworks of popular thinking about the Muslim community, the individual, and the state within which the appeal for Pakistan was made. This selection of pro-Pakistan Muslim League election posters from the Punjab provides a glimpse into this world.

A few words are necessary on the political background to these elections and on the demand for Pakistan in the Punjab. Though League members had in the late 1930s discussed proposals for Pakistan, or for a separate Muslim state or states in India, the League formally adopted the demand for a separate state (or states) only in 1940 in the so-called Lahore Resolution, which articulated the demand for separate Muslim states in India (Poster 9). Though the resolution did not clearly spell out the nature of Pakistan (indeed, the word "Pakistan" was not even used), the demand for Pakistan, however ill-defined, subsequently became the rallying cry of the League, particularly in conflict and negotiation at the all-India level with the British and the Indian National Congress.

Political conflict in the Muslim-majority province of the Punjab, however, was shaped far more directly by growing regional tension in the province between the League and the Punjab Unionist Party, a party of rural interests including Hindus, Muslims, and Sikhs, led largely by Muslim landlords, that had ruled Punjab with a strong majority in the provincial assembly since the elections of 1937. From late 1937 until 1944, the Muslim League and the Unionist Party had been in loose alliance in the Punjab, based on a 1937 pact between Muhammad Ali Jinnah, the all-India leader of the League, and the Unionist Premier, Sir Sikander Hyat Khan. The Unionists had supported the League in all-India affairs, in exchange for the League not challenging the position of the Unionists in the Punjab. But with the league increasingly committing itself to popular mobilization based on the Pakistan demand in the mid-1940s, this agreement broke down in 1944. The League then expelled the new Unionist Premier, Malik Khizr Hyat Khan Tiwana, and the two parties openly split. Though a faction of Unionist landlords (including Mumtaz Daultana, Shaukat Hyat, and Iftikhar Husayn Khan Mamdot, who were the sons of former Unionist leaders) at that time sided with the League, the Unionist Party retained their majority in the Punjab Assembly. From 1944 until the elections of 1946, politics in Punjab were thus marked by sharp opposition between the Muslim League and the Unionists.

At the all-India level, the demand for Pakistan pitted the League against the Congress and the British. In Punjab, however, the electoral clash over Pakistan focused largely on contests between candidates of the League and candidates of the Unionist Party. Key to the struggle was the structure of "separate electorates" within which the elections were conducted. British colonial electoral structures separated Hindus, Muslims, and Sikhs in the Punjab into separate constituencies in which co-religionists voted only for candidates of their own religion. This arrangement guaranteed that Muslims would contest the 1946 provincial assembly elections not against candidates of other communities but against each other. In the electoral arena, debate over the creation of Pakistan thus became primarily a debate among Muslims. In the rural areas, where the overwhelming majority of Muslim constituencies were contested, the League's main adversaries in the election were Muslim candidates of the Unionist Party. In the cities, League candidates contested primarily against candidates of the Khaksar and Ahrar parties, two regional Muslim movements with a largely urban base.

What, then, was the nature of the Muslim League's appeal in these circumstances? In the context of competition among Muslims, the League stressed the *unity* of Muslims as the overriding issue, with Pakistan as a powerful symbol of that unity. Earlier constitutional negotiations around the demand for Pakistan (such as those conducted at the Simla conference in July 1945) had foundered precisely on Jinnah's claims to be the "sole spokesman" for the Muslims. But in these election appeals, the commitment to Muslim unity emerges not just as a tactic in constitutional negotiations, but as an imperative deriving from Muslim principle and Muslim history. To support Pakistan as a symbol of Muslim unity, was not only to support the Muslim League in electoral competition with other political parties, but also to demonstrate a personal commitment to Islamic ideals under challenge from those who would divide the community for self-interested reasons at a critical juncture. The League painted the Unionists (and to a lesser degree the Ahrars and the Khaksars as well) as parties of worldly interest. To support the League was to place commitment to the community first, even in the context of the divisions among Muslims made manifest by the electoral process itself.

League posters thus presented support for the Unionist Party as a threat to the

unity of the community, primarily because it rested on the powerful ties of kinship, faction, *biradari* (clan), and interest operating in the everyday lives of Punjab's Muslims. These were ties that had long played critical roles in electoral politics, and that had linked Punjabi Muslims to the administrative structure of the
British government. But the League now attacked such ties as dividing the community (Posters 8 and 10), and as being manipulated by the British and the
Unionists for their own worldly ends (Poster 12). This is not to suggest, of course,
that the manipulation of *biradari*, faction, and economic interest were missing
from the League's own electioneering in 1945–1946. They were not. The very
structure of elections in British Punjab meant that successful electioneering required attention to local allegiances and divisions. But rhetorically, the League
stressed the importance of Pakistan as a symbol that transcended the everyday
politicking that even the Muslim League's own candidates engaged in. To identify
with Pakistan was to symbolically transcend the everyday pressures of politics in
the name of a higher personal commitment to Muslim community (and Muslim
unity) (Poster 11). Pakistan thus symbolized the importance of the state as a symbol of the community's unity, whatever the divisions of interest, kinship, and faction that defined society itself.

    This image of Pakistan of course contrasted sharply with the realities of politics
under the existing British colonial state. Muslims and Hindus alike were "slaves"
of colonial domination, as one poster put it (Poster 6). Jinnah thus took strong exception to the old image of the Muslim League as a party of "Nawabs, Nawabzadas,
and titleholders," allied to the British, which he portrayed as a product of Congress
propaganda (Poster 6). Though many Punjab Muslim League leaders were in fact
scions of ex-Unionist, landlord families, the League's campaign continued in 1946
to contain echoes of the more radical provincial Muslim League Manifesto of
1944, which had called for the overturning of structures of colonial, bureaucratic
domination and the establishment, under Pakistan, of a more socially just society.

    But as the elections of 1946 approached, even this populism was cast less as an
appeal for social justice than as an appeal to an idealized vision of Muslim community and unity embodied by an idealized Muslim state. The contrast was thus
not only with the British colonial state, but also with the corruption and division
associated with worldly state power in Islamic history. This emerges clearly, for example, in the posters commemorating the martyrdom of Husayn at Karbala as a
model for the Pakistan struggle. The struggles of Husayn against the worldly corruption of Yazid, commemorated at Muharram, serve as a backdrop in these
posters for the ongoing struggles of Punjabi Muslims to escape the snares of "*jagirs*, offices, and squares of land," offered by the Unionist Party and the British government (Poster 5). Pakistan as an Islamic state thus symbolized resistance to colonial domination—and to the political manipulation of society's divisions. It also
symbolized the need for individuals to rise above all their inherited ties to family,
biradari, caste, and tribe and to link their personal honor to the image of unity embodied by Pakistan (Posters 8, 9, and 10).

    Even the appeals of the 'ulama that appeared as part of the Muslim League's election campaign stress Pakistan's meaning as a symbol, and offer little vision of a distinctive blueprint for Islamic state authority. As the reprinted comments from the prominent Deobandi scholar, Maulana Ashraf Ali Thanavi, who had died in 1943, suggest, there were many 'ulama in India, particularly within the Jamiat-i Ulama-i Hind, who opposed the Muslim League and supported the Congress, largely out of strong anti-colonialism and uncertainty about the commitment of League leaders to the shariat (Poster 4). But many other 'ulama, such as Maulana Shabbir Ahmad Usmani, supported Pakistan in spite of such concerns. For Usmani, personal commitment to Muslim unity transcended even adherence to the shariat. He invokes the model of Harun, who was temporarily willing even to tolerate *shirk* (or giving partners to God), a clear violation of shariat, in order to preserve the unity of the community (Poster 1). The same concern appears in statements of Sufi pirs, an example of which comes in these documents from the Sajjada Nishin (Chief Successor) of the shrine at Ajmer (Poster 3).

None of this is to imply, of course, that the structure of law was irrelevant to the campaign for Pakistan, for the very structure of the elections within which the appeal for Pakistan was made in early 1946, was one defined by colonial law. That this was a "constitutional war," as Usmani put it, was something the posters generally recognized. "In place of bullets and gunpowder," he noted, "votes are being used" (Poster 2). Some of the posters thus appealed directly to colonial election law to protect the free conscience of the individual voter, which was necessary to make possible the individual's transcendence of worldly coercion and worldly ties (Poster 7).

Still, despite this concern with law, it is not the image of Pakistan as a legally constituted state, whether rooted in colonial or Islamic law, that dominates the images created in these posters. Rather, Pakistan appears most often as a pure symbol. It is in this context that these posters throw light not only on the campaign for Pakistan's creation in the mid-1940s, but on the longer-term dynamics of Muslim state-building and its popular legitimation. As several of these posters suggest, the tensions between Islamic community ideals—and Islamic unity—and the realities of power politics, with its tribal, sectarian, and worldly divisions, were deeply ingrained in Muslim thinking, dating in the sacred imaginary all the way back to the very origins of the Muslim community amidst *fitna* (disorder) and *jahiliya* (the pre-Islamic era of ignorance) (Posters 8 and 10). Such tensions were, of course, ever-present in electoral competition. In these appeals, it is this tension, more than anything else, that drives the moral imperative to choose sides in the campaign for Pakistan.

Punjab Muslim League election propaganda for Pakistan, as illustrated in these posters, thus suggests not only the particularities of the distinctive Punjabi political context preceding the provincial elections of 1946, but also the important conceptual structures that underlay the League's attempts to mobilize popular support for Pakistan as a symbol of Muslim community. To understand the practical role played by the concept of Pakistan as an Islamic symbol, one must understand the specific political context in which it was invoked. The structure of the electoral arena under British rule was critical to the way that arguments for Pakistan were framed in these flyers. Elections were predicated on the free choice (and the free conscience) of the individual voter. Yet elections were also defined by the competition among Muslims that was inherent in the structuring of separate electorates, often based on local, tribal, factional, and sectarian divisions. The appeal to Pakistan played off these tensions, defining a symbol of unity and personal commitment that transcended the world of divisive and self-interested politics that inescapably shaped elections. It is in looking at this intersection between political context and Islamic paradigms that we can most clearly see in these posters Islam in practice in the creation of a Muslim state.

TRANSLATIONS OF FLYERS/POSTERS

1. A MESSAGE FROM A SERVANT OF THE FAITH IN THE NAME OF THE MUSLIMS OF PUNJAB AND SARHAD (NORTH WEST FRONTIER PROVINCE)

Everyone already knows the importance of the present elections. According to an announcement of the British government, the future structure of government in India will be created by those people who are selected at this time and go into the Assemblies. Therefore, the greatest need of the moment is that the voters recognize well their national duty (*qaumi farz*) and in this matter take no heed of any pressure, greed, personality, or connection. At this time we have before us only two goals. One is that the Muslim *qaum* should put before the government, the Congress, and other interested communities its true and just demand for Pakistan in agreed upon words and with one voice. The second is that the great organization of the Muslim *qaum* should be sufficiently clear and complete that, with whatever other community it makes peace or war, it should do so not on behalf of some people, but so that it is understood to speak for the community as a whole. By good fortune, the grace and power of Allah after much time has provided the wherewithal that today the Muslim community is collected on the All-India Muslim League platform under the green crescent flag, and the Pakistan idea has taken possession of their hearts and minds. The importance of what God has provided we should respect. That which is truly deserving of thanks is that a collective spirit (*ijtima'i ruh*) pervades the thinking and ideals of every Muslim individual. To be unanimous in agreement on some right purpose for Muslims is a magnificent gift. Look at when the Bani Israel from their folly became caught up in cow worship (*gosala parasti*). Harun (Aaron) remonstrated with them but the Bani Israel did not take heed of his good advice and continued to say they would not stop until Musa (Moses) returned. Finally, filled with anger, Musa came back, threatening his community, and furiously demanding of Harun why he had not attempted to prevent these idolatrous actions? At this point, Harun made this excuse: I worried that you would come and blame me, saying "You caused division in the Bani Israel and did not wait for my word." Note that Harun could not tolerate dividing the community and for a short while even ignored their idolatry (*shirk*).

My request also at this important and critical time is that Muslims not create divisions among themselves and for a little while leave their other discussions aside. Becoming all of one heart and one voice, they can raise the Pakistan slogan, strengthen the community's organization, and make the voice of the Muslim League successful.

Every voter should recognize his national duty and teach others also that they should not neglect theirs, and whatever difficulties Punjab's plan of action has created, they should try to overcome with national (*qaumi*) unity.

Janishin-i Shaykh al-Hind (The Successor to the Shaykh of India [i.e., Maulana Mahmud Hasan, d. 1920]) Hazrat Allama Maulana (The Elevated Learned Presence) Shabbir Ahmad Usmani

2. APPEAL OF THE 'ULAMA AND SUFIS (*MASHA'IKH*) OF ISLAM

To Punjab Assembly Voters

> *Beyond the stars there are still more worlds*
> *Now there are still more tests of love.*

(Iqbal)

In the capacity of president of the All-India Jamiat al-Ulama-i Islam and after consultations and unity of opinion from more than three hundred 'ulama, Sufis and *masha'ikh* of Hindustan who took part in a meeting at Lahore on 25–27 January,

I make the appeal below to all you voters on the basis of those meetings:

You are well aware of the reality that at this time in Hindustan there is a great and decisive constitutional war going on in which the fate of both Hindustan and the Muslims will be decided. This is not a war of guns and ditches, but an election war, and in this war, in place of bullets and gunpowder, votes are being used.

In the Central Assembly election, you used your votes well, and by the grace of God in this first battle you achieved 100% success. It was the sort of success that in the present age no political party in the world has been able to show, and, without exaggeration, this struck the opponents of the Muslim League dumb. *Al-hamdulillah* (Praise be to God). But the war is not now over; to the contrary, the battle of the provincial elections is harder than this previous battle. Therefore, I appeal to you that in this battle also you achieve 100% success and forever finish off the candidates of the opposition, laying their schemes forever in the dust.

Even though nowadays in the Punjab the real opposition to the Muslim League does not come from the Congress, yet there are numerous other parties, among whom the Unionist Party is foremost, so that Congress has announced for certain that the decision for Pakistan will depend on the Punjab provincial elections.

Therefore I strongly appeal to you, the live-hearted of the Punjab, to make such a grand demonstration of the oneness of the *qaum* and the unity of the *millat* that after the election in every corner of the Punjab a second day of victory can be celebrated, just as on 11 January 1946. And in the name of our national and party glory, all opposing parties should be made so unsuccessful that every candidate opposing the Muslim League may lose their deposit just as has already happened now in Bengal. [To prevent frivolous candidacies, the law required that candidates make a refundable deposit with the government; if they failed to draw a certain minimum percentage of votes, then their deposit was lost.] Remember that if the Muslim League should be unsuccessful, then the Congress and all opponents will have the opportunity to say that the Muslims of Punjab do not want Pakistan and the result of this will be that the consideration of the independence of the Muslims of India will, on the basis of the negligence of the Muslims themselves, be finished for a long time. It is clear that these provincial elections are not only elections, but also a question of the life and death of India's Muslims. If in this battle, God forbid, you are unsuccessful, then no other manifestation of the glory of the Muslims is possible. Therefore I once again appeal to you to try to recognize the delicacy of the times and try to make 100% of the candidates of the Muslim League successful in the provincial elections, and even to create success by such a glorious majority that all opponents will forfeit their deposits. It is clear that after the success of the Muslim League in the provincial elections, both the British and the Congress will have no choice other than to accept Pakistan. *Insha'llah* (God willing).

Long live the Muslim League, Long live Pakistan (Zindabad Muslim League, Paindabad Pakistan)

Shaykh al-Islam Maulana Shabbir Ahmad Usmani, President, All-India Jamiyat al-Ulama-i Islam

3. A MESSAGE OF SHAYKH AL- MASHA'IKH (SHAYKH OF SHAYKHS) HAZRAT DIWAN SAYYID AL-I RASUL ALI KHAN, SAJJADA NISHIN (CHIEF SUCCESSOR), DESCENDANT OF HAZRAT KHWAJA-YI KHWAJAGAN (HONORABLE MASTER OF MASTERS) SULTAN AL-HIND (SULTAN OF INDIA) KHWAJA MU'INUDDIN CHISHTI AJMERI

In the Name of the Muslims of Punjab and Sarhad

Noble Brothers: A very critical time has now come for the Muslims of India. The political struggle that is going on at this time in the form of elections is so important that if the Muslims in this constitutional war work with inattention or let some form of greed or fear influence them and do not recognize their common duty (*jama'ati farz*), then perhaps the chance to raise up the Islamic *millat* will not come. Unfortunately illness prevents me, otherwise I would myself come to your province and make all efforts in aid and support of the Muslim

League. Now from the confinement of my sick bed, I appeal to the Muslims of Punjab and especially to those bound to the Ajmeri shrine in the name of the ancestral honor of Khwaja Gharib Nawaz that they keep in mind the honor and reputation of the Muslim *qaum*. They should not be influenced by any fear or greed, but rather launch an organized struggle to make the community's organization strong for gaining Pakistan, on which rests the prosperity and place of the Muslims. They should make every effort under the direction of the Indian Muslims' beloved Quaid-i Azam Muhammad Ali Jinnah to gain in the battle of the provincial elections also the level of success that was won in the Central Assembly, and prove once more in the world that Muslims are vigilant, organized, and will not draw breath without the acceptance of the Pakistan demand, which is based on the essence of justice.

It is your obligation for the prosperity of the community and for Islamic honor that you vote only for that candidate who is nominated by your sole representative party, the Muslim League. At this time, do not bring up the question of someone's caste (*zat*), nor raise conflicts of *biradari*, but give your vote, which is a responsibility (*amanat*) of the Muslim *qaum*, to the Muslim League candidate.

Understand Well

To give your vote to the candidate of the Muslim League is to support the glory of Islam and the *qaumi* honor of the Muslims.

And to give your vote to someone other than the Muslim League candidate, whether he is standing for a well-known organization or standing as an independent, is to oppose the great majority, to cut at the root of the organized life of the Muslims, and to fulfill the plans of the enemies of the *millat*.

If you felt the delicacy of the times, and, giving your vote in favor of the Muslim League, laid the wishes of those who would disorganize Islam in the dust, then, *insha'llah* the stage of the Islamic *millat's* glory will be near.

God may guide you to recognize your Islamic duty and act on this without fear or peril.

4. THE LOFTY PROCLAMATION OF JANAB HAKIM AL-UMMAT (PHYSICIAN OF THE COMMUNITY) MUJADDID-I MILLAT (RENEWER OF THE NATION) MAULANA ASHRAF ALI THANAVI [FROM A PAMPHLET BY MAULANA THANAWI]

Words of Truth (Kalimat al-Haq)

In the Congress, those people whom the public at large calls 'ulama are of two kinds. Of one kind are those who by reason of speeches and articles are famous and popular among particular classes but are not learned in the shariat. Since they are not learned, therefore not many complaints can be made about their approach to (religious) problems, etc. The other kind are those people who in truth are educated and regular 'ulama, but, having annihilated themselves in the Congress (*fana f'il Kangres ho kar*), have exceeded the limits of the shariat. By reason of hatred of the British, they have sided with the Congress and have not paid attention to limits and restrictions even though they are in the holy *hadis*.

[Arabic with Urdu translation:] *Love and animosity should both be balanced; their positions can be reversed. Friends can be enemies and enemies can be friends.*

This second type of people say clearly that when the English leave India then peace and contentment will be the fate of all 'ulama. Therefore, (they say), we need to make forceful efforts, even if the very faith (*iman*) of Hindustan and Hindustani Muslims may be ruined. Likewise, some men of learning say that we should participate in the Congress for the reason that Congress might be brought under the control and influence of the Muslims. If this is the true purpose, then such a purpose would be easier to attain in the Muslim League, because the Muslim Leaguers are prepared to follow them. In accord with this, very important workers of the League have written to me that we are ready to obey the opinion of the revered 'ulama, while Congress workers themselves are trying to create their own conditions. To obtain mastery over them is difficult. Now the only choice is to join the League to bring it under control and to reform those who are worthy of reform. Similarly they can expel the worthless people.

The rest of the Hindus on no account want the British to leave India; their advantage is in the very establishment of the British. Their mode is that under the supervision and protection of the British they may gain official and legal power and exercise government authority. (*al-Fusul al-wasul*, 136)

5. 'ASHURA OF MUHARRAM AND THE DUTY OF MUSLIMS

The day of commemorating the memory of the Great Martyr Imam Husayn came. In the court of the pure Imam, the time for Muslims to offer tears of love and faith has come. From the pure memory of the Great Martyr the ideals of sacrifice, purity and righteousness are again becoming fresh.

History repeats itself. It is not a comparison of personalities. "What relation is there between earth and the pure world." But see the amazing similarity of events: those very same weapons that were used at that time are being used even today to break the followers of Husayn's name away from the Islamic *millat*.

The Partisanship of Error. At that time offices and gifts of land (*inams*) were given by the government. Today *jagirs*, offices, squares of land, and *inams* are being given. The enemy powers of Islam and the Muslims are prodigal in conspiracies. Today, in place of the imam, it is a test of the followers of the imam's name.

The Collective Glory of the Muslims is on one side and conspiracies to tempt, deceive, and lead Muslims astray are on the other. At the *'ashura* of Muharram the eyes of Muslims are opening. The mention of the pure (*pak*) Husayn is warming faithful hearts. Spurning every fear, incitement or worldly greed, Muslims are arrayed in an Islamic army under an Islamic banner.

Keepers of the Prestige of the Name of Husayn. Tell the world and the world's powers that for the glory of the Muslims we will come out successfully in every test, through the model provided in Karbala by our pure exemplar.

6. CONGRESS IS A COWARD

Sardar Patel [a Congress leader] Should Answer Quaid-i Azam's Truth

For years Congress has been making this untrue propaganda that the Muslim League is a party of Nawabs, Nawabzadas, and titleholders. By means of workers with money and other means, Congress in other countries also is making propaganda that the Muslim people are not with the League. I ask where was the Congress at that time when the Central Assembly elections were going on? When they published their first list of candidates for the Central Assembly, no names of Muslim candidates were included. When I announced that the Congress had fled from the field, then in a second list the names of two or three Muslim candidates were included. The Congress expended hundreds of thousands (*lakhs*) of black market rupees on non-League candidates. The money gained in this hypocritical way was spent for hypocritical purposes. But what was the result? The Muslim League gained a 100% success in those elections.

Sardar Patel's Bombay Speech

Sardar Patel said in a speech in Bombay that it was true that the Muslim League was successful in the Central Assembly elections but that the decision on the future of Hindustan will not be made in those elections. The Congress did not contest the League in the Central Assembly elections. I ask the leaders of the Congress, who had stopped you from contesting against the League? You are for the last seven or eight years telling and deceiving the world that you represent the Muslims. Now why didn't you put up Muslim candidates? Now why did you show such cowardice?

From Whom will Pakistan Come? Or, What is Pakistan?

Quaid-i Azam announced that we will not beseech the Hindus for the attainment of Pakistan and we are not. They themselves are slaves. We want to grab Pakistan from the hands of the British who are in power. It is not just Pakistan's freedom, it is the freedom of the Muslims of the whole subcontinent of Hindustan. If Hindus agree, then we will immediately end this slavery. If they do not agree, then they themselves are putting an obstacle in the path to freedom.
    (Lahore, 17 January 1946, Habibia Hall speech)

7. BROTHERS OF THE COUNTRYSIDE, REMEMBER, NO GOVERNMENT OFFICER CAN COERCE YOU

Brothers of the Countryside Remember
No Government Officer Can Coerce You

You may Give Your Vote to Whomever you Want

The government of Punjab, in its announcement number 10786 issued on the 3rd of November 1945, instructed government officers that they may not interfere in elections. Officers of the Department of Police, the Revenue Department, the Department of Education, the Department of Agriculture, the Cooperative Department, the Panchayat Department cannot tell anyone giving his vote for whom he should vote. If an officer from one of these Departments tells you to vote in favor of some candidate, you should immediately report it to your District Muslim League or to the Punjab Provincial Muslim League, Lahore.

In the Countryside

Asamidar, Khatadar, Mazdur, Kisan, Nambardar, Sufedposh, Zaildar, Inamdar, Jagirdar, Sarpanch [These titles all refer to rural occupations, status designations, offices, or forms of landholding] — All these people are free. You may give your vote to whomever you want.

No Government Officer Can Coerce You

8. WHETHER YOU ARE A SAYYID, A MIRZA, OR AN AFGHAN; WHATEVER YOU MAY BE, SAY THAT YOU ARE ALSO A MUSALMAN

Whether you are a Sayyid, a Mirza, or an Afghan
Whatever you May Be, Say that you are also a Musalman

(Iqbal)

The Enemies of the Muslims are two:
Color and genealogy (*rang o nisab*), that is, the disorder (*fitna*) of tribes and biradaris
And
Country and homeland (*mulk o watan*), that is, the idols of nationalism (*qaumiyat*) and attachment to country (*wataniyat*)

The *fitna* of color and genealogy is a product of the era of ignorance before Islam (*jahiliya*), and is being provoked in the name of power in government. Nationalism and attachment to country (*qaumiyat o wataniyat*), that is, the *fitna* of separating politics and religion, (are being provoked) in the name of India's independence. Muslims! Break the idols of color and genealogy and country and homeland. Your honor (*izzat*), the honor of your *biradari* and tribe, the honor of your family are all from the honor of Islam and the Muslims. That Muslim, that tribe, that *biradari*, that family is deserving of honor who advances in the service of Islam and the Muslims. The Muslim League has taken and raised up this purpose. It is for this purpose that the demand for Pakistan is being made.

Support only Pakistan and the Muslim League

9. AN ISLAMIC STATE WILL SURELY BE ESTABLISHED

I see that if nowhere else a strong Islamic state will surely be established in northwest India.

—Hazrat Allama Iqbal

This was the statement of the Hakim al-Ummat [Physician of the
   Community]
This political insight and perceptivity was the result of faith (*imani*)
In view of which the Muslims of India have always continued to try
   to protect their Islamic constitution and community existence
   (*milli hasti*)
Under which, after the bloody uprising of 1857, the late Sayyid [Sayyid
   Ahmad Khan] took up the leadership of the Muslims
Under which Muhammad Ali [Jauhar]established the principles of the
   Khilafat movement
Which is the single demand of the Muslim League, and now the "Lahore
   Resolution," known as Pakistan, is on the tongue of every Muslim
Which is the single path
To live as a Muslim, for a Pakistan of freedom, steadfastness, honor, and
   self-respect
Break all the idols of name, lineage, country, homeland, community
   (*qaum*), pedigree
Error and love of ambiguity are the same; Truth is without partner
Do not accept error, partners (of God) or moderation of the truth
The Time of Establishing Pakistan Has Come
Go, and for the honor of your faith and religion (*din o iman*), vote for
   Pakistan and the Muslim League

10. BECOME ONE

Hold fast together to the rope of Allah and do not be divided [Qur'an 3:103]

Remember, all Muslims are Brothers

Destroy casteism, sectarianism, faction and bondage
These are all matters of ignorance (*jahalat*)

Islam has interpreted all of these as the zeal of the era of ignorance
   (*jahiliyat*)

Coming together, all should become one

Keep before you one organization, one goal, one constitution
Islam only is your constitution
The *millat* only is your *qaum*
The League only is your representative organization
Pakistan only is your goal

Come— All becoming one, you may gain the good fortune of taking
    part in the Pakistan struggle
Today is our test of honor (*izzat* and *ghairat*), our self-respect, our zeal
Come— Tell the world the Muslims are alive

One has seen last night, not tomorrow
Only today is your new era

11. ENEMIES ARE FLEEING

Enemies are Fleeing
Coercion and intimidation are helpless

Treachery, Untrustworthiness, Community selling, and Community killing
must suffer disgrace

Live-hearted of the Punjab
From your one attack, the ranks of the unrighteous were scattered
Praise be
On your passion of faith (*jazba-yi iman*), your community honor
    (*ghairat-i milli*), and your determination and steadfastness

Brave Lion-hearted of Pakistan
Go Forward
The field is in your hands
Establish your organization and let no differences affect your
    organization and discipline
With full peace (*sakun*), full patience (*itminan*), and full tranquility
    (*amn o aman*)
Vote for the Muslim League

12. NAWAB MAMDOT, MIAN MUMTAZ DAULTANA, SARDAR SHAUKAT HYAT, AND RAJA GHAZANFAR ALI KHAN'S APPEAL TO THE MUSLIMS OF THE PUNJAB (BEFORE THE ELECTIONS)

The Government's Improper Interference in the Elections

The Muslims of the Punjab know well that in view of the critical and decisive
status of the coming elections, the provincial Muslim League made full efforts
to the best of its ability that the official government of the Punjab would fully
understand its duties and create a perception of performing with honesty. In

protest against that shameful interference which the official government's workers are making in the affairs of the political parties, and against that disgraceful pressure of high officials which has taken the form of an organized conspiracy for suppressing the designs of the Muslims of Punjab, we wrote letters, sent telegrams, and published appeal on appeal to the Vazir-i Hind [Secretary of State for India], the Viceroy Bahadur, and the Governor of the Punjab. But we are afraid that the lords of the government, closing their eyes to every concern, have decided that no reason will be heard; therefore we are forced, in the way of every party in the world which has connections with the people, to turn to the steadfastness and wakefulness of those people who, as they say, are the sculptors of our fate, that is, the masses (*jamhur*) of the Punjab.

An Appeal to the Muslims of the Punjab

In this internal situation, we strongly request the Muslims of Punjab, in the name of their great traditions, past legacies and future greatness, that they themselves take the reins of their fate in their hands and not allow some form of fear, wavering or weakness to enter their hearts. In this way truly will come to them the glory and dignity that the times has laid before them. We have already taken a step in the direction of Pakistan, and it is not possible for the intoxicated (*majnunana*) strategies of a destructive power to stop us or hold us back from these steps. We will trample under foot those who divert us from this path. The Muslim League in India is gaining victory everywhere. The pride of its enemies is already broken and they are confounded with fear. It is a reality that no one can deny and our fighting success in the Central Assembly elections is a great proof of that.

What is the Direction of the Wind?

Today some straws are telling us the direction of the wind. *Insha'llah*, this very wind will take the form of a storm, a storm the example of which Hindustan has never seen. The Muslims of Punjab understand well that Government officers cannot do anything. Only cowards would fear them. They know that if they, with purity of intention and cleansing of the heart, struggle and raise their voice against evil and injustice, all the powers of reaction will be dispersed just as the light of the sun coming out of mist and fog.

Be Wary of the Unionist Ministers

The duty of Punjab's Muslims is to beat down with contempt those efforts of the Unionist Ministry whose aim, at this final time, is nothing else but to encourage the greed for squares of land, salaries, and *jagirs*, to turn us away from our faith (*iman*). For us, the status of these pieces falling from the table of the official government is like someone giving a check in the name of a bank that is insolvent. Those people who drew up the Government of India Act did not intend that, with the dissolution of the Assemblies, the ministers of the country, instead of fulfilling their customary duties, would use their authority to sacrifice government lands and the agricultural income of the country in giving bribes to their supporters and partisans. We warn them that after the defeat of the Assembly these powers do not have the support of the people. Further, once the Assembly elections were announced, these highhanded actions were wholly illegal, and it is appropriate that, in going forward, what was done at the whim of the government should be criticized in independent proceedings. Only those grants will be excepted that were given to some person who, under the administrative constitution of the province, had, as they say, a right to them.

The Last Breath of the Unionist Party

We reassure our Muslim brothers: After one or two months you will not hear the Unionist Party's name. This Party is, practically speaking, already finished and has fled from the field. For us there is no delight in the last rays of a setting sun, nor anxiety of too much heat.

The Muslims of the Punjab should Stand Up

Finally, we request that the Muslims of the Punjab forget *biradaris*, tribes, personal animosities, and rivalries, and having become united, stand up for achieving freedom and Pakistan, that is, the desire and object of their own fate.

Acknowledgments

I would like to thank Afroz Taj for assistance with some problems in the translations.

Further Reading

For good background reading on the political and intellectual background to the creation of Pakistan, see Peter Hardy, *The Muslims of British India* (London: Cambridge University Press, 1972). There is a very large literature on Partition, but critical for the political background to the negotiations is Ayesha Jalal, *The Sole Spokesman* (Cambridge: Cambridge University Press, 1985), and Mushirul Hasan, ed., *India's Partition: Process, Strategy, Mobilization* (Delhi: Oxford University Press, 1993). For an overview of the politics leading to Partition in the provinces, see Ian Talbot, *Provincial Politics and the Pakistan Movement: The Growth of the Muslim League in North-West and North-East India, 1937–1947* (Karachi: Oxford University Press, 1988). For specific background on the 1946 elections in Punjab, see Ian Talbot, "The 1946 Punjab Elections," *Modern Asian Studies* 14, no. 1 (1980): 65–91; and David Gilmartin, "A Magnificent Gift: Muslim Nationalism and the Election Process in Colonial Punjab," *Comparative Studies in Society and History* 40, no. 3 (1998): 415–436.

— 32 —

Advocating a Secular Pakistan:
The Munir Report of 1954

Asad Ahmed

In 1953 there were mass demonstrations and violent riots in Lahore and elsewhere in West Pakistan against the minority Ahmadis, members of a much-excoriated Muslim sect that had emerged in late nineteenth-century Punjab. The Report of the Court of Inquiry established to investigate the causes of the riots, popularly known as the Munir Report after the senior presiding judge, Muhammed Munir, also examined whether Pakistan was intended as a liberal democratic or an Islamic state. The question of the degree to which Islam would inform political and constitutional arrangements in the new Muslim state was part of ongoing public debates. The Court sought to flesh out what this much-expressed desire, but undertheorized project, for an Islamic state actually entailed in terms of institutional political arrangements and policy prescriptions. It concluded that an Islamic state was anathema to the ideals of political modernity and that Pakistan ought to be a liberal secular state.

The Court's uncompromising defense of secular liberalism has ensured its lasting political relevance, and it continues to be cited by Pakistani liberals as the clearest exposition of the dangers of an Islamic state. Despite the judges' advocacy of a secular state, the Report, in fact, exhibits considerable textual ambivalence in its discussion of Islam. On the one hand the judges understand Islam as a comprehensive religio-political totality, as what they take to be a traditional religion that encompasses all aspects of life. On the other, they valorize a modern secular conception of religion as a private individual matter of faith that has nothing to do with "the business of the state." These two conceptions of religion set up a constitutive tension between Islamic history and theology on the one hand, and contemporary political theory on the other. Throughout the Report, the discussion of Islam constantly moves between these registers of theology, history, and political theory. Stretched across these domains, Islam's signification becomes ambivalent—as doctrinally inflexible, historically anachronistic, and therefore incommensurable with political modernity—and yet the basis of the putative nation. The judges sought to demonstrate that this incommensurability consisted in a political willingness to compromise with the 'ulama over fundamental differences which, they argued, could only foster further political confusion and religious agitation. Not surprisingly, they concluded that only in a secular order could Islam shed the "dead weight of centuries" and become transformed, revitalized, and once again a dynamic religion.

Although famous for its excursus into political theory, the Court's actual terms of reference were to examine the circumstances leading to the riots and assign legal responsibility for the breakdown in law and order. The majority of the Report provides a chronological account focused on the key actors: the religious parties, the media, politicians, and the bureaucracy. It describes the process through which the religious parties unanimously formulated their three demands: that the Ahmadis be declared a non-Muslim minority; that Chaudhri Zafrullah Khan, a prominent Ahmadi politician appointed foreign minister by Mohammed Ali Jinnah, be dismissed; and thirdly, that Ahmadis be excluded from holding senior state office. The judges found that the hesitant, equivocal, and vacillating response of the politicians— in the face of increasing religious agitation—was the principal reason for the riots. In contrast to the unreasonable 'ulama and unprincipled politicians, the Report's state-centered law-and-order narrative portrays bureaucrats and the civil administration as the voice of reason. In its conclusion the Court assigns primary responsibility to the religious parties, with particular emphasis on the Ahrar and the Jama'at-i Islami (Society of Islam), led by the Islamist thinker, Abul Ala Maududi, both of which had long opposed the demand for Pakistan. The Report also criticizes the responses of the central and provincial governments.

Had the judges restricted themselves to determining legal culpability, the Report would have been of little interest except to historians studying the emergence of, and links between, sectarianism and the state in Pakistan. However, the judges argued that the principal demands of the religious parties that the Ahmadis be declared as non-Muslims and removed from state office had two important implications. First, it presumed a theological means through which a Muslim could be genuinely identified and distinguished from other self-professed Muslims. Secondly, it implied a religious justification for denying senior positions in an Islamic state to non-Muslim communities. It was, therefore, necessary to understand the 'ulama's conception of an Islamic state from which these demands were derived. Central to the Court's response was the delineation of two antagonistic conceptions of Islam—traditional and retrogressive as opposed to progressive and modern—as noted above.

In seeking to assign responsibility for the political causes of the disturbance, the judges examined many 'ulama who had played a role in the protests. The 'ulama had to insist that their demands were solely based on religion. If they admitted to the political character of the demands, they could be held criminally responsible for the disturbances. In effect, the terms of inquiry forced the 'ulama to voice a pure doctrinal religion and prevented them from pragmatically addressing and engaging with questions of the contemporary relationship between religion and politics. In so doing, the judges foreclosed the possibility of any distinction between "Islam" and the "Islamic state" and thereby acceded to the religious parties' theological depiction of Islam as a religio-political totality. Unsurprisingly, the Jama'at-i-Islami, while contesting many other aspects of the Report, was delighted that the Court agreed with their conception of Islam. As their *Analysis* put it, "the Court itself holds the view that Islam is a religio-political system and not merely a religious system" (Ahmad 1956, p. 143). Methodologically, the judges synthetically consolidated the responses of diverse 'ulama thereby giving greater coherence and intellectual rigor to the hitherto theoretically underdeveloped notion of the "Islamic state." This double move of disabling the 'ulama's political speech and deductively constructing a theory of the state from their disparate statements led the judges to ventriloquize the 'ulama's doctrinal pronouncements. The result was to give the Court's 'ulama-inflected elaboration of the Islamic state both religious and judicial sanction.

This methodology that stressed similarities in the 'ulama's positions in order to construct a theory of the Islamic state could, however, equally be used to exaggerate their differences. This was manifest in the judges' discussion of sectarian differences that, they asserted, would inevitably lead to reciprocal and endless accusations of apostasy between the various sects. Profound sectarian differences among Muslims are one of the striking and distinctive characteristics of Islam in modern South Asia (and the sectarian orientations referenced below—Deobandi, Barelvi, Ahl-i Hadith, and Jama'at Islami—appear in several entries included in this book).

In the Court's view religious difference would invariably undermine the unity of the Muslim community and the incipient nation. This argument was all the more persuasive against the background of the riots. The differences that the Report focused on derived from a question the judges put to the various 'ulama, a question that was deceptive in its simplicity. The judges asked the clerics to define a Muslim, and they stipulated that "the definition was to be on the principle on which a term in grammar is defined" (*Report*, p.215). This was necessary, they argued, because in an Islamic state rights were to be differentially distributed on the basis of religious affiliation. Such a state would have to devise methods and procedures for distinguishing Muslims from non-Muslims.

The Report reproduced the relevant portions of transcripts in which nine leading religious scholars representing the spectrum of religious thought in Pakistan, attempted to define a "Muslim." Some sought to abide by the Court's request for a minimal definition and stated that anyone who pronounces the *kalimah* (Muslim profession of faith) and follows the example of the Holy Prophet should be considered a Muslim. The Ahmadis also stipulated the minimal conditions of professing the *kalima* and belonging to the Holy Prophet's community. Others were not quite as succinct and provided various additional requirements, such as belief in all the prophets up to Muhammad, the Day of Judgment, and angels. Still others found it impossible to enumerate all the requirements for being a Muslim or to distinguish between "Muslim" as a nominal legal identity and *Momin,* the true virtuous Muslim.

After elaborating what it regarded as a veritable panoply of religious difference and demonstrating the 'ulama's inability to agree on even a minimal definition, the Court made its much celebrated and oft reiterated comment invoking the consequences of sectarian differences, which has become a staple of secular critique, polemics, and scholarship:

> Keeping in view the several definitions given by the 'ulama, need we make any comment except that no two learnèd divines are agreed on this fundamental. If we attempt our own definition as each learnèd divine has done and that definition differs from that given by all others, we unanimously go out of the fold of Islam. And if we adopt the definition given by any one of the 'ulama, we remain Muslims according to the view of that *alim* (religious scholar), but *kafirs* according to the definition of everyone else. . . . The net result of all this is that neither Shias nor Sunnis nor Deobandis nor Ahl-i-Hadith nor Barelvis are Muslims, and any change from one view to the other must be accompanied in an Islamic State with penalty of death if the Government of the State is in the hands of the party which considers the other party to be *kafirs.* (*Report,* pp. 218–219)

Nevertheless, a cursory analysis of the 'ulama's responses demonstrates that either they did not fully understood that the language of the law required irreducible minimum conditions for the purpose of definition or, if they had, they were not equipped to translate their theological discourse (and its concern with piety) into a liberal juridical discourse (with its concern with definition and legal identity). Most of the 'ulama merely enunciated the numerous beliefs and acts required to be a virtuous Muslim subject. Nor did any one understanding necessarily exclude the others. The Jama'at-i-Islami, in its subsequent critique, noted that definitional differences were hardly unknown in politics and the social sciences, and that there was no real difference between the scholars in "the real concept and meaning of the word 'Muslim'" (Ahmad, p. 163). They contended that none of them would actually declare the definition provided by any of the others as wrong. Indeed, it would be hard to, since none of the beliefs and practices specified was controversial.

Through this strategy of confining the 'ulama to inflexible doctrinal pronouncements, of over-emphasizing certain similarities and exaggerating differences, the judges constructed an 'ulama version of the Islamic state as inflexible, intolerant, and anachronistic. However, by conflating Islam with the Islamic state they effectively conceded that the 'ulama's doctrinal understanding of Islam as a sociopolitical system was correct. By way of counter they could only express their desire that Islam become a revitalized and privatized faith for the individual; in a word, modern. Only when Islam was freed from the dead hand of clerical authority, they said, could it once again become a dynamic force in Muslim life. Thus the only choices were either to support the 'ulama's Islam or adopt the Court's secularist stance. This clear and unequivocal assertion, notwithstanding a certain textual ambivalence, remains. This is a consequence of the judge's authoritative rendering of the 'ulama's version of Islam/Islamic State as historically "real" and theologically "true" which, ironically, militated against their wish that Islam be transformed, through a secular strategy, into a modern religion.

EXCERPTS FROM THE MUNIR REPORT

THE IDEOLOGY BEHIND THE DEMANDS

With this statement of the doctrinal differences between the Musalmans and the Ahmadis and of the activities of the latter, we are in a position to understand the grounds on which the three demands were put forward. . . . And throughout the inquiry every one has taken it for granted that the demands were the result of the ideology on the strength of which the establishment of an Islamic State in Pakistan was claimed and had been promised from certain quarters. The point which must be clearly comprehended to appreciate the plausibility or otherwise of the demands is that in an Islamic State or, what is the same thing, in Islam there is a fundamental distinction between the rights of Muslim and non-Muslim subjects, and one distinction which may at once be mentioned is that the non-Muslims cannot be associated with the business of administration in the higher sphere. Therefore if the Ahmadis were not Muslim but *kafirs*, they could not occupy any of the high offices in the State, and as a deduction from this proposition, two of the demands required the dismissal of Chaudhri Zafrullah Khan and other Ahmadis who were occupying key positions in the State, and the third required the declaration of Ahmadis as a non-Muslim minority to ensure that no Ahmadi may in future be entrusted with any such position in the State. As this issue which the demands directly raised was fundamental, and of the greatest importance to the future of Pakistan, we have, with the assistance of the 'ulama gone closely into the conception of an Islamic State and its implications which we now proceed to state.

THE ISLAMIC STATE

It has been repeatedly said before us that implicit in the demand for Pakistan was the demand of an Islamic State. Some speeches of important leaders who were striving for Pakistan undoubtedly lend themselves to this construction. These leaders while referring to an Islamic State or to a State governed by Islamic Laws perhaps had in their minds the pattern of a legal structure based on or mixed up with Islamic dogma, personal law, ethics, and institutions. No one who has given serious thought to the introduction of a religious State in Pakistan has failed to notice the tremendous difficulties with which any such scheme must be confronted. . . .

Before the Partition ... the Quaid-i-Azam said that the new State would be a modern democratic State, with sovereignty resting in the people and the members of the new nation having equal rights of citizenship regardless of their religion, caste, or creed. When Pakistan formally appeared on the map, the Quaid-i-Azam in his memorable speech of 11th August 1947 to the Constituent Assembly of Pakistan, while stating the principle on which the new State was to be founded, said:

> Now, if we want to make this great State of Pakistan happy and prosperous we should wholly and solely concentrate on the well-being of the people, and specially of the masses and the poor. If you will work in cooperation, forgetting the past, burying the hatchet, you are bound to succeed. If you change your past and work together in a spirit that every one of you, no matter to what community he belongs, no matter what relations he had with you in the past, no matter what is his color, caste, or creed, is first, second and last a citizen of this State with equal rights, privileges, and obligations, there will be no end to the progress you will make. I cannot emphasize it too much. We should begin to work in that spirit and in course of time all these angularities of the majority and minority communities—the Hindu community and the Muslim community—because even as regards Muslims you have Pathans, Punjabis, Shias, Sunnis, and so on and among the Hindus you have Brahmins, Vashnavas, Khatris also Bengalis, Madrasis and so on—will vanish. Indeed if you ask me this has been the biggest hindrance in the way of India to attain its freedom and independence and but for this we would have been free peoples long ago. ... We are starting with this fundamental principle that we are all citizens and equal citizens of one State .... Now, I think we should keep that in front of us as our ideal and you will find that in course of time Hindus would cease to be Hindus and Muslims would cease to be Muslims, not in the religious sense, because that is the personal faith of each individual, but in the political sense as citizens of the State.

The Quaid-i-Azam was the founder of Pakistan, and the occasion on which he thus spoke was the first landmark in the history of Pakistan. The speech was intended both for his own people, including non-Muslims, and the world, and its object was to define as clearly as possible the ideal to the attainment of which the new state was to devote all its energies. ...

We asked the 'ulama whether this conception of a State was acceptable to them and every one of them replied in an unhesitating negative, including the Ahrar and erstwhile Congressites with whom before the Partition this conception was almost a part of their faith. If Maulana Amin Ahsan Islahi's evidence correctly represents the view of Jama'at-i-Islami, a State based on this idea is the creature of the devil, and he is confirmed in this by several writings of his chief, Maulana Abul Ala Maudoodi, the founder of the *jama'at*. None of the 'ulama can tolerate a State which is based on nationalism and all that it implies; with them *millat* and all that it connotes can alone be the determining factor in State activity.

FOUNDATIONS OF THE ISLAMIC STATE

If the true scope of the activities of the State is the welfare, temporal or spiritual or both, of the individual, then the first question directly gives rise to the bigger question: What is the object of human life and the ultimate destiny of man? On this widely divergent views have prevailed, not at different times but at one and the same time. . . . Islam emphasizes the doctrine that life in this world is not the only life given to man but that eternal life begins after the present existence comes to an end, and that the status of a human being in the next world will depend upon his beliefs and actions in this world. As the present life is not an end in itself but merely a means to an end, not only the individual but also the State, as opposed to the secular theory which bases all political and economic institutions on a disregard for their consequences on the next life, should strive for human conduct which ensures for a person better status in the next world. According to this theory Islam is the religion which seeks to attain that object. Therefore the question immediately arises: What is Islam, and who is a *momin* or a Muslim? We put this question to the *'ulama* and we shall presently refer to their answers to this question. But we cannot refrain from saying here that it was a matter of infinite regret to us that the *ulama* whose first duty should be to have settled views on this subject, were hopelessly disagreed among themselves. Apart from how these learnèd divines have expressed themselves, we conceive of Islam as a system that covers, as every systematic religion must, the following five topics:

1. the dogma, namely, the essentials of belief;
2. the cult, namely, religious rites and observances which a person must perform;
3. ethics, i.e. rules of moral conduct;
4. institutions, social, economic and political; and
5. law proper.

The essential basis of the rules on all these subjects is revelation and not reason, though both may coincide. This coincidence, however, is accidental because human reasoning may be faulty and ultimate reason is known only to God, Who sends His message to humanity through His chosen messengers for the direction and guidance of the people. One must, therefore, accept the dogma, observe the cult, follow the ethics, obey the law, and establish the institutions that God has revealed, though their reason may not be apparent—nay even if they be opposed to human reason. Since an error by God is an impossibility, anything that God has revealed, whether its subject be something occult or preternatural, history, finance, law, worship, or something which according to human thought admits of scientific treatment as for instance the birth of man, evolution, cosmology, or astronomy, has got to be accepted as absolute truth. The test of reason is not the acid test and a denial of this amounts to denial of the supreme wisdom and designs of Allah—it is *kufr*. . . .

At this stage another principle, equally basic, comes into operation, and that is that Islam is the final religion revealed by God, complete and exhaustive in all respects, and that God will not abrogate, detract from, or add to this religion (*din*) any more than He will send a fresh messenger. . . . As the ultimate test of truth, whether the matter be one of a ritual or political or social or economic nature, is revelation and revelation has to be gathered from the Qur'an and the *sunna* carries almost the same degree of inerrancy as revelation and the only evidence of *sunna* is hadith, the first duty of those who desire to establish an Islamic State will be to discover the precise rule applicable to the existing circumstances whether that rule is to be found in the Qur'an or hadith. Obviously the persons most suited for the purpose would be those who have made the Qur'an and hadith their life-long study, namely, among the Sunnies, the 'ulama, and among the Shias, the *mujtahids* who are the spokesmen of the hidden Imam, the ruler *de jure divino*. The function of these divines would be to engage themselves in discovering rules applicable to particular situations, and they will be engaged in a task similar to that in which Greek philosophers were engaged, with only this difference that whereas the latter thought that all truth lay in nature and had merely to be discovered by individual effort, the 'ulama and the *mujtahids* will have to get at the truth that lies in the holy Book and the books of hadith.

THE ESSENTIALS OF THE ISLAMIC STATE

Since the basis of Islamic law is the principle of inerrancy of revelation and of the Holy Prophet, the law to be found in the Qur'an and the *sunna* is above all man-made laws, and in case of conflict between the two, the latter irrespective of its nature, must yield to the former. . . . Therefore if Pakistan is or is intended to be converted into an Islamic State in the true sense of the word, its Constitution must contain the following five provisions:

1. that all laws to be found in the Qur'an or the Sunna shall be deemed to be a part of the law of the land for Muslims and shall be enforced accordingly;
2. that unless the Constitution itself is framed by *ijma-i-ummat*, namely by the agreement of the 'ulama and *mujtahids* of acknowledged status, any provision in the Constitution which is repugnant to the Qur'an or *sunna* shall to the extent of the repugnancy be void;
3. that unless the existing laws of Pakistan are adapted by *ijma-i-ummat* of the kind mentioned above, any provision in the existing law which is contrary to the Qur'an or *sunna* shall to the extent of the repugnancy be void;
4. that any provision in any future law which is repugnant to Qur'an or *sunna* shall be void.

5. that no rule or International Law and no provision in any convention or treaty to which Pakistan is a party, which is contrary to the Qur'an or the *sunna* shall be binding on any Muslim in Pakistan.

SOVEREIGNTY AND DEMOCRACY IN THE ISLAMIC STATE

That the form of Government in Pakistan, if that form is to comply with the principles of Islam, will not be democratic is conceded by the 'ulama. . . . When it is said that a country is sovereign, the implication is that its people or any other group of persons in it are entitled to conduct the affairs of that country in any way they like and untrammeled by any considerations except those of expediency and policy. An Islamic state, however, cannot in this sense be sovereign, because it will not be competent to abrogate, repeal, or do away with any law in the Qur'an or the *sunna*. Absolute restriction on the legislative power of a state is a restriction on the sovereignty of the people of that state and if the origin of this restriction lies elsewhere than in the will of the people, then to the extent of that restriction the sovereignty of the State and its people is necessarily taken away. In an Islamic State sovereignty, in its essentially juristic sense, can only rest with Allah. In the same way, democracy means the rule of the *demos*, namely the people, directly by them as in ancient Greece and Rome, or indirectly through chosen representatives as in modern democracies. If the power of the people in the framing of the Constitution or in the framing of the laws or in the sphere of executive action is subject to certain immutable rules, it can not be said that they can pass any law that they like, or in the exercise of executive functions, do whatever they like. Indeed, if the legislature in an Islamic State is a sort of *ijma*, the masses are expressly disqualified from taking part in it because *ijma-i-ummat* in Islamic jurisprudence is restricted to 'ulama and *mujtahids* of acknowledged status and does not at all extend, as in democracy, to the populace.

OTHER INCIDENTS OF THE ISLAMIC STATE ACCORDING TO 'ULAMA

In the preceding pages we have attempted to state as clearly as we could the principles on which a religious state must be built if it is to be called an Islamic state. We now proceed to state some incidents of such State, with particular reference to the *ulama's* conception of it.

LEGISLATURE AND LEGISLATION

Legislature in its present sense is unknown to the Islamic system. The religio-political system, which is called *din-i-Islam,* is a complete system that contains in itself the mechanism for discovering and applying law to any situation that may arise. During the Islamic Republic [the period of the early caliphate] there was no legislature in its modern sense, and for every situation or emergency that arose law could be discovered and applied by the 'ulama. The law had been made and was not to be made, the only function of those entrusted with the administration of law being to discover the law for the purposes of the particular case, though when enunciated and applied it formed a precedent for others to follow . . . .

Since Islam is a perfect religion containing laws, express or derivable by *ijma* or *ijtihad*, governing the whole field of human activity, there is in it no sanction for what may in the modern sense be called legislation. Questioned on this point Maulana Abul Hasanat, President, Jamiat-ul-ulama-i-Pakistan says:

Q. Is the institution of legislature as distinguished from institution of a person or body of persons entrusted with the interpretation of law, an integral part of an Islamic State?

A. No. Our law is complete and merely requires interpretation by those who are experts in it. According to my belief no question can arise in law which cannot be discovered from the Qur'an or the hadith.

Maulana Abul Ala Maudoodi, however, is of the opinion that legislation in the true sense is possible in an Islamic state on matters which are not covered by the Qur'an, the *sunna*, or previous *ijma*, and he has attempted to explain his point by reference to the institution of a body of persons whom the Holy Prophet, and after him the *khulafa* (caliphs) consulted on all matters relating to affairs of State. The question is one of some difficulty and great importance because any institution of legislature will have to be reconciled with the claim put forward by Maulana Abul Hasanat and some other religious divines that Islam is a perfect and exhaustive code wide enough to furnish an answer to any question that may arise relating to any human activity and that it does not know of any "unoccupied field" to be filled by fresh legislation. There is no doubt that Islam enjoins consultation and that not only the Holy Prophet but also the first four caliphs and even their successors resorted to consultation with the leading men of the time, who for their knowledge of the law and piety could well be relied upon. In the inquiry not much has been disclosed about the Majlis-i-Shura (consultative council) except what is contained in Maulana Abul Ala Maudoodi's written statement which he supplied to the Court at its request. That there was a body of men who were consulted is true, but whether this was a standing body and whether its advice had any legal or binding force, seems somewhat doubtful. These men were certainly not elected in the modern way, though their representative character cannot be disputed. Their advice was certainly asked *ad hoc*, but that they were competent to make law as the modern legislatures make laws is certainly not correct. The decisions taken by them undoubtedly served as precedents and were in the nature of *ijma*, which is not legislation but the application of an existing law to a particular case. When consulted in affairs of State, their functions were truly in the nature of an advice given by a modern cabinet, but such advice is not law but only a decision.

Nor can the legislature in a modern state correspond to *ijma* because, as we have already pointed out, the legislature legislates while the 'ulama of Majlis-i-Shura, who were called upon to determine what should be the decision on a particular point which was not covered by the Qur'an and the *sunna*, merely sought to discover and apply the law and not promulgate the law, though the decision when taken had to be taken not only for the purpose of the particular case but for subsequent occasions as a binding precedent. An intriguing situation might arise if the Constitution Act provided that any provision of it, if it was inconsistent with the Qur'an or the *sunna* would be void, and the *intra vires* ["within the powers," Latin] of a law made by the legislature were questioned before the Supreme Court on the ground that the institution of legislature itself was contrary to the Qur'an and the *sunna*.

THE POSITION OF NON-MUSLIMS

The ground on which the removal of Chaudhri Zafrullah Khan and other Ahmadis occupying key positions in the State is demanded is that the Ahmadis are non-Muslims and that therefore like *zimmies* in an Islamic state they are not eligible for appointment to higher offices in the State. This aspect of the demands has directly raised a question about the position of non-Muslims in Pakistan if we are to have an Islamic Constitution. According to the leading 'ulama, the position of non-Muslim in the Islamic state of Pakistan will be that of *zimmies*, and they will not be full citizens of Pakistan because they will not have the same rights as Muslims. They will have no voice in the making of the law. No right to administer the law and no right to hold public offices. . . .

During the Islamic Republic, the head of the state, the *khalifa*, was chosen by a system of election, which was wholly different from the present system of election based on adult or any other form of popular suffrage. The oath of allegiance (*ba'it*) rendered to him possessed a sacramental virtue, and on his being chosen by the consensus of the people (*ijma ul ummat*) he became the source of all channels of legitimate Government. He and he alone then was competent to rule, though he could delegate his powers to deputies and collect around him a body of men of outstanding piety and learning, called *Majlis-i-Shura* or *Ahl-ul-Hall-wal-Aqd*. The principal feature of this system was that the *kuffar*, for reasons which are too obvious and need not be stated, could not be admitted to this *majlis*, and the power which had vested in the *khalifa* could not be delegated to the *kuffar*. The *khalifa* was the real head of the State, all powers vesting in him and not a powerless individual like the President of a modern democratic state who is merely to sign the record of decisions taken by the Prime Minister and his Cabinet. He could not appoint non-Muslims to important posts and could give them no place either in the interpretation or the administration of the law, the making of the law by them as already pointed out, being a legal impossibility.

This being the position, the State will have to devise some machinery by which the distinction between a Muslim and non-Muslim may be determined and its consequences enforced. The question, therefore, whether a person is or is not a Muslim will be of fundamental importance, and it was for this reason that we asked most of the leading 'ulama to give their definition of a Muslim, the point being that if the 'ulama of the various sects believed the Ahmadis to be *kafirs*, they must have been quite clear in their minds not only about the grounds of such belief but also about the definition of "Muslim," because the claim that a certain person or community is not within the pale of Islam implies on the part of the claimant an exact conception of what a Muslim is. The result of this part of the inquiry, however, has been anything but satisfactory, and if considerable confusion exists in the minds of our 'ulama on such a simple matter, one can easily imagine what the difference on more complicated matters will be. . . . This definition was asked after it had been clearly explained to each witness that he was required to give the irreducible minimum conditions which a person must satisfy to be entitled to be called a Muslim and that the definition was to be on the principle on which a term in grammar is defined. . . .

Keeping in view the several definitions given by the 'ulama, need we make any comment except that no two learnèd divines are agreed on this fundamental. If we attempt our own definition as each learnèd divine has done and that definition differs from that given by all others, we unanimously go out of the fold of Islam. And if we adopt the definition given by any one of the 'ulama, we remain Muslims according to the view of that *alim* but *kafirs* according to the definition of everyone else.

APOSTASY

Apostasy in an Islamic State is punishable with death. On this the 'ulama are particularly unanimous. . . . The net result of all this is that neither Shias nor Sunnis nor Deobandis nor Ahl-i-Hadith nor Barelvis are Muslim, and any change from one view to the other must be accompanied in an Islamic State with the penalty of death if the Government of the State is in the hands of the party which considers the other party to be *kafirs*. And it does not require much imagination to judge of the consequences of this doctrine when it is remembered that no two 'ulama have agreed before us as to the definition of a Muslim . . . [and that] . . . the death penalty for *irtidad* (apostasy) has implications of a far-reaching character and stamps Islam as a religion of fanatics, which punishes all independent thinking. The Qur'an again and again lays emphasis on reason and thought, advises toleration and preaches against compulsion in religious matters, but the doctrine of *irtidad* as enunciated . . . strikes at the very root of independent thinking when it propounds the view that anyone who being born a Muslim or having embraced Islam, attempts to think on the subject of religion with a view, if he comes to that conclusion, to choose for himself any religion he likes has the capital penalty in store for him. With this implication Islam becomes an embodiment of complete intellectual paralysis. . . .

―――――

We have dwelt at some length on the subject of Islamic State not because we intended to write a thesis against or in favor of such State but merely with a view to presenting a clear picture of the numerous possibilities that may in future arise if true causes of the ideological confusion which contributed to the spread and intensity of the disturbances are not precisely located. That such confusion did exist is obvious because otherwise Muslim Leaguers, whose own Government was in office, would not have risen against it; sense of loyalty and public duty would not have departed from public officials who went about like maniacs howling against their own Government and officers; respect for property and human life would not have disappeared in the common man who with no scruple or compunction began freely to indulge in loot, arson and murder; politicians would not have shirked facing the men who had installed them in their offices; and administrators would not have felt hesitant or diffident in performing what was their obvious duty. If there is one thing that has been conclusively demonstrated in this inquiry, it is that provided you can persuade the masses to believe that something they are asked to do is religiously right or enjoined by religion, you can set them to any course of action, regardless of all considerations of discipline, loyalty, decency, morality, or civic sense.

Pakistan is being taken by the common man, though it is not, as an Islamic State. This belief has been encouraged by the ceaseless clamor for Islam and Islamic State that is being heard from all quarters since the establishment of Pakistan. The Phantom of an Islamic State has haunted the Musalman throughout the ages and is a result of the memory of the glorious past when Islam rising like a storm from the least expected quarter of the world—the wilds of Arabia—instantly enveloped the world, pulling down from their high pedestal gods who had ruled over man since the creation, uprooting centuries old institutions and superstitions and supplanting all civilizations that had been built on an enslaved humanity. What is one hundred and twenty-five years in human history, nay in the history of a people? And yet during this brief period Islam spread from the Indus to the Atlantic and Spain, and from the borders of China to Egypt, and the sons of the desert installed themselves in all old centers of civilization—in Ctesiphon, Damascus, Alexandria, India, and all places associated with names of the Sumerian and the Assyrian civilizations. Historians have often posed the question, what would have been the state of the world today if Muawiya's siege of Constantinople had succeeded or if the proverbial Arab instinct for plunder had not suddenly seized the *mujahids* of Abdur Rahman in their fight against Charles Martel on the plains of Tours in Southern France. Maybe Muslims would have discovered America long before Columbus did and the entire world would have been Moslemized; maybe Islam itself would have been Europeanized. It is this brilliant achievement of the Arabian nomads, the like of which the world had never seen before, that makes the Musalman of today live in the past and yearn for the return of the glory that was Islam. He finds himself standing on the crossroads, wrapped in the mantle of the past and with the dead weight of centuries on his back, frustrated and bewildered and hesitant to turn one corner or the other. The freshness and the simplicity of the faith, which gave determination to his mind and spring to his muscle, are now denied to him. He has neither the means nor the ability to conquer, and there are no countries to conquer. Little does he understand that the forces which are pitted against him are entirely different from those against which early Islam had to fight, and that on the clues given his own ancestors human mind has achieved results which he cannot understand. He therefore finds himself in state of helplessness, waiting for someone to come and help him out of this morass of uncertainty and confusion. And he will go on waiting like this without anything happening. Nothing but a bold re-orientation of Islam to separate the vital from the lifeless can preserve it as a World Idea and convert the Musalman into a citizen of the present and the future world from the archaic incongruity that he is today. . . .

The sublime faith called Islam will live even if our leaders are not there to enforce it. It lives in the individual, in his soul and outlook, in all his relations with God and men from the cradle to the grave, and our politicians should understand that if Divine commands cannot make or keep a man a Musalman, their statutes will not.

Sources

Excerpts in this essay were edited from *The Report of the Court of Inquiry into the Punjab Disturbances of 1953* (Lahore: Government Printing Press, 1954), pp. 200– 220, 231–232.

Further Reading

For an account of the anti-Ahmadi riots and their aftermath, see Leonard Binder, *Religion and Politics in Pakistan* (Berkeley, CA: University of California Press, 1963). On Maudoodi's conceptualization of Islam as ideology, see Seyyed V. R. Nasr, *Mawdudi and the Making of Islamic Revivalism* (New York: Oxford University Press, 1996). The Jama'at-i Islami's critique of the Munir Report can be found in Khursid Ahmad, ed., *An Analysis of the Munir Report* (Karachi: Jamaat-i-Islami Publications, Herald Press, 1956). For an account of Ahmadi theology and history, see Yohanan Friedmann, *Prophecy Continuous: Aspects of Ahmadi Religious Thought and Its Medieval Background* (Berkeley, CA: University of California Press, 1989); and Spencer Lavan, *The Ahmadiyah Movement* (New Delhi: Manohar, 1974).

Maulana Yusuf Ludhianvi on the Limits
of Legitimate Religious Differences

Naveeda Khan

Maulana Muhammad Yusuf Ludhianvi (1932–2000) was a well known, some would say infamous, scholar, jurist, author, and political leader based in Pakistan and associated with the Deobandi *maslak* (path), a denomination discussed in several of the preceding chapters (especially Chapter 17). Maulana Ludhianvi taught at the famous Binori Town madrasa in Karachi and wrote a Q&A column in the national Urdu daily *Jang* for over a decade. He was a leading figure in the Alami Majlis-i Tahaffuz-i Khatam-i Nabuwwat (International Committee for the Protection of the Finality of Prophethood), an international outfit that reported on and targeted the activities of the Ahmadiyya movement, the subject of the Munir report of 1954 (see Chapter 32) and ultimately the target of a 1974 constitutional amendment defining members of the group as non-Muslim. Later Maulana Ludhianvi became well known for his anti-Shia polemics and activities. On May 18, 2000, he was ambushed and killed by persons unknown in Karachi, a possible victim of the two decade long Shia-Sunni conflict in Pakistan. His death coincided with efforts by the then military government of General Pervez Musharraf to introduce certain procedural changes in the infamous Blasphemy Law (Section 295-C) within the Pakistan Penal Code, which would have limited the ease of application of the law. The crowds that gathered nationwide to mourn the death of Maulana Yusuf Ludhianvi protested these changes in his name, successfully staying the course of the government.

The translations below are of a letter inquiring into legitimate religious differences within the Muslim community (*ummah*), which was sent to Maulana Muhammad Yusuf Ludhianvi, and of Maulana Ludhianavi's letter written in reply to the query. These form part of the introduction to a well-known and oft-published book titled *Differences within the Community and the Right Path* (1995), written by the Maulana himself, who explains that the naïve ignorance displayed in the letter of inquiry was the motivating factor for his writing the book. The subtitle of the book is "Part One, in which, through the correct pointing out of the straight path, the differences within the Shia, Sunni, Hanafi, Deobandi, Barelwi, and Maududi sects (*firqa*) as displayed in their texts are reviewed in light of the *sunnah* (the prophetic tradition)."

The 1954 Munir Report provided us a picture of the 'ulama as fractious and divided (see Chapter 32). This internal divisiveness was the reason forwarded by the judges who authored the report for discounting the speech and, therefore, the participation of the 'ulama in any state-building projects. Yet, it can be argued, the Report misrepresents the 'ulama in that it takes differences in opinion to amount to disagreement over a form of life. The phrase "forms of life" (following the anthropologist Veena Das) captures both the diversity of social life—that is, "forms" of life—as well as the upper and lower limits of what is considered human within a given society—that is, forms of "life." If we attend closely to the language of the 'ulama within the Munir Report we see that irrespective of their differences in opinion in no way would they discount one another's claim to be a Muslim, even if they may view the other to be misguided or ignorant. Furthermore, their language captures something like an agreement over what constitutes the form of "life" within their society, that is, the upper and lower limits of what it is to be both human *and* Muslim. The definition of these limits allows for the exclusion of Ahmadis, and possibly the Shias, from the community of Muslims and underwrites violence against them, at least in the case of Pakistan.

To see how such exclusion is enacted, one can usefully follow the distinction that Maulana Yusuf Ludhianvi draws between *ijtihadi ikhtilaf* (interpretive difference) and *nazariyati ikhtilaf* (ideological difference). We see how the first coincides with differences in opinion and is, as he says, a blessing to the community. The second, however, may exceed the outer limits of what it is to be human; for instance, he writes that the person who has been bitten by ideological difference descends to non-human behavior himself and cannot concede flesh-and-bloodedness to others. Here we see how a person drops out of the human race or, as Maulauna Ludhianvi suggests, ceases being human on account of holding not simply erroneous but potentially fatal ideological positions.

Maulana Ludhianvi not only distinguishes between interpretative and ideological differences but also seeks to differentiate correct shades of opinion from false. He does so to delimit the scope of disputation. Above all, his repetitive insistence upon the singularity of the Prophet and his Companions does not simply re-inscribe Sunni normative perspectives but is also aimed against the Ahmadis and Shias, who are said to compromise the Prophet Muhammad's uniqueness by their elevation of the founder of the Ahmadiyya movement and the Shi'i imams, respectively. He also excludes Sunnis who do not value the historical schools (*mazhab*) of Sunni jurisprudence and the traditions of commentary based on them. These include the modernists (from Saiyid Ahmad Khan to Iqbal), as well as the Ahl-i Hadith ("Salafis") and the Islamists (above all those of Maududi's Jama'at-i Islami). Thus the only groups within the limits of legitimate differences of opinion are Deobandis such as himself and "Barelwis," including presumably those mentioned in the query, who follow the practices he labels as *shirk* (associationism). Thus his writings give expression to a central paradox within public religious life in Pakistan in which arguments in favor of transcending sectarian divides, or at least delimiting the scope of disputation, have gone hand in hand with increased sectarian divisiveness.

However, there is more to texts like this than their obvious polemical intent and the support they provide to sectarian division, even possibly to violence. Such texts evince sophistication in understanding the dynamics of everyday life; in particular, tensions within inter-subjective relations, and the frailties of the human spirit. The excerpt below demonstrates the problem of difference as not just an issue in religious life but as intrinsic to modern existence. Maulana Yusuf Ludhianvi's suspicion of public enthusiasm for religious debate and disputation, and his fear that those who engage in such not only risk their mind and body but their human-ness, suggests his intuition that in modern life one continually flirts with skepticism towards one's own existence and that of others. In speaking of religious doubt, Ludhianvi gestures toward the specter of modern skepticism in the lines describing the state of the person lost in his own ideological point of view, to whom the whole world appears to be one of bad fiction, living as though everything and everyone is unreal. This is not an uncommon description of modern life lived under the deluge of media, for instance. The question that I pose to the readership, but which remains unanswered is: Do we have the intellectual and spiritual resources to take on such polemical texts in all their vitality, inclusive of both their attunement towards alienation in modern life and their pernicious effects on mutual co-existence within that life?

LETTER TO MAULANA MUHAMMAD YUSUF LUDHIANVI

In the name of God, the Compassionate, the Merciful

Most Venerable Maulana Sahib! Many best respects! My own brother, my cousin brother, five uncles and many of our closest relatives including myself have been residing in Dubai and Sharjah for a long time. All, except for one or two of us, are strict in the performance of our prayers and spend much of our free time occupied in lengthy religious reflection and judgment, debate and disputation. Most of us are educated and maintain some learning in religious issues as well. Almost all of us have books written by various great 'ulama espousing different religious tenets (*aqai'd*, pl. of *aqidah*), which we study closely. Our close kinship is equalled only by our religious differences. We bitterly carp at each other's religious tenets, just as others do in our beloved homeland. We criticize each other's favored great 'ulama, holding forth on their imperfections. The majority of us subscribe to the Sunni tenets of those who call themselves the true lovers of the Messenger (Peace be upon Him [hereafter, PBUH]), and thus imagine themselves to be the most favored (just as in Pakistan these days Noorani Mian Sahib [Maulana Shah Ahmed Noorani, d. 2003] considers himself or rather his party [the Jamiat-i-Ulama-i-Pakistan] [another] "Mecca" [*sawaad-i azam*]. The remaining few maintain relations with those sects in which they only perform the obligatory prayers in imitation of the Arabs, and they cite as their proof the fact that since Islam originated in this area these people are in the right. There is even one such "group" amongst us who claim that Maulana Maududi Sahib is the only learnèd scholar in Pakistan. They further claim that saying the *fatiha* [the first chapter of the Qur'an] during *ziarat* [visitation of the graves of saints], doing *gyarhawin* [commemorative rituals] for Hazrat Ghawth Pak (Divine blessing be upon him) and doing *khatam sharif* [recitation of the Qur'an] are all *shirk*, etc. At any rate, whenever all of us debate an issue, I am made the mediator because I never speak ill of any sect or of any scholar. As a result, my companions happily accept my decision, and we are able to reach somewhat of a conclusion in our debates. However, there are some questions that I am not able to solve on account of not having sufficient knowledge. As I follow your column in *Jang* [the Urdu daily] quite closely, I have taken the advice of all my companions in posing to you a few urgent problems (*masa'il*) upon which we have not as of yet reached an agreement:

1. What are the differences in religious tenets among the Sunni, Shia, Deobandi, Barelwi, and Wahhabi sects? What is the discord amongst them? Which amongst them is the best, and how many sects are there within that one? Please provide us the titles of books of respected imams.

2. How correct is it to perform only the obligatory portions of the prayer? I asked a *khatib sahib* [one who delivers the Friday sermon], an Egyptian, who is well regarded here, "Why do you undertake only two *rakat farz* [obligatory rotation within the prayer] during the Friday prayers when there are *sunnat* (recommended) and *nafal* (supererogatory) *rakat* (rotations) as well?" This was his reply: "The house of the Messenger of God (PBUH) was at the door of The Mosque of the Prophet (PBUH). He would get up from his house, go to the mosque and perform two *rakat* along with the congregation there, whereupon he would return to his house. No one knows what he would do once he returned to his house. For this reason I simply follow the *sunnah* (way) of the Prophet (PBUH)."

    Kindly write in detail about this problem, shedding light upon whether the *khatib sahib* is correct or not? If not, please inform us what is correct.

3. Is it *shirk* to say the *fatiha* during *ziarat*, do *gyarhawin* and have *khatam sharif* (Qur'anic recitation) or recitation of God's name (*zikr*) towards asking for someone's absolution? Please clarify this problem with reference to the Qur'an and *sunnah*.

It is our submission that your answer can change our lives because we have all reached a decision to act upon whatever you write with reference to the Qur'an and *sunnah*. That is why in all your kindness please show us a straight path.

Your well-wisher,
Muhammad Karim, Dubai (UAE)

MAULANA MUHAMMAD YUSUF LUDHIANVI'S REPLY

The pleasure that you and your companions espouse in religion (*din*) is worthy of congratulations. However, it is my advice that you turn this face of pleasure from debate and disputation towards learning and teaching about religion, towards recasting yourself in accordance with the practical debts you owe your religion and towards bringing our Prophet (PBUH), his felicitous way, into your life and that of others. This request of mine is based upon two reasons. One reason is that debate and disputation depletes a man's vigor in undertaking practice. It is our Prophet (PBUH)'s excellent instruction, duly attributed in Ahmed, Tirmizi, Ibn Maja and different authoritative books [hadith collections], that:

> The gift of wrangling is given to that nation (*qaum*) that has strayed.

If so, a nation's entanglement in disputatiousness and wrangling cannot be said to be a good omen for it.

The second reason is that during debate and disputation it is commonly the case that the passion to understand another and to make oneself understood is subdued, overpowered by the passion to have everyone agree only with you. Particularly when a person is not fully acquainted with the knowledge of the *shari'ah* they are unable to properly uphold the punitive aspects of it. It is often times the case that something is wrong and unjust (*na haqq*), but the disputant will try to prove that it is just. It is also often times the case that during debate and disputation the disputant may find fault with God's favored servants, and through such extended and uncalled for censure, blacken his own account. All these factors together will not only deprive him of the passion for religious practice but they will also weaken the capacity of the structure of his mind to accept the truth. For these reasons my brief advice to you, gentlemen, is that each of you immerse yourself in religious works in accordance with the instructions of the religious scholar whom you trust and sincerely believe to be a God-fearing and true scholar who spreads the message of God and the instructions of our Prophet (PBUH) amongst the people only for the sake of God's pleasure. And instead of wasting your time in debate and disputation, keep yourselves preoccupied in remembrance and recitation of God's names (*zikr o tasbih*), *durud sharif* (praise of the Prophet), recitation of the glorious Qur'an, and other pious works.

Although your first question is brief, its response would be the subject of a bulky book. This worthless person has neither capacity nor leisure to do what is right in writing such a book. Nevertheless, I write a few lines to satisfy your request. It will be this worthless person's good fortune if these lines bring profit to you and your friends or else:

> Worthless merchandise is returned!
> [Persian: "Bad goods are before the master's beard."]

We should first acquaint ourselves with what is "the rightful religion" (*din-i haqq*) to be used as our measure against which to evaluate which sect is rightful or close to rightful. I, you, and every Muslim knows that "the rightful religion" is that divine message from God which our Prophet (PBUH) brought to us, upheld by the Prophet (PBUH) and his Companions (*sahaba*) under the Prophet (PBUH)'s own supervision, and which God has vowed to protect till the Day of Resurrection (*qiyamat*). God has secured this rightful religion in the countenance of the glorious Qur'an, the commands of our Prophet (PBUH), the practice of the great Companions (With whom God is pleased), and the exposition of the interpretive jurists (*a'ima mujtahidin*). Thanks be to God that these are still securely available to our community as though this religion was revealed in our present age.

The second thing that is necessary for us to understand is that two kinds of differences have emerged within the community. Our Prophet (PBUH) had been informed of both kinds of differences and he advised the community accordingly.

The first kind of difference emerged over those problems requiring *ijtihad* (interpretation) among the Companions (With whom God is pleased) and the generation directly after them (Divine blessing be upon them), the interpretive jurists who are famous under the names of Hanafi, Shafii, Maliki and Hanbali. This kind of difference sometimes used to come to light during the blessed era of our Prophet (PBUH). For example, on one occasion the Prophet (PBUH) bid his Companions (With whom God is pleased) to reach the settlement of the Banu Kuraiz, giving them the following instruction:

> Let no man amongst you say the '*asr* (late afternoon) prayer until you reach Banu Kuraiz [in Arabic and Urdu]

By chance the Companions (With whom God is pleased) were delayed in reaching the settlement and the time for the '*asr* prayer was waning. So the Companions (With whom God is pleased) consulted one another as to what should be done. During the consultation, two groups emerged. It was the opinion of one group that if the Prophet (PBUH) had clearly ordered that the '*asr* prayer not be said before reaching Banu Kuraiz, then they had no authority to say the prayer on the way. For this reason, and regardless of the fact that the prayer fell wanting, it was important to implement the Prophet (PBUH)'s instructions. Now it was the opinion of the second group that the blessed intention of this order was that they should reach Banu Kuraiz before the time for the '*asr* prayer and say the prayer there. But since they were not going to be able to arrive there before sunset, there was no point leaving the prayer wanting. "Although we have been delayed in reaching there, it does not necessarily follow that we should leave our prayer wanting, thus adding further to our deficiency." In short, the first group agreed to fall short on their prayer in order to implement the Prophet (PBUH)'s command and would not be diverted from the explicit form of the Prophet (PBUH)'s command. But the second group thought it best to implement the intention behind the Prophet (PBUH)'s command. They stopped along the way to perform their 'asr prayer and then continued on to Banu Kuraiz. When this event was presented in the divan of the Prophet (PBUH), our Prophet (PBUH) did not reprimand any one group; rather he considered them both worthy of approval as each had struggled to implement the Prophet (PBUH)'s intention. Many such examples may be found.

In a word, there is therefore one kind of difference that can be called "interpretative (ijtihadi) difference." This difference is not only natural and inescapable, rather it is considered a "blessing" and the person who has been granted even the slightest light of intelligence will see that this is so. Time permitting, I would have shed more light upon this kind of difference. All said, this difference is completely correct. The command regarding this form of difference is that one act upon the interpretations of the jurist in whom one has confidence and that one view with regard and courtesy the remaining wise men because these gentlemen were both religious experts of the highest level and internal devotees of God. There is no one among those who have come after them who can either be their equal in scholarship or in insight (ma'rifat). This is the reason why men of stature amongst the saints of God, for example, Hazrat Pir of all Pirs Syed Shaykh 'Abd al-Qadir Gilani (Blessed of God), Sayyid Hazrat Junayd Baghdadi (Blessed of God), Shaykh Muhyi al-Din Ibn al-'Arabi (Blessed of God), Khwaja 'Ali Hujwiri (Blessed of God), Ganj Baksh Farid al-Din Shakharganj (Blessed of God), were all followers of these interpretive imams.

The second kind of difference is known as "ideological difference" and this is the subject of your query. Our Prophet (PBUH) also forecast this kind of difference and he set up the standard to distinguish truth from falsehood within it. Consequently, the advice of the Prophet (PBUH) is:

> The Banu Israel split into seventy-two sects and my community will split into seventy-three sects. All of them except for one will go to Hell. He was asked: Oh Messenger of God (PBUH), which is the sect which is to get salvation? He declared it to be those people who stay the course on which I am and my Companions (With whom God is pleased).

There is one more hadith:

> Seventy-two will go to hell and one to heaven. And this one will be that party (jamaat), that is, the party that is in the right. Other people will emerge amongst whom desires and wrongful ideologies are as widespread as in the constitution of a man bitten by a rabid dog, whose disease contaminates his every joint, and every vein and fiber.

There is another hadith:

> Those men who outlive my era will see many differences emerge. You should grip tightly with your teeth onto my ways and those of the duly instructed Rightfully Guided Caliphs [a point of difference with the Shia] (With whom

God is pleased)! And see that you guard against those sayings that are newly invented because everything that is invented (in the name of religion) is reprehensible innovation (*bidat*) and every *bidat* is error.

In yet another hadith, our Prophet (PBUH) drew a line and declared: "This is God's path." Then he drew some branches to the right and left of the line and declared: "These are those paths upon each of which sits a Satan tempting people to their paths by saying that this is the right path." After that our Prophet (PBUH) recited the following verse from the glorious Qur'an:

This is my straight path. Just continue on it.

(All of the above are to be found in the *Mishkat* hadith collection.)

There are many other instances of such advice from our Prophet (PBUH). However it is neither possible nor necessary for me to gather them. These sacred commands very clearly inform us of the following points:

1. Our Prophet (PBUH) forecast the emergence of ideological differences.
2. This kind of difference was declared to be not to his liking and other than one party he threatened the rest with hell.
3. To reach the right and wrong within this kind of difference the Prophet declared the following as the standard measure: That person or group that follows in the ways brought by our Prophet (PBUH) and that was followed by the noble Companions (With whom God is pleased), is in the right, and those who proceed against this standard are in the wrong. Consequently the right standard is the path of the Prophet (PBUH) and his Companions (With whom God is pleased). . . .
4. The Prophet (PBUH) declared as reprehensible innovation all those actions and instructions that were invented in the name of religion.
5. The Prophet (PBUH) also detailed the disease arising from the invention of such innovation, namely that of following wrongful desires. . . .
6. Our Prophet (PBUH) has instructed the community during the appearance of these differences to keep strong and steadfast in the observance of the Prophet (PBUH) and the Rightfully Guided Caliphs (With whom God is pleased). To be guided by their instructions is to be above doubt and suspicion. Firmly hold on to the right path with your canine teeth such that should thousands of gales of innovation and desire blow, and hundreds and thousands of flashes of lightning of new and seemingly beautiful ideologies flash, this firm relationship within the grasp of the community ought not to break loose.
7. The Prophet (PBUH) has also said that the path of God is that one held on to by the Prophet (PBUH) and that has also been traveled by the Companions (With whom God is pleased). Except for this path, all else is invented by the Satan and any person who gives invitation to these paths is an "agent" of Satan, or is rather an incarnation of Satan. Any person who leaves the straight path shown by God and sets off on these other paths

then he should know that he is heading to a dark cave, to the mouth of sorcery, and will undoubtedly become the food of some stray sheep in a desolate desert.

As these principles and tenets are mentioned in the Qur'an and in the hadith, and can be cast into the mind, then it should not be difficult for a person of intelligence to understand which of the sects of the ones you mentioned are in the right.

Sources

These excerpts were translated from Maulana Muhammad Yusuf Ludhianvi's *Ikhtilaf-i Ummat awr Sirat-i Mustaqeem* (Differences within the Community and the Right Path) (Karachi: Maktab-i Ludhianvi, 1995).

Further Reading

For a historical background on the Deobandi movement, see Barbara D. Metcalf, *Islamic Revival in British India: Deoband, 1860–1900* (Princeton, NJ: Princeton University Press, 1982). For a description of the Barelwi movement, see Usha Sanyal, *Devotional Islam and Politics in British India: Ahmed Riza Khan Barelwi and His Movement* (Delhi: Oxford University Press, 1996). An intellectual background on the Ahmadiyya movement can be found in Yohanan Friedmann, *Prophecy Continuous* (Berkeley, CA: University of California Press, 1989). A good overview of the rise of Mawdudi's Jama'at-i Islami is available in Seyyed Vali Nasr, *Mawdudi and the Making of Islamic Revivalism* (New York: Oxford University Press, 1996). For a discussion of the Ahl-i Hadith in South Asian religious politics, see Daniel Brown, *Rethinking Tradition in Modern Islamic Thought* (Cambridge: Cambridge University Press, 1996). A discussion of Shia-Sunni relations in Pakistan is available in Muhammad Qasim Zaman, *The Ulama in Contemporary Islam: Custodians of Change* (Princeton, NJ: Princeton University Press, 2002). Kenneth Jones, *Religious Controversy in British India: South Asian Dialogues* (Albany: State University of New York Press, 1992) explores the changing contours of religious disputation in colonial India. See Naveeda Khan, "Of Children and *Jinn*: An Inquiry in an Unexpected Friendship during Uncertain Times," in *Cultural Anthropology* 21(2) 2006: 234–264, for a discussion of the relationship between sectarian differences and everyday life.

— 34 —

The Indian Jama'at-i Islami Reconsiders
Secular Democracy

Irfan Ahmad

Most studies of Islamic movements focus on "Islamist" parties in the mostly undemocratic, Muslim-majority societies of the Middle East, the so-called heartland of Islam. Such studies typically contend that "Islam" is opposed to secular democracy and that Islamic movements are inhospitable to change. The experience of the foremost Islamist movement in the secular democracy of India makes plain, however, that the nature of the polity in which a movement operates makes a decisive difference. The history of that movement, the Jama'at-i Islami Hind ("Islamic Party of India," hereafter "Jama'at") further makes clear that far from being hostile to change, an Islamist movement can, in fact, undergo fundamental transformation.

The two selections below are intended to demonstrate the substantial ideological transformation the Jama'at has undergone since Partition on the issue of secular democracy. The first selection is from a collection of responses by Maulana Maududi to a set of questions posed by the readers of his journal *Tarjumanul Koran*, published on the eve of independence in 1945. It depicts the Jama'at's uncompromising opposition, at that time, to secularism and democracy. It shows that the Jama'at considered it to be an open violation of *shari'a*, the divine Islamic law, as well as of monotheism itself, to participate in elections and accept employment in what it called an "infidel (*kafirana*) state." This was the position at the time of the founding of the Jama'at in 1941. Jama'at continued to adhere strictly to this position throughout the 1950s and 1960s. From the early 1960s on, however, there began to be an internal debate about whether or not it should continue to characterize secular democracy as *haram* (religiously forbidden). The debate—intensely fierce and continued over two decades—was eventually resolved in 1985 with the decision to take part in elections. The second selection, from the published proceedings of the meeting of the consultative council of the Jama'at in 1985, shows the Jama'at's acceptance of secular democracy and its decision to allow its members to participate in the elections of the national parliament and state assemblies.

Like many of his contemporaries, Syed Abul Ala Maududi (1903–1979), the founder of the Jama'at, was concerned with the fall of the Mughal Empire and what was seen as the loss of Muslim power. Maududi's own family had served the Mughals and, subsequently, the princely state of Hyderabad. Maududi grew up in the shadow of the ever-declining state of the Nizams. Something of an autodidact in Islamic studies as well as English, Western philosophy, and Marxism, he was a consistent opponent of British rule. He began his career as an Urdu journalist. While still in his teens, he became a staunch advocate of the Indian National Congress. During this phase of his career, Maududi published a laudatory biography of Gandhi (confiscated by the British), as well as a panegyric biography of Madan Mohan Malaviya, a Congress leader later remembered as an architect of a specifically Hindu nationalism. He served as editor of the *Muslim*, the Urdu organ of the Jamiat-'Ulama-i Hind, an organization of 'ulama allied to the Congress and in support of a united, secular India.

During the late 1930s, however, Maududi turned from support of the Congress to an Islamist ideology resonant with the other totalitarianisms of his day, such as Fascism and Communism. His ideas were in tune, broadly speaking, with authoritarian political and theological theories. He developed a novel political theology, for example, two main features of which stand out. At the core lay an unwavering belief that the true divine religion—and he considered only Islam to be such—should be the guiding force for organizing each and every domain of life, including the affairs of the state. He strongly believed that the reason why Muslims had lost power was due to their deviation from "pure" Islam. Further, he held that Islam asked its followers to institute a state based on *shari'a*. He thus argued that the mission of all the prophets of Islam had been the establishment of an Islamic state. In his numerous writings, most important of which was *Four Fundamental Koranic Terms* (1941), an Urdu tract that later became the bible of his ideology, Maududi contended that the word *din* (religion) meant state. He interpreted the word "Allah" in a similar fashion. Rejecting the division between the metaphysical and worldly political life, he argued that Muslims should worship Allah not just in the metaphysical life but also in the political life, because He was a "ruler, dictator (*aamir*) and legislator" of the latter domain as well. Central to such a formulation was Maududi's contention that Islam was an organic, indivisible whole. It was a complete system of life whose nerve center was the Islamic state. So foundational did the pursuit of the *shari'a* state become in his ideology, that he declared that true Muslims could not even breathe under an un-Islamic state.

Second, under the synthetic influence of both Hegel and Marx at once, Maududi offered a remarkably novel approach to reading Islamic history. All of human history, he maintained, was the story of a perennial battle between Islam and *jahiliat*, the term typically used to describe the historical period of "ignorance" before the advent of the Prophet Muhammad and the Qur'an. For Maududi, *jahiliat*, like Islam, was an indivisible organic system. And the two could never coexist. According to Maududi, Islam obligated its followers to eliminate *jahiliat* and implant an Islamic state. By *jahiliat*, Maududi meant an order or perspective that was metaphysical as much as political. In particular, he cited two of its forms: pure (*khalis*) and polytheistic (*mushrikana*). The ultimate expression of "pure *jahiliat*" was the atheistic Western civilization which, having denied the divine truth, relied on reason, the senses, and experience. Politically, it expressed itself in human sovereignty—be it monarchy or secular democracy. He described "secular states" in particular as the exact opposite of what he called the true Islamic ideology. In the educational arena, the Aligarh Muslim University (AMU), the premier institution of Western-style learning for Muslims founded in 1875, was its prime example, which he called a "slaughterhouse" (*qatalgah*). "Polytheistic *jahiliat*" was characterized by speculation and superstition. Ancient civilizations like Babylon, India, and Greece represented polytheistic *jahiliyat*, as did, he argued, several beliefs and practices of Sufism and the Ahl-i-Sunnat wa Jama'at (popularly called Barelvi) sect. Although pervasive, he did not consider polytheistic *jahiliat* a potent force, given its lack of a political system.

Based on this newly crafted political theology, Maududi dismissed all the Muslim parties of his day as un-Islamic because the pursuit of an Islamic state was absent from their agenda. Maududi argued that the Qur'an (61, 9) enjoined the political domination of Islam. This, he argued, was the goal that "pure Muslims" (*asli musalman*) had no choice but to pursue. From this perspective, he wrote, "all [parties]—the Muslim League, the Ahrar, the Khaksar, the Jamiat 'Ulama[-i-Hind], and the Azad [Muslim] Conference—represent erroneous positions (*baatil* [*jahiliat*]) to be obliterated." He underlined the need for forming a party with a "pure Islamic goal."

In August 1941, Maududi's clamor for "pure Islam" found expression when he founded the Jama'at-i Islami (Islamic Party). As President (*amir*) of the Jama'at, he described its mission as the "establishment of an Islamic state/Allah's Kingdom (*hukumat-i ilahiyya ka qayaam*)." Interestingly, the Constitution of the Jama'at called for Allah's Kingdom to include the whole world and kept its membership generously open to any inhabitant "in any part of the world." Clearly, this was a utopian hope. Maududi believed it realistic to establish Allah's Kingdom in the whole of India. He dismissed concern that Muslims were a minority as a corrupting notion of *jahiliat*. Maududi instead argued that they were a party in the same sense as the Communists were. And if the Communists, despite being a numerical minority, could dream of inaugurating a Communist state, Muslims should likewise, he believed, strive for a *shar'ia* state.

Maududi urged Muslims to shun secularism and democracy, which he saw as the preeminent symptoms of *jahiliat*, or *taghut*, because they denied the divine laws of Allah by promulgating man-made laws. The Jama'at Constitution clearly stated that it would not grant membership to those who were members of legislative bodies that framed laws in violation of *shari'a*. It further stated that Jama'at members would be obliged to resign their positions in the army, judiciary, banking, and other institutions of an un-Islamic state. Likewise the Jama'at members were not permitted to study in universities such as the AMU, because they were "institutions of *jahiliat*."

The fiercest target of Jama'at's boycott was, however, the elections. Thus, when Maududi founded the Jama'at, he asked Muslims in general, and his party members in particular, not to participate in elections because they authorized elected representatives to legislate human, as opposed to divine, laws. Participating in elections of secular assemblies, he warned, would lead to Muslims' denial of the very creed of monotheism whose recitation made them believers. The first selection below articulates this position.

It was precisely on this ideological ground that Maududi also opposed the Muslim League and its demand for Pakistan as a separate state of Muslims. Since the League did not desire a *shari'a* state and its leaders were Westernized, he described Pakistan as *na-Pakistan* (un-holy land), *faqistan* (famished land), and an "infidel state of Muslims." He called the League "the Party of Pagans (*Jama'at-i jahilia*)." However, the vagaries of politics eventually pushed Maududi to endorse the demand for Pakistan. He increasingly came to realize that converting the whole of India into an Islamic state was an unrealistic goal, and he sought instead to snatch Pakistan's leadership away from the League. History did not favor his dream. In 1947 he migrated to Pakistan.

With the partition of India, the Jama'at was divided into Jama'at-i Islami Hind (India) and Jama'at-i Islami Pakistan. In 1951, the nascent Indian Republic held the first-ever elections to form a government. Muslims outside of the Jama'at fold participated enthusiastically, but the Jama'at did not. In an Urdu pamphlet, *The Issue of Elections and Indian Muslims*, published on the eve of the first general elections, Abullais Islahi Nadwi (1931–1990), the first amir of the Jama'at in independent India, justified the boycott of elections on the following grounds:

> A Muslim believes in the *sovereignty of Allah* as the straightforward and primary demand of his fundamental kalimah (credo, belief). And it is an open matter that the entire hullabaloo about elections is the spectacle of the *sovereignty of man*, whose relation . . . in no way can be linked with the sovereignty of Allah. If you go into detail, you will realize that in whatever form you participate in elections, you are flouting the commandments and guidance of sharia at every step. [italics added]

Nadwi refused to participate in the election of even local village bodies (*panchayat*), saying that however independent they might be, they were nonetheless "a department of an un-godly system," and Muslims' participation was simply "wrong" and "lethal." No other Islamic organization or scholar outside the Jama'at agreed.

Continuing its policy of boycott, the Jama'at did not participate in the second general elections, held in 1957. However, on the eve of the third general elections in 1962, there began a debate in the Markazi Majlis-i Shura (the central consultative council, hereafter "Shura") of the Jama'at. The debate centered on the (il)legitimacy of democracy and secularism. In July 1961, the Shura set up a Committee to determine whether elections could be used for pursuing *iqaamat-i din* (establishment of religion). The Qur'anic phrase "*iqaamat-i din*" was the new mission statement that the Jama'at had inserted into its Constitution after Partition to replace its earlier mission of *hukumat-i ilahiyya* (Allah's kingdom). The Committee concluded that the

Jama'at could compete in elections if the purpose was to make the Indian Constitution "Islamic" rather than to sustain the current "ungodly system" (*ghayr ilahi nizam*). The Committee further said that the Jama'at could participate in elections only when there was a real possibility of change in favor of establishing an Islamic system. The Shura unanimously accepted the recommendation and went on to pass two separate resolutions that had no reference to *iqaamat-i din* but rather to the legitimacy of participating in the elections, both as voters and candidates, "in the vital interests of Islam and Muslims." It did not, however, lift the ban on voting in the 1962 elections or in the elections of 1967. In 1967, however, it approved a set of criteria under which members could vote. The most important of these criteria were that the candidate "must believe in the *kalimah* [i.e., he must be a Muslim]" and regard legislation against Allah as *haram*. Under these criteria the Jama'at endorsed voting for a single candidate for the Bhopal Constituency where Aftab, a Muslim candidate, was in the fray. This was the first time the Jama'at lifted the ban on voting.

Debate continued with many in the Shura favoring a lifting of the ban without reference to the earlier conditions. The issue, however, remained in limbo until the crisis of civil liberties nationwide brought on by the Emergency imposed by Mrs. Indira Gandhi in the summer of 1975. When the Emergency was lifted and elections announced, the Jama'at ended its ban, disregarding its earlier conditions (e.g., that the candidate must believe in *kalimah*), and participated actively. The foremost criterion now was that the candidate must be committed to the "restoration of democracy," because Mrs. Gandhi had suspended civil liberties and banned all political parties, including the Jama'at. Debate continued, however, until February 1985, when the Shura permanently lifted the ban against voting.

As the second selection below indicates, when the final decision to lift the ban on voting was taken, the original objective of *iqaamat-i din* was not mentioned. The previous conditions had disappeared, including even the requirement that the candidate must be a Muslim. The only criterion was that a candidate must not be "clearly" opposed to Islam and Muslims. As a matter of fact, it categorically mentions that the candidate could be a "non-Muslim."

Before the Jama'at decided to participate in elections, it already had begun to accept employment by the Indian government as legitimate. As a prominent national leader of the Jama'at recently told me, "All Muslims as well as Jama'at people should now try to get every government position, from the post of a peon to that of the President of India."

VOTING IN THE ELECTIONS FOR SECULAR ASSEMBLIES IS *HARAM* AND TAKING EMPLOYMENT IN AN INFIDEL GOVERNMENT ILLEGITIMATE (1945)

Question: Is membership in assemblies legitimate (*ja'iz*) for Muslims, and if not, why not? Representatives of two big Muslim organizations here are contesting elections for membership in the Assembly. They are putting pressure on me to get my vote. Even ulema are also making the same demand [for Muslims to vote for these candidates]. . . . Also please clarify the status of the government jobs. . . .

Maududi's Response: You should clearly understand the principle that all the democratic systems that have been developed in the present age, among them the present assemblies of India, are based on the assumption that, in worldly affairs, inhabitants of a country themselves possess the right to formulate principles and frame comprehensive laws and rules about civic issues, politics, economics, morality, and society. For this legislation, there is no necessity for any authority higher than that of public opinion. This ideology is absolutely the opposite of the ideology of Islam. Integral to the creed of monotheism in Islam is that Allah is the Lord and Ruler of people and the whole world. Issuing orders and guidance is His job. The job of the people is to derive laws of life from His order and guidance. Moreover, if they exercise their independent thought, they do so within the parameters in which Allah Himself has given them autonomy (*azadi*). From this ideological standpoint, the source of law and foundation in all the affairs of life recognizably are the Book of Allah and the tradition (*sunnat*) of his Prophet, and to accept the above-mentioned democratic ideology by deviating from this ideological standpoint is tantamount to deviating from the creed of monotheism. We, therefore, say that membership in such assemblies and parliaments, which are based on the democratic principles of the present age, is *haram,* and to vote for them is also *haram.* Because to vote means that we elect an individual whose job under the present Constitution is to make legislation that stands in absolute opposition to the creed of monotheism. If somebody from among the 'ulama says that [voting] is *halal* and legitimate, then, ask him his justification. If you wish to understand the details of this problem, read my books: *Muslims and the Present Political Predicament*, Volume Three (*Musalman aur maujudah siyasi kashmakash, hissa 3*) and *The Political Theory of Islam* (*Islam ka nazaria-i siyasi*).

For issues like this, it is not an argument at all that since [an un-Islamic polity] has been imposed upon us, and all the affairs of life are connected therewith, if we do not participate in elections, and do not try to take part in the system of government, we would be severely disadvantaged. This argument does not make something *haram halal* (unlawful, lawful). If that were so, there would not be a single *haram* thing in the *shari'a* that could not be justified as *halal* on the logic of expediency and necessity. In accordance with the principle of dire necessity (*izterar*), *shari'a* does permit what is *haram.* But this principle does not mean that because you have neglected your own duties, you create the condition of dire necessity yourself, and then make that dire necessity a justification for declaring each and every *haram* thing *halal.* . . . The system [of government] that is now imposed on Muslims, and whose imposition they offer as an argument of dire necessity, is after all the result of their own negligence. Instead of investing their energy in overthrowing this system and establishing a pure Islamic system, they are making this dire necessity the basis for participating in, and prospering under, this [un-Islamic] system.

The answer to your second question is that as far as individual affairs are concerned there is no problem if an individual Muslim strikes a deal for a particular service or job in return for a wage or a salary with an individual non-Muslim, provided that the job does not directly entail something *haram*. But following this logic, the effort of a large group of 'ulama to justify positions in an infidel (*kafirana*) government as legitimate is not correct. These people ignore the essential difference that exists between the personal business of a non-Muslim individual and the collective business of a non-Islamic system. The purposes of a non-Islamic system permeate all its affairs under every condition, and in every aspect, and that purpose is that there prevail non-Islam (*ghayr Islam*) in place of Islam in all of human life, disobedience in place of obedience, rebellion against Allah in place of the caliphate of Allah. It is evident that [a non-Islamic polity] is the sum of all that is *haram*. Therefore, no distinction whatsoever can be maintained among the different departments of such a system on the grounds that the job of a given department is of a legitimate nature while the job of another department is illegitimate. All these departments are jointly establishing a greater disobedience or sin. In order to understand the exact nature of the issue, the following example should be sufficient. If an institution was set up with the objective of spreading disbelief (*kufr*) among the common people, and propagating apostasy (*murtad*) among Muslims, then, for any Muslim to take up employment in that institution in return for wages, even if that job in itself might be of a *halal* nature cannot be legitimate.

Muslims still advance the logic of dire necessity: If we do not become part of the machinery of this [un-Islamic] government, then non-Muslims will capture it and all power will be in their hands. The response to this argument is exactly the response given to the first question about dire necessity.

FOR PARTICIPATION IN THE ELECTIONS OF A SECULAR NATIONAL PARLIAMENT AND STATE ASSEMBLIES (1985)

It is clear from the policy statements and mission of the Jama'at-i Islami Hind that it wants the elimination of all types of evils (*buraiyon*) and the development of human values in the country. It seeks to end tyranny and injustice, and to establish justice. It wants fundamental human rights, particularly the safety of life and dignity, to be thoroughly safeguarded; economic and social justice should be readily available to all; communalism and cultural aggression should be obliterated; totalitarian and dictatorial tendencies should be wiped out; and democratic values should flower and prosper. All paths to economic exploitation in the country should be blocked, and poverty and hunger, and disease and illiteracy ought to be wiped out. Social evils such as inequality, hierarchy and [caste-related] untouchablity should be ended, and the lot of the downtrodden classes and collectivities should be uplifted in economic and social terms.

Provincial and linguistic biases, prejudices and hatred against religious, linguistic, and cultural minorities should disappear.

Our country is the cradle of multiple cultural and religious units where, in accordance with our Constitution, they enjoy the guaranty of safeguarding and advancing their identity, language, and distinct culture. However, it is quite unfortunate that in the path of these fundamental rights cultural aggression and hateful communalism are becoming strong impediments that are severely harmful to communal integration and may endanger the unity and integrity of the nation. In this context, the narrow-mindedness, oppositional attitude, and sheer recklessness with which important problems, especially Muslim Personal Law, religious education, [religious] endowments, language, and so forth, are approached hardly needs to be spelt out. The agenda of certain elements, which favor totalitarian and dictatorial methods and practices and often display such tendencies, need to be taken into proper account. For the Jama'at, the restoration and continuation of democracy is one of the foremost needs.

In order to pursue its objectives, purposes and goals, the Jama'at-i Islami Hind adopts moral, peaceful, constructive, and democratic and constitutional means, and it abstains from all methods that are against honesty and candor or that risk communal hatred, class antagonism, and disorder on earth (*fasad fi al-ard*). Included in the concept of democratic and constitutional means is participation in electoral politics. Therefore, for important objectives such as promotion of popular human values, elimination of evils (*munkiraat*), establishment of equity, pursuit of social and economic justice, and elimination of totalitarian and dictatorial tendencies, in its meeting held in February 1985, the Markazi Majlis-i Shura of the Jama'at-i Islami Hind has, with certain terms and conditions, decided to lift the ban on its members against voting. In this context, Markazi Majlis-i Shura has laid down the following criteria that Jama'at members should take into account.

1. The candidate promises that on getting elected he [or she] would try his best to work for the promotion of common human values; elimination of evils; pursuit of economic and social justice; checks against totalitarian and dictatorial tendencies; eradication of untouchability; biases against religious, linguistic, and cultural units; stemming of communalism and cultural aggression; purification of national society from corruption, particularly evil and wicked practices like gambling, lottery, and alcohol-drinking; and the purging the national economy of the curse of interest.

2. [The candidate] is on the whole, familiar with, and sympathetic to, the stands and demands of Muslims on such issues as the protection of their life and property, dignity and honor, religious education, [Muslim] Personal Law, language, endowments and so forth.

3. [The candidate] promises that on having been elected, he would support our stands and demands and not endorse any legislation that harms them.

4. He should not be from a party
   a. whose ideology is clearly against Islam and Muslims or whose practices are antithetical to the stands and demands of Islam and Muslims.
   b. which intends to establish a totalitarian and dictatorial system in the country.
5. In his circle of acquaintances, he should be recognized and known as a good and truthful person.
6. He should be expected to keep his promises.
   Note: These criteria would also apply to non-Muslim candidates.
7. In the country or in a state [province], if a situation arose in which the decisive contest was between only those parties which, based on our criteria, were not eligible for our votes, then the vote could be used in favor of a less detrimental party.

Sources

The titles for both excerpts are my own. The first is translated from Syed Abul Ala Maududi, *Rasa'il-o-Masa'il* (New Delhi: Markazi Maktaba Islami Publishers, 1999) 1, 303–306. The second excerpt is translated from Jama'at-i Islami Hind, *Rudad-e-majlis-e-Shura, May 1967–May 1989* (Proceedings of the Advisory Council, May 1967–May 1989) (Delhi: Markazi Maktaba Islami, 1989) 2, 383–384, 483–485.

Futher Reading

For an analysis of the Jama'at's ideological transformation, see my *From Allah's Rule to Secular Democracy: The Transformation of the Jamaat-e-Islami in North India* (Princeton, NJ: Princeton University Press, 2009); "Genealogy of the Islamic State: Reflections on Maududi's Political Thought and Islamism," *Journal of the Royal Anthropological Institute* (2009, Special issue on Islam, Politics and Modernity, forthcoming); and "Between Moderation and Radicalization: Transnational Interactions of Jamaat-e-Islami of India," *Global Networks: A Journal of Transnational Affairs* 5.3 (2005): 279–299. For the earliest account of the Indian Jama'at in English, see Chapter 4 of M. S. Agwani's *Islamic Fundamentalism in India* (Chandigarh: Twenty-first Century Indian Society, 1986). For a thorough and rich biographical account of Maududi, see Syed Vali Reza Nasr, *Maududi and the Making of Islamic Revivalism* (New York: Oxford University Press, 1996); on the Pakistani Jama'at, see his *The Vanguard of Islamic Revolution: The Jamaat-e-Islami of Pakistan* (Berkeley, CA: University of California Press, 1994).

GLOSSARY

---

abjad — Scheme in which each letter of the Arabic and Persian alphabet corresponds to a numerical value; used in chronograms, etc.

Ali, 'Ali — Son-in-law and cousin of the prophet Muhammad, the rightful successor of the Prophet according to the Shi'a.

'alim (pl. 'ulama) — Scholar, learned man; in particular, one learned in Islamic legal and religious studies.

amir — Person with authority; i.e., general, commander, political leader.

'ashura — Tenth day of the month of Muharram (q.v.), commemoration of the martyrdom of Imam Husayn (q.v.)

avatara, avatar — Sanskrit term for divine incarnation.

barkat, baraka — Blessing, holiness; inherent spiritual power.

batin — Inner, hidden, or esoteric aspect of reality; a major focus of Sufi mystical thought and practice.

bhagvan — Hindi term for god.

bhajan — Devotional songs in the bhakti (q.v.) traditions.

bhakti — Hindi term for devotion; religious traditions that emphasize personal devotion to a deity.

Chishti, Chishtiyya — Major Sufi order.

darbar — Court of a king or ruler.

dargah — Seat of spiritual authority represented by Sufi lodge or shrine; *lit.*, court.

darshan — Hindi term for seeing and being seen by a holy person or an image of a deity.

darwesh, dervish — Sufi mendicant.

du'a — Personal prayer; *lit.*, asking.

faqih — Jurist, scholar of Islamic law.

faqir (pl. fuqara) — Sufi mendicant.

fatiha — Opening chapter of the Qur'an, commonly recited as part of canonical and personal prayers.

fatwa — Advisory legal opinion issued by a qualified mufti (q.v.) in response to a question.

guru — Spiritual teacher and guide.

hadith — Reliably transmitted reports of words and deeds by the Prophet Muhammad.

hajj — Annual pilgrimage to Mecca, required of all able Muslims at least once in their lifetimes.

halal — Legitimate according to Islam, ritually pure; *opposed to* "haram."

Hanafi — One of the four schools of jurisprudence in Sunni Islam, named after founder Imam Abu Hanifa (d. 767).

haqiqat, haqiqa — Spiritual truth; *lit.* truth, reality.

haram — Illegitimate according to Islam, ritually unclean; *opposed to* "halal."

Husayn — Grandson of the prophet Muhammad and son of Ali, martyred in 680 C.E. at Karbala; third Shi'i Imam (q.v.).

imam — Leader of prayer; founder of a major law school in Sunni Islam; in Shi'i Islam, those descendants of the prophet Muhammad considered to be the legitimate hereditary leaders of the Muslim community.

jihad — Struggle to control base desires, just war; *lit.*, struggle.

kafir — Unbeliever.

kalimah — Basic expression of Muslim faith; i.e., "There is no god but Allah, and Muhammad is his messenger."

khalifa — Caliph, successor, representative.

Krishna — A major Hindu deity, the eighth avatar (q.v.) of Vishnu.

ma'arifat, ma'arifa — Mystic or esoteric knowledge.

madhhab — *See* "mazhab."

madrasa — School, place of learning.

Mahdavi, Mahdawiyya — Pertaining to the mahdi (q.v.), a messianic movement founded by Sayyid Muhammad Jaunpuri (d. 1505) in the region of Jaunpur in northern India.

mahdi — A spiritual personage or messiah who will appear on the last day.

maktab — Muslim elementary school; Qur'anic school.

masnavi — A long poem; a genre of poetry in Persian, Turkish and Urdu.

maulvi, mawlawi — Term of respect for scholars of the Islamic religious sciences; *lit.*, my lord.

mazhab — Sect, school of thought, school of jurisprudence.

millat — A people, a community, often of co-religionists.

muezzin, mu'azzin, mu'addin — One who gives the formal call to prayers at the mosque.

mufti — One qualified to give an opinion on a point of Islamic law.

Mughal Dynasty — A dynasty of Turko-Mongol origin that ruled a large part of South Asia from 1526 to 1857; *also known as the* Timurid Dynasty.

Muharram — First month of the Islamic calendar; occasion of Shi'a commemoration of the martyrdom of Imam Husayn (q.v.)

murid — Sufi disciple, devotee of a murshid (q.v.)

murshid — Sufi master who guides murids (q.v.); pir (q.v.)

Mussalman — Muslim; a Persian and Urdu variant of the Arabic word "Muslim"

namaz — Muslim canonical prayer.

Naqshbandi, Naqshbandiyya — A major Sufi order.

pandit — A Brahman learned in the Hindu religious sciences.

pir — Spiritual guide and elder; murshid (q.v.).

Qadiri, Qadiriyya — A major Sufi order.

qaum — Nation; community; ethnicity.

qawwali — Devotional Sufi song.

qazi, qadi — Muslim judge.

Ramadan — Holiest month in the Islamic calendar when Muslims are supposed to fast from dawn to dusk.

Safavid Dynasty — Iranian dynasty (1501–1736) that imposed Shi'ism.

sant — Spiritual leader and teacher in the bhakti (q.v) traditions.

sayyid, syed (f. sayyida) — Descended from the prophet Muhammad.

Shafi'i — One of the four schools of jurisprudence in Sunni Islam, named after founder Imam Shafi'i (d. 820 C.E.).

sharia, shariat, shari'at, shari'a, shari'ah — Islamic law; the totality of the exoteric revelation.

shaykh — An elder, a head, a saint; a descendant of Muhammad's companions.

Shia, Shi'a. Shi'i, Shiite, Shi'ite — Member of the Islamic sect that holds Ali and his lineage to be the lawful successors to the prophet Muhammad as leaders of the Muslims; *lit.*, sect, party.

shirk — Sin of polytheism in Islam.

Sikh — A follower of Guru Nanak (d. 1539); member of the Sikh religion.

Sufi — Follower of a mystic path.

sultan — King, ruler.

sunnat, sunna — The normative practice of the prophet Muhammad and the early community, embodied in the hadith (q.v.) literature.

Sunni — The majority tradition in Islam; excludes the minority Shi'a (q.v) sect.

surah — Any of the 114 chapters or sections or the Qur'an.

Tamil — A Dravidian language spoken in the south of India.

tariqat, tariqa — A system of doctrine or training associated with, and transmitted by, particular Sufis or schools of Sufis.

tazkira — Biography or biographical dictionary of saints, scholars, poets, etc.

'ulama, 'ulema — *See* " 'alim."

'urs — Death anniversary of a saint; *lit.*, marriage, referring to the desired union with God.

Vishnu (*adj.* Vaishnava) — A major Hindu deity. *See* "avatar," "Krishna."

Wahhabi — Term used to describe a follower or Muhammad ibn 'Abd al-Wahhab (1702–1792), an Arabian reformer who urged a return to pristine prophetic teachings; often used pejoratively to suggest radical iconoclasm and Arab influence.

waqf — Property trust or endowment according to Islamic law.

wazir — Minister; chief secretary.

yoga — Ancient Indic discipline of meditation and mental and spiritual training.

zikr — Recollection of God, often through the repetition of specified formulas.

INDEX

'Abd al-Haqq Dihlawi, Shaykh, 390

'Abd al-Hayy Lakhnawi, Mawlawi/Maulana, 343–44, 346–47

'Abd al-Qadir Badayuni, 372, 390–401

'Abd al-Qadir Gilani (Ghawth-ii a'zam), Shaikh, Syed/Sayyid, 101, 106, 167, 344, 444

'Abdul 'Aziz, Shah, 21, 201

'Abdullah Muhaddith Ropari, 342–43, 349

'Abdu'l Latif, Shah, *Risalo*, 50

abjad, 79, 457

Abu Bakr al-Siddiq (caliph), 237, 307, 313, 324

Abu Dawud, Imam, 307

Abu al-Fazl ibn Mubarrak, 14, 15, 77, 79, 390

Abu Hanifa, Imam, 227, 231, 285, 298, 300, 301, 302, 303, 307, 312, 321

Abu'l A'la Maududi/Abul Ala Maududi/Abul Ala Mawdudi/Abul ala Maudoodi, Maulana/Mawlana, 28–29, 189, 242, 252, 253, 319, 425, 429, 433, 441, 447, 448

Abul Hasan 'Ali /Hujwiri, Shaykh, 5

Abu'l Kalam Azad, Maulana, 372–73

Abul Mahasin Muhammad Sajjad, Maulana, 269, 317–25

Afghanistan, xvii, xx, 6, 17–18, 27, 29–30, 77, 243, 270

Agra, 17, 82

agriculture, 4, 371, 375–89

Ahl-i Hadith, 101, 226, 342–43, 426, 427, 435, 439

Ahl-i-Sunnat wa Jama'at/Ahl-i Sunnat va Jama'at (Barelvi/Barelwi) sect, 45, 101–3, 106, 226, 329, 342, 426, 427, 435, 439, 441, 449

Ahmad, Imtiaz, xxii, xxiii

Ahmadabad, 10

Ahmad Barelvi/Barelwi Shahid, Sayyid, 21, 201–2

Ahmadiyya movement, 372, 373–74, 438, 439; Ahmadis, 373, 424, 425, 426, 428, 434, 435, 439

Ahmad Khan, Syed, Sir Saiyid/Saiyyid, 22–23, 24, 294, 420, 439. *See also* Aligarh Muslim University

Ahmad Riza/Rada Khan/Ahmad Rada Khan/ Ahmad Rida Khan, Maulana/Mawlana, 101, 169, 170, 171, 342, 344–48

Ahmad Shah Abdali, 17

Ahmad Sirhindi, Shaikh/Shaykh, 136, 158–65, 390

Ahrar party, 410, 425, 429, 449

Ajmer, 6, 9, 14, 45, 77, 80, 81, 82, 124; Ajmeri shrine, 416. *See also* Mu'inuddin Chishti, Khwaja

Akbar, Jalal al-Din Muhammad (Emperor), 13–14, 15, 22, 77–78, 80, 85, 155, 266, 331, 372, 390, 391

Akbar Allahabadi, 330

Akbarnama, 81–82

'Ala al-Din, Sultan, 286–90

'Ala' al-Din 'Ali Sabir, 213

'Ala al-Din Khalji/Khilji, 280–81, 331

'Alauddin Khalji, Sultan (character), 66

'Ali/'Ali ibn Abi Talib, Hazrat, 43, 48, 55, 113, 331, 457, 458, 459; as avatar of Vishnu, 43; and ginans, 51; in Hashim Khudawand Hadi, 90; and Kalki, 49; and names, 343, 347, 348; and poster art, 124; and Prophet Muhammad, 213; relics of, 167; robe (*khirqa*) of, 168; and *Saloko Nano*, 52; in Shi'ism, 124; in Suman, 60; sword of, 213; and *Taqwiyyat al-Iman*, 207; and truck art, 131

'Ali Bin Usman 'Ali Hujwiri (Data Ganj Bakhsh), Khwaja, 124–26, 127, 444

Aligarh Muslim University/Muhammadan Anglo-Oriental College, 21–23, 294, 449

Allah, 207–8, 350; and Abul Ala Maududi, 448, 452, 453; Allah's Kingdom, 449; Allah's light, 66; ceremonies and beliefs owed only to, 205; and *charkhi-namas*, 90, 91; fundamental beliefs about, 257–60; and Hindavi Sufi romance, 63; intercessor with, 210; and Islamic state, 432; obedience to, 258–59; in poster art, 128; power of, 257–58, 261; praise for, 65; and qawwalis, 96; and Qur'anic

Allah (*continued*)
  exegesis, 253; responsibility from, 259–61;
  striving in path of, 255; and *Taqwiyyat al-Iman*,
  205, 206, 207; unity of, 46; worship of, 208,
  209. *See also* God
Allahabad, 294
All-India Muslim League. *See* Muslim League
All-India Muslim Personal Law Board (AIMPLB),
  317, 356, 362
Ameer Ali, Syed, 295
Amin Ahsan Islahi, Maulana, 429
amin/amen, 296, 297, 298, 299, 300, 301–2, 303
amir, 241, 242, 244, 245, 320, 322–33, 450, 457
angels, 66, 121, 204, 207, 210, 223
Anglo-Mohammedan/Muhammadan law,
  266–67, 295
Anwarshah Kashmiri, Maulana, 227, 228–31
apostasy, 31, 242, 244, 245, 246, 247, 267,
  268, 329, 435–36. *See also* conversion
'aqiqa, 341–42
Arabia, 215, 319
Arabic, 2; Arabic names, 341
Arabs, 13, 256, 257, 342, 372, 436–37
Arberry, Arthur J., 361, 362–63
Arya Samaj, 25, 241, 328
Asani, Ali, 10
asceticism, 65, 68, 284, 383, 384, 396; and
  Ahmad Sirhindi, 159; and Chishti Sufi order,
  213; and Hindavi Sufi romance, 63–64; and
  Ibn Battuta, 136; and Malik Muhammad
  Jayasi, 64
'ashara, 247
Asher, Catherine, 15
Ashoka, 282; Ashokan Pillars, 290–91
Ashraf 'Ali Thanavi/Thanawi, Maulana, 135,
  305–16, 328, 343, 412, 416–17
'ashura, 417–18, 457
astrology, 391, 395, 396
astronomy, 391, 392
Ataturk, Mustafa Kemal, 25
Aurangzeb, 'Alamgir (Emperor), 14, 15, 17, 19,
  158, 166
Avadh, Awadh, 17, 63; Avadhi, 41, 46
avatar, avatara, 49, 50, 457, 458, 459
Ayodhya, xxi, 31

Babri Majid, Ayodhya, 31
Babur, Muhammad Zahiruddin (Emperor), 12,
  13
Badruddin Tyabji, Faiz Muhammad, 295; Muslim
  law [Principles of Muhammadan Law], 361
Bahlol Lodhi, 144, 145, 148–49, 152, 155–56
Bahmanis, 11, 45

Baluchistan, 27
Bangladesh, 30–31, 240, 250–55
Banne Miyan (Muhammad A'zam Khan), 137,
  174–84
Barelvi/Barelawis. *See* Ahl-i-Sunnat wa Jama'at/
  Ahl-i Sunnat va Jama'at (Barelvi/Barelwi) sect
barkat/baraka, 8, 79, 120, 208, 400, 457
beauty, 46, 56
Begley, Wayne, 14
Behl, Aditya, 188
beloved, the, 52, 53, 56, 58, 59, 64, 94, 98
Bengal, 8, 10, 13, 17, 18, 30, 373; administrative partition of, 25; Bay of Bengal, 376;
  Bengali Muslims, 372; colonial economy of,
  20–21; deities of, 376; forest clearing and
  growth of Islam in, 375–89; and Hinduism,
  375–76; and Ibn Battuta, 139, 140; and Jalal
  al-Din Tabrizi, 377; and reform, 373; revenue documents from Mughal period,
  386–88
bhajans, 58, 96, 457
bhakti tradition, 49, 51, 58, 93, 95, 97, 457,
  458; *bhakti* poetry, 43, 51, 59, 96. *See also*
  devotion
Bhutto, Zulfiqar Ali/'Ali, 46, 373
bid'a (deviant innovation), 204. *See also* names
Bihar, 63, 318, 320, 323, 324, 386
Bijapur, 11, 88
al-Biruni, Abu Rayhan, 5–6, 392
body, 64, 187; as a city with nine gates, 65; as
  fort, 66; four humors within, 214; and Hajji
  Imdadullah, 212, 213, 218–19, 220, 221;
  and macrocosm-microcosm, 188, 214; in
  ritual, 214; subtle, 65, 66, 214; Sufi ascetic,
  66; tenth door or *dasama dvara* of, 65; yogic,
  65
Bollywood, 32, 58
Bombay, 31
Brahmans/Brahmins, 4, 5, 6, 13, 266, 282, 284,
  371, 375, 405, 406, 407, 429; brahmanic
  rituals, 203; Brahman's egg, 72
Brahmaputra River, 140, 385
Brahmo Samaj, 203
breath/breathing, 213, 214, 219–21, 222–23
Buddha, the, 397, 398
Buddhists, 4, 272, 334
Bukhara, 81
Bukhari, Imam, 231, 233, 234, 235, 312, 321

Calicut, 1, 2, 372, 403, 404, 407
caliphs/caliphate, 5, 319–20, 433, 445, 453
caste, 5
charisma. *See barkat/baraka*

charismatic image, 14

Chatterjee, Partha, xxii, xxiv

children, 124, 147; destitute, 354; education of, 329–30, 336–37; marriage of, 203, 267; rearing of, 329; travel by, 313, 314, 315; wealth of, 312, 313, 314, 315; and women, 114, 329–30, 331, 335–36

China, 20, 139, 141, 142

Chishtis/Chishtiyya, 11, 18, 81, 83, 166, 167, 176, 188, 212, 415, 457; and ʻAli, 43, 213; and Bahmani rulers, 45; Chishti-Nizamis, 213; Chishti-Sabiri lineage, 213, 215; Chishti shaykhs, 64, 88; and Delhi sultanate, 8–9; founder of, 124; on God and Creation, 89; and Hajji Imdadullah, 215, 220; and Malik Muhammad Jayasi, 63, 65; and music and song, 77; poetry of, 88; recitation of, 217–23. See also Muʻinuddin Chishti, Khwaja; Nizamuddin/Nizam al-Din Auliya/Awliya Delhi, Hazrat Shaykh; Salim Chishti, Shaykh

Chola Dynasty, xxi

Christians, 194–95, 243; and Anglo-Muhammadan Law, 295; Arab conquests of, 4; and Ayira Macala, 190; and Malabar society, 406; and Sayyid Ahmad Khan, 23

civil union, 352

Cochin, 372, 403

colonialism, xix–xxii. See also Great Britain

Communism, 448, 449

Congress Party. See Indian National Congress

conversion, 4, 5, 8, 87, 154, 194, 240, 268, 328. See also apostasy; proselytism

Coromandel coast, 403

cosmic regeneration, 392

cosmology, 376, 393

cosmos, 72, 214

courtesan singer (tawaʼif), 182

crime, 209, 266, 270, 274. See also law

Criminal Procedure Code, 296, 354, 356, 358, 360, 361

custom, 265, 314

Dacca/Dhaka, 20, 376

Dakhni/Dakani, 11, 45, 50, 87–88

Dallal, Ahmad, 19–20

dance, 57, 273, 275

dargah(s) (graves), 8, 36, 44, 79, 150, 457; of Barkatiyya family, 167, 170, 171; of great ancestors, 136; of Haider Shaykh, 145; and literature, 88; of saints, 441; of Sayyid Husayn Khing Sawar, 80–81; of Sufis, 14. See also tombs

darshan, 51, 457

darul harb, 21

Dar al-ʻUlum/Uloom. See Deoband

darwesh/dervish, 140, 141, 142, 151, 153, 162, 273, 275, 284, 457

Das, Veena, xxii, xxiii, 439

daʻwa (preaching movement), 187

death, 203, 216, 405. See also funeral customs

Deccan, 6, 11, 13, 17, 87

Delhi, 11, 13, 17, 18, 19, 45, 139, 149, 201, 202, 213

Delhi Sultanate, 6–9, 10, 63, 77, 279, 281, 376, 377, 385

democracy, 319, 432, 447–55; and Abul Ala Maududi, 449, 452; in India, 31, 32; and Jamaʻat-i Islami, 450, 451, 453, 454; and Jinnah, 26

Deoband, 226; Dar al-ʻUlum/Deoband madrasa/school/Academy, 188, 212, 226, 227, 228, 229, 234, 241, 305, 306, 317, 328, 343; NWFP Deobandi seminary, 29

Deobandis, 36, 188, 226–28, 318, 342, 343, 373, 412, 441; and Gilani, 227; and Muhammad Yusuf Ludhianvi, 438, 439; and Munir Report, 426, 427, 435

Deogir, 288

Devanagari script, 24

devotion, 43, 51, 371; devotional objects, 120; devotional songs, 43, 45–46; devotional stories, 43; and Hajji Imdadullah, 212; and Hindavi Sufi romance, 63; and naʼt, 101; and personal voice, 57; and Taqwiyyat al-Iman, 204. See also bhakti tradition

Dharma, 376

Digambaras, 68

disciple, 51, 159, 161–62, 169

divorce, 268, 308, 310–11; and Dissolution of Muslim Marriages Act, 268; and fatwas, 340; and Ibn Battuta, 274, 276; and Imarat-i Shariʻat, 317; and Muslim Personal Law, 352–53; and Shah Bano Case, 352–66; and triple talaq, 353. See also marriage

dress, 4, 272, 273, 276, 405

duʻa, 457

Dudu Miyan, 21

al-Durr al-Mukhtar, 301, 307, 312, 313

East Africa, 58

East Bengal, 27

East Pakistan, 30

ecstasy/rapture, 9, 45, 56, 162, 173, 176, 396

education, 23–24, 25, 203, 236, 328, 329–30, 449

Ellenborough, Lord Edward Law, xx

Elliot, Henry Miers, *History of India as Told by Its Own Historians*, xix–xx
emotion, 255, 258, 260, 261
English East India Company, 20, 21, 22, 166, 188, 203, 293. *See also* Great Britain
eroticism, 64, 94

fairy, 204, 207, 208
faith, 54, 206; profession of, 159, 161, 212, 213
family, 135, 241, 268, 272, 305, 308. *See also* law
faqih (pl. *fuqaha*), 306, 457
faqir, 145, 152, 153, 154, 457
Farangi Mahall, 14; seminary at, 342
Farid al-Din Shakarganj, Shaykh, Ganj Baksh, 81, 213, 444
farz/fard (pl. *fara'iz*), 319; *Fara'izi* movement, 21; *fard 'ayn/farz al-'ain* (a personal obligation), 189, 241, 313; *fard kifayah/farz al-kifaya* (communal obligation), 189, 241, 313; *jama'ati farz* (common duty), 415; *qaumi farz* (national duty), 413
fasting, 194, 217
Fatawa Hindiyya/Fatawa-yi 'alamgiri, 14, 313
Fatehpur, 81
fatiha ceremony, 168, 204, 441, 457
Fatima/Fatima al-Zuhra, 48, 53, 55, 124, 131, 171
Fatimid Empire, 49
fatwa, 265; and British authorities, 293, 294; characteristics of, 339–40; in colonial period, 340; and names, 269–70, 339–50; and parental rights, 305–16; structure of, 340–41
fez, 22, 23
film, 32, 58, 103
Firoz/Firuz Shah Tughluq, 10, 281, 282, 290–91
First Afghan War, xx
food, 175, 221
forests, 371, 386, 388
forgiveness, 216
fortune-telling, 192–93, 194
funeral customs, 168, 196, 203, 407. See also *dargah*(s) (graves); death; relics (*tabarrukat*); shrine(s); tombs
Fyzee, A.A.A., 267

Gabriel (angel), 96, 98, 210
Galenic ideas, 214
Gandhi, Indira, 451
Gandhi, Mahatma, 25, 269, 318, 448
Ganges River, 140, 376, 378
gardens, 14, 61, 64, 70
gems, 69, 71

gender roles, 93–94, 272, 329, 336, 353. *See also* women
Ghazali, Imam, 310
Ghaznavids, xxi, 5, 6, 138
Ghiyas al-Din Balban, 279, 280, 282–86
Ghosh, Amitav, 2
Ghulam Ahmad, Mirza, 372, 373
Gnostics, 49
Goa, 12
God, 55, 77; and *Ayira Macala*, 196; and *chakki-namas*, 88, 89; and *charkha-namas*, 88, 89, 91; consent to will of, 217; elevation of word of, 322; guidance of, 215–16; and Hajji Imdadullah, 214, 215–16, 217, 218, 219, 220, 221; and *hamd* (praise of God), 93, 94; and holy fools, 173–74; and kingship, 283; meeting with, 51; memory of, 217; mosque as property of, 302; and names, 342, 345, 347, 348, 349; names of, 80, 442; oneness of, 103; and poster art, 124, 126; presence of, 214; and qawwalis, 94, 95–96; and Qur'an, 230; repudiation of, 311; spiritual union with, 77; and Tablighi Jama'at, 242, 246, 247, 248; Throne of, 214; and truck art, 130; way of (*fi sabil allah*), 241; and *zikr*, 213. *See also* Allah
Golconda, 11
Gorakhnathi yogis, 63, 66
Great Britain, 24, 202, 205, 269; and Abul Ala Maududi, 448; and Afghanistan, 18; and Banne Miyan, 175; and colonial narratives, xix–xx; colonial rule by, 20–26, 174, 194, 225, 228, 293, 354, 373; and elections, 413; and Hajji Imdadullah, 212; and Hasan Nizami, 328; and holy fools, 174; judges of, 293, 294; and law, 267, 293–303; and models for mental illness, 174; and Muslim League, 417; and Pakistan, 409, 410, 411; and Punjabi Muslims, 411; Queen's Proclamation of 1858, 22, 267; and religious pluralism, 326–27; and rule of law, 20, 266; and sense of justice, 293; and transmission of learning, 188. *See also* English East India Company
Gujarat, 10, 13, 32, 49

hadith, xviii, 21, 94, 123, 242, 245, 265, 307, 350, 444, 446, 457, 459; and Ashraf 'Ali Thanawi, 305–6; and *Ayira Macala*, 190; and Barani, 281; and *dars al-Qur'an*, 251, 252, 253; and Deoband madrasa, 305; and fatwas, 339, 341, 342; and Gilani, 227–38; and Hajji Imdadullah, 216, 217, 218–19; and Muhammad Gesudaraz, 45; and Muhammad Yusuf Ludhianvi, 442, 444, 445, 446; and Munir Report, 431, 433; and names, 344, 346, 349; and Nuri Miyan, 169; and parental rights, 310–14, 315, 316; provenance of, 229; and qawwalis, 93; and Qur'an study, 254, 258, 259, 260, 261; and Sayyid Ahmad Khan, 23; and Shah Waliullah, 19, 201; six early collections of, 225; study of, 225–38; and Sufis, 10; and *Tablighi Nisab*, 241; and *Taqwiyyat al-Iman*, 207, 209, 210, 211; of 'Umar, 308

hajj, 79, 184, 202, 205, 240, 313, 314, 342, 457. *See also* pilgrimage; pilgrims

Hajjaj ibn Yusuf, 396

halal, 452, 453, 457

Hamid Nagore/Nagori, Shahul, in Tamilnad, 2, 44, 191

Hammad, 312

Hanafi/Hanifis, 33, 296, 298, 299, 302, 303, 342, 443, 457

Hanafi school of law/*madhab*/*mazhab*, 2, 14, 159, 164, 226, 227, 230, 231, 268, 271, 300, 301, 307, 342

Hanbal, Ahmad ibn, Imam, 300, 301

Hanbali school of law, 443

haqiqa/haqiqat, 65, 95, 386, 457

haram, 193, 289, 307, 457

Hari Shyam, 96

Harun al-Rashid, 280, 284–85

Hasan, Imam, 53, 55, 124, 131, 167

Hasan Nizami, Khwaja, 135, 269, 326–27, 328, 329–34

Hastings, Warren, 266, 267

heart, 213, 218–19, 220, 223

Hegel, G.W.F., 448

hell, 192–99, 283

Hidaya/Hedaya of al-Marghinani, 230, 267, 300–301

Hidayat Ali, 342

Hidayatullah, M., *Mulla's Mahomedan Law*, 363

hijrah, 256, 257, 260

Hind, 269

Hinduism, 36, 240; and *Ayira Macala*, 193, 194; as central to Indian nationalism, 267; deities in, 193; epics of, 15; and Hindu Adoption and Maintenance Act, 353, 359; and Hindu Marriage Act, 353; and Hindu Succession Act, 35; and law, 266, 267; as monolithic, 187; and Muslim Personal Law, 353; and paradise, 397; and poster art, 120; and remarriage of widows, 267; and shared customs and sacred sites, 194

Hindu Kush, 3

Hindu-Muslim riots, 241

Hindu nationalism, 31, 32, 44, 66, 357, 448

Hindus, 31, 44, 144, 272, 286, 334; ancient, xxii; and Anglo-Muhammadan Law, 295; and Delhi sultans, 281; as enemies of Prophet Muhammad, 287; and Haider Shaykh, 145; Hindu pandits, 293; Islamization of, 87; and Muslim League, 417; and names, 341; and personal law, 353; in Punjab, 410; separate codes for, 266; and *shari'a*, 279; and Shaykh Sadruddin Sadr-i Jahan, 146, 155; and *Taqwiyyat al-Iman*, 207

Hindu temple(s), 15, 203; at Somnath, xx, xxi

Hir Ranjha, 18

holy fool, 9, 24, 173–84. *See also* saints

holy men, 68, 177, 188, 273, 371, 384; burial sites of, 204; and doctrine of Unity (tauhid), 201; and Ibn Battuta, 139; and Tablighi Jama'at, 243; and *Taqwiyyat al-Iman*, 204, 205, 206. *See also* saints; Sufis

homosexuality, 193, 194, 195–96

hospitality, 58

houris, 69

Hudud Ordinances, 270

Humayun (Emperor), 13

Husayn, Imam, 53, 55, 101, 106, 113, 114, 124, 131, 167, 207, 411, 417, 418, 457

Husayn Ahmad Madani, Maulana, 178–79, 228, 235, 373

Hyder, Syed Akbar, 96

Hyderabad, 17, 27, 174, 175

hypocrisy, 193–94, 197, 255, 257, 284

Ibn al-'Arabi, Muhyiddin, 45, 392

Ibn Battuta, 8, 10, 135–36, 371, 383; as ambassador to China, 271; and Jalal al-Din Tabrizi, 138–42; and Maldive Islands, 271–72, 273–77; as qadi/qazi, 139, 265–66, 271–77; *Rihla*, 138, 140–42, 273–77

idolatry, 193, 196, 284, 414. *See also* paganism

Ijma'/ijma, 341, 431–34

ijtihad, 433, 439, 443, 444

ijtihad-i ikhtilaf, 439

Ikram, Shaikh Muhammad, xxii–xxiii

Iltutmish, Shams al-Din, 279, 284

imam, 53, 114, 165, 229, 342, 457, 458; authority of, 48; devotion to, 49; and doctrine of unity (*tauhid*), 201; and ginans, 50, 51; and gits, 57, 58; and *na't*, 103; role of, 58; and *Taqwiyyat al-Iman*, 207, 210; undue honor to, 270; veneration of, 204

imambara, 18
Imdadullah, Hajji, Muhajir-i makki, 135, 188, 212–23
Inayat Khan, Hazrat, 35, 36, 135, 268, 326, 327–28, 329
Indian National Congress, 25–26, 27, 31, 269, 318, 356, 372, 409, 414–15, 417, 448
India/Republic of India, xvii–xviii, 58, 120, 124, 215, 295, 374, 450; and Abul Ala Maududi, 449, 450; administration of, 24; anti-Muslim pogroms in, 31–32; Arab dynasty in, 3–5; and Barkatiyya Sayyids, 166; and Bengal, 30, 201; colonial, xix, 20–22, 174, 294; colonial economy of, 20–21; and colonial history, xix–xx; Constitution of, 360, 364, 366, 451, 454; conversion in early, 5; cultural pluralism in, 32; eighteenth century, 18; freedom of, 25; holy places shared in, 273; home rule movement in, 328; and Ibn Battuta, 138, 139; independent, 26, 353, 354, 419; Indian Councils Act (1909), 25; Indian Law Reports, 293, 294, 295; Indian Penal Code, 267, 296, 297, 299, 301, 302; integration of Muslims into, 354; Islamic law in, 293–303; Islamic life in, 32; Islam in colonial, 20–22; and Jama'at-i Islami, 32, 447; kingship in, 279; land revenue in colonial, 20–21; law in, 266, 352; and Muhammad Zahiruddin Babur, 12; Muslim interests in independent, 31–32; Muslim League in, 409; Muslim-majority provinces of, 27; and Pakistani military, 28; partition of, 26, 27, 30, 31, 189, 240, 242, 245, 328, 354, 409, 450; and pilgrimage, 77; post-independence, 317; post-Mutiny period, 24; post-partition, 320; power of Muslim rulers in, 281; precolonial, 173; president of, 32; reformers in, 308; *shari'at* governance in, 317–25; and Shaykh Sadruddin Sadr-i Jahan, 148; Sufism in, 13; and Tablighi Jama'at movement, 240–41; and trade, 1, 3, 138; traditions of, xxii; united, secular, 448
Indra, 67, 70, 71, 72, 73, 75, 378
Indus River, 4
infidels. See *kafirs*
inheritance, 317, 340, 352, 357, 405
inscriptions, 45, 79, 83–85
insha'llah, 416
intercession (*shafa'a*), 101, 102
Iran, 27, 29
Islam, 187; and Abul Ala Maududi, 448, 449, 452, 453; basic rules and regulations of, 261; beliefs fundamental to, 257–60; communica-
tion of doctrine of, 187; and criminal law, 267; and fatwas, 340; first millennium of, 390, 391; four schools of, 300; and Hinduism, 194; and Malabar, 404, 405, 406, 407; and Munir Report, 424–25, 427, 428, 430–31, 433, 437; and Muslim League, 373; in new nation states, 26–35; pillars of, 330; regulations of, 270
Islamic fidelity, 205
Islamic history, 448–49
Islamic law, 169, 293–303, 317, 356, 364, 371; and Anglo-Mohammedan law, 267; and colonial state structure, 318; and Deoband Academy, 212; and Deobandis, 226; five major categories in, 307; in Malabar, 407; in Pakistan, 270; and Shaykh Ahmad Sirhindi, 158. See also *shari'a/shari'at*
Islamic modernists, 294
Islamic state/Republic, 424, 426, 427, 432, 434, 448, 449
Islami Oikya Jote, 31
Islamization, 87, 270
Ismai'il Shahid, Maulana/Shah, 201–4, 270; *The Taqwiyyat al-Iman (Support of the Faith)*, 201–11
Isma'ilis/Ismailis, 11, 43–44, 46, 48, 49, 58
Israel, 413–14, 444

Jahangir Nur al-Din Salim (Emperor), 13, 14, 15, 136, 158
jahiliyyat/jahiliyya/jahiliat, 242, 318–19, 321, 448–49
Jains, 4, 68, 155, 282
Jalal al-Din Tabrizi, Shaykh, 140–41, 376–82
Jalal Mujarrad of Sylhet, Shah, 135, 136, 139–40, 371–72
Jama'at-i Islami, 29, 30, 31, 187, 189, 252, 373, 425, 426, 427, 429, 439, 449
Jama'at-i Islami Bangladesh, 250
Jama'at-i Islami Hind, 374, 447–55
Jama'at-i Islami Pakistan, 450
jama'at khanas (houses of congregation), 49
Jami'at-i 'ulama Bihar, 320, 323
Jamiat-i-Ulama-i Hind/Jamiat 'ulama (JUH), 318, 412, 448, 449
Jamiat-i-Ulama-i-Pakistan, 440, 443
Jats, 4, 5, 17
jauhar, 66
Jaunpur, 10
Jesus, 97, 394, 395, 396, 399
Jews, 4, 191, 194–95, 256, 334
jihad, 21, 22, 23, 28, 202, 205, 318, 458; and Afghanistan, 29; anti-Russian, 29; as armed

resistance (*jihad bi al-sayf*), 318; in colonial period, 21; and Tablighi Jama'at, 242, 243, 244
Jinnah, Muhammad Ali, 25, 28, 48, 318, 409–10, 416
jizya, 4, 287
judge, 8, 340. See also *qazi*
jurisprudence (*usul-i fiqh*), 229
jurist. See *faqih* (pl. *fuqaha*)

Ka'ba/Kaaba, 84, 85, 124, 128, 129, 130, 214, 301, 330
kafirs, 165, 318, 435, 458
kalimah, 426, 451, 458
Kalki, 49
Kanauj, 6
Karbala, 46, 106, 247, 411
Karim al-Husseini, Shah, Aga Khan IV, 48, 61
Kashmir, 13, 27
Kerala, 190
Khaksar party, 410, 449
khalifa, 90, 151, 152, 155, 434, 458
Khilafat movement, 25, 269, 420
Khuda Bakhsh, S., 295
Khurasan, 81, 140
Khusrau/Khusraw Dehlavi, Amir, xvii, 9, 46, 81, 230
kings/kingship, 8, 279; regulations of, 208–9, 265, 280, 282–86, 287, 290
Koran. See Qur'an
Krishna, 51, 63, 95, 96, 98, 382, 458
Kumar, Sunil, 6, 8
Kwajah Gharib Nawaz. See Mu'inuddin Chishti

Lahore, 5, 424, 425, 426
Lahore Resolution, 409
landlords, 20, 21, 22, 372, 382, 409, 410, 411
law: and case law, 267; civil, 293, 295, 299, 359; criminal, 267, 293, 294; customary, 268; of evidence and procedure, 267; family, 317, 352; and family lands, 268; inheritance, 268; and marriage, 267; medieval schools of, 226; Muhammadan Ecclesiastical Law, 300, 302; personal, 360; positive (*fiqh*), 229–30; procedural, 293; traditional schools of/*madhhab*, 23, 307, 458. See also Hanafi school of law; Hanbali school of law; Islamic law; Maliki law school; Shafais/Shafi'i school; *shari'a/shari'at*
law courts: informal, 265, 270; non-governmental, 25; official colonial and postcolonial secular, 265
Law Reports Act (1875), 294
Lewis, Samuel, 327

liberalism, 424
light, 51, 53, 55, 79
Lodhis, 10, 12, 136
lotus, 65, 75
lotus-women, 71
love, 52, 56, 61, 64, 68, 69, 94, 95, 98, 124
Lucknow, 14, 18, 342

ma'arifat, 458
macrocosm-microcosm, 188, 213, 214
Madan Mohan Malaviya, 448
madhhab. See law
madrasa(s), 24, 29, 187, 267, 458; and Ashraf 'Ali Thanawi, 268; in Bengal, 31; and Deobandis, 188, 226, 227, 228, 229, 241, 305, 306, 328; and Gilani, 227; and Mughals, 388; and 'ulama, 265
Madrasa Subhaniyya (Allahabad), 317. *See also* Deoband; Farangi Mahall
magic, 140, 194
Mahabharata, 148
Mahdavi, Mahdawiyya, 9, 11, 63, 393, 458
Mahmood, Justice Syed, 294–95, 297–303
Mahmood Tahir, 295
Mahmud Ghaznavi/Mahmud of Ghazna, Sultan, xviii, xx, xxi, 5, 44, 331
Mahmud Hasan, Shaykh al-Hind, 227, 228, 229, 231–35, 236, 237–38
Mahmud Jaunpuri, Amir Sayyid. See Muhammad/Mahmud Kazimi Jaunpuri, Amir Sayyid
mahr, 354, 355, 356, 357, 358, 361, 363, 365
majazi, 64, 95
majzub, 9, 137, 173–84
maktab, 168, 458
Malabar, 1, 372, 403–8
Maldives, xvii, xxi, 139, 271–72, 273–77
Maliki law school, 268, 271, 443
Malwa, 10
Mamdani, Mahmood, xxiv
Manazir Ahsan Gilani, 188, 226–38
Mandhakar, 81
Mandu, 10
Manicheans, 49
Man Singh, Raja, 15
Mansur al-Hallaj, 95, 97
Marathas, 13, 17, 18, 22
marriage, 32, 51, 329; and adultery, 276; advertisments for, 332; ceremonies at, 204; to Christian or Jewish women, 333; to European women, 333–34; and fatwas, 340; and Ibn Battuta, 274, 275; and Imarat-i Shari'at, 317; and law, 267; and Malabar society, 405; and

marriage (continued)
  Muslim Personal Law, 352; polygamous, 333, 352, 355; and Shah Bano case, 352–66; spousal rights in, 305, 307, 308, 309; Sunni-Shi'a, 333; temporary, 272, 274. See also divorce
marsiyas, 18, 113
martyrs, 46, 204, 207, 208, 210, 411
Marx, Karl, 448
Mary, virginity of, 96–97
masnavi, 44, 458
Mathura, 15
Maududi sect, 439
Mauritius, 45, 102, 103, 104, 343
Mecca, 85, 218, 221, 257
mediation, 207
medicine, 214
Medina, 105, 257
meditation, 68, 161, 214
messiah, 392, 393, 395, 396, 399, 400
military/army, 30, 188, 274, 283, 289; and Banne Miyan, 174–75; and Malabar society, 406; and military fiscalism, 18; and military slaves (mamluks), 5, 6; and Shah Jahan, 386; and zimmi, 4
millat, 416, 417, 421, 430, 458
millennium, 11, 14, 136, 372, 390, 391, 392, 393, 394–95
miracles, 81, 396; and Banne Miyan, 175, 176; and Haider Shaykh, 147, 148; and poster art, 33; and Prophet Muhammad, 106; and saints, 383; and Sayyid Ahmad, 23; of Shah Jalal, 139; and Shaykh Sadruddin Sadr-i Jahan, 156; stories about, 151, 152; and Sufis, 8, 243
Mishkat (al Masabih), 231, 310, 311, 312, 445
modernism, 24, 26, 28, 188, 306
modernity, 22, 341
Mohammed/Mohammad Ali Jinnah, 26, 270, 373, 411, 418, 425, 429
momin, 427, 430
monasticism (rahbaniyyat), 319, 321
Mongols, 8, 12
monotheism, 65, 204
morality, 44, 165, 189, 243, 255, 268
Moses, 95, 97, 256, 413
mosques, 1, 14, 84; behavior of worshippers in, 294–303; in heart, 216; of Imam Abu-i Laith of Samarqand, 81; of Imam Sahib, 245; and Jalal al-Din Tabrizi, 377–78, 379–82; and markaz, 241; and Mughals, 387, 388; as property of God, 302; protection of, 24; and Shah Jalal Mujarrad, 385; and Tablighi Jama'at movement, 241

mourning, 18, 46. See also nauha
muftis, 286, 293, 294, 339, 340, 341, 458
Mughals/Mughal India, 12–17, 77, 166, 266, 371, 376, 383, 387–88, 390, 391, 448, 458
Muhammad, Imam, 312, 313
Muhammad, Sultan, 140, 280
Muhammad Ali (Jauhar), 420
Muhammadan Anglo-Oriental College. See Aligarh Muslim University/Muhammadan Anglo-Oriental College
Muhammad Ghauri/of Ghor, 6
Muhammad Husain, 296, 297, 298
Muhammad Ilyas, Maulana, 328
Muhammad/Mahmud Kazimi Jaunpuri, Amir Sayyid, 10–11, 372, 393, 399, 400, 458
Muhammad Shafi', Maulana Mufti, 244
Muhammad the Prophet, 48, 53, 54, 55, 88, 113, 151, 312; and Ahmad Sirhindi, 158, 159, 165; ansar (helpers) of, 243, 244; as avatara of Vishnu, 96; and Ayira Macala, 190, 192, 193–94, 195; birthday of, 204, 329; as bridegroom, 96; call toward Islam, 256; and chakki-namas, 90; and charkhi-namas, 90; and children's wealth, 313, 315; Companions (Sahabah) of, 307, 396, 439, 443, 445; devotion to, 101–2; family of, 106, 113, 123; and ginans, 50; greatness of, 204; green dome of tomb of, 105; and Hajji Imdadullah, 216, 221; hijrah to Medina, 256, 257; Hindus as enemies of, 287; and historical context of Qur'an, 256–57; as human model vs. source of miracles or conduit of revelation, 201; as intercessor, 204; and Jama'at-i Islami, 452; khulafa/caliph (successors) of, 243, 244; as mediator, 102, 103; and millennium, 394, 395, 397; and Mirza Ghulam Ahmad, 373; and modernism, 23; mosque of, 124, 128, 129, 130; Muhammad Yusuf Ludhianvi on, 439, 442, 443–45; in Munir Report, 433; and names, 204, 344, 345, 348, 349; and na't, 101, 102, 104–5, 170; and Nuri Miyan, 168; and parents, 310, 311; and partition of India, 373; as perfect human, 94, 96; and poster art, 120–24, 126, 128; and praise poetry, 106; as primordial human being, 130; and proselytism, 237; and qawwalis, 96; relics of, 166–67; and rights of self, 308, 309; and seclusion of women, 335; spiritual presence of, 102, 105; and Sufism, xviii, 8; and Tablighi Jama'at, 244; and Taqwiyyat al-Iman, 206, 207, 210; and truck art, 130, 131; and veiling, 335

Muhammad Yusuf, Maulana/Hazratji, 241, 244, 245, 247–48
Muhammad Yusuf Ludhianvi, Maulana, 244, 374, 438–46
Muharram/Muhurram, 18, 46, 113–18, 203, 247, 411, 458
Muhyi al-Din Ibn al-'Arabi, Shaykh, 395, 444
Mu'inuddin Chishti, Khwaja, (Khwaja Gharib Nawaz), 8, 13, 77–78, 81–82, 101, 124–26, 147, 221, 416; *dargah* of, 77, 79, 80. *See also* Ajmer
Mujibur Rahman, Shaykh, 30
Multan, 148
Mumtaz Daultana, 410
Mumtaz Mahal, 14
Munir Report, 29, 373–74, 424–37, 438, 439
murshid, 8, 91, 144, 329, 458. *See also* spiritual guides/spiritual preceptor (pir, *murshid*)
Murshidabad, 20
Musalman Waqf Validating Act, 268
Musharraf, Pervez, 28, 30, 438
music, xxii, 9, 45, 77, 158, 187, 197, 327; and Ahmad Sirhindi, 159, 164; and *Ayira Macala*, 193; and Banne Miyan, 182
Muslim, Imam, 244, 312
Muslim Brotherhood (Egypt), 319
Muslim League, 26, 268, 372, 412, 413, 450; and Abul Ala Maududi, 449; election posters of, 373, 409–23; electoral support for, 25; foundation of, 25; in India, 409; and Islam, 373; and Munir Report, 436; and Pakistan, 409–23; and Sajjad, 318
Muslim League Manifesto (1944), 411
Muslim Personal Law (MPL), 32, 252–53, 267, 270, 295, 354, 355, 357, 359, 360, 361, 454
Muslim Personal Law (Shari'at) Application Act, 268
Muslim reformist movements, 201–5
Muslims, 344; definition of, 426–27, 435, 439; as foreign conquerers, xx–xxi; separate political identity for, 25
Muslim state, 372, 373. *See also* Islamic state/ Republic
Muslim Women (Protection of Rights on Divorce) Act (MWA), 356–58, 364–66
mysticism, 51, 97, 334, 336, 396, 398, 400; and Hindavi Sufi romance, 63; and love, 45; and mystic way (*tariqa*), 170; and preceptor, 284; and qawwalis, 94, 95; and seclusion, 334, 335; and Sufi romances, 64; and union, 66. *See also* *bhakti* tradition; Sufis; Sufism

names, 341–50; and association with God, 343; of children, 269–70; choice of, 265; and equivocation, 347, 348; and God, 341; of God, 13, 85, 158, 159; and *Taqwiyyat al-Iman*, 207
Nanak, Guru, 10
Naqshbandi/Naqshbandiyya, 13, 136, 158, 159, 165, 166, 188, 215, 220, 458
na't (praise of the Prophet), 45, 93, 94, 101–11, 168, 171
Nath yogis. *See* yogis
nationalism, 341, 373, 419; Bengali, 25; and English East India Company, 20; Hindu, 31, 32, 44, 66, 357, 448; and historiography, 17; and Ibn Battuta, 272–73; and Indian tradition, xxii; and Munir Report, 429; and Qutb Minar, 6, 8; religiously based, 37; and Tariqa-i Muhammadiyya and jihad, 205
nauha, 113–18
Nayar, 405, 406, 407
Nehru, Jawaharlal, xx
Neo-Platonism, 49, 213
Nepal, xviii
9/11 attacks, 29, 242
Nishapur, 81
Nizam of Hyderabad, 22, 137, 148, 448
Nizamuddin, Basti (Delhi neighborhood), 32–35, 37, 244, 245
Nizamuddin/Nizam al-Din Auliya/Awliya Delhi, Hazrat Shaykh, 9, 13, 32, 44, 81, 213, 241, 268–69, 280
Nizari Ismailis, 48, 49, 50, 57
nonviolence/pacifism/non-cooperation, 25, 27, 66, 318
Nurbakhsh /Nurbakhshiyya Sufi order, 393, 399

Orissa, 13
Ottomans, 12, 14, 24, 25, 269, 391

pacifist war (*harb-i silmi*), 318. *See also* nonviolence/pacifism/non-cooperation
Padmavat /Padmavati (character), 64, 66, 188
Padmini, 69
paganism, 256, 257. *See also* idolatry
Pakistan, xvii, 31; and Abul Ala Maududi, 450; and Ahmad Sirhindi, 158; Bengali citizens of, 26; debate over creation of, 410; democratic failures of, 28; devotional image in, 120–32; formation of separate state of, 373; ideological path of, 27–29; independent, 354; and India, 31; and Islam, 373–74; Islamic law in, 270, 270; as Islamic state, 28, 411, 424–37; as liberal secular state, 424; military in, 27–28;

Pakistan (continued)
  and Muhammad Yusuf Ludhianvi, 440; and
    Munir Report, 424; and Muslim community,
    412; and Muslim League, 409, 411–12, 450;
    Muslim political and economic interests in,
    28; and Muslim population of, 30; as Muslim
    state, 409; and Muslim unity, 410, 411; and
    national institutions, 27; and official ideology,
    xxii; and Punjab, 410; and secular liberalism,
    374; secular position in, 28; as state for Mus-
    lims vs. Islamic state, 26; as symbol, 410, 411,
    412, 413; and Tablighi Jama'at movement,
    240; as U.S. ally, 28
Pakistan Penal Code, 438
Pandavas (characters), 290
pandit, 72, 458
paradise, 44, 61, 64, 66, 83, 192, 392, 397
parda/porda, 258, 261, 333. See also veiling
parents, 309–11, 314, 315
Parsi Matrimonial Act, 359
Parsis, 334
Pashtuns/Pathans, 27
Patel, Alka, 10
Patel, Sardar, 418
paths (tariqa). See tariqa/tariqat
patience, 216, 217
pearls, 66, 69, 73, 79
peasantry, 21, 372, 376
Persian, 2, 12, 13, 15, 63, 87, 88, 96, 191
Persians, 13, 17
Perso-Turkish rulers, 281, 282
Pickthall, Marmaduke, 362
piety, 265, 328
pilgrimage, 168, 247, 313, 314, 330; and Hajji
    Imdadullah, 212; to Mecca, 205; mementos
    of, 120; and poster art, 120, 124; to shrines
    of Ajmer, 77–85; sites of, 203; and Taqwiyyat
    al-Iman, 204, 208; to tomb of Ghalib, 35; to
    tombs of holy men, 8, 43, 194. See also hajj
pilgrims, 77, 79, 80, 167; and Haider Shaykh,
    145; and Nuri Miyan, 171; to Shaykh
    Sadruddin Sadr-i Jahan, 146
pir (spiritual master), 81, 90, 146, 153, 458;
    and chakki-namas and charkha-namas, 88, 89;
    and ginans, 48, 49–50, 51; and Haider Shaykh,
    145; life stories of, 144; Nuri Miyan as, 169;
    Sufi elder as, 8; and Taqwiyyat al-Iman, 207,
    208, 210. See also murshid; spiritual guides/
    spiritual preceptor (pir, murshid)
Portugal, 1, 2, 12, 187, 190–91, 195, 372,
    403, 404, 407
praise poems. See na't (praise of the Prophet)

Prasad, Rajendra, xx
prayer(s), 84, 260; and Ahmad Sirhindi, 159,
    160–61, 162–64, 165; and Ayira Macala, 194;
    and Banne Miyan, 177; and Barkatiyya
    Sayyids, 167; call to (adhan), 342; as dedi-
    cated to God alone through pir, 154; five
    daily, 258; and Hajji Imdadullah, 216, 217;
    and Ibn Battuta, 276; and kingship, 283–84;
    Muhammad Yusuf Ludhianvi on, 443–44;
    and Nuri Miyan, 168; obligatory portions of,
    441; and Queen Empress v. Ramzan, 296,
    298, 299, 300, 302; and responsibility,
    259–60; to Shaykh Sadruddin Sadr-i Jahan,
    146; and Tablighi Jama'at, 241, 246; tahajjud,
    330; and women, 330
preaching, 236, 242, 244, 245–48. See also
    proselytism; sermons
printing, 21, 24, 36, 202, 214, 340
prophets, 204, 210, 270, 376
proselytism, 25, 237–38. See also conversion;
    preaching
Punjab, 8, 17, 18, 30, 31, 49, 202, 245; voters
    of, 409–23
Punjabi devotional poetry, 46
Punjab Unionist Party, 409, 410

Qadiri, Qadiriyya, 166, 176, 215, 220, 458
al-Qaeda, 29
qalandar, 9
Qarmatians, xxi
qaum, 413, 414, 415, 416, 421, 458
qaumiyat, 419
qawwali, 34, 45, 77, 93–99, 170, 182, 458
qazi, qadi, 265, 266, 273, 274, 286, 340, 458;
    Ibn Battuta as, 139, 255–56, 271–77; Mughis
    as, 281, 286–90. See also judge
qul ki fatiha, 171
Qur'an, 146, 223, 243, 248, 274, 330, 350, 391,
    398, 400, 420, 457, 459; and Abd al-Qadir
    Gilani, 227; and Abul A'la Maududi, 28, 449;
    and Ahmad Sirhindi, 159, 160–61, 162, 163,
    164; and Anwarshah Kashmiri, 230; and
    Ayira Macala, 192; and Banne Miyan, 180;
    and Bukhari, 234; defined, 458; descent of,
    396; and equivocation, 347; exegesis of, 227,
    230–31, 250; and fatwas, 339, 341, 343; and
    fulfillment of trusts, 309; and ginans, 50;
    and gits, 58; and hadith, 225; and Hajji
    Imdadullah, 212, 214, 215, 216, 217, 218,
    222; and heaven, 66; historical context of,
    256–57; and holiness, 136; and Ibn Battuta,
    139; and Islamic principles, 23; and Jama'at-i

Islami, 450; and kingship, 284; lessons on, xix, 31, 189, 250–61; Madani surahs, 256; in madrassa, 229; Makki surahs, 256; and Malabar society, 405; and Malik Muhammad Jayasi, 64–66; and Muhammad Yusuf Ludhianvi, 442, 443, 445, 446; and Munir Report, 431, 432, 433, 434, 435; and names, 346, 349; and na't, 102, 104; and Nuri Miyan, 167, 168, 169, 171; and paradise, 66; and poster art, 122, 125, 126; and qawwalis, 93, 95, 96; revelation of, 256; and Shah Bano case, 356, 357, 361–62, 363; and Sufis, 10; and Tablighi Jama'at, 243; and *Taqwiyyat al-Iman*, 206, 207, 210; and 'Ubayd Allah Sindhi, 236–37; in Urdu, 202; and *zikr*, 213
Qur'anic omen (*istikhara*), 276, 277
qutb, 168
Qutb, Sayyid, 319
Qutb Minar, 6, 7, 8
Qutbuddin Bakhtiyar Kaki, Khwaja/Hazrat, 6–9, 44, 81, 271

rain, 58, 60, 61
Rajasthan/Rajasthani, 13, 15, 49, 77, 147
Rajputs, 13, 15, 17, 66, 281
Ramadan/Ramzan, 164, 296, 298, 458
Ramayana/Ramcharitmanas, 44, 155, 390
Ram Mohun Roy, 203, 204
Rampur, 167–68
Ram/Rama/Ramacandra/Ram Chandra, xx–xxi, 31, 44, 65, 68, 155
recollection. See *zikr*
reincarnation/rebirth, 14, 51, 391, 392–93
relics (*tabarrukat*), 120, 136, 166–67, 168, 175, 208. See also funeral customs
renunciation, 68, 216, 217
repentance, 216
revenue/*kharaj*, 282–83, 288, 289, 376. See also taxation
rituals, 32, 50, 113, 159, 167, 187, 267
Rumi, *Masnavi*, 50
Russo-Turkish war (1878), 269

Sachar Report, 32
Sadruddin Sadr-i Jahan, Shaykh (Haider Shaykh), 10, 136, 144–56
Safavids, 12, 17, 391, 393, 458
Said, Edward, xix
saints, 44, 81, 120, 144, 146, 158–65, 175, 329, 384; and charisma, 13; graves of, 441; and hagiography, 383; and Ibn Battuta, 138, 139; and kingship, 284; and *Taqwiyyat al-Iman*,

204–5, 207–8; undue honor to, 270. *See also* holy fool; holy men; Sants; Sufis; 'urs
Salafis, 439
Salim Chishti, Shaykh, 77–78
sama', 77, 146. *See also* music
Samarqand, 81
sandal ritual, 170–71
Sanskrit, 88, 203
Sants, 10, 49, 51, 58, 458
Sarkhej complex, Ahmadabad, 10–11
Satan, 209, 212, 244, 283, 445
sati, 203, 267
satpanth (true path), 43, 49, 51, 53
Saudi Arabia, 29
sayyid, syed, 458
Sayyid Ahmad Khan Rizwi, 177–78
sayyids, 48, 49, 50
Schimmel, Annemarie, 26
scholars, xxiii, 14, 205. *See also* 'ulama/'ulema
sect/sectarianism, 29, 36, 46, 204, 266, 322, 340, 342, 365, 373, 374, 425, 426, 440
secularism, xx, 26, 424, 447–55
seekers, 68, 82
self/ego, 51, 53, 55, 95, 213, 217
self-mortification, 64, 65
Sen, Amartya, xxii
Sena dynasty, 377
Sepoy Rebellion (1857), 22
sermons, 50, 244. *See also* preaching
Shabbir Ahmad Usmani, Maulana, 414–15
Shafais/Shafi'i school, 164, 300, 301, 302
Shafi'i/Shafai/Shafii, Imam, 301
Shahada, 126–27. *See also* kalimah
Shah Bano, 267, 270, 295, 352–66
Shahbaz Qalandar, 124, 126, 130
shahid (martyr), 242
Shah Jahan (Emperor), 14, 15, 16, 22, 79–80, 82–83, 85, 386; mosque of, 80
Shah Jalal Mujarrad, 376, 383–85
sharia/shari'at, 65, 90, 168, 320, 359; and Abul Ala Maududi, 448, 449; and 'Ala al-Din, 286–90; and Anglo-Mohammedan law, 267; defined, 458; and early Perso-Turkic sultans of Delhi, 279; five objectives of, 319; and Hindus, 286–87; and Jama'at-i Islami Hind, 447; and Nuri Miyan, 170; as proper path, 265; shari'at order (*tanzim-i shar'i*), 319; and state, 279–80, 281, 282, 286, 287–89. *See also* Islamic law; law
Shari'at Act, 360
Shari'at Governance Council, Imarat-i Shari'at, 319–20

Shari'atullah, Haji, 21

Shaukat Hyat, Sardar, 421

Shi'as, 36, 48, 124, 427, 441, 459; of Awadh and Bengal, 166; efflorescence of, 18; exclusion of, 439; and imams, 46, 439; and Muhammad Yusuf Ludhianvi, 438, 439; and Muharram, 32, 113–18, 203; and Munir Report, 435; in Pakistan, 29, 438; ritual traditions of, 106; Shi'i Isma'ili, xxi; and *Taqwiyyat al-Iman*, 187–88

Shihab al-Din Suhrawardi, Shaykh, 81, 377, 385

Shikarpur, 17

shirk, 204, 208, 209, 210, 459

shrine(s): of Adam's footprint in Ceylon, 272, 273, 275; at Ajmer, 412; of Banne Miyan, 175; of dead saints, 120; of Mu'inuddin Chishti, 9, 44–45; of Nizam al-Din Auliya, 34, 328; of Sufis, xxi, 44, 45, 64, 93; and *Taqwiyyat al-Iman*, 205, 208. *See also* funeral customs

Siddiq Hasan Khan, Nawwab, 342

Sikhs, 17, 21, 144, 202, 205, 459; dynasties of, 128; gurus of, 120; and Haider Shaykh, 145; in Punjab, 410; and Sadruddin Sadr-i Jahan, 146, 155; and Tablighi Jama'at, 247

silsila, xviii, 8

Simla Conference, 410

sin, 54, 192, 193, 195, 196, 197–99, 209, 210, 216, 309–10, 346

Singhala (Sri Lanka), 44, 65, 66, 70, 71, 72–76. *See also* Sri Lanka

Singhala-dipa, 64, 65, 71

Sistan, 81

Siva, 65, 71, 272

slaves, 267, 273, 275, 276

Solomon, 283

Somnath, xx, xxi

song/singer, 50, 175, 182, 273

soul, 44, 51, 52, 56, 60, 212, 397; and *maya*, 51; quest of, 63–76; transmigration of, 393, 397, 398–99, 401

South Africa, 350

Soviets, 29, 270

Special Marriage Act, 352

spiritual guides/spiritual preceptor (pir, *murshid*), 24, 51, 305, 326. See also *murshid*; pir (spiritual master)

spirituality, 44, 51, 176, 187

spiritual leaders, 322

spiritual vision (*didar*), 58

Sri Lanka, xviii, 1, 26, 190–91, 373. *See also* Singhala (Sri Lanka)

Stoicism, 213

Sufi love mysticism, 51

Sufi master (*shaykh*), 170

Sufi Order of the West, 327

Sufi romance, 10, 11

Sufis, xxiii, 5, 8, 17, 45, 145, 151, 152, 158, 166, 371–72, 398, 459; and Ahmad Sirhindi, 159; and ascetic body, 66; and Barkatiyya family, 167; and Brahmo reform movement, 203; conversions by, 126; as counterbalance to 'ulama, 279; and Delhi sultans, 8–9; devotionalism of, 43; Ghazi Miyan of Bahraich, xxiii; and holy fools, 173; and hospices, 64; and Ibn Battuta, 136, 140; and Iltutmish, 279; as mediators, 371; of medieval India, 87; missionary activities of, 87; and Mughals, 13; and Muslim League, 373; and Pakistan, 414; and poster art, 124; and Sadruddin (Haider Shaykh), 136; shrines of, xxi, 44, 45, 64, 93; and Tariqa-i Muhammadiyya, 205; and yogis, 151. *See also* holy men; *murshid*; pir; saints; tombs

Sufi seeker, 66

Sufi *shaykhs*, 64

Sufism, xviii, 2, 5, 49, 132, 184, 384; and Abul Ala Maududi, 449; and Ahl-i Sunnat, 101; American, 327; and Ashraf 'Ali Thanawi, 305; and *Ayira Macala*, 194; debates about, 77; and Deobandis, 188, 226; four stages of path, 65; and Hajji Imdadullah, 216; and Hazrat Inayat Khan, 35, 268, 327; and Hinduism, 46; and Jalal al-Din Tabrizi, 377; and Kashf al-Mahjub, 5; and *nur-i muhammadi*, 105; and qawwalis, 97; and Shah Waliullah, 20; to Shaykh Sadruddin Sadr-i Jahan, 146; succession of masters of, 167; suspect as superstition, 137; symbols in, 214; and Tablighi Jama'at, 242–43; and *Taqwiyyat al-Iman*, 187–88, 205; and *zikr*, 89, 188, 213

Sufi teachers, 10

Sufi way (*suluk*), 169

Suhrawardi order/Suhrawardiyya, 9, 144, 166, 385

sultan, 10, 269, 459

Sultana Khadija, 277

sunnah/sunnat/sunna, 102, 136, 204, 349, 431, 432, 433, 434, 439, 441, 452, 459

Sunnis, 49, 124, 300, 301, 341, 427, 440, 441, 459; and Badayuni, 390; and hadith, 225; and jurisprudence, 439; and Muhammad Yusuf Ludhianvi, 439; and Munir Report,

435; and *na't*, 106; in Pakistan, 29; and sectarianism, 36

Supreme Court of India, 355, 356, 357

surah. *See* Qur'an

Surat al-Ikhlas, 217

Sylhet, 385

syncretism, xxi, xxii, xxiii, 14, 372, 403

Tablighi Jama'at movement, 25, 31, 33–34, 36, 188–89, 240–48, 269, 327–28, 373

Taj Mahal, 14

Talbot, Cynthia, 12

Taliban, 28, 29

Tamil, 2, 190, 459

Tamil literature, 3, 187

taqavi loans, 282

Taqi Usmani, Mufti, 343, 349–50

taqiyya (dissimulation of religious beliefs), 49, 346

Taqwiyyat Iman/al-Iman, 21, 46, 187–88, 205–11

Tariqa-i Muhammadiyya, 201, 204, 205

tariqa/tariqat, xviii, 8, 65, 101, 206, 459

tauhid (unity). *See* unity (*tauhid*), doctrine of

taxation, 4, 5, 15, 22, 272, 281, 287, 407–8. *See also* revenue/*kharaj*

ta'zias (replicas of tombs of martyrs), 18, 19

tazkira, 168–70, 459

teachings: and Shaykh Sadruddin Sadr-i Jahan, 150–51; and Tablighi Jama'at, 244, 246; and teaching *shaykhs*, 44

terrorism, 242, 243

Thapar, Romila, xxi

theft, 287, 288

Theosophical Society, 327

Thubbat [Tibet], 141

time, 14, 391, 392, 398

Timur, 6, 12, 331

Timurid Dynasty, 458

Timurid heritage, 266

Tipu Sultan, 331

Tirmidhi/Tirmadhi/al-Tirmidhi, Imam, 229, 232, 234, 344

Titu Mir, 21

tolerance, xxi, 14, 46

tombs, 8, 18, 19, 35, 43, 194. See also *dargah*(s) (graves); death; funeral customs

Tonk, 201

Torah, 256

trade, 17

traditionalists, 24

trance (*sama*), 9, 45

translation, 15, 202, 203, 293, 295

transnationalism, 35–36, 101, 269

trust, 216, 217

truth, 52, 55, 223

Tughluq Dynasty, 6

Turkestan, 384

Turko-Afghans, 5, 138

Turko-Mongol lineage, 14

Turks, 5, 12

'Ubayd Allah Sindhi, Maulana, 236, 237, 238

'ulama/'ulema, 236, 237, 396, 457, 459; and Abul A'la Maududi, 28, 29, 452, 453; and 'Ala al-Din, 286; Barelwi sectarian orientation among, 137; in colonial period, xxiii; and Delhi sultanate, 279; different religious tenets of, 440–41; and family obligations, 268; fatwas of, 269; and form of life, 439; and Gilani, 228; and hadith, 225; and Hindus, 287; and Iltutmish, 279; as interpreters of law, 318; and Islamic state, 28, 425, 428; and Jami'at 'Ulama-i Hind, 25, 318; and kingship, 284, 289; and Mughals, 14; and Munir Report, 425–27, 428, 429, 430, 431, 432, 433, 434, 435, 439; and Muslim League, 373, 416–17; and Nuri Miyan, 168, 169, 170; and Pakistan, 28, 29, 411–12, 414; and print, 24; professionally trained, 188; and relics, 166; roles of, 265–66; and Sajjad, 318, 319; and Sayyid Ahmad Khan, 23; and *shari'at* governance, 322–33, 334; and social change, 306; and spousal rights, 308; Sufis as counterbalance to, 279; and Tablighi Jama'at movement, 241; teaching by, 189, 241. *See also* scholars

'Umar ibn al-Hazrat (caliph), 307, 308, 321, 323, 331

Umayyids, 4

ummat, 321, 322, 323, 391, 394

Uniform Civil Code (UCC), 352, 353, 356, 357, 363

Unionist Party, 410–11, 414, 423

United States, 29–30

unity (*tauhid*), doctrine of, 201, 204, 205, 206, 207

Upanishads, 204

Urdu, xxii, 18, 24, 25, 30, 35, 58, 96, 101, 103, 104, 202, 318

'urs, 9, 45, 80, 81, 167–68, 170–71, 459. *See also* saints

Uzbeks, 12

Vaishnava/Vaishnavite tradition, 10, 49, 50

van der Veer, Peter, xxii, xxiii

Varanasi, 15
veiling, 258, 329, 334–35, 405. See also
   parda/porda
vernacular, 57, 93, 96, 202, 203
Vijayanagar, 11, 12
virahini, 51, 58–59, 94, 96, 97
Vishnu, 49, 50, 459
Vivekananda, Swami, 268, 326, 327

Wahhabis, xxiii, 20, 205, 296, 302, 342, 441,
   459
Wahhabiyya, 346
wajib (legally incumbent), 307
wakf/waqf, 302, 459
Waliullah/Wali Allah, Shah, 18–20, 21, 201, 227,
   233–34, 342
Washbrook, David, 20
wealth, 55, 310, 311, 330
West Pakistan, 27, 30, 424
West/Western civilization, 188, 226, 306, 326,
   327, 349, 449
widows, 203, 267
women, 23, 32, 51, 69, 89, 135, 269; and
   Ashraf 'Ali Thanawi, 305; and *Ayira Macala*,
   192, 193, 194, 195, 197–98; and Bangladesh
   Islami Chatri Sangstha meetings, 251, 255;
   and *chakki-namas* and *charkha-namas*, 88; and
   children, 114, 329–30, 331, 335–36; and
   conversation, 331–32; destitute, 354; in devotional Dakhni poems, 45; and divorce, 270,
   352–66; and dress, 8, 272, 335; and feminism, 353, 357; and gits, 57; and grinding
   and spinning songs of devotion, 87–91; and
   Hajji Imdadullah, 214; and Ibn Battuta, 272,
273, 274, 276; and Inayat Khan, 268, 329;
   and law, 267, 268; maintenance of divorced,
   353, 354–66; and Malabar society, 405; and
   marriage, 268, 352–66; and misogyny, 357;
   as mothers, 308, 335; and Mughals, 14; and
   Muslim Personal Law, 252–53; and Muslim
   religious identity, 353; and outward life, 336;
   Parsi, 334; and qawwalis, 94, 97; in Rajput,
   13; residence for, 313–14; rights of, 307–8,
   313–14; as rulers, 272, 274; seclusion of,
   334–37; and separation from beloved, 43;
   and Shah Bano Case, 352–66; soul symbolized as, 18; as spiritual leaders, 329; and
   Sufism, 326; in Sufi verse, 11; and Tablighi
   Jama'at movement, 241; and veiling, 335;
   as *virahini*, 58. *See also* gender roles
World War I, 269

Yazid ibn Mu'awiyya, 106, 110, 396, 411
Yemen, 384
yoga, 459
yogis, 10, 44, 49, 63, 64, 65, 66, 68, 154, 214,
   334, 406

Zafrullah Khan, Chaudhri, 425, 428, 434
zakat (alms-tax) collectors, 311–12
Zia al-Din Barani, 279–80, 281, 282–90
Ziaul Haq/Zia al-Haq, General, 29, 30, 46, 270
zikr, 91, 146, 152, 158, 159, 188, 213, 214,
   216–20, 222–23, 459
zimmi, 4, 5, 287, 434
Zionism, 243
Zoroastrians, 4, 49
Zum Zum, 85